Interrogating Race and Racism in Postsecondary Language Classrooms

Xiangying Huo
University of Toronto, Canada

Clayton Smith
University of Windsor, Canada

A volume in the Advances in Educational Marketing, Administration, and Leadership (AEMAL) Book Series

Published in the United States of America by
    IGI Global
    Information Science Reference (an imprint of IGI Global)
    701 E. Chocolate Avenue
    Hershey PA, USA 17033
    Tel: 717-533-8845
    Fax: 717-533-8661
    E-mail: cust@igi-global.com
    Web site: http://www.igi-global.com

Copyright © 2024 by IGI Global. All rights reserved. No part of this publication may be reproduced, stored or distributed in any form or by any means, electronic or mechanical, including photocopying, without written permission from the publisher. Product or company names used in this set are for identification purposes only. Inclusion of the names of the products or companies does not indicate a claim of ownership by IGI Global of the trademark or registered trademark.

                    Library of Congress Cataloging-in-Publication Data

Names: Huo, Xiangying, 1973- editor. | Smith, Clayton, 1959- editor.
Title: Interrogating race and racism in postsecondary language classrooms /
  edited by Xiangying Huo, Clayton Smith.
Description: Hershey, PA : Information Science Reference, 2024. | Includes
  bibliographical references and index. | Summary: "This book investigates
  race and racism in postsecondary language classrooms, how race
  intersects with language, how power impacts and shapes language teaching
  and learning, and how hegemony and ideology perpetuate linguistic
  injustice and discrimination against racially minoritized students"--
  Provided by publisher.
Identifiers: LCCN 2023037547 (print) | LCCN 2023037548 (ebook) | ISBN
  9781668490297 (hardcover) | ISBN 9781668490334 (paperback) | ISBN
  9781668490303 (ebook)
Subjects: LCSH: English language--Study and teaching (Higher)--Foreign
  speakers. | Racism in higher education. | Racism in language. | LCGFT:
  Essays.
Classification: LCC PE1128.A2 I66 2024 (print) | LCC PE1128.A2 (ebook) |
  DDC 428.0071/1--dc23/eng/20230914
LC record available at https://lccn.loc.gov/2023037547
LC ebook record available at https://lccn.loc.gov/2023037548

This book is published in the IGI Global book series Advances in Educational Marketing, Administration, and Leadership (AEMAL) (ISSN: 2326-9022; eISSN: 2326-9030)

British Cataloguing in Publication Data
A Cataloguing in Publication record for this book is available from the British Library.

All work contributed to this book is new, previously-unpublished material. The views expressed in this book are those of the authors, but not necessarily of the publisher.

For electronic access to this publication, please contact: eresources@igi-global.com.

Advances in Educational Marketing, Administration, and Leadership (AEMAL) Book Series

Siran Mukerji
IGNOU, India
Purnendu Tripathi
IGNOU, India

ISSN:2326-9022
EISSN:2326-9030

Mission

With more educational institutions entering into public, higher, and professional education, the educational environment has grown increasingly competitive. With this increase in competitiveness has come the need for a greater focus on leadership within the institutions, on administrative handling of educational matters, and on the marketing of the services offered.

The **Advances in Educational Marketing, Administration, & Leadership (AEMAL) Book Series** strives to provide publications that address all these areas and present trending, current research to assist professionals, administrators, and others involved in the education sector in making their decisions.

Coverage

- Governance in P-12 and Higher Education
- Technologies and Educational Marketing
- Students as Consumers
- Enrollment Management
- Educational Leadership
- Marketing Theories within Education
- Academic Pricing
- Faculty Administration and Management
- Advertising and Promotion of Academic Programs and Institutions
- Educational Management

IGI Global is currently accepting manuscripts for publication within this series. To submit a proposal for a volume in this series, please contact our Acquisition Editors at Acquisitions@igi-global.com or visit: http://www.igi-global.com/publish/.

The Advances in Educational Marketing, Administration, and Leadership (AEMAL) Book Series (ISSN 2326-9022) is published by IGI Global, 701 E. Chocolate Avenue, Hershey, PA 17033-1240, USA, www.igi-global.com. This series is composed of titles available for purchase individually; each title is edited to be contextually exclusive from any other title within the series. For pricing and ordering information please visit http://www.igi-global.com/book-series/advances-educational-marketing-administration-leadership/73677. Postmaster: Send all address changes to above address. Copyright © 2024 IGI Global. All rights, including translation in other languages reserved by the publisher. No part of this series may be reproduced or used in any form or by any means – graphics, electronic, or mechanical, including photocopying, recording, taping, or information and retrieval systems – without written permission from the publisher, except for non commercial, educational use, including classroom teaching purposes. The views expressed in this series are those of the authors, but not necessarily of IGI Global.

Titles in this Series

For a list of additional titles in this series, please visit: www.igi-global.com/book-series/advances-educational-marketing-administration-leadership/73677

Challenging Bias and Promoting Transformative Education in Public Schooling Through Critical Literacy
Lyndsey Aubin Benharris (Fitchburg State University, USA) and Katharine Covino (Fitchburg State University, USA)
Information Science Reference • copyright 2024 • 300pp • H/C (ISBN: 9781668496701) • US $230.00 (our price)

Promoting Quality Hybrid Learning Through Leadership and Educational Management
Edgar Oliver Cardoso Espinosa (Instituto Politécnico Nacional, Mexico)
Information Science Reference • copyright 2024 • 264pp • H/C (ISBN: 9798369300947) • US $220.00 (our price)

Handbook of Research on Critical Issues and Global Trends in International Education
Megel R. Barker (TASIS England, UK) Robyn Conrad Hansen (Northern Arizona University, USA) and Liam Hammer (International School of Lusaka, Zambia)
Information Science Reference • copyright 2024 • 744pp • H/C (ISBN: 9781668487952) • US $270.00 (our price)

Socio-Economic Implications of Global Educational Inequalities
Gamze Sart (Istanbul University-Cerrahpaşa, Turkey) Pınar Tokal (Netkent Mediterranean Research and Science University, Turkey) and Nursel Aydıntuğ Myrvang (Biruni University, Turkey)
Information Science Reference • copyright 2024 • 314pp • H/C (ISBN: 9798369306932) • US $230.00 (our price)

Leading and Managing Change for School Improvement
Nadire Gülçin Yildiz (Istanbul Medipol University, Turkey)
Information Science Reference • copyright 2024 • 300pp • H/C (ISBN: 9781799839408) • US $215.00 (our price)

Strategic Opportunities for Bridging the University-Employer Divide
William E. Donald (University of Southampton, UK & Ronin Institute, USA)
Information Science Reference • copyright 2024 • 300pp • H/C (ISBN: 9781668498279) • US $225.00 (our price)

Exploring Meaningful and Sustainable Intentional Learning Communities for P-20 Educators
Susan R. Adams (Butler University, USA) and Angela Breidenstein (Trinity University, USA)
Information Science Reference • copyright 2024 • 340pp • H/C (ISBN: 9781668472705) • US $230.00 (our price)

Tools, Exercises, and Strategies for Coping With Complexity
Rune Storesund (Storesund Consulting, Kensington, USA) and Ian I. Mitroff (Mitroff Crisis Management, Berkeley, USA)
Information Science Reference • copyright 2024 • 209pp • H/C (ISBN: 9781668465639) • US $110.00 (our price)

701 East Chocolate Avenue, Hershey, PA 17033, USA
Tel: 717-533-8845 x100 • Fax: 717-533-8661
E-Mail: cust@igi-global.com • www.igi-global.com

Table of Contents

Preface xiv

Acknowledgment xix

Section 1
Language and Race

Chapter 1
Introduction: Interrogating Race and Racism in Postsecondary Language Classrooms 1
    Xiangying Huo, University of Toronto, Canada

Chapter 2
The Terrorized Experiences of Latina Bilingual Preservice Teachers With Language and Race 28
    Lucy Arellano Jr., University of California, Santa Barbara, USA
    Ana K. Soltero López, Fresno City College, USA
    Delia M. Carrizales, Texas Tech University, USA

Chapter 3
Overcoming Racism and Discrimination: Experiences of Vietnamese ESL Teachers in Canada........ 52
    Elena Tran, Niagara College, Toronto, Canada & Sheridan College, Canada
    Thu Thi-Kim Le, Ho Chi Minh City University of Technology and Education, Vietnam &
        University of Windsor, Canada

Chapter 4
Coloniality and Whiteness in Evangelical ESL Classrooms 73
    Ruthanne Hughes, University of South Carolina, USA

Section 2
Language and Identity

Chapter 5
Backing Into Race: Immigration, Identity, and Social Movement Theory in English Language
Teacher Education... 98
    Tonda Liggett, Linfield University, USA

Chapter 6
Belonging and Legitimacy for French Language Teachers: A Visual Analysis of Raciolinguistic
Discourses 116
    Mimi Masson, Université de Sherbrooke, Canada
    Simone Ellene Cote, Independent Researcher, Canada

Chapter 7
Expanding Understandings of Race in Postsecondary Language Classrooms: A Call for
Multiraciality in Teacher Identity Research 150
    Marcela Hebbard, The University of Texas Rio Grande Valley, USA

Chapter 8
Language, Identity, and Racism in Postsecondary Classrooms 172
    Michael Olayinka Gbadegesin, Lead City University, Nigeria
    Rachel Oluwafisayo Aluko, Lead City University, Nigeria

Section 3
Interrogating Race and Racism in Postsecondary Language Classrooms

Chapter 9
Empowering Linguistic Diversity: Theory Into Practice in Multilingual Writing Classrooms 193
    Anita Chaudhuri, University of British Columbia, Canada
    Jordan Stouck, University of British Columbia, Canada

Chapter 10
Writing Centers' Praxis Is Not Neutral but Raced: Collaborative Ethnography 218
    Daniel Chang, Simon Fraser University, Canada
    Qinghua Chen, The Education University of Hong Kong, Hong Kong
    Angel Mei Yi Lin, Simon Fraser University, Canada

Chapter 11
A Textbook Case of Antiracism: Course Readings and Critical Pedagogy for Multilingual First-
Year University Writers 241
    Srividya Natarajan, King's University College, Canada
    Emily Pez, King's University College, Canada

Chapter 12
Implications of Multilingual Students' Stories for Promoting Linguistic Justice in Higher
Education: Insights From Oral History Interviews 265
    Kamila Kinyon, University of Denver, USA

Chapter 13
Translanguaging or English Monolanguaging? Exploring Postsecondary Students' Perceptions of
Linguistic Human Rights in Pakistan's Sindh Province 290
    Ameer Ali, Government Arts and Commerce College, Larkano, Pakistan
    Maya Khemlani David, University of Malaya, Malaysia
    Shahnawaz Tunio, Government Arts and Commerce College, Larkano, Pakistan

Chapter 14
A Systematized Review of Anti-Racist Pedagogical Strategies 306
    Teresa Holden, University of Windsor, Canada
    Clayton Smith, University of Windsor, Canada

Compilation of References 325

About the Contributors 362

Index 367

Detailed Table of Contents

Preface xiv

Acknowledgment xix

Section 1
Language and Race

Chapter 1
Introduction: Interrogating Race and Racism in Postsecondary Language Classrooms 1
    Xiangying Huo, University of Toronto, Canada

The introductory chapter interrogates race and racism in postsecondary language classrooms by mainly exploring Critical Race Theory, raciolinguistics, and Critical Language and Race Theory to examine race, racism, and racialization, as well as intersectionality between language and race, language and ideology, language and identity, and race and pedagogy. Chapter 1 discusses the importance of these theoretical frameworks, their integration with one another, and the connections of these frameworks with the volume, explores the links of language with ideology and identity, investigates seven antiracist and decolonial pedagogies (i.e., translingual pedagogy, multilingual pedagogy of writing, plurilingual approach, translanguaging, culturally responsive, relevant, and sustaining pedagogies, critical language awareness pedagogy, and multiliteracies pedagogy), and calls for action on combatting racism in higher education language classrooms to advance racial equity and enact linguistic and social justice.

Chapter 2
The Terrorized Experiences of Latina Bilingual Preservice Teachers With Language and Race 28
    Lucy Arellano Jr., University of California, Santa Barbara, USA
    Ana K. Soltero López, Fresno City College, USA
    Delia M. Carrizales, Texas Tech University, USA

The United States is a multilingual country, yet there continues to be a deficit view of languages spoken in classrooms other than English. The purpose of this study is to examine the lived experiences of Latina bilingual preservice teachers in relationship to language and race. Specifically, the authors consider how linguistic terrorism and racism influence future career decision-making for these students. This qualitative study considers the lived experiences of eight bilingual preservice teachers in California and Texas. Utilizing narrative inquiry from a grounded theory perspective, the study examines the experiences surrounding their use of Spanish and how they are treated as racialized beings. Findings demonstrate how the participants turned these negative experiences into motivation and fuel to become bilingual classroom teachers. Conclusions suggest the need to restructure educator preparation programs addressing the challenges faced by future teachers as they navigate raciolinguistic spaces in their educational journeys. Implications for research, policy, and practice are presented.

Chapter 3
Overcoming Racism and Discrimination: Experiences of Vietnamese ESL Teachers in Canada........ 52
    Elena Tran, Niagara College, Toronto, Canada & Sheridan College, Canada
    Thu Thi-Kim Le, Ho Chi Minh City University of Technology and Education, Vietnam &
        University of Windsor, Canada

Although the global workforce becomes increasingly diverse, many minority groups are still standing in the path of multiple forms of exclusion. Among them are the non-White and non-native English-speaking teachers who are striving to prove their credentials and secure their careers throughout the world. The purpose of this paper is to examine the challenges faced by two Vietnamese ESL teachers pursuing their careers in Ontario, Canada. The researchers utilized a collaborative autoethnography approach developed by Ngunjiri et al. (2010) to share and analyze their experiences. This involved four key steps: preliminary data collection, subsequent data collection, data analysis and interpretation, and report writing. Through this iterative process, they engaged in both individual and team activities, revisiting previous steps to enhance data collection, analysis, or interpretation as needed. The findings revealed the unique obstacles that they encountered from various sources, including society, schools, students, and native-speaking colleagues. These challenges encompassed systemic discrimination against minority Asian professionals when recrediting their credentials, marginalizing the hiring process and being treated as outsiders within the field. By amplifying their unheard voices, the researchers aim to contribute to a more inclusive and equitable English as a Second Language (ESL) industry in Ontario.

Chapter 4
Coloniality and Whiteness in Evangelical ESL Classrooms 73
    Ruthanne Hughes, University of South Carolina, USA

This chapter ethnographically investigates how ideologies of whiteness and missions interact in an evangelical English language school in South Carolina. Using discourse analysis of classroom observations and interviews with five teachers across eleven classes, the chapter explores how whiteness is central to but unmarked in the presentation of American culture that students are socialized into, and how legacies of colonialism and assimilationist strategies are upheld in the presentation of white evangelical culture as equivalent to American culture. The ideologies described here demonstrate how contemporary practices of evangelical ESL programs continue to reflect a lingering history of colonialism and white supremacy in which the field of English teaching has long been implicated (Han & Varghese, 2019; Kim, 2019; Kubota, 2001, 2021; Pennycook, 2002; Vaccino-Salvadore, 2021; Vandrick, 1999). It is important to note where the legacy of these movements remains so that biases and harmful practices can be confronted and ameliorated.

Section 2
Language and Identity

Chapter 5
Backing Into Race: Immigration, Identity, and Social Movement Theory in English Language
Teacher Education..98
    Tonda Liggett, Linfield University, USA

This chapter focuses on more accurate and in-depth analyses of immigration in relation to individual identity factors as a way to better understand the specific role of race in broader relations of power within English language teaching. Using data from a narrative case study to account for various positionalities, this chapter proposes a general framework for English language teacher education that draws on aspects of social movement theory to analyze contextual factors of immigration, such as migration channels, settlement in urban/rural localities and human capital, and transnationalism. By incorporating specific aspects of social movement theory, an intersectional approach to ELT education holds promise of preparing teachers to identify racism, power, and gaps in support for their multilingual students.

Chapter 6
Belonging and Legitimacy for French Language Teachers: A Visual Analysis of Raciolinguistic
Discourses 116
    Mimi Masson, Université de Sherbrooke, Canada
    Simone Ellene Cote, Independent Researcher, Canada

With the ongoing French as a second language (FSL) teacher shortage crisis driving multi-million-dollar expenditures from governments, professional associations, and school boards, little attention has turned towards identifying systemic issues, rooted in racial ideologies, which may be impacting FSL teachers' desire to stay (or even enter) into the profession. In this chapter, using visual narratives and arts-based research methods, the authors applied LangCrit and raciolingusitics to examine future FSL teachers' discourses about French as a language/culture and learning French and teaching French. The data collected over a year, showcasing three participants, reveal the vastly different positionalities entrenched in complex interactions with language standard ideologies, native-speakerism, colonialism and racism. The authors ask, then, how stakeholders and teacher education programs might account for these differing lived realities when it comes to recruiting and preparing future FSL teachers for long-term success in the profession.

Chapter 7
Expanding Understandings of Race in Postsecondary Language Classrooms: A Call for
Multiraciality in Teacher Identity Research.. 150
    Marcela Hebbard, The University of Texas Rio Grande Valley, USA

While issues of race in relation to teacher identity have been addressed in language education research, they have often been confined to special issues. Factors contributing to the "absent-present" nature of race include an imbalanced focus on intersectionality which tends to prioritize the teacher's linguistic identity over other social categories, such as race and the persistent dichotomy between the idealized native speaker and non-native speaker. To broaden the understandings of race in teacher identity research within postsecondary language classrooms, this chapter advocates for considering the notion of multiraciality. To support these arguments, results from a critical discourse analysis (CDA) of four empirical studies are presented. The analysis demonstrates that race is often perceived as fixed and singular. The findings suggest that language educators and researchers should engage in critical thinking about how they describe and racially classify students and participants.

Chapter 8
Language, Identity, and Racism in Postsecondary Classrooms 172
Michael Olayinka Gbadegesin, Lead City University, Nigeria
Rachel Oluwafisayo Aluko, Lead City University, Nigeria

Language, identity, and racism are three concepts that define people's attitudes in all facets of relationship. The system of interrelatedness which exists among the three concepts of language, identity, and racism can therefore be said to be reflective. This study investigated elements of language used in foregrounding identity and racism in multiracial classroom settings. The study gathered data through a self-designed Google questionnaire of a mixed structure. Forty Nigerian graduate students studying in different parts of the world were selected for the research. The study shows that use of language to establish identity and racism is covert in postsecondary classrooms of the selected respondents; hence, expression of racism among learners is mostly done unconsciously and basically unintended.

Section 3
Interrogating Race and Racism in Postsecondary Language Classrooms

Chapter 9
Empowering Linguistic Diversity: Theory Into Practice in Multilingual Writing Classrooms 193
Anita Chaudhuri, University of British Columbia, Canada
Jordan Stouck, University of British Columbia, Canada

The chapter uses the case of multilingual students to discuss how teaching and learning practices in Canadian writing classrooms must examine "systems and structures of linguicism, racism, and classism, which are interrelated and continuously shaping one another" to develop an understanding of linguistic racism. A critical dialogic approach was used to listen to the study participants and explore strategies to promote decolonial practice in the writing classroom and inform literature on Canadian multilingual pedagogy. The chapter identifies themes of diversity, curriculum design and instructional practice aligned with linguistic justice practices, and perceptions of success and challenges to recommend theoretical standpoints and examples of classroom practice. Through this process of negotiating theory into practice, the authors move from a focus on linguistically and culturally responsive pedagogy toward sustaining and revitalizing pedagogy. They conclude with macro-level strategies and a call to promote and sustain linguistic justice.

Chapter 10
Writing Centers' Praxis Is Not Neutral but Raced: Collaborative Ethnography 218
Daniel Chang, Simon Fraser University, Canada
Qinghua Chen, The Education University of Hong Kong, Hong Kong
Angel Mei Yi Lin, Simon Fraser University, Canada

This chapter begins by questioning the existing practices of writing centre tutoring. Based on the first author's writing centre tutoring experience and some artifacts, such as consultation notes, consultation forms, and feedback on student essays, the authors question whether the writing centre is truly a safe and neutral space for post-secondary writers and whether writing tutoring feedback contains some Eurocentric racial discourses that are complicit and coded in a way that sounds so called objective. Drawing on Lemke's principle of intertextuality, the authors highlight how standardized academic writing expectations have been unconsciously normalized and naturalized in writing centre tutoring discussions, thereby reinforcing the tutor's authority. In the end, we are in the position to look for an alternative, transformative change in the writing centre tutoring practice and a structural shift that can go beyond "remedial writing service provider."

Chapter 11
A Textbook Case of Antiracism: Course Readings and Critical Pedagogy for Multilingual First-Year University Writers 241
    Srividya Natarajan, King's University College, Canada
    Emily Pez, King's University College, Canada

The pedagogic assumption that English is not only a target language for international students and other L2 English users, but also a metonym for the desirable culture to which they must assimilate is still prevalent in many Canadian institutions. This chapter discusses how two teacher-practitioners wrote a first-year writing (FYW) textbook for multilingual students, drawing on critical pedagogy to resist this form of white linguistic and epistemic supremacy while also empowering multilingual writers and resolving the vexed question of content in writing textbooks. In this chapter, the authors describe their fruitless search for a suitable textbook, their decision to write their own, their articulation of the principles that would guide their composing process, the frameworks they drew upon, and the secondary research that supported their choices as they created FYW learning materials that were antiracist and anti-linguicist but supportive of the academic success of multilingual students within the prevailing assessment ecologies in their institution.

Chapter 12
Implications of Multilingual Students' Stories for Promoting Linguistic Justice in Higher Education: Insights From Oral History Interviews 265
    Kamila Kinyon, University of Denver, USA

This chapter explores multilingual students' experiences and addresses ways that institutions of higher learning can best celebrate and support multilingual learners. Challenging the long-standing deficit model, many researchers have used raciolinguistic and translingual concepts to reframe multilingualism as an asset. The author draws on these frameworks in contextualizing her oral history research collecting multilingual students' stories. This year-long study conducted in 2022-23 was funded by an internal grant at a private U.S. university in the Rocky Mountain region. Eleven multilingual students with diverse native languages and countries of origin were interviewed about their perceptions of their native languages as heritage languages, their academic experiences, and other aspects of their lived experiences. After documenting and analyzing these stories, the author offers suggestions for what institutions of higher learning can do to best institute linguistic justice on their increasingly multilingual campuses.

Chapter 13
Translanguaging or English Monolanguaging? Exploring Postsecondary Students' Perceptions of
Linguistic Human Rights in Pakistan's Sindh Province 290
    Ameer Ali, Government Arts and Commerce College, Larkano, Pakistan
    Maya Khemlani David, University of Malaya, Malaysia
    Shahnawaz Tunio, Government Arts and Commerce College, Larkano, Pakistan

This study explores postsecondary students' perceptions of translanguaging and its nexus with linguistic human rights in Pakistan's Sindh province. English monolanguaging policy in higher educational institutions in Sindh has been seen as a ladder for upward social mobility. This monolingualism has posed challenges to linguistic diversity and linguistic human rights in the province (Sindh) that is multilingual. Interviews conducted via WhatsApp with postsecondary students in Sindh showed the popularity of translanguaging in contrast to English monolanguaging. Responses provided by participants were coded and qualitatively analyzed. Findings demonstrated how translanguaging could help provide and protect linguistic human rights.

Chapter 14
A Systematized Review of Anti-Racist Pedagogical Strategies 306
    Teresa Holden, University of Windsor, Canada
    Clayton Smith, University of Windsor, Canada

Racism permeates postsecondary language classrooms around the world which affects the experiences and learning outcomes of language students, namely those who study English as an additional language and English as a foreign language, referred to as additional language learners (ALLs), English as a second language (ESL), or English language learners (ELLs). Through an interrogation of the connection between race and language instruction, this chapter discusses anti-racist practices that interfere with language teaching in higher education. It presents a systematized review that aims to critically examine existing literature on the interrogation of racism within higher education with a focus on anti-racist pedagogical strategies. Critical Race Theory (CRT) guides the analysis and highlights the underlying power structures and systemic racism that shape language education. This review finds evidence of epistemological racism, linguistic biases, White supremacy, and English language dominance in the higher education language classroom. Recommendations for teacher practice are made.

Compilation of References 325

About the Contributors 362

Index 367

Preface

In this increasingly globalized world, national boundaries are getting increasingly blurry. Globalization calls on applying pluralistic insights to moving from "uniform knowledge and hierarchical communities" to hybridity (McGroarty 2010, p. 20), shifting from homogeneity to heterogeneity, from Eurocentrism to decolonialization (Kramsch, 1993), and from "ethnocentrism" to "ethnorelativism" (Bennett, 1993, p. 22) to challenge global inequalities.

Interrogating Race and Racism in Postsecondary Language Classrooms is a timely and much-needed book in the scholarly inquiry and language education in the contemporary world. The book was born in the post-pandemic era and in times of wars, violence, and injustice. It investigates race and racism in postsecondary language classrooms, how race intersects with language, how power impacts and shapes language teaching and learning, and how hegemony and ideology perpetuate linguistic injustice and discrimination against racially minoritized students and teachers. It examines how racism has created institutional, structural, and individual barriers for language teachers and learners in higher education, as well as proposing potential strategies to combat racism, colonialism, and linguicism. *Interrogating Race and Racism in Postsecondary Language Classrooms* contributes to the existing raciolinguistic research with data-driven studies to investigate race, racism, language, as well as the interplay between race and language by offering valuable alternative pedagogies for teaching the dominant language (e.g., English and French) for empowerment and emancipation. As well, *Interrogating* employs diverse perspectives from instructors, students, faculty, and teacher candidates, not only in teacher education, but also in ESL, EFL, TESOL, FSL, writing classrooms, and at writing centers.

CHAPTER OVERVIEW

There are 14 chapters in this book, including research-based studies, stories, counter-stories, and racialized experiences through multiple research methods, such as narrative inquiry, critical discourse analysis, visual analysis, narrative case study, critical dialogic approach, collaborative ethnography, systematic literature review, collaborative autoethnography, document analysis, interviews, observation, surveys, and introspective method. Three major sections are interconnected with one other: "Language and Race," "Language and Identity," and "Interrogating Race and Racism in Postsecondary Language Classrooms." We originally planned to solicit manuscripts related to the English language teaching only in this collection. To our joy, we later received an interesting chapter on French as a Second Language (FSL) teachers. After the breakout of the riots in France in summer 2023, we decided to include the non-English language (e.g., French) in this volume to hear diverse voices in different language and social settings.

Preface

Section 1: Language and Race

Section 1, "Language and Race," starts with an introductory chapter to provide an overview of the volume, by exploring the concepts of "race," "racism," and "racialization," as well as major conceptual frameworks and key themes in race and language studies, with seven anti-racist pedagogies proposed at the end of the chapter. Then, contributors in Section 1 examine racism, linguicism, and discrimination that raciolinguistically minoritized students, English/French as a Second Language (ESL/FSL) teachers, and teacher candidates have suffered from in the dominant society.

Chapter 1, Xiangying Huo's "Introduction: Interrogating Race and Racism in Postsecondary Language Classrooms," mainly explores Critical Race Theory, raciolinguistics, and Critical Language and Race Theory to examine race, racism, and racialization, as well as intersectionality between language and race, language and ideology, language and identity, and race and pedagogy. Chapter 1 discusses the importance of these theoretical frameworks, their integration, and the connection of these frameworks with the volume, explores the links of language with ideology and identity, investigates seven antiracist and decolonial pedagogies, and calls for action on combatting racism in higher education language classrooms to advance racial equity and enact linguistic and social justice.

Chapter 2, "The Terrorized Experiences of Latina Bilingual Pre-Service Teachers With Language and Race," by Lucy Arellano Jr., Ana K. Soltero López, and Delia M. Carrizales, involves a study informed by the raciolinguistic framework and the Critical Race Theory, with a narrative inquiry study—English and Spanish bilingual Latina pre-service teachers in California and Texas. This chapter has well explained how systemic oppression manifests into teacher shortages with a compelling conclusion—"You terrorize and racialize them" which will leave many thought-provoking questions about teacher candidates' educational praxis.

Chapter 3, "Overcoming Racism and Discrimination: Experiences of Vietnamese ESL Teachers in Canada," is an inquiry paper, written by Elena Tran and Thu Thi-Kim Le, with a collaborative autoethnographic method that explores the linguistic, sociopolitical, and hiring challenges which internationally trained ESL teachers experienced when seeking employment in Ontario, Canada. It contributes to the development of a more equitable ESL industry in Canada.

Chapter 4, "Coloniality and Whiteness in Evangelical ESL Classrooms," by Ruthanne Hughes, is a South Carolina based study with the ethnographic research design to explore the ideologies of Whiteness and missions in ESL classrooms. The research speaks critically of the connection between Whiteness and missionary efforts in the ESL classroom to integrate students into Eurocentric, White evangelical culture. It includes a lot of interesting discussion of how colonial practices are present and used in ESL classrooms to promote White Christianity.

Section 2: Language and Identity

In Section 2, "Language and Identity," our authors employ various approaches to investigate the intersectionality between language and identity, identity and race/racism, and legitimacy and belonging.

In Chapter 5, "Backing into Race: Immigration, Identity, and Social Movement Theory for English Language Teacher Education," Tonda Liggett adopts a robust theoretical framework grounded in the social movement theory. This chapter resorts to a narrative case study with in-depth discussion and intersectionality between racism, immigration, and other positionalities. It makes an important contribution to teacher education by debunking racist assumptions and providing valuable strategies.

Chapter 6, "Belonging and Legitimacy for French Language Teachers: A Visual Analysis of Raciolinguistic Discourses," employs an arts-based approach and visual narratives to examine French as a second language (FSL) teachers' belonging and legitimacy in Canada. Mimi Masson and Simone Ellene Côté link FSL teacher identity to race which has not yet to be explored. The contributors also challenge native speakerism and standard ideology with valuable implications. Their unique perspective and the visual analysis research method make this chapter original.

Chapter 7, "Expanding Understandings of Race in Postsecondary Language Classrooms: A Call for Multiraciality in Teacher Identity Research," written by Marcela Hebbard, employs critical discourse analysis and the raciolinguistic lens to call for the incorporation of multiraciality with identity research by examining four recent empirical studies on teacher identity and making insightful recommendations for language educators and researchers.

Michael Olayinka Gbadegesin and Rachel Oluwafisayo Aluko, in Chapter 8, "Language, Identity, and Racism in Postsecondary Classroom," examine the interconnectivity of language and identity as elements of racism and uses the raciolinguistic perspective and the intersectional theory, with a comprehensive questionnaire and literature search with the involvement of 40 Nigerian students studying in seven different countries across five continents.

Section 3: Interrogating Race and Racism in Postsecondary Language Classrooms

Section 3, "Interrogating Race and Racism in Postsecondary Language Classrooms," includes an assortment of theories—Critical Race Theory, Critical Language and Race Theory, and the raciolinguistic perspective with a rich collection of innovative and liberatory anti-racist, anti-oppressive, decolonial pedagogies.

Chapter 9, "Empowering Linguistic Diversity: Theory Into Practice in Multilingual Writing Classrooms," by Anita Chaudhuri and Jordan Stouck, is a well-conceived chapter with mixed methods to examine a writing course at a Canadian university that allows the course development journey to be told. There are strong research findings, as well as guiding principles to promote linguistic justice along with pedagogical and assessment practices for instructors to consider. This chapter has great potential for enhancing teaching in this field by implementing culturally responsive pedagogy and especially culturally sustaining pedagogy.

Daniel Chang, Qinghua Chen, and Angel Mei Yi Lin, using a collaborative ethnographic research design at a Canadian postsecondary writing center, have proposed an anti-deficit, non-remedial writing assessment approach—intertextuality in Chapter 10, "Writing Centers' Praxis Is Not Neutral but Raced: Collaborative Ethnography." This chapter contributes to the decolonial writing assessment by deconstructing writing centers, dismantling the standard English norm, and advocating linguistic justice to the development of student voice and authorship in the "co-journeying" tutoring sessions.

Chapter 11, "A Textbook Case of Antiracism: Course Readings and Critical Pedagogy for Multilingual First-Year Writers," by Srividya Natarajan and Emily Pez, discusses the journey that the two authors went on to create their own textbook for international students who took first-year writing courses at Canadian universities that will represent diverse cultures and linguistic backgrounds and address international students' raciolinguistic predicaments for international students. This chapter is helpful to writing instructors to rethink about their teaching materials and redesign curriculum for equity, diversity, and inclusion.

Chapter 12, "Implications of Multilingual Students' Stories for Promoting Linguistic Justice in Higher Education: Insights From Oral History Interviews," written by Kamila Kinyon, aims to enact linguistic justice and advocate pedagogical changes through multilingual students' stories, as well as perceiving these students' languages as resources instead of deficits. It uses oral history interviews with a focus on creating better teaching practices and space where multilingual students' voices can be heard which promises a solid set of recommendations for professional and teaching practice.

Chapter 13, "Translanguaging or English Monolanguaging? Exploring Postsecondary Students' Perceptions of Linguistic Human Rights in Pakistan's Sindh Province," by Ameer Ali, Mya Khemlani David, and Shahnawaz Tunio, is based on a well-developed study that lends itself to more fully understanding of student perceptions of translanguaging and how translanguaging connects with human rights with carefully crafted research questions through interviews with thematic analysis and careful discussion. It identifies the significant role that translanguaging can play in shaping equitable and inclusive language policies in education.

Chapter 14, "A Systematic Review of Anti-Racist Pedagogical Strategies," written by Teresa Holden and Clayton Smith, explores second language education globally and emphasizes the potential impact of language education on societal dynamics, advocating for pedagogies that contribute to a just and inclusive educational environment. This chapter underscores the oppression faced by non-White and non-native English speakers in language education and serves not only as a systematic review of anti-racist pedagogical strategies but also integrates a critical examination of language education's role in perpetuating or challenging existing power structures.

TARGET AUDIENCE

This book is intended for scholars, researchers, faculty, instructors, and professionals in English language teaching, non-English language education, higher education, applied linguistics, sociolinguistics, educational linguistics, anti-racist education, critical multilingual studies, translingual studies, and those who are interested in the research of race, language, and the area of teaching English cross-culturally and translingually in postsecondary classrooms, such as faculty, instructors, and educational developers who design the inclusive, anti-racist, and anti-colonial curriculum, and administrators and policy makers who oversee academic especially language programs. The book will also be useful for teacher candidates, non-native English-speaking students, undergraduates, and graduate students in TESOL/ESL/EFL and French as a Second Language (FSL) programs.

SIGNIFICANCE OF THIS BOOK

First, the volume has seamlessly applied and integrated major theoretical frameworks (e.g., Critical Race Theory, raciolinguistics, Critical Language and Race Theory, Latinx Critical Race Theory, Social Movement Theory, Intersectional Theory, and intertextuality) to study race and language, and adopted original research methods (mentioned earlier) with contributors' empirical studies for scholarly, critical, and novel inquiries to enrich the conceptual frameworks and the research methods of raciolinguistic research.

Second, the volume embraces various discourses, narratives, stories, and counter-stories in different geographic and language teaching contexts. As an African proverb goes, "Until lions have their historians, tales of the hunt shall always glorify the hunter." In this volume, marginalized voices and different perspectives are heard from Africa, Asia, and North America, including Nigeria, Malaysia, China, Pakistan, Vietnam, Canada, and the United States. Such marginalized and unique voice acts as a "retaliatory weapon" (Ladson-Billings, 2023, p. 376) and "a manifestation of humanity… through resistance to oppression" (Bell, 1990, p. 379) to refute White superiority, power, hegemony, and unjust society for racial equity and linguistic human rights.

Thirdly, this volume includes the collection of liberatory and emancipatory anti-racist, anti-oppressive pedagogies in global postsecondary language teaching contexts to call for inclusive and multimodal modes of learning (e.g., multilingual and translingual approaches, culturally responsive pedagogy, culturally sustaining pedagogy, critical pedagogy, and translanguaging) and thus to raise fundamental questions about the role of universities in challenging racism and implementing ethical internationalization to tackle global hierarchy and hegemony (Huo, 2020). These innovative pedagogies embrace multiple anti-racist and anti-oppressive approaches, with effective pedagogical practices and valuable recommendations, will make a significant contribution to language education and raciolinguistic studies.

Last but not least, the book uses the perspective of intersectionality between language and race in higher education classrooms by problematizing raciolinguistic injustice and hierarchy with the monolingual and monocultural norm as a frame a reference, combating racism, colonialism, linguicism, linguistic terrorism, and native speakerism, as well as advocating changes and pedagogical paradigm shifts. Thus, the volume has important theoretical, methodological, and pedagogical implications for language teaching and raciolinguistic research, and will thus provide researchers, policy makers, educators, and practitioners with effective strategies and possible alternatives to interrogate race and language in postsecondary language classrooms so as to teach the dominant language for justice and liberation (Huo, 2020).

Xiangying Huo
University of Toronto, Canada

Clayton Smith
University of Windsor, Canada

REFERENCES

Bell, D. (1990). Racial realism—after we're gone: Prudent speculations on America in a post-racial epoch. *Saint Louis University Law Journal, 34*(3), 393–406.

Bennett, M. J. (1993). Towards ethnorelativism: A developmental model of intercultural sensitivity. In R. M. Paige (Ed.), *Education for the intercultural experience* (pp. 21–71). Intercultural Press.

Huo, X. Y. (2020). *Higher education internationalization and English language instruction: Intersectionality of race and language in Canadian universities*. Springer. doi:10.1007/978-3-030-60599-5

Kramsch, C. (1993). *Context and culture in language teaching*. Oxford University Press.

Ladson-Billings, G. (2023). Critical Race Theory—What It Is Not! In E. Taylor, D. Gillborn, & G. Ladson-Billings (Eds.), *Foundations of critical race theory in education* (3rd ed., pp. 369–380). Routledge.

McGroarty, M. E. (2010). Language ideologies. In N. H. Hornberger & S. L. Makay (Eds.), *Sociolinguistics and language education* (pp. 3–39). Multilingual Matters. doi:10.21832/9781847692849-003

Acknowledgment

We would like to acknowledge the help of all people involved in this project, particularly our authors and reviewers who took part in the review process. Our book would not have been completed without their support.

First, we would like to thank our authors for their hard work and contributions. Our heartfelt gratitude goes to each chapter's author(s) who dedicated their time and expertise to this book.

Second, we wish to acknowledge the valuable contributions of the reviewers regarding the improvement of quality, coherence, and content presentation of our chapters. Most of the authors also served as reviewers and we highly appreciate their double tasks. We would also like to thank our external reviewers for their knowledge, wisdom, and devotion of their time to our book.

Thirdly, we would like to thank the IGI Global team for its assistance with the whole process.

Last but not least, our sincere thanks go to every colleague we know or do not know all over the world to spread the word about our book and to help promote our call for proposals. We deeply appreciate their encouragement and support.

Section 1
Language and Race

Chapter 1
Introduction:
Interrogating Race and Racism in Postsecondary Language Classrooms

Xiangying Huo
https://orcid.org/0000-0001-8165-1486
University of Toronto, Canada

ABSTRACT

The introductory chapter interrogates race and racism in postsecondary language classrooms by mainly exploring Critical Race Theory, raciolinguistics, and Critical Language and Race Theory to examine race, racism, and racialization, as well as intersectionality between language and race, language and ideology, language and identity, and race and pedagogy. Chapter 1 discusses the importance of these theoretical frameworks, their integration with one another, and the connections of these frameworks with the volume, explores the links of language with ideology and identity, investigates seven antiracist and decolonial pedagogies (i.e., translingual pedagogy, multilingual pedagogy of writing, plurilingual approach, translanguaging, culturally responsive, relevant, and sustaining pedagogies, critical language awareness pedagogy, and multiliteracies pedagogy), and calls for action on combatting racism in higher education language classrooms to advance racial equity and enact linguistic and social justice.

This chapter discusses the intersectionality between language and race, language and ideology, and language and identity, as well as calling for antiracist, decolonial pedagogies in language education. The first section introduces the concepts of "race," "racism," and "racialization." It then discusses Critical Race Theory (CRT), raciolinguistics, and other conceptual orientations (e.g., cohesive theory of race and Critical Language and Race Theory), as well as their integration with one another, links to this volume, and critiques of CRT. In the second section, the intersection of language and ideology is explored. The chapter turns to the examination of the interplay of language and identity in its third section. The last section explores race and pedagogy by discussing seven key antiracist and anti-oppressive pedagogies in the field.

DOI: 10.4018/978-1-6684-9029-7.ch001

LANGUAGE AND RACE

From Quijano's (2000) "coloniality of power" [i.e., superiority versus inferiority based on power relations and social hierarchies (Maldonado-Torres, 2007)] to "coloniality of language" referring to linguistic power relations (Veronelli, 2015, p. 113), English has become a "colonial language" (Kachru, 1986, p. 5) and a "language for oppression" (Kachru, 1986, p. 13). With a colonial history and as an imperial legacy, English has created a hegemonic construct that assumes monolingualism and monoculturalism as frames of reference (Kiczkowiak & Lowe, 2018). Language is raced and race is languaged (Alim et al., 2016). Race and language are historically interweaved and have co-constructed to subordinate raciallinguistically minoritized people (Hudley, 2016). Language and race embrace language and racism, and language and racialization (Alim et al., 2020), as well as entailing "racial politics" (Alim, 2016b, p. 36). Roth-Gordon (2016) summarizes that deep-rooted racism and the disenfranchised class "cannot afford to ignore language as a critical resource for the construction of racial meaning" (Alim, 2016a, p. 27). There has also been awareness of the link between race and language in non-English languages (Talburt & Stewart, 1999).

Race, Racism, and Racialization

Race

DuBois (1989) declares that "the problem of the 20th century is the problem of the color line" (p. 29). Hesse (2016) contends that "[R]ace is not in the eye of the beholder or on the body of the objectified"; it is "an inherited western, modern-colonial practice of violence, assemblage, superordination, exploitation, and segregation… demarcating the colonial rule of Europe over non-Europe" (p. viii). Condon (2007) manifests that the society is structured and stratified based on how people are raced. Race is not isolated from the setting where it was produced — colonialism (Esch et al., 2020); race has been used to justify colonialism as "a by-product," "an intrinsic part," and "part of the intestines of empire" (Pieterse, 1990, p. 223).

Racism

"Racism is a global White supremacy and is itself a political system, a particular power structure of formal and informal rule, privilege, socioeconomic advantages, and wealth and power opportunities" (Mills, 1997, p. 3). Consequently, racism obstructs "our liberal democratic ethos" (Hochschild, 1984, p. 3). Hudley (2016) suggests that "racism-based language is one of the last acceptable forms of racism" (p. 361). Alim (2016a) argues that instead of "erasing race," scholars should make joint efforts to eradicate "all forms of language-based racism and discrimination" (p. 27). There are different types of racism as categorized by different scholars. According to Hudley (2016), racism takes the forms of internalized racism (e.g., Racially minoritized people doubt their cultures' value influenced by the distorted information conveyed to them), personally mediated racism (i.e., biased perceptions and stereotypic assumptions based on race), and institutional racism (at the societal, governmental, or global level). Following Kubota and Lin (2009), there are institutional/structural racism and epistemological racism (based on epistemological knowledge that values White culture).

Introduction

Racialization

Racialization, synonymous with racial classification, is "markedness...operating against an unmarked background of what social actors perceive as normative" (Uriciuoli, 2011, p. E113) and is socially constructed (Luke & Lin, 2006). It is the root of marginalization and exclusion of racially minoritized people (Flores & Garcia, 2020). Racialization, stemming from colonialism and capitalism, has produced racial discrimination and social injustice (Alim et al., 2020). Alim (2016b) asserts that "ethnoracially minoritized" (p. 48) people are "ideologically positioned and racialized as 'people of color'" (p. 35). The "racialization of language" (Pimental, 2011) subjugates, subordinates, and dehumanizes racialized communities. Scholars indicate intersectionality between language and race (Alim et al., 2016a; Kubota & Lin, 2009) and racially minoritized people are victims of racism, linguicism (Kubota et al., 2021), and "raciolinguicism" (Esch et al., 2020, p. 401).

Linguicism (i.e., linguistic racism), similar to racism (Skutnabb-Kangas, 1998), refers to "ideologies, structures, and practices which are used to legitimate, effectuate, and reproduce an unequal division of power and resources (both material and immaterial) between groups which is defined on the basis of language" (Phillipson, 1992, p. 47). Holliday (2005) shows that linguicism takes the forms of both consciousness and subconsciousness, explicitly and implicitly, abstraction and concreteness. English linguistic imperialism, as a sub-category of linguicism which "operates globally as a key medium of Centre-Periphery relations" (Phillipson, 1992, p. 56) with the "dominance of English" "asserted and maintained by the establishment and continuous reconstitution of structural and cultural inequalities between English and other languages," has led to "Anglocentricity," ethnocentrism, and monolingualism (Phillipson, 1992, p. 47). Linguistic imperialism and linguicism have switched from "sticks, carrots, ideas" (p. 55) in colonialism to language ideology imposed by the Center on the Periphery to strengthen the Center's imperialist power and dominant status (Phillipson, 1992). Such linguistic injustice, grounded on race, class, or ethnicity, others minority languages and cultures (Breckner, 2019; Wood, 2019). Skutnabb-Kangas (1998) describes the danger of linguicism in this way: "we are still living with linguistic wrongs… Unless we work fast, excising the cancer of monolingual reductionism may come too late, when the patient, the linguistic (and cultural) diversity in the world, is already beyond saving" (p. 12). Rosa (2016) suggests that further research needs to study the relationship between "minute linguistic forms" and "ethnoracial categories across contexts and scales" to probe into "visible" and "audible" racialization "in everyday interactions" (p. 79).

Theoretical Frameworks in Race and Language Research

This section examines major theoretical frameworks in race and language research, including Critical Race Theory (CRT), raciolinguistics, and other conceptual orientations (i.e., cohesive theory of race and Critical Language and Race Theory). This part defines and explains these conceptual frameworks, discusses their connection, significance of these frameworks, their relevance to education as well as to this volume, and critiques on CRT.

CRITICAL RACE THEORY

Critical Race Theory (CRT) interrogates racial discrimination by examining the root of racial inequality and proposing strategies to redress social injustice. There are several key tenets of CRT.

Key tenets of CRT

Racism is normal. CRT scholars point out that "ordinariness" makes racism invisible and unidentifiable to White people (Delgado & Stefancic, 2023, p. 8). Taylor (2023) clarifies that the erasure of racism is a result of White supremacy which other systems are evaluated against. Because the persuasive influence of racism and normalization of White superiority, White people are unconscious of "whiteness as a construction" (Gillborn, 2023, p. 45), or the privilege which they enjoy, or the racial oppression that subordinate groups have suffered from.

Race as social construction. Race is a social construct and a signifier (Morrison, 1992). Delgado and Stefancic (2023) declare that "race and races are products of social thought and relations" and that "races are categories that society invents, manipulates, or retires when convenient" (p. 9). That means "the power of a social reality" generates inequity and inequality (Ladson-Billings, 2023b, p. 373).

Interest convergence. Critical Race Theory researchers make commitments to social justice by critiquing interest convergence and Whiteness as a property (Solorzano, 1997; Solorzano & Yosso, 2001) which are two important concepts and tools in CRT (Charles, 2008). Interest convergence relates to "alignment"—converging the interests of the dominant class with those of the underclass (Ladson-Billings, 2023b, p. 372), implying that minoritized people may succeed only when their interests align with those of Whites (Bell, 2004). The second tool Whiteness as property is regarded as "the legal legitimation of expectations of power and control that enshrine the status quo as a neutral baseline, while masking the maintenance of white privilege and domination" (Harris, 1993, p. 1715). Whiteness as property ensures that White people are the sole beneficiaries (Gillborn, 2023), enjoying the exclusive rights belonging to the dominant class.

Differential racialization and its consequences. CRT scholars recognize that the dominant society racializes minoritized groups (Delgado & Stefancic, 2023). Since Whiteness is the standard, all other racialized groups are evaluated againt the White norm (Ladson-Billings, 2023a). Minority people are marginalized as "outsiders," "unknown entities," and "strangers" (James, 2010, p. 231). Two notions "intersectionality and antiessentialism" are entailed. Oftentimes, due to polar divisions in the society, it is difficult to study intersectionality (Ladson-Billings, 2023b) that connects race with class, gender (James, 2012; Solorzano & Yosso, 2001), and "religion, ethnicity, national origin, and/or birthplace" (Delgado & Stefancic, 2023, p. 231). Essentialism over-generalizes and stereotypes the attributes of a single group (Ladson-Billings, 2023b), yet everybody has multiple identities instead of as being categorized as one fixed group or entity (Delgado & Stefancic, 2023) despite their "group identities" (Ladson-Billings, 2023b, p. 374).

Narrative and voice. Narrative, storytelling (Bell, 1987), and counter-storytelling (Solorzano, 1997), as powerful weapons, counter racial hierarchy with the unique voice (Delgado & Stefancic, 2023) and experiential knowledge (Solorzano & Yosso, 2001) from people of color. Such "positioned perspective" (Lawrence, 1992) or "subjectivity of perspective" (Taylor, 2023, p. 7) serves as a "distinct political strategy" (Crenshaw, 1988, as cited in Taylor, 2023, p. 7) and "transformative resistance strategy" (Bell, 2023, p. 35) to problematize racial injustice. Delgado (1995) identifies noticeable differences between White people's and non-Whites' vantage points as Whites see it as "real history," "truth," or "objective science" (Ladson-Billings, 2023, p. 376) instead of as the "perspective" (Delgado, 1995). By contrast, minority people's narrative, being "a form of knowing" (Lawrence, 1992, p. 2283), challenges the notions of meritocracy and color blindness—the main components of the dominant ideology (Solorzano, 1997; Solorzano & Yosso, 2001). Consistent with Delgado and Stefancic (2023), Black, Asian, Latina, and other racialized contributors in this volume depict their subordinate experiences with narratives and refute race and racism in their language teaching as "resistance to oppression" to "struggle for freedom" (Bell, 1990, p. 379).

Links of CRT to Education and this Volume

Ladson-Billings (2023b) notices close links between CRT and education in that CRT emphasizes the intersectionality of class, gender, and national origins, and challenges dominant ideologies, such as objectivity and race neutrality (Solorzano, 1997; Solorzano & Yosso, 2001), using counter-stories and narrative as a "pedagogical tool" through intentional and reflective "listening techniques" to invigorate and validate education (Taylor, 2023, p. 8). CRT's tenets are aligned with "equal opportunity" and "equal treatment" schools and civil rights that activists strive for (Ladson-Billings, 2023a, p. 22). Additionally, CRT scholars' interdisciplinary perspective of curriculum, instruction, assessment, funding, and desegregation is also relevant to education (Solorzano, 1997; Solorzano & Yosso, 2001). Besides the connection between CRT and education theories (Taylor, 2023), Gillborn (2023) denounces "Education Policy as an Act of White Supremacy" in the chapter title to battle with racial inequity and social injustice and call for educational reforms. The inclusion and reinforcement of the Critical Race Theory in this volume mainly lie in CRT's intersectionality between race, class, and "other forms of oppression" (Taylor, 2023, p. 8). As a powerful tool to challenge injustice and an impactful educational theory to guide the scholarly inquiries in this volume, CRT is used to advocate liberatory and emancipatory pedagogies and practices. It is highly relevant to postsecondary language classrooms. Since CRT represents racialized teachers' and students' perspectives, this collection of raciolinguistically minoritized contributors garner those subordinate experiences through narratives, stories, and counter-stories to "redirect the dominant gaze, to make it see from a new point of view what has been there all along" (Taylor, 2023, p. 6). These narratives challenge the dominant discourse and problematize racialized paradigms, let the dominant class hear underprivileged voices, and to readdress raciolinguistic inequity and injustice so as to call for pedagogical and social changes.

Critiques of CRT

Despite its great impact on race related studies, CRT is criticized for its "pessimistic" feature by treating racism as unconquerable. However, Gillborn (2023) has quoted Delgado and Stefancic's (2001) words: "Is medicine pessimistic because it focuses on diseases and traumas?" (p. 13) to refute those critiques and stress the CRT scholars' endeavor for greater equity. CRT has also received critiques regarding its devaluation of class. Instead of focusing on the intersection between race and class, scholars contend that an emphasis should be placed on how race, racial distinctions, and racism are deep-rooted in the sociopolitical system, generating racialized class relations (Darder & Torres, 2004). In addition, critiques on CRT are mainly surrounding its absence of the link of language to race, racialization (Anya, 2021), and language discrimination derived from racism (Baker-Bell, 2020). The raciolinguistic perspective proposed in recent years (Alim et al., 2016; Rosa & Flores, 2017) has complemented CRT by integrating race with language and interrogating power, racialization, and linguistic racism with race as the root cause.

Raciolinguistics

Grounded in the interconnection between race, identity, language, and teaching (Alim et al., 2016b; Flores & Rosa, 2015), the raciolinguistic perspective (Alim et al., 2016; Rosa & Flores, 2017) indicates the close intersection between language and race by investigating "how language is used as a means of social, political, and economic oppression" (Alim, 2016a, p. 27). There are five principles of raciolinguistics: 1) historical and contemporary co-naturalizations of race and language as part of the colonial formation of modernity, 2) perceptions of racial and linguistic difference, 3) regimentations of racial and linguistic categories, 4) racial and linguistic intersections and assemblages, and 5) contestations of racial and linguistic power formations (Rosa & Flores, 2017). Rosa and Flores (2017) point out that the raciolinguistic approach examines "how structures of privilege and power are reproduced or disrupted" to fight against White domination, "racial capitalism," and "racial and class inequities" (p. 21).

Informed by the raciolinguistic lens, the notion of "raceclass" was raised which "not only challenges the co-constitution of racial and class hierarchies, but also forges a joint critique of white supremacy and capitalism," uncovering power imbalance between the White, dominant class and the subordinate, racialized people (Rosa & Flores, 2017, p. 18) in "hyperracial times" (Alim, 2016a, p. 1). Lo (2016) also clarifies how "White Raciolinguistic Imaginaries" (p. 100) view Asian Americans as "racial others" (p. 99). Alim (2016b) further insists that the raciolinguistic perspective can help researchers think about alternative approaches to resisting racialization.

Links of Raciolinguistics to this Volume

As this volume concerns race and racism in language classrooms, the raciolinguistic framework fits the volume seamlessly by interrogating co-naturalization of language and race, racialization of minority students, teacher candidates, and language teachers in postsecondary language contexts, how power dominates raciolinguistic ideologies and impacts identity, how race shapes the way we view language, and "How language shapes our ideas about race" as indicated in Alim et al.'s (2016) book title. Multiple contributors in this volume have adopted the raciolinguistic framework to account for systemic racism and subordination of raciolinguistically minoritized students, in-service teachers, and preservice teachers in teacher education, and postsecondary writing, TESOL, and ESL classrooms for racial equity, linguistic justice, and social justice.

Other Conceptual Orientations

Hudley (2016) proposes the "cohesive theory of race" (p. 382) from educational, theoretical, and methodological perspectives by using mixed research methods and advocating the "racial linguistic social justice approach" (p. 399) to critique racialization and prevent the reproduction of racialization from occurring.

There is another important framework: "LangCrit"— a critical language and race theory. Incorporating a critical lens of race similar to CRT and aligned with the raciolinguistic perspective on "hearing language gaps" (Rosa & Flores, 2015, p. 77) by "listening subjects" impacted by raciolinguistic ideologies (Rosa & Flores, 2015, p. 78), LangCrit, according to Crump (2014), emphasizes the "intersection of the subject-as-heard and the subject-as-seen" (p. 207). It examines the "ways in which race, racism, and racialization intersect with issues of language, belonging, and identity" (pp. 207-208). LangCrit recognizes that racism is part of daily life and socially contrived. LangCrit connects different facets of identities and indicates that language [including (counter)storytelling] is interwoven with politics, history, and the society. LangCrit is linked to this volume as it supports the view that racialized people are first seen and judged by their colors, but not by their languages (Hill, 2010) which is helpful to challenge power which permeates language education and the dominant society and thus to reexamine language policies, practices, ideologies, and pedagogies in the racialized space. LangCrit resonates with the chapters collected in this volume which investigate "power in linguistic resources and spaces" to "understand how individuals do language" (Swift, 2020, p. 61). LangCrit also contributes to rethinking about language ideology that shapes identity in the ways how people view their identities by engaging with language and how "linguistic racialization" (Swift, 2020, p. 61) intertwines "racialized positionings" (Crump, 2014, p. 220), identity, and belonging which this volume deals with. As well, LangCrit is conductive to language studies, teaching, and pedagogies; besides, its critical perspective is particularly useful to this volume.

Intersection of Theoretical Frameworks

Critical Race Theory, raciolinguistics, and Critical Language and Race Theory intersect at the following junctions. First, CRT stresses race and other forms of oppression and is related to education especially with its salient feature of intersectionality (e.g., gender, nationality, and so on). Intersectionality is also exhibited in both raciolinguistics and LangCrit (e.g., between race and language) which is instrumental to language education and language studies. Hence, the intersectional lenses make these three frameworks converge. Second, all three frameworks acknowledge that race and racism produce injustice and discrimination. CRT places race and racism at the core by attributing persecution of racialized groups to color while the raciolinguistic framework stresses co-naturalization between race and language and LangCrit highlights the interplay between race and language as well. Thirdly, all the above frameworks problematize essentialism and normalization of racism in daily life while raciolinguistics added the layer of the essentialized "linguistic assumptions" (Rosa & Flores, 2023, p. 105) and LangCrit researchers refute essentialized concept of belonging (Crump, 2014). Fourthly, all three frameworks combat power, ideology, and White privilege. Furthermore, these frameworks address the important part that language plays. In CRT and LangCrit, narratives are used to help the subordinate class articulate its suppressed and forbidden voices. By comparison, through the raciolinguistic lens, language is the major ingredient of raciolinguistic studies. Last but not least, all these three frameworks concern identity, such as linguistic identity, racial identity, and social identity, and cultural identity. In the following section, raciolinguistic ideologies will be examined by fusing racial ideology with linguistic ideology.

LANGUAGE AND IDEOLOGY

Power and hierarchy, as discussed in previous conceptual frameworks, are maintained through raciolinguistic ideologies (Esch, 2020). Language is closely related to ideology, as well as identity (which will be explored in the next section: "Language and Identity"). In this part, raciolinguistic ideologies and standardization as ideology are discussed.

Raciolinguistic Ideologies

Ideology is relational with the close linkage between race and language (Rosa, 2019a) and between race and class (Valdes, 2017) — "Looking like a Language, Sounding like a Race" (Rosa, 2019a). Mackenzie (2014) demonstrates that "Within traditional EFL methodology there is an inbuilt ideological positioning of the students as outsider and failure—however proficient they become" (p. 8). Barrett (2006) also finds the connection between language ideology and racial inequality. The "deficit ideologies" justify the rectification of the languages used by racialized minority people to fix the "mismatch" between their languages and the normalized academic language (Flores & Garcia, 2020, p. 181). Consequently, based on Seidlhofer (2011), racialized people are forever losers "in an inescapable double bind" since they can neither obtain the prestigious status of native speakers, nor can they revise the language for their own use. They are "told that they got it wrong because they have the misfortune not to be native speakers" (p. 34).

Gorham (1999) contends that ideology is a key concept in stereotypical representation since ideology has economic, social, and political dimensions (James, 2010). Language is a commodity linked to linguistic, cultural, economic capital for social mobility and symbolic capital (Bourdieu, 1986). As sociopolitical power is shaped by White supremacy, Western superiority, and hegemony, entrenched in stereotypes about race, class language, and ethnicity (Fiske, 2018), Rosa and Burdick (2016) argue that power and privilege have created social class and linguistic hierarchy associated with global capitalism and political economy. As a result, subjectification (Shankar, 2006), materiality (Rosa & Burdick, 2016), and commodification of language (Block, 2008) perpetuate language ideology and regard the dominant language as a markable commodity (Block, 2008).

Standardization as Ideology

As English is the language of the elite in a lot of countries, it becomes a "natural language of higher education" and acts as a gatekeeper to minorities (Joseph & Ramani, 2006, p. 193). Seidlhofer (2011) notes that "Standard English ideology is a special case of standard language ideology," linked to "ethnopolitical, socioeconomic, and other interests" (p. 42). Standard English, equivalent to White English (Wheeler, 2016), is "an idea in the mind rather than a reality" and the mainstream strives to "keep the notion of a standard language alive in the public mind" (Tagg, 2012, p. 313). Milroy (1999) states that language ideology of "appropriateness" of English exits in the United Kingdom (based on class), in the United States (displayed by race), and is also pervasive in Canada (p. 178). Hegemony-related language ideologies are political and influential, affecting people's "common sense" and entrench norms (McGroarty, 2010, p. 4) by making "language correctness and purity" (p. 314) standards, codifying "politically correct" language (Seidlhofer, 2011, p. 57), and devaluing "politically incorrect language" (Hewings & Tagg, 2012, p. 1). Consequently, "Monoglossic Language ideologies" (by upholding monolingualism), converged with "Raciolinguistic ideologies" (Flores & Garcia, 2020, p. 180), or "raciolinguicism" (Esch et al., 2020, p. 401), caused by language hegemony and White supremacy (Huo, 2020) dominated by English or European languages (e.g., French) (Esch et al., 2020), other minority groups by treating racialized students as deficient learners (Flores & Rosa, 2015, p. 150) and non-native English-speaking teachers of color as illegitimate "imposters" (Lin et al., 2005, p. 214, as cited in Bourdieu, 1991). Such language-as-entity paradigm excludes multilingual speakers who do not "have" the standardized language (Flores & Garcia, 2020, p. 179).

Similarly, Kubota et al. (2021) recognize that "linguistic hierarchy" (p. 5) and "racial hierarchy" (p. 17) include native English-speaking students inside the "White box" and "linguistic space" while excluding non-native outsiders out of the "White box" (p. 17) and resulting in racialized otherness (Lee, 2015). Although bilingualism (i.e., English and French as two official languages) is the national policy of Canada, neither NES (Nonnative English Speakers) nor NFS (Nonnative French Speakers) fit this *White box* despite their high English proficiency. Native speakerism is pronounced especially in English and European language teaching (Saraceni, 2015). Rosa (2019) uses the raciolinguistic framework to probe into the "ethnoracial category" (p. 1) and examine how Latinxs have become "racial others" (p. 4). Rosa (2019b) puts forward that such racialized ideology of "languagelessness" stigmatizes Latinxs as "producing neither English nor Spanish legitimately" (p. 6) "based on their ethnoracial positions rather than their linguistic practices" (Rosa, 2016, p. 65) "and/or the subordination of" minority languages (e.g., Spanish) "to English in White public space" (Rosa, 2016, p. 68).

Like their minority students, racialinguistically minoritized teachers are also marginalized as "strangers in the academy" as described in Li and Beckett's study (2011) given their perceived "illegitimate" language proficiency and non-native English-speaking status in the host society (Huo, 2020). Researchers have debunked "homogenizing ideologies" and "hegemonic ideologies" (Alim et al., 2020, p. 6) which are detrimental to language teaching and learning. Thus, there is also a call for the delegitimation of racialized teachers (Esch et al., 2020). Since racialized ideologies are entrenched in language teaching and identity is "racialized ideological construct" (Esch et al., 2020, p. 404), identity will be discussed in the following session, as well as its intersectionality with language.

LANGUAGE AND IDENTITY

The interplay between language and identity is explored in this part, including racialized teachers' and students' identities. Language is not neural (Brand, 1990), symbolizing one's identity (Steinman, 2009a, 2009b). Rosa and Burdick (2016) articulate that language and identity are "contingent and co-constructed" (p. 114) and that linguistic identities co-naturalize other social identities" (p. 110). Paralleling Alim et al.'s study (2016b), Rosa and Burdick (2016) explain that identity is not stable or monolithic and that "language does not simply reflect preexisting identities—it actually participates in the construction, reproduction, and transformation of identity" (p. 110). Alim (2016a) highlights the influence of language on "the construction, maintenance, and transformation of racial and ethnic identities" (p. 8). Given that linguistic identities are racialized (Rosa, 2019), Makoni et al. (2003) highlight "the linguistic construction of ethnoracial identities, the role of language of racialization and ethicization, and the language ideological process" (Alim et al., 2020, p. 2). Furthermore, racialized identities are supposed to sound like native-speaking speakers (NSS). When speaking objects "perform race" in communication, race "becomes an intelligible category" since listening subjects tell what they hear (Alim et al., 2020, p. 2). Such "ideologization of identities" (Rosa, 2014) impacts racial authenticity (Chun, 2011) which aligns with Alim and Smitherman's (2012) notions of "languaging race"—to "examine the politics of race through the lens of language" (p. 3) and "racing language"—to theorize "language from the lens of race" (Alim, 2016, p. 13).

Following Canagarajah (2015), the standard native speaker norm has negative effects on raciolinguistically minoritized students' identities. Such "deficient identification" (p. 417) neglects multiple capital and linguistic repertoire that multilingual students possess by merely assessing these students' proficiency against the monolingual standard. However, the "native speaker identity" may not be the goal of multilingual students as they want to "embrace the differences" of "English as part of" their identities (p. 417). Moreover, the native speaker "identity label" is static, linked to "racialized attributes" and thus caused "conceptual problems" (p. 417). What Anglo people think as accepted and unaccepted in their norm only shows the interpretations from the perspective of one culture which is apart from the objective of higher education that diversity is encouraged (Steinman, 2009a). Take writing as an example, ESL/EFL writing contains multi-layered meanings and connotations to convey one's "textual, contextual, cognitive, emotional and political" values (Basta, 2022, p. 155). The omission of multilingual perspectives gives rise to acculturation and assimilation. Rogers et al. (2020) illustrate that as identity is regarded as "a conduit for learning" and plus both identity and learning are indispensable to human development (p. 62), the "identity-relevant" approaches (p. 64) to helping construct and navigate learners' multiple identities is of great significance to counter deficit mindsets and turn racialized minority students from "passive recipients of an oppressive culture" to "active agents," ultimately able to "radically transform their identities" (p. 73).

Akin to learner identity, "teacher identity is a racialized ideological construct" (Esch et al., 2020, p. 404). Impacted by raciolinguistic ideologies, non-White, non-native teachers struggle to teach the dominant language in the society where English is a societal language as depicted by a body of literature (see Esch et al., 2020; Holliday, 2005; Huo, 2020). Based on native speakerism and NS-NNS dichotomy, racialized teachers face linguistic, sociopolitical, and hiring challenges (Huo, 2020). Kramsch (1997) explains that "Native speakers are made rather than born," inferring cultural capital, the middle class, and dominant value enjoyed by native speakers (p. 363). Akin to protectionism in business (Canagarajah, 1999), "native insiders" (Norton, 1997)—the "owners of a language" (Medgyes, 2001, p. 417) are unwilling to grant the membership to "non-native outsiders" (Medgyes, 2001, p. 431). Therefore, native speakerism produces division between privileged native speakers and disenfranchised non-native speakers by placing NS in a superior position to NNS speakers (Kramsch, 1997).

Liggett (2009) indicates that studying Whiteness in teachers' identities is useful in language teaching. There are inextricable links between ideologies, teachers' racial, colonial, and linguistic identities, and their teaching (Kubota & Lin, 2009; Motha, 2014). Thus, when teacher identities are associated with race, teachers' identity formation and practice may also influence their pedagogies and learning outcomes (Vitanova, 2016). An example is from Canagarajah's (2016) study where he implemented the concept of *identity-as-pedagogy* in his study to regard "teacher identity as a nexus of membership" to counter raciolinguistic membership (p. 68). Contributors in this volume also investigate language and identity and reflect critically on the impact of language on teacher and learner identities. Despite limited studies focusing on the influence of teachers' (racial) identities on their pedagogies, there has been some indication of such links between identity and pedagogy (e.g., Ligget, 2009; Motha 2014; Taylor, 2017) and race and pedagogy (Kubota & Lin, 2009).

RACE AND PEDAGOGY: ANTIRACIST APPROACHES

This section examines seven antiracist, anti-oppressive, decolonial pedagogies including translingualism (Canagrajah, 2013b), multilingualism (May, 2014), plurilingualism (Flores, 2013), translanguaging (Crump, 2014), culturally responsive (Ladson-Billings, 1994), relevant (Ladson-Billings, 1995, 2021), and sustaining pedagogies (Alim et al., 2020; Paris, 2012), critical language awareness (Alim, 2010), and

Introduction

multiliteracies pedagogy (New London Group, 1996) to counter deficit models and biased pedagogies (Kubota, 2021). Laurence (1992) regards "pedagogy as scholarship as struggle" (p. 2231). When race and pedagogy are concerned, Lin (2006) affirm that language teaching was "in dire need of an explicit exploration of race" (p. 472) and argue that there is a paucity of research into race and second language teaching (Also see Esch et al., 2020). Kubota and Lin (2009) also address the link and intersection between race and second language teaching at "the multi/plural turn in applied linguistics" (Kubota, 2016). Most of the proposed or implemented pedagogies do not address race or racism directly or openly (without mentioning the name of "race"/"racism") (Jorge, 2012), but with the inference from race, such as critical or culturally responsive pedagogies (Hone, 2007) while some use "euphemisms for race" without combating racism explicitly (Esch et al., 2020, p. 411, as cited in Lee, 2015) and some others are race-centered (e.g., translanguaging approach and culturally sustaining pedagogy). This section will explore these seven major pedagogies to decenter Whiteness and dismantle hegemonic standard English.

Translingual Pedagogy

Canagarajah (2013b) defines "translingual" as "the ability to merge different language resources in situated interactions for new meaning construction" (p. 2). Translingualism refers to a theory "about language tends to highlight hybridity, multiplicity, and porousness, as well as intercultural and transnational aspects of language" (Shapiro, 2022, p. 70, as cited in Canagarajah, 2013b). Following Canagarajah (2015), different from the 1) subtractive (i.e., seeing L1 and L2 as conflicting with each other), 2) additive (e.g., believing that one language can be built on the other, but L1 and L2 are still deemed as two separate linguistic entities), and 3) recursive approaches [("languages in one's repertoire are treated as enabling the learning of each other, reconfiguring the competence of each in complex ways" (p. 422)], the translingual orientation perceives languages as a whole. Such orientation treats language acquisition as multi-dimensional, and regards competence as being fluid, developing, and "integrated with all languages in one's repertoire making up a synthesized language competence" (p. 423). Rather than rejecting the standard norm, the translingual model proposes "deconstructing Standard English to make students aware that it is a social construct" (p. 425). Canagarajah (2015) comments that multilingual students "feel intimidated" or their creativity will be impacted if they are required to follow those standard English (SE) criterion and that SE works best when student "shuttle between different dialects or language repertoires" (p. 425). The translingual approach thus calls for multilingual students' "keen sensitivity to the norms operative in specific communicative contexts" (p. 525) and encourages students to become "commuters," exchanging writing strategies (Steinman, 2009a) between different linguistic communities, as well as negotiating various norms (Huo, 2018). Another similar approach is the multilingual pedagogy of writing.

Multilingual Pedagogy of Writing

Akin to translingual pedagogy, the multilingual pedagogy emphases and celebrates multilingualism and language repertoire, mobilizing students' multiple linguistic resources and developing their different voices and multiple identities to dismantle the standard norm of English. The multilingual pedagogy of writing, put forward by Canagarajah (2006a), contains three tenets. First, not all deviation from norms is erroneous. Such decentering thoughts are helpful to multilingual writers' "rhetorical negotiation so that they can modify, resist, or reorient themselves to the rules in a way favorable to them" (p. 602), confirmed by Garcia (2009) that students can better comprehend the standard if they diverge from it. Second, move writing merely as "constitutive" "text construction" to "performative" "social acts," full of "social meanings and functions" (p. 602). Thirdly, change writing from its "objective and transparent" function of conveying messages to represent identity. Hence, multilingual students are encouraged to negotiate their values, interests, and identities formed in their writing (p. 602). Canagarajah (2006a) also advocates changing written discourses from being "context-bound or context-sensitive" to "context-transforming" by connecting to writers and deploying writing in various ways. Hence, the aim of the teaching of writing is to facilitate students' critical thinking by demystifying dominant conventions, "to critically engage with" rhetorical contexts, and to link writing practice to the social environment (p. 603) in order to adapt writing to students' voices and identities. Canagarajah (2023) extends the multilingual pedagogy of writing to the decolonizing pedagogy through the ecological approach by representing "embodiment" (e.g., selecting readings and resources from racialized writers to adapt to students' needs and Canagarajah's own "identity-as-pedagogy": stressing his identity as a multilingual scholar of color, p. 22, as cited in Morgan, 2004) and "relationality" (i.e., "building knowledge and resources together", as opposed to the one-way colonial approach by imparting language to learners, p. 23) in his teaching of multilingual writing (p. 1). Our contributors in this volume have advocated both multilingual and translingual approaches to address diversity. Paralleling the multilingual writing pedagogy, the plurilingual approach, to be discussed in the next section, reinforces differences instead of deficiencies.

Plurilingual Approach

Similar to the first two pedagogies (i.e., translingual and multilingual approaches), the plurilingual approach, continues to problematize monolingualism with the native speaker English as the sole norm by encouraging pluralism and diversity to reconstruct English with the use of English varieties. According to Flores (2013), the concept of plurilingualism, as a "policy ideal" in TESOL (p. 501), refutes "nationalist framings of language that privilege monolingualism in terms of a standardized variety of a national language" (p. 508) at the "dynamic turn in TESOL" (p. 502) and "social turn in applied linguistics" (Flores, 2013, p. 508). Upheld by the Council of Europe, plurilingualism is regarded as "a response to the need for a new language ideology for the changing sociopolitical context" (Flores, 2013, p. 510). Contrary to monolingualism, plurilingualism includes the communicative dimension of language (Beacco, 2007) by including cultural competence in multiple language varieties—the key feature of plurilingualism and "enterprising-self" which regards "plurilingualism as part of the reconceptualization of citizenship" in globalization" (Flores, 2013, p. 512). This new addition embraces a more global lens (Breidbach, 2003) to accommodate diversity and "produce a new citizenship and develops a new solidarity and a more democratic society" (Flores, 2013, p. 512). The plurilingual approach is a "democratic behavior" by recognizing "speakers' plurilingual repertoires and language diversity in inter-regional and international communication" (Beacco, 2007, p. 36). The next pedagogy to be explored is translanguaging.

Translanguaging Pedagogy

Following Gracia and Li (2018), despite some connection with plurilingualism and translanguaging in that both approaches involve several languages used by the speaker, they are not the same. Unlike plurilingualism, mainly aiming to protect "the ability of all citizens of European nations to communicate in named languages, although to varying degrees" (p. 3, as cited in Hélot & Cavalli, 2016), translanguag-

Introduction

ing means speakers' added "linguistic and semiotic features to their communicative repertoire" for the meaning-making purpose beyond their named languages or sociopolitical defined borders (p. 3). Translanguaging, called as "transformative pedagogy for inclusion and social justice" (2023, p. 1), "a Practical Theory of Language" (Li, 2018, p. 9), and "a critical sociolinguistic theory" (Gracia & Li, 2018, p. 1), as compared with multilingualism, it has gone farther by treating bilinguals' "translanguaging being" to counter raciolinguistic ideologies (Li, 2023, p. 1). The translanguaging pedagogy places learners at the core of education instead of the named languages (Gracia & Li, 2018) in the translanguaging space (Li, 2011) through "co-learning" and "transpositioning" (i.e., considering bilinguals' languages and their racial identities together) (Li, 2023, p. 2). The translanguaging pedagogy, with "multimodal and multisensory" features (Li, 2018, p. 9), draws on students' existent linguistic resources to master the target language (Lin, 2012). On the teachers' part, the translanguaging needs teachers to change their language pedagogies in scaffolding and in a "transformative" way for flexibility, creativity, bilingualism, and seeing learners as themselves instead of judging their languages with monolingualism as the norm. The translanguaging pedagogy is beneficial to language education, particularly useful to linguistically minoritized learners (Gracia & Li, 2018, p. 4). The translanguaging approach has also been proposed our contributors in this volume for linguistic human rights. The multiliteracies pedagogy will be discussed next for agency and voice.

Multiliteracies Pedagogy

What is in common among translingual, multilingual, plurilingual, translanguaging, and multiliteracies pedagogies is to center on multilingual students' voices by highlighting learner-centeredness, self-autonomy, and agency. Criticality is also highlighted in multiliteracies pedagogy. Multiliteracies pedagogy focuses on a "burgeoning variety of text forms" and "a multiplicity of discourses" (New London Group, 1996, p. 61), integrates old and new literacy practices and pedagogies, celebrates "minority and marginalized voices," and embraces sociocultural and individual lenses (Rowsell et al., 2008, p. 112). Rowsell et al. (2008) clarify that multiliteracies pedagogy is an "inclusive, critical to literacy" (p. 112) and "a constructivist, dialogical approach" (p. 114), raising students' consciousness of power dynamics and inequity (Gee, 2000) and fostering learner-centered "'inquiry' or 'discovery' learning" (Kalantzis & Cope, 2000, p. 129). Rowsell et al. (2008) also emphasize the effects of multiliteracies pedagogy on teacher education. Similarly, transcultural pedagogy (Andreotti & Souza, 2008) and "critical transcultural literacy" (de Souza, 2016, p. 276) approaches are also proposed with the heterological and alternative thinking (Wulf, 2010).

Critical Language Awareness Pedagogy

Critical Language Awareness (CLA) Pedagogy, conceptually based on critical pragmatism (Pennycook, 1997), following Shapiro (2022), has succeeded as "an approach to language and literacy education that focuses on the intersections of language, identity, power, and privilege, with the goal of promoting self-reflection, social justice, and rhetorical agency among student writers" as a "both/and" approach (p. 12). That means students should know both "writing processes" and "products," as well as teacher feedback focused on "growth and transfer of Learning" (p. 70). Critical Language Awareness Pedagogy includes several key principles: language awareness (i.e., consciousness of how language works), discourse (pragmatic way of language use rather than rules in textbooks), critical discourse analysis (CDA), power (i.e., "the ability to achieve purpose and effect change" [Brown, 2018]), prescriptivism, descriptivism, variety (i.e., dialect), standard(ized) language (i.e., ["what powerful people do to language" (p. 44]), and language ideology (i.e., language beliefs). In this sense, critical discourse analysis stresses power dynamics and how the use of language empowers and disempowers others. Instead of "prescribing how people should use language" as supported by prescriptivism regarding standard English as the only correct norm to abide, descriptivism advocates stress "what people actually do with language" (p. 43). Alim (2005) regards CLA as the pedagogy to raise students' awareness of problematizing the unjust society and make social change.

The CLA pedagogy is espoused by McKinney (2017) who proposes the transformative language and literacy pedagogies by teaching CLA at school. McKinney (2017) adds that the pedagogy should center on learners' "metalinguistic awareness" and "their linguistic repertoire" and empower racialized students to become "knowers" and legitimate learners" (Esch et al., 2020, p. 409, as cited in McKinney, 2017). McKinney (2017) implies that the language and literacy pedagogies should aim to turn racially minoritized learners into "creative multilingual and multidialectal languagers, critically aware of the relationship between language and power" (p. 139).

Culturally Responsive, Relevant, and Sustaining Pedagogies

As compared with the former six pedagogies which stress minoritized students' linguistic strengths, culturally responsive, relevant, and sustaining pedagogies focus more on culture by placing culture at the center of teaching and learning in culturally responsive and relevant pedagogies (Ladson-Billings, 1994) and advocating sociopolitical consciousness. Besides problematizing monolingualism and monoculturalism, culturally sustaining pedagogy openly racism (Alim et al., 2020, p. 262) and racism.

Culturally responsive pedagogy positions students' "cultural references" in every dimension of teaching and learning (Ladson-Billings, 1994) which has proved effective, impactful, and transformative for racially and linguistically minoritized students (Huo & Khoo, 2022; Khoo & Huo, 2022a, 2022b). Developed from culturally responsive pedagogy, culturally relevant pedagogy encompasses three tenets: student attainment, cultural competence, and critical/socio-political awareness to challenge social injustice (Ladson-Billings, 2021). Ladson-Billings (2014) infers that culturally sustaining pedagogy "uses culturally relevant pedagogy as the place where the beat drops" (p. 76). Following Alim et al., (2020), Culturally Sustaining Pedagogy (CSP) is a "critical, anti-racist, anti-colonial framework" (p. 262), challenging colonialism and "whiteness (including white normativity, white racism and ideologies of white supremacy)" (p. 261) and countering "white settler capitalist gaze" and "other hegemonic gazes" (p. 262). CSP advocates changes from assimilation to cultural pluralism (Alim et al., 2020), from monolingualism and monoculturalism to "linguistic and cultural dexterity and plurality" (Paris, 2009), and from culture and identity to "process of learning" (Alim et al., 2020, p. 271), as well as sustaining and revitalizing "the linguistic, literate, and cultural practices" of racially minoritized students (Paris, 2012, p. 93) as opposed to "dehumanizing deficit approached to education (Paris, 2012, p. 96). Such "shifting culture of power" (Delpit, 1988) switches from the White, dominant class to *collective third space*, or "forward-looking third space" (Gutierrez, 2008) with *funds of knowledge* (Moll & Gonzalez, 1994). Culturally sustaining pedagogy, as a liberatory and emancipatory pedagogy, celebrates multilingualism and multiculturalism by "sustaining lives and reviving souls" (Wong, 2019). Contributors in this volume also advocate the implementation of culturally responsive pedagogy and culturally sustaining pedagogy for equity, diversity, and inclusivity.

Introduction

Connection of these Seven Antiracist Pedagogies

These seven pedagogies are interwoven with one another. First of all, as language is a social act, most of these pedagogies emphasize rhetorical engagement and agency for ownership, voice, and identity to empower and liberate racialized learners (Khoo & Huo, 2023). In addition, people from racialized communities are encouraged to negotiate norms—to deconstruct standard English norms and enact linguistic justice (Canagaragh, 2007; Huo, 2018). The goal is to implement the pedagogies with multiple norms and muti-dimensional perspectives. Further, in these decolonial approaches language is fluid and mutifaceted, treated as repertoire and resources. So are the cultures, such as culturally responsive, relevant, and sustaining pedagogies. Therefore, differences and diversity are celebrated and valued, according to Joseph and Ramani (2006), as "walking with two legs" (e.g., multilingual, translingual, and plurilingual pedagogies, and so on) which will be more beneficial than the mainstream implementation of "hopping with one leg" (p. 194) [i.e. "English-only" policy (p. 195)]. Although not all these pedagogies address race openly or explicitly, they have all called for the teaching with pluralistic and international lens, as well as using critical, antiracist, decolonial strategies to teach dominant languages for equity, empowerment, democracy, and social justice. In this volume, our contributors have implemented many of these antiracist pedagogies, including but not limited to multilingual and translingual approaches, translanguaging, culturally responsive pedagogy, and culturally sustaining pedagogy.

CONCLUSION

This chapter has interrogated race and racism in language education by discussing the main theoretical frameworks in race and language, explores the intersection between language and ideology, and language and identity, by challenging racism, linguicism, power, hegemony, and White supremacy, as well as proposing seven antiracist, decolonial pedagogies in postsecondary language classrooms. Alim (2016a) concludes that raciolinguistics goes beyond academic inquiry to a "critical, progressive linguistic movement that exposes how language is used as a means of social, political, and economic oppression" (p. 27) in examining the relationship and interconnectedness between language and race, language and identity, and race and pedagogy. Rubdy and Saraceni (2006) reveal that English has become a "hybrid language, mixed with elements from other languages" (p. 202) and that English symbolizes "identities, voices and interests" of speakers in various linguistic communities (p. 203), so it has enhanced more consciousness of the necessity for multilingual students and teachers to build new identities to resist "monolithic, monolingual" perspective of the English language and culture (Joseph & Ramani, 2006, p. 197) and to embrace "linguistic and cultural hybridity" (Kachru, 1992a, p. 105). In the globalization era, Zamel (1998) foresees multi-models in future writing communities and readership as multiliteracies are resources instead of deficiencies. Scholars have envisioned the interconnected pedagogies between the global and the local, such as Canagarajah's "worldliness of English" as a "resistance of perspective," Pennycook's "appropriation" (p. 15) paradigm, and Lin et al.'s (2005) theoretical reconfiguration from TESOL to TEGCOM (Teaching English for Glocalized Communication) to deconstruct hegemony and reconstruct ideology.

Informed by Canagarajah (2006b), it is time to reorient English from being a "target language" (p. 209) to "a repertoire of language competence" (p. 210), from the deficit models to "treat language proficiency as a pragmatic endeavor of developing their already-available translingual competence for specific genres, activities, and purposes in a situated manner" (Canagarajah, 2015, p. 430), from hegemonic "monolingual ideologies" to translingualism between languages and across "multilingual communities" (Canagarajah, 2015, p. 437), and from the "us/them" distinction (between the inner circle and the rest of the world, or native speakers and non-native speakers) (Holliday, 2003) to a "we" (or "we are all in this together") position where all English-speaking communities come to negotiate their norms on equal footing (Canagarajah & Said, 2009, p. 170). Flores and Rosa (2015) comment that these critical perspectives and pedagogies provide alternatives to "shifting language education from inadvertently perpetuating the racial status quo to participating in struggles against the ideological processes associated with the white speaking and white listening subject" (p. 169), and ultimately change multilingual students' and teachers' "subordinate" status (inferior to native speakers) to "autonomous" status (i.e., independent stance with NNSs' own standards) (Seidlhofer, 2011). There are also needs for non-English language education. For example, affected by the Eurocentric view and language ideologies, diversity is not addressed in FSL (French as Second Language) curriculum and teaching (Faroogh, 2021) as echoed by Masson (2021).

Although the consciousness of and sensitivity to varieties of English have been raised (Kachru & Nelson, 2006), the paradigm shifts have challenges ahead because the powered always hope to go on controlling the powerless in our world (Kachru, 1992b). The goal of language teaching is not to sacrifice one language as the price to obtain the other, but to integrate diverse student writers' L1 with L2 to help them find their voices and individuality (Canagarajah, 2007), as well as exploring their identities which is also true with teacher identity: "The identity, while challenging a monolithic, monolingual view of culture, will also create a new form of globalism, which values and upholds diversity" (Joseph & Ramani, 2006, p. 197). Such pedagogical possibilities and alternative approaches are also crucial to reconstructing learning as "a genuine multiplicity of trajectories, and thus potentially of voices" (Massey, 2005, p. 55) by highlighting the key role of language in racism and discrimination (Alim, 2016), shifting from the stigmatized perception of "speaking subjects," viewed as illegitimate and deficient speakers, to problematize "white culture and linguistic hegemony" (Alim & Paris, 2015, p. 79) that "orient the ears of listening subjects" (Rosa & Flores, 2015, p. 78) and the eyes of White readers, shifting from language to languaging (Garcia et al., 2016), and placing language education as "a small piece of a larger movement for social transformation" (Flores & Garcia, 2020, p. 187), as well as emancipation of racialized groups from racism, structural barriers, and oppression. This is what this book is for; I hope this volume will be a step forward for these conversations, possibilities, and changes.

REFERENCES

Alim, H. S. (2005). Critical language awareness in the United States: Revisiting issues and revising pedagogies in a resegregated society. *Educational Researcher, 34*(7), 24–31. doi:10.3102/0013189X034007024

Alim, H. S. (2010). Critical language awareness. In N. H. Hornberger & S. L. McKay (Eds.), *Sociolinguistics and language education* (pp. 205–231). doi:10.21832/9781847692849-010

Alim, H. S. (2016a). Introducing raciolinguistics: Racing language and languaging race in hyperracial times. In H. S. Alim, J. R. Rickford, & A. F. Ball (Eds.), *Raciolinguistics: How language shapes our ideas about race* (pp. 1–30). Oxford University Press. doi:10.1093/acprof:oso/9780190625696.003.0001

Introduction

Alim, H. S. (2016b). Who's afraid of the transracial subject? Raciolinguistics and the political project of transracialization. In H. S. Alim, J. R. Rickford, & A. F. Ball (Eds.), *Raciolinguistics: How language shapes our ideas about race* (pp. 33–50). Oxford University Press. doi:10.1093/acprof:oso/9780190625696.003.0002

Alim, H. S., & Paris, D. (2015). Whose language gap? Critical and culturally sustaining pedagogies as necessary challenges to racializing hegemony. *Journal of Linguistic Anthropology, 5*(1), 79–81.

Alim, H. S., Paris, D., & Wong, C. P. (2020). Culturally sustaining pedagogy. In N. S. Nasir, C. D. Lee, R. Pea, & M. M. de Royston (Eds.), *Handbook of the cultural foundation of learning* (pp. 261–276). Routledge. doi:10.4324/9780203774977-18

Alim, H. S., Rickford, J. R., & Ball, A. F. (Eds.). (2016). *Raciolinguistics: How language shapes our ideas about race*. Oxford University Press. doi:10.1093/acprof:oso/9780190625696.001.0001

Alim, H. S., & Smitherman, G. (2012). *Articulate while Black: Barack Obama, language, and race in the U.S.* Oxford University Press.

Andreotti, V., & de Souza, L. M. (2008). *Learning to read the world through other eyes*. Global Education.

Anya, U. (2021). Critical race pedagogy for more effective and inclusive world language teaching. *Applied Linguistics, 42*(6), 1055–1069. doi:10.1093/applin/amab068

Baker-Bell, A. (2020). Dismantling anti—Black linguistic racism in English language arts classrooms: Toward an anti-racist Black language pedagogy. *Theory into Practice, 59*(1), 8–21. doi:10.1080/00405841.2019.1665415

Barrett, R. (2006). Language ideology and racial inequality: Competing functions of Spanish in an Anglo-owned Mexican restaurant. *Language in Society, 35*(2), 163–204. doi:10.1017/S0047404506060088

Basta, H. (2022). Beyond welcoming acceptance: Re-envisioning consultant education and writing center practices toward social justice for multilingual writer. In B. R. Schreiber, L. Eunjeong, J. T. Johnson, & N. Fahim (Eds.), *Linguistic justice on campus: Pedagogy and advocacy for multilingual students* (pp. 105–121). Multilingual Matters. doi:10.21832/9781788929509-008

Beacco, J. (2007). *From linguistic diversity to plurilingual education: Guide for the development of language education policies in Europe*. Council of Europe.

Bell, D. (1987). *And we will not be saved: The elusive quest for racial justice*. Basic Books.

Bell, D. (1990). Racial realism—after we're gone: Prudent speculations on America in a post-racial epoch. *St. Louis Law Journal, 34*, 393–405.

Bell, D. (2004). *Silent covenants: Brown vs board of education and the unfulfilled hopes for racial reform*. Oxford University Press. doi:10.1093/oso/9780195172720.001.0001

Block, D. (2008). Language education and globalization. In S. May & N. H. Hornberger (Eds.), *Encyclopedia of language and education. Volume 1: Language policy and political issues in education* (2nd ed., pp. 31–43). Springer Science & Business Media LLC. doi:10.1007/978-0-387-30424-3_3

Bourdieu, P. (1986). The forms of capital. In J. G. Richardson (Ed.), *Handbook of theory and research for the sociology of education* (pp. 241–258). Greenwood Press.

Brand, D. (1990). *No language is neutral*. Coach House Press.

Breidbach, S. (2003). *Plurilingualism, democratic citizenship in Europe and the role of English*. Council of Europe.

Britton, E. R., & Lorimer Leonard, R. (2020). The social justice potential of critical reflection and critical language awareness pedagogies for L2 writers. *Journal of Second Language Writing, 50*, 100776. doi:10.1016/j.jslw.2020.100776

Brown, B. (2018). *Dare to lead: Brave work. Tough conversations. Whole hearts*. Penguin Random House.

Canagarajah, A. (2013b). *Translingual practice global Englishes and cosmopolitan relations*. Routledge.

Canagarajah, A. S. (1999). Interrogating the "native speaker fallacy": Non-linguistic roots, nonpedagogical results. In G. Braine (Ed.), *Non-native educators in English language teaching* (pp. 77–92). Lawrence Erlbaum Associates.

Canagarajah, A. S. (2006a). Toward a writing pedagogy of shuttling between languages: Learning from multilingual writers. *College English, 68*(6), 589–604. doi:10.2307/25472177

Canagarajah, A. S. (2006b). Negotiating the local in English as a lingua franca. *Annual Review of Applied Linguistics, 26*, 197–218. doi:10.1017/S0267190506000109

Canagarajah, A. S. (2007). Lingua franca English, multilingual communities, and language acquisition. *Modern Language Journal, 91*(4), 923–938. doi:10.1111/j.1540-4781.2007.00678.x

Canagarajah, A. S. (Ed.). (2013a). *Literacy as translingual practice: Between communities and classrooms*. Routledge. doi:10.4324/9780203120293

Canagarajah, A. S. (2015). Clarifying the relationship between translingual practice and L2 writing: Addressing learner identities. *Applied Linguistics Review, 6*(4), 415–440. doi:10.1515/applirev-2015-0020

Canagarajah, A. S. (2016). Multilingual identity in teaching multilingual writing. In G. Barkhuizen (Ed.), *Reflections on language teacher identity research* (pp. 67–73). Routledge.

Canagarajah, A. S., & Said, S. B. (2009). English language teaching in the outer and expanding circles. In J. Maybin & J. Swann (Eds.), *The Routledge companion to English language studies* (pp. 157–170). Routledge.

Canagarajah, S. (2023). Decolonizing academic writing: Pedagogies for multilingual students. *TESOL Quarterly*, tesq.3231. Advance online publication. doi:10.1002/tesq.3231

Cavanaugh, J. R. (2005). Accent matters: Material consequences of sounding local in northern Italy. *Language & Communication, 25*(2), 127–148. doi:10.1016/j.langcom.2005.02.002

Charles, H. (2008). Toward a critical race theory of education. *Contemporary Justice Review, 11*(1), 63–65. doi:10.1080/10282580701850413

Chun, E. (2011). Reading race beyond Black and White. *Discourse & Society*, *22*(4), 403–421. doi:10.1177/0957926510395833

Chun, E., & Adrienne, L. (2016). Language and racialization. In N. Bonvillain (Ed.), *The Routledge handbook of linguistic anthropology* (pp. 220–233). Routledge.

Condon, F. (2007). Beyond the known: Writing centers and the work of anti-racism. *Writing Center Journal*, *27*(2), 19–38. doi:10.7771/2832-9414.1628

Crenshaw, K. W. (1988). Race, Reform, and Retrenchment: Transformation and legitimation in antidiscrimination law. *Harvard Law Review*, *101*(7), 1331–1387. doi:10.2307/1341398

Crump, A. (2014). Introducing LangCrit: Critical language and race theory. *Critical Inquiry in Language Studies*, *11*(3), 207–224. doi:10.1080/15427587.2014.936243

Darder, A., & Torres, R. D. (2004). *After race: Racism after multiculturalism*. New York University Press.

de Souza, L. M. (2016). Multiliteracies and transcultural education. In G. Ofelia, N. Flores, & M. Spotti (Eds.), *The Oxford handbook of language and society* (pp. 261–280). Oxford University Press.

Delgado, R. (1995). *Critical race theory: The cutting edge*. Temple University Press.

Delgado, R., & Stefancic, J. (2001). *Critical race theory: An introduction*. New York University Press.

Delgado, R., & Stefancic, J. (2023). *Critical race theory: An Introduction* (4th ed.). New York University Press.

Delpit, L. (1988). The silenced dialogue: Power and pedagogy in educating other people's children. *Harvard Educational Review*, *58*(3), 280–298. doi:10.17763/haer.58.3.c43481778r528qw4

DuBois, W. E. B. (1989). *The souls of Black folks*. Bantam. (Original work published 1903)

Esch, K. S. V., Motha, S., & Kutoba, R. (2020). Race and language teaching. *Language Teaching*, *53*(4), 391–421. doi:10.1017/S0261444820000269

Faroogh, N. (2021). Beyond baguettes and berets. Imagining an anti-racist and culturally relevant FSL curriculum. *The Monitor*. https://monitormag.ca/articles/beyond-baguettes-and-berets-imaginingan-anti-racist-and-culturally-relevant-french-curriculum

Fiske, S. T. (2018). Controlling other people: The impact of power on stereotyping. In S. Fiske (Ed.), *Social cognition* (1st ed., pp. 101–115). Routledge. doi:10.4324/9781315187280-5

Flores, N. (2013). The unexamined relationship between neoliberalism and plurilingualism: A cautionary tale. *TESOL Quarterly*, *47*(3), 500–520. doi:10.1002/tesq.114

Flores, N., & Garcia, E. S. (2020). Power, language, and bilingual learners. In N. S. Nasir, C. D. Lee, R. Pea, & M. M. de Royston (Eds.), *Handbook of the cultural foundation of learning* (pp. 178–191). Routledge. doi:10.4324/9780203774977-12

Flores, N., & Rosa, J. (2015). Undoing appropriateness: Raciolinguistic ideologies and language diversity in education. *Harvard Language Review*, *85*(2), 149–171. doi:10.17763/0017-8055.85.2.149

Garcia, O. (2009). *Bilingual education in the 21st century: A global perspective*. Wiley-Blackwell.

Garcia, O., Flores, N., & Spotti, M. (2016). Conclusion: Moving the study of language and society into the future. In O. Garcia, N. Flores, & M. Spotti (Eds.), *The Oxford handbook of language and society* (pp. 545–552). Oxford University Press. doi:10.1093/oxfordhb/9780190212896.001.0001

Garcia, O., & Li, W. (2018). Translanguaging: Introduction. In C. A. Chapelle (Ed.), *The Encyclopedia of Applied Linguistics* (pp. 1–7). John Wiley & Sons. doi:10.1002/9781405198431.wbeal1488

Gee, J. P. (2000). New people in new worlds: Networks, the new capitalism, and schools. In B. Cope & M. Kalantzis (Eds.), *Multiliteracies: Literacy learning and the design of social futures* (pp. 43–68). Routledge.

Gillborn, D. (2023). Education policy as an act of White supremacy: Whiteness, critical race theory, and education reform. In E. Taylor, D. Gillborn, & G. Ladson-Billings (Eds.), *Foundations of critical race theory in education* (3rd ed., pp. 42–58). Routledge.

Gorham, B. W. (1999). Stereotypes in the media: So what? *The Howard Journal of Communications*, *10*(4), 229–247. doi:10.1080/106461799246735

Grant, R. A., & Lee, I. (2009). The ideal English speaker: A juxtaposition of globalization and language policy in South Korea and racialized language attitudes in the United States. In R. Kubota & A. Lin (Eds.), *Race, culture, and identities in second language education* (pp. 44–63). Routledge.

Gutierrez, K. (2008). Developing a sociocritical literacy in the third space. *Reading Research Quarterly*, *43*(2), 148–164. doi:10.1598/RRQ.43.2.3

Hélot, C., & Cavalli, M. (2016). Bilingual education in Europe: Dominant languages. In O. García & A. Lin (Eds.), *Bilingual and multilingual education* (pp. 471–488). Springer. doi:10.1007/978-3-319-02324-3_26-1

Hesse, B. (2016). Counter-racial formation theory. In P. K. Saucier & T. P. Woods (Eds.), *Conceptual aphasia in Black: Displacing racial formation* (pp. vii–x). Lexington Books.

Hewings, A., & Tagg, C. (2012). General introduction. In A. Hewings & C. Tagg (Eds.), *The politics of English: Conflict, competition, co-existence* (pp. 1–3). Routledge.

Hill, J. H. (2010). Language, race, and white public space. In L. Wei (Ed.), *Bilingualism and multilingualism: Critical concepts in linguistics* (Vol. 3, pp. 394–409). Routledge.

Hochschild, I. J. (1984). *The new American dilemma: Liberal democracy and school desegregation*. Yale University Press.

Holliday, A. (2005). *The struggle to teach English an international language*. Oxford University Press.

Hone, D. E. (2007). "A meeting place for us": Milpera, a newcomer high school. *Multicultural Education*, *14*(4), 8–15.

Hudley, H. C. A. (2016). Language and racialization. In *The Oxford handbook of language and society*. Oxford University Press.

Huo, X. Y. (2018). Negotiation of writing norms. *Literacy Information and Computer Education Journal, 9*(4), 3033–3036. doi:10.20533/licej.2040.2589.2018.0397

Huo, X. Y. (2020). *Higher education internationalization and English language instruction: Intersectionality of race and language in Canadian universities.* Springer. doi:10.1007/978-3-030-60599-5

Huo, X. Y., & Khoo, E. (2022). Effective teaching strategies for Chinese international students at a Canadian University: A reading-writing online program. In C. Smith & G. Zhou (Eds.), *Successful teaching strategies for culturally and linguistically diverse international students* (pp. 241–264). IGI Global., doi:10.4018/978-1-7998-8921-2.ch013

James, C. E. (2010). *Seeing ourselves: Exploring race, ethnicity and culture* (4th ed.). Thompson Educational Publishing.

James, C. E. (2012). Students at risk: Stereotyping and the schooling of Black boys. *Urban Education, 47*(2), 464–494. doi:10.1177/0042085911429084

Jorge, M. (2012). Critical literacy, foreign language teaching and the education about race relations in Brazil. *The Latin Americans. SECOLAS Annals, 56*(4), 79–90.

Joseph, M., & Ramani, E. (2006). English in the world does not mean English everywhere: The case for multilingualism in the ELT/ESL profession. In R. Rubdy & M. Saraceni (Eds.), *English in the world: Global rules, global roles* (pp. 186–199). Continuum.

Kachru, B. B. (1986). *The alchemy of English: The spread, functions and models of non-native Englishes.* Pergamon.

Kachru, B. B. (1992a). Introduction: The other side of English and the 1990s. In B. B. Kachru (Ed.), *The other tongue: English across cultures* (2nd ed., pp. 1–15). University of Illinois Press.

Kachru, B. B. (1992b). Teaching world Englishes. In B. B. Kachru (Ed.), *The other tongue: English across cultures* (2nd ed., pp. 108–121). University of Illinois Press.

Kachru, B. B., & Nelson, C. L. (1996). World Englishes. In S. L. MaKay & N. H. Hornberger (Eds.), *Sociolinguistics and language teaching* (pp. 71–102). Cambridge University Press.

Kachru, Y., & Nelson, C. L. (2006). *World Englishes in Asian contexts.* Hong Kong University Press.

Kalantzis, M., & Cope, B. (2000). Changing the role of schools. In B. Cope & M. Kalantzis (Eds.), *Multiliteracies: Literacy learning and the design of social futures* (pp. 121–148). Routledge.

Khoo, E., & Huo, X. Y. (2022a). The efficacy of culturally responsive pedagogy for low-proficiency international students in online teaching and learning. *The Journal of Teaching and Learning, 16*(2), 67–85. doi:10.22329/jtl.v16i2.7022

Khoo, E., & Huo, X. Y. (2022b). Toward transformative inclusivity through learner-driven and instructor-facilitated writing support: An innovative approach to empowering English language learners. *Discourse and Writing/Rédactologie, 32*, 394-404.

Kiczkowiak, M., & Lowe, R. J. (2018). *Teaching English as a lingua franca: The journey from EFL to ELF.* DELTA Publishing.

Kleyn, T. (2010). Cultural mismatch in Honduran Garifuna communities: The role of culture, race, and language in schools. *Diaspora, Indigenous, and Minority Education, 4*(4), 217–234. doi:10.1080/09636412.2010.513229

Kramsch, C. (1993). *Context and culture in language teaching*. Oxford University Press.

Kramsch, C. (1997). The privilege of the nonnative speakers. *PMLA, 112*(3), 359–369. doi:10.1632/S0030812900060673

Kubota, R. (2016). The multi/plural turn, postcolonial theory, and neoliberal multiculturalism: Complicities and implications for applied linguistics. *Applied Linguistics, 37*(4), 474–494. doi:10.1093/applin/amu045

Kubota, R. (2021). Critical antiracist pedagogy in ELT. *ELT Journal, 75*(3), 237–246. doi:10.1093/elt/ccab015

Kubota, R., & Corella, M., Lim, K., & Sah, K. P. (2021). "Your English is so good": Linguistic experiences of racialized students and instructors of a Canadian university. *Ethnicities, 0*(0), 1–21.

Kubota, R., & Lin, A. (2006). Race and TESOL: Introduction to concepts and theories. *TESOL Quarterly, 40*(3), 471–193. doi:10.2307/40264540

Kubota, R., & Lin, A. M. (Eds.). (2009). *Race, culture, and identities in second language education: Exploring critically engaged practice*. Routledge. doi:10.4324/9780203876657

Ladson-Billings, G. (1994). *The dreamkeepers: Successful teachers of African American children* (1st ed.). Jossey-Bass.

Ladson-Billings, G. (1995). Toward a theory of culturally relevant pedagogy. *American Educational Research Journal, 32*(3), 465–491. doi:10.3102/00028312032003465

Ladson-Billings, G. (2014). Culturally relevant pedagogy 2.0: A.k.a. the remix. *Harvard Educational Review, 84*(1), 74–84. doi:10.17763/haer.84.1.p2rj131485484751

Ladson-Billings, G. (2021). I'm here for the hard re-set: Post pandemic pedagogy to preserve our culture. *Equity & Excellence in Education, 54*(1), 68–78. doi:10.1080/10665684.2020.1863883

Ladson-Billings, G. (2023a). Just what is Critical Race Theory and what's it doing in a nice field like education? In E. Taylor, D. Gillborn, & G. Ladson-Billings (Eds.), *Foundations of critical race theory in education* (3rd ed., pp. 13–29). Routledge.

Ladson-Billings, G. (2023b). Critical Race Theory—What it is not! In E. Taylor, D. Gillborn, & G. Ladson-Billings (Eds.), *Foundations of critical race theory in education* (3rd ed., pp. 369–380). Routledge.

Lawrence, C. R. III. (1992). The word and the river: Pedagogy as scholarship as struggle. *Southern California Law Review, 65*, 2231–2298.

Lee, E. (2015). Doing culture, doing race: Everyday discourse of "culture" and "cultural difference" in the English as a second language classroom. *Journal of Multilingual and Multicultural Development, 36*(1), 80–93. doi:10.1080/01434632.2014.892503

Introduction

Li, G., & Beckett, G. H. (2011). "Strangers" of the academy: Asian women scholars in higher education. *Stylus (Rio de Janeiro)*.

Li, W. (2011). Moment analysis and translanguaging space: Discursive construction of identities by multilingual Chinese youth in Britain. *Journal of Pragmatics, 43*, 1222–1235.

Li, W. (2018). Translanguaging as a practical theory of language. *Applied Linguistics, 39*(1), 9–30. doi:10.1093/applin/amx039

Li, W. (2023). Transformative pedagogy for inclusion and social justice through translanguaging, co-learning, and transpositioning. *Language Teaching*, 1–12.

Ligget, T. (2009). Unpacking White racial identity in English language teacher education. In R. Kutoba & A. M. Y. Lin (Eds.), *Race, culture, and identities in second language education: Exploring critically engaged practice* (pp. 27–43). Routledge.

Lin, A., Wang, W., Akamatsu, N., & Riazi, M. (2005). International TESOL professionals and teaching English for glocalized communication (TEGCOM). In A. S. Canagarajah (Ed.), *Reclaiming the local in language policy and practice* (pp. 197–222). Routledge.

Lin, A. M. Y. (2012). Multilingual and multimodal resources in L2 English content classrooms. In C. Leung & B. Street (Eds.), *English'—A changing medium for education* (pp. 79–103). Multilingual Matters.

Lo, A. (2016). "Suddenly faced with a Chinese village": The linguistic racialization of Asian Americans. In S. H. Alim, J. R. Rickford, & A. F. Ball (Eds.), *Raciolinguistics: How language shapes our ideas about race* (pp. 97–112). Oxford University Press. doi:10.1093/acprof:oso/9780190625696.003.0006

Luke, A., & Lin, A. (2006). Coloniality, postcoloniality, and TESOL…Can a spider weave its way out of the web that it is being woven into just as it weaves? *Critical Inquiry in Language Studies, 3*(2-3), 65–73. doi:10.1080/15427587.2006.9650840

Mackenzie, I. (2014). *English as a lingua franca: Theorizing and teaching English*. Routledge. doi:10.4324/9781315890081

Makoni, S., Ball, A., Smitherman, G., & Spears, A. K. (Eds.). (2003). *Black linguistics: Language, society, and politics in Africa and the Americas*. Routledge.

Makoni, S., & Pennycook, A. (Eds.). (2006). *Disinvesting and reconstituting languages*. Palgrave Macmillan. doi:10.21832/9781853599255

Maldonado-Torres, N. (2007). On The coloniality of being. *Cultural Studies, 21*(2-3), 240–270. doi:10.1080/09502380601162548

Massey, D. (2005). For space. *Sage (Atlanta, Ga.)*.

Masson, M. (2021). On working with racialized youth in French as a second language: One teacher's culturally responsive practice. *Revue scientifique des arts-communication, lettres, sciences humaines et sociales, 1*(4), 164-189.

Matha, S. (2014). *Race, empire, and English language teaching*. Teachers College Press.

May, S. (Ed.). (2014). *The multilingual turn: Implications for SLA, TESOL and bilingual education*. Routledge.

McGroarty, M. E. (2010). Language ideologies. In N. H. Hornberger & S. L. Makay (Eds.), *Sociolinguistics and language education* (pp. 3–39). Multilingual Matters. doi:10.21832/9781847692849-003

McKinney, C. (2017). *Language and power in post-colonial schooling: Ideologies in practice (language, culture, and teaching)*. Routledge.

Medgyes, P. (2001). When the teacher is a non-native speaker. In M. Celce-Murcia (Ed.), *Teaching English as a second or foreign language* (3rd ed., pp. 429–442). Heinele & Heinele.

Mills, C. (1997). *The radical contract*. Cornell University Press.

Milroy, J., & Milroy, L. (1999). *Authority in language: Investigating standard English* (3rd ed.). Routledge.

Moll, L., & Gonzalez, N. (1994). Lessons from research with language minority children. *Journal of Reading Behavior*, *26*(4), 23–41. doi:10.1080/10862969409547862

Morgan, B. (2004). Teacher identity as pedagogy. *International Journal of Bilingual Education and Bilingualism*, *7*(2-3), 172–188. doi:10.1080/13670050408667807

Morrison, T. (1992). *Playing in the dark: Whiteness and the literary imagination*. Harvard University Press.

Motha, S. (2014). *Race, empire, and English language teaching*. Techers College Press.

New London Group. (1996). A pedagogy of multiliteracies: Designing social features. *Harvard Educational Review*, *66*(1), 60–92. doi:10.17763/haer.66.1.17370n67v22j160u

Paris, D. (2009). "They're in my culture, they speak the same way": African American language in multiethnic high school. *Harvard Educational Review*, *79*(3), 428–447. doi:10.17763/haer.79.3.64j4678647mj7g35

Paris, D. (2012). Culturally sustaining pedagogy: A needed change in stance, terminology, and practice. *Educational Researcher*, *41*(3), 93–97. doi:10.3102/0013189X12441244

Park, J., & Wee, L. (2012). *Market of English: Linguistic capital and language policy in a globalized world*. Routledge.

Pennycook, A. (1997). Vulgar pragmatism, critical pragmatism, and EAP. *English for Specific Purposes*, *16*(4), 253–269. doi:10.1016/S0889-4906(97)00019-7

Pennycook, A. (2003). Beyond homogeny and heterogeny: English as a global and worldly language. In C. Mair (Ed.), *The Politics of English as a world language: New horizons in postcolonial cultural studies* (pp. 3–17). Rodopi. doi:10.1163/9789401200929_003

Phillipson, R. (1992). *Linguistic imperialism*. Oxford University Press.

Pieterse, J. (1990). *Empire & emancipation: Power and liberation on a world scale*. Pluto Press.

Pimentel, C. (2011). The color of language: The racialized educational trajectory of an emerging bilingual student. *Journal of Latinos and Education*, *10*(4), 335–353. doi:10.1080/15348431.2011.605686

Quijano, A. (2000). The coloniality of power and social classification. *Journal of World-systems Research*, 6(2), 342–386. doi:10.5195/jwsr.2000.228

Rogers, L. O., Rosario, J. R., & Cielto, J. (2020). The role of stereotypes: Racial identity and learning. In N. S. Nasir, C. D. Lee, R. Pea, & M. M. de Royston (Eds.), *Handbook of the cultural foundation of learning* (pp. 62–78). Routledge. doi:10.4324/9780203774977-5

Rogers, L. O., & Way, N. (2018). Reimaging social and emotional development: Accommodation and resistance to dominant ideologies in the identities and friendships of boys of colors. *Human Development*, 6, 1–2.

Rosa, J. (2014). Learning Ethnolinguistic Borders: Language and Diaspora in the Socialization of U.S. Latinas/os. In R. Rolón-Dow & J. G. Irizarry (Eds.), *Diaspora Studies in Education: Toward a Framework for Understanding the Experiences of Transnational Communities* (pp. 39–60). Peter Lang Publishing.

Rosa, J. (2016). From mock Spanish to inverted Spanglish: Language ideologies and the racialization of Mexican and Puerto Rican youth in the United States. In S. H. Alim, J. R. Rickford, & A. F. Ball (Eds.), *Raciolinguistics: How Language Shapes Our Ideas About Race* (pp. 65–80). Oxford University Press. doi:10.1093/acprof:oso/9780190625696.003.0004

Rosa, J. (2019). *Looking like a language, sounding like a race: Raciolinguistic ideologies and the learning of Latinidad*. Oxford University Press. doi:10.1093/oso/9780190634728.001.0001

Rosa, J., & Burdick, C. (2016). Language ideologies. In O. García, N. Flores, & M. Spotti (Eds.), *The Oxford Handbook of Language and Society* (pp. 103–124). Oxford University Press.

Rosa, J., & Flores, N. (2015). Hearing language gaps and reproducing social inequality. *Journal of Linguistic Anthropology*, 5(1), 77–79.

Rosa, J., & Flores, N. (2017). Unsettling race and language: Toward a raciolinguistic perspective. *Language in Society*, 46(5), 621–647. doi:10.1017/S0047404517000562

Rosa, J. & Flores, N. (2023). Rethinking language barriers & social justice from a raciolinguistic perspective. *Dædalus, the Journal of the American Academy of Arts & Sciences, 152*(3), 99-114.

Roth-Gordon, J. (2016). *Race and the Brazilian body: Blackness, Whiteness, and everyday language in Rio de Janeiro*. Palgrave Macmillan. doi:10.1525/california/9780520293793.001.0001

Rowsell, J., Kosnik, C., & Beck, C. (2008). Fostering pedagogy through preservice teacher education. *Teaching Education*, 19(2), 109–122. doi:10.1080/10476210802040799

Rubdy, R., & Saraceni, M. (2006). An interview with Canagarajah. In R. Rubdy & M. Saraceni (Eds.), *English in the world: Global rules, global roles* (pp. 200–211). Continuum.

Saraceni, M. (2015). *World Englishes: A critical analysis*. Bloomsbury Academic.

Seidlhofer, B. (2011). *Understanding English as a lingua franca*. Oxford University Press.

Shankar, S. (2006). Metaconsumptive practices and the circulation of objectifications. *Journal of Material Culture*, 11(3), 293–317. doi:10.1177/1359183506068807

Shapiro, S. (2022). *Cultivating critical language awareness in the writing classroom*. Routledge.

Skutnabb-Kangas, T. (1998). Human rights and language wrongs—A future for diversity? *Language Sciences, 20*(1), 5–28. doi:10.1016/S0388-0001(97)00008-9

Solorzano, D. G. (1997). Images and words that wound: Critical race theory, racial stereotyping, and teacher education. *Teacher Education Quarterly, 24*(3), 5–19.

Solorzano, D. G., & Yosso, T. J. (2001). From racial stereotyping and deficit discourse toward a critical race theory in teacher education. *Multicultural Education, 9*(1), 2–8.

Steinman, L. (2009a). Contrastive rhetoric and university classroom. In R. D. Trilokekar, G. A. Jones, & A. Shubert (Eds.), *Canada universities go global* (pp. 154–167). James Lorimer & Company Ltd.

Steinman, L. (2009b). Academic writing and the international imperative. *Collected Essays on Learning and Teaching, 2*, 33–39. doi:10.22329/celt.v2i0.3200

Swift, M. (2020). "First they Americanize you and then they throw you out": A LangCrit Analysis of Language and Citizen Identity. *Journal of Belonging, Identity, Language, and Diversity, 4*(1), 57–80.

Tagg, C. (2012). Ideologies of English. In A. Hewings & C. Tagg (Eds.), *The politics of English: Conflict, competition, co-existence* (pp. 297–338). Routledge.

Talburt, S., & Stewart, M. A. (1999). What's the subject of study abroad? Race, gender, and living culture. *Modern Language Journal, 83*(2), 163–175. doi:10.1111/0026-7902.00013

Taylor, A. (2017). Putting race on the table: How teachers make sense of the role of race in their practice. *Harvard Educational Review, 87*(1), 50–73. doi:10.17763/1943-5045-87.1.50

Taylor, E. (2023). The foundations of critical race theory in Education: An introduction. In E. Taylor, D. Gillborn, & G. Ladson-Billings (Eds.), *Foundations of critical race theory in education* (3rd ed., pp. 1–10). Routledge.

Uriciuoli, B. (2011). Discussion essay: Semiotic properties of racializing discourses. *Journal of Linguistic Anthropology, 21*(s1), E113–E122. doi:10.1111/j.1548-1395.2011.01100.x

Valdes, G. (2017). From language maintenance and intergenerational transmission to language survivance: Will "heritage language' education help or hinder? *International Journal of the Sociology of Language, 243*(243), 67–95. doi:10.1515/ijsl-2016-0046

Veronelli, G. A. (2015). Five: The coloniality of language: Race, expressivity, power, and the darker side of modernity. *Wagadu: A Journal of Transnational Women's and Gender Studies, 13*, 108-134.

Vitanova, G. (2016). Exploring second-language teachers' identities through multimodal narratives: Gender and race discourses. *Critical Inquiry in Language Studies, 13*(4), 261–288. doi:10.1080/15427587.2016.1165074

Wheeler, R. (2016). So much research, so little change: Teaching standard English in African American classrooms. *Annual Review of Linguistics, 2*(1), 367–390. doi:10.1146/annurev-linguistics-011415-040434

Wong, C. P. (2019). *Pay you catch me: A critical feminist and ethnographic study of love as pedagogy and politics for social science*. Stanford University.

Wulf, C. (2010). Education as transcultural education: A global challenge in educational studies in Japan. *International Yearbook*, 5, 33–47.

Yosso, T. J. (2005). Whose culture has capital? A critical race theory discussion of community wealth. *Race, Ethnicity and Education*, 8(1), 69–91. doi:10.1080/1361332052000341006

Zamel, V. (1998). Questioning academic discourse. In V. Zamel & R. Spack (Eds.), *Negotiating academic literacies* (pp. 187–197). Lawrence Erlbaum.

Chapter 2
The Terrorized Experiences of Latina Bilingual Preservice Teachers With Language and Race

Lucy Arellano Jr.
University of California, Santa Barbara, USA

Ana K. Soltero López
Fresno City College, USA

Delia M. Carrizales
Texas Tech University, USA

ABSTRACT

The United States is a multilingual country, yet there continues to be a deficit view of languages spoken in classrooms other than English. The purpose of this study is to examine the lived experiences of Latina bilingual preservice teachers in relationship to language and race. Specifically, the authors consider how linguistic terrorism and racism influence future career decision-making for these students. This qualitative study considers the lived experiences of eight bilingual preservice teachers in California and Texas. Utilizing narrative inquiry from a grounded theory perspective, the study examines the experiences surrounding their use of Spanish and how they are treated as racialized beings. Findings demonstrate how the participants turned these negative experiences into motivation and fuel to become bilingual classroom teachers. Conclusions suggest the need to restructure educator preparation programs addressing the challenges faced by future teachers as they navigate raciolinguistic spaces in their educational journeys. Implications for research, policy, and practice are presented.

DOI: 10.4018/978-1-6684-9029-7.ch002

"So, if you want to really hurt me, talk badly about my language. Ethnic identity is twin skin to linguistic identity—I am my language. Until I can take pride in my language, I cannot take pride in myself" (Anzaldúa, 1999, p. 81).

INTRODUCTION

The United States is a multilingual country, yet despite numerous languages represented in rural and urban areas, there continues to be a deficit view of languages other than English spoken in classrooms. As the country becomes more diverse, the demand for Spanish bilingual teachers has steadily increased. However, subtractive schooling policies and practices (Valenzuela, 1999) and second language misconceptions have negatively influenced the way language learning is viewed which has led many Spanish-speaking emergent bilinguals to lose their language. In fact, often once emergent bilinguals start school, they "learn to develop negative views of themselves and their linguistic dexterity as racialized individuals" (Fallas-Escobar, 2023, p. 3). One outcome of the systemic disruptive view of language has resulted in bilingual teacher shortages (Horn et al., 2021).

The purpose of this chapter is to examine the lived experiences of Latina bilingual preservice teachers from California and Texas and how their educational trajectories are shaped by language and race. Building from Anzaldúa's (1999) work, we operationalize linguistic terrorism to disentangle problematic experiences around the Spanish language. As the opening quote reminds us, language is inextricably linked to race. We define linguistic terrorism as actions that produce feelings of intimidation, shame, and fear for individuals that speak a "minority" language, which creates a hierarchy of power dictating what is acceptable behavior and what is not (Anzaldúa, 1999). The conceptual frameworks are presented next followed by a review of literature.

CONCEPTUAL FRAMEWORKS

This study is informed by a raciolinguistic framework and Latinx Critical Race Theory.

Raciolinguistic Framework

The first framework focuses on the co-naturalization of race and language and the intersectionality of other categories, such as class, gender, and sexuality (Alim, 2016). Raciolinguistics contends that historical and structural processes that maintain institutionalized hierarchies which continue to subordinate minoritized races and languages need to be interrogated, decolonized, and eradicated to achieve authentic diversity discourse (Rosa & Flores, 2017). In education, Flores and Rosa (2015) point out that additive approaches to bilingual education subscribe to a discourse of "appropriateness," (p. 150) which they argue is rooted in the standardization of language practices that result in the conceptualization and acceptance of "academic English" or what Flores and Rosa refer to as "Standard English" (p.151) and for this context "academic Spanish." This standardization of language is an ideological practice adopted and practiced in schools today that maintains the conflation of racialized bodies and attributed linguistic deficiency. In other words, when observing the rich linguistic repertoires of diverse youth in school, racialized students are overwhelmingly viewed as linguistically deviant in comparison to their White counterparts, when practicing linguistic repertoires that are innovative. For example, when a White person does not speak proper academic English, this digression can be viewed as a one-time instance and does not get attributed as a fixed language practice. Black, Indigenous, or person of color is heard speaking Spanglish and/or does not speak proper academic English, they are much more likely to be viewed as practicing nonconformist languages which is viewed as a fixed characteristic based on who they are, neither a proper Spanish nor a proper English speaker. Rosa (2016) jarringly reminds us about the truth regarding such societal language beliefs, in which it is more likely for a White person who does not speak properly to ascend to powerful high societal positions as in the case of George W. Bush, while Black, Indigenous, and People of Color (BIPOC) continue to be stigmatized, discriminated against, and marginalized for their linguistic practices. This underscores the significant influence that one's race, language practices, and intersection of both, play in the impressions we leave on others.

Flores and Rosa's (2015) raciolinguistic perspective expands on the concept of the White gaze which privileges the White perspective, and allows for the examination of the White gaze through the "eyes"—racialization, "mouth"—linguistic practices, and "ears"—how the language practices of racialized subjects are heard. Within the context of this study, this framework contributes new knowledge about the raciolinguistic epistemologies of Latina bilingual preservice teachers and how it helps them reflect on their own experiences with linguistic terrorism and as racialized subjects. Moreover, it provides them with a critical analysis of the education system that further fuels their aspirations to become transformative teachers.

Latinx Critical Race Theory

Furthermore, we ground this work on a critical race theory (CRT) framework which recognizes that White supremacy, and the racial hierarchy it perpetuates, is enabled within multiple systems including education, health care, criminal justice, and law (Delgado & Stefancic, 2023). Specifically, we invoke Latinx Critical Race Theory (LatCrit) as it expands on the work of CRT scholars and addresses directly the unique elements situated within a Latinx context like language, immigration, ethnicity, culture, identity, phenotype, and sexuality (Hernández-Truyol, 1997). Villalpando (2004) summarizes the components of both CRT and LatCrit as: 1) focus on race and racism, 2) contest dominant ideology, 3) enact social justice and social justice practices, 4) recognize experiential knowledge, and 5) focus on historical context. In this present study of language and racism, LatCrit provides a complementary lens to understand the confluence of Spanish and anti-Latinx racism.

LITERATURE REVIEW

We present a brief literature review situated within the concepts of deficit ideology and linguistic terrorism. In this review, we discuss policies and mandates implemented from a deficit perspective, bilingual education and teacher preparation programs, and racism in educational settings.

Guiding Concepts

A deficit framework refers to an ideology that views students, particularly BIPOC students, as responsible for the challenges they experience (Gorski, 2011; Sleeter, 2004; Solórzano & Yosso, 2001). For example, many non-English speaking students struggle with English acquisition throughout their schooling, and it is common for their teachers, and other educators, to blame them for not learning English quickly enough. Additionally, these students commonly get shamed for speaking their native language in school. Their lack of academic success is pinned squarely on their inability or perceived unwillingness to speak English. However, what often fails to occur in schools is the recognition of the lack of resources such as bilingual texts, qualified bilingual teachers, and affirmation of native languages, all of which have strong evidence of being effective in supporting English-language learners.

Anzaldúa's (1999) concept of linguistic terrorism speaks powerfully about a common experience many speakers of languages other than English experience throughout their lives. She describes how in U.S. society, multilingual and multicultural individuals struggle with acceptance. They neither feel they belong in the U.S. or in their ancestral homeland. Language practices are at the core of identity, and it is also leveraged as a source of shame and power to dominate and when pervasive rise to the level of terrorism. Anzaldúa discusses how vernaculars such as Spanglish, Chicano Spanish, Tex-Mex, etc. are frowned upon, shamed, and constantly critiqued as "improper" and "incorrect," which are acts of linguistic terrorism. Anzaldúa (1999) states:

Deslenguadas. Somos los del español deficiente. We are your linguistic nightmare, your linguistic aberration, your linguistic mestisaje, the subject of your burla. Because we speak with tongues of fire we are culturally crucified. Racially, culturally, and linguistically somos huerfanos – we speak an orphan language. (p. 38)

Anzaldúa poetically shares the sentiments that arise from experiencing constant othering due to language that exemplifies linguistic terrorism. The power and domination that go hand in hand with terrorism have historically been codified into policies that dictate language and are imbued with deficit notions.

Implementation of Deficit Policies

The effective implementation of theory-based bilingual education programs that support the linguistic development of emergent bilinguals in their native language and English is imperative. Historically, the politicization of bilingual education has negatively impacted policy implementation in schools that materializes as inadequate education of emergent bilinguals. For example, Proposition 187 (1994) in California ruled that undocumented immigrants could not attend public school. Thus, undocumented emergent bilinguals were denied the opportunity to become fluent in English in an academic setting. Additionally, Proposition 187 mandated school districts with the responsibility of questioning families' immigration status and reporting them to the agency formerly known as Immigration and Naturalization Services (INS) if they suspected they were undocumented. Although later ruled unconstitutional, this proposition placed undue burden, fear, and unnecessary stress on teachers, parents, and students and had a direct impact on bilingual education. Proposition 187 was a policy that legalized both linguistic terrorism and racism.

Ignoring decades of research, Proposition 227 (1998) was passed in California under the guise that English immersion was intended for students to learn English quicker; thus, requiring schools to teach only in English (Wright, 2019). Once again, emergent bilinguals were faced with discriminatory policies that viewed their native language as a limitation instead of an asset in acquiring a second language. As in the case of Proposition 187, teachers' jobs were politicized and threatened if they did not abide by policy. For instance, under Proposition 227, parents could sue teachers if they spoke a language other than English to their children. While Proposition 187 was deemed unconstitutional nearly three years after it passed, Proposition 227 was in place for nearly 20 years and codified linguistic terrorism into sanctioned educational practices. Students who spoke a language other than English were strategically targeted during the era of proposition 187 and 227. Thus, the linguistic terrorism and racism experienced as a result of these policies continues to negatively impact emergent bilinguals, their families, and teachers to this day.

Politicizing education hurts students and while linguistically intolerant policies were overturned in the late 1960s in Texas, other state mandates continue to negatively impact emergent bilinguals. For example, funding per emergent bilingual in Texas has not changed since 1984 (Skies & Villanueva, 2021). Furthermore, elementary schools where the majority of bilingual programs are implemented experienced significant cuts in 2011 (Skies & Villanueva, 2021). Research in bilingual programs has indicated dual language programs are the most effective for teaching a second language and maintaining a native language (Wright, 2019). Yet, most emergent bilinguals are in ESL programs that do not promote bilingualism.

Educator Preparation Programs and Bilingual Education

Given the deficit policies emergent bilinguals have endured for decades, perhaps Latinx bilingual preservice teachers who come from similar marginalized communities are better situated to teach current emergent bilinguals (Paris & Alim, 2017). The need to train and recruit bilingual Spanish teachers was imperative long before the implementation of the Bilingual Education Act (1968). However, specific objectives in educator preparation programs do not always reflect the needs of preservice teachers of color, thus leaving many to feel invisible (Anderson & Aronson, 2019).

Bilingual preservice teachers continue to grapple with the nuances of language "appropriateness." Fallas-Escobar and Treviño (2021) find that Latinx bilingual preservice teachers are preoccupied with the perceptions and comments of others about their language skills. This fixation influences their own self-perceptions of their bilingual proficiency and a policing of language modification based on social settings (Fallas-Escobar, 2023). Fallas-Escobar and Treviño (2021) argue that it is imperative for bilingual teacher education programs to guide Latinx bilingual preservice teachers to unpack such perceptions, critically analyzing the language ideologies and hierarchies that still dominate and determine language proficiency.

In their study of bilingual teachers, Babino and Stewart (2023) found that their language practices were sanctioned (privileged) or subaltern (invisibilized) depending on the social setting. For example, one of the participants spoke Spanish at home, and Spanglish in community spaces and at home sometimes; however, English was the preferred and dominant language during their schooling. The daily maneuvering of social spaces and gauging the appropriateness of language practices is a skill possessed by multilingual speakers. Babino and Stewart (2023) assert the importance of practicing decolonizing strategies in bilingual teacher education programs and dual immersion programs that validate and welcome all language practices. It is crucial for teacher education programs and professional development for in-service teachers to consider adopting pedagogical approaches that guide teachers to interrogate language, race, and their intersection. Doing so will assist with recognizing and addressing the internalized deficit views and preoccupation with self-policing of language practices observed among preservice and in-service teachers. This will ensure that we begin producing teachers who adopt a stance as critical educators who will authentically validate and nurture the diverse language practices among the multicultural and multilingual students in our schools.

Unfortunately, focusing on a student's assets and providing validation to them does not always occur. For instance, throughout their childhood, many emergent bilinguals are told to focus on learning English, yet for those who want to become Spanish bilingual teachers the expectation is to have an advanced level of fluency in reading, writing, listening, and speaking in Spanish. In Texas, for example, one of the licensure exams requires bilingual preservice teachers to be able to write lesson plans in Spanish over any given content area. These licensure exams focus on standard language ideologies (Briceño et al., 2018; Ciriza, 2023). However, bilingual preservice teachers are given limited opportunities to fully develop their biliteracy skills (Gauna, 2023; Musanti, 2014). For instance, most bilingual teacher preparation programs offer few opportunities to foster high levels of language development (Caldas, 2021; Guerrero, 2023). Additionally, some faculty are unable to support bilingual preservice teachers linguistically thus Arroyo-Romano (2022) recommends institutions should ensure faculty are biliterate and can serve as language models. Nonetheless, the success of teacher preparation programs is measured by accreditation institutions that examine the number of times bilingual preservice teachers take a licensure exam (Gauna et al., 2022). Which begs the question, if course work is designed for White preservice teachers with English dominance in mind, how are bilingual preservice teachers expected to meet state mandated Spanish licensure exams? Thus, linguistic discrimination continues to impact bilingual preservice teachers in educator preparation programs when they do not adequately prepare them to pass the state mandated licensure exams.

Racism in Educational Settings

The concept of "Whiteness" is utilized as a frame to examine racism in educational settings. Whiteness is racial power that advantages White people while disadvantaging BIPOC (Bonilla-Silva, 2012; Cabrera, 2019; Matias, 2016). As a structure, Whiteness is a racial discourse that serves to make racist systems seem natural, objective, justified, and normalized (Cabrera, 2019; Gusa, 2010). A study focused on the actions of White teachers in group conversations found that White teachers de-racialized conversations, prioritized politeness, and affirmed the intentions of colleagues without critiquing actions that perpetuated racial dominance, and failed to challenge colleagues' racist statements (Yoon, 2012). Considering the experiences of White teacher candidates, Matias (2013) found that when White people did not engage in their own self-learning about their racial identities, they carried a sense of authority, superiority, and purity that perpetuated racial oppression. Furthermore, they normalized their White positionality and perceived themselves as having no racial impact in the educational environment and remained emotionally distant from racial injustice (Matias, 2013). Even as White teachers strive to increase equity and employ culturally responsive practices, they maintain the racialized system of dominance that impedes equity (Matias, 2013; Yoon, 2012).

It is important to further complicate the conversation and posit that the outcomes of Whiteness are not solely ascribed to White people. BIPOC can also perpetuate the system of domination founded on

Whiteness. Examples of this are embedded throughout the history of education including the assimilation of Native Americans, racial segregation perpetuated by the notion of "separate but equal," corporal punishment for speaking languages other than English in schools, and more recently "racist nativism" (Pérez Huber et al., 2008). Racist nativism is defined as

The assigning of values to real or imagined differences in order to justify the superiority of the native, who is perceived to be White, over that of the non-native, who is perceived to be People and Immigrants of Color, and thereby defend the native's right to dominance. (Pérez Huber et. al., 2008, p.43)

The opening excerpt of this manuscript is from Gloria Anzaldúa's "How to Tame a Wild Tongue," in which she describes the complex internal and external struggles of being bicultural and bilingual in the United States embodies the tension of racist nativism. Her influential work translates to teacher education, specifically, the preparation of bilingual teachers, as identity is tied to language. Research on preservice bilingual teachers details their challenges with the internalization of racism and deficit language views imposed by others and the impact it has on their journeys towards becoming teachers (Babino & Stewart, 2023; Cho, 2014; Fallas-Escobar & Treviño, 2021; Galindo & Olguín, 1996; Musanti, 2014).

METHODOLOGY

We examined the lived experiences of eight bilingual Latina preservice teachers in California and Texas via a narrative inquiry qualitative study (Mertova & Webster, 2020). As an under-researched area of study, a grounded theory approach (Cresswell & Poth, 2018) was selected due to the minimal knowledge on the raciolinguistic terrorism experienced by bilingual Latina preservice teachers. Grounded theory promotes systematic comparative analysis, a methodological approach that is appropriate when little is known about a phenomenon. Grounded theory seeks to construct an explanatory theory that reveals an intrinsic process in the area of inquiry (Bryant & Charmaz, 2007).

Research Questions

Specifically, this study seeks to answer the following research questions:

1) What experiences with language and race influence future career decision-making for Latina bilingual preservice teachers?
2) How do raciolinguistic epistemologies inform understanding of the education system?
3) What is the process of turning experiences with linguistic terrorism and racism into fuel and drive for their careers as Latina bilingual preservice teachers?

Study Setting

California participants (n=4) were preparing to become bilingual/dual-immersion teachers. They had completed their undergraduate degree and were enrolled in a post-baccalaureate Multiple Subject credential program at a public state university in California. In addition to their credentials, they were also seeking a bilingual authorization in Spanish which would make them eligible to teach in Spanish-English

Table 1. Bilingual preservice teachers' demographics

Participant	Year in College	Grade Level Placement	State
Lety	Senior	1st	Texas
Yesenia	Senior	1st	Texas
Patricia	Senior	1st	Texas
Jazmin	Senior	1st	Texas
Lily	Post-baccalaureate	2nd	California
Julieta	Post-baccalaureate	3rd	California
Olivia	Post-baccalaureate	2nd	California
Maria	Post-baccalaureate	3rd	California

dual immersion programs. In this three-semester credential program, participants fulfilled the required hours of student teaching in addition to their coursework. Participants were conducting their clinical hours in two 2nd grade and two 3rd grade classrooms.

Texas participants (n=4) were undergraduate bilingual preservice teachers enrolled in a teacher preparation program in a state university. Bilingual preservice teachers in this teacher preparation program complete two years at a community college and one year of online teacher preparation courses. As part of their licensure requirements for this teacher preparation program, bilingual preservice teachers completed one academic year of student teaching in a bilingual dual language classroom. Participants were completing their student teaching in 1st grade bilingual/dual-language classrooms. All study participants were in placements with bilingual children. Please refer to Table 1 for additional demographic information.

Approval by the Institutional Review Boards (IRB) at both institutions was granted. The target population for this study that was sought included matriculated teaching credential students who self-identified as Latina and bilingual. In the end, four credential candidates from California, and four from Texas participated in the study, for a total of eight English/Spanish Latina bilingual preservice teachers. The course modality for all participants in the study was online with face-to-face clinical placements. They all also identified as first-generation college students (not a requirement to participate).

Data Collection

A detailed email about the study objectives was sent to potential California participants via a listserv of students enrolled in the credential and bilingual authorization program at one state university. Similarly, Texas potential participants were recruited via an email sent to bilingual preservice teachers enrolled in the teacher preparation program at a state university. In both recruitment approaches, California and Texas preservice teachers who identified as Latina and bilingual were instructed to contact the researcher to express their interest in participating in this study and schedule the interviews. Upon acceptance to be in the study, participants were provided with the consent forms and interview questions ahead of time. They were interviewed one-on-one by a member of the research team, one for California participants and one for Texas participants. The interview sessions lasted approximately one hour, with each session conducted and recorded over Zoom and later transcribed. The interview questions are included in the Appendix.

Data Analysis

We applied a multistep approach to data analysis. First, each member of the research team read each transcript numerous times and immersed themselves in the data of each participant. The team then came together to discuss their individual notations of tentative codes. The codes reflected the overarching research questions which included language, race, linguistic terrorism, racism, and career aspirations. Next, the researchers utilized techniques related to both grounded theory and narrative coding. Grounded theory calls for repeated comparative analysis for the production of coding and category development. In this secondary analysis stage, event to event was compared across transcripts for each code. These initial codes were then compared to other codes. These codes were then collapsed into categories. The new data that emerged was then compared with the original data scheme produced in the early stages of the analysis process. This iterative process involves both inductive and deductive reasoning in data analysis (Charmaz, 2006). Narrative coding is "appropriate for exploring intrapersonal and interpersonal participant experiences and actions to understand the human conditions through narrative" (Saldaña, 2016, p. 296). The researchers created a list of codes utilizing a narrative coding approach, then collaboratively wrote detailed descriptions for each code in a codebook in subsequent meetings. After this process, the research team re-read the transcriptions in their entirety, and individually critically examined the narratives. As a result of a thorough discussion and mutual agreement, the classifications were finalized. Two distinct areas emerged–racism and linguistic terrorism–in reviewing the codes, categories, and themes generated via the data analysis stages. These dominant themes are presented in the findings section.

Positionality Statement

We offer a positionality statement to provide context to our relationship with the participants and by extension to the data. We identify as Latina scholars and educators and are bilingual–fluent in Spanish. At the time of writing this chapter, we held faculty ranks of assistant and associate professors. Our academic disciplines are Education and Ethnic Studies. All of us share research interests and perform scholarly work on the experiences of Latinx students. Two of us were responsible for coordinating bilingual education teacher certification programs. We all have experience teaching both undergraduate and graduate students at the collegiate level and also all taught in the K-12 sector and thus understand first-hand classroom experiences of the participants in the study. Our life experiences and positionalities allowed us to connect with participants facilitating the recruiting, consenting, and interviewing processes. It further allowed a deeper understanding to interpret the findings when reading the transcriptions of the participant interviews.

FINDINGS

The findings are organized in three different sections. We first present participant experiences with linguistic terrorism. Next, we share examples of how race, racialization, and racism showed up in the participants' day-to-day lives. Finally, we consider how both these experiences were transformed into fuel in pursuing their educational and career trajectories.

The Terrorized Experiences of Latina Bilingual Preservice Teachers

Linguistic Terrorism

The Latina bilingual preservice teachers shared experiences with linguistic terrorism in their interviews. The majority of their experiences stemmed from their educational settings. Lety from Texas indicated people pretended not to understand her when she spoke English. She ascribed this behavior to her,

Having an accent or having a different culture than someone else because they see you different... Knowing that you have an accent, knowing that it is like a barrier [to receiving] the same treatment as others. When people tell you "Oh I don't understand you." And although everyone else can understand you, but there are certain people who tell you "I don't understand." That makes you kind of scared, that you are scared to stand out, not to stand out, but to speak because you say, "What if I am not accepted?" The fact that you go to the university and see that everyone understands everything well, and that you are on the side like "Oh, well, what is that thing?" That, I think, has been one of the hardest things.

Lety notes that feeling like an outsider is exacerbated when people tell her that they do not understand her even though she truly believes that they do. Similarly, Lily, a bilingual preservice teacher from California started learning English as an adult and she expressed she had felt frustrated and lacked support as she acquired a second language.

Well, it's not easy. Because people look at you, "Oh how come she can't write?" "She doesn't know how to read and write! You're in the United States!" And that's just like, okay yeah you go to my country and try to write and read in that short time. I don't think so. It's not easy. You need to make connections; you need to build relationships. Every time somebody told me, "You don't say it like that," please tell me, how can I say it. Because I don't know. You have the knowledge, and I don't, so tell me how I can improve. Because that will be the only way to get better. They say, "Rome wasn't built in one day." or "The world wasn't built in one day." It's true, nothing is built right away, it takes time. Little grains at a time. And eventually we get to where we need to be. There has been a lot of struggling, because when I was a kid, I couldn't really comprehend a lot of stuff. I could read some of it, but I couldn't capture the idea of it. So I had to struggle to learn English, that's the same struggle and it was so frustrating.

Lily's passage highlights how emergent bilinguals have to deal with the misconception that others have of them. They believe because Lily could not read or write in English, she is completely illiterate. This then leaves the learner to question her own capacity and intelligence.

Olivia from California shared that she was not allowed to speak Spanish anywhere which led her to feeling isolated–even in her own home. The sentiment shared by her parents illustrates the internalized narrative of the "English only" movement that erroneously perpetuated the idea that speaking Spanish was a detriment to learning English.

We weren't allowed to speak Spanish. We were told, you know, you need to practice your English at home. For the longest time, it was me and my cousin who were very isolated in-in that language and just English-with our-our parents had that mentality of solamente en Inglés porque así van aprender (only in English, because that is how you will learn).

Patricia, a bilingual preservice teacher from Texas, indicated she struggled academically before moving to the United State at the age of 14. Moreover, she experienced lack of support from one teacher and bullying from her classmates due to her low English proficiency.

I already struggled, I was already struggling at school in Mexico and coming here and having to learn, not only the content but the language at the same time, was a really big challenge. I struggled a lot because I was really insecure of myself in a lot of ways so that really didn't help me a lot to practice what I was learning and that was one of the things. Also, at first, I had one teacher that denied the support that I was supposed to have because I was coded as a newcomer student because of my language. So he didn't give me the accommodations that he was supposed to in the classroom and I had to go to summer school because of that. Because of course, I was putting in my name, I ended up just going to his class, putting my name on the papers and not answering any of the questions because I was not comprehending anything and that was one of the challenges as well.

Particia articulates the multiple layers that she had to navigate in her new environment. First, she had to learn a new language. Second, she had to gain content knowledge in the new language. Third, she had to learn how to navigate a new school system without knowing the language. This last challenge shows up as bullying discussed below. But before going there, one additional point to be made is that Patricia was denied opportunities to learn. All she could do was put her name on a piece of paper which resulted in her being held back and forced to attend summer school. She continues,

Bullying was another thing that was really hard for me in school because not knowing the language, you might be in trouble with older students especially when working in teams. That happened to me in two different classes, one of them was P.E. and the other was science. In my P.E. classes, there was this group of students and they were Black and I was placed on their team. Didn't like that we lost because I didn't understand what I was supposed to do in the game. So they started bullying me at the gym and they [would] talk, but of course I didn't understand what they were saying. Someone else will translate for me and they would tell me to go to the office and go to the principal's and let them know what they were doing to me, but I really never [did] anything about it.

Terrorizing linguistic practices experienced by mentor teachers when they were students continue to impact preservice teachers today and emergent bilinguals in current K-12 classrooms. The linguistic trauma inflicted on a child decades ago has persisted (in this example) for at least three generations. Julieta, a bilingual preservice teacher from California, shared the following regarding her mentor teacher:

He was reprimanded for speaking Spanish, because I've seen him with the other teachers. I have other teachers at my same grade level that are also originally from Mexico or were Spanish speaking at home before they went to school, and they don't speak Spanish at school. When I start to speak Spanish, a lot of the times, they reply in English. Once in a while I'll start speaking a little bit of Spanish, but they say, "Oh when I was younger, we would get in trouble at school if we spoke Spanish." So they don't like it... I feel like maybe they have that negative connotation of translanguaging at the classroom so they only let the kids speak English.

The Terrorized Experiences of Latina Bilingual Preservice Teachers

Most bilingual preservice teachers experienced a form of linguistic terrorism in their educational journeys. These included people pretending not to understand their English, their own feelings of isolation, their intelligence being questioned, bullying from peers and most importantly missed learning opportunities in the classroom. Next, we present lived experiences with race, racialization and racism.

Race, Racialization, and Racism

The participants shared numerous stories about race, racism, and racialized events that happened to them or directly impacted them. These experiences occurred both within and outside of an academic setting. We begin by sharing three examples of racism from Maria, Jazmin and Yesenia. Maria from California shared that she was driving one day and a person in another car was trying to draw her attention.

We stopped at a red light and my music was not loud and so I just ignored it and I had a lot of things going on too, so I-I hear this person. She's talking fairly loudly and I'm like, oh okay, well probably she's having a hard day or whatever. I ignored it. She eventually pulled up a little bit closer to me and my window was slightly rolled down and she looked at me and just, based on the color of my skin and what I was listening to she said straight out, "I fucken hate Mexicans!" And I just turned, I looked at her, and she said it again. And she said "You guys don't like Black people. You guys are..." you know, this and that and, in my head, I'm like, "What happened? Did I do something wrong?" Umm...I'm like well it's not fair that she just, based on skin or my color, what I'm listening to, that I'm Mexican.

Maria goes on to share more of her internal narrative describing all of the feelings that she is experiencing which are a combination of confusion, anger, and hurt. She was trying to make sense of what happened. In her thinking of what to do, she shares,

I'm like well, you know, we can all be racist, right? At some point in your life, whether it's just because, or, I don't know. We all have our reasons, right? Umm...but I'm like, okay, what should I do? So I just keep going and that lady was following me, and I'm like, okay relax, everything's going to be okay. We are not all the same, right? We don't all believe or feel the same way towards other races.

This experience stayed with Maria well after it had occurred. Even though it may not have happened within an educational setting, it influenced her educational journey. The impact of this racist attack while driving was significant because when asked about it in an academically related interview, it still comes up for her.

Other participants also shared traumatic events that affect their self-perceptions. Jazmin from Texas remembered back to when Latinxs were being targeted with racial slurs and derogatory images particularly centered around immigration. She shared that those sentiments really hit home for her because she identifies with the immigrant experience.

[There was] a good while where Latinos themselves were being targeted with racial slurs, pictures, and immigration [status] itself. Immigration has always been a big part of me because that's just who I am. That's who my family is. That's who my parents are. So whenever it came to like people saying, "Oh well go back to your country. You don't belong here." That really hit home because that's-I mean we-I've-I've grown up here. My parents have been here for 22 years, and we've built a life here. My dad goes to work

every day. He never misses a day even if he's sick. So, yeah, it really did hit home because I get it, you know. I get that there's people that don't agree with there being immigrants. But at the same time these people come to make a better life, not just for themselves, but also for their families.

The xenophobic comments made Jazmin feel like she had to defend her and her family's presence in the United States. The "go back to your country" comment is infused with racist and nativist sentiments. Another participant recounted an event that occurred under similar circumstances and left a lasting impact, yet it did not involve the participant directly. Yesenia shared her perspective on the El Paso, Texas shooting that happened at Walmart in August of 2019 where a White supremacist targeted Latinxs and killed 23 people in that mass shooting. While describing the event in her conversation with the researcher, she is referring to the hypocrisy (her word) of the media in coverage between the George Floyd murder and this mass shooting event.

I did notice how much attention they brought to that, towards African Americans and I noticed how they did not do that with us Mexicans. They never made, we have never made such national news on what has happened to many Mexicans. Before it wasn't something that made news. I guess maybe because it happens so often that people wouldn't consider it important to other people, but it is important. For example, the El Paso shooting, it was a big mass shooting and it made news for like, I would say maybe a week and it was over with. People didn't talk about it anymore. Although it was centered specifically on the guy who was shooting, he was centered basically on killing Hispanics. He said that he went specifically to El Paso to shoot Hispanics. So, even though that was his cause, even though that was his center to attack Hispanics, that wasn't a big deal to anybody. It wasn't national news, and a lot of people died. But many people saw that as okay cuz, I guess, we weren't... as sad as it sounds, we weren't important enough to make news.

Given a chance for further reflection, Yesenia is able to summarize her feelings.

I feel like, although myself, I wasn't personally attacked, I feel as though, together as a race/ethnicity, we were attacked in that way. Looking at the news, they were making a big deal out of other things but when it came to the race of us, Hispanics, Mexicans or Latinas or Latinos, it wasn't such a big deal.

The three examples of racism presented in this section thus far, shared by Maria, Jazmin, and Yesenia, are all examples of how external events impact higher education experiences. Digging a little deeper we would also be remiss if we did not at least acknowledge the sentiment of anti-Blackness in the Latinx community, and tension between Black and Brown communities that sometimes emerge during challenging events. Although unpacking this dynamic is beyond the scope of this project, three participants shared stories in relation to Black individuals. Patricia experiences bullying from Black peers, Maria gets yelled at while driving her car, and Yesenia compares the El Paso shooting with the murder of George Floyed. These references further complicate the race, racialization, and racism discussion.

Next, we hear from Patricia and Oliva whose racialized experiences occurred within the context of an educational learning environment. Patricia from Texas problematizes the stigma she feels when others hear her accent and the assumptions that they make:

The Terrorized Experiences of Latina Bilingual Preservice Teachers

People assume that I'm here illegally because of my accent. I don't think my accent is that strong, but I still have it, you know, that accent when I speak English. I get questions when I speak English a lot. "Um, are you here... How did you get into university if, if you were born in Mexico?" And some people will just go straight up to me and ask me if I'm here legally or illegally.

Patricia's experience is tied to linguistic terrorism discussed in the previous section because of her accent, but here, it takes on an added layer of racism by questioning her legal status and presence at her university. Similar to Jazmin's experience that is imbued with xenophobia and nativist rhetoric, this event hits Patricia more directly because it brings into question her intelligence and ability to be a university student due to the assumptions made by a third party merely due to her accent. The same level of racialization is inflicted on Olivia from California, but in her case, it is a teacher that expresses these sentiments. She shares,

In high school, I wasn't very open about being undocumented. But I remember a teacher saying, "Oh those aliens are never going to be more than farm workers." And I'm like getting upset about it, just thinking about it. And that just kind of blew my mind that this teacher said that knowing that there's students who are undocumented and como yo (like me). It just makes me emotional 'cause it's something that I always think about. He praised everyone else on being smart and...umm...I feel like because I'm Latina, because I sometimes spoke Spanish with my friends... and I'm pretty sure he heard me at one point. I remember him saying, "Oh those aliens are never going to be more than that."

Even in her retelling this story, she gets emotional and upset because of the multiple layers of oppression being inflicted upon her. And the most egregious is that they come from an authority figure–a teacher–that has the power to shape her future life trajectory. As painful and traumatic as these experiences were, the participants still found the strength to transform them into positive outcomes. The next section discusses how the participants turned these negative experiences into motivation to become bilingual classroom teachers.

Turning Linguistic Terrorism and Racism Into Fuel

Despite these negative experiences with racism and linguistic terrorism–or more accurately–because of these experiences, several of the participants asserted that they developed raciolinguistic epistemology that served as fuel and motivation to become bilingual teachers. Raciolinguistic epistemologies refers to the ways of knowing the world and maneuvering in everyday society that results from the recognition of the interrelationship between being a minoritized BIPOC and speaking a non-dominant language. Participants' epistemological standpoints were deeply anchored in the sacrifices and dreams of their immigrant parents and families.

Julieta from California expresses that during hardships when she feels like she cannot keep moving forward, she reflects on the sacrifices of her cousins in Mexico.

My mom would always tell me tus primos en Mexico fueron a la escuela, se subieron al camión a las 5 de la mañana para llegar a la escuela a las 6 y luego cruzar el cerro (your cousins in Mexico went to school, they caught the bus at 5 in the morning, to get to school at 6, and then they crossed the hill) and it was true because I have cousins that they're now attorneys, they're business owners, agronomos (agronomists).

The challenges of her cousins reminded Julieta of the privileges she had in the U.S.

I always felt like my life was so much easier because I had a car to drive myself to school. I didn't have to go on a bus and I have my family here...I just feel like I was given so many opportunities because like I said, I had to leave school and then come back but it was never like 'I'm not gonna finish', it was always 'I'm gonna finish, eventually'... I think the perseverance within my family, the ones in Mexico still, and the ones here too.

As a U.S. citizen, Julieta recognizes that the racist nativism her undocumented family members face on a day-to-day basis is a driving force for the collective family perseverance that propels them to keep pushing forward to accomplish the American dream.

I have family that's here illegally and no les falta nada (they have everything they need) because they work hard and yes, they have fear of deportation. I do have family members that have been deported and they have that fear, but it's never stopped them. It's never stopped them from having their families and getting their homes and making their businesses and working and doing the best that they can. I think about that. One of my uncles told me no se cuanto tiempo voy a tener aqui, voy a hecharle ganas todo el tiempo que este aqui (I don't know how long I'm going to be here, I'm going to give it my all the time that I'm here). I was born here so obviously I don't have that feeling of, "What if something happens? What if I have to leave tomorrow or next month or next year?" I don't have to worry about that in the way that they do, but I should because if it helps them, it could help me. I feel like it's really inspiring to see how much someone can accomplish with so little, and me who was given so much, even if I didn't have school paid for, I'd go every day to work. I have my car, I have family support, so why would I not take advantage of that?

Patricia from Texas, who was born in Mexico and migrated to the U.S. at age 14, had similar racist nativist experiences as Julieta's family.

I've gone through a lot of racism since I've came... now I'm more realistic [knowing] that I'm gonna find somebody on my way, who is gonna make comments about my color, about my ethnicity... I had an officer being really racist with me. He even told me that if he wanted, he could send me back to Mexico. Um, so I think something that I've learned, and the only thing I do basically is just being realistic, and just get my mindset ready for when that happens to me again, and being able to know how to handle it.

Despite the draconian language and racist experiences that participants were impacted by, they transformed such encounters into the impetus that drives their goal of becoming bilingual Latina teachers. Precisely because of their own lived experiences in U.S. schooling and society, they are motivated by their passion and commitment to validate, empower, and uplift the students and families they will serve in the ways they wish they would have received. Patricia shared this:

Seeing all the parents that needed that support. Not only the students, but the community as well [motivated me]. It's something I really like to do, to help others and I think that's a really good way to [help] parents and students. I didn't really have good experiences as a student until I got to college. My whole childhood in elementary, middle, and high school were not really the best experiences I've had. Espe-

The Terrorized Experiences of Latina Bilingual Preservice Teachers

cially those [when I was] trying to learn the language. So that was something that really pushed me to give others what I never got in my classroom.

As aspiring dual immersion teachers, Jazmin, like Patricia, shared characteristics and experiences with her students that allowed her to authentically understand her students and support them in their educational journeys. She said,

I think about the students all the time and I've met students that actually have lived similar lives to how I grew up as a child. That really helps me put myself in their shoes and see what they're going through and better understand who they are as a student. I can better understand the parents and be able to help them, and provide the resources that they need to make it a little bit easier for them-for their students to be successful in their education.

The desire to support their students holistically and nurture their multilingual skills was often interrupted by the harsh realization of the dominance of English hegemony among veteran teachers. In their preparation as bilingual preservice teachers, participants observed the dissonance in language ideologies. Mentor teachers like Julieta's, emigrated to the U.S. at eleven years old and had experienced strictly enforced English-only instruction, in which he was punished for speaking Spanish and thus internalized that speaking Spanish at school was bad. Whether consciously or unconsciously, he adopted such beliefs, and they were reflected in his pedagogy as a current teacher. Julieta shared her thoughts on this phenomenon, especially in dual immersion programs.

It's hard for me to see that because I don't want him to instill those kind of negative views on them [students] speaking Spanish in the classroom, they can learn in whichever language. They can learn in English and Spanish when they're learning about science or math, you can learn that in any language, it's the same thing...There's that aspect of how many of these teachers are stigmatizing being bilingual in the classroom. There's a limited amount of dual immersion programs, there's a limited amount of bilingual classrooms, so it's been hard for me to communicate to my students because it's not my classroom. At the end of the day, it's not. It's hard to communicate with them that it's okay to speak two languages, that it's better to speak two languages, that it's important to.

In Anzaldúa's seminal book *Borderlands/La Frontera: The New Mestiza*, she eloquently describes the challenges of maneuvering *la frontera* (the border) of English-dominant and Spanish-dominant worlds, both of which subscribe to language purist ideologies and negate Spanglish and other "impure" vernaculars. Thus, as the opening quote to this chapter asserts, until one is able to take pride in one's language skills in its various forms, one will not be able to take pride in oneself. It is evident from the participant stories that Anzaldúa's acuity on language, ethnic identity, and their intersectionality continue to be relevant topics today. Straddling, but most importantly, dismantling the borderland continues to be a skill that many multilingual speakers continue to grapple with as articulated by Julieta.

I was able to learn great English at school and great Spanish with my mom because my mom went to school in Mexico...puedo hablar los dos idiomas muy bien (I can speak both languages very well) but part of it is because my family never told me that I needed to speak only English at school, which is what a lot of Hispanic families do tell their kids. You need to speak the language that they speak at school and it's hard. Es difícil darle la contra al maestro en el salon, es difícil darle la contra a los papas que dicen que no quieren que sus hijos hablen español en el salon (it's hard to counter the teacher in the classroom, it's hard to counter the parents who say they don't want their kids to speak Spanish in the classroom)...I think one of the challenges that Latinas face is that we're expected to speak properly in either language. If you hear a Latina speak fluent English, you think maybe their Spanish isn't that good. If you speak fluent Spanish maybe their English isn't that great. Actually that's a similar experience I personally see. It's hard to say yo estudie y aunque estudié en otro idioma, puedo tener el aprendizaje en los dos idiomas (I went to school, and although my schooling was in one language, I can have the learning in both languages)...It is challenging as a bilingual to be able to express yourself in the language that you're comfortable in, which could be either English or Spanish and comfortable in both... That's why I'm gonna start educating children to help the next generation know that this is not the case, that we can speak both languages.

Our study findings reveal how blatant experiences with linguistic terrorism and racism have impacted the lives of Latina bilingual preservice teachers. Participants shared stories about linguistic terrorism and racist nativism in their educational, societal, and professional experiences. Despite these lifelong experiences, participants have proclaimed that these epistemologies have influenced their career aspirations to be transformative bilingual educators– who uplift and holistically nurture the multilingual and multicultural students they will serve.

DISCUSSION AND CONCLUSION

Summary of Study Findings

Latina bilingual preservice teachers follow their career trajectory as a result of a myriad of influences. A powerful factor was the impact of state-dictated propositions that framed bilingualism as a deficit and pushed English-only rhetoric into the public domain especially within public schooling. While these propositions have since been overturned (e.g., Prop 187, 227 in California), the impact they left behind endures. Specifically, the sociopolitical landscape that these propositions have validated is still perpetuating racism and linguistic terrorism in the dynamics of bilingual classrooms throughout the nation. These women's testimonies, their stories, provide powerful and graphic examples of linguistic terrorism and racism.

The findings of this study illustrate the intersectionality of language and race in the experiences of Latina bilingual preservice teachers and its influence on their chosen career. Several of the participants in this study experienced disparaging remarks from primary school teachers around their Spanish-speaking activities in the classroom at a young age. These events left traumatic memories and have shaped how they experience their own bilingual identities. Racism further complicates this language dynamic by adding a layer of oppression forcing the participants to navigate racialized spaces within both the K-12 and higher education environments. Nevertheless, finding themselves at the intersection of linguistic terrorism and racism, these participants find the motivation and transform these negative experiences into a strong driving force fueling aspirations to become bilingual classroom teachers. Despite, or more accurately, because of these traumatic experiences they take on anti-oppressive and decolonizing pedagogies in teaching the next generation of students. The raciolinguistic epistemology developed as a result of primary schooling socialization (around language and race) informs their motivation and teaching philosophies.

Implications

We offer implications to inform research, policy, and practice. While the Latina bilingual preservice teachers from California and Texas that participated in our study are only a small sample of all bilingual teachers, their experiences can inform wider audiences across the country and at all levels of the education system (K-20).

Research

As the findings of this study illustrate, the experiences of the participants lie at the intersection of language, race, ethnicity, immigration, gender, education, and socioeconomic status. All participants were enrolled in credential and certification higher education programs pursuing bilingual authorization at public state universities. Further research should focus on the experiences of students in educator preparation programs. As Fallas-Escobar and Treviño (2021) argue, teacher candidates should be provided the space in their programs to critically analyze language ideologies and hierarchies. This speaks directly to the need in higher education to include intentional curricular requirements to facilitate candidates' understanding of their positionalities with identity, language, and race.

The Latina participants in this study were native Spanish speakers and shared the same identity as some of their classroom students. It is important to point out that there are other Latina Spanish-speaking preservice teachers that choose to not pursue the bilingual authorization. Why not? Further research on Latina preservice teachers could illuminate the career choice of those potential educators. In addition, the participants in this study were the ones that persevered despite experiencing attacks on their language and identities. They have come full circle in their educational journeys and are now transforming the system they had to endure by practicing decolonizing strategies (Babino & Stewart, 2023; Rosa & Flores, 2017). Yet, a future research question to pursue is: How many other potential Latina bilingual preservice teachers have been pushed out due to linguistic imperialism, accentism, xenophobia, and racism?

Another future line of inquiry that this study provokes is that of racial/ethnic identity and linguistic identity. As Anzaldúa (1999) reminds us, "Ethnic identity is twin skin to linguistic identity—I am my language" (p. 81). What does that connection of ethnic and linguistic identity look like? Findings of this study demonstrate how the participants endured linguistic terrorism and racism and turned it into motivation to fuel their teaching careers. But what if they did not have to endure attacks on their race and language? What if they were subjected to empowering and nurturing spaces that allowed the use of Spanglish and translanguaging? How much further would the field of bilingual education be (both in the K-12 and higher education levels) if these students did not have to battle these slights and instead could focus on their passion?

Policy

Policies have had a direct and enduring impact on the field of education. One of the most influential to the bilingual education movement was California's Proposition 227 that was passed in 1998. It single-handedly turned the entire state's educational system into English-only instruction. Other states followed, implementing similar policies. It took 18 years for California to overturn it with Proposition 58 in 2016. Even today, 25 years later, its effects are still felt on a national level. It galvanized racist nativism (Pérez Huber et al., 2008), xenophobia, and fueled an anti-immigrant flame. This is embodied by the comments made by one of Olivia's teachers: "Oh those aliens [referring to undocumented immigrants, not actual aliens] are never going to be more than farm workers" (Olivia, California). Societal norms are replicated in the classroom and internalized by students.

Even today we are witnesses to the broad impact state policies have on the national psyche. Those specifically targeting education include anti- "critical race theory" policies, the "Don't Say Gay or Trans" bill in Florida, and the resurgence of banning books within local and school libraries. In Texas, postsecondary institutions have eliminated offices of diversity, equity, and inclusion. The importance of policy and the effect it has on the education of its students cannot be overstated. The results of this study demonstrate the dire need of policies that empower and humanize teacher candidates and the communities they come from. What if more K-12 systems employed policies implementing dual-language immersion programs? What if future policies recognized the value in multilingualism? What if higher education teacher education programs were more purposeful in developing policies that truly serve their students and by proxy the next generation of leaders?

Practice

The most important practice that the results of this study speak to is that of teacher recruitment. There is a national shortage of teachers, and an even more dire paucity of bilingual teachers. In Texas and California, there are higher numbers of individuals that are bilingual than in other states–yet they are not turning to education as an option to pursue a career. Could linguistic terrorism and racism in schools influence career choices? The participants in this study provide some insight. It is heartbreaking to hear that one of the systems that has the power to educate and dispel stereotypes is the one that is perpetuating them. Education has often and historically been considered the means to a better life. Gonzalez (2001) shares, "Education is the great equalizer in a democratic society, and if people are not given access to a quality education, then what we are doing is creating an underclass of people who will challenge our very way of life" (as cited in Growe & Montgomery, 2003, p. 23). The participants in this study are challenging the way of life, they are ringing the life; they are alerting us of the trauma, racism, sexism, xenophobia, and linguistic imperialism they are subjected to in the public education system. Ironically, it is this same system perpetuating the "isms" that has the power to eradicate them.

If teacher education programs truly want to bring about transformational change, the everyday practices need to be re-thought. Minds need to be liberated and decolonial practices implemented (Babino & Stewart, 2023) to reimagine the powerful role teachers hold. It is beyond simply recruiting more BIPOC bilingual teachers into the classroom (although that would be a great start). It requires innovation within the higher education setting that trains the teachers who will serve future generations in the K-12 educational system. Leaning on the conceptual framework utilized in this study, the raciolinguistic framework highlights the standardization of race and language practices that reinforce hierarchical systemic oppression. Moreover, LatCrit, provides some recommendations as to how educational practices can be evolved: 1) recognize the racialization endemic in the education system, 2) contest dominant ideology, 3) employ social justice practices, 4) value and incorporate experiential knowledge, and 5) teach the historical context.

In sum, future research should focus on students in educator preparation programs uncovering the ways they understand their positionalities with identity, language, and race. Postsecondary institutions must implement policies that empower and humanize teacher candidates and the communities they come from. Liberatory and decolonial practices must be implemented so that no future Latina bilingual preservice teachers have to endure the trauma of racism, sexism, xenophobia, and linguistic imperialism. Finally, the results of this study explicate how systemic oppression manifests into teacher shortages. At face value, the results of this study can help answer the question, "How do you recruit future Latina bilingual teachers?" You terrorize and racialize them. This cannot be a practice that continues.

REFERENCES

Alim, H. S., Rickford, J. R., & Ball, A. F. (2016). *Raciolinguistics: How language shapes our ideas about race*. Oxford University Press. doi:10.1093/acprof:oso/9780190625696.001.0001

Anderson, A., & Aronson, B. (2019). Teacher education, diversity, and the interest convergence conundrum. How the demographic divide shapes teacher education. In K. T. Han & J. Laughter, (Eds.), *Critical race theory in teacher education informing classroom culture and practice* (pp. 26-35). Teachers College.

Anzaldúa, G. (1999). *Borderlands/La Frontera: The new mestiza*. Academic Press.

Arroyo-Romano, J. E. (2022). My Spanish feels like my second language: Addressing the challenges of the academic language of bilingual teachers. *Journal of Latinos and Education*, 1–21. doi:10.1080/15348431.2022.2146118

Babino, A., & Stewart, M. A. (2023). Whose bilingualism counts? Juxtaposing the sanctioned and subaltern languaging of two dual language teachers. *Journal of Language, Identity, and Education*, 1–18. Advance online publication. doi:10.1080/15348458.2023.2169697

Bonilla-Silva, E. (2012). The invisible weight of whiteness: The racial grammar of everyday life in contemporary America. *Ethnic and Racial Studies*, *35*(2), 173–194. doi:10.1080/01419870.2011.613997

Briceño, A., Rodriguez-Mojica, C., & Muñoz-Muñoz, E. (2018). From English learner to Spanish learner: Raciolinguistic beliefs that influence heritage Spanish speaking teacher candidates. *Language and Education*, *32*(3), 212–226. doi:10.1080/09500782.2018.1429464

Bryant, A., & Charmaz, K. (2007). Grounded theory research: methods and practices. In A. Bryant & K. Charmaz (Eds.), *The Sage handbook of grounded theory* (pp. 1–28). Sage. doi:10.4135/9781848607941

Cabrera, N. L. (2019). *White guys on campus: Racism, White immunity, and the myth of "post-racial" higher education*. Rutgers University Press. doi:10.36019/9780813599106

Caldas, B. (2021). Spanish language development and support in a bilingual teacher preparation program. *Journal of Language, Identity, and Education*, *20*(1), 18–29. doi:10.1080/15348458.2021.1864206

Charmaz, K. (2006). *Constructing grounded theory: A practical guide through qualitative analysis*. Sage (Atlanta, Ga.).

Cho, H. (2014). Enacting critical literacy: The case of a language minority preservice teacher. *Curriculum Inquiry, 44*(5), 677–699. doi:10.1111/curi.12066

Ciriza, M. del P. (2023). Comparing Spanish certification exams for bilingual teachers: Test design and other pedagogical considerations. *International Journal of Bilingual Education and Bilingualism, 26*(2), 114–130. doi:10.1080/13670050.2020.1791046

Collins, B. A., Sánchez, M., & España, C. (2023). Sustaining and developing teachers' dynamic bilingualism in a re-designed bilingual teacher preparation program. *International Journal of Bilingual Education and Bilingualism, 26*(2), 97–113. doi:10.1080/13670050.2019.1610354

Creswell, J. W., & Poth, C. N. (2018). *Qualitative inquiry & research design: Choosing among five approaches* (4th ed.). Sage.

Delgado, R., & Stefancic, J. (2023). *Critical race theory: An introduction* (4th ed.). NYU Press.

Fallas-Escobar, C. (2023). "Se me sale el Español y se me pega el Spanglish!": Latina/o bilingual teacher candidates' racialized notions of bilingualism. *Critical Inquiry in Language Studies*, 1–20. Advance online publication. doi:10.1080/15427587.2023.2218507

Fallas-Escobar, C., & Treviño, A. (2021). Two Latina bilingual teacher candidates' perceptions of language proficiency and language choice options: Ideological encounters with listening and speaking others. *Bilingual Research Journal, 44*(1), 124–143. doi:10.1080/15235882.2021.1877213

Flores, N., & Rosa, J. (2015). Undoing appropriateness: Raciolinguistic ideologies and language diversity in education. *Harvard Educational Review, 85*(2), 149–171. doi:10.17763/0017-8055.85.2.149

Galindo, R., & Olguín, M. (1996). Reclaiming bilingual educators' cultural resources: An autobiographical approach. *Urban Education, 31*(1), 29–56. doi:10.1177/0042085996031001002

Gauna, L. M., Beaudry, C., & Cooper, J. (2022). The leaking Spanish bilingual education teacher pipeline: Stories of PK-20 challenges told by Latinx becoming bilingual teachers in the U.S. *Journal of Latinos and Education, 22*(5), 1885–1899. doi:10.1080/15348431.2022.2057989

Gauna, L. M., Márquez, J., Weaver, L., & Cooper, J. (2023). Bilingual teacher candidates and their professors: Efforts to pass a Spanish proficiency certification exam. *Bilingual Research Journal, 46*(1-2), 158–175. doi:10.1080/15235882.2023.2225460

Gonzalez, G. (2001). *Education is the great equalizer in a democratic society*. https://www.indiana.edu/~ocmhp/092801/text/gonzalez.htm

Gorski, P. C. (2011). Unlearning deficit ideology and the scornful gaze: Thoughts on authenticating the class discourse in education. *Counterpoints, 402*, 152–173. https://www.jstor.org/stable/42981081

Growe, R., & Montgomery, P. S. (2003). Educational equity in America: Is education the great equalizer? *Professional Educator, 25*(2), 23–29.

Guerrero, M. D. (2023). State of the art: A forty-year reflection on the Spanish language preparation of Spanish-English bilingual-dual language teachers in the U.S. *International Journal of Bilingual Education and Bilingualism, 26*(2), 146–157. doi:10.1080/13670050.2020.1865257

Gusa, D. L. (2010). White institutional presence: The impact of Whiteness on campus climate. *Harvard Educational Review, 80*(4), 464–489. doi:10.17763/haer.80.4.p5j483825u110002

Hernández-Truyol, B. E. (1997). Borders (en)gendered: Normativities, Latinas, and a LatCrit paradigm. *New York University Law Review, 72*, 882–927.

Horn, C., Burnett, C., Lowery, S., & White, C. (2021). *Texas Teacher Workforce Report.* https://www.raiseyourhandtexas.org/wp-content/uploads/2020/11/Texas-Teacher-Workforce-Report.pdf

Matias, C. E. (2013). Check yo'self before you wreck yo'self and our kids: Counterstories from culturally responsive White teachers? ... to culturally responsive White teachers! *Interdisciplinary Journal of Teaching and Learning, 3*(2), 68–81.

Matias, C. E. (2016). *Feeling White: Whiteness, emotionality, and education.* Sense Publishers. doi:10.1007/978-94-6300-450-3

Mertova, P., & Webster, L. (2020). *Using narrative inquiry as research method: An introduction to critical event narrative analysis in research, teaching and professional practice.* Routledge.

Musanti, S. I. (2014). "Porque sé los dos idiomas:" Biliteracy beliefs and bilingual preservice teacher identity. In Y. Freeman & D. Freeman (Eds.), *Research on preparing preservice teachers to work effectively with emergent bilinguals.* Emerald Group Publishing Limited. doi:10.1108/S1479-368720140000021002

Paris, D., & Alim, H. S. (2017). What is culturally sustaining pedagogy and why does it matter? In D. Paris & H. S. Alim (Eds.), *Culturally sustaining pedagogies: Teaching and learning for justice in a changing world* (pp. 1–21). Teachers College Press.

Pérez Huber, L., Benavides Lopez, C., Malagón, M., Velez, V., & Solórzano, D. (2008). Getting beyond the "symptom," acknowledging the "disease": Theorizing racist nativism. *Contemporary Justice Review, 11*(1), 39–51. doi:10.1080/10282580701850397

Rosa, J. (2016). Standardization, racialization, languagelessness: Raciolinguistic ideologies across communicative contexts. *Journal of Linguistic Anthropology, 26*(2), 162–183. doi:10.1111/jola.12116

Rosa, J., & Flores, N. (2017). Unsettling race and language: Toward a raciolinguistic perspective. *Language in Society, 46*(5), 621–647. doi:10.1017/S0047404517000562

Saldaña, J. M. (2016). *The coding manual for qualitative researchers* (3rd ed.). Sage.

Skies, C. L., & Villanueva, C. (2021). Creating a more bilingual Texas: A closer look at bilingual education in the Lone Star State. *Every Texan*, 1-32. https://files.eric.ed.gov/fulltext/ED614323.pdf

Sleeter, C. E. (2004). Context-conscious portraits and context-blind policy. *Anthropology & Education Quarterly, 35*(1), 132–136. doi:10.1525/aeq.2004.35.1.132

Solórzano, D. G., & Yosso, T. J. (2001). From racial stereotyping and deficit discourse toward a critical race theory in teacher education. *Multicultural Education, 9*(1), 2–8.

Valenzuela, A. (1999). *Subtractive schooling: U.S.-Mexican youth and the politics of caring.* State University of New York Press.

Villalpando, O. (2004). Practical considerations of critical race theory and Latino critical theory for Latino college students. *New Directions for Student Services, 105*(105), 41–50. doi:10.1002s.115

Wright, W. E. (2019). *Foundations for teaching English language learners: Research, theory, policy, and practice* (3rd ed.). Caslon.

Yoon, I. H. (2012). The paradoxical nature of whiteness-at-work in the daily life of schools and teacher communities. *Race, Ethnicity and Education, 15*(5), 587–613. doi:10.1080/13613324.2011.624506

KEY TERMS AND DEFINITIONS

Bilingual Licensure: Sought by bilingual preservice teachers who wish to become eligible to teach in dual immersion programs.

Bilingual Preservice Teacher: A bilingual student enrolled in an accredited teacher education program seeking a teaching credential alongside a bilingual licensure.

Latina: A person who self-identifies as female with origins in Spanish-speaking countries.

Linguistic Terrorism: Verbal and nonverbal actions that lead to feelings of fear and shame for individuals that speak a minoritized language.

Racism: Overt and covert acts of discrimination and antagonism toward a person or people based on their racial/ethnic affiliation.

APPENDIX

Interview Questions for Participants

1) How did your desire to become a teacher emerge?
2) What are some struggles, barriers, or challenges that you have faced as a Latina student?
3) In what ways are you still struggling, or has it been hard to overcome these challenges?
4) Do you think your experience as a student has changed due to COVID-19? Or is it different from those who were not being trained during the COVID-19 pandemic?
    a) If yes, how?
    b) If not, why not?
5) If you had to explain "trauma" to someone else, how would you describe it?
6) Do you think you have experienced trauma?
    a) If yes, please describe (at your own level of comfort)?
    b) If not, have you witnessed others around you endure trauma? Can you describe their situation?
7) Have you experienced trauma in the online setting?
    a) What were the conditions where this took place?
    b) Is this an ongoing issue, or has there been resolution?
8) Have you experienced trauma in an educational setting?
    a) General schooling
    b) Credential courses
9) News outlets and social media often depict traumatic events (such as the murder of Geroge Floyd, mass shootings, etc.). What defense strategies (if any) do you practice to prepare yourself for future trauma?
10) During the pandemic, have you ever felt personally attacked based on your identities (such as race/ethnicity, gender, class, age, etc.) from content that you saw online?
11) If a close friend came to you and shared that they are experiencing challenges in their mental health, what would you advise them to do?
12) In your role as a pre-service teacher, do you think about these challenges for your own students? Particularly within the last two years?
    a) How do you address these concerns?
    b) What does your mentor-teacher do?

Chapter 3
Overcoming Racism and Discrimination:
Experiences of Vietnamese ESL Teachers in Canada

Elena Tran
https://orcid.org/0000-0002-6839-1584
Niagara College, Toronto, Canada & Sheridan College, Canada

Thu Thi-Kim Le
Ho Chi Minh City University of Technology and Education, Vietnam & University of Windsor, Canada

ABSTRACT

Although the global workforce becomes increasingly diverse, many minority groups are still standing in the path of multiple forms of exclusion. Among them are the non-White and non-native English-speaking teachers who are striving to prove their credentials and secure their careers throughout the world. The purpose of this paper is to examine the challenges faced by two Vietnamese ESL teachers pursuing their careers in Ontario, Canada. The researchers utilized a collaborative autoethnography approach developed by Ngunjiri et al. (2010) to share and analyze their experiences. This involved four key steps: preliminary data collection, subsequent data collection, data analysis and interpretation, and report writing. Through this iterative process, they engaged in both individual and team activities, revisiting previous steps to enhance data collection, analysis, or interpretation as needed. The findings revealed the unique obstacles that they encountered from various sources, including society, schools, students, and native-speaking colleagues. These challenges encompassed systemic discrimination against minority Asian professionals when recrediting their credentials, marginalizing the hiring process and being treated as outsiders within the field. By amplifying their unheard voices, the researchers aim to contribute to a more inclusive and equitable English as a Second Language (ESL) industry in Ontario.

DOI: 10.4018/978-1-6684-9029-7.ch003

Overcoming Racism and Discrimination

Higher education studies, over the past decades, have explored different issues regarding being a non-native English-speaking teacher (NNESTs) in different English as a Second Language (ESL) teaching markets. Many of them (Amin, 1997, 2000; Braine, 2013; Butler, 2007) have shown that there is an intrinsic connection between race and teachers' credibility. Particularly, it is evident that NNESTs in different parts of the world have not shared the same status as their native English-speaking colleagues (NESTs). The discrimination has carried undue influences at societal and global levels (Braine, 2013; Butler, 2007). For example, knowledge and ability of NNESTs in Hong Kong are questioned because of the belief that non-native English teachers are inferior, threatening their authority and confidence in classrooms (Norton & Tang, 1997). In Japan, NNESTs are discredited by parents who want their children to be taught by NESTs (Takada, 2000). Students studying English also want NESTs in classrooms because these teachers are considered better models for students since they have native pronunciation, cultural knowledge, better vocabulary and understanding of grammar (Clark & Paran, 2007; Silva, 2009).

In Canada, NNESTs have also experienced students' negative attitudes, unfair treatment, and complicated regulations from the government (*Ontario Helping Newcomers Start Their Careers,* 2021). In her study interviewing adult ESL students from different racial, cultural, and linguistic backgrounds, Amin (1997) concluded that students' assumptions and stereotypes, such as only White people are *real*, *proper*, *Canadian*, or only White people can be native speakers of English, disempowered NNESTs as authentic ESL teachers (p. 580). These challenges highlight the need for empirical studies to address the unique difficulties NNESTs encounter in their profession. As an act of protest against discrimination towards NNESTs, we voice our direct experiences and sentiments in trying to find our place in the Ontario ESL industry. To do that in the most authentic way possible, we would like to employ the method of collaborative autoethnography and embark on a conversational tone, using personal pronouns throughout this chapter.

We came to Canada as "federal skilled workers" and one of us is a "Ph.D. scholarship holder" with extensive international teaching experience and official ESL training and degrees, but we both struggled to enter and develop in the Canadian ESL industry. The greatest challenges we face are *Canadian credentials* and *Canadian work experience*. It is neither *how much* nor *how relevant* credentials and experience we have; the key word here is *Canadian*. We need to find jobs to finance our education in Canada, but we need Canadian degrees to apply for professional employment. Anyone with common sense could see the inherent "Canadian credentials" versus "Canadian work experience" trade-off. The crucial criterion of having Canadian work experience further compounds our challenge of finding jobs as many ESL teaching positions require at least two years of teaching history *inland*. Like many other internationally trained colleagues in Canada, we are stuck in a never-ending loop, desperately trying to break free.

Inspired by Thomas's (1999) study, we identified our key challenges and grouped them into three levels: institutional – from society, organizational – from schools, and interpersonal – from students and native-speaking colleagues. The minority voices like ours need to be shared to complete the current equity, diversity, and inclusion (EDI) picture. By deeply discussing this topic, we hope that policymakers, educational institutions, and teacher training programs can gain valuable insights into challenges, as well as specific needs of non-native ESL teachers. This knowledge can inform the development of inclusive policies, training programs, and support structures that empower non-native educators, foster intercultural competence, and improve the quality of ESL education in Ontario multicultural classrooms.

LITERATURE REVIEW

As the primary objective of this study pertains to investigating the experiences of two minority teachers within the context of Ontario, Canada, the literature review predominantly concentrates on this specific setting. An overview of career prospects in Ontario, especially for internationally trained workers, will be presented, followed by a closer look at the opportunities and challenges in the educational sector. Lastly, the problem that ESL teachers face will be discussed in greater detail.

Overview of Career Prospects in Ontario and Challenges Faced by Immigrant-Skilled Workers

According to a report from Statistics Canada (2022), Canada has the highest percentage (57.5%) of working-age people with tertiary credentials, thanks to internationally-trained immigrants and international students. However, the educated workforce is underused, while Canadian labour market shortages remain. There is a substantial gap between the Canada-educated population and the actual numbers of working professionals.

One reason for this situation is that skilled immigrants and international graduates are likely to be stuck in survival jobs. Instead of continuing their careers as doctors, nurses, engineers, or educators, they take entry-level jobs at restaurants, fast-food chains, and call centers. According to CBC News, 60% of the 372,000 job vacancies in Ontario during the third quarter of 2022 required no more than high-school education, paying, on average, less than $20 an hour, and more than one-third of them are in sales and services (Crawley, 2023).

Figure 1. Job Vacancies in Ontario for the third quarter of 2022
Source: Crawley (2023)

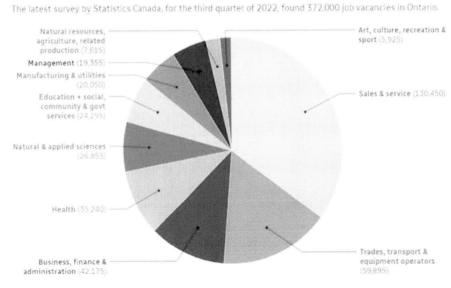

With record high inflation of more than 5%, living costs have become unaffordable (Bank of Canada, 2023). Survival jobs may cover the basic living expenses, but keep internationally-trained workers further away from their career trajectory. According to Spillane (2023), the main barriers that skilled workers face in breaking free from the cycle of survival jobs are credential recognition, official language proficiency, and a fixation on having local work experience. These barriers hinder their abilities to fully utilize their skills and potential in Canada, thereby limiting their contributions to the country's society and economy. The government of Ontario also acknowledges this fact:

In 2016, only one-quarter of internationally trained immigrants in Ontario were employed in the regulated professions for which they trained or studied. Currently, internationally trained immigrants face multiple barriers to getting licensed in their field including unfair requirements for Canadian work experience, unnecessary, repetitive and costly language testing, and unreasonable processing times. At present, licensing time in some regulated professions takes up to 18 months or more, while workers wait in limbo, wasting valuable time when they could be contributing to the economy (Ontario Helping Newcomers Start Their Careers, 2021).

Systemic Discrimination Against Internationally Trained Teachers in Ontario, Canada

Internationally-trained teachers in Ontario face the same problems. Schmidt (2010) has confirmed that the major obstacle to immigrant teachers' integration is systemic discrimination. According to the Ontario Human Rights Commission (n.d.), "systemic discrimination can be described as patterns of behaviour, policies or practices that are part of the structures of an organization, and which create or perpetuate disadvantage for racialized persons" (para. 2). It leads to the situation that immigrant teachers, no matter how skilled, are still excluded from professional opportunities.

In the same vein, Schmidt and Block (2010) emphasized that "employment equity is a distant goal for many internationally educated teachers who report much lower rates of employment than Canadian-born peers" (p. 2). Despite over a decade of advocating for equity and inclusion, the statistics remain discouraging. According to the latest report released by the Ontario College of Teachers (2021), new-to-Canada teachers licensed in Ontario experience "by far the highest rate of unemployment at 37%" (p. 48). This report also documented the voice of an unemployed intermediate-senior English/History teacher qualified in 2020 with more than six years teaching experience prior to immigrating to Canada (p. 48):

I am a teacher with many years of experience. It's very challenging for new teachers from other countries. We bring a lot of international experience that can help contribute to diversity. I feel let down by the Permanent Resident Immigration process as I still find myself two years later in non-teaching, survival jobs.

It is obvious that immigrant teachers who choose to relocate and establish themselves in Canada encounter a multitude of challenges and face discrimination within the education system. Specifically, they often have significant difficulties in securing teaching positions, leading some to take a detour to the workplace by volunteering and getting familiar with the school culture (Mindzak, 2016). This path, however, can come at a considerable cost in terms of both time and money. CBC News covered one such story: Thirukumaran, a chemistry teacher with 20 years working experience internationally, finally got a paid teaching position after spending two years volunteering for TDSB and 10,000 dollars borrowed from friends and family to appeal the initial denial from the Ontario College of Teachers. He urged other teachers to be resilient; nevertheless, he acknowledged that discrimination against internationally trained teachers remains an ongoing issue (Balintec, 2023). This discrimination against this population hinders their career progression and financial stability, ultimately limiting the quality and inclusivity in the education system.

Discrimination Faced by Internationally Trained ESL Teachers in Ontario, Canada

Navigating a career as an internationally trained educator in Canada, as analyzed above, is hard, and these challenges are particularly difficult for international trained English teachers when they are non-native and non-White teachers. This situation is described by Thomas (1999), who indicates that "they must establish their credibility as teachers of the English language before they can proceed to be taken seriously as professionals" (p. 5). The layers of social prejudice and stereotypes have been extensively examined in studies such as "Native and Non-Native EFL Teachers Dichotomy: Terminological, Competitiveness, and Employment Discrimination" (Mersad & Senad, 2019). The study casts light upon aspects of terminological distinctions, competitiveness disparities, and pertinent employment discrimination against non-native teachers of the English language. The findings of this study were that although "both types of teachers can be equally successful and useful in teaching the English language" (p.124), the propaganda such as native speaker fallacy, ownership, and native speakerism prevented non-native teachers' equality with native teachers and that "this is certainly the right time (…) for the whole world to add 'linguistic discrimination' to the list of unacceptable discriminatory policies" (p. 124).

The notion of nativism and discrimination against immigrant ESL teachers were confirmed in the context of Ontario, Canada by Amin's work (2000) as follows: "In Canada, teachers are expected to adhere to the native speaker norm" (p. 237). As a case in point, one participant in her study was reported to be "shocked and depressed by her initial experiences in Canada, due to people's nonacceptance of her English" (p. 233). Amin concluded that ESL teachers in Canada resist not only linguistic nativism, but also its collusion with colonialism, imperialism, sexism, and racism. She argued that these "multilayered determinants... regulate the lives of ESL teachers who are seen as non-native speakers of English" (p. 245). Amin's thesis (2000) clearly showcased the hardships faced by immigrant English teachers. In reflection, for internationally trained ESL teachers who are non-white and non-native, maintaining their jobs and teacher identities necessitate joining the fight to decenter nativism and decolonize English.

Confusing Reaccreditation Process in Ontario, Canada

To teach ESL in Ontario, an applicant must hold a valid Ontario College of Teachers' Certificate of Qualification and be certified as either an Ontario Certified English Language Teacher (OCELT) or an Internationally Certified Teacher of English as an Additional Language (ICTEAL) (OCELT&ICTEAL certification, n.d.). The applicant needs to go through a lengthy reaccreditation process that may take up to a few years and around 10,000 dollars, depending on the applicant's current profile.

There are two main paths to obtain certification: Application Path 1 for graduates of TESL Ontario accredited training programs, and Application Path 2 for Competency-and-Credit Based Prior Learning Assessment & Recognition (CCPLAR). However, both paths require additional training in the form of CLB Bootcamp and Introduction to PBLAE. The accreditation process for TESL Ontario programs is

Overcoming Racism and Discrimination

rigorous, and not all programs meet the requirements for certification. The majority of internationally trained ESL teachers are not eligible to apply through Path 1, and should opt for the CCPLAR path which requires extensive documentation of prior experience, education, and training.

Even after earning certification, ESL teachers in Ontario face ongoing obligations: They must meet annual renewal requirements which involve completing forms, fulfilling professional development (PD) requirements, and paying renewal fees. Failing to meet these requirements can result in the suspension or revocation of certification. If certification lapses, teachers must go through a reinstatement process.

Limited Career Prospects and an Unfair Hiring Process

ESL teachers typically receive lower pay and fewer work benefits compared to teachers in other fields, due to several factors, including less secure and contract-nature positions.

First, many ESL teachers work in privately funded language schools or community centers where salaries are usually lower than those in public schools. According to ONTESOL, "most English teaching jobs in Canada are found in private language schools, which offer ESL immersion classes to international students living in Canada between 1 and 12 months" (*Teach English in Canada | TESOL Teaching Canada*, n.d.). This arrangement leads to unstable income, as it depends on factors, such as the number of students enrolled and the availability of classes. The best ESL jobs in the field are typically found

Figure 2. A Job Posting for a Part-Time Supply Language Instructor Position
Source: https://ca.indeed.com

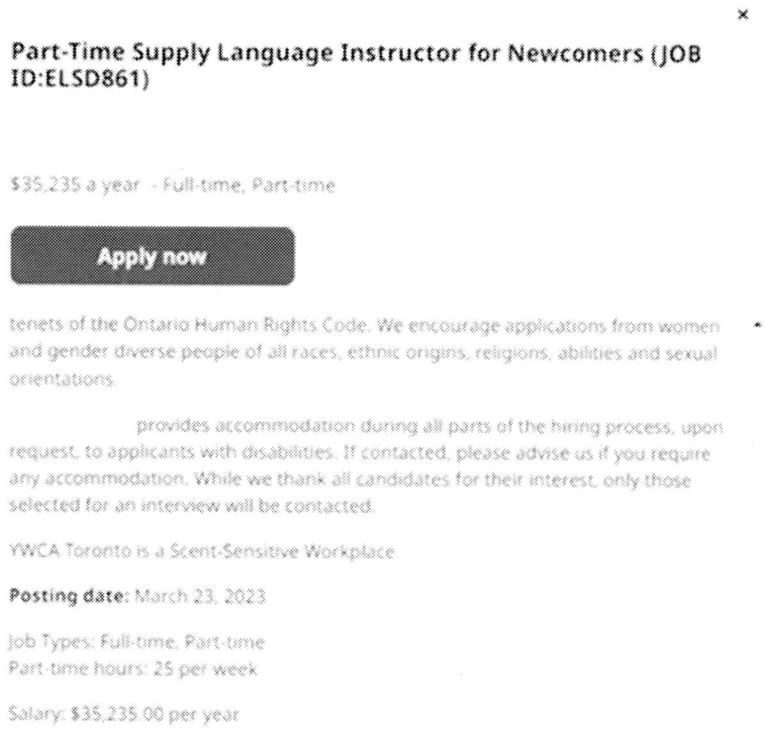

Part-Time Supply Language Instructor for Newcomers (JOB ID:ELSD861)

$35,235 a year - Full-time, Part-time

Apply now

tenets of the Ontario Human Rights Code. We encourage applications from women and gender diverse people of all races, ethnic origins, religions, abilities and sexual orientations.

_____ provides accommodation during all parts of the hiring process, upon request, to applicants with disabilities. If contacted, please advise us if you require any accommodation. While we thank all candidates for their interest, only those selected for an interview will be contacted.

YWCA Toronto is a Scent-Sensitive Workplace.

Posting date: March 23, 2023

Job Types: Full-time, Part-time
Part-time hours: 25 per week

Salary: $35,235.00 per year

at the Language Instruction for Newcomers to Canada (LINC), a program operated by Citizenship and Immigration Canada (CIC). While these positions offer higher payment compared to others, they still do not provide completely secure employment. According to a CIC report (2010), the temporary or contractual nature of teaching positions has been a longstanding issue, with nearly half of the LINC teachers being NNESTs. Supposedly, the issue stems from the uncertain number of newcomers enrolling in LINC classes and the short-term contracts between CIC and LINC program delivery organizations (CPOs). However, scholars such as Moussu (2006) and Canagarajah (1999) argue that the problem of job instability for NNESTs is rooted in politics and driven by financial gains as NESTs can ensure their "trade privilege" (Rajagopalan, 2005, p. 284).

As a case in point, a recent job posting for a Part-Time Supply Language Instructor for Newcomers in Etobicoke, Ontario with one of the biggest non-profit organizations in North America and 150 years history shows that the successful candidate can earn about $35,000 a year (See Figure 2). This means that a teacher's earnings are less than $3,000 a month, while renting a one-bedroom apartment in the city costs around $2,501 a month (Fox, 2023).

Linguistic and Racial Discrimination

Linguistic and racial discrimination manifests itself in students' resistance to learn English with non-native, non-white teachers:

The report from CIC (2002) highlights the dissatisfaction of students with NNESTs in their classes. The students expressed two primary concerns through learner surveys and focus groups. Firstly, they believed that they would learn English more effectively from NSs. Secondly, they questioned whether teachers with less-than-ideal command of English, in terms of vernacular and pronunciation, were serving them adequately.

This preference for NESTs and dissatisfaction with NNESTs is rooted deeply and given different names: "native speaker fallacy" as described by Phillipson (2009, p. 218) and "native speakerism" coined by Holliday (2013, p. 6). Essentially, it is the belief that NNs are inherently the ideal models and teachers of English, due to their birthplace and cultural background. Despite being challenged in the literature for decades, this misconception remains prevalent and widespread among students, institutions, and societies worldwide.

Medgyes (1992, 2001) has conducted studies exploring the effectiveness on NNESTs and found that they provide more realistic models for learners, understand potential learning problems, offer more suitable teaching-learning strategies, and demonstrate empathy, sensitivity, and responsiveness to students' needs. NNESTs are believed to excel in "accuracy" (Norton & Tang, 1997) and possess rich grammatical knowledge (Medgyes, 1994). NNESTs are generally considered more "culturally and linguistically aware and more "insightful" than NESTs. With all of these advantages, NNEST should not be considered inferior to their native colleagues (Medgyes, 2001).

Nevertheless, stakeholders often blindly uphold the misguided belief that NESTs are more ideal (Floris & Renandya, 2020) and exhibit preferences for White teachers (Amin, 1994, 1999). This often results in discriminatory practices towards NNEST and international-trained ESL teachers who are viewed as inferior, due to "accent discrimination" (Derwing & Munro, 2009; Matsuda, 1991; Munro, 2003), NNESTs' "self-perceived prejudice based on ethnicity or nonnative status" (Kamhi-Stein, 2000, p.10), and scrutiny from their native coworkers (Morita, 2004). The following section will closely analyze each of the three factors.

Accent Discrimination and Racism

It is important to note that everyone speaks with an accent, and "how you speak is who you are" (Kinzler, 2020). Accents reflect the speakers' original backgrounds, cultures, class, and social identities. In her book, Kindzler (2020) provides evidence that the voices of minorities have been dismissed in the media, and their credibility has been undermined and stigmatized in workplaces and court cases. In movies, protagonists often speak with native-like accents, while antagonists are given foreign accents. In court cases, witnesses who speak with accents are not trustworthy for the jury. Additionally, teachers with the slightest accents are considered incapable of communicating in English. In Chapter 6 of her book, she concludes that accent discrimination is a significant issue with both racial and social implications. Similariy, Amin (2000) argued that "accents, like race, are socially organized, are a linguistic manifestation of nativism, and constitute a new and effective form of racism" (p. 4). Kachru (1992) also observed that the "accent bar" hindered the recognition of NNESTs. Matsuda (1991) further explains that the people whose English is viewed as purified and standardized hold the power and the status of the dominant culture, while those who do not speak with the right accent are considered inferior. As a result, NNESTs' credibility and legitimacy are questioned. This accent discrimination perpetuates the notion that NNSs are inadequate language instructors which has reinforced the preference for NESTs in education settings.

The intertwining of accent discrimination and discrimination based on race is evident in the Canadian context (Munro, 2003), and English second language (L2) users are the victims of both (Derwing & Munro, 2005). James (2001) revealed the discrimination against Black teachers in Canada. He found that black teachers were consistently subjected to negative perceptions and constant scrutiny by students. The students in his study expressed their surprise at having a black teacher, as they associated Black individuals with lower socioeconomic status, limited education, and criminality. Unfair treatment against Asian teachers was also examined by Derwing and Munro (2005). In their study, teacher candidates of Asian descent were even bullied by students from Eastern Europe due to their race. Additionally, racial and linguistic identities were further explored by Liu (1999). Native-speaking teachers were sometimes perceived as non-native speakers because of their Asian ethnicity, while Caucasian teachers were often assumed to be native speakers even if they were not. The association of Whiteness with privilege and authority perpetuates discrimination against non-native, non-White teachers, further marginalizing their experiences and contributions in educational settings.

NNESTs' Self-Perceived Prejudices Based on Ethnicity or Non-Native Status

The consequence of the prevailing belief that NESTs are superior, and NNESTs are inferior language instructors is the eternal linguistic fear and anxiety among NNESTs. In Huo's book (2020, p. 63), such anxieties have two stages: "linguistic insecurity," as coined by Kachu and Nelson (1996), and "inferior complex," as highlighted by Liu (2015), Medgyes (1994), and Rajagopalan (2005). Both outline the internalized feelings of inadequacy and self-doubt experienced by NNESTs as a result of societal and institutional bias. They can also shatter NNESTs' confidence, resulting in self-evaluation to the point where they are "panicked" or "intimidated" (Liu, 1999, p. 162). According to Kamhi-Stein (2000), NNESTs' low self-esteem is not just because of the "self-perceived challenges to professional competence," but also the "self-perceived prejudice based on ethnicity or nonnative status" (p. 10).

Such negative emotions are fueled by the students' intolerance. In a study in Toronto, Ontario, Amin (2000) proved that students' attitudes differ substantially toward NESTs and NNESTs. They are tolerant of the mistakes made by NESTs, but they readily challenge and question NNESTs right away if they detect an error. For teachers influenced by the Confucian doctrine in which teachers are expected to be infallible, and become a threat to authority, the anxieties can be exacerbated (Paine, 1990). They are more self-conscious of their mistakes and fixated on maintaining a favorable image of themselves as teachers among students.

Workplace Skepticism or Judgment Against NNESTs

Teacher identities are not solely shaped by their own self-perceptions, but also by how they are perceived and treated by their coworkers in the field of ESL education (Farrell, 2016; Wong et al., 2022; Wong & Turkan, 2022). The opinions and attitudes of their colleagues play a significant role in shaping the professional identity and sense of belonging of ESL teachers. When non-native, non-White teachers are subjected to prejudice and discrimination from their coworkers, it can have profound implications for their self-esteem, confidence, and overall professional well-being.

NNESTs felt unworthy due to their embarrassment over their past experiences as language learners (Johnson, 2006; Kim, 2011). Morita's study (2004) revealed that NNESTs faced skepticism or judgment from their native colleagues, further exacerbating their challenges in establishing credibility and fostering a supportive work environment. Wong (2022) showcased the challenges faced by a new ESL teacher who ultimately decided to leave the profession. The lack of support from colleagues and the marginalization of non-native backgrounds presents systemic barriers that deter individuals from entering and remaining in the ESL teaching field. Experiencing isolation and being looked down upon at work can be a deeply demotivating and dissatisfying experience, often leading to a loss of drive and job satisfaction, and in some cases, exiting the field altogether.

In conclusion, non-native English-speaking ESL teachers frequently encounter discrimination and are often paid less, despite possessing equivalent qualifications and experiences compared to their native English-speaking counterparts. The bias, rooted in the notions of native-speakerism and accent discrimination, can compel them to accept lower-paying positions or even leave the teaching profession which is a significant loss considering their valuable contributions to language education.

METHODOLOGY

Research Question

The existing literature extensively explores various facets of discrimination faced by internationally trained teachers in Canada. However, limited attention has been given to the distinct experiences of Vietnamese ESL teachers, resulting in their voices being further marginalized. Through the exchange of personal narratives and reflection on individual life circumstances, our aim is to investigate the following research question:

How does discrimination manifest in the Canadian ESL industry, particularly against Vietnamese ESL teachers?

Collaborative Autoethnography

Autoethnography (AE) is a qualitative research method that focuses on self as a study subject, so researchers who employ this method use their personal stories, which are situated in sociocultural contexts, as data to hone an understanding of society through the unique lens of self (Chang, 2008, 2011). By adding another dimension: *Collaboration,* Chang et al. (2016) defined *Collaborative autoethnography* (CAE) as a research method that involves "researchers pooling their stories to find some commonalities and differences and then wrestling with these stories to discover the meanings of the stories in relation to their socio-cultural contexts" (p. 17). Thus, CAE still explores personal narratives, but does so collectively and cooperatively within a group of researchers, gaining "a meaningful understanding of sociocultural phenomena reflected in their autobiographical data" (Chang et al., 2016, p. 24). Both AE and CAE are self-focused, context-conscious, researcher-visible, and critically dialogic. Other common key features of AE and CAE include emotional resonance, experience specificity, analytic reflexivity, and inter-subjectivity.

This study employs CAE as a research methodology and is based on two autoethnographic accounts of personal narratives in collaboration. Personal narratives, also referred as the personal experiences, opinions, and thoughts, are shared qualitatively in the narrative research design (Ellis & Bochner, 1996). The purpose of this methodology is to provide individuals with a sense of self in a cultural context, allowing them to reflect meaningfully on their experiences (Ellis & Bochner, 2003). By reflecting on our situations and writing about our stories, we are expected to heal our wounds, since writing personal stories can be therapeutic. It allows us to make sense of ourselves and our experiences (Richardson, 2000), and hopefully make peace with them. The study will also empower us, NNETs, as the minority group in the Canadian ELS industry (Amin, 1997), since we can "speak against, or provide alternatives to, dominant, taken-for-granted, and harmful cultural scripts, stories, and stereotypes" (Adams et al., 2017, p. 3), and "describe moments of everyday experience that cannot be captured through more traditional research methods" (Adam et al., 2017, p. 4).

The Process of Collaborative Autoethnography

The process of this CAE is guided by Ngunjiri et al.'s (2010) project, composed of the following four phases (Figure 1). This iterative process allows researchers to combine both individual and team activities and return to a previous step that enhances data collection, analysis, or interpretation by using as many iterations as necessary.

Figure 3. The Iterative Process of Collaborative Autoethnography (Ngunjiri et al., 2010)

Phase 1: Preliminary Data Collection

Since we often shared with each other our challenges being non-native ESL teachers in Canada, we collectively decided to conduct this study with a general direction, scope, focus, and topics of the research to explore at this beginning stage. This initial converging step was followed by our official weekly meetings, via Zoom, to share our experiences. These meetings were audio-recorded and transcribed to add to our pool of data.

Phase 2: Subsequent Data Collection

Initially, each of us read the transcripts and reflected on our experiences individually. Then, we continued meeting online to review, discuss, and pose questions to each other, sharing and adding more data, if necessary. This convergent step enabled us to shape the path of our study together, whereas the divergent step created the space for us to collect our data free of one another's influences.

Phase 3: Data Analysis and Interpretation

We met again to collectively explore preliminary analysis, create open coding, and identify and develop key themes. After this theme-search step, we interpreted and made meanings based on the analyzed data, honing a comprehensive picture of our experiences. We alternated between individual (divergent) and collaborative (convergent) activities multiple times throughout the initial three phases, persistently working towards achieving agreement and mutual consensus.

Phase 4: Report Writing

As a group, we reached a collective decision regarding the structure of the final report. Subsequently, each member took on the task of individually writing different sections that had been discussed. Following this, we meticulously proofread, edited, and revised the paper. Finally, we met online to bring all the components together and finalize the report.

FINDINGS AND DISCUSSION

Subject 1: Elena came to Canada in 2019 as a skilled worker. She earned a master's degree from Victoria University (Melbourn, Australia). She is currently teaching at Sheridan College and Niagara College Toronto. With her broad background in International Studies, TESOL, Publishing and Management, she has shaped the minds of thousands of students from diverse cultural backgrounds.

Subject 2: For 10 years working as an ESL lecturer for a Vietnamese prestigious university, Thu completed a competitive thesis-based master program in TESOL. Now, she is pursuing a Ph.D. program in Educational Studies at the University of Windsor and working as a graduate teaching and researcher assistant.

Overcoming Racism and Discrimination

Our voices as NNESTs in the Ontario ESL labor market are key to the discussion on the unique challenges that we, as Vietnamese teachers and scholars, have encountered in the Canadian social and institutional system. In this section, we narrated our personal stories and broke them into three levels, guided by Thomas's (1999) study: institutional – from society, organizational – from schools, and interpersonal – from students and native-speaking colleagues. While Elena's data represents challenges from society at the institutional level, Thu provides more specific data explaining her organizational obstacles. We both experienced difficulties from students and colleagues on an interpersonal level.

Institutional level: Being Trapped in the Systemic Discrimination Against Minority Asian Professionals

Elena: The story I am about to share is a personal account of my costly and perplexing journey to reaccredit my credentials, and the unfortunate discrimination I faced during my re-training time. It was a challenging and disheartening experience that left me questioning the fairness of different Canadian institutions.

After attaining my permanent residency status for one year, my family migrated to Canada in 2020 during COVID. My strongest wish was to continue working in the ESL field, and to provide financial support for my family. It was challenging to work as an ESL teacher right away, as I had to navigate a new country, a different culture, and a totally different hiring system.

After doing a lot of research, I learned that the document from World Education Services which verified my honors master's degree in TESOL (Test of English to Speakers of other Languages) seemed to hold little value in Canada because the hidden job market here favored individuals with Canadian credentials. Therefore, the first thing I needed to do was to get the appropriate accreditation, and then

Figure 4. Email Rejecting Elena's PLAR Assessment Application

Dear Elena,

Thank you for submitting your PLAR Assessment Application for TESL Ontario Accreditation.

I regret to tell you we cannot accept your application for assessment at this time due the following reason:

- An 18-month full-time in-class Masters education with Victoria University (Melbourne, Australia) does not meet the English language proficiency (ELP) requirement of accreditation. ELP option 1 reads as follows:

"A **minimum-three-year** full-time in-class **bachelor's degree** program completed with English as the language of instruction in an English speaking country

You should take a recognized ELP test and obtain the required bands/scores to be eligible for PLAR assessment.

Once your proof of ELP is in place, we will reconsider your application.

If you have any questions, please let me know.

Best,

become an Ontario Certified ESL teacher. I worked as an on-the-phone interpreter with a meager income, while waiting to be re-accredited to work as an ESL teacher.

I applied through the Prior Learning Assessment and Recognition (PLAR) process, highlighting the fact that my master's degree was obtained from a well-known Australian university, where I received the honor of being the valedictorian during the graduation ceremony. I also spent two months self-studying the CLB and the PBLA systems and attained all of the necessary certificates. However, the response I received was disheartening:

I was shocked. So, a master's degree held less value than a bachelor's degree? Was my master's, postgraduate diploma, and bachelor's degree, along with over 10 years of teaching experience, not sufficient? And if someone studying a PhD program in TESOL even in Canada for three years, would they have to wait another one to four years until it is completed, or was it simply because the Canadian system was more superior?

With all of these doubts, I decided to pursue a Canadian TESL diploma to understand what I was lacking. I started an online TESL diploma course when my third daughter was two months old. She was born with a hip dislocation, and I put her next to me when I attended lessons. I turned off my camera when I needed to breastfeed her. Despite all my sacrifices, the learning experience was not worthwhile. It was actually horrible. I had the feeling that my teachers and my classmates, most of whom were native Canadians, looked down on me. One incident that stands out is when my teacher made a general statement in class, claiming that Vietnamese-speaking students spoke the most unintelligibly. She showed a YouTube video of a funny English lesson to illustrate her point (See Figure 5). When I tried to tell her that the video was not in Vietnamese but Thai, she ignored me. From that point on, it seems as if everybody could dismiss my voice.

Figure 5. Comedy YouTube Video Shown to Make Fun of Vietnamese Accent
Source: https://youtube.ca

Funny Learning English Lessons Class Ep.1

Overcoming Racism and Discrimination

Contrary to their belief, I was one of the first ones to graduate, again with straight A's. I got a job in a college even before I completed my degree. When I shared some job postings on our students' WhatsApp's group, some questioned how I knew about college jobs. I told them that I worked at college then. They said that the pay was too good to be true, and that these positions required managerial experience, so, what they were implying was that being Vietnamese meant that I could not secure decent jobs, and that I should not have had managerial experience, or that I was telling lies. I only told them that the links were there for them to check, and if they were interested, they could apply.

After a year of working, I finally obtained my OCELT & ICTEAL certificates and professional designations. However, despite my $6,000 and two-year investment, these credentials did not significantly enhance my standing or credibility as a teacher. Instead, this whole experience brought me feelings of regret and shame, as I found myself subjected to discrimination from my classmates, teachers, and the whole system. The bitter irony is that I, the one who was bullied, is the only one who remembers and carries the burden of shame.

It is not and will not be an isolated story. This systematic discrimination, perhaps unconscious, has been affecting not just me. My story is just another validation of the unfair treatment and bullying shared by many Asian educators examined by Derwing and Munro's research (2005). We have been subjected to bullying, marginalization, and hostility. The symmetric nature of this kind of discrimination underscores the need for collective awareness and understanding.

Now, Thu is taking on a similar journey to mine. Although she had ten years of experience teaching English in Vietnam, and her master's degree is assessed by World Education Services (WES) as having Canadian equivalency to a master's degree in Canadian institutions, she must set aside her international training and degrees and start over from scratch to land an ESL teacher job in Ontario. This sustainably impacts her self-esteem and confidence. She must carefully manage time and financial resources, while trying to adapt to the requirements. This often involves making difficult and costly sacrifices and striking a balance among various priorities. I sincerely hope that she will not have to endure any further bullying along this already arduous path.

Organizational Level: Being Marginalized

Thu: With an aim to continue my career as an ESL teacher in the new labor market – Canada, my story communicates challenges pertaining to the feelings of inadequacy, inferiority, and competitive labor market during the hiring process. Coming to Canada as a PhD scholarship holder, I bring my prior professional and academic background, credentials, and experiences, but they are often not recognized and valued by employers and institutions of higher education in Ontario as these lack "Canadian" elements. Knowing that "when in Rome, do as the Romans do," I got my master's degree assessed by World Education Services (WES). Fortunately, my three-year English-training program is a Canadian equivalency to a master's degree in Canadian institutions.

However, even though I submitted so many applications to various colleges and English centers, I never heard back from them, nor did I receive any calls for an interview. I recognized that WES, mentioned as an official verification organization for degrees, has no real value in Canada. Elena learned this after she spent money verifying her honor master's degree, but it did not help with her journey of reaccrediting her credentials. One simple explanation for this is that we still need "Canadian credentials" and "Canadian experience." Picot and Hou (2003) indicate that international credentials have little to do with access to professional environments in a foreign land. As a result, to seize a Canadian employment opportunity, internationally-trained immigrants often seek education and training in new fields (Chassels, 2005).

With the feeling that my prior educational qualifications and experiences are inadequate in Canada, I started working as a teaching assistant in my university to have Canadian teaching experience. I was offered this job, as this is a guaranteed funding resource for my doctoral program. I have been teaching for two years at this Canadian institution; however, things have not changed, and my challenges seeking the position of an ESL course instructor remain. I have never heard from any employers after my emails and applications were sent. Similar to Lanying who shared stories as a newcomer in Canada (Chassels, 2010), I felt that my self-worth and self-esteem were diminishing, due to my inability to access employment related to my education and experience.

Although facing the feelings of inadequacy and inferiority, I refused to give up. Fortunately, I received one response: the first interview with a program coordinator from a college in Toronto. The interview went so well that I had a chance to discuss my qualifications, teaching experience, and philosophy further. The coordinator provided me with detailed information regarding the job for a new teacher, such as office hours, hourly pay, different teaching shifts, number of courses per semester, first assessment for teaching skills, or requirements for follow-up semesters. The interview ended with "I will send you the teaching materials and requirements for your demo teaching with the academic manager in the afternoon." My heart was dancing at that moment, and I thought "Yeah, my time comes, and my patience pays off." However, two days later, the email I got from her was a big shock for me.

Figure 6. Email Rejecting Thu's Job Application before the Demo Teaching

Hello Thu

Thank you for taking the time to speak with me and allowing us to consider you for a position with

While you have an impressive background, we have ultimately decided to move forward with other candidates for the role.

I'm happy to stay in touch should anything change or other opportunities with us come about that might fit your background as we continue to scale.

Again, thank you so much for your interest in and all the best in your future endeavors.

This refusal email would make sense if I had performed poorly in my demo-teaching. However, I was not even given a chance to showcase my skills and teaching techniques. They promised to arrange a demo section for me, but they broke their words. This decision was not made based on my performance, but on unseen reasons, so I wonder, then, if they were because of my gender, ethnicity, race, or nationality. It is unfair to me, not only because they broke their promise, but also because they did not take into account how much effort, time, energy, and money that I had devoted to reaching this point to meet the Canadian ESL industry requirements.

All of the painful feelings that I have experienced, and my limited access to the Ontario ESL labor market are closely linked to the concept of power, knowledge, and anti-racism education (Dei, 2000). Dei (2000) express consideration for opportunities available to immigrant minorities and that "race, class and gender conspire to determine which people are allowed into Canada where they are permitted to work once admitted and the conditions under which they work" (p. 32). According to Public Policy Forum (2004), the hiring process of immigrant teachers is significantly influenced by the privilege of Canadian credentials and experience. This hiring process can be categorized as racist because employers are reluctant to accept these teachers on board just due to their lack of "Canadian" elements (Goldberg, 2006).

Interpersonal Level: Being an "Outsider"

The accents, skin color, and ethnicities of minority teachers hold political significance (Bulamur, 2013). Among these factors, skin color determines whether they are recognized as insiders in academia. Zamel (1995) also demonstrate that non-native individuals are often "othered" (p. 519) and marginalized as "strangers in academia" (p. 506). We, being both non-native and people of color, truly found it difficult to fit in, despite our continuous efforts to connect with others. Our expertise is belittled by our colleagues and managers who do not even attempt to listen to our perspectives. The feeling of being present, but blocked by an unseen, yet unbreachable barrier, is profoundly demoralizing, leading to a sense of isolation and mediocrity. Below are our stories of being the invisible party in an organization.

Elena: I vividly remember the conversation I had with a White native teacher who worked as an ESL for the Toronto District School Board. We were having a casual dinner with a group of friends, and he might have had a few too many beers. We were practically strangers. However, I thought it was a good opportunity to network with people from a different background, so I asked him about his job and the prospects of working at the school board. His response caught me off guard. He said, "I've got a good ear. Judging by the way you speak: your English is really good. You definitely have a chance. I have a Chinese co-worker who teaches CLB 1-2. I couldn't understand a single f... word she said in our meeting."

I regretted initiating that conversation. It was so awkward. I did not know how to respond to his remark. So many questions raced through my mind: "What if his colleague is not Chinese, but only looks Chinese? Maybe she is Vietnamese, or from somewhere else entirely." However, one thing is clear: accented Asian teachers are often looked down upon by their native colleagues. Honestly, it made me question whether I really wanted to be part of that environment even if I had the chance.

Thu: As a teaching assistant, I usually grade students' papers, make them informed, and send them their scores together with comments or feedback in a way that clarifies their perceived scores. I remember once, when a group of students were not satisfied with the scores that they received. They sent an email to the course instructor without carbon copying me. I did not know about the email, until the instructor forwarded it to me and asked me to address their questions. I was happy to give further explanations, based on the given rubric. However, my name and contact information were also provided at the beginning of the semester, in class, in person, and included in the syllabus. In prior emails to this incident, it was transparent that I was the one who graded their assignments and communicated the feedback. Moreover, this group of students were pursuing their master's degrees. They are all professional communicators and email users. They should not have been that ignorant, not knowing how to send messages to the right audience. The only possible explanation for sending it to the instructor, and skipping me, was to deliberately keep me out of the loop. Deep down, I felt like my evaluation was not acknowledged, my credibility was dismissed, and my voice was ignored. I bet if I were a White native teaching assistant, they would never have done that.

This lonely, isolated sentiment is supported by the research of Canagarajah (1999) and Ren (2018) as they elucidated the struggles non-native English-speaking teachers face in establishing their professional identities as legitimate educators. However, we are living in the twenty-first century, an era focused on equity, diversity, and inclusion (EDI). How is our legitimacy as teachers possibly still judged based on race, nativeness, and ethnicity? If it is not racism or discrimination, then what else could it be?

CONCLUSION

In conclusion, our experiences as Vietnamese ESL teachers in Ontario, Canada have been disheartening, but we recognize that we are not alone in facing racism and discrimination based on our race, ethnicity, and language abilities. Similar to some participants in Amin's thesis (2000), our identities as ESL teachers, immigrant women, minority Asians from former colonized nation intersect. While we may feel powerless to change our reality, we firmly believe in the importance of contributing our voices to create a difference. Despite all those attempts to silence and belittle us, we choose to present our cases and seek out like-minded individuals who share our personal integrity, professional aspirations, and desire for legitimacy.

Thankfully, we have been fortunate enough to find each other and have formed a supportive network. Through collaborating on this chapter, we have actively engaged in our professional development, leveraging our collective experiences to reason and navigate the challenges we encounter. Our motivation to persevere and never give up remains unwavering. We are committed to amplifying our voices and working towards a more inclusive and equitable future within our field.

REFERENCES

Adams, T. E., Ellis, C., & Jones, S. H. (2017). Autoethnography. In J. Matthes, C. S. Davis, & R. F. Potter (Eds.), *The international encyclopedia of communication research methods* (1st ed., pp. 1–11). Wiley. doi:10.1002/9781118901731.iecrm0011

Amin, N. (1997). Race and the identity of the N=nonnative ESL Teacher. *TESOL Quarterly, 31*(3), 580. doi:10.2307/3587841

Amin, N. (2000). *Negotiating nativism, minority immigrant women ESL teachers and the native speaker construct* [Thesis]. https://tspace.library.utoronto.ca/handle/1807/14099

Balintec, V. (2023, January 26). *This teacher hopes his 2-year battle to get certified in Ontario inspires other skilled immigrants | CBC News*. CBC. https://www.cbc.ca/news/canada/toronto/oct-internationally-educated-teacher-update-1.6724231

Bank of Canada. (2023). *Monetary policy report—April 2023*. Author.

Braine, G. (Ed.). (2013). *Non-native educators in English language teaching*. Routledge. doi:10.4324/9781315045368

Bulamur, A. N. (2013). Legitimacy of teaching English composition as a non-native speaker. *Universal Journal of Educational Research*, *1*(3), 170–174. doi:10.13189/ujer.2013.010305

Butler, Y. (2007). How Are nonnative-English-speaking teachers perceived by young learners? *TESOL Quarterly*, *41*(4), 731–755. Advance online publication. doi:10.1002/j.1545-7249.2007.tb00101.x

Chang, H., Ngunjiri, F., & Hernandez, K.-A. C. (2016). *Collaborative autoethnography*. Routledge., doi:10.4324/9781315432137

Chassels, C. (2010). Participation of internationally-educated professionals in an initial teacher education Bachelor of Education degree program: Challenges and Supports. *Canadian Journal of Educational Administration and Policy*, 100.

Chassels, C. J. (2005). Internationally-educated adults: Issues of access to university undergraduate degree programs. *American Educational Research Association Annual Meeting*.

Clark, E., & Paran, A. (2007). The employability of non-native-speaker teachers of EFL: A UK survey. *System*, *35*(4), 407–430. doi:10.1016/j.system.2007.05.002

Crawley, M. (2023, January 30). *Noticing a labour shortage? Here's what's really going on in Ontario's job market*. CBC News. https://www.cbc.ca/news/canada/toronto/ontario-workers-shortage-1.6727310

Dei, G. J. (2000). Towards an anti-racism discursive framework. In D. George & C. Agnes (Eds.), *Power, knowledge and anti-racism education: A critical reader* (pp. 23–40). Fernwood.

Dervic, M., & Becirovic, S. (2019). Native and non-native EFL teachers dichotomy: Terminological, competitiveness and employment discrimination. *Journal of Language and Education*, *5*(3), 114–127. doi:10.17323/jle.2019.9746

Derwing, T. M., & Munro, M. J. (2009). Putting accent in its place: Rethinking obstacles to communication. *Language Teaching*, *42*(4), 476–490. doi:10.1017/S026144480800551X

Ellis, C., & Bochner, A. P. (1996). Talking over ethnography. In C. Ellis & A. P. Bochner (Eds.), *Composing Ethnography: Alternative Forms of Qualitative Writing* (pp. 13–45). Alta Mira Press.

Ellis, C., & Bochner, A. P. (2003). Autoethnography, personal narrative, reflexivity: Researcher as subject. *Collecting and Interpreting Qualitative Materials*, *2*, 199–258.

Farrell, T. S. C. (2016). Surviving the transition shock in the first year of teaching through reflective practice. *System*, *61*, 12–19. doi:10.1016/j.system.2016.07.005

Floris, F. D., & Renandya, W. A. (2020). Promoting the value of non-native English-speaking teachers. *PASAA: Journal of Language Teaching and Learning in Thailand, 59*, 1–19.

Goldberg, M. P. (2006). Discursive policy webs in a globalization era: A discussion of access to professions and trades for immigrant professionals in Ontario, Canada. *Globalisation, Societies and Education, 4*(1), 77–102. doi:10.1080/14767720600555103

Holliday, A. (2013). *The Struggle to teach English as an international language*. Oxford University Press.

Huo, X. (2020). Review of Research on Teachers of English as an International Language. In *Higher Education Internationalization and English Language Instruction*. Springer., https://doi.org/10.1007/978-3-030-60599-5_4

James, C. E. (2001). I've never had a black teacher before. Talking about identity. *Encounters in Race, Ethnicity, and Language*, 150–167.

Johnson, K. E. (2006). The sociocultural turn and its challenges for second language teacher education. *TESOL Quarterly, 40*(1), 235–257. doi:10.2307/40264518

Kachru, B. B. (1992). *The other tongue: English across cultures*. University of Illinois Press.

Kachru, B. B., & Nelson, C. L. (1996). World Englishes. *Sociolinguistics and Language Teaching, 11*, 71–102.

Kamhi-Stein, L. D. (2000). Adapting U.S.-based TESOL education to meet the needs of nonnative English speakers. *TESOL Journal, 9*(3), 10–14. doi:10.1002/j.1949-3533.2000.tb00261.x

Kim, H.-K. (2011). Native speakerism affecting nonnative English teachers' identity formation: A critical perspective. *English Teaching, 66*(4), 53–71. doi:10.15858/engtea.66.4.201112.53

Kinzler, K. D. (2020). *How you say it: Why you talk the way you do? And what it says about you*. Houghton Mifflin Harcourt.

Liu, J. (1999). From their own perspectives: The impact of non-native ESL professionals on their students. In G. Braine (Ed.), *Non-native educators in English language teaching* (pp. 159–176). Routledge.

Matsuda, M. J. (1991). Voices of America: Accent, antidiscrimination law, and a jurisprudence for the last reconstruction. *The Yale Law Journal, 100*(5), 1329–1407. doi:10.2307/796694

Medgyes. (2001). When the teacher is a non-native speaker. *Teaching English as a Second or Foreign Language, 3*, 429–442.

Mindzak, M. W. (2016). *Exploring the working-lives of unemployed and underemployed teachers in Ontario* [Ph.D., The University of Western Ontario (Canada)]. https://www.proquest.com/docview/2701131028/abstract/161BF75B4A6D49B6PQ/1

Morita, N. (2004). Negotiating participation and identity in second language academic communities. *TESOL Quarterly, 38*(4), 573–603. doi:10.2307/3588281

Munro, M. J. (2003). A Primer on Accent Discrimination in the Canadian Context. *TESL Canada Journal, 20*(2), 38–51. doi:10.18806/tesl.v20i2.947

Ngunjiri, F. W., Hernandez, K.-A. C., & Chang, H. (2010). Living Autoethnography: Connecting Life and Research. *Journal of Research Practice*, *6*(1).

Norton, B., & Tang, C. (1997). The identity of the nonnative ESL teacher on the power and status of nonnative ESL teachers. *TESOL Quarterly*, *31*(3), 577–580. doi:10.2307/3587840

OCELT & ICTEAL certification. (n.d.). TESL Ontario. Retrieved Dec 31, 2023, from https://teslontario.org/certification/teacher-certification/

Ontario College of Teachers. (2021). *Transition to teaching 2021: 20th annual survey of Ontario's early-career elementary and secondary teachers.* Ontario Colleges of Teachers.

Ontario Helping Newcomers Start Their Careers. (2021). King's Printer for Ontario. https://news.ontario.ca/en/release/1001014/ontario-helping-newcomers-start-their-careers

Paine, L. W. (1990). The Teacher as Virtuoso: A Chinese Model for Teaching. *Teachers College Record*, *92*(1), 49–81. https://doi.org/10.1177/016146819009200105

Phillipson, R. (2009). *Linguistic imperialism continued.* Routledge.

Picot, G., & Hou, F. (2003). *The rise in low-income rates among immigrants in Canada.* Analytical Studies Branch, Statistics Canada.

Public Policy Forum. (2004). *Bringing employers into the immigration debate: The public policy implications of findings.* https://policycommons.net/artifacts/1203936/bringing-employers-into-the-immigration-debate/1757046/

Ren, K. (2018). "I was refused an ELT job for being non-native" An Insight into the Native Speaker Ideology in ELT. *Journal of English Language and Literature*, *10*(1), 940–945. Advance online publication. doi:10.17722/jell.v10i1.379

Richardson, L. (2000). Evaluating ethnography. *Qualitative Inquiry*, *6*(2), 253–255. doi:10.1177/107780040000600207

Schmidt, C. (2010). Systemic discrimination as a barrier for immigrant teachers. *Diaspora, Indigenous, and Minority Education*, *4*(4), 235–252. doi:10.1080/15595692.2010.513246

Schmidt, C., & Block, L. A. (2010). Without and within: The implications of employment and ethnocultural equity policies for internationally educated teachers. *Canadian Journal of Educational Administration and Policy*, 100.

Silva, L. P. (2009). *Students' expectations and attitudes towards nonnative-English-speaking teachers in ESL and EFL Settings: Teachers' and students' own perspectives.* https://researchrepository.wvu.edu/etd/10152

Spillane, R. (2023, March 30). *To win the battle for newcomer talent employers need to engage early.* Thestar.Com. https://www.thestar.com/opinion/contributors/2023/03/30/to-win-the-battle-for-newcomer-talent-employers-need-to-engage-early.html

Statistics Canada. (2022, November 30). *Canada leads the G7 for the most educated workforce, thanks to immigrants, young adults and a strong college sector, but is experiencing significant losses in apprenticeship certificate holders in key trades.* https://www150.statcan.gc.ca/n1/daily-quotidien/221130/dq221130a-eng.htm

Takada, T. (2000). The social status of L1 Japanese EFL teachers. *TESOL Matters, 10*(3). http://www.tesol.org/s_tesol/sec_document.asp?CID=195&DID=854

Teach English in Canada | TESOL Teaching Canada. (n.d.). On TESOL. Retrieved June 29, 2023, from https://ontesol.com/teach-english-in-canada/

Thomas, J. (1999). Voices from the periphery: Non-native teachers and issues of credibility. In G. Braine (Ed.), *Non-native educators in English language teaching* (pp. 5–14). Lawrence Erlbaum.

Wong, C.-Y. (2022). "ESL teachers are looked down upon": Understanding the lived experience of a first-year ESL teacher with culturally and linguistically diverse background. *Journal of Educational Research and Practice, 12*(1). Advance online publication. doi:10.5590/JERAP.2022.12.1.20

Wong, C.-Y., & Turkan, S. (2022). "NO ONE KNOWS WHO I AM": What school leaders can learn from ESL teachers' voices. *NYS TESOL Journal, 9*(1), 30–38.

Wong, C.-Y., Pompeo-Fargnoli, A., & Harriott, W. (2022). Focusing on ESOL teachers' well-being during COVID-19 and beyond. *ELT Journal, 76*(1), 1–10. doi:10.1093/elt/ccab069

Zamel, V. (1995). Strangers in Academia: The experiences of faculty and ESL students across the curriculum. *College Composition and Communication, 46*(4), 506–521. doi:10.2307/358325

KEY TERMS AND DEFINITIONS

Collaborative Autoethnography: A qualitative research approach that combines elements of autoethnography (auto-, ethno-, and graphy-) with collaboration among multiple researchers. Applying this approach, researchers come together to explore their personal experiences and stories, sharing their narratives and interpretations.

Employment Discrimination: Discrimination in the workplace where internationally trained teachers are treated unfairly and barred from getting jobs and work-related benefits.

Institutional Challenges: Obstacles or difficulties that non-native English-speaking teachers (NNESTs) encounter caused by society or systems, for example Canadian credentials and experience.

Interpersonal Challenges: Obstacles or difficulties that NNESTs encounter caused by students and native-speaking colleagues, for example linguistic discrimination.

Nativism: Protecting interests, including workplace interests of native-born against immigrants.

Organizational Challenges: Obstacles or difficulties that NNESTs encounter caused by schools, for example the hiring process and being treated as outsiders.

White Supremacy: White people are superior to those of other races, so in the context of this study, white ESL teachers are better than others.

Chapter 4
Coloniality and Whiteness in Evangelical ESL Classrooms

Ruthanne Hughes
University of South Carolina, USA

ABSTRACT

This chapter ethnographically investigates how ideologies of whiteness and missions interact in an evangelical English language school in South Carolina. Using discourse analysis of classroom observations and interviews with five teachers across eleven classes, the chapter explores how whiteness is central to but unmarked in the presentation of American culture that students are socialized into, and how legacies of colonialism and assimilationist strategies are upheld in the presentation of white evangelical culture as equivalent to American culture. The ideologies described here demonstrate how contemporary practices of evangelical ESL programs continue to reflect a lingering history of colonialism and white supremacy in which the field of English teaching has long been implicated (Han & Varghese, 2019; Kim, 2019; Kubota, 2001, 2021; Pennycook, 2002; Vaccino-Salvadore, 2021; Vandrick, 1999). It is important to note where the legacy of these movements remains so that biases and harmful practices can be confronted and ameliorated.

INTRODUCTION

An often underdiscussed component of hegemony present and transmitted in the English as a Second Language (ESL) classroom is that of white[1] American evangelicalism. It is a poorly kept secret that the field of Teaching English to Speakers of Other Languages (TESOL) has strong connections to missions work[2]. Religion has always been intimately tied to colonialism (de los Ríos et al., 2019; Gearon et al., 2020; Lachenicht et al., 2016; Veronelli, 2015; Winchcombe, 2021), as the motivations of European explorers and conquerors can be described by the motto "Gold, God, and Glory." As the arm of colonialism reached out, so did the church, with missionaries quickly establishing posts and schools. In order to transmit the gospel, the missionaries and indigenous people needed to have a common language. While some missionaries elected to learn the language(s) of the indigenous people and translate the Bible into those languages, others instead focused on teaching the indigenous people English so as to teach them

DOI: 10.4018/978-1-6684-9029-7.ch004

Christianity. Today, many ESL and English as a Foreign Language (EFL) teachers are missional evangelical Christians, and many missions-focused evangelical Christian universities offer TESOL degrees and certificates with the express intention of offering teaching English as a platform for missions work. Even in schools that are not explicitly Christian, the ideologies of missions work and evangelical theology often perpetuate colonialism and linguistic injustice in the ESL classroom. Students are socialized into "American culture"; however, white evangelical culture is often presented as representative of American culture in an effort to evangelize to and convert students.

This chapter investigates how ideologies of whiteness and missions interact in the ESL classroom through an ethnographic look at an English language school in South Carolina, marketed as a secular university-prep school, but with a Christian affiliation and missions-work orientation. The present study engages in discourse analysis in order to discuss how whiteness is central to but unmarked in the presentation of American culture that students are socialized into, and how legacies of colonialism and assimilationist strategies are upheld in the presentation of white evangelical culture as equivalent to American culture. The ideologies described in this chapter demonstrate how contemporary practices of evangelical ESL programs continue to reflect a lingering history of colonialism, Anglocentrism, and white supremacy in which the field of English teaching has long been implicated (Han & Varghese, 2019; Kim, 2019; Kubota, 2001, 2021; Pennycook, 2002; Vandrick, 1999). It is important to note where the legacy of these movements is still present in ESL today so that biases and harmful practices can be confronted and ameliorated.

COLONIALISM AND THE CHURCH

While the project of colonialism was largely an economic venture, the dominance that colonial powers maintained for centuries, and still maintain today, was not achieved by economic control alone. In conjunction with the competition for resources was the pursuit of cultural dominance and civilization of the colonized: colonial nations achieved and maintained economic dominance through cultural, religious, and linguistic promotion that was predicated on the erasure of indigenous cultures, religions, and languages. Religion was a critical vehicle for the imposition of the colonizer's culture onto the colonized. At first, the religion being exported was Catholicism, but with the Protestant Reformation, Protestantism became more culturally relevant and ultimately replaced Catholicism as the primary source of missionaries. In particular, Protestant missionaries became intrinsically linked with British imperialism (Gearon et al., 2020). In this context, teaching literacy was highly valued, as the doctrine of *sola scriptura* (Gearon, 2013) stated that God's written word is the only authority and only means of revelation from God, and thus reading God's word was crucial to salvation. This value resulted in the teaching of English reading and writing being strongly promoted across the vast British empire. Oftentimes, missions work and the teaching of English were one and the same pursuit as the lines between the pursuit of colonial dominance, Christian proselytization, and civilization of the native[3] blurred.

The results of this intertwining between English education, religion, and colonialism are still being felt throughout the fields of ESL and EFL (Gearon et al., 2020; Pennycook & Makoni, 2005). Indeed, English's status as the current lingua franca cannot be divorced from the history of colonialism and capitalism (O'Regan, 2021). The fact that many people consider English to be a necessary skill for economic advancement is rooted in the economic dominance of first the colonial British empire and then the neocolonial United States. While the global status of English is one result of colonialism, it also feeds further coloniality, as the demand for English begets continued exportation of the English language and Western culture. Protestant missionaries continue to be a key part of this exportation, with many missionaries teaching EFL as a platform to allow them to enter foreign countries and spread their religion (Johnston, 2017; Johnston & Varghese, 2006; Kim, 2019; Varghese & Johnston, 2007), or teaching ESL as a means to evangelize to foreign nationals residing in the United States (Han & Varghese, 2019). Evangelical Protestants are at the forefront of this work, as denominations considered to be evangelical are characterized by their dedication to evangelizing, or spreading the news of the Christian gospel (Edwards, 2015).

THE WHITE LISTENING SUBJECT

Whiteness has historically been at the core of colonialism, but as it operates as the unmarked, it is necessary to bring it into focus through raciolinguistic frameworks and concepts such as the white listening subject. The white listening subject is an extension of Inoue's concept of the listening subject. Inoue (2003) argued that the listening subject was instrumental in the *creation* of a category of Japanese woman who speaks Japanese women's language. During the late 19th and early 20th centuries, intellectual men wrote about the reported speech of schoolgirls, criticizing their speech as a corrupt form of language. Despite the small number of girls and women speaking in the reported ways, this ideology of schoolgirl language became so common that it eventually came to be synonymous with Japanese women's language and shifted in connotation, considered a sign of desirable Japanese womanhood. The listening subject in this case held great power to shape not only the way Japanese women were perceived, but the ideologies surrounding women's language and the identities of Japanese women in modernity. Similarly, the white listening subject holds power to shape the way white and non-white speakers are perceived, filtering language through a lens of hegemonic power that equates white speakers' English with the standard. On the converse, the white listening subject may perceive non-white speakers to be deviating from standard English when they are in fact producing standard language (Flores & Rosa, 2015).

The white listening subject is not necessarily a white person, nor even an individual (Rosa & Flores, 2017). Rosa and Flores (2017) argue that "racially hegemonic perceptions can be enacted […] not simply by white individuals but rather by whiteness as an historical and contemporary subject position that can be situationally inhabited both by individuals recognized as white and nonwhite" (Rosa & Flores, 2017, p. 628). People of many positionalities can embody the white listening subject because the term describes the act of listening with the white subject position in focus. Hegemonic systems derive their power from the actions of both the oppressors and the oppressed, self-replicating through internalized oppression that resists an examination of the default paradigms of what is accepted as normal.

Institutions infused with raciolinguistic ideologies may also act as white listening subjects, perceiving and judging student speech according to racialized standards irrespective of the attitudes of individual teachers (Rosa & Flores, 2017). Even when individual teachers hold reflexive attitudes and work against racism in aspects of their private lives, they may take on the role of the white listening subject in the school setting in response to raciolinguistic ideologies circulating in the broader discourse. An example of this can be seen in Flores, Lewis, and Phuong (2018). Their article proposed a raciolinguistic chronotope perspective, using data from an ethnographic study conducted over several years in a bilingual English/Spanish K-8 charter school. One particularly telling interview displays a teacher's anxiety regarding the future of Spanish in the United States:

I've noticed, especially my children who are lower in both languages, they have a struggle of kind of like turning that switch off of when English stops, when Spanish starts and vice versa. A lot of times what I see when we are learning letter sounds or interpreting them in the reading and decoding, I get a lot of Spanish sounds. You know for, for instance the word "yellow." A lot of times they have that accent on the /y/, reading /j/ jellow you know, so it sounds "jellow" in English. It puts a lot of pressure on me as an English teacher because if they are not performing in my class, you know potentially 20 years down the road, English being the language of America, what is that gonna look like? (Teacher Interview, 6/11/15). (Flores et al., 2018, p. 19)

This teacher expressed a sense of obligation toward listening to her students as future members of society, anticipating the judgments they might cast on her students. At other points in interviews, this teacher "expresse[d] ambivalence about the fairness of broader society" (Flores et al., 2018, p. 19). However, she still embodied a white listening subject in her perceptions and assessment of her students, drawing on raciolinguistic chronotopes and institutional norms to justify her judgements. This teacher was not an anomaly but represented more broadly circulated ideologies. Even if individual teachers do not wish to judge a student or might not judge the student's language if they encountered it outside of the classroom, within the institution, they may take on the role of the white listening subject that will judge them in the future, believing it to be their job to prepare their students for this eventuality (Flores et al., 2018).

The orientation to the white listening subject can also be observed in nonhuman actors. Language learning institutions often adopt school-wide curricula or pedagogical policies and stances that reinforce raciolinguistic ideologies. Alim (2007) stated that "language pedagogies are inherently ideological" (p. 166). Culture is taught alongside language, transmitting existing power structures. Ideologies about what kind of language is acceptable circulate explicitly in language learning environments. However, these ideologies are also implicitly tied to ideologies about what kinds of *speakers* are acceptable. It is common for teachers' language ideologies to elevate Standardized American English (SAE), a dialect inherently tied to forms of power in the United States (U.S.), to the exclusion of other varieties spoken by native speakers in the U.S. and abroad, as well as varieties of World English. Even if teachers' personal beliefs differ from the standards expressed in the curriculum, these ideologies have power in affecting how the school operates and how teachers act as white listening subjects, both when teaching and assessing.

METHODOLOGY

Overview

This project investigated whiteness through the white listening subject at an evangelical ESL school, utilizing data drawn from ethnographic observation I conducted between November 2021 and May 2022 and supplemented by recorded classes from the 2020-2021 school year. Classes and teacher interactions were observed in order to investigate school culture, language rating norms, and circulating ideologies and discourses. Following the period of observation, I also conducted individual interviews with each teacher. Transcription conventions are included in Table 1.

Coloniality and Whiteness in Evangelical ESL Classrooms

Table 1. Transcription conventions

–	Unfinished word or utterance
,	Short pause in conversation
(.)	Longer pause
(1)	Number indicates the number of seconds of silence.
CAPITAL LETTERS	Increase in volume
!	Emphasized utterance; shows excitement
?	Rising intonation
.	Falling intonation
=	Latching or a continuous utterance
:	Lengthening of the sound immediately preceding; The length of the sound is proportional to the number of colons.
____	Redacted; used for people and places that do not have assigned pseudonyms.
XXX	Laughter; number of Xs corresponds to length of laughter.
italics	Emphasis
{ }	When annotations correspond to only part of the utterance, the corresponding part is enclosed in { }.
{{ }}	Used when a single utterance has more than one annotation referring to different parts of the utterance; the second instance is enclosed in two sets of brackets corresponding to its annotation, also enclosed in two sets of brackets. Additional sets of brackets may be used as needed.
> <	Rate of speech is faster than surrounding speech.
< >	Rate of speech is slower than surrounding speech.

Research Questions

This chapter addresses the following research question: How are institutional practices of language assessment by ESL instructors at an evangelical Christian school potentially shaped by, and how do they contribute to the shaping of, locally circulating ideologies of language, race, and religion?

Researcher Positionality

As the researcher, my positionality is particularly relevant to my engagement with and analysis of this data. I am a young white woman raised primarily in the U.S. south, with a few years of my early childhood spent in South Korea. I was raised inside evangelical Christianity in circles where ESL was frequently used as a tool of ministry and/or missions work[4], and I was steeped in missionary culture from the day I was born. Both sets of my grandparents were career missionaries and my parents were missionaries for 2.5 years when I was young. After my parents returned from the mission field, my father began teaching at an evangelical Bible college with a particular focus on missions work.

While I did not initially set out to study the religious environment of my childhood, my faith background is extremely relevant to the communities I have studied. I came into contact with my participants at the site introduced below expressly through the missionary contacts of my family, as the founder knows my grandmother and father in their capacities as missionaries and granted me access after I reached out to him, identifying myself as their kin. Additionally, my own experiences with evangelical Christianity and with missionary culture provided my participants and me with common ground and a sense of familiarity and affinity. While my faith has changed as I have grown older, I still navigated my research with much of the knowledge and proficiency of an insider, understanding the Biblical references and speaking the coded language used to safely refer to missionary efforts.

Research Site

The site, denoted by the pseudonym Omega Language School, or Omega, was an English language school with campuses in two major South Carolina cities. They recruited students internationally and advertised themselves as an option to prepare students to enter higher education institutions in the U.S. They also recruited what they termed "local students," meaning non-American, nonnative English speakers already living in South Carolina who wished to improve their English, primarily in order to attain new

Table 2. Affiliations of schools listed on Omega's website

School	Affiliation	Racial Demographics
University of South Carolina Aiken	State school, satellite campus	61.4% white 23.1% Black 6.54% Hispanic [a]
University of South Carolina Upstate	State school, satellite campus	52.1% white 29.7% Black 7.06% Hispanic [a]
Clemson Graduate School	State graduate school	62.4% white 21.3% international 7.1% Black [b]
Greenville Technical College	City community college	59.4% white 17.6% Black 12.5% Hispanic [a]
Midlands Technical College	Regional community college	44.9% white 34.5% Black 7.37% Hispanic [a]
Bob Jones University	Private university; Self-described as "Orthodox, historic fundamentalist, non-denominational Christian liberal arts university"	70.5% white 7.32% Hispanic 2.54% Asian [a]
Charleston Southern University	Private university; Affiliated with South Carolina Baptist Convention	63.9% white 17.9% Black 4.61% two or more races [a]
Erskine College	Private Christian college and graduate seminary	49.0% white 29.9% unknown 16.3% Black [c]
Limestone University	Non-denominational Christian university	45% white 37% Black 10% unknown [d]
North Greenville University	Private university; Affiliated with South Carolina Baptist Convention	63% white 23% unknown 7% Black [a]

Note. Only the top three racial/ethnic categories for each school are provided in the Racial Demographics column. Data are from Data USA [a], College Factual [b], Forbes Magazine [c], and US News [d].

job opportunities. At the time of data collection, a large percentage of their students were local students, and had been since the Covid-19 pandemic.

As their website was a primary recruitment tool for students, the contents of the site are particularly relevant to the institution's image and culture. The school's mission statement and goals emphasized a commitment to friendliness and to meeting student needs. The site also promoted a multicultural image, recruiting from and appealing to students from a wide variety of national backgrounds. On their home page, they included testimonials from students from Vietnam, Brazil, Taiwan, China, Spain, Chile, and Venezuela. Their application was available in several languages including English, Spanish, Chinese, Korean, Vietnamese, Portuguese, Japanese, Arabic, Turkish, and Russian,[5] and the website had a built-in tool that allowed it to be translated into 20 languages.

Omega had a "no-TOEFL" conditional admission agreement with several colleges, universities, and high schools. This means that students who had passed Level 5 at Omega could transfer to one of these schools without having to take the TOEFL or IELTS exam. The schools included three private Christian high schools, along with three state schools, two community colleges, and five Christian-affiliated colleges or universities. The affiliations of the universities are in Table 2 below.

The two campuses of Omega were run similarly, but the City A campus was more robust in terms of student enrollment and numbers of teachers. At the time of data collection, City A employed four teachers who each taught three classes a day, five days a week. The City B campus employed one teacher who taught two classes, five days a week. The school tailored the classes offered to the needs of the students enrolled, with levels determined by the Common European Framework of Reference for Languages (CEFR). Classes in Grammar, Speaking and Listening, and Reading and Writing were provided for each level, or for a combination of levels, such as Level 3-4 Reading and Writing.

Participant Demographics

I observed five teachers at Omega for a total of 28 hours. Three white women taught at the City A site, one white man taught at the City B site, and one white woman was currently acting as an administrator but provided recordings of herself teaching virtually during the Covid-19 pandemic. Two of the City A teachers additionally provided videos of themselves teaching virtually during the pandemic. The teachers and their pseudonyms, along with the level/class designation taught and how many hours I spent directly observing their class are depicted in Table 3. Teachers self-selected their pseudonyms, with the exception of Bob, who requested I select for him.

Students in these courses (N=50) represented multiple countries and first languages (L1s), with many students coming from Latin America (at least 22) and East Asia (at least 13). Student information for each class is included in Table 4 below. Class sizes were small, varying between three and seven students. Students' religious backgrounds included Catholic Christianity, Islam, Buddhism, and atheism. Students were not asked to provide their religious affiliation; however, students occasionally brought up their religious backgrounds in class, and that information is noted here. Other students may have practiced additional religions that were not mentioned.

Omega gave me access to virtual recordings made in 2020/2021, also included in Table 4. However, the school did not consent to give me students' contact information, so students could not be reached to obtain their demographic information. In these classes, denoted with an asterisk in the table below,

Table 3. Participant information

City	Pseudonym	Demographics	Class(es) Taught	Hours of Direct Observation
Omega City B	Bob	White man, 63	Level 3, Speaking & Listening/ Level 4 Reading & Writing	10
Omega City A	Kay	White woman, 52	Level 4, Grammar	3
			(Virtual) Level 4 Grammar	1.25
Omega City A	Cheryl	White woman, 61	Level 4, Speaking & Listening	1.5
			(Virtual) Level 5 Grammar	1
			(Virtual) Level 6 Speaking & Listening	1.25
			(Virtual) Level 3 Reading & Writing	1.25
Omega City A	Christi	White woman, 41	Level 2, Reading & Writing	1.5
Omega Virtual	V	White woman, 42	(Virtual) Beginner Pronunciation	4
			(Virtual) Intermediate Pronunciation	0.75
			(Virtual) Conversation, Low Advanced	2.5

demographic information is based on my perception (particularly for gender) and on what information was mentioned in class. Some students made explicit reference to their first language or home country, but some did not. The information in the table is therefore not parallel or complete, but as much detail as possible is provided. Where race and country of origin information were not available but religious information was, "Muslim" appears in lieu of nationality or race/ethnicity.

RESULTS AND DISCUSSION

Throughout the period of ethnographic observation, several dynamics at play in the culture of Omega Language School emerged: the predominance of whiteness, the goal of assimilation and conversion to white American evangelicalism, and simultaneously the opacity of white American evangelicalism. Language ideologies were intertwined throughout these dynamics, privileging (white) Standardized American English over other English dialects and other non-English languages as the school and teachers oriented towards a white listening subject. These dynamics and ideologies were produced, reproduced, and reified in a multitude of ways in the culture of the school and in the teaching policies and practices of the institution and of individuals, as will be discussed in excerpts from classroom observations and individual interviews below. These excerpts are analyzed utilizing discourse analysis to highlight how the language in context exemplifies and contributes to the circulating institutional ideologies.

Table 4. Omega student demographics by class

Teacher	Class	Number of Students	Student Demographics
Bob	Level 3 Speaking & Listening/ Level 4 Reading & Writing	3	1 Chinese woman 1 Colombian man 1 Hispanic woman
Kay	Level 4, Grammar	3	2 Hispanic women 1 Brazilian woman
Kay	(Virtual) Level 4 Grammar	4*	1 East Asian woman 3 women
Cheryl	Level 4 Speaking & Listening	6	2 Turkish women 2 Colombian women 1 Brazilian woman 1 Japanese woman
Cheryl	(Virtual) Level 6 Speaking & Listening	7*	1 Vietnamese woman 1 East Asian woman 1 Brazilian man 1 Peruvian woman 1 Muslim woman, perhaps Arab 1 man, perhaps Italian 1 woman, speaks Russian and mentioned returning to Israel
Cheryl	(Virtual) Level 5 Grammar	5*	1 Brazilian man 1 Arab man 2 men, likely Italian 1 woman
Cheryl	(Virtual) Level 3 Reading & Writing	3*	1 East Asian man, perhaps Korean 1 Muslim woman 1 Black man, perhaps Caribbean
Christi	Level 2 Reading & Writing	6	3 Hispanic women 1 Black Hispanic woman 1 Hispanic man 1 East Asian woman
V	(Virtual) Beginner Pronunciation	4*	4 Chinese women
V	(Virtual) Intermediate Pronunciation	3*	1 Colombian man 1 Muslim woman, perhaps Arab 1 East Asian man
V	(Virtual) Conversation Low-Advanced	6*	2 Colombian men 1 Colombian woman 1 Venezuelan woman 1 Taiwanese woman 1 Argentinian woman

Whiteness in Evangelical Christian Culture

To understand how whiteness operated at Omega, it is first important to discuss whiteness in evangelical Christian culture in general. In evangelical Christian culture, whiteness is ever-present but often unmarked. It is often commented from the pulpit that "the most segregated hour in America is 11 am on Sunday,"[6] and if asked, white evangelicals would agree that the Black church in America does things differently. These differences emerge in practices, such as what clothing to wear, what types of movements are acceptable during worship, and the normativity of call-and-response during sermons, as well as in theology, such as in the theology of suffering, orientations to social justice, and the role of the Holy Spirit. Despite passing calls for integration, little attention is given to these differences. If differences are acknowledged, they are peripheral within the culture of white American evangelicals. This culture is defined primarily by negative definitions of who is *not* included in the group. For example, many evangelicals do not consider Catholics or Mainline Protestants to be *true* Christians. Yet, when drawing lines between who counts as a true Christian and who does not, members of the Black church and other nonwhite churches are often left out of the calculation completely—not counted as either true Christians or as apostates. Whiteness is presumed to be the default of evangelical culture. Thus, evangelical culture as a whole orients towards the white listening subject in a way that privileges and normalizes whiteness.

Whiteness at Omega

Omega was founded by a man of color who came to the United States as an international student, but all the teachers employed at the time of this study were white Americans, and the school oriented towards the white listening subject (Rosa & Flores, 2017) in the varieties of English it taught and prepared students to engage with. Although it was not the stated goal of the majority of the students, the school's primary mission was to prepare students with English skills that would allow them to enter American higher education. When interviewed, teachers identified SAE as the target language which they hoped to help their students acquire. Multiple teachers linked this to the fact that the curriculum was designed to teach students academic English and to facilitate their integration into an American, and likely a South Carolinian, university. Notably, seven of the ten universities Omega partnered with to funnel students into their programs were predominantly white institutions (PWIs), as evidenced by student demographics in Table 2. Of the three schools in Table 2 that were not strictly PWIs, two of them, Limestone College and Erskine College, had high numbers of unreported data, with the race/ethnicity being unknown for 10% and 23% of their students, respectively, which may have skewed this data. At both Limestone and Erskine, as well as the third school, Midlands Technical College, white students still made up the largest racial demographic, even if they did not comprise over 50% of all students.

Some teachers discussed with me that most of the students enrolled in the school at the time were not those who hoped to attend university, but rather immigrants and refugees already living locally who hoped to improve their English in order to better navigate daily life and find better jobs. When I followed up on this and asked if the teachers therefore focused on Southern American dialects or other dialects the students might be encountering, teachers affirmed that students needed help understanding the dialects they heard in the community, including African American language and Southern English, but said that beyond answering specific questions students asked, they did not incorporate these dialects into the curriculum. However, multiple teachers pointed to non-American dialects that students were exposed to in upper levels of the curriculum, as can be seen in example (1) below. This example highlights the extent to which American dialects were not emphasized at Omega, despite being the dialects students encountered in their daily lives. This points to an imagined listening subject that does not align with students' needs.

Coloniality and Whiteness in Evangelical ESL Classrooms

(1) Interview with Cheryl

1	Researcher:	what kind of, um *dialects* are really being emphasized *in* the curriculum?
2		like is it academic, like Midwestern newscaster? English? or like a southern variety: or.
3	Cheryl:	starting in level--*not* a southern I-pretty pretty newscaster but
4		starting in level fi:ve or! (3) I'd have to ask!--I usually teach five and six. I thi:nk? that's where it starts but it might even start in four.
5	Researcher:	okay
6	Cheryl:	um, but I know for *sure* it's in the C E F R for five and six
7		is that they purposefully like they'll have an Austra*li*an, or they'll have, uh you know, *diff*erent accents they'll have a British person they'll have an, Indian person who s- speaks English with an Indian {accent you know and} {getting quieter}
8		UM (1) and they'll have (1) loud *noise* like you're in an airport
9	Researcher:	[ah:
10	Cheryl:	[so it's not this clear
11	Researcher:	yeah
12	Cheryl:	they'll purposefully make it you're talking over the *tele*phone, so that they have to practice listening with *those* things (2)
13	Researcher:	cool (1)
14	Cheryl:	but because they live *here* they *will* sometimes come in and ask me
15		you know my neighbor sai:d [I'm fixin' tuh, such and such, *what does that mean*!
16	Researcher:	[XXX
17		yeah
18	Cheryl:	or they will *ask* me *southern* things
19	Researcher:	yeah
20	Cheryl:	but we don't *have* it in class.

In line 3, Cheryl was adamant that Southern American dialects were not a part of the curriculum, interrupting her own thought to negate my suggestion. In line 4, she offered that other accents were presented in the curriculum in later classes. Although she was unsure when it started, I confirmed that these accents do start being presented in level 5, which was the highest level required in order to be accepted to one of the partner schools. Cheryl referenced the CEFR standards as she reflected on when these accents were introduced (line 6). This is telling—Omega's curriculum was based on the CEFR framework, and as a European standard, the CEFR framework does not emphasize American regional varieties. Cheryl then provided examples of the accents students were exposed to, first listing broad prestige dialects frequently associated with white speakers: Australian English and British English (line 7). She then mentioned an Indian English accent, and this time added a qualifying phrase: "Indian person who speaks English with an Indian accent" (line 7). This additional qualification highlights that Indian English is not an unmarked dialect, like the previous two were. In lines 14-15, Cheryl offered that students did ask about Southern American features, but then stated that Southern dialects were not covered in class (line 20). However, the speech sample she provided as an example of Southern speech ("fixin' tuh") was not only a feature of Southern American English, but also of African American Language (AAL). Although she recognized the gap in the curriculum in regard to Southern American English, she did not recognize the gap concerning white English versus AAL.

The school culture at Omega heavily valued meeting student needs, but the need of students to understand community members in their daily lives was not met due to the orientation toward the white listening subject. The curriculum and expectations of the teachers were oriented towards white academics as the future listeners they needed to prepare their students for, at the expense of the current listeners students, were actually engaging with. When students were finally introduced to other dialects, the dialects the curriculum presented were affected by the European bias inherent in the CEFR framework. This may be a reflection of elitism, prestige, and even colonialism, with European standards being viewed as more academic or foundational. Additionally, race and class intersect here, as when students were exposed to dialect variety, they were presented with varieties relevant to world travelers, but not relevant to local working-class students. Students were not provided samples of AAL, nor of white Southern American English or white working-class varieties. The white listening subject was imagined not only as white, but also as educated and middle class. Students were expected to learn the language of this subject, regardless of the language contexts they actually found themselves in.

Another visible effect of the white listening subject can be seen in Omega's English only policy. Despite their touted valuation of multiculturalism, school policy prohibited student L1s in the classroom. Each classroom of the City A campus had a posted sign that read "English Only" in big black letters. Underneath it in smaller black letters were two lines reading, "This includes phone conversations. Please step outside if you need to talk in your native language." Not every teacher enforced this rule, but it was posted prominently for all students to see and was a part of the school culture. In City B, there was no sign, but the instructor frequently reminded students to speak in English instead of their native languages although he did allow students to talk on the phone in their native languages during breaks. However, on one occasion, after a student finished talking on the phone, he gently chided the student that if he kept speaking his L1, he would not learn English. At both campuses, this policy is a sign of their orientation toward the white listening subject. It reflects a monolingual bias and reveals an imagined future where students will be required to speak English and only English, rather than a multilingual world where translanguaging is a reality and an asset. This imagined future privileges the white listening subject, preparing students for the types of language deemed appropriate by white monolingual listeners.

Assimilation and Conversion to White Evangelicalism

In the absence of students' native languages at Omega, SAE and white evangelical culture were positioned as a unifying middle ground where various cultures could meet. This was exemplified on Omega's website, the front page of which featured student quotes endorsing and promoting the program. Of the eight testimonials provided, the first four mentioned international experiences and friendships, using phrases like "make friends from all over the world," "get to know different cultures and people," "great international experience," and "students…from all over world [sic]." Students were recruited with the allure of international experiences through the shared medium of English. However, despite touting the value of multiculturalism, many school practices ultimately promoted assimilation to white American evangelical Christian culture, such as with book clubs that studied religious materials and a field trip to watch a religious movie or with religious decorations presented as cultural artifacts. Omega inserted Christianity into the school environment as if it simply represented American culture. Although religion was not included in marketing materials for prospective students at all, once students arrived at the school, American culture acted as a proxy for the proselytization of Christianity. The valuation of multiculturalism shaped their approach to evangelism; since students came from many backgrounds, their L1s were prohibited in the classroom, and white evangelical culture and SAE were promoted as the neutral meeting space for various cultures.

School practices promoted assimilation to white evangelical Christian culture. One piece of evidence for this is in the use of a British book as part of an American cultural enrichment activity. Kay's students, who were high level grammar students, talked about a book club that focused on *The Chronicles of Narnia* by C.S. Lewis, who, despite being an Anglican, is beloved in evangelical circles for the way his novels were written to "pre-baptize the imagination," (as my father always described it[7]), meaning they introduce people to concepts of Christianity through stories so that the seeds of faith have already been planted and may be more likely to grow the next time the reader hears about Christianity more explicitly. The book club was marketed merely as an after-class enrichment activity and was not identified as being related to Christianity either in the way I heard it talked about or in flyers. It was instead grouped with other cultural and social enrichment opportunities, such as conversation partners and out-of-class field trips. However, it is not the author nor the culture depicted in the book that provide an American experience, as C.S. Lewis was British and the novel depicts British children during World War II. Instead, because of how strongly associated Lewis is with white evangelical culture, American culture acted as a proxy for what students were really being exposed to: white evangelicalism.

Christian cultural artifacts were offered to students as examples of American media in other situations as well. In one class I observed, Kay was arranging to take students to watch *Christmas with The Chosen* in theaters after class in order to practice English listening skills. *The Chosen* is a TV series about the life of Jesus from a Christian perspective. They also released a Christmas special about the birth of Christ which came out in theaters. In the class period before the student went to the movie, the students expressed concern to Kay about how hard it would be to understand English movies without subtitles. Kay told them that there might be glasses available with subtitles, but also said, "well, since you *know* the story, that'll make it easier to understand. It's a good first one to watch without subtitles." Students agreed with both her assessment that they knew the story, and that knowing the story would make understanding the English easier. It is likely that Kay knew the students were aware of the story because she had told them the story or had witnessed others telling them.

Kay was intentional in bringing Christian artifacts into the classroom. I asked her about the movie and Christmas decorations shown in example (2).

(2) Classroom observation with Kay

1	Researcher:	>I was just gonna ask< what's the movie you guys are seeing?	
2	Kay:	we're going to see um Christmas with The Chosen?	
3	Researcher:	oh cool	
4	Kay:	um I don't know if you've seen it	
5	Researcher:	no I haven't (.) I- I >really don't watch movies very frequently XX<	
6	Kay:	yeah its um uh the Christmas story	
7	Researcher:	cool!	
8	Kay:	uh yeah, on the big screen. So	uncomfortable
9	Researcher:	nice. yeah I was noticing the: advent calendar do you guys add to this every day?	friendly
10	Kay:	So ugh I forgot to do that today [yeah] I brought that from ho:me and I=	
11	Researcher:	[XX]	
12	Researcher:	=that's awesome yeah	
13	Kay:	yeah.	
14	Researcher:	yeah I really like all the little felt XXX	
15	Kay:	yeah, my kids. we did that at- at church one year	
16	Researcher:	nice	
17	Kay:	an intergenerational event. [and	
18	Researcher:	[oh that's great	
19	Kay:	they feel like they've outgrown it. [unintelligible] take it to school	
20	Researcher:	someone will appreciate it XXXXXX	
21	Kay:	but it's a fun way to you know talk about sto:rie:s Bible stories.	

In line 8, Kay seemed slightly uncomfortable. As I interacted with her, I interpreted this as her not knowing what else to say, but not being unwilling to keep talking. In my attempt to get her to elaborate, I switched to a related topic and asked about the advent calendar hanging on the wall (line 9). During the Christmas season, a nativity scene and advent calendar were present in Kay's classroom. Kay referenced forgetting to add to the advent calendar on a day I observed (line 10), indicating that the advent calendar was usually used as a part of classroom activities.

A bit of context is necessary to understand the calendar, which was a type of advent decoration known as a Jesse tree. Although in the broader American culture, advent calendars are used to count down the days to Christmas with small gifts or treats, Jesse trees instead add a new piece of the story of the Bible each day, ultimately culminating in the story of the birth of Christ. These advent calendars are valued because the holistic narrative of the Bible is viewed as a necessary part of understanding why humanity needed God to come to earth in the form of a baby to redeem humanity from their sins.

Jesse trees are designed to be used in Christian homes as a way to teach children the stories of the Bible. However, after Kay's children had outgrown it, she brought it into the classroom (line 19), highlighting that she was not sharing a culturally relevant or age-appropriate artifact as much as she was using the artifact as a means to spread evangelicalism. Kay made it explicit in line 21 that it was in the classroom as an opportunity for her to share Bible stories with the class. At first, she just termed these "stories." As a coded term, this would have been enough to indicate that she really meant Bible stories, but she did not rely on coded language alone, and immediately clarified for me that she did mean stories from the Bible (line 21).

The ways in which American culture and white evangelical Christian culture were conflated in Kay's classroom were emblematic of the school's attitudes toward religion as an institutional actor. Although religion was not included in marketing materials for prospective students at all, once students arrived at the school, American culture seems to be a method some teachers used to evangelize to students. The religious ties of the institution were not transparent, and although the curriculum the school used did not involve Christian beliefs, individual teachers did bring evangelism into their teaching and interactions with their students, with the backing of the school's administration that viewed the school as missions work. Religion was not overtly present at Omega, but was a constant factor motivating teachers to engage with their students with the ultimate goal of converting them to Christianity.

Opacity of White American Evangelicalism

Religion went without saying at Omega, with consistent religious undercurrents going unnoticed by students. As discussed above, recruitment materials made no mention of religion. However, for in-group members, the religious commitment of the organization was immediately visible through the name of the school. *Omega* is a pseudonym, but their true name is a word easily understood as associated with Christianity to other Christians, having a deep meaning connected the way God interacts with humanity. However, this meaning is opaque to those outside of Christianity and the evangelical sphere, and especially to the students they recruit. In interviews, I asked the teachers whether they thought their students recognized the meaning of the school's name. All answered that they did not discuss the meaning and expected students probably did not know. Kay mentioned that students who were Christians were probably aware, but also expressed surprise when I told her that the website had no information about the meaning of the name, nor any mention of Christianity at all.

Christianity was not an overt presence at Omega: the physical buildings looked like any other small school, and the curriculum was not religiously based. However, it was a constant undercurrent to the interactions between students and staff. As the school administrator, V, put it, the school tried to hire teachers and staff that were Christian, saying, "we like to have teachers that are like-minded." "Like-minded" is a coded term denoting evangelical Christians who share the goal of spreading Christianity. In describing this purpose to me, V revealed a missional mindset that underlay the stated goal, using coded language and pauses as she constructed this meaning. This is shown in example (3).

(3) Interview with V

1	Researcher:	okay so I know Omega also is like (.) <Christian connected, affiliated>	
2		like omega being like the word for _____ or whatever<	Definition is redacted to not reveal the name of the school
3		how exactly do you describe that? like are the teachers at Omega all Christians? like is it viewed as a ministry? orr.	
4	V:	yeah so:: (.)	
5		um _____ is obviously Christian. and so we try to get (.) teachers and administration that are also Christian.	Redacted name is the president of the school
6		and so we like to have (.) {<um teachers that ar::e>} like-minded!	{Hesitatingly}
7		nd that like (.)um (.) we::, like we *want* to see the best *for* our students?	
8		and so that can be um academically, um lifestyle um uh *spiritually* that kind of thing.	
9	Researcher:	yeah	
10	V:	and so yeah, and like, we pray for the students like we want them to do *well* and and thrive and that kind of thing. so.	

In this conversation, both V and I were delicately negotiating meaning (lines 1, 4, 5, 6, 7). I was navigating the tension between invoking insider knowledge (line 2) in order to elicit specific information while also asking questions that an insider would not have to or want to ask (line 3). This negotiation perhaps cast doubt on whether I was an insider to missionary culture and would be receptive to missions oriented goals. In response, V paused repeatedly to search for words (lines 4, 5, 6, 7) that would truthfully convey the mission of the school while also not coming off as too strongly evangelically motivated. In line 6, she settled on a coded term ("like-minded") that in-group members use to identify other in-group members.

Kay also used coded language along with circumlocution as she discussed the way she saw the mission of the school. Kay described her motivation for teaching at Omega: "I started volunteering here as a conversation partner, and fell in love with the students and just felt like I was called to do this. So I got an ESL certification." She later elaborated, in example (4) below.

V and Kay both showed their hesitancy to directly label their motivations as the desire to evangelize, V through pauses and lengthened sounds as she searched for the right words and Kay through circumlocution (lines 6, 8, 10, 16, 20). V emphasized that she and other staff wanted what is best for the students holistically (line 7): they cared for students' overall well-being in ways that extend beyond the spiritual (line 8). In this local context, V's expression of a broad scope of concern for students distanced her from the type of missions ideology that focuses on the soul at the expense of the body and uses physical needs as a way to entice people into hearing the missionaries' message. Instead, V aligned with a more progressive ideology that wants to meet students' felt needs for language skills, as well as their (possibly unfelt) spiritual needs. Kay, however, was more open about having a direct spiritual motivation for teaching. She was not a teacher previously and became one at Omega because she felt the call of God to have "real relationships" (line 8) with the students. She did not directly state why having real relationships is so meaningful to her. Instead, through her pauses (lines 8, 10, 11, 12, 14, 15), she displayed a careful stance that managed the delicate boundary between being truthful while not directly revealing her mission mindset. I joined her in this delicate work when I provided the phrasing "the door…opened,"

Coloniality and Whiteness in Evangelical ESL Classrooms

(4) Interview with Kay

1	Kay:	so I mean it was all providential.
2		I um
3		one of my friends was volunteering (.) here
4		and (.) I was (.) um I can't remember oh! I think I was between or I had had some health issues and had to stop my other job because it was stressful? and um just concentrate on my health for a while and then and *she* said well why don't you volunteer at Omega?
5		and um
6		so yeah, fell in love with my first conversation partner
7		and then and she was from Spain, and then I had two conversation partners from Saudi Arabia.
8		and (.) was just eye-opening for me to um (.) have *real* relationships? with (.) *Muslims*!
9	Researcher:	yeah
10	Kay:	and um yeah and so then I just (.) kept feeling like this nagging thing of (.) ya need to (.) you might enjoy doing this
11		and um (.)
12		so I did I went and got the certification (.)
13		and I subbed? here first
14		and then (.)
15		the rest (.)
16		I feel like God's done that
17	Researcher:	yeah
18	Kay:	my whole life
19	Researcher:	yeah
20	Kay:	I didn't go seeking something necessarily but
21	Researcher:	the door just kinda [opened
22	Kay:	_____ [the door just kinda opened. nodding, smiling

(line 21) an evangelical phrase related to how God directs a person towards the mission God has for their life or to particular missions opportunities. Kay took up the phrase quickly and cheerfully (line 22), acknowledging that I had understood what she was tacitly saying.

V and Kay's usage of coded evangelical language reveals the presence of missions ideologies within the school. Missionary culture necessitates coded language because oftentimes missionaries' conversion efforts are looked down upon, if not outright illegal. While proselytization is not illegal in the U.S., there is still a sense that one must hide one's evangelism efforts so as not to scare off the people being evangelized. One way to hide this is through having a platform: a legitimate business that allows a missionary entry into communities they hope to evangelize, such as a language school. Although the U.S. is not a dangerous context for Christians or missionaries, this paradigm is relevant to the way Omega was presented: Omega was simultaneously "just" an English school—a legitimate and accredited educational institution—and a mission field where Christianity could be shared with the nations. Whether intentional or not, the opacity of religion served to further evangelism goals as religious ties were concealed in the presentation of the school's mission and its selection of teachers.

CONCLUSION

The project of evangelism, no matter how well intentioned, echoes the long colonial history of religious erasure. Evangelism pairs with the school's strategy of assimilation, which is itself another arm of coloniality, seeking to replace diverse culture, languages, and religions with American culture, Standardized American English, and white evangelical Christianity. Omega obfuscated their goal of evangelism by conflating white evangelical Christianity and American culture and by institutionally focusing on the integration of students into English-centric, white evangelical culture. All teachers employed by Omega were white native English speakers, with the only person of color also being the only non-native English speaker. The non-native English speaker was employed in a support role—she communicated with students about scheduling, visas, and college applications and acted as an intermediary for Spanish-speaking students when their English was not at a level to easily facilitate administrative conversations. Although this may not be a conscious choice on the part of the school's administrators, having only white native English speakers in the authoritative roles as teachers reified the hegemonic understanding of both English and whiteness as dominant. Race, native language, and religion were all interconnected. While the school may not have intentionally hired only native English speakers, they did deliberately hire evangelical Christians. Given the racial segregation of Christianity in America, this resulted in a de facto hiring preference for white teachers. The presence of only white teachers, only Christian teachers, and only native-English speaking teachers was due to the same goal—immersing students in white evangelical culture. Ultimately, this served the purpose of evangelizing students, with the aim of converting them to evangelical Christianity and replacing their previous religions. The assimilationist tactics the school used, particularly the fact that the intention for evangelism was hidden from students, drew on long legacies of the relationship between colonialism and the church that have caused great harm to indigenous cultures, religions, and languages. Despite the school's official goals of friendliness and welcome for students, their actions still worked to perpetuate coloniality and hegemonic whiteness in the classroom.

Missions work and the field of ESL are prone to reproduce whiteness and coloniality in insidious ways. Well-intentioned people in both fields can easily cause harm while working to help. Critical discussions of the ways whiteness is reproduced in English classrooms are crucial, alongside careful reflections on the historic baggage and dynamics that come with missionary efforts. This discussion of whiteness and missionary efforts in the ESL classroom is important for English language teachers, professionals, and researchers to engage with because understanding the raciolinguistic ideologies of religion, language, and race circulating in these communities and the ways in which these evangelical programs relate to students is the first step in determining where the harmful legacies of colonialism and white supremacy still affect the field of ESL and the students it purports to serve. This discussion may also be useful to non-native English-speaking students. Highlighting disingenuous practices that ultimately serve to promote white Christianity may allow students to recognize programs that participate in these behaviors, giving them the opportunity to opt out.

This study reveals several practical pedagogical implications. First, it echoes the call of others for a translanguaging lens in the language classroom (see García, 2009, 2014). Second, it suggests that schools and teachers should consider the dialects that they are privileging in the classroom: do the dialects taught match with the dialects students will reasonably encounter in their daily lives? What power dynamics do the dialects being taught uphold? The choice of curriculum or testing standard can impact what dialects students are being exposed to and whether they are being prepared for the language skills they desire, or the language skills the white listening subject desires. Relatedly, student needs should be regularly and intentionally assessed so that adjustments can be made to the curriculum as necessary. Particularly at an evangelical school which functions primarily as a means of meeting student needs in order to have an avenue to share Christianity with them, building in regular needs assessments would help ensure that these goals are being met. Additionally, schools and teachers should be reflexive about how whiteness, coloniality, or cultural dominance may have slipped into teaching practices, such as with English-only policies or choices of cultural lessons. This reflexivity should include an examination of power dynamics in the classroom. In order to avoid reproducing colonial ideologies and other harmful biases, it is imperative that those with the power to make rules and policies question whether those rules are coming from a place of personal, cultural, or hegemonic preference. Recognizing how the teaching of ESL can be used as a tool of missions work and the ideologies of assimilation that can be a part of that work is critical in order to push the field of ESL towards greater inclusivity, sensitivity, and diversity. The harmful legacies of colonialism, ethnocentrism, and white supremacy do not dissipate by themselves; instead, ingrained biases must be intentionally identified and confronted if there is to be hope of change.

REFERENCES

College factual. (n.d.). *Clemson University graduate school report.* https://www.collegefactual.com/graduate-schools/clemson-university

Data, U. S. A. (n.d.-a). *Bob Jones University.* https://datausa.io/profile/university/bob-jones-university

Data, U. S. A. (n.d.-b). *Charleston Southern University.* https://datausa.io/profile/university/charleston-southern-university

Data, U. S. A. (n.d.-c). *Greenville Technical College.* https://datausa.io/profile/university/greenville-technical-college

Data, U. S. A. (n.d.-d). *Midlands Technical College.* https://datausa.io/profile/university/midlands-technical-college

Data, U. S. A. (n.d.-e). *North Greenville University.* https://datausa.io/profile/university/north-greenville-university

Data, U. S. A. (n.d.-f). *University of South Carolina Aiken.* https://datausa.io/profile/university/university-of-south-carolina-aiken

Data, U. S. A. (n.d.-g). *University of South Carolina Upstate.* https://datausa.io/university-of-south-carolina-upstate

de los Ríos, C. V., Martinez, D. C., Musser, A. D., Canady, A., Camangian, P., & Quijada, P. D. (2019). Upending colonial practices: Toward repairing harm in English education. *Theory into Practice, 58*(4), 359–367. doi:10.1080/00405841.2019.1626615

Edwards, J. J. (2015). *Superchurch: The rhetoric and politics of American fundamentalism.* doi:10.5860/CHOICE.191900

Flores, N., Lewis, M. C., & Phuong, J. (2018). Raciolinguistic chronotopes and the education of Latinx students: Resistance and anxiety in a bilingual school. *Language & Communication, 62,* 15–25. doi:10.1016/j.langcom.2018.06.002

Forbes Magazine. (n.d.). *Erskine College*. Forbes. https://www.forbes.com/colleges/erskine-college-and-seminary/?sh=5f6b126465dc

García, O. (2009). Education, multilingualism and translanguaging in the 21st century. *Social Justice through Multilingual Education*, 140-158.

García, O. (2014). Countering the dual: Transglossia, dynamic bilingualism and translanguaging in education. In R. Rubdy & L. Alsagoff (Eds.), *The global-local interface, language choice and hybridity* (pp. 100–118). Multilingual Matters. doi:10.21832/9781783090860-007

Gearon, L. (2013). The King James Bible and the politics of religious education. *Religious Education (Chicago, Ill.)*, *108*(1), 9–27. doi:10.1080/00344087.2013.747838

Gearon, L., Kuusisto, A., Matemba, Y., Benjamin, S., du Preez, P., Koirikivi, P., & Simmonds, S. (2020). Decolonizing the religious education curriculum. *British Journal of Religious Education*, *43*(1), 1–8. doi:10.1080/01416200.2020.1819734

Han, H., & Varghese, M. (2019). Language ideology, Christianity, and identity: Critical empirical examinations of Christian institutions as alternative spaces. *Journal of Language, Identity, and Education*, *18*(1), 1–9. doi:10.1080/15348458.2019.1569525

Inoue, M. (2003). The listening subject of Japanese modernity and his auditory double: Citing, sighting, and siting the modern Japanese woman. *Cultural Anthropology*, *18*(2), 156–193. doi:10.1525/can.2003.18.2.156

Johnston, B. (2017). *English teaching and Protestant mission: The case of Lighthouse School*. Multilingual Matters.

Johnston, B., & Varghese, M. (2006). Neo-imperialism, evangelism, and ELT: Modernist missions and a postmodern profession. In J. Edge (Ed.), *Re-)locating TESOL in an age of empire* (pp. 195–207). Palgrave Macmillan.

Kim, E. Y. (2019). English as a site of evangelical contact: A critical ethnography of missionary English teaching between South and North Koreans. *Journal of Language, Identity, and Education*, *18*(1), 10–24. doi:10.1080/15348458.2019.1575739

Kubota, R. (2001). Discursive construction of the images of U.S. classrooms. *TESOL Quarterly*, *35*(1), 9–38. doi:10.2307/3587858

Kubota, R. (2021). Critical antiracist pedagogy in ELT. *ELT Journal*, *75*(3), 237–246. doi:10.1093/elt/ccab015

Lachenicht, S., Henneton, L., & Lignereux, Y. (2016). Spiritual geopolitics in the early modern imperial age. An introduction. *Itinerario*, *40*(2), 181–187. doi:10.1017/S0165115316000309

Lewis, C. S. (1956). *Surprised by joy: The shape of my early life*. Harcourt Brace.

O'Regan, J. P. (2021). *Global English and political economy*. Routledge. doi:10.4324/9781315749334

Pennycook, A. (2002). *English and the discourses of colonialism*. Routledge., doi:10.4324/9780203006344

Pennycook, A., & Makoni, S. (2005). The modern mission: The language effects of Christianity. *Journal of Language, Identity, and Education*, *4*(2), 137–155. doi:10.120715327701jlie0402_5

Prince, Z. (2016, June 15). Eleven o'clock on Sundays is still the most segregated hour in America. *The Louisiana Weekly*. http://www.louisianaweekly.com/eleven-oclock-on-sundays-is-still-the-most-segregated-hour-in-america/

Rosa, J. D., & Flores, N. (2017). Unsettling race and language: Toward a raciolinguistic perspective. *Language in Society*, *46*(5), 621–647. doi:10.1017/S0047404517000562

US News Best Colleges. (n.d.). *Limestone University*. US News. https://www.usnews.com/best-colleges/limestone-college-3436

Vandrick, S. (1999). ESL and the colonial legacy: A teacher faces her 'missionary kid' past. In G. Haroian-Guerin (Ed.), *The personal narrative: Casting ourselves as teachers and scholars* (pp. 63–74). Calendar Islands. doi:10.4324/9781410606273-34

Varghese, M., & Johnston, B. (2007). Evangelical Christians and English language teaching. *TESOL Quarterly*, *41*(1), 5–31. doi:10.1002/j.1545-7249.2007.tb00038.x

Veronelli, G. A. (2015). The coloniality of language: Race, expressivity, power, and the darker side of modernity. *A Journal of Transnational Women's & Gender Studies*, *13*, 108–134.

Winchcombe, R. (2021). *Commercializing America: Religion, trade, and the challenges of English colonialism*. Encountering Early America. doi:10.7765/9781526145789.00007

KEY TERMS AND DEFINITIONS

Assimilation: An ideology that promotes conformity to a particular cultural norm, at the expense of one's original culture, language, religion, etc.

Colonialism: The system of domination of one power, or group of powers, over other nation(s) and people(s), historically related to the West's domination and exploitation of the Global South.

Common European Framework of Reference: A six-point scale used to rate language ability, originally and primarily used in Europe.

Hegemony: The system of influence by which the dominant cultural group maintains its power.

Missionary: An individual who engages in the work of missions as a dominant activity.

Missions: The intentional work of evangelizing people who are not Christians, especially non-Westerners.

Multiculturalism: The coexistence of multiple cultures in one society or dynamic.

Raciolinguistic: Of or relating to the co-construction of race and language.

Translanguaging: The multilingual act of accessing one's full repertoire of linguistic resources and/or moving fluidly between languages; a pedagogical framework that honors multilingual students' full linguistic repertoires as valid and valuable within the classroom.

White Listening Subject: An ideological position that reflects the dominance and normativity of whiteness as the standard by which and for which language must be produced.

ENDNOTES

1. There is debate about whether "white" should be capitalized or lowercase. In previous work, I have chosen to capitalize "White," with the intention to work against implications of lowercase white that might serve to normalize whiteness as the unmarked standard. The use of capitalized white in those works was intended to bring whiteness into focus as an object of study and to interrogate its influence upon social relationships. However, in the present social climate, "White" is often capitalized in the writings of white supremacists online. Although I still value the work of normalizing whiteness as a category of study, I have chosen not to capitalize "white" in this chapter in order to avoid the semblance of participating in their aims of elevating whiteness above other races and racialized people.

2. Within the evangelical community, "missions work" may also be referred to as "missionary work," "mission work," or simply "missions." I use "missions work," as this is the term most commonly used in the community I was raised in.

3. While this is quite problematic and offensive language, it must be stated that this was the project that colonialism undertook and the language that was often used to describe it.

4. Ministry and missions work are very similar, but distinguished by whether one is reaching out to individuals who are already within the church (ministry), or proselytizing to non-churched people (missions).

5. It appears that there was intended to be an application available in the following languages, but the link was not active at the time of data collection: French, German, Indonesian, Italian, and Thai.

6. This is a paraphrase of a quote from Dr. Martin Luther King, Jr, regarding a phenomenon which still holds true in the present day (Prince, 2016).

7. That this concept is not specific to my father but is instead common throughout evangelicalism was demonstrated in the frustratingly long time it took me to determine that although dozens of articles, blogs, sermons, and videos refer to *The Chronicles of Narnia* as the work of baptizing the imagination, C.S. Lewis did not himself say this. Rather, he used the concept when talking about his own experience reading *Phantastes* by George MacDonald: "that night my imagination was, in a certain sense, baptized" (Lewis, 1956, p. 172). This concept has since been taken up to describe the work Lewis's fantasy books engage in.

APPENDIX

Interview Questions

Demographic Questions

1. Where are you from?
2. How long have you lived in South Carolina?
3. What has your time living in South Carolina been like?
4. Have you lived in any other places? What was your time living there like?
5. What language(s) do you speak?
6. What language(s) are you most comfortable speaking?
7. What language(s) does your community usually speak?
8. What language(s) do your close friends speak?
9. What language(s) does your family speak?
10. How long have you been teaching?
11. What training did you receive before you started teaching?
12. Do you think that training was helpful to prepare you for the situations you encounter in the classroom?
13. Do you think any of your training was unhelpful for the situations you encounter in the classroom?
14. What are the demographics of your students?

Classroom Dynamics and Perception of Student Identity

1. What are some of the challenges you face in the classroom?
2. What are some of the challenges you face with your students?
3. What backgrounds do your students usually come from?
4. What challenges do your students bring into the classroom?
5. Are there any tensions in the classroom between students from different backgrounds?
6. Have you ever experienced conflict or tension in the classroom between yourself and student(s)?

School Culture

1. Have you taught at other schools, besides the one you currently teach out?
2. How does the culture of this school compare to cultures at other schools you've been at, either as a student or a teacher?
3. Do you feel that teachers are connected to students' lives and problems?
4. Do you feel that administrators are connected to students' lives and problems?
5. Do you feel that administrators are connected to teachers' lives and problems?
6. For teachers at Omega: Are students aware of the Christian meaning of the name of the school? Do you ever discuss it with them?

Language Assessment Norms

1. What are some of the norms of English that you and the school are trying to teach your students?
2. Do teachers in your school generally assess students in similar ways?
3. What do you personally rely on when you assess students' English skills?
4. What do you personally rely on when you assess students' pronunciation?
5. If you assess students differently than others in your school, how do you think your practices are different from theirs?

Language Beliefs

1. What are your goals for students who successfully complete your class(es)? What makes them successful?
2. What kind(s) of language skills do your students need to learn in order to be successful?
3. Are there certain varieties of English that are more important for your students to learn?
4. When you think of an ideal English speaker, what do you think of?
5. When you think of an ideal English student, what do you think of?
6. What kinds of skills or personality traits go into making someone a good language learner?
7. Are there skills, lack of skills, or personality traits that contribute to someone struggling with language learning?

Section 2
Language and Identity

Chapter 5
Backing Into Race:
Immigration, Identity, and Social Movement Theory in English Language Teacher Education

Tonda Liggett
https://orcid.org/0000-0002-0955-0960
Linfield University, USA

ABSTRACT

This chapter focuses on more accurate and in-depth analyses of immigration in relation to individual identity factors as a way to better understand the specific role of race in broader relations of power within English language teaching. Using data from a narrative case study to account for various positionalities, this chapter proposes a general framework for English language teacher education that draws on aspects of social movement theory to analyze contextual factors of immigration, such as migration channels, settlement in urban/rural localities and human capital, and transnationalism. By incorporating specific aspects of social movement theory, an intersectional approach to ELT education holds promise of preparing teachers to identify racism, power, and gaps in support for their multilingual students.

English language teacher (ELT) education programs in the U.S. have included research on teacher identity as a way to unpack and problematize implications for classroom instruction (e.g., Ajayi, 2011; Liggett, 2009; Motha, 2014; Taylor, 2017; Vitanova, 2016). Indeed, when we look at the intersections of race and language, we see how previous research has informed the field and worked to incorporate inquiry into identity in teacher education programs (e.g., Alim, 2010; Lee, 2015; Kubota & Lin, 2009; Liggett, 2014; Varghese et al., 2016; Von Esch et al., 2020) often through culturally responsive pedagogy; diversity, equity, inclusion (DEI); or social justice education. However, over the past several years, the topic of race and immigration has intensified in the U.S., often with harmful, false, and denigrating rhetoric about immigrants and immigrant groups. The linguistic and cultural diversity of English learners (ELs) suggests that more and more teachers serve as intercultural and interlinguistic educators, in effect, educators who reach out to learners from a variety of backgrounds to provide effective strategies

DOI: 10.4018/978-1-6684-9029-7.ch005

for rigorous academic learning (Garcia & Kleifgen, 2018; Snyder & Fenner, 2021). For teachers, this involves not only making curricula relevant and understandable but also expanding perspectives beyond second language acquisition.

Because ELs have parents, grandparents, relatives, friends or themselves who have experienced immigration first hand, a focus on more accurate and in-depth analyses of the factors that influence migration in relation to identity factors could lead to better understandings of the specific role of race in broader relations of power within English language teaching. This relationality expands within the various contexts of political, economic, and social issues that determine opportunity and possibility for multilingual students and their families. To account for this relationality, I propose a general framework for ELT education that incorporates contextual factors of immigration, such as political relationship between sending and receiving countries, economic opportunities based on human capital, and social connections to family abroad, along with individual identity factors and aspects of social movement theory. Incorporating specific aspects of social movement theory provides an intersectional approach to ELT education, which holds promise of preparing teachers to identify gaps in support for their multilingual students.

Burns and Robert (2010) emphasize the importance of social theory in English language education stating that, "More nuanced theoretical approaches reframe ESOL research, shifting away from simply what works in the classroom to what could work if language and migration were better understood,

Figure 1. A general framework: Three focal areas for ELT education

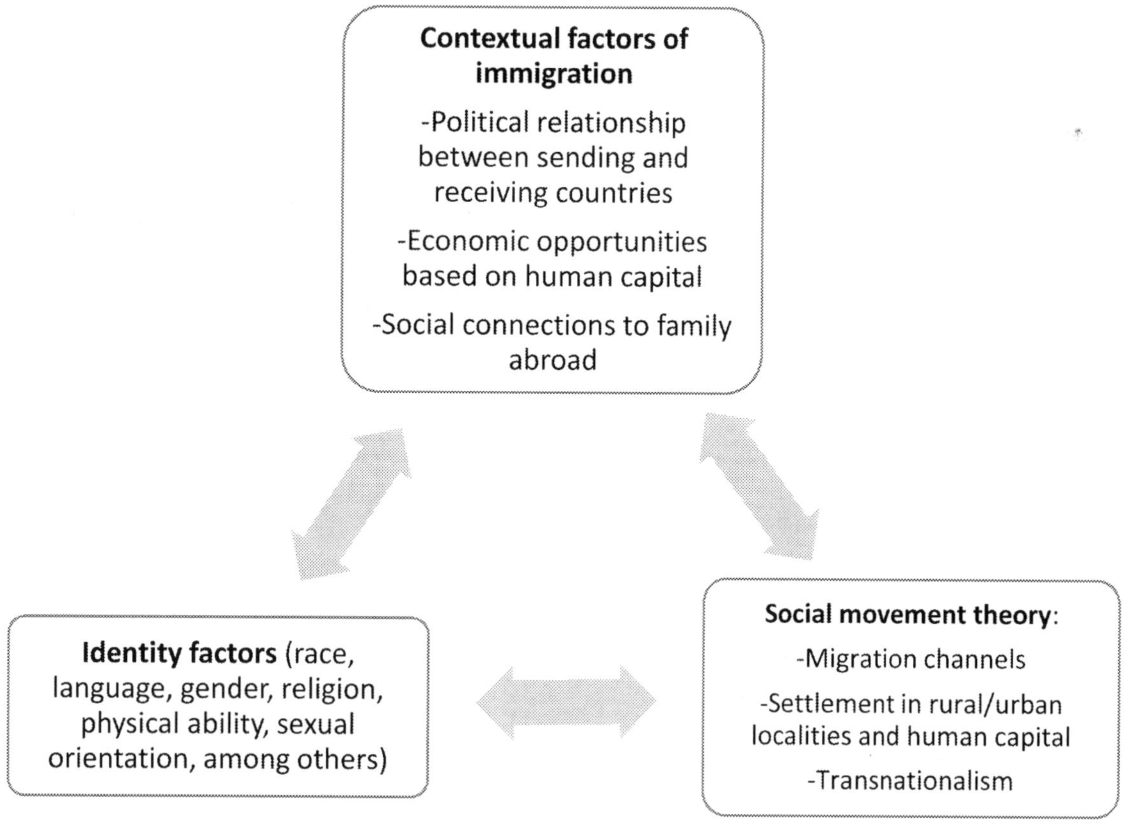

Contextual factors of immigration
- Political relationship between sending and receiving countries
- Economic opportunities based on human capital
- Social connections to family abroad

Identity factors (race, language, gender, religion, physical ability, sexual orientation, among others)

Social movement theory:
- Migration channels
- Settlement in rural/urban localities and human capital
- Transnationalism

holistically, through the lens of social theory" (p. 415). Within the context of this research study, I draw specifically on three aspects of social movement theory for analysis: 1) migration channels; 2) settlement in rural/urban localities and human capital; and 3) transnational ties abroad (See Figure 1).

CONTEXTUAL FACTORS OF IMMIGRATION IN THE UNITED STATES

Throughout this chapter, I use the term "immigrant" to refer to people residing in the U.S., but not citizens at birth. This population includes naturalized citizens, lawful permanent residents, persons on certain temporary visas, those people limited under refugee or asylee status, and unauthorized immigrants. (Migration Policy Institute [MPI], 2023). Immigration has fluctuated throughout U.S. history when it peaked to nearly 15 percent of the population in 1890 and then plummeted to 5 percent in 1970. In 2021, according to the most recent census records, the immigrant population comprised 13.6% of the U.S. population, nearly 45.3 million people, living in the United States (MPI, 2023). These immigrant groups come from many different countries with varied social and economic backgrounds, and for multiple reasons. The diversification of immigrant populations over the past 40 years has changed considerably due to economic markets, political relationships between countries, and social willingness to integrate immigrants into existing communities.

Since 2010, new arrivals are more likely to come from Asia, with India and China as the top sending countries. In addition, immigration from the Dominican Republic, the Philippines, Cuba, Venezuela, Guatemala, and El Salvador also increased between 2010 and 2019. By contrast, immigrants from Mexico declined by more than 779,000 during the same period, representing the biggest absolute decline of all immigrant groups. In fact, as recently as 2013, India and China surpassed Mexico as the top origin countries for new arrivals, displacing Mexico's longstanding number one sending position (MPI, 2023).

When we analyze immigration to the U.S. in 2020, there emerges a pattern of a nearly unprecedented focus on reducing the number of immigrants, along with the COVID-19 pandemic, which drastically froze travel and immigration throughout the world. Prior to 2020, the immigrant population in the U.S. was growing at much slower rates than in 2010 and recent arrivals shifted to being mostly from Asia rather than other regions. The year 2020 was also notable in that 1) illegal immigration declined, 2) the U.S. resettled the smallest number of refugees in the history of refugee resettlement programs, and 3) nearly 50% of recently arrived immigrants (between 2014 and 2019) had a bachelor's degree or higher compared to 33% of U.S. born citizens (MPI, 2023). These trends are notable because negative press and social media would have us believe that the opposite is true: that the number of illegal immigrants is soaring, that refugees are straining social services, that immigrants are uneducated. In fact, such misinformation permeates social narratives and negatively influences perspectives about immigrants as they relocate to various urban and rural locations across the U.S. Their reception in these locales determines chances for upward mobility, educational attainment, and acceptance in their new context.

ENGLISH LEARNERS IN THE UNITED STATES

The focus on English learners (ELs) in the context of this chapter is on first or second-generation immigrants. First-generation meaning a person born in a country outside of the U.S. with at least one parent also born in another country, while second-generation refers to any person born in the U.S. with at least one parent born outside of the U.S. (MPI, 2023). I use the term English Learner (EL) to refer to non-native English speakers who are learning English in K-12 schools (Peregoy & Boyle, 2017). Between 2010 and 2019, the EL population grew from approximately 4.5 million students (9.2%) to approximately 5.1 million students (10.4%). This slow growth follows the decline in illegal immigration and refugee resettlement outlined in the section above. It is also important to note that this growth varied significantly depending on the location of settlement. For example, the percentage of students who were ELs was higher for school districts in more urbanized locations with 14.8% in cities, 10% in suburban areas, 7% in towns, and 4.4% in rural areas (National Center for Education Statistics (NCES), 2023).

According to the U.S. Census Bureau (2021), 26.6% of the total U.S. population speaks a language other than English; Spanish comprises 13.2%, followed by Indo-European languages 3.8%, Asian and Pacific Islander languages 3.5%, and other languages 1.2%. For K-12 education in the fall of 2019, more than 5.1 million ELs were enrolled in public elementary and secondary schools, which represents 10 percent of total student enrollment (MPI, 2023). In addition to these numbers, other key factors influence current migration trends such as educational attainment and poverty. Poverty and low income play a significant role in the economic status and upward mobility. Data from the National Center for Children in Poverty (2019) indicates that 45% of children of immigrant parents live in low-income families compared to 35% for children of native-born parents. As I discuss the multiple topics involved in issues of immigration and education, I am mindful of the complexity of legal status that each category of people categorized as "immigrant" carries. I examine this in more detail as I unpack the migration channels available to people as they enter the U.S.

THEORETICAL FRAMEWORK

I address three contemporary social movement theories—cosmopolitanism, popular cosmopolitanism, and super-diversity—to identify how they may highlight other positionalities in relation to race and ELT education. I also draw on the tenets of critical race theory to expand critical approaches to teaching and to better understand how the intersectionality of racial, linguistic, and cultural identity factors are foregrounded and backgrounded in educational contexts. One tenet of critical race theory is the notion that society accepts racism as an ordinary, permanent fixture of life (Taylor et al., 2009). In this sense, racism is part of the daily landscape throughout the United States. This implies that inequitable conditions occur in covert ways, e.g. systemically at the policy level as well as in overt acts of racism. Thus, any remedy to be pursued comes from the unmasking and exposing of racism in all of its various permutations and intersections with the contextual factors of immigration and social movement theory.

Cosmopolitanism/Popular Cosmopolitanism

Cosmopolitanism refers to a global sense of place as well as a synergy between collective and personal cultural identities that nurture the recognition of individual positionality and worldview (Delanty, 2006; Massey, 1994). A cosmopolitan disposition means that individuals draw on their country of origin as a source of identity (Appiah, 2006; Guardado, 2010; Kastoryano, 2000) while at the same time promoting a personal "stance of openness towards divergent cultural experiences" (Hannerz, 1990, p. 239). Appiah (2006) identifies two strands of thinking that intertwine within the notion of cosmopolitanism; one is that we have obligations to others that extend beyond our family bonds or shared citizenship, and two, that we take seriously the value of particular human lives, i.e., the practices and beliefs that lend them significance. These two ideals—universal concern, and respect for legitimate difference—become fertile ground for difference and values to be sorted out. In looking at the ways in which cosmopolitanism intertwines universal obligations and individual beliefs, we begin to recognize the dynamic and shifting nature of identity construction in the lives of multilingual students, and how these layered and complex structures inform ways of knowing for interactions, behavior, and academic work.

Contemporary scholars of social movement theory (e.g., Compton, 2023; Heidemann, 2019; Wise, 2016) argue for a definition of cosmopolitanism that includes unprivileged individuals (such as those in this study) who hold a variety of experiences that reflect increasing migration and movement across geographic and virtual spaces, but also have local orientations that influence knowledge construction. That point of reference, or global-local dynamic, is an important component of interconnectivity in English language teacher education as it ties abstract global perspectives to local schools and student populations. Even within similar localities (e.g., the same state), two individuals do not necessarily have the same social borders that bind them or inhabit the same life experiences (Roudometof, 2020; Shiller & Irving, 2014).

A modified and updated ideology of cosmopolitanism, has evolved in an effort to more specifically connote the mobility of people, ideas, cultures, images, or objects across space in relation to local, national, and global influences (Ergas, 2020; Roudometof, 2020; Tedeschi 2022). These modifications highlight the pluralization of borders where people from within the same state can inhabit markedly different orientations and connections. This allows for nuance within cultural groups based on local context and what Wise (2016) identifies as the "micro-nature of cosmopolitan practices" (p. 2289). Being able to consider and incorporate local orientations is germane to truly representing the lived reality and global diversity of the multilingual students who populate schools and communities today. As educators try not to box in students from the same cultural or ethnic background, highlighting this aspect of popular cosmopolitanism is key for ELTs to develop nuanced understandings of intragroup differences and the important factors that affect them.

Super-Diversity

As considerations of local and global populations have become increasingly more nuanced and complex, the theory of super-diversity has gained notoriety (Blommaert, 2013; Charalambous et al., 2015; Crul, 2016; Lin, 2018; Meisser & Vertovec, 2014). Vertovec (2007) introduced the concept of super-diversity as a way to demonstrate that the paradigm of the multicultural city falls short in understanding social and cultural diversity because of the one-dimensional focus on ethno-cultural identity. Unlike the 1960s when fairly homogeneous groups of foreign workers migrated from a limited number of countries, the past few decades have indicated that the number of countries of origin as well as the diversity within the diversity has gradually increased (Vertovec, 2019). This transition represents changes in migration patterns worldwide where people from more places now migrate to more places, causing unprecedented forms of social and cultural diversity especially in the largest urban centers of the world (Vertovec, 2019).

The concept of super-diversity is not just additional categories to consider when discussing social identity, rather, it is a call for greater recognition of the multiple variables and configurations that underpin migration, and most importantly, it considers their intersections (Meisser & Vertovec, 2014). Vertovec uses the term to mean "the search for better ways to describe and analyze new social patterns, forms and identities arising from migration driven diversification" (2019, p. 125). The inclusion of migration in the definition of superdiversity is particularly helpful for ELT education as a way to better understand the changing contexts of multilingual student experiences in the U.S. and the various factors that influence upward mobility and educational attainment/opportunity. Key to this interchange is connecting individual identity construction to broad contextual factors that work to frame worldviews and ideas about individual possibilities. In this study, the student participants' positionalities directly shaped their sense of agency, access to educational opportunities, and participation in local and global communities.

METHODOLOGY

This research study is a narrative case study (Sonday et al., 2020) with two participants, Natalia and Leo (pseudonyms). In conducting a narrative case study, I began with the experiences and life stories of these two students as a way to account for the intersections of multiple identity factors in relation to aspects of social movement theory to capture detail and nuance. The use of case study as a method offered the opportunity for greater understanding of the ways that specific aspects such as migration channel, location of settlement, human capitol, and border crossing played out for these two participants. Narrative inquiry (Clandinin & Connelly, 2000) provided deeper insight into the complexity of their individual migration experiences while recognizing the impact of their political, economic, and social contexts (Sonday, Ramugondo & Kathard, 2020). I followed a grounded theory method of data analysis that focuses on the process of understanding where knowledge and theory are constructed through social interaction (Charmaz, 2005). This necessitates relationships with research participants that are less formal with longer interviews as a way to get at how participants make meaning of their new social contexts (Charmaz, 2005; Azulai, 2020). Being able to generate themes from their life stories and experiences, highlighted the processes of resettlement and adjustment to a new language and culture (Azulai, 2020). In addition, this allowed me to emphasize two very diverse local and global worlds, and the multiple realities and complexities within them. With the themes, I developed a general framework that integrated contextual factors of immigration in relation to social movement theory and identity factors. In this sense, any theories generated from the data are grounded in the narratives of the participants. Throughout my analyses, I focused on theory development that makes visible hierarchies of power and assumes that any theory put forth from this research is incomplete (Charmaz, 2005; Sonday et al., 2020).

Research Question

How could the intersections of immigration, identity, and social movement theory inform a general framework for ELT education that works to highlight the relationships between racism and other positionalities?

Each student was part of an educational program that worked to support economically disadvantaged students in K-12 and postsecondary academic and social learning. They had been active in the program for at least three years. Each had research permissions, field notes, an educational portfolio, attendance records, and interview data that described their individual lives and educational biographies. Both were postsecondary English learners and first-generation immigrants who had come to the U.S. as children. Natalia and Leo's stories were among several students who shared a common story with narratives that were woven through the complications of poverty, racism, marginalization, and access to resources.

Participants

When Leo came to the U.S. as a kindergartener, he was a fluent Spanish-speaker and began school as an English learner. Over the years, he became fluent in English reading and speaking, but eventually became less and less fluent in Spanish. As an older student, he began to struggle and became increasingly disenfranchised with school and other social involvements, which eventually resulted in a record as a juvenile offender. At about age 16, officials threatened to return him to Mexico, but there was no one in his small village able to take him in. By this time, his oral Spanish consisted of only a few phrases and he was not easily understood by his relatives in Mexico. This further isolated him not only from his extended family but also his immediate family who moved freely back and forth across the border between his mother's village and their home in the U.S. His mother became a citizen when she remarried and his siblings were born in the U.S., so their movement was not a political obstacle; whereas, Leo's unauthorized status carried the constant fear of being detained, punished, and returned permanently to Mexico.

Natalia also came to the U.S. at about the same age as Leo, but she came from Russia. She spoke fluent Russian and eventually became fluent in English reading, writing, and speaking. She did well in school and was able to retain her fluency in both Russian and English to obtain higher paying jobs where she could use both languages to navigate various social settings. In addition, she was able to travel freely because of her legal status and was hired for a part-time position by a Korean-owned arts business that catered to a sophisticated clientele. Indeed, she had traveled in several European countries and stayed with relatives in Germany with side-trips to London and Paris. She had also been to China with her mother on a business trip. However, in her local context in the U.S., she struggled to make ends meet. As a young wife, married at 19, she had obligations to care for her younger siblings and maintain her mother's household where they all lived.

FINDINGS

My original research question focuses on the intersectionality of immigration, identity, and social movement theory in an effort to highlight the relationships between racism and other positionalities. In this research it became clear that racism wove through the various contexts that were germane to Natalia and Leo's lives in the U.S. With ethnic bias against Mexicans and racism against people of color, Leo's economic opportunities and access to employment were negatively impacted. Natalia, on the other hand was positively impacted by the economic opportunities through the privilege of being a light-skinned woman of Russian descent. She was able to fully participate in the same summer program based on federal funding that marginalized Leo because of his juvenile record, which was a key networking opportunity for future work. Their experiences were importantly shaped by existing measures of race that were mapped onto each of them and intersected with other determinant identity factors such as education and class.

While family networks informed each immigrant group on how to participate in and navigate various governmental systems, the U.S. dynamics of racialization came into play with the Russian population, which favored Natalia and allowed her to circumvent the racial and linguistic discrimination that Mexicans often experience. Because of this, Leo and the other Mexican students experiences with governmental systems was fear based; whereas, the Russian and Ukrainian youth were able to get official documents together utilizing family knowledge frameworks that reflected a more empowered stance in negotiating such systems—a very different scenario than the Latino students who struggled to get these same documents.

One's experience with their individual identity can play out as an assemblage of positions (i.e., status/role) where narratives and discourse are constructed by the subject from relations (and therefore experiences) of one's positionality (Shiller & Irving, 2014). This implies that the notion of identity should not be approached simply as the coexistence of a plurality of positions or as an aggregate of factors, but as a contextually dependent interchange of material and symbolic positionality (Varghese et al., 2016). Such an approach takes into consideration the push/pull factors that intersect and reflect the dynamic nature of individual and societal contexts. Key to this intersection is identity (re)construction in relation to broad contextual factors that work to frame worldviews and ideas about individual possibility. In this study, the difference between Natalia and Leo's positionality directly shaped their sense of agency, thoughts about future job markets, access to educational opportunities, and participation in local and global communities.

In addition, the role of transnationalism highlighted some ways in Natalia and Leo's lives that made clear the nuanced ways that multilingual students can be a part of home country and new country. In this study, they often didn't have a choice of building a life on two separate continents as a "cosmopolitan citizen" because it was too expensive to do so. Even though Natalia, as a U.S. citizen, was able to travel abroad for work, she wasn't able to afford this on her own. Leo's limited ability to cross back and forth to his family's town in Mexico meant that his enactment of transnationalism played out quite differently than Natalia. His displacement as a transnational person unfolded according to a series of circumstances beyond his control despite his mother, stepfather, and two younger siblings being legal residents. Both Leo and Natalia were capable of producing and expressing a form of cosmopolitanism that is representative of working-class people and their lives (Rogaly, 2020; Wise, 2016). Within these multidimensional spaces, today's cosmopolitanism involves new formulations of people whose jobs and political situations include the positionalities illustrated by Natalia and Leo where socioeconomic status and one's ability to cross borders can account for both privileged and less privileged populations.

SOCIAL MOVEMENT THEORY AND AN ELT FRAMEWORK

There are three aspects of social movement theory that are particularly informative for a general framework for ELT education that highlight how immigration weaves through many multilingual students' lives: 1) migration channels, 2) location of settlement and human capitol, and 3) transnationalism. Understanding the relationship between these three is important to understanding the broader political, economic, and social context wherein multilingual students and their families build their lives. Indeed, in relation to racism and other positionalities, these factors determine access to employment, schooling, and possibilities for upward mobility.

1)   Migration Channels

Migration channels and the various legal statuses are fundamental to understanding the ways in which people group themselves, where they live, how long they can stay, how much autonomy they have (versus control by an employer), whether their families can join them, what kind of livelihood they can undertake and maintain, and to what extent they can make use of public services and resources such as, schools, health care, job training, social benefits, and other public funds (Vertovec, 2019; Wise, 2016). An individual's migration pattern influences their length of residency and frequency of visiting their home country, and consequently, the ability to understand and adapt to the new country's dominant practices. Work status in the new country comes with restrictions on movement and access to support services depending on the economic-driven logic of selective immigration policy, H1B professional visas, H2 agricultural visas, refugee and asylee status, and benefits that may come with each classification such as, housing allowance, job training, healthcare, among others. One's immigration status is key to determining the relationship they can have with the state in terms of access to resources, the legal system, and employment, all of which are important means of social capital and economic viability (Meisser & Vertovec, 2014).

Most notable about Leo's situation is that his status underscores the complexity of social movement of immigrant populations. Because of his immigration status and the complications of his language and legal status, he lives in limbo, unable to access the city-to-city migratory routes that characterize current social networks of connection between cities in Mexico and the U.S.

For Natalia, the distance between the U.S. and Russia prohibits frequent visits to family and friend networks, so despite being able to travel freely, she is limited by the economic realities of her life and family obligations.

Migration channels are also nuanced by gender and the ways that gendered flows of immigration impact labor divisions, both within the household and in the public realm. The type of work that immigrant women and girls engage in when living in the context of a new country, and the ways in which the family structure within the household changes are important aspects for ELTs to consider as a way to engage and connect with their multilingual female students who may be struggling to make sense of new cultural norms in the midst of retaining a sense of normalcy and familiarity with their family and home community (Liggett, 2010; Vitanova, 2016). For example, a restructuring can occur based on the advanced language proficiency of a daughter, which suddenly casts her into a role that is different or unfamiliar from her previous context. This can shift one's status in the school or community, yet it could also cause disequilibrium in the family structure at a challenging time of adjustment if such a shift involves the woman becoming the main (or sole) breadwinner, or the daughter suddenly having the most cultural capitol because of her language proficiency. English language teachers are in a position to ameliorate such change when they are aware of the ways that gender role shift can impact family life in a new cultural context and then can enact strategies/methods that utilize this information in their teaching practice.

2) Location of settlement and human capitol

Where immigrants settle is determined by their social networks, their individual human capital, and their access to employment. One's ability to obtain work depends on their background, professional, and educational experiences. In terms of human capital, educational attainment in the context of the U.S. is highly valued and is often a key pull factor in attracting immigrants to various urban, suburban, or rural communities. In fact, 50% of recent immigrants arrive in the U.S. with a Bachelor's degree compared to 33% for the native population (MPI, 2023). Locality is also related to material conditions as well as to the nature and extent of other immigrant and ethnic group presence. When looking at urban and rural settlement patterns, contemporary immigration remains largely an urban phenomenon, concentrated in the most populated cities: New York/New Jersey, Los Angeles, Miami, Chicago, Houston, San Francisco, and Washington, D.C. (MPI, 2023). This pattern has occurred regularly over the last several decades with the same cities emerging as the preferred destinations. In particular, there has been a gradual end to rural-bound groups coming to settle empty lands or work as farm laborers, which was a significant component of pre-World War I immigration. While many undocumented immigrants begin as rural workers, they gradually move into the larger cities, attracted by higher wages and better working conditions (Portes & Rumbaut, 2014).

Like native [English speaking] youth, newly arrived immigrants, as newcomers to the labor market, tend to search for immediately available opportunities. Regardless of their qualifications and experience, recent immigrants generally enter at the bottom of their respective occupational ladders, whether manual workers, professionals, or entrepreneurs. (p. 104)

On every level, Leo's access to employment intersects with his human capitol, which in turn, challenges his potential to realize economic capital. Leo's individual experience mirrors a larger pattern in the findings of a longitudinal study by Telles & Ortiz (2008) who constructed a 35-year longitudinal data set covering the integration of original respondents and their descendants. They found that the primary responsibility for the dismal results in educational attainment and economic mobility for Mexican American children was due to their racialization in the U.S. In the U.S., they are stereotyped by teachers and school authorities as innately inferior to white and Asian students and are treated accordingly (Telles & Ortiz, 2008). Such treatment becomes a self-fulfilling prophecy, as Mexican origin youth try to defend themselves against discrimination and a threatened sense of self by abandoning aspirations for high academic achievement and rejecting members of their own group who attempt to do so as "acting white" (Portes & Rumbaut, 2014, pp. 295). The signals and racial stereotypes that educators and society send to students impact the extent to which they will engage and persist in school, and while racial stereotypes may produce a positive self-identity for white and Asian students, they produce a negative one for Blacks and Latinos (Telles & Ortiz, 2008). Leo's disinterest in formal post-secondary education was an obstacle for obtaining his general education diploma (GED) as he had not been successful in school-based educational settings and struggled with written language in English and spoken language in Spanish. He is, however, an accomplished artist whose paintings quickly sold at a local gallery event and who has interpersonal skills that allowed him to be the leader of a successful mural-painting project. Unfortunately, this event had little crossover to the broader art field as a way to access and maintain economic gain for him.

Natalia's ability to become upwardly mobile in the context of the U.S., intersected with other aspects of her identity including race and language proficiency. She did not have the negative mapping of race onto her as a white Russian and was able to graduate from high school, attend a local community college, and attain work that tapped into her fluent language skills in both Russian and English. These factors were foundational to maintaining her economic ability to (re)locate to cities/towns and continue her educational pursuits if she chose.

Examining the multiple layers of complexity involved in location of settlement and human capitol can assist ELT educators to deconstruct negative stereotypes about immigrants' educational attainment and to better understand how different immigrant groups get racialized in the context of the U.S. This factor plays a significant role in integration and reception by local communities. Learning about this could further impress upon ELTs to hold high expectations for their students as teachers' expectations for student achievement is a significant factor to their academic success and well-being as illustrated in even more research with students of color (Milner, 2020; Pollock, 2017; Sensoy & DiAngelo, 2017) and English language learners (Garcia & Kleifgen, 2018; Snyder & Fenner, 2021).

3) Transnationalism:

Trans denotes both moving through space or across lines, as well as changing the nature of something... to refer to the cultural specificities of global processes, tracing the multiplicity of the uses and conceptions of 'culture'. (Ong, 1999, p. 4)

Ong captures the sense that not only the physical movement between the old and new country but also that in the process, one is changed from the experience, modifying cultural ways of knowing through the intersections germane to each context. Lives are affected by border crossings, ongoing connections to family and friends, along with the ability to maintain relationships, native language, and support networks in the homeland. These may be ties across countries, not only with communities, but other types of social formations such as transnationally active networks, groups, and organizations. It is possible to maintain such support systems more intensely in an array of links with places of origin and diasporas elsewhere because of improved modes of communication, access to the internet, less expensive travel, and increased cell phone usage (Vertovec, 2019).

With contemporary migration, more frequent border-crossings and time spent in both the host and home countries, transnational migrant parents, may find it challenging to understand, appreciate and enact the expectations of the host country's educational settings (Chan, 2020). As Chan's research shows, transnational migrants express their perspectives regarding their children's education based on their home country's practices as terms of reference; in fact, some have no intention of adopting the practices of the host country but have adhered to the familiar practices of their homeland, which they still visit often (Chan, 2020). Conversely, there are migrant families who intend to settle permanently in the host country and acculturate or assimilate within it. Such a range of heterogeneous parenting practices demonstrates the new configurations of social groupings where groups are not necessarily defined by ethnicity or country of origin, but increasingly by common language, English language proficiency, locality, socio-economic position, or immigration status (Spoonley & Bedford, 2012).

Both Leo and Natalia spent little time in their home country, though for different reasons. Leo's ability to express transnationalism was limited to the virtual connections that he had with family members and friends in Mexico because of the risks of border crossing as a person without legal status. This made his connections to his immediate family and friends in the U.S. become more dominant. Similarly, though for different reasons, Natalia spent little time in her home country because of the distance and cost of travel to it. She was able to enact a sense of transnationalism through her fluency in English and Russian, educational background, immigration status, and family/professional networks and organizations. These two examples of students' transnational experiences could help raise ELT awareness of the complex ties and connections that their students maintain as central parts of their identity development. Better understandings could assist in developing responsive pedagogical orientations that support multilingual student engagement and integration in the school community.

MOVING FORWARD: STRATEGIES TO DEEPEN UNDERSTANDINGS OF IMMIGRATION

Immigration is increasingly about the ability to cross borders, to communicate between relatives/friends from home and new contexts. We see how political, economic, and social issues come into play to influence access and opportunity for the students in this study within their respective postsecondary settings. These dynamic and changing factors challenge ELT educators to consider the influence on learning, participation, engagement, motivation, and understanding of instruction for the English language learners in their classrooms. While these students may have significantly different experiences than their teachers and peers, as teacher educators we need to choose materials that help ELTs think about student experience in ways that are unimaginable to them, especially if they are monolingual and monocultural (Liggett, 2017; Sensoy & DiAngelo, 2017). In other words, we need to provide them with readings, documentary films, podcasts, and other historical/current data on immigration that reflects and locates a broad spectrum of immigrant experiences. This presses ELTs to think outside of the box, outside of their own experiences in education, so that they have a better idea of what factors in a child's life might greatly influence the ways they approach their schooling.

As ELTs prepare to go into the classroom and work with multilingual students, more in-depth understandings of the complex issues surrounding immigration will better prepare them to advocate on behalf of students and their families not only to improve students' academic achievement but also to change the hearts and minds of the school community, so that substantive integration can occur and everyone has a better chance to lead fulfilling lives. I look to social theory and contemporary theories of immigration as *another* lens to inform our work with immigrant English learners. ELT educators are in an important position to expand preservice and inservice teachers thinking by using material that centers alternative perspectives in relation to the context of race and various positionalities in U.S. society. Through the use of storytelling, narratives, multimedia, and longitudinal data, teachers/teacher candidates' perspectives widen and various positionalities are better understood. Below is a list of materials that I have found to be helpful for students to make more nuanced connections between the individual identity factors that we discuss in class to the broader political, economic, and social issues that we see arise in our readings and multimedia resources.

Resources for incorporating immigration in ELT curricula:

- *Immigrant America, 4th edition* by Portes & Rumbaut (2014): Contains individual narratives of immigrants' stories settling in various cities across the U.S. as well as longitudinal data on education, second-generation, status, economic, and political push-pull factors that effect where immigrants settle, find jobs, and go to school.
- The *Migration Policy Institute* website, features a variety of resources, research data, and free webinars to address specific topics of immigrant ethnicity, language(s), religious tradition, age, among others. This website is also helpful to update gaps from the longitudinal data in *Immigrant America* (2014) above to current year data. https://www.migrationpolicy.org

For information on DACA: https://www.migrationpolicy.org/programs/data-hub/deferred-action-childhood-arrivals-daca-profiles

For information on individual state immigration data: https://www.migrationpolicy.org/programs/data-hub/state-immigration-data-profilesS

For U.S. immigration trends: https://www.migrationpolicy.org/programs/data-hub/us-immigration-trends

- The documentary film, *Rain in a Dry Land,* by Anne Makepeace (2006), follows two Somali Bantu families as they transition from the Kakuma Refugee Camp in Kenya to two different cities in the United States. The film conveys the struggles, hardships, and growth of family members as they enter school, work, and society in the United States. Updating the information from this film to the current Kakuma Refugee population (https://www.unhcr.org/ke/kakuma-refugee-camp) is a great way to examine migration channels and the mapping of race onto African people as they settle in various cities across the U.S.
- The documentary film, *Maid in America,* by Anayansi Prado (2005) follows three women who have immigrated from Central America and Mexico to find better paying work to support the families that they left behind. Each woman finds employment as a domestic worker while struggling to reconcile their life and roles in a new country with the absence and loss from their native country.
- The United We Dream website has current DACA information for undocumented students, along with resources, and toolkits to use in classrooms and school communities. https://unitedwedream.org/tools/
- The Colorin Colorado website is a bilingual site for educators and families of English language learners that has teaching videos and extensive information on ways for teachers to support immigrant students and families. https://www.colorincolorado.org/immigration/guide/issues
- The Learning for Justice website has resources (including lesson plans) to teach about immigration with information on how to support undocumented and EL students. https://www.learningforjustice.org/topics/immigration

With increased polarization on views of immigration, it becomes increasingly important for teachers to deconstruct negative stereotypes about immigration and immigrant populations. English language teacher educators are in an important position to reverse these negative stereotypes by using material and instruction that value the knowledge and skills that immigrant students and their families bring to local communities. Multilingual students can experience daily microaggressions that work to denigrate and put into question their intelligence, integrity, and trustworthiness in broader society and teachers can play an important role in reversing such treatment.

An important area to address when using these resources is the potential for them to be triggering events for students who have experienced trauma in their lives or they could work to further racialize and stigmatize immigrant populations. To avoid this, I recommend that ELT educators consistently locate the individual narratives/stories within broader political and social contexts in order to underscore different levels of influence (e.g., institutional, cultural, individual). In addition, pointing out the intersectionality of identity and the various context specific ways that these factors are foregrounded or backgrounded in relation to external influences beyond students' control, such as relationship between home and new country, economic market forces, or local reception of multiple immigrant groups.

Moving forward, as educators adapt and modify the suggestions that I have put forth here, another area of examination includes the impact of climate change. The rapid onset of events such as natural disasters and heavy rainfall mix with slow onset events like sea level rise and deforestation to drive displacement across borders. Since climate is not included under the 1951 United Nations Convention as grounds for asylum, there is a legal gap and a lack of social protections for these vulnerable populations. The future will inevitably see an increase in climate refugees.

CONCLUSION

I have laid out a general framework here for incorporating aspects of social movement theory in ELT education as a way to better understand the intersections with racism and other positionalities for English learners in the U.S. The aspects that I discuss in this chapter have changed significantly in the last decade making inquiry into migration channels, location of settlement and human capitol, and transnationalism areas that offer much potential to more accurately prepare ELTs to work with their multilingual students. Burns & Roberts (2010) remind us that, "The classroom is a globalized social space, with students whose reasons for migration, desires and dreams, linguistic and cultural resources, and functional goals may all differ from that of other class members" (p. 411). ELT educators prepare their students for an increasingly global and mobile K-12 population. The creation and implementation of curricula that speak to these realities fosters new venues for access and engagement with topics that are germane to multilingual students and their families. An intersectional approach to incorporating aspects of social movement theory in relation to identity factors can work to highlight the relationship between the role of racism with other positionalities for more nuanced understandings in ELT education.

REFERENCES

Ajayi, L. (2011). Exploring how ESL teachers related their ethnic and social backgrounds to practice. *Race, Ethnicity and Education, 14*(2), 253–275. doi:10.1080/13613324.2010.488900

Alim, H. S. (2010). Critical language awareness. In N. H. Hornberger & S. L. McKay (Eds.), *Sociolinguistics and language education: New perspectives on language and education* (pp. 205–231). Multilingual Matters. doi:10.21832/9781847692849-010

Appiah, A. (2006). *Cosmopolitanism: Ethics in a world of strangers*. Norton.

Azulai, A. (2020). Are grounded theory and action research compatible? considerations for methodological triangulation. *The Canadian Journal of Action Research, 21*(2), 4–24. doi:10.33524/cjar.v21i2.485

Blommaert, J. (2013). Citizenship, language, and superdiversity: Towards complexity. *Journal of Language, Identity, and Education, 12*(3), 193–196. doi:10.1080/15348458.2013.797276

Burns, A., & Roberts, C. (2010, September). Migration and adult language learning: Global flows and local transpositions. *TESOL Quarterly, 44*(3), 409–419. doi:10.5054/tq.2010.232478

Chan, A. (2020). Superdiversity and critical multicultural pedagogies: Working with migrant. *Policy Futures in Education, 18*(5), 560–573. doi:10.1177/1478210319873773

Charalambous, C., Zembylas, M., & Charalambous, P. (2015). Superdiversity and discourses of conflict: Interaction in a Greek-Cypriot literacy class. *Working Papers in Urban Language & Literacies*.

Charmaz, K. (2005). Grounded theory in the 21st century: Applications for advancing social justice studies. In N. K. Denzin & Y. S. Lincoln (Eds.), *Sage handbook of qualitative research* (pp. 507–535). Sage Publications.

Clandinin, D. J., & Connelly, F. M. (2000). *Narrative inquiry: Experience and story in qualitative research*. Jossey-Bass Publishing.

Compton-Lilly, C., & Hawkins, M. R. (2023). Global flows and critical cosmopolitanism: A longitudinal case study. *Harvard Educational Review*, *93*(1), 26–52. doi:10.17763/1943-5045-93.1.26

Crul, M. (2016). Super-diversity vs. assimilation: How complex diversity in majority-minority cities challenge the assumptions of assimilation. *Journal of Ethnic and Migration Studies*, *42*(1), 54–68. doi:10.1080/1369183X.2015.1061425

Ergas, O. (2020). Education and cosmopolitanism: Liberating our non-cosmopolitan minds through mindfulness. *Policy Futures in Education*, *18*(5), 610–627. doi:10.1177/1478210319876512

Garcia, O., & Kleifgen, J. A. (2018). *Educating emergent bilinguals: Policies, programs, and practices for English learners*. Teachers College Press.

Guardado, M. (2010). Heritage language development: Preserving a mythic past or envisioning the future of Canadian identity? *Journal of Language, Identity, and Education*, *5*(9), 329–346. doi:10.1080/15348458.2010.517699

Hannerz, U. (1990). Cosmopolitans and locals in world culture. In M. Featherstone (Ed.), *Global culture: Nationalism, globalization, and modernity* (pp. 237–252). Sage Publications.

Heidemann, K. A. (2019). Close, yet so far apart: Bridging social movement theory with popular education. *Australian Journal of Adult Learning*, *59*(3), 309–318.

Kastoryano, R. (2000). Global trends and issues: Settlement, transnational communities and citizenship. *International Social Science Journal*, *52*(165), 307–312. doi:10.1111/1468-2451.00261

Kubota, R., & Lin, A. (2009). *Race, culture, and identities in second language education: Exploring critically engaged practice*. Routledge. doi:10.4324/9780203876657

Lee, E. (2015). Doing culture, doing race: Everyday discourses of 'culture' and 'cultural difference' in the English as a second language classroom. *Journal of Multilingual and Multicultural Development*, *36*(1), 80–93. doi:10.1080/01434632.2014.892503

Liggett, T. (2009). Unpacking white racial identity in English language teacher education. In R. Kubota & A. Lin (Eds.), *Race, culture, and identities in second language education: Exploring critically engaged practice* (pp. 27–43). Routledge.

Liggett, T. (2010, September). Postpositivist realist theory of identity: Expanding notions of gender in teacher education. *Journal of Curriculum Theorizing*, *26*(2), 90–101.

Liggett, T. (2014). The mapping of a framework: Critical race theory and TESOL. *The Urban Review*, *46*(1), 112–124. doi:10.100711256-013-0254-5

Liggett, T., Watson, D., & Griffin, L. (2017, March). Language use and racial redirect in the educational landscape of "just good teaching." *Teaching Education*, *28*(4), 393–405. doi:10.1080/10476210.2017.1306506

Lin H. (2018). *Super-diversity*. doi:10.6191/JPS.201812_57.0003

Massey, D. (1994). *Space, place, and gender*. University of Minnesota Press.

Meissner, F., & Vertovec, S. (2014). Comparing super-diversity. *Ethnic and Racial Studies*, *38*(4), 541–555. doi:10.1080/01419870.2015.980295

Migration Policy Institute. (n.d.-a). *Largest Immigrant Groups Over Time*. Retrieved May 5, 2023, from https://www.migrationpolicy.org/programs/data-hub/charts/largest-immigrant-groups-over-time

Migration Policy Institute. (n.d.). [Frequently Requested Statistics-Immigrants Now Historically]. Retrieved May 5, 2023, from https://www.migrationpolicy.org/article/frequently-requested-statistics-immigrants-and-immigration-united-states#immigrants_now_historically

Migration Policy Institute. (n.d.-b). *Frequently Requested Statistics-Demographic-Educational-Linguistic*. Retrieved May 17, 2023, from https://www.migrationpolicy.org/article/frequently-requested-statistics-immigrants-and-immigration-united-states-2020#demographic-educational-linguistic

Migration Policy Institute. (n.d.-c). *ELL Information Center*. Retrieved June, 21, 2023, from https://www.migrationpolicy.org/programs/ell-information-center

Migration Policy Institute. (n.d.-d). *ELs K-12 per State*. Retrieved on July 13, 2023, from https://www.migrationpolicy.org/programs/data-hub/charts/english-learners-k-12-education-state

Migration Policy Institute. (n.d.-e). *Immigrant Population Metro Area*. Retrieved July 13, 2023 from https://www.migrationpolicy.org/programs/data-hub/charts/us-immigrant-population-metropolitan-area?width=1000&height=850&iframe=true

Milner, H. R. IV. (2020). *Start where you are, but don't stay there* (2nd ed.). Harvard Education Press.

Motha, S. (2014). *Race, empire, and English language teaching*. Teachers College Press.

National Center for Children in Poverty. (n.d.). *Children Living in Poverty*. Retrieved July, 7, 2021, from www.nccp.org

National Center for Education Statistics. (n.d.). *English Learners in Public Schools*. Retrieved May, 17, 2023, from https://nces.ed.gov/programs/coe/indicator/cgf

Ong, A. (1999). *Flexible citizenship: The cultural logics of transnationality*. Duke University Press.

Peregoy, S. F., & Boyle, O. F. (2016). *Reading, writing, and learning in ESL: A resource book for teaching K-12 English learners* (7th ed.). Pearson.

Pollock, M. (2017). *Schooltalk: Rethinking what we say about and to students every day*. The New Press.

Portes, A., & Fumbaut, R. G. (2014). *Immigrant America: A portrait* (4th ed.). University of California Press. doi:10.1525/9780520959156

Rogaly, B. (2020). *Stories from a migrant city: Living and working together in the shadow of Brexit*. Manchester University Press. ProQuest Ebook Central, https://ebookcentral.proquest.com/lib/linfield/detail.action?docID=6144184

Roudometof, V. (2020). Globalization, cosmopolitanism and 21st century populism. *Protosociology*, *37*(165).

Sensoy, O., & DiAngelo, R. (2017). *Is everyone really equal? An introduction to key concepts in social justice education* (2nd ed.). Teachers College Press.

Shiller, N. G., & Irving, A. (2014). *Whose cosmopolitanism? Critical perspectives, relationalities and discontents*. Berghahn Books.

Snyder, S., & Fenner, D. S. (2021). *Culturally responsive teaching for multilingual learners: Tools for equity*. Corwin Publishing.

Sonday, A., Ramugondo, E., & Kathard, H. (2020). Case study and narrative inquiry as merged methodologies: A critical narrative perspective. *International Journal of Qualitative Methods, 19*. doi:10.1177/1609406920937880

Spoonley, P., & Bedford, R. (2012). *Welcome to our world? Immigration and the reshaping of New Zealand*. Dunmore Publishing.

Taylor, A. (2017). Putting race on the table: How teachers make sense of the role of race in their practice. *Harvard Educational Review, 87*(1), 50–73. doi:10.17763/1943-5045-87.1.50

Tedeschi, M., Ekaterina, V., & Jauhiainen, J. S. (2022). Transnationalism: Current debates and new perspectives. *GeoJournal, 87*(2), 603–619. doi:10.100710708-020-10271-8

Telles, E. E., & Ortiz, V. (2008). *Generations of exclusion: Mexican-Americans, assimilation, and race*. Russell Sage Foundation.

United States Census Bureau. (n.d.). *Bachelor's Degree or Higher*. Retrieved June, 21, 2023, from https://data.census.gov/cedsci/profile?g=0100000US

Varghese, M., Motha, S., Trent, J., Park, G., & Reeves, J. (2016). Language teacher identity in multilingual education. *TESOL Quarterly, 49*(1), 219–220. doi:10.1002/tesq.221

Vertovec, S. (2007). Super-diversity and its implications. *Ethnic and Racial Studies, 30*(6), 1024–1054. doi:10.1080/01419870701599465

Vertovec, S. (2019). Talking around super-diversity. *Ethnic and Racial Studies, 42*(1), 125–139. doi:10.1080/01419870.2017.1406128

Vitanova, G. (2016). Exploring second-language teachers' identities through multimodal narratives: Gender and race discourses. *Critical Inquiry in Language Studies, 13*(4), 261–288. doi:10.1080/15427587.2016.1165074

Von Esch, K. S., Motha, S., & Kubota, R. (2020). Race and language teaching. *Language Teaching, 53*(4), 391–421. doi:10.1017/S0261444820000269

Werbner, P. (1999). Global pathways: Working class cosmopolitans and the creation of transnational ethnic worlds. *Social Anthropology, 7*(1), 17–35. doi:10.1017/S0964028299000026

Wise, A. (2016). Becoming cosmopolitan: Encountering difference in a city of mobile labour. *Journal of Ethnic and Migration Studies, 42*(14), 2280–2299. doi:10.1080/1369183X.2016.1205807

KEY TERMS AND DEFINITIONS

English Language Teacher Education: Teachers of multilingual students learning English.

Identity: They way one perceives themselves in terms of race, ethnicity, culture, language, gender, sexual orientation, religion, physical ability, and other affinity groups in relation to society.

Immigration: The movement of people/groups from one country to another because of political, economic, or social forces.

Positionality: One's social standing/status in relation to other people within a given context.

Race: A socially constructed concept in the United States that categorizes people based on their skin color.

Social Movement Theory: Theoretical frameworks that identify key factors about the movement of migrant populations from one country to another.

Chapter 6
Belonging and Legitimacy for French Language Teachers:
A Visual Analysis of Raciolinguistic Discourses

Mimi Masson
https://orcid.org/0000-0002-1516-4601
Université de Sherbrooke, Canada

Simone Ellene Cote
Independent Researcher, Canada

ABSTRACT

With the ongoing French as a second language (FSL) teacher shortage crisis driving multi-million-dollar expenditures from governments, professional associations, and school boards, little attention has turned towards identifying systemic issues, rooted in racial ideologies, which may be impacting FSL teachers' desire to stay (or even enter) into the profession. In this chapter, using visual narratives and arts-based research methods, the authors applied LangCrit and raciolingusitics to examine future FSL teachers' discourses about French as a language/culture and learning French and teaching French. The data collected over a year, showcasing three participants, reveal the vastly different positionalities entrenched in complex interactions with language standard ideologies, native-speakerism, colonialism and racism. The authors ask, then, how stakeholders and teacher education programs might account for these differing lived realities when it comes to recruiting and preparing future FSL teachers for long-term success in the profession.

INTRODUCTION

In response to the ongoing French as a second language (FSL) teacher shortage crisis in Canada (Masson et al., 2019), governmental and educational institutions have been focusing on recruiting more French language speakers to the profession. While specifics vary across provinces and territories, teacher educa-

DOI: 10.4018/978-1-6684-9029-7.ch006

tion programs are generally about two years in length, after an initial four years at university. They offer general pedagogical and subject-specific methodology (didactics) courses, often in English and when possible in French, as well as practicum in schools where future teachers can practice teaching in FSL programs (see Smith et al, 2023 for a detailed pan-Canadian comparison of programs). Recruits are usually either graduates of French immersion programs, or individuals from French-speaking nations around the world with whom the government is forging agreements so that French-speaking individuals may immigrate to Canada to become practicing teachers. This signals a shift in the make-up of the French teacher population, with large numbers of FSL learners becoming French teachers and an increasing number of potential French teachers immigrating from Africa, South America, the Caribbeans and Asia, some of whom may speak non-standard forms of French. Standard forms of French considered 'appropriate' or 'correct' those from France, Belgium, Switzerland or Québec. In Canada, while research has focused on the professional needs and linguistic profiles of FSL teachers (Jack & Nyman, 2019; Masson et al., 2019), it has overlooked their intersections with racial identity. In fact, there is little understanding of who are FSL teachers and what issues they must negotiate as they develop their practice (Byrd Clark, 2010; Tang, 2020), particularly through a raciolinguistic lens. Indeed, the ways in which issues of race, racism and colonialism are tied up in FSL teaching and learning is just emerging as a field of research in Canada (Wernicke et al., forthcoming). With this chapter, we seek to examine how raciolinguistic issues might have a bearing on future FSL teachers' identity formation, and how well they are able to establish a sense of belonging and legitimacy which may shed light on another dimension affecting their long-term desire to remain in the profession.

While we reference the literature on the FSL teacher shortage across Canada, our study took place in Ontario (a province in Canada) where many of the issues identified in the pan-Canadian literature also surface. Our intention is to challenge and nuance general discourses about who are FSL teachers in Canada using a raciolinguistic lens. Below, we outline key socio-historical and socio-political realities in the Canadian context. Having these in mind, it is important to facilitate the process of looking at the intersection of racializing discourses associated with French and the professional identity construction of novice FSL teachers and the possibilities of them developing a sense of belonging in the French-speaking community.

SITUATING FRENCH WITHIN THE CANADIAN COLONIAL PROJECT

Embarking on an exploration of FSL teacher identity requires imagining possibilities for becoming a professional who teaches language within intersections of language and race in Canada. It also requires an understanding of the socio-historical context of French in Ontario and Canada more broadly. A few pertinent facts stand out.

First, we will study the unique history of French in Canada. Longstanding fighting between the British and the French for dominance of stolen Indigenous lands in Canada, and the subsequent dominance of English-speaking peoples, contributed to the progressive marginalization and oppression of French speaking communities by the British and their settler descendants (Haque, 2012; Makropoulos, 2004). At the same time, its status as one of the first colonizing languages on Canadian soil is also what afforded French its official language status. Second, historical conceptualization and theorization of the French language and second language acquisition rely on deficit-oriented perspectives towards competency, fluency and legitimacy. These epistemes have carried on in the field of FSL education (Wernicke et al., forthcoming). In fact, linking back to the intertwining of French/English colonization in Canada, rationales for British and French domination in Canada were founded on the 'superiority' of White Western Europeans, giving credence to the idea that those who were not part of the Franco-British racio-culturo-linguistic groups faced linguistic and cultural deficits, and therefore were not 'worthy' or 'capable enough' of governing (Haque, 2012). Third, colonizing ideologies have led to the prevailing association of French with Whiteness, contributing to the construction of Canadian Francophone identity as White and of European descent (Madibbo, 2021). In effect, the education system has been reinforcing this association of French and Whiteness in the selection of classroom materials, topics of discussion, and representations of French language and culture (Kunnas, 2019; Masson et al., 2022). To illustrate the ways in which Whiteness is reinforced as the racial norm with French, a study examining the current Ontario FSL curriculum identified the erasure of Indigenous French-speaking population, and exoticization non-White French speaking regions and peoples around the world (Masson, et al., 2023).

Canada was first confederated as a nation in 1867, with the provinces of New Brunswick, Nova Scotia and the 'province of Canada' (now made up of Ontario and Quebec) (The Canadian Encyclopedia, 2023). Much of the tension between English- and French-speaking populations are embedded in the emergence of Canada as a nation, as French and British colonial powers fought for control of this territory, and maintained through the provincial linguistic policy. For instance, in Ontario, English is the official and dominant language. French, which is not an official language at the provincial level (only at the federal level), is a minoritized language. Meanwhile in Quebec, the reverse is true: French is the only official language at the provincial level and English is a minoritized language. In both provinces, the minority language is taught as the default second language across schools.

Central to discussions in this chapter are the notions of Eurocentrism and Whiteness. We define Eurocentrism as a sustained and intentional focus and valorization of cultural norms emanating from a European tradition. This is not to say that Eurocentric norms do not have their own merits. Simply, they become an issue when they are promoted to the exclusion of other forms of knowledge and ways of being, such as Afro-Caribbean and Indigenous ways of knowing. We define Whiteness as a socializing process, transmitted through culture, language, customs, beliefs, and world views, which emanate from White people as a group. This concept is useful to understand racial hierarchies that emerge in a postcolonial context such as Canada, since White-dominant culture is normalized and used as a standard for what is socially appropriate and expected. Whiteness is a set of socialization processes, however, historically, due to the economic, social and capital domination of White people in the North American context, it has been erroneously equated as superior to other racialized groups' beliefs and practices (e.g., Indigenous people and people from the African diaspora), and used to reinforce racial hierarchies. Both Whiteness and Eurocentrism are intertwined in the Canadian context (Haque, 2012; Vigouroux, 2017).

BELONGING TO THE FRENCH AS A SECOND LANGUAGE TEACHING PROFESSION

In this section, we outline the notions of belonging and legitimacy, important processes in successful teacher identity formation (Alsup, 2006; Schaefer & Clandinin, 2019). Teachers' sense of belonging and legitimacy can be examined by a combination of things, including their beliefs and experiences with a given language, shaped by both internal emotional and intellectual forces, and external social forces. We first examine these concepts broadly and explicitly tie them back to racial ideologies.

Belonging

Having a sense of belonging is a fundamental human desire (Baumeister & Leary, 2017). Vallente (2020) uses 'alignment as a mode of belonging" (p. 4) to describe it. Taken from Wenger's (1998) model of Communities of Practice (CoPs), alignment refers to "an individual's activities within broader structures and enterprises, allowing the identity of a larger group to become part of the identity of the individual participants." (Vallente, 2020, p. 3). For FSL teachers, we can think of two groups with which it might be important to develop alignment as a mode of belonging: French teaching professionals and French speakers. FSL teachers need to develop a shared sense of what it means specifically to be a French teacher in Canada. Vallente (2020) found that misalignment in language teachers' identity formation led to reproducing ideologies and practices rooted in monolingualism, native-speaker norms, and subtractive multilingualism: all key frames of reference have been shown to intersect with racial ideologies (Flores & Rosa, 2015) which we explore further below. If FSL teachers are meant to teach French which is an entry point into French languages and cultures for students, then understanding their relationship with the target language becomes important. Particularly their relationship to the target language will also influence how they teach in ways that reproduce or subvert inclusive and oppressive ideologies.

Linguistic identity has been an important marker for belonging and professionalism in the second language teaching profession. For instance, Riches and Parks (2021) found that language teachers categorize each other according to their perceived sense of linguistic belonging (in this case, anglophone, francophone, and allophone). This affected not only their sense of belonging in their schools but also their potential for collaboration with other colleagues, just like the feeling of not belonging to the English-speaking community undermines English teachers' teaching identities (Menezes de Oliveira e Paiva, 2016).

Davey (2013) identified belonging as one of the five specific, intertwined areas of identity (i.e., becoming, doing, knowing, being, and belonging). For Davey, teacher belonging is reflected through the CoPs that teachers are involved in, and their awareness of the similarities and differences that exist with other teachers. Xu (2017) discusses this in terms of pursuit of membership in a community:

Identity is inevitably relational, which suggests that individual teachers need to join the community to which they desire to belong. Being part of the community will generate a sense of belonging, which enhances participation and performance. However, becoming a full member of a community is not a straightforward matter, nor is it a guarantee of success. (Liu & Xu, 2011, p. 123)

Legitimacy

In Communities of Practice, new members must develop legitimate peripheral participation (Lave & Wenger, 1991) which is the ability to participate incrementally in ways that promote opportunities to experiment with new forms of learning, being and doing (Davies, 2005). This is important to establish social standing, validity and emotional ties in a professional community, and to transition from a less experienced to a more experienced member. For language teachers, it is essential to feel seen, heard, and accepted as legitimate teachers (Miller, 2009), particularly as the way language teachers legitimate their identities involves a complex and subtle (re)negotiation of raciolinguistic and neoliberal ideologies (Ho, 2023). Language teachers have reported struggling with their professional legitimacy (Widodo et al, 2020) regarding questions of authenticity and competence in the target language. For English language teachers, questions of social status as it relates to native-speakerism (as a form of ultimate legitimacy as a speaker of the target language) permeate language teacher identity formation (Matsuda, 2017). We hypothesize that a similar phenomenon is in effect for FSL teachers. Language teachers may struggle to establish legitimacy in their profession if they feel a sense of insecurity relative to their language competence (Wolff & De Costa, 2017). Identity formation among individuals can be weakened when certain types of discrimination are perceived as legitimate (Freynet & Clément, 2019). For FSL teachers, this would mean that internalizing ideas that their French is not correct, good enough, or beautiful, etc. On the other hand, when discrimination against individuals is considered illegitimate (that is, not grounded in facts or evidence), they are able to draw on cognitive strategies to reject these perceptions, by developing resilience, as a coping mechanism (Fletcher & Sarkar, 2013). Discrimination has also been found to encourage stigmatized individuals to think more deeply about their own identities and positions in society (Freynet et al, 2018; Pilote & Canuel, 2013). In the case of linguistic discrimination, this entails, for example, reconsidering the status of their accent in relation to other varieties.

Questions of legitimacy among FSL learners and teachers in Canada have been framed in terms of linguistic (in)security (Culligan et al, 2023; Roy & Galiev, 2011; Séror & Weinberg, 2021; Wernicke, 2020). Filtering this construct through a critical lens, we can see that the notion of linguistic insecurity is deeply rooted in deficit-oriented perspectives that place the burden of inclusion on the French teacher themselves, and serves as a mode of policing and excluding teachers from developing a sense of belonging within French speaking communities (Fedoration & Tang, 2023; Tang & Fedoration, 2022). This is emblematic of a deficit-oriented perspective towards FSL teachers, who bear the brunt of the blame for not feeling 'secure' enough to be able to teach well or stay in the profession (M. Tang, November 4, 2022, personal communication). It ignores the deep-seated colonial ideologies about language that underpin this mindset. Indeed, the focus seems to be on how closely FSL teachers can sound like native speakers (associated erroneously with better quality teaching capacity) and how well they can use language 'correctly'. Of course, European or Quebecois varieties of French, both of which are strongly entangled with Whiteness, are the varieties considered as standard and 'correct' (Kunnas, 2019).

As we can see, it is very difficult to disentangle what legitimacy and belonging to these two groups might mean for FSL teachers, since both these constructs influence and co-create each other. Our work aims to respond to Xu's (2017) call to illuminate the 'dark zones' of Language Teacher Identity (LTI) research by paying attention to the tensions and reconciliation among teachers' multiple identities and sub-identities, particularly in the ways that different identities become prioritized or shifted in different settings/contexts. Inspired by Xu (2017), we argue for a holistic view of FSL teacher identities in which we examine the interactions of both their personal and professional identities. This is particularly important given that interactions and experiences from their personal life contribute to forming beliefs about language, language learning and language teaching that will seep into their professional practice.

UNDERSTANDING OF LANGUAGE TEACHER IDENTITY

First, we view teacher identity through a post-structural and discourse analytic lens, as a social process of becoming, where a teacher's identity is always evolving and in interaction with social discourses. Concepts such as identity-as-pedagogy (Morgan, 2004), that is, the fact that what teachers do in the classroom impacts their sense of self and their relationships with their students, and that those interactions in turn transform them, highlight the ineffable link between the personal and the professional.

This creates a sense of urgency for understanding their beliefs, attitudes and experiences as these shape teachers' future practice.

Literature on French language teacher identity in Canada has addressed FSL teachers' identities as plurilingual (Byrd Clark, 2010; Wernicke, 2018) and their marginalization in the workplace (Masson, 2018), but what is absent from the discussion has been the issue of race (Wernicke et al., forthcoming). Some literature is beginning to center race in the conversation of FSL teacher identity. A recent paper by Wernicke (2022) highlights how official French-English bilingualism policy in Canada reinforces monoglossic ideologies, constricting possibilities for racialized FSL teachers to draw on the multilingual funds of knowledge that they bring. Masson et. al. (2022) observe that some teacher education programs preparing future FSL teachers struggle to adequately address issues of race, Whiteness and colonization during those formative years. In addition, the programs, in some cases, end up reinforcing oppressive practices and ideologies, while alienating potential future FSL teachers of color. In essence, we have only been getting a partial picture of FSL teacher identities. This is an ongoing trend in FSL research, where issues of race and how they interact with policy, curricula and student learning (e.g., Davies, 2023; Kunnas, 2019; Lavoie, 2015) are becoming more central to our understanding of FSL education as a system in Canada. Research focusing on French teachers' identities needs to go beyond language and include race and other social identities, such as culture, gender, socioeconomic status, and (dis)ability.

LANGCRIT AND RACIOLINGUISTIC CONCEPTUAL FRAMEWORKS FOR EXPLORING FSL TEACHER IDENTITY

Given our interest in looking at the intersection of racializing discourses associated with French and the professional identity construction of FSL teachers, we draw on raciolinguistics and Critical Language and Race Theory (LangCrit) to highlight how "race, racism, and racialization intersect with issues of language" (Crump, 2014, p. 207). Specifically, we seek to avoid masking race (Crump, 2014a; Von Esch et al., 2020) when exploring how future FSL teachers develop a sense of professional identity. We conceive of race as a social construct that functions ideologically as a racializing force when certain characteristics, such as skin color, accent, and ancestry, are used as the basis for justifying who is and is not a legitimate and competent user of French (Wernicke et al., forthcoming)

LangCrit emphasizes the way in which linguistic identities interact with racialized identities and its implications for individual identity performance and negotiation. It makes explicit the intersection of subject-as-heard and subject-as-seen (Sarkar et al., 2007). In our case, how FSL teachers, as racialized beings, are perceived, by the way they look or sound, reveals the external expectations of what French speakers/teachers should look and sound like, and by extension, how these teachers may or not fit those expectations, creating possibilities for misalignment when trying to develop a sense of legitimacy and belonging to the profession. We also examine FSL teacher candidates' internal personal perceptions of their linguistic and racial identities, and how racialized positionings or racialized spaces intersect with an individual's investment in or affiliation to a language, and ultimately, their professional identities as language teachers (Crump, 2014b). We use the constructs of the White listening subject from raciolinguistics (Flores & Rosa, 2015; Rosa & Flores, 2017) to unpack ideologies. The White listening subject is "an ideological position and mode of perception" (Flores & Rosa, 2015, p. 151) which filters language practices through the idealized linguistic practices valued and normalized by the White middle class. Accounting for the White listening subject, we examine its intersection with two language ideologies: the native speaker ideology and the standard language ideology. Language ideologies are broader interconnecting beliefs and attitudes about something pertaining to language, which will shape one's disposition towards (working with) that language. We see how (often unspoken) racial ideologies reinforce colonial patterns of thought implicitly in the discourses surrounding language use and teacher identity.

Intersections of Native Speaker Ideology and Racial Ideology

The native speaker is an idealized version of what a speaker of a given language sounds like (Cook, 1999). Its operational premise is that native speakers are the best / truest models for speaking a target language. Adding the physical dimension of what the idealized native speaker looks like, in English, this speaker is constructed as White (Flores & Rosa, 2022). Similarly, in Canada, the construction of an ideal French native speaker is White and of European origin or ancestry (Madibbo, 2021). The ability to look and sound like the idealized White native speaker provides opportunities for upward social mobility and inclusion, adding a power dimension to that language, which ultimately reinforces racial hierarchies that maintain associations with Whiteness as a norm for signaling professionalism, legitimacy and competence. Racialized students and professionals face real consequences of exclusion and marginalization in academic institutional settings due to raciolinguistic ideologies (Fallas-Escobar & Herrera, 2022; Holliday & Squires, 2021; Sekaja et al, 2022). Yet, professionals also note that they need English (or in our case French) to succeed in their chosen careers.

Intersections of Standard Language Ideology and Racial Ideology

Standard language ideology represents the bias towards an idealized 'standard' form of a given language (Lippi-Green, 1997). Its operational premise is that standard varieties of a language are the "best/purest/truest" forms of the language. French European varieties, also associated with Whiteness, are constructed as superior (i.e., more "beautiful," "authentic," "correct") (Vigouroux, 2017). This standard often becomes normalized and even imposed on language learners. It is also often tied to the protectionist idea of linguistic purism: that a certain variety of a language is the "best," "purest" form of that language. Those who do not conform to the standard can be seen (or heard) as less capable or deficient in their language competency. Discourses rooted in what is the "appropriate" standard to use when speaking the target language as a second language positions racialized speakers as deficient in their language production (Flores & Rosa, 2015). Going beyond discourses of linguistic insecurity, the standards of appropriate language use are constructed around the needs and expectations of white listening subjects (Inoue, 2006, as cited in Flores & Rosa, 2015), normalizing White native speakers' linguistic practices as the desired goal. For racialized speakers of French, conforming to language standards associated with Whiteness as a norm creates a raciolinguistic tension, placing them at the margins of target language production.

Deep theorizing between language ideologies and racial ideologies is a means to counter contemporary epistemology, the content and ways in which we teach that are currently steeped in Whiteness (Meighan, 2023; Von Esch et al., 2020). The entanglement of language and racial ideologies persist and contribute to the ongoing colonial project in Canada. Although French is a minoritized language in Canada, it is also a colonial language that was made official. It is through the colonial project that French has established its legitimacy, status and power in the Canadian context, and in other contexts such as African countries that some FSL teachers might come from (Makropoulos, 2004; Vigouroux, 2017).

METHODOLOGY

Data was gathered during a project conducted in a Teacher Education program with FSL teacher candidates, which received approval from the Ethics Review Board. The project drew on arts-based research (ABR) methodologies to examine how FSL teachers negotiate their personal and professional identities throughout their pre-service years. ABR is an effective tool for gathering information about teachers' beliefs and experiences with a given language. There is a long tradition of using ABR in teacher education in Europe (e.g., Melo-Pfeifer, 2019; Molinié, 2011; Rocafort, 2019). ABR framework enables researchers to address the process of self-actualization and reflection during teacher preparation (Melo-Pfeifer, 2019; Molinié, 2009), while engaging in a dialectical process during teacher education (Fillol, et al., 2019; Onițǎ, et al., 2021). Artistic research practices (visual and narrative) (Barkuizen, 2014; Barone & Eisner, 2011; Leitch, 2006) also allow researchers to reach thoughts, beliefs, and ideas that are less tangible and not always consciously accessible to unspoken things.

Over the course of a year, teacher candidates in a two-year teacher education program worked with their professor in the context of their FSL methodology course to create visual and artistic narratives about themselves to explore, for example, their beliefs about language learning, their vision of the 'ideal' French teacher, their hopes and fears in becoming French teachers, and their understanding of translanguaging and plurilingualism. They created poems, Venn diagrams, collages, and digital identity texts.

Research Question

Using a raciolinguistic lens, what issues related to developing a sense of belonging and legitimacy as French as a second language teachers emerge for teacher candidates during their teacher preparation program?

Participants

Seven participants took part in the study. We asked participants to self-identify how they would characterize their profiles, represented in Table 1, either by completing the table or by gathering information from their data. Pseudonyms were self-selected by participants. Although we focused on three specific participants in the data analysis below (indicated with an * in Table 1), we felt it relevant to contextualize these focal participants within the broader group of participants (n=7). We note, in particular, the prevalence of White, female, Canadian-born participants. The choice of our three focal participants was made intentionally to amplify perspectives from Black and Asian immigrant perspectives.

The categories in Table 1 are meant to be a snapshot of how participants identified at the time of the study. They do not account for a fully nuanced view of the complex unique backgrounds of the participants.

Data Collection

In this chapter, we will examine the plurilingual portraits that our participants created following the prompt: "Please draw a silhouette to represent your linguistic and cultural repertoires. You may draw both inside and outside your silhouette." Teacher candidates were invited to participate in the study once the course was over and their final grades were submitted. They then participated in three 90-minute life story interviews over the course of three consecutive weeks during which we reviewed their artwork

Table 1. Participant profiles in alphabetical order

Name	Racial/Ethnic Identifier	Gender	Citizenship Status
Jade	White Canadian of European heritage (Scottish/Hungarian)	Female	Born in Canada; Canadian citizen
Jane	Questioning racial identity; possibly White and Middle Eastern; Egyptian franco-Arabic heritage	Female	Born and raised in Canada
Lisa	White Canadian (European - German and Irish heritage)	Female	Canadian citizenship
Lucy*	White Canadian of European heritage (French/British)	Female	Born and raised in Canada; Canadian, French, British citizenships
Lyne*	Black African	Female	Born and raised in Cameroon but now a Permanent Resident in Canada
Nawa*	Southeast Asian and Minority Chinese in Diaspora	Male	Recent Permanent Resident of Canada (4th year at time of giving the interview) Born and raised in Southeast Asia but spent a few years in his adolescence and young adulthood in multiple countries including Canada (Quebec)
Ryan	White; Irish-Canadian	Female	Born and raised in Canada. Grandparents immigrated to Canada

collaboratively and their thinking around the aforementioned topics. The interview protocol template is available in Appendix 1. The interviews were conducted in French, English or both, based on what the participants felt most comfortable speaking.

DATA ANALYSIS

We used an iterative approach to the coding (Srivastava & Hopwood, 2009). First, we ran an initial visual analysis of the portraits by detailing the colors, shapes and iconography the participants used. We noted some possible interpretations of these drawings. From this initial preliminary visual analysis, we tailored the interview protocols of each participant for their life-story interviews to be able to ask clarification and probing questions about the meaning participants encoded in their artwork and how they made sense of their personal and professional experiences relating to French. We then used participants' descriptions of their drawings to establish connotative meaning – what Van Leeuwen (2011) describes as the concepts, ideas and values present in the drawings. After the interviews were completed, we conducted discursive analysis (Gee, 2014) of the life-story narratives to tease out their language representations, language attitudes and language ideologies. Finally, we conducted an iconographical analysis based on participants' interpretations of their drawings and our own (Van Leeuwen, 2011). We used the elements of design (point, line, shape, value, form, texture, space and color) and principles of design (balance, proportion, contrast, repetition, rhythm, pattern, movement, emphasis and unity) to inform our analysis (Field, 2018). We contrasted our interpretations with what the participants had expressed discursively during the interviews. In a final step in the analysis process, we shared our analysis with the participants and noted any agreement, disagreements or tensions that surfaced.

Using an interpretive iterative process to work on the data with participants, our interpretations were challenged (i.e., our interpretation of francophone as a neutral term, devoid of racial significance), as were the participants' (i.e., their understanding of 'culture'), who were asked to justify their responses. In some cases, they revised their interpretations after more reflection on the topics of conversations between the interviews (which took place over three weeks). Our view of data collection and analysis is deeply iterative, and we consider data not to be static, but simply one representation at a given point in time. This collaborative back and forth between the visual and oral narratives allowed us to capture the nuances of teachers' identities in becoming, specifically, how they negotiated their beliefs and experiences, how they made sense of what they learned in the program and saw in their practicum. It also served to highlight the complexity and competing ideologies that exist within teachers' representations. Many expressed contradictory ideas (i.e., one was born francophone and one can become francophone through practice), which we consider very natural and fundamentally human, indicating identity formation is dynamic and always develops within a specific context.

Researcher Positionalities

As a team of White settler women, we recognize that our positionality within Canadian society is one of privilege aligned with the dominant group. With White women being over-represented in the teaching profession, and in the field of education, it is more important for us to trouble the ways in which we might be reproducing hegemonic discourses and practices. We take a critical stance in our work to disrupt what might seem like "common-sense" and be "taken-for-granted" in our interpretations. For this, we draw from readings rooted in Critical Race Theory and anticolonial feminism (Dei & Asgharzadeh, 2001; Ladson-Billings, 2020; Mendoza, 2016; Patel, 2014), we engaged in critical conversations with colleagues, and we used a dialogic process of member-checking with participants to ensure did not impose a biased view on their data. We recognize that there are limits to this and take full responsibility for any shortcomings.

FINDINGS

In this section, we present four themes that emerged across all participants' identity formation during our analysis: 1) their relationship to French, 2) their experiences with standard varieties of French, 3) how they identify themselves as French speakers, and 4) how they identify themselves as French teachers. To illustrate the unique interaction of participants' social and racial positioning with French languages and cultures, we used the portraits of three focal participants: Lucy, Lyne and Nawa (presented in alphabetical order). Instances of convergence and divergence of the themes will be developed in the discussion section below. The aim is not to compare them but to consider the salient features of each that mark their relationship with French (i.e., the geographical dimension of where they come from, and where they have lived), the family dimension (i.e., was French transmitted and how or learned?), and the place of French among their other languages, all through a raciolinguistic lens.

Lucy

Lucy identifies herself as a White Canadian anglophone woman. Her mother is English (UK) and French (France) and immigrated to Canada as a child. Her father's family is anglophone and settled in Canada over 200 hundred years ago. Her relationship with French is complicated. Growing up, her mother did not speak French to her and she learned it at school (mandatory in Canada). At the time of the study, she had a strong English accent when she spoke French which she was self-conscious about.

In her drawing (Figure 1), Lucy uses repetition of blue and red to represent and emphasize English and French as her dominant languages. Lucy uses line and shape to make a distinction between her body and the languages/cultures she speaks or studies.

Figure 1. Lucy's linguistic and cultural portrait

She uses visual quotes to make patterns and repetition with natural free-form shapes, such as the maple leaf to represent Canadian English culture, and the fleur de lys to represent French culture from France and Quebec. Their placement behind her creates a backdrop, or environment that she is immersed in, that of Canadian French-English bilingualism.

Relationship to French

Lucy does not express a strong sense of closeness with the French, mainly due to how she was introduced to it through her family. For her, as a child, French is somewhat of an exclusionary language, a mysterious code spoken by mother and grandmother, not transmitted to the children. Instead, she builds a strong connection with another European language: Spanish.

I just don't feel super attached to [French] at all. . . . I know I should learn French because I am French, and I'm going to be a French teacher. But, like, Spanish I really love. (Lucy)

Throughout her life experience and her schooling, Lucy has built a strong eurocentric linguistic repertoire, represented in her drawing with the Italian, Russian and Spanish flags at the bottom right corner and the Union Jack, used to represent languages and cultures ideologically. When asked to elaborate on this Eurocentric focus, particularly with French, Lucy explains that it is due to a combination of heritage and the varieties of French she was exposed to when she grew up:

I do definitely think too much about France and Quebec. But that's maybe not so much just because I'm white, but because I lived in both places. I'm French, I have a French passport and everything. But I do try my best to listen to things about other places and read things, and listen to music from other places as well, but again it's always hard to find. (Lucy)

In justifying her focus on Eurocentric varieties of French, Lucy claims her identity as a French person and rejects its associations with Whiteness, instead focusing on the fact that these were the only varieties she was exposed to at school and with her family. Throughout our discussions with White participants, this was a recurring discourse. Many either rejected or had not thought about this connection between language and race (to their credit, this was a connection we were only beginning to explore as well at the time of the study, and our discussions with participants greatly helped to cement our understanding of raciolinguistic research). As Madibbo (2021) has shown, in the Canadian context, French is constructed as a White language and culture. While a growing minority of Black and Middle Eastern people exist in Canada, the strong association of Whiteness, Eurocentricity and French work to erase Blackness from *la francophonie* (a term commonly used to refer to the French-speaking communities around the world).

Experiences With Standard French

Lucy's use of national flags to represent languages/cultures in her repertoire speaks to her association of nation-statehood with standard language ideologies in the construction of her linguistic identity. Although a standard gives Lucy some kind of goal or aspiration to work towards with her French, it is also a source of great anxiety when it comes to establish a sense of legitimacy when she speaks French, particularly when she speaks to other French speakers. This seems to be a cultural particularly of French, as Lucy explains the difference in the encounters she has had with Spanish speakers:

I think all the Spanish speakers I've met... like, everyone was super like, "Wow! You're learning Spanish! You're so good at Spanish!" Like, "This is so amazing you're learning!". So they're really encouraging. But French people, they're like, "I can't understand you. . . ." "What are you saying. . . ?" Even though I was saying it properly, just because I have an accent. And yeah, it's just kind of frustrating, because I know I'm saying the words with an accent, but I'm still saying the words, so that's not super fun. (Lucy)

Indeed, a characteristic in many French-speaking cultures is a hyper corrective attitude towards the use of standard French. As Klikenberg (2001) states, "Un francophone est d'abord un sujet affecté d'une hypertrophie de la glande grammaticale" (*A francophone is first and foremost a person with an enlarged grammatical gland*, our translation). This attitude is applied to learners of French as well. It comes from a deeply entrenched ideology of linguistic purism that has been constructed throughout European nationalistic endeavors in the late 19th and the early 20th century, which have been reproduced by the ensuing education system that was established (Bourdieu & Passeron, 1970). With this understanding, we can link this (self-)policing attitude of standard language use as a form of control and status signaling, as the practice is most common among middle and upper classes. It works as a form of classism by establishing and maintaining the status quo among dominant groups.

Identifying as a French Speaker

While we do not take the position that FSL teacher candidates must identify themselves as francophones, we do believe it is essential to discuss this notion with future FSL teachers. Presumably, for French teachers to function effectively and be linguistic and cultural models for their students, they should be identified as French speakers on some level. During the interviews, we asked participants whether they regarded themselves as francophones. Interestingly, none of them said they did. Lucy's response exemplifies one aspect of this rejection of the term francophone:

I just don't feel like I would count myself as someone who speaks French fluently so I wouldn't say I am francophone. . . . Maybe I would have felt more francophone if my mom had kept speaking to me in French. (Lucy)

While we initially defined the term francophone as 'someone who speaks French', over the course of the study this definition evolved, particularly when taking into account the national context and personal background of the speakers and their relationship with French. Our Canadian-born participants, like Lucy, expressed a great deal of resistance to adopting the label of 'francophone'. Like many of our White Canadian-born participants, Lucy defines being francophone as a mix of having 'high enough' proficiency, heritage and feeling close to the language, echoing native speaker ideologies. When asked whether someone who has attained a 'high enough' proficiency can become francophone, the Canadian-born participants felt conflicted. Results differed for our internationally educated Asian and Black participants (discussed below).

Identifying as a French Teacher

Closely tied to this notion of identifying as a French speaker is participants' abilities to identify themselves as a French teacher. For us, part of the impetus of this project was noticing the resistance of Canadian-born teacher candidates to perceive themselves as French speakers. Given that having a strong professional identity is one of the key predictors of long-term success in the profession (Alsup, 2006), in light of the ongoing FSL teacher shortage crisis (Masson et al., 2019) understanding this particular facet of FSL teacher candidates' identity formation seemed particularly urgent. Lucy expresses a commonly shared sentiment among our participants:

Well, I want to improve my French before I become a French teacher, so I wouldn't want to teach French where I'm at now but I definitely plan on fixing that and then becoming a French teacher and history as well. (Lucy)

Lucy's response is indicative of a deficit-based perspective towards her identity as a French teacher; one that has been noted and investigated by Tang and Fedoration (2022, 2023). Without asset-based, positive, self- and other-regulated forms of legitimation, FSL teachers risk chipping away at their sense of belonging in the profession over the long-run. To us, this negative valuation stems from a combination of linguistic purism and standard language ideologies. As we have demonstrated above, these ideologies are closely linked to Eurocentrism and Whiteness as the norm when speaking French varieties. They are also ideologies which allow for perpetuating control over populations that can be marked as coming from outside of White French-born, European-heritage, middle- and upper-class norms. While our White teacher candidates did not necessarily think of or experience exclusion based on the criteria of Whiteness, the following narratives from Lyne and Nawa will demonstrate how this criterion also has an important bearing on the identity construction of FSL teachers.

Lyne

Lyne comes from Cameroon, which has an officially bilingual policy (French-English), like Canada. Hundreds of local languages are spoken there, such as Yemba, Ngwa, Bulu and Ewondo. Lyne comes from the (south-western) English-speaking region, which is a minoritized community. Her parents moved to the French-speaking region when she was young. Lyne grew up plurilingual, speaking Ngwa at home with her parents, English at school and French and Camfranglais with her friends and in the community. Although Lyne conducted her interview in French, her responses were translated to English.

Relationship to French

In her portrait (Figure 2), Lyne uses the colors yellow, green, and red specifically to represent her home country, Cameroon. Blue, white and red also represent French culture from France. In her explanation Lyne highlights the overlap of the color red (present in both countries' national flags) can be seen as the intersection of these two cultures because her home country was colonized by France. Lyne also uses overlapping colors in her drawing to represent how French was imposed on her people. She explains: *"I would say, in Cameroon, when I spoke French, it was much more out of compulsion, or to be accepted. To have more opportunities, because it's the dominant language."* (Lyne). Growing up, Lyne's

Figure 2. Lyne's linguistic and cultural portrait

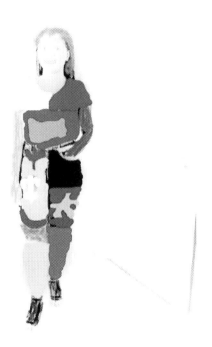

relationship to French is constructed through a legacy of colonialism; its economic, social and political ramifications still at play to this day.

Experiences With Standard French (at School)

Lyne expresses great love for French language, linguistics and literature. At school, her teachers fostered a great passion and appreciation for European literature and poetry. At the same time, her teachers emphasized using 'proper' grammar, adopting French European as the standard. Hence, similarly to Lucy, Lyne displays strong standard language ideologies. From school, she learned that Eurocentric varieties of French are the 'correct' French, and this creates tension for her when she expresses that her accent in French does not correspond to that standard. She says:

As a Black woman, I would say that initially, before I came from Cameroon I thought my accent was not correct. . . . I used to tell myself that I had to speak in a certain way. . . . Then me, personally, before, I was thinking there was something wrong with my accent, and I had to change, it wasn't beautiful enough. (Lyne)

For Lyne, this is an ongoing process of deprogramming negative associations made between her way of speaking French and her racial identity. As she explains, it was not until leaving Cameroon and moving to Canada that she identified herself as a Black woman. Being repositioned as a Black woman in the Canadian context has allowed Lyne to reflect on how she was positioned by the White listening subject (Rosa & Flores, 2015) in this context, and by extension how she was being positioned by the White listening (colonial) subject throughout her schooling in Cameroon.

Identifying as a French Speaker

Lyne uses orange to represent her home language, Ngwa, which she places on her belly – the center of her being – to represent that it is a core part of her identity. By overlapping her local language (orange) onto French (blue), she is expressing that it supersedes and mediates her connection with French. In this way, she is expressing resistance and defiance towards the colonial project. When asked explicitly if she identifies herself as francophone, Lyne says:

Given my background . . . I wouldn't say I'm a francophone, (I would say I'm Cameroonian and for me a Cameroonian identifies by the local languages). So I don't identify myself by French or English because – as we have been colonized, (I would have a problem) when someone claims to be a francophone in Cameroon. They say you don't know your origins. You are not proud of your origins. So to say that I am a francophone for me would be to endorse colonization and to deny even who I am. So I don't like to say I'm a francophone. (Lyne)

The linguistic purism we alluded to in Lucy's portrait takes on a new form for racialized population from former colonies: it works to uphold the colonial project. Even here, the native-speaker identity is tied up with the colonial project. As Lyne explains, in Cameroon, some youth growing up in big cities have French as their mother tongue, because their parents are not able to maintain child-rearing in their local language, or even perceive having French as the mother tongue as a form of social prestige.

Identifying as a French Teacher

Lyne is the only participant to use colors to represent non-standard varieties of French from Africa. She explains that blue, red, green, and yellow, also represent the flags from places such as: Mali, Senegal, Gabon and Equatorial Guinea. So here, like Lucy, Lyne is relying on nation-state ideology to represent linguistic identity. In her case, it represents marginalized communities within *la francophonie*. In her portrait, she physically makes space for these non-standard varieties of French, but when it comes to using them in her teaching practice, she paints a different picture:

So I always worry about that: Does the other person understand? And I, in turn, I also have to ask myself, will the students understand what I'm saying when I'm talking? First of all, the fact that I'm Black, are they going to accept me when I walk into a classroom? How are they going to look at me? And besides being Black, I speak French not the way they do, not the French they know. . . . I have concerns about how the students perceive me, the way I teach, the way I speak, and looking at me first. I know that some people have been asking questions. (Lyne)

Lyne expresses her worry about her non-standard variety of French being understood by the White listening subject in the Canadian context. Not only that, but she worries that her standard of French will delegitimize her as a French teacher in the eyes of her students, their parents and her colleagues.

Nawa

Nawa is from a South-Eastern Asian country (which he requested not be identified). He grew up in an urban environment, in a small city. He enjoys learning languages and has studied French, English, Japanese and Chinese. He learned English and French at school and through his study-abroad experiences. He traveled to Canada as part of a study abroad program when he was 16 and lived in Quebec for a year.

In his portrait (Figure 3), Nawa uses colors to represent the different languages in his repertoire: Red for his home language (which also represents blood), blue for French (like the Quebec flag), green for English (like Robin Hood's hat), and orange for Japanese (like the Japanese oranges that are "sweet and bright").

Figure 3. Nawa's linguistic and cultural portrait

Experiences With French

Nawa used free-form shapes and bold lines to create three distinct faces of himself that represent the different personalities he has in each language (he explains there was not enough room to represent Japanese). Interestingly, his facial expressions also seem to express his comfort level with his languages. His home language face (in red) is happy and joyous, his English face (green) is confident and smiling and his French face (blue) looks uneasy and apprehensive. In his interview, Nawa explains that he feels "not good enough" when speaking French because of the strict standard language ideologies. The drawing could be interpreted as capturing the level of linguistic (in)security Nawa feels. Nawa explains how he rejects linguistic discrimination that could prevent him or his students from developing a sense of legitimacy and belonging as French speakers:

I have recently looked up an FSL learning video . . . and it was comparing France and Québec vocabulary. And, oh my God, watching that made me anxious. Like, the video was so bad: the French lady [in it] was so condescending. (Nawa)

Nawa seems to be aware of the discriminatory nature of standard language ideologies, which have angered him. This may be due to his experiences learning French in Quebec as a teenager and returning to his home country in Asia where European French standard is more valued. Nawa explains how Asian speakers of French reproduce language hierarchies in his home country:

You know, an Asian speaking Parisian French being condescending to other Asian people speaking other variations of French IS the reality in French language education in [my home country]. (Nawa)

Having potentially faced linguistic discrimination in his home country, Nawa is also hyper-aware of the ways in which standard language ideologies intersect with racial ideologies. He explains how during his exchange in Quebec as a teenager, because he presented as an Asian man, people had low expectations about his language abilities:

Like back in [Quebec], I think people had low expectations, when [I] speak French. And I mean, if [I] were a Caucasian teenager coming from somewhere to spend a year in Quebec, people would probably think that I would be able to speak French because of how I look. . . . You would have to witness that first reaction. When you meet a new person and they'd be like, "Oh wow. Lui, il parle pas français," (Oh, wow, this guy doesn't speak French), right? [about a White learner of French]. So, but that almost never happened to me. People would assume that I was from somewhere else. Maybe it's my appearance, maybe it's the way that I walk. Maybe, it's my mannerism. So, in a way it helped a little bit. (Nawa)

This excerpt illustrates the complex nature of intersecting linguistic and racial ideologies. On the one hand, the language politics in Quebec lead to a very strong 'pressure' to speak French, which could foster a sense of linguistic insecurity for a learner of French who cannot conform. It must be noted, however, that in the region where Nawa stayed, there was a great sense of pride in the variety of regional French spoken and a European language standard would likely be rejected by locals. The pressure in the context comes from the expectation that French, rather than English, should be spoken in the public and private sphere (not that 'proper' European French must be spoken). On the other hand, for Nawa, the low expectations towards his French, due to racial ideologies about who speaks French, created a sense of relief. Because of these racist ideologies, as a learner of French at the time, he was able to escape the judgment associated with not speaking French fluently in that context. From this experience, Nawa is able to identify and play with people's expectations in a way that benefitted his identity construction as a French speaker.

Identifying as a French Speaker

Nawa's composition of the drawing creates unity within the drawing via repetition of the faces captures three points of interest for the viewer to focus on. The faces also have different proportion sizes. The English face is larger than the French face, which might represent Nawa's stronger sense of comfort as an English speaker than a French speaker. The English face is making eye contact and holding a gaze, whereas the French face is averting its gaze. Similar to the severity of French speakers that Lucy has expressed, Nawa also expresses that English speakers are more tolerant of accents and different word choices than French speakers. When asked if he identifies himself as francophone, Nawa responds:

I would call myself, I don't know, yeah, so many things, a new Canadian, an immigrant. I don't know, an Asian guy . . . but francophone, I don't know. Probably not because there seems to be a very high standard that you have to attain before calling yourself francophone. Hmm, so no. (Nawa)

Contrary to Lucy and other Canadian-born participants, Nawa does not make reference to heritage as an identifier for the term francophone. Coming from outside Canada, this makes sense given the historical relationship between French- and English-speaking populations in Canada. However, we can see how pervasive the notion of 'native speaker' is, which is extended to speakers of French throughout the world. Nawa explains an incident he had when walking around with a group of friends:

In the market area . . . there was this Black woman who was lost. And so she went to this Black friend of mine to ask for directions and she asked in French. So that sort of told me that she probably . . . just recently came to Canada. And I turned out to be the only person who was able to communicate with her. She was looking for a particular location. Yeah so, you can see, like, in the eyes of the rest of the group. It's like, "Wow! Did you grow up in Quebec?" You know, there were things like that, and, I don't know, I feel kind of special. [laughs] (Nawa)

Presumably, coming from an African country where she was used to seeing Black people speak French, this woman approached Nawa's Black friend to speak French. Here, Nawa was able to help the woman while also challenging her idea that most Black people speak French in Canada (while many do, it is not the case for everyone), and introduce the idea that an Asian person can speak French fluently. As the only person who spoke French in this situation, it provided him with cultural capital that legitimated him as a French speaker in this instance. His friends, being impressed with his French skills, may also have had their expectation that fluent (or 'native', from Quebec) speakers of French present as White challenged. Nawa seems to enjoy challenging people's preconceived notions, even if they are founded in racist ideologies. This is an outlook he brings to his approach to teaching French in the Canadian context as well.

Identifying as a French Teacher

In his professional context, Nawa experiences the same low expectations towards his linguistic abilities in French. He is questioned about his ability to speak French because he presents as Asian. He says: "the way that I look probably makes me less credible for many parents. And that has an impact on me as a future French teacher" (Nawa), indicating that "there's always the feeling of not being good enough when I have to use French in a professional setting" (Nawa).

Nawa understands the implications of racial ideologies of his perceived sense of legitimacy. He resists by explaining that legitimacy is not going to come from outside. It has to come from within:

Yeah, so for myself, and what I have learned as a teacher, if I still think that way, I will never be able to be proud of myself, right? As a speaker, as a teacher, or even as a learner, because I'm not going to get to the point where my skin color changes, right? So yeah, I like that my presence in school, as a French teacher, started to matter. For many schools, cause a MALE teacher, an Asian male teacher who speaks French? Yeah and I think this is something that, you know, has to happen, has to start. (Nawa)

As an individual who learned French, Nawa is aware about the negative impacts standard language ideologies can have, as we demonstrated above. This personal journey of reflection manifests in his professional identity formation as well. As illustrated by the story of the video he watched on YouTube, Nawa makes pedagogical decisions based on his personal experiences. He explains that as a teacher he feels it would be inappropriate to use and reproduce negative stereotypes about non-European French language varieties in his classroom. He also demonstrates a strong sense of self (as an individual and as a teacher) by recognizing that the world around him is where the problem lies, not with his own linguistic abilities or his racial identity. Nawa is able to identify, challenge and reject ideologies that position him as deficient and make choices to empower himself and his students.

DISCUSSION

What these participants have in common is that they have chosen at a certain stage in their lives to become French teachers. It supposes at once that their relationship to the French language is going to be very different. As teacher educators, we wondered why and in what way? Our aim was to understand how they construct the notion of legitimacy as French speakers and teachers, and see how they position themselves, personally and professionally, within the French-speaking community to develop a sense of belonging.

ESTABLISHING LEGITIMACY (AS A FRENCH SPEAKER AND TEACHER)

All seven participants show evidence of the negative impact of standard language ideology. This affects the ways in which they construct legitimacy as French speakers, leaving it at that is reminiscent of common discourses around the linguistic insecurity that FSL teacher candidates experience. However, upon closer examination, we can see some key differences emerge.

The White teacher candidates, like Lucy, seem more concerned with the question of establishing legitimacy in the French-speaking community. Whereas the racialized TCs either renegotiate what it means to be a French speaker (like Lyne) or reject the possibility of achieving legitimacy as French speakers (like Nawa). Adding a raciolinguistic lens to the analysis reveals how this idea of legitimacy intersects with the White listening subject. Similar to the ways in which raciolinguistic intersections normalize the standards of Whiteness in academic language with academic performance (Keicho, 2021), for racialized FSL teachers, Whiteness is considered as a necessary condition for professional excellence and legitimacy in the teaching profession. Racialized speakers in these situations may choose to conform to the standard, or create their own space and reject standards that reinforce linguistic associations with Whiteness by legitimizing their own perspectives about and practices with the target language. For each participant, the notion of legitimacy as a French speaker is constructed around the idea of the 'White native-speaker' of European descent as the truest form of a French speaker. This echoes the findings presented by Ho (2023), who found that language teachers may use the concept of 'nativeness', which they may associate with their birthplace, their heritage or their upbringing, as a means of establishing legitimacy. This speaks to the need for more critical and in-depth discussions with future FSL teachers about native-speakerism and its negative impact on constructing a strong sense of self as a speaker of French.

In terms of establishing legitimacy as French teachers, both Lyne and Nawa speak to the intersection of subject-as-seen and subject-as-heard (Crump, 2014; Sarkar, et al, 2007). Lucy, despite her accent (subject-as-heard), like other White teacher candidates, has never experienced being questioned about her legitimacy as a French teacher, or her capacity to teach French. Her identity of subject-as-seen conforms to the expectation about speakers of French being White. In fact, our data showed that White teacher candidates were most concerned about making a mistake, and thus treated this worry as an opportunity to redefine the role of errors in the classroom and model linguistic risk-taking for their students. Although we have heard of White French learners who become teachers being questioned about their language proficiency, for these teachers, there is always a *possibility* of accessing a space where they can be legitimized (by 'working hard enough' on their French) which is not always the case for French speakers of color. Lyne and Nawa, as early as during their practicum experience, both question or are questioned about their capacity to teach French. Their physical bodies (subject-as-seen) do not fit into the vision of the ideal French speaker as White. They worry about how their accents and colors will determine whether students, colleagues and parents will accept them as French teachers. There are lessons to be learnt from Nawa's understanding of legitimacy for teacher education. Affirmation of professional identity is a journey in critical self-reflection. His remarks and critical reflection could be very useful to use in teacher preparation programs where future FSL teachers could analyze what is happening personally and professionally to Nawa and the other participants.

BELONGING (TO THE FRENCH-SPEAKING COMMUNITY AND THE TEACHING PROFESSION)

All participants rejected their identities of being francophone. We can see how this rejection is tied to interactions with native-speaker ideologies. But if we add the raciolinguistic lens, again, more nuances behind the reason for rejecting the francophone identity emerges. Lucy, like many of the White participants, constructs francophone identity as tied to proficiency and heritage. Examining this rejection purely through a linguistic lens invisibilizes the fact that the ideal French speaker is constructed as White in Canada (Madibbo, 2021). Thus, a sort of racial privilege emerges. By this logic, that we also fell prey to when we started this work, Lucy has the possibility of gaining access to 'francophone-ness' if she works hard enough on her proficiency and develops a feeling of closeness to the language. Whereas for the racialized teacher candidates, there is no possibility of 'alignment as mode of belonging'.

For Lyne, there are socio-historical implications tied to colonialism and imperialism. Lyne constructs her identity of francophone as a colonial subject. For her, this identity marker is irreconcilable with her experience as a Black woman from a post-colonial African nation. For Nawa, the color of his skin does not fit into the construction of the idealized French speaker as White, which means that he will never be able to access the French language community (at least not from external validation). We would argue it should be part of their training that teacher candidates learn to identify and possibly address raciolinguistic ideologies and offer their students a chance to understand that being a francophone can be redefined in a less simplistic way. Professional standards steeped in Whiteness and expectations have geared towards the White-listening subject, whether intended or not, intersect with racializing processes that position racialized speakers as deficient, as has been shown in the ESL context (Darbes, 2023; Flores & Rosa, 2015). The same phenomenon emerges from the data for FSL teachers. For teacher candidates in preparation programs, such efforts would serve to highlight how 'francophone' as a categorizing label can exclude some people. It may also create possibilities and space for more teachers with diverse linguistic, racial and cultural backgrounds. As we have demonstrated, Canadian-born teacher candidates are immersed within the local histories between English-French people and a complicated relationship between different varieties of Canadian French. Previous research has also shown that in many instances, FSL preparation programs, the educators and teacher candidates have reinforced or exacerbated White supremacist, Eurocentric beliefs and practices (Masson et al., 2022). For international students coming into these programs, it is key to acknowledge how their relationship to French may differ, oftentimes mediated by France's colonial history.

Through our discussions with participants, opening up the definition of francophone to remove this notion of heritage as a form of legitimacy seemed to create new possibilities for the TCs to access a sense of belonging in their profession. On some level, if the definition of francophone is limited to 'someone who speaks French', then becoming francophone must be possible for them as teachers and for their future students. At the same time, we recognize that ignoring the heritage component of being francophone in the Canadian context can be problematic. For linguistic minority communities in Canada who have faced systemic oppression and violence from English-speaking communities and have fought for their rights to be recognized and speak their own language, the identity of francophone is much more than just 'speaking French'. It is our belief that the oppressor/oppressed status of French is unique to the Canadian context. As such, the lived realities of French-speaking communities, both inside and outside of Quebec, need to be reconciled with the experiences of English-speaking communities, Indigenous communities and other linguistic communities present in Canada. At the very least, this unique point should be addressed in French teacher preparation programs so that future generations may be more aware of what it means to speak French in Canada, why it is taught in schools, and what linguistic responsibilities ensue.

In the next section, we outline some considerations for FSL teacher education, research and those involved in the teaching profession more broadly.

FOR FSL TEACHER EDUCATION

Given the findings in this chapter, it is important to raise critical multilingual language awareness (CMLA) among teacher educators and future FSL teachers to understand the pervasiveness of racial, colonial and imperial ideologies and how they intersect with our ideas about languages, language users and learning/teaching languages. For instance, FSL teacher educators can critically re-think the professional contexts (i.e., classrooms at the Faculty of Education, practicum settings, schools they visit, and special outings, etc.) being offered to FSL teacher candidates, and how these might be reproducing colonial ideologies. Additionally, in terms of constructing legitimacy, all teachers need to identify their beliefs about native-speakerism, their experiences with it, and how they might reinforce this ideology in the classroom. The same applies to standard language ideologies. FSL teacher candidates need to consider what standard they use, why, and how they challenge that (if at all). For instance, a common argument might be that it is easier to teach the French European standard for understandability, but teacher educators can explore with FSL TCs: easier for whom? Teacher educators can help teachers establish a sense of empowerment, legitimacy and professional agency (Pavlenko, 2012) to think critically about how they position themselves for others to be seen or heard.

FOR FSL RESEARCH

As we have argued elsewhere (Wernicke et al., forthcoming), and demonstrated in this paper, it is important to establish new lines of inquiry in FSL research. While much of the research on FSL teacher identity has focused on their linguistic identity, current research needs to go beyond language and include race and other social identity markers, such as culture, gender, socioeconomic status, ability, etc. which are fundamental parts of social discourses that mediate teachers' experiences, beliefs and attitudes with and towards language (Von Esch et al., 2020). One particular area of interest that has garnered a lot of attention in the research community, school boards, faculties and professional associations is the notion of linguistic insecurity. With research and other professional initiatives informing professional learning policies, and federal and provincial funding agendas in the millions of dollars, we see a great need to revisit the idea of linguistic insecurity by adding a racial lens and moving away from a colonial, deficit-based view of language ability. In the current state of affairs, the framing of linguistic insecurity in the field is complicit in reproducing a mode of policing and excluding teachers from developing a sense of belonging within French-speaking communities. Forging new directions in this area would require a deeper and more explicit questioning around the notion of language, adopting a sociolinguistic approach focused on speakers/users of language, possibly even calling into question the frontiers between languages (i.e., not viewing languages as closed and bounded entities) (Makoni & Pennycook, 2006).

FOR FSL TEACHER PROFESSION

Within the FSL teaching profession, it is important to think about who we are focusing our attention on and who we are speaking to (or ignoring) to ask ourselves what message we are sending to racialized people in FSL, including parents, students, teacher candidates, and teacher educators. Lucy's case is important, and members of the racially dominant group (i.e., White teachers) need to take accountability for the ways in which they benefit from and reproduce oppressive ideologies. However, if we just focus on White Canadian-born teacher candidates in the profession, we are missing out on all these other people striving to become FSL teachers who move within and beyond the realm of whiteness. Given what we have seen about the impact of racial ideologies, are we truly content to continue as is? Building on what we discussed previously in terms of where funding is being allocated, are we making ethical decisions by offering teacher preparation and spending millions launching recruitment and retention efforts, without really understanding these teachers' experiences more broadly? In this sense, it is important for teacher education programs and other institutional powers to take responsibility for perpetuating a very narrow view of who can become an FSL teacher.

CONCLUSION

We take the position that teachers' personal and professional life experiences inform their classroom practice, their relationship with students and the learning environments they create for their students. Contextualizing our findings on FSL teacher identity within local discourses and histories of French in Canada and abroad, leads us to consider, as teacher educators, how we prepare teachers to teach in a language minority context (as is the case in Ontario, Canada). What sorts of relationships are FSL teachers building with French and how might that affect their practice and the kinds of relationships they can help their students build with French?

Future research agendas might also consider gathering data from students and parents to further this exploration of the intersection between linguistic and racial ideologies. Student discourses on their French teachers might reveal whether or not feelings of linguistic legitimacy and belonging to French-speaking communities are being mirrored in the classroom. It might also be worth investigating the media discourses on French language learning and French teachers in Canada and how these might contribute to the sense of (il)legitimacy and (lack of) belonging teachers report feeling.

While we have tried to contextualize feelings of legitimacy and belonging within socio-historical contexts of French in Ontario, as teacher educators and researchers, we wonder what that means for future FSL teachers' capacity to teach French and help their students build relationships with French. Is it even necessary to feel a sense of belonging and legitimacy in French-speaking communities? What are the ramifications of that? What do we want to strive for in Teacher Education programs?

In this chapter, we have shown the need for more in-depth investigation into FSL teachers' professional identities that include a racial dimension, particularly as linguistic ideologies interact with racial ideologies. We have also demonstrated the link between personal and professional life experiences in the identity formation of FSL teachers in Canada, and the great variance within that process of identity formation within and across FSL TCs due to their different backgrounds. Based on this analysis, we suggested how we can rethink certain aspects of French teacher preparation in Canada. Ultimately, this work is a call to develop teacher preparation pathways from a perspective that legitimizes all speakers in their linguistic, racial and social differences for the express purpose of supporting strong linguistic and professional identities among future FSL teachers.

ACKNOWLEDGMENT

We would like to thank Samantha Van Geel for the work she did developing our method of visual analysis and Dr. Christine Hélot for her insightful feedback on initial drafts of the paper.

REFERENCES

Alsup, J. (2006). *Teacher identity discourses: Negotiating personal and professional spaces*. Routledge. doi:10.4324/9781410617286

Barkhuizen, G. (2014). Narrative research in language teaching and learning. *Language Teaching*, *47*(4), 450–466. doi:10.1017/S0261444814000172

Barkhuizen, G. (2016). Language teacher identity research: An introduction. In G. Barkhuizen (Ed.), *Reflections on language teacher identity research* (pp. 9–19). Routledge. doi:10.4324/9781315643465-5

Barone, T., & Eisner, E. W. (2011). Arts based research. *Sage (Atlanta, Ga.)*.

Baumeister, R. F., & Leary, M. R. (2017). The need to belong: Desire for interpersonal attachments as a fundamental human motivation. *Interpersonal Development*, 57-89.

Bourdieu, P., & Passeron, J.-C. (1970). *La reproduction: éléments pour une théorie du système d'enseignement*. Édition Minuit.

Butler-Kisber, L. (2010). *Qualitative inquiry: Thematic, narrative and arts-informed perspectives*. Sage Publications. doi:10.4135/9781526435408

Byrd Clark, J. (2010). Making "wiggle room" in French as a Second Language/Français langue seconde: Reconfiguring identity, language, and policy. *Canadian Journal of Education*, *33*(2), 379–406.

Cook, V. (1999). Going beyond the native speaker in language teaching. *TESOL Quarterly*, *33*(2), 185–209. doi:10.2307/3587717

Crump, A. (2014a). Introducing LangCrit: Critical language and race theory. *Critical Inquiry in Language Studies*, *11*(3), 207–224. doi:10.1080/15427587.2014.936243

Crump, A. (2014b). *"But your face, it looks like you're English:" LangCrit and the experiences of multilingual Japanese-Canadian children in Montréal* [Unpublished doctoral thesis]. McGill University.

Culligan, K., Battistuzzi, A., Wernicke, M., & Masson, M. (2023). Teaching French as a second language in Canada: Convergence points of language, professional knowledge, and mentorship from teacher preparation through the beginning years. *Canadian Modern Language Review*, *79*(4), 352–370. doi:10.3138/cmlr-2022-0059

Darbes, T. (2023). Constructing deficit from diversity: Assessment and placement networks and the raciolinguistic enaction of ESL. *Language and Education*, 1–15. doi:10.1080/09500782.2023.2239774

Davey, R. (2013). *The professional identity of teacher educators: Career on the cusp?* Routledge. doi:10.4324/9780203584934

Davies, B. (2005). Communities of practice: Legitimacy not choice. *Journal of Sociolinguistics*, *9*(4), 557–581. doi:10.1111/j.1360-6441.2005.00306.x

Davis, S. (2023). Multilingual Learners in Canadian French Immersion Programs: Looking Back and Moving Forward. *Canadian Modern Language Review*.

Dei, G. J. S., & Asgharzadeh, A. (2001). The power of social theory: The anti-colonial discursive framework. *The Journal of Educational Thought*, *35*(3), 297–323.

Fallas-Escobar, C., & Herrera, L. J. P. (2022). Examining raciolinguistic struggles in institutional settings: A duoethnography. *Linguistics and Education*, *67*, 101012. doi:10.1016/j.linged.2022.101012

Fedoration, S., & Tang, M. (2023, February 14). *The contradiction of being a French L+ teacher: Issues to consider to support immersion teachers.* CASLT Online Professional Learning Webinars.

Field, J. (2018). *An illustrated field guide to the elements and principles of art + design.* Lulu.com.

Fillol, V., Razafimandimbimanana, E., & Geneix-Rabault, S. (2019). La créativité en formation professionnalisante: un processus émancipateur. *Contextes et didactiques: Revue semestrielle en sciences de l'éducation*, (14). doi:10.4000/ced.1497

Fletcher, D., & Sarkar, M. (2013). Psychological resilience. *European Psychologist*, *18*(1), 12–23. doi:10.1027/1016-9040/a000124

Flores, N., & Rosa, J. (2015). Undoing appropriateness: Raciolinguistic ideologies and language diversity in education. *Harvard Educational Review*, *85*(2), 149–171. doi:10.17763/0017-8055.85.2.149

Flores, N., & Rosa, J. (2022). Undoing competence: Coloniality, homogeneity, and the overrepresentation of whiteness in applied linguistics. *Language Learning*. Advance online publication. doi:10.1111/lang.12528

Freynet, N., & Clément, R. (2019). Perceived accent discrimination: Psychosocial consequences and perceived legitimacy. *Journal of Language and Social Psychology*, *38*(4), 496–513. doi:10.1177/0261927X19865775

Gee, J. P. (2014). *An introduction to discourse analysis: Theory and method.* Routledge. doi:10.4324/9781315819679

Haque, E. (2012). *Multiculturalism within a bilingual framework: Language, race, and belonging in Canada.* University of Toronto Press. doi:10.3138/9781442686083

Ho, W. Y. J. (2023). Discursive construction of online teacher identity and legitimacy in English language teaching. *Learning, Media and Technology*, 1–16. doi:10.1080/17439884.2023.2259295

Holliday, N. R., & Squires, L. (2021). Sociolinguistic labor, linguistic climate, and race (ism) on campus: Black college students' experiences with language at predominantly white institutions. *Journal of Sociolinguistics*, *25*(3), 418–437. doi:10.1111/josl.12438

Jack, D., & Nyman, J. (2019). Meeting labor market needs for French as a second language instruction in Ontario. *American Journal of Educational Research*, *7*(7), 428–438. doi:10.12691/education-7-7-1

Keicho, M. (2021). *Raciolinguistic socialization and subversion at a predominantly white institution* [Unpublished bachelor's thesis]. Swarthmore College.

Kunnas, R. M. (2019). *Inequities in black et blanc: Textual constructions of the French immersion student* [Unpublished master's thesis]. University of Toronto.

Ladson-Billings, G. (2020). Just what is critical race theory and what's it doing in a nice field like education? In L. Parker & D. Gillborn (Eds.), *Critical race theory in education* (pp. 9–26). Routledge. doi:10.4324/9781003005995-2

Lah, M. (2017). "Vous avez un petit accent": Enseignement de la prononciation aux apprenants de Français langue étrangère. *Lingüística, 57*(1), 171–183. doi:10.4312/linguistica.57.1.171-183

Lave, J., & Wenger, E. (1991). *Situated learning: Legitimate peripheral participation*. Cambridge University Press. doi:10.1017/CBO9780511815355

Lavoie, C. (2015). Trois stratégies efficaces pour enseigner le vocabulaire: Une expérience en contexte scolaire innu. *Canadian Journal of Applied Linguistics, 18*(1), 1–20.

Leitch, R. (2006). Limitations of language: Developing arts-based creative narrative in stories of teachers' identities. *Teachers and Teaching, 12*(5), 549–569. doi:10.1080/13540600600832270

Lippi-Green, R. (1997). *English with an accent: Language, ideology, and discrimination in the United States*. Routledge.

Madibbo, A. (2021). *Blackness and la Francophonie: Anti-black racism, linguicism and the construction and negotiation of multiple minority identities*. Presses de l'Université Laval. doi:10.2307/j.ctv23khnb5

Makoni, S., & Pennycook, A. (Eds.). (2006). *Disinventing and reconstituting languages*. Multilingual Matters. doi:10.21832/9781853599255

Makropoulos, J. (2004). Speak White! Language and race in the social construction of Frenchness in Canada. In C. Nelson & C. Nelson (Eds.), *Racism, eh? A critical inter-disciplinary anthology of race and racism in Canada* (pp. 242-257). Captus Press.

Masson, M. (2018). Reframing FSL teacher learning: Small stories of (re)professionalization and identity formation. *Journal of Belonging, Identity, Language, and Diversity, 2*(2), 77–102.

Masson, M., Grant, R., & Keunne, E., & Carroll, S. (2023, April 13). *Anticolonial feminist critical discourse analysis: Race, gender, culture and capitalism in the second language curriculum*. American Educational Research Association (AERA).

Masson, M., Knouzi, I., Arnott, S., & Lapkin, S. (2021). A critical interpretive synthesis of post-millennial Canadian French as a second language research across stakeholders and programs. *Canadian Modern Language Review, 77*(2), 154–188. doi:10.3138/cmlr-2020-0025

Masson, M., Kunnas, M., Boreland, T., & Prasad, G. (2022). Developing an anti-biased, anti-racist stance in second language teacher education programs. *Canadian Modern Language Review, 78*(4), 385–414. doi:10.3138/cmlr-2021-0100

Masson, M., Larson, E. J., Desgroseilliers, P., Carr, W., & Lapkin, S. (2019). *Accessing opportunity: A study on challenges in French-as-a-second-language education teacher supply and demand in Canada.* Office of the Commissioner of Official Languages. https://www.clo-ocol.gc.ca/en/publications/studies-other-reports/2019/accessing-opportunity-study-challenges-french-second

Matsuda, A. (Ed.). (2017). *Preparing teachers to teach English as an international language.* Multilingual Matters. doi:10.21832/9781783097036

Meighan, P. J. (2023). Colonialingualism: Colonial legacies, imperial mindsets, and inequitable practices in English language education. *Diaspora, Indigenous, and Minority Education, 17*(2), 146–155. doi:10.1080/15595692.2022.2082406

Melo-Pfeifer, S. M. (2019). Comprendre les représentations des enseignants de langues à travers des récits visuels. La mise en images du développement professionnel des futurs enseignants de français langue étrangère. *EL. LE, 8*(3), 587-610.

Mendoza, B. (2016). Coloniality of gender and power: From postcoloniality to decoloniality. In L. Disch & M. Hawkesworth (Eds.), *The Oxford handbook of feminist theory* (pp. 100–121). Oxford University Press.

Menezes de Oliveira e Paiva, V. L. (2016). Language teaching identity: A fractal system. In G. Barkhuizen (Ed.), *Reflections on language teacher identity research* (pp. 258-263). Routledge.

Miller, J. (2009). Teacher identity. In A. Burns & J. Richards (Eds.), *The Cambridge guide to second language teacher education* (pp. 172–181). Cambridge University Press. doi:10.1017/9781139042710.023

Molinié, M. (2009). *Le dessin réflexif: élément d'une herméneutique du sujet plurilingue.* Encrages-Belles Lettres.

Molinié, M. (2011). *Démarches portfolio en didactique des langues et des cultures. Enjeux de formation par la recherche-action.* Encrages-Belles Lettres.

Morgan, B. (2004). Teacher identity as pedagogy: Towards a field-internal conceptualisation in bilingual and second language education. *International Journal of Bilingual Education and Bilingualism, 7*(2-3), 172–188. doi:10.1080/13670050408667807

Office of the Commissioner of Official Languages. (2022). *Cross-Canada Official Languages Consultation 2022.* https://www.canada.ca/en/canadian-heritage/campaigns/consultation-official-languages-2022/report.html

Oniță, A., Guéladé-Yaï, L., & Wallace, L. (2021). Walking the talk: Three language educators Engage in a walking-based art inquiry for anti-racist education. *Journal of the Canadian Association for Curriculum Studies, 18*(2), 80–102. doi:10.25071/1916-4467.40642

Patel, L. L. (2014). Countering coloniality in educational research: From ownership to answerability. *Educational Studies (Ames), 50*(4), 357–377. doi:10.1080/00131946.2014.924942

Riches, C., & Parks, P. (2021). Navigating linguistic identities: ESL teaching contexts in Quebec. *TESL Canada Journal, 38*(1), 28–48. doi:10.18806/tesl.v38i1.1367

Rocafort, M. C. (2019). The development of plurilingual education through multimodal narrative reflection in teacher education: A case study of a pre-service teacher's beliefs about language education. *Canadian Modern Language Review*, *75*(1), 40–64. doi:10.3138/cmlr.2017-0080

Rosa, J., & Flores, N. (2017). Unsettling race and language: Toward a raciolinguistic perspective. *Language in Society*, *46*(5), 621–647. doi:10.1017/S0047404517000562

Roy, S., & Galiev, A. (2011). Discourses on bilingualism in Canadian French immersion programs. *Canadian Modern Language Review*, *67*(3), 351–376. doi:10.3138/cmlr.67.3.351

Sarkar, M., Low, B., & Winer, L. (2007). "Pour connecter avec les peeps": Quebequicité and the Quebec hip-hop community. In M. Mantero (Ed.), *Identity and second language learning: Culture, inquiry, and dialogic activity in educational contexts* (pp. 351–372). Information Age Publishing.

Schaefer, L., & Clandinin, D. J. (2019). Sustaining teachers' stories to live by: Implications for teacher education. *Teachers and Teaching*, *25*(1), 54–68. doi:10.1080/13540602.2018.1532407

Sekaja, L., Adams, B. G., & Yağmur, K. (2022). Raciolinguistic ideologies as experienced by racialized academics in South Africa. *International Journal of Educational Research*, *116*, 102092. doi:10.1016/j.ijer.2022.102092

Seror, J., & Weinberg, A. (2021). Exploring the longitudinal impact of university immersion: Bilingual spaces, multilingual values. *System*, *99*, 102523. doi:10.1016/j.system.2021.102523

Smith, C., Masson, M., Spiliotopoulos, V., & Kristmanson, P. (2023). A course or a pathway? Addressing French as a Second Language teacher recruitment and retention in Canadian BEd programs. *Canadian Journal of Education*, *46*(2), 412–440.

Srivastava, P., & Hopwood, N. (2009). A practical iterative framework for qualitative data analysis. *International Journal of Qualitative Methods*, *8*(1), 76–84. doi:10.1177/160940690900800107

Statistics Canada. (2023). *Key facts on the French language in Ontario in 2021*. https://www150.statcan.gc.ca/n1/pub/89-657-x/89-657-x2023017-eng.htm

Tang, M. (2020). *D'apprenant à enseignant: la construction identitaire et l'accès à la communauté professionnelle des enseignants de français en Colombie-Britannique* [Unpublished Doctoral thesis]. Simon Fraser University.

Tang, M., & Fedoration, S. (2022, November 3). *The contradiction that is an L+ teacher: A guide to help me thrive*. Congrès de l'ACPI.

The Canadian Encyclopedia. (2023). *Confederation*. https://thecanadianencyclopedia.ca/en/article/confederation-plain-language-summary

Vallente, J. P. C. (2020). Framing pre-service English language teachers' identity formation within the theory of alignment as mode of belonging in community of practice. *Teaching and Teacher Education*, *96*, 103177. doi:10.1016/j.tate.2020.103177

Van Leeuwen, T. (2011). Semiotics and iconography. In T. Van Leeuwen & C. Jewitt (Eds.), *The Handbook of Visual Analysis* (pp. 92–118). Sage.

Vigouroux, C. B. (2017). The discursive pathway of two centuries of raciolinguistic stereotyping: 'Africans as incapable of speaking French'. *Language in Society*, *46*(1), 5–21. doi:10.1017/S0047404516000804

Von Esch, K. S., Motha, S., & Kubota, R. (2020). Race and language teaching. *Language Teaching*, *53*(4), 391–421. doi:10.1017/S0261444820000269

Wenger, E. (1998). Communities of practice: Learning as a social system. *The Systems Thinker*, *9*(5), 2–3.

Wernicke, M. (2018). Plurilingualism as agentive resource in L2 teacher identity. *System*, *79*, 91–102. doi:10.1016/j.system.2018.07.005

Wernicke, M. (2020). Orientations to French language varieties among Western Canadian French-as-a-second-language teachers. *Critical Multilingualism Studies*, *8*(1), 165–190.

Wernicke, M. (2022). "I'm trilingual–so what?": Official French/English bilingualism, race, and French language teachers' linguistic identities in Canada. *Canadian Modern Language Review*, *78*(4), 344–362. doi:10.3138/cmlr-2021-0074

Wernicke, M., Masson, M., Kunnas, M., & Adatia, S. (forthcoming). Moving beyond erasure of race in French second language education. In R. Kubota & S. Motha (Eds.), *Race, racism and antiracism in Language Education*. Routledge.

Widodo, H. P., Fang, F., & Elyas, T. (2020). The construction of language teacher professional identity in the Global Englishes territory: "we are legitimate language teachers". *Asian Englishes*, *22*(3), 309–316. doi:10.1080/13488678.2020.1732683

Xu, Y. (2017). Becoming a researcher: A journey of inquiry. In G. Barkhuizen (Ed.), *Reflections on Language Teacher Identity Research* (pp. 120–125). Routledge.

KEY TERMS AND DEFINITIONS

Arts-Based Research: Research methods that utilize multimodal forms art as a mode of expression, interpretation and/or data collection.

French as a Second Language: A subject taught in Anglophone K-12 schools in Ontario (Canada). French is taught as an additional language either as a subject (Core French) or as a medium of instruction (French Immersion).

LangCrit: A theoretical framework used to examine the interaction of physical and social norms with racializing discourses.

Language Teacher Identity: The professional identity that language teachers develop over the course of their career. Their professional identity will inform multiple aspects of their job, for instance, how they teach, how they relate to students, colleagues and parents, and how they understand their subject-matter.

Raciolinguistics: A theoretical framework used to examine the interaction of linguistic ideologies with racial ideologies.

Teacher Education: Learning over teachers' careers that generally begins in a teacher preparation program and continues on throughout a teacher's career in the form of professional development.

APPENDIX

Life-story interview: Session 1: Experiences and beliefs about French language learning
<u>Themes</u>: Self, Family, Attitude Towards Education & Educational Experiences in French, Relationship to the French Language, Linguistic Background, Future Plans, Intercultural experiences.

Personal Background

Self

- Tell me about yourself.
    - Place of birth
    - Current living situation

Family

- Tell me about your family.
    - Siblings
    - Current location

Intercultural experiences

- Let's look at your Plurilingual Portrait.
- How would you describe your cultural background?
- What cultures did you represent in your Plurilingual Portrait? Please explain.
- What new cultures have you encountered? How have they influenced you? Explain how they are a part of you (or not)?

Linguistic Background

- What language(s) do/did you speak at home?
    - With whom?
- Let's look at your Venn diagram, tell me about how you use the different languages you speak and with whom?

Relationship to the French language

- When did you begin studying/learning French?
    - School / private lessons / other
    - Program (French immersion, Core French, etc.)
- Why did you choose (start studying?) to study French?

- Did you enjoy studying French?
- Tell me more about that experience.
- How did it affect you? / How has studying French affected your life? / How has it affected your future career/academic plans?
- Do you feel you are francophone? Why (not)? How would you describe yourself?

Attitude towards education & educational experiences with French

- Tell me about your elementary school experience learning French. Describe a typical day.
- Tell me about your high school experience learning French. Describe a typical day.
- Who was your favorite French teacher in elementary or high school? Why?
  - What was this teacher like?
- Tell me about your university experience learning French.
  - Location / with or without family
  - What did you study?
  - Favorite / least favorite subjects
  - How many years did you study in university?

Future plans

- What are your career goals?
- Where would you like to live? Why?

Life-story interview: Session 2: The experience of entering the FSL teaching profession

<u>Themes:</u> Teacher Preparation, Teaching in practicum, Post-teaching and learning
   uOttawa Teacher Education program

- Why did you choose to study at the University X Bachelor of Education program?
- Did your choice have anything to do with the linguistic context at the university, or your own linguistic and cultural background?

Teacher Preparation

- Tell me about your experience preparing to teach French.
- How did you prepare to become a French teacher before entering the B.Ed program?
- Were there any things that you worried or wondered about?
- What were some things you felt confident about/ looked forward to?
- What has been your overall experience so far in the B.Ed program? Do you feel prepared to teach French in schools?

Languages and language teaching

- Let's look at your Plurilingual poem, how did it affect your perception of language teaching?
- Did it affect how you understand the role of other languages in the FSL classroom?

Imagined Teacher self

- In the collage activity you were asked to complete a collage portrait of your ideal FSL teacher, tell me about your vision of the ideal FSL teacher.
  - Where / why did you get these ideas?
- Are there qualities represented in your collage that reflect how you currently approach your teaching practice?
  - Are there qualities represented in your collage that reflect how you envision approaching your teacher practice in the future?

Teaching in practicum (Actual teacher self)

- Tell me about your experience so far with teaching French.
- Can you describe a typical day for me in practicum?
- Tell me about your overall practicum experience in the B.Ed program.
- Were things as you expected? What was different? What expectations were (not) met?
- How did your French language skill impact your teaching?
  - Did you feel confident about certain things?
  - Were there some challenges in certain areas? Which ones?
  - How did you address any challenges you faced?

Post-teaching and learning

- Now that you have taught FSL in schools and finished your FSL methodology course, tell me about how you feel about teaching French?
- Are there any areas where you feel unprepared? Any things that worry you? Please describe.
- How do you feel about addressing these challenges? What steps will you take to address them?
- Is there anything else you would like to share about preparing to teach French in Ontario schools?

Life-story interview: Session 3 Collaborative reflection on artistic creation

Themes: Current Life. There are a few questions we will definitely ask, but this session will mostly consist of **follow up questions** based on answers from Sessions 1 & 2. A sample of potential questions has also been included.

  Reflection on Interview session 1 and 2 *(Sample questions. These will be adapted based on findings from Interview 1 and 2)*

- In Interview 1 you mentioned [XYZ], how does this compare to what you talked about in Interview 2?
- In interview 1 you mentioned [XYZ], this seems to expand upon what you talked about in Interview 2. Can you please tell me more about that?

Current Situation

- What was your experience of completing the arts-based activities?
    - Did you have a favourite or least favourite activity? Why?
- How did it feel expressing yourself using the medium of art?
- How might you integrate creative expression into your teaching practice?
    - What can this teach us about students' experiences communicating about their identity?
- Do you feel integrating arts-based activities promote professional development and/or mental wellbeing as a FSL TC? How so (or not)?
- After completing all the arts activities, how do you feel in your position as an FSL teacher?
- Do you think it has helped you in any aspect of your life as a French speaker? As a French teacher? If so, how? If not, why not?

Chapter 7
Expanding Understandings of Race in Postsecondary Language Classrooms:
A Call for Multiraciality in Teacher Identity Research

Marcela Hebbard
https://orcid.org/0000-0002-1523-8957
The University of Texas Rio Grande Valley, USA

ABSTRACT

While issues of race in relation to teacher identity have been addressed in language education research, they have often been confined to special issues. Factors contributing to the "absent-present" nature of race include an imbalanced focus on intersectionality which tends to prioritize the teacher's linguistic identity over other social categories, such as race and the persistent dichotomy between the idealized native speaker and non-native speaker. To broaden the understandings of race in teacher identity research within postsecondary language classrooms, this chapter advocates for considering the notion of multiraciality. To support these arguments, results from a critical discourse analysis (CDA) of four empirical studies are presented. The analysis demonstrates that race is often perceived as fixed and singular. The findings suggest that language educators and researchers should engage in critical thinking about how they describe and racially classify students and participants.

INTRODUCTION

Literature on teacher identity in language-related fields, including applied linguistics, Teaching English to Speakers of Other Languages (TESOL), and Second Language Acquisition (SLA), has long shown that teachers construct multiple identities across space and time through discursive, narrative, and concrete socially situated practices (Braine, 1999; Cheung et al., 2015; Choe & Seo, 2021; Hallman, 2009;

DOI: 10.4018/978-1-6684-9029-7.ch007

Expanding Understandings of Race

Kubota & Lin, 2009; Nagamoto, 2012; Trent, 2015; Varghese et al., 2005). While contextual influences impact teacher identity construction, self-knowledge is a crucial dimension for identity development because it prompts teachers to interrogate how their linguistic and social identities, including their racial identity, interact with and influence their pedagogical practices (Alsup, 2006; Motha et al., 2012; Santoro, 2009). From this perspective, racialization is inevitably salient in the teaching of language (Charles, 2019; Flores & Rosa, 2015; Ladson-Billings, 1995b; Motha, 2014; Paris & Alim, 2017; Park et al., 2023; Shuck, 2006). However, although issues of race in connection to teacher identity have been addressed in language education research, they have often been relegated to special issues (Kubota & Lin, 2006; Varghese et al., 2016). At least two factors have obscured the complex notion of race in teacher identity research. The first is an overt focus on intersectionality—a framework for understanding how a person's subjectivities and characteristics (e.g., class, gender, roles) intersect with unequal systems and structures shaping the person's experience (Crenshaw, 1989; Loden & Rosener, 1990). In teacher identity work, there has been an imbalanced focus on intersectionality that tends to privilege the teacher's linguistic identity over other social categories like race, class, and gender (Ellis, 2016; Varghese et al., 2016).

The second factor is the hierarchical dichotomy of the idealized native speaker teacher (NST) and non-native speaker teacher (NNST), which continues to serve as a guiding principle for conducting teacher identity research (Moussu & Llurda, 2008; Shuck, 2006; Yazan & Rudolph, 2018). This dichotomy, when viewed through a critical racial perspective, operates within a mono-ideological framework (e.g., monoracial and monolingual). It typically assumes the NST as having one race (White) and being English monolingual, and the NNST as having one race (non-White) and being non-English monolingual, without questioning the logic behind that assumption (Charles, 2019; Motha, 2014; Ruecker & Ives, 2015). Even critical perspectives such as Critical Race Theory (CRT) and Raciolinguistics, used to inform our work on language teacher identity research, operate in a bicolored fashion—either/or—classifying people as either people of color or having White identities (Alim et al., 2016; Daniel et al., 2014; Rosa & Flores, 2015). As a result, critical perspectives have unintentionally perpetuated monoraciality, a belief that prohibits individuals from identifying with more than one racial group or background on the basis that racial differences are necessary for maintaining solidarity within a group and its identity (Jordan et al., 2014; Ladson-Billings, 1995b).

The above discussion underscores the importance of continuing to interrogate, uncover, problematize, and eliminate the pervasiveness of mono-ideologies such as monolingualism, monoraciality, and racism in teacher identity work. To carry out this task, it is crucial that we critique our critical perspectives and incorporate underrepresented groups (Rudolph & Yazan, 2023). One population of language educators overlooked in language identity research is individuals who identify as multiracial or mixed race, defined as having two or more racial backgrounds (Patton et al., 2016). Therefore, in this chapter, I argue that, to enhance our understanding of the powerful role racialized mono-ideologies play in the postsecondary language classroom, the field should include the notion of multiraciality in teacher identity research.

The goal of this chapter is threefold: 1) to provide an overview of how the socio-historical mechanisms of hypodescent and anti-miscegenation laws helped normalize a monoracial ideology in the U.S. context; 2) to discuss how the legacy of these mechanisms extended monoracial ideologies in education, specifically in language teacher identity research and critical perspectives; 3) to propose the notion of multiraciality in teacher identity research as a way to challenge the colonial 'common sense' of maintaining a racial dichotomy mentality. To support these claims, I discuss the critical analysis of four empirical studies that explore teacher identity in language instruction. I drew on Critical Discourse Analysis (CDA) and the notion of multiraciality as the theoretical framework to guide the analysis. The research question guiding analysis included does the researcher explicitly disclose their positionality? How are participants classified linguistically and racially? What assumptions about race do authors make either implicitly or explicitly? Given that racial identity is inextricably tied to other social categories, what other social categories do the authors consider, if any?

Audiences that can benefit from reading this chapter include students, instructors, program coordinators, and administrators. They can learn that multiraciality has been a constant phenomenon since the beginning of the United States (and abroad) (Masuoka, 2018; Pascoe, 2009b), yet its visibility has been suppressed through the colonial laws of hypodescent and anti-miscegenation (Callister & Didham, 2009; Daniel et al., 2014). Knowing this can help committed individuals to combat racial institutional, structural, and individual barriers by devising reconciling strategies among ethnic groups, to further challenge or question the notion of native speakerism, the belief that a 'native speaker' embodies "not only the English language but also Western teaching methodology" (Lowe & Kiczkowiak, 2016, p. 2), and to propose novel pedagogical strategies against raciolinguistic discriminatory practices in the postsecondary classroom.

DEFINING TERMS

Before proceeding, it is important to define a few key terms that this chapter utilizes to assist the reader's understanding of the theoretical framework guiding the discussion.

Mixed Race Individuals

The term 'mixed race' refers to individuals who identify as having two or more racial or ethnic heritage backgrounds (e.g., Black/White, Japanese/Hispanic (Patton et. al., 2016). Mixed race individuals are often exposed to multiple cultures and linguistic practices, and many are perceived as racially ambiguous (Tsai et al. 2021). Other terms commonly used include biracial, multiracial and blended (Patton et al., 2016). In this chapter the terms mixed race and multiracial are used interchangeably.

Interracial Individuals

The term interracial is used in this work to refer to individuals who are in committed long-term relationships with someone from a different racial and/or ethnic group.

Race/Ethnicity

The concepts of race and ethnicity are contentious terms (Kubota & Lin, 2009). Both terms lack biological determinism, meaning they do not denote "innate or inherent attributes of human beings" (Kubota & Lin, 2009, p. 4). Nevertheless, the impact of race and ethnicity on people's everyday lives is a *real* social fact (Törngren et al., 2021). Throughout history, these constructs have been strategically used to mark differences between people, setting them apart from one another (Kubota & Lin, 2009; Lewis & Phoenix, 2004). Some scholars conceptualize race and ethnicity as identical for many communities (Patton et al., 2016), while others see them as related but different. They argue that race is an arbitrary system of classification based on power and privilege, whereas ethnicity distinguishes groups based on cultural

Expanding Understandings of Race

patterns, ancestry, and traditions (Kubota & Lin, 2009; Patton et al., 2016). For clarity, this work relies on the American Psychological Association (APA) definition of race, which integrates both constructs. According to the APA online dictionary, race is a socially constructed concept used to classify a segment of the human population based on shared physical features, ancestry, or language. Self-reported race can change in different social contexts, and individuals may identify with more than one race. In contrast, ethnicity involves social categorization based on an individual's membership in or identification with a specific cultural or ethnic group (APA Online Dictionary, n.d.).

In sum, acknowledging the variability within people's groups (e.g., Asian or Asian American encompasses different ethnic groups such as Hmong, Han Chinese, and Gujarati Indian) and the contested meanings of these concepts, this work uses the terms race and ethnicity interchangeably (Patton et al., 2016).

This chapter draws connections from various theoretical bodies of work, including critical cultural studies, history, legal studies, sociology, language education, and writing studies. The remainder of the chapter is organized as follows: First, a brief history details how anti-miscegenation laws and the one-drop rule developed and normalized the ideology of monoraciality in American society. This ideology, however, was not without resistance. Next, the discussion explores how the legacy of these laws extended to higher education in the 1960s and 1970s, shaping critical perspectives, specifically Critical Race Theory and its different pedagogical iterations. Following that, the chapter presents an analysis of four empirical studies on teacher identity, utilizing Critical Discourse Analysis and the notion of Multiraciality as a theoretical framework. The chapter concludes with suggestions for teaching and further research on teacher identity.

A BRIEF HISTORY OF ANTI-MISCEGENATION LAWS AND THE ONE-DROP RULE

Origins and Definitions

This section discusses how anti-miscegenation laws and the one-drop rule developed and helped normalize monoraciality. The term 'miscegenation' was coined in 1862 by two anti-Lincoln and pro slavery Democratic pamphleteers who wanted to be satirical about the supposed consequences of racial equality in America between Whites and Blacks (Pascoe, 2009b). Miscegenation refers to the mixture of two or more races (Pascoe, 2009b) whereas the Principle of Hypodescent racially classifies anyone with a single drop of African ancestry as a Black person. These two notions are an American invention and historically developed in parallel (Hollinger, 2003; Pascoe, 2009b; Reginald et al. 2014; Washington, 2008). Miscegenation laws against racial mixing toward interracial sex and marriage developed as early as 1662, the same year the state of Virginia established the principle of hypodescent also known as the One-Drop rule (Daniel et al., 2014; Hickman, 1997). Combined, these laws not only establish a racial hierarchy and segregation between enslaved African people and their descendants and the White slaveholding group, but also the ideology of monoraciality, the 'common' belief that prohibits individuals from identifying with more than one racial group or background on the basis that racial differences are necessary for maintaining solidarity within a group and its identity (Hannah-Jones, 2019; Hollinger, 2003; Jordan et al., 2014; Washington, 2008). It was until 1924 that the one-drop rule became law when the "Preservation of Racial Integrity Act" was passed mandating that any individual with a single drop of African ancestry be categorized as Black (Hickman, 1997; Washington, 2008).

Racial Mixing: A Product of Colonization

Monoraciality assumes no racial mixing, however, racial mixing or multiraciality is not a new phenomenon, it is a product of colonization (Hickman, 1997; Hollinger, 2003; Pascoe, 2009b; Weaver, 2009). Colonization, defined as the displacement and undermining of societies including their values, cultures, and ways of life by outside people, values and incites violence against the lives of the colonized people (Clements, 2011). Violence can take many forms including physical aggression, public humiliation, slavery, and the development of a racial stratification system where the colonizer group creates social constructions like legal codes to limit the rights and privileges of other ethnic groups so the colonizer group becomes the majoritized group exerting control over the minoritized groups (Clements, 2011; Gonzalez, 2011; Omi & Winant, 1994; Pascoe, 2009b; Patton et al., 2016).

In colonial America, the first people being violated were the Native people who had lived in these lands for thousands of years. It is estimated that more than ten million Native people lived in North America at the time settlers from Europe came to colonize (Jordan et al., 2014; Russell, 2006; Weber, 1992). Of the different Western European colonizers that settled these lands, the English and the Spanish had the greatest impact (Gonzalez, 2011). Large colonies from both groups took root in separate regions; the English in the northeast region and the Spanish in the southern region (Gonzalez, 2011). However, in comparison with Spanish conquistadores who carried the legacy of racial and cultural mixing experienced under the long period of Arab domination, the English maintained a stricter separation from Native people fueled by religious, economic, and racial beliefs (Gonzalez, 2011; Hannah-Jones, 2019; Menchaca, 2008, Pascoe, 2009b).

This apparent separation does not mean that there was no racial intermixture between the British European colonizers and the colonized people. There was. In fact, it did not take long for a mixed race population to develop. Hickman (1997) notes that there are legal records ordering punishment for fornication between a White and Black person as early as 1632. However, because the British settlers needed to become the majoritized racial group, they spent time unifying both non-British as well as British colonists across social class and region (Clements, 2011; Goebel, 1938; Gonzalez, 2011; Hannah-Jones, 2019; Johnson, 1931; Jordan, 2014; Washington, 2011). Once the wealthy and intellectual British colonists became the majoritized slave-holding group, they codified laws to force social reorganization that favored them (Gonzalez, 2011; Hannah-Jones, 2019; Kendi, 2017). They also crafted and exported a public history of America according to their own image - an America that is White, monoracial, monolingual and monocultural (Hollinger, 2003; Hannah-Jones, 2019).

While race mixing occurred between Whites and Native women, the largest race intermixture happened between White men and enslaved African women and their descendants (Braveheart-Jordan & DeBruyn, 1995; Clements, 2011; Hannah-Jones, 2019; Kendi, 2017; Kuhlmann, 1992). It is estimated that more than 12.5 million African men, women and children were violently unrooted from their communities, stripped of their human value, and objectified, and about 1.8 million perished while being subjugated to cross the Atlantic Ocean (Basu, 2022; "Diving with a Purpose," n.d.; Gabaccia, 1989; Hannah-Jones, 2021).

As the dehumanizing enslavement of African people grew, African women and their offspring were sexually exploited and objectified as property (Cruz & Berson, 2001; Hannah-Jones, 2919; Kendi, 2017; Pascoe, 2009b). Johnson explains that "White men did not think of their actions as immoral—for how could the white man be morally wrong to a piece of property?" (Johnson, 2010, p. 35). Even mixed race children who resembled the phenotype of their White progenitors were subjected to oppression

Expanding Understandings of Race

and were assigned the status of the subjugated group (Davis, 1972, Hickman, 1997). This is known as the hypodescent principle, when mixed-origin people are racially assigned to the lower-status parental group (Iverson et al., 2022).

However, Western European colonizers were not the only ones creating laws against racial mixing, Native Nations did too, especially where Indian leaders were also slaveholders. It is estimated that the Cherokee tribe enslaved about 4,000 Black individuals prior to the Civil War (Gonzalez, 2011; Parker, 2022; Pascoe, 2009b). American Indian nations banned marriages to Blacks but not to Whites and linked its concerns directly to property. The Cherokee tribe passed a law that said that if White men fathered children with Indian women, they were obligated to leave the property for the children, but if an Indian person married a Black individual, they were charged with committing a disgraceful act to the Nation (Pascoe, 2009b; Parker, 2022).

Racial Mixing After the American Revolution

By the time of the American Revolution in 1765, there was a growing multiracial population. Some historians estimate that there were between 60,000 to 120,000 people of mixed ancestry including White-Black, White-Indian, and Black-Indian unions residing in the colonies and far fewer with a three-way racial intermixture (Cruz & Berson, 2001; Jordan, 2014). However, instead of recognizing these interracial unions and their mixed race descendants, the elites continued to codify laws to prevent interracial sex and marriage (Pascoe, 1996a). These legislative actions were arbitrary and did not stop the exploitation of enslaved women and their offspring by White masters and overseers. On the contrary, these laws reinforced the social idea to normalize a monoracial ideology that viewed race as hierarchical, monolithic, and in need to be maintained separate despite the reality that Black-White mixing was taking place (Hollinger, 2003; Pascoe, 2009b).

Claiming that all White European settlers raped and exploited their female slaves, however, would be an inaccurate generalization. Some White European men married Black women for life. There is legal evidence that before the American civil war, White men sought to form interracial committed relations with Black women and Indian women but faced opposition by White lawmakers ruling the U.S. legal system (Menchaca 2008; Pascoe 2009b). John Ferdinand Webber, for instance, a second-generation immigrant from England, moved to Austin, Texas in 1826 to serve as a private in the War of 1812. There, he had sexual relationships with his neighbor's black enslaved woman named Silvia Hector. He eventually paid for her freedom and married her. They left Austin and relocated to the Rio Grande region due to the constant prejudice by Whites and Blacks alike because of their eleven mulatto children and mixed marriage. In the Rio Grande Valley, Webber bought land and built his family homestead. To assimilate to the Mexican culture dominant in the area, he changed his name to Juan Fernando Webber and along with Silvia, played a key role in the Underground Railroad movement by aiding slaves seeking freedom in Mexico (Bacha-Garza et al., 2019).

The end of slavery juxtaposed two possible racial realities. On the one hand, racial equity seemed a possibility when the U.S. Congress passed, in 1866, the Civil Rights Act and later in 1868, the Fourteenth Amendment which promised equal protection of the laws to all U.S. citizens (Pascoe, 2009b). On the other hand, the descendants of Western European colonists, mostly White men who had assumed the label "native" Americans to distinguish themselves from the immigrants who arrived later, wondered where their privileges and responsibilities as the majoritized racial group begin and end (Marinari et al., 2019; Pascoe, 2009b). Unsurprisingly, the courts sided with White men and claimed that the Civil Rights Act of 1866 provided the same rights of marriage to Blacks and Whites, but what it did not provide was a "superior right of a negro to marry a white woman, when a white man *can not* marry a negro" (Pascoe, 2009b, p. 43 *italics in the original*). In doing this, the U.S. legal system solidified the separation of the races as the "natural law" mostly between Black and White persons, but not without the complexity in determining who counts as Black or White (Pascoe, 2009b; Törngren et al., 2021).

Racial Mixing, Whiteness, and Monoraciality

Codifying the separation of races contributed to normalizing the ideology of monoraciality even though as noted earlier, historically, mixed race individuals constituted the majority of the population in the United States. Historians estimate that 70 to 80% of African Americans are of mixed race and hundreds of thousands, if not millions, of classified Whites have Black blood (Hickman, 1997; Pascoe, 2009b; Washington, 2008). African American scholars have noted that a reason why mixed race Black/White individuals have gone unrecognized is that the one-drop rule gave enslaved Africans and their descendants a reason to claim a Black group identity despite that the rule has its origins in racist notions of White purity (Daniel, 2002; Hickman, 1997). Historians have also claimed that many "White" Americans from the majoritized group intermarried when southern and eastern European immigrant groups such as Italians, Irish, Hungarian, and Greeks were viewed as White or were acknowledged as White when political need arose to disenfranchise Blacks and non-European people in local governments (Barrett & Roediger, 2016; Hickman, 1997; Rothenberg, 2016). Furthermore, the annexation of territories in the American Southwest also complicated the state of Whiteness. For example, when Mexico lost vast territories to the United States in 1848, the predominantly White American government adopted laws prohibiting people of European blood and their descendants from marrying Africans and their descendants (Menchaca, 2008). These codes placed Spanish-speaking Mexican settlers of Spanish, Indian, Black ancestry in an ambiguous position since during Mexican rule, intermarriage was common between Spanish/Indian (mestizos), Spanish/African (mulatos) and White/Mulatos (Ruiz & Sánchez Korrol, 2006).

While anti-miscegenation laws were ruled unconstitutional in 1967, the ongoing legal codification against interracial sex and marriage and their descendants over hundreds of years contributed to the American society to develop a monothetical view of race instead of a polythetical one. The term polythetical refers to assigning different weights to one's ancestry, physical appearance, and sociocultural status, whereas monothetical means defining race through the hypodescent principle and keeping races separate (Washington, 2008).

The monothetical view of race, created in large part by anti-miscegenation laws and the principle of hypodescent, was contingent on garnering a collective will for American society to embrace it as a 'social fact' (Washington, 2008). To spread, the monothetical view of race needed support from large social institutions. One of these institutions is the U.S. Census, which social scientists call "the primary arm of our public racial categorization system" (Rockquemore et al., 2009, p. 20). Each census has been shaped by the given historical period and the existing race relations of that particular period (Omi & Winant, 1994, p. 11). Nonetheless, the two main racial categories that have appeared since the first census in 1970 are White and Black (Hickman, 1997). It was not until the 2000 U.S. census, after a decade-long debate on how persons with parents of different races should be racially categorized, that individuals who identify as having two or more races were presented with that option for the first time (Rockquemore et al., 2009; U.S. Census). This option was included in the 2010 and 2020 census, respectively. The 2020 U.S. Census results show that individuals who identify as multiracial grew considerably from 9 million people in 2010 to 33.8 million in 2020, a 276% increase (Census.gov). In the next section, I will explain how the ideology of monoraciality extended to higher education, shaping critical perspectives, specifically Critical Race Theory and its pedagogical iterations.

THE LEGACY OF ANTI-MISCEGENATION AND HYPODESCENT

Mono-Ideologies, Critical Perspectives, and Teacher Identity

The normalization of a monoracial ideology, a legacy of the mechanisms of anti-miscegenation and hypodescent, extended to the critical perspective of Critical Race Theory (CRT). In the 1970s, scholars of color and students in legal studies voiced dissatisfaction with race reforms, arguing that these laws were premised on ideals of assimilation, integration, and color blindness (Ladson-Billings & Tate, 1995; Martinez, 2020; Omi & Winant, 1994). They called for positioning race as the center of the legal arguments (Olson, 2003). In doing so, these scholars shifted the attention from how Americans had historically looked at Blacks and other minoritized groups to how they have looked at Whites, placing the construct of Whiteness as a central component of racial ideology (Kennedy et al., 2005; Kolchin, 2009; Rothenberg, 2016). While this action marked a major paradigm shift by making White a racial category, CRT scholars unintentionally and perhaps unknowingly perpetuated a monoracial dichotomy that continued to conceptualize race as fixed and singular, dividing it into two main groups: Whites vs. People of Color (Ladson-Billings & Tate, 1995a; Martinez, 2020b; Ruecker, 2011a).

As the CRT movement grew, it informed pedagogical practices such as Culturally Relevant Pedagogy (Ladson-Billings, 1995b) which encourages educators to help their students accept and affirm their cultural identity critically as a way to challenge institutional inequities, and Culturally Sustaining Pedagogies (Paris & Alim, 2015) which calls educators and schools to support and sustain the cultural ways of being of communities of color as a way to foster positive social transformation. More recently, Flores and Rosa (2015) offered a Raciolinguistic perspective that calls to reframe language diversity in education. This approach examines the ways the dominant White culture has co-constructed language and race since the colonial era (Flores & Rosa, 2019). To challenge the monoglossic and monoracial ideologies that permeate schools, the raciolinguistic approach seeks to make visible how despite the fact that many language-minoritized students produced the linguistic practices after their white speaking subject, the white listening subject continues to label their linguistic practices as deficient "based on their racial positioning in society as opposed to any objective characteristics of their language use" (Flores & Rosa, 2015, p. 151). Raciolinguistic ideologies stigmatize non-dominant linguistic practices thus defining an individual or group linguistic capacity in terms of race (Alim et al., 2016; Rosa, 2016).

While these critical perspectives have greatly contributed to uncover inequalities, they have operated from a raciolinguistic binary. Racially, these perspectives mostly focus on inequalities between Whites and People of Color. For instance, Flores and Rosa (2015) claim that the white speaking and listening subject should not be understood as a biographical individual, that is someone who is racially White, but as an ideological position (p. 151). However, the examples these authors present in several of their publications suggest otherwise (Flores & Rosa, 2015; Rosa, 2016; Rosa & Flores, 2017). In their seminal 2015 article, the racialized participant populations highlighted include a student born in the United States but whose both parents were born in Mexico, a second-generation Chicana student from Texas, and former President Barack Obama who is racially categorized as African American even though he is of mixed heritage (Flores & Rosa, 2015).

Linguistically, these critical perspectives operate within the dichotomy of native speaker (NS) and nonnative speaker (NNS) (Alim et al., 2016; Flores & Rosa, 2015a; Kazan & Rudolph, 2018; Ruecker & Ives, 2015b). In teacher identity work, language scholars have advocated moving beyond this dichotomy since at least the 1990s (Canagajarah, 1999). However, disrupting and removing the belief that teachers whose identities correspond with the idealized native speaker "might, practically and/or theoretically, serve as better teachers" has proven difficult (Yazan & Rudolph, 2018, p. 5). Recently, language scholars have called to grant idealized nativeness to both NEST and NNEST alike by juxtaposing the NNEST's nativeness and knowledge of the local language(s) against the non-nativeness of the NEST of the local language(s) (Yazan & Rudolph, 2018). This juxtaposition then places both NNEST and NEST in superior and inferior categories leveling the field. However, what happens when the NNESTs are not local? This model does not consider those NNESTs who are not local and whose variety of English is different from the local varieties. This model also assumes that NEST cannot be native speakers of a local language.

To address this new binary distinction, scholars have called to reconceptualize the nature and purpose of local language use in classroom practice by distinguishing the "local" and "non-local" NNESTs while avoiding falling into deficit-oriented models and the universalized NS fallacy (Yazan & Rudolph, 2018). In other words, by contending that "*all* learners, users, and teachers may potentially experience degrees of fluid privilege-marginalization relating to their identities, talents, training and experiences, as per essentialized binaries of Self-Other within a given setting, and Self-Other in terms of a given context and the "world beyond," scholars think is possible to problematize the binaries of learner, user, and instructor identity (Yazan & Rudolph, 2018, p. 8). While this model seems promising, I argue that multiracials, as one of the fastest growing demographic groups in the United States, can also help further disrupt and challenge the colonial 'common sense' of maintaining a racial and linguistic dichotomy mentality. In the next section, I discuss the critical analysis of four empirical studies that explore teacher identity in language instruction in relation to race.

THEORIZING MULTIRACIALITY IN TEACHER IDENTITY RESEARCH THROUGH CDA

To explore whether the concept of race, including multiraciality, is "absent present," that is, implied but not explicitly represented in teacher identity literature (Prendergast, 1998), I conducted a critical discourse analysis (CDA). CDA as a theory is concerned with the relationships of language, discourse, and power in the construction of and representation of the social world (Rogers, 2004). Two principles that guide this approach include the understanding that discourse is an integral aspect of power and control (Bloor & Bloor, 2007; Fairclough & Wodak, 1997; Huckin et al., 2012), and the expectation that the researcher will ethically interrogate their own positions, beliefs, and attitudes as members either of the same social group being investigated or as observers of it (Bloor & Bloor, 2007).

To guide the critical discourse analysis, I drew on the growing interdisciplinary field of Critical Mixed Race Studies (CMRS). As noted earlier, the phenomenon of multiraciality is not new. Multiracial individuals have been present in the United States since its beginnings (Hickman, 1997; Pascoe, 2009b; Washington, 2008). However, it was until the 1980s, that the disciplines of sociology, anthropology, and ethnic studies began to pay attention to an 'overlooked group' - the multiethnic and multiracial descendants of mixed couples (Törngren et al., 2019). Informed by CRT, the work of Paul Spickard (1989) and Maria Root (1992, 1996) on multiracial people in America, among others, served to lay the foundation for multiracial studies (Daniel et al., 2014; Törngren et al., 2019). By the early 2000s, mixed race scholarly publications had grown exponentially, but it was until 2014 that mixed race studies became formally defined as the interdisciplinary area of inquiry named - *Critical Mixed Raced Studies* (CMRS) (Daniel et al., 2014).

As a field, CRMS places mixed race and multiracials as "subjects of historical, social, and cultural processes rather than simply objects of analysis" (Daniel et al., 2014, p. 8). Its objective is to critically study the world in which racially mixed people live including the ideological, social, economic, and political forces. Theoretically, CRMS operates within an intersectional framework, that is, race is always connected to other social categories such as gender, sex, class, and religion (Daneil et al. 2014). However, CMRS departs from CRT in that it calls to questioning, critiquing, and challenging racial issues beyond the American context and its focus on white supremacy (Harper et. al. 2009). CMRS does not negate white supremacy. Instead, in addition to interrogating whiteness, it also questions "the equally profound investment communities of color have in preserving monoracial identities" (Daniel et al., 2014, p. 13). In other words, while CMRS scholars note that acknowledging the whiteness in blackness is useful, "in relation to multiracial theory, race mixing cannot be an issue relegated to blackness alone," there is a need to research issues among races "of color" (McKibbin, 2014, p. 197).

Furthermore, in contrast with CRT's implicit assumption that racial identity is stable or fixed, CRMS views racial identity as something that often changes over the life course, it does not develop in a predictable linear process, it does not have an end point, and it varies depending on the racial composition of social networks, where the individuals are and whom they are interacting with (Patton et al., 2016; Renn, 2004; Rockquemore & Brunsma, 2002; Rockquemore et al., 2009). So, some of the aspects I paid attention to while analyzing the selected studies were how the researchers classified their participants linguistically and racially and whether there were multiracial or interracial participants present in their study. Question guiding analysis included does the researcher explicitly disclose their positionality? How are participants classified linguistically and racially? What assumptions about race do authors make either implicitly or explicitly? Given that racial identity is inextricably tied to other social categories, what other social categories do the authors consider, if any?

To select the studies on language teacher identity an intersectional criteria was used which included: date of publication (within the last 15 years), authors self-identified or were identified as being from Inner Circle countries (countries where English has had a long-standing presence such as Australia, the United States, Canada, the United Kingdom and New Zealand), focus (the attention of the study is on teacher identity), mention and discuss implicitly or explicitly the NEST and NNEST dichotomy, mention of gender of the teacher population investigated (broad representation), and whether racial identities were implied or explicitly stated. At the end, two studies from TESOL Quarterly, one study from TESOL Journal, and one study from an edited collection were selected. Table 1 below summarizes the information of the four studies.

Table 1. Selected articles

Author	Title	Year of Publication	Publisher/Editors	Concept of Race
Tonda Liggett	Unpacking White Racial Identity in English Language Teacher Education	2009	Kubota, R. & Lin, A. M. (Eds.). Race, culture and identities in second language education.	Explicit
Roslyn Appleby	Researching Privilege in Language Teacher Identity.	2016	TESOL Quarterly	Absent-Present
Elizabeth M. Ellis	I May Be a Native Speaker but I'm Not Monolingual: Reimagining All Teachers' Linguistic Identities in TESOL.	2016	TESOL Quarterly	Absent-Present
Quanisha D. Charles	Black Teacher of English in South Korea.	2019	TESOL Journal	Explicit

Brief Overview of Selected Studies

Tonda Liggett (2009)

Liggett examines the racial and cultural assumptions and perspectives of a group of six pre-service and in-service White English-language teacher candidates. Liggett's goal is to counteract social inequality by raising awareness in teacher candidates, so they enter their classrooms "with broadened perspectives on how racial identity influences the ways they approach their teaching and understand their diverse student population" (p. 28).

Using a qualitative research methodology, Liggett interviewed and observed six white female English Language Teachers. Three participants teach in rural schools, whereas the other three participants teach in an urban setting. Data revealed that participants avoided talking about their own white racial identity, and in some cases, spoke of it negatively. None of the participants considered the role cultural and historical conditioning play in how they understand their racial identity. Liggett concludes that English language teacher programs should expose white teacher candidates to materials that problematize relations of domination, racial privilege, and white racial membership.

Roslyn Appleby (2016)

Appleby investigates the experiences of white native-English-speaker teachers who enjoy significant professional benefits and privileges. According to Appleby, the vectors of privilege alluded to NESTs include being White, from an Inner Circle country, middle-class, usually male, and heterosexual. Appleby self-identifies as having some of the vectors of privilege as a white, native-speaker English language teacher in an international setting. She notes that studying herself and privilege is not difficult, but studying other White NESTs is complex because of the "potential alignment with - and resistance toward - institutional racial privilege" (p. 759).

Appleby interviewed 34 white Western men teaching English in Japan over a period of 3 years. Data revealed that most of her participants reflected vectors of privilege. However, these vectors of privilege were invisible to them. Data also showed that contrary to research that positions White males as "the object of romantic and sexual desire by Japanese women" (p. 760), the participants' identities were complex, fluid, and fragmented. Participants reported that schools exploited their whiteness and used it to attract customers, and that academic benefits offered to Japanese academics were not extended to them.

Elizabeth M. Ellis (2016)

Ellis' study seeks to problematize the dichotomy of the NEST/NNEST binary by showing that the linguistic identities of TESOL teachers are varied and complex. Ellis claims that teacher linguistic identity presumes the NEST as monolingual and NNEST as deviant. She sees as crucial the need to move beyond teachers' identities in relation to English and, instead, examine teachers' identities in relation to their *languaged lives*, "the language-learning and language-using experiences that inform their identities and positioning as teachers of English" (p. 599). Twenty-nine graduates from a linguistics master's program in a public university in Australia who live and teach English across seven countries agreed to participate in her study. Instead of categorizing their participants' identities as NEST/NNEST, she analyzed the participants' language experiences through the notions of circumstantial bilingual (individuals that learn another language in order to survive), elective bilingual (individuals that learn another language by choice), and monolingual experience. Findings revealed that all 29 language teachers had acquired, learned, or had contact with an additional language. Twenty-four participants were classified as bilingual. Only five participants had monolingual experiences. All participants claim English as their dominant language, but only 19 said they acquired English as a first language, and the remaining 10 had a childhood language other than English. Only five participants self-described as nonnative speakers. Ellis concluded that these findings "go some way to debunking the myth of the "monolingual native speaker teacher" who is usually imagined in opposition to the "bilingual" nonnative speaker teacher" (p. 611). To support her claims, Ellis discusses the languaged lives of two of her participants: Stan, born in Britain and teaching in Japan, and Virginia, born in Malaysia and teaching in Canada.

Quanisha D. Charles (2019)

Charles' study explores the teaching experiences and influence of Black teachers of English (BTEs) working in South Korea. She notes that scholarship on BTEs and their teaching experiences is limited. While avoiding essentializing the experiences of BTEs in South Korea, Charles explains that typically, ELTs are imagined as White. To get employment there, applicants need to be citizens of countries predominantly recognized as racially White, such as Australia, Canada, Ireland, New Zealand, the United States, Britain, and South Africa, and have a bachelor's degree. Even though all of these countries are historically racially, ethnically, and linguistically diverse, Charles notes that citizenship signals to the employer that the prospective applicant is White and speaks English as their dominant language.

Charles explains that many BTEs are native English speakers, yet they "face marginalization due to their racial background and/or skin color" (p. 4). Drawing on CRT and inquiry narrative, Charles explores how context shapes the experiences of BTEs in South Korea. Data revealed that participants view race as an important element in how they are perceived in South Korea. Charles concluded that an implication of her study is to encourage BTEs to be aware of their role as cultural ambassadors. That is, to be "mindful that they are both learning and teaching about cultures and that their job is not only to educate but also to become educated" (p. 13). Being a cultural ambassador, cautioned Charles, is complex because when culture and race merge, one needs to ask themselves which culture gets represented and if the representation is accurate.

DISCUSSION

Authors' Raciolinguistic Positionalities

Analysis revealed that two out of the four authors explicitly disclosed their positionalities. Appleby and Liggett both identify racially as white, gender as women, and both acknowledge a degree of linguistic privilege as self-described NES. As stated earlier, one of the principles in CDA is for the researcher to interrogate their own positions, beliefs, and attitudes as members either of the same social group being investigated or as observers of it (Bloor & Bloor, 2007).

Disclosing positionalities nowadays is important because it can help the teacher-scholar be alert, recognize, and address the assumptions made about people and how these unexamined stereotypes might influence their pedagogies and research (Liggett, 2009). For example, I infer that Charles might identify as a Black NES scholar. If that's the case, Charles used CRT as her analytical lens to capture the experiences of Black teachers of English in Korean society. CRT honors experiential knowledge of minoritized people as truth. Had Charles disclosed her racial identity in connection to CRT, the reader would have gained a deeper understanding of the discussion about hierarchical paradoxes of power (e.g., BTEs recognized as NES, yet marginalized because of their race).

Here, it is appropriate to disclose my raciolinguistic positionality. I am a Mexican-born multiracial woman with Central Mexico Indigenous, French, and Spanish ancestry. Regarding my linguistic identity, I see myself as a forever-sequential bilingual (Kalashnikova & Mattock, 2014). Even though I speak, read, and write with high proficiency in Spanish, English, as my additional language, has become my dominant academic language in writing and speaking. I find myself constantly expanding my vocabulary and knowledge in both of my languages.

Participants' Described Raciolinguistic Positionalities

Holliday (2019) notes that educators and researchers alike should think critically about how they describe and classify students and participants racially. I extend Holliday's call to include participants' linguistic positionalities. For example, the goal of Ellis' study is to problematize the dichotomy of the NEST/NNEST binary by demonstrating that "being a native speaker does not equate to being monolingual" (p. 612). However, upon closer analysis, the language Ellis uses to describe and classify Stan and Virginia, two of her participants, seems to reinforce rather than problematize the NEST/NNEST dichotomy and the underlying power structures.

To describe Virginia, Ellis uses the following phrases: she "describes herself as having a native speaker's competence in spoken and written English" (p. 612), "considers herself a native speaker of English" (p. 612), "thinks of herself as a native speaker of English" (p. 617), "claims that [English] is her first written language" (p. 622), and "now regards herself as a native speaker of English" (p. 623). Only once does Ellis write, "Virginia is, then, a native or near-native speaker of [...] English" (p. 618).

In contrast, Ellis uses the phrase "[Stan] describes himself as a native speaker" only once and classifies Stan as certainly a native speaker of English more than five times, emphasizing his near-native fluency in spoken Japanese. In comparison, Ellis asserts that Virginia's accent and her Chinese appearance cause others to perceive her as a nonnative speaker of English. If the purpose of Ellis' piece is to reimagine teachers' identities, why not refer to Virginia also as a native English speaker but with a vastly different *languaged life* experience than Stan from the beginning? How would Stan's appearance in relation to his 'near-native accent' in Japanese cause others to perceive him long term?

While my intention in this chapter is not to discount Ellis' important work, from a critical perspective, experiences with immigration, gender, power, and race are implied in Ellis' data; however, these experiences are not explored. For instance, comparing Stan's survival in Japan does not equate to the survival experiences that the majority of non-English speaking immigrants go through (Marinari et al., 2019). Stan has a secure teaching job and social status because of his racial appearance and spoken language (Ruecker & Ives, 2015). These factors do not depend on whether he speaks Japanese or not (p. 622). This is evident in the example that Ellis gives about Stan being so immersed in Japanese that during the interview, he came up with a Japanese term to express his idea instead of the English word. While Ellis claims that Stan's example demonstrates "his strong identity as a Japanese speaker" and his linguistic giftedness (p. 614), one can only wonder if Virginia had done the same — that is, to replace an English word with a Chinese term — would her linguistic practices be perceived the same as Stan's? She is, after all, a native speaker of Chinese and English. According to Flores and Rosa (2015), the answer is no. Virginia would be subjected to raciolinguistic ideologies. That is, even if she achieves near-native accent in English like Stan did in Japanese, she will continue to be racialized and labeled a nonnative speaker of English (Flores & Rosa, 2015).

Monoraciality and Linguistic Dichotomies

Analysis also revealed that all four studies reflect a monoracial and linguistic dichotomy framework. For example, Appleby's (2016) study is framed around the NEST/NNEST binary and seems to essentialize race by assuming that Inner Circle countries are White. This assumption is evident when she states that "thirty-three male participants were NESs from Inner Circle countries" and ties the participants' privilege to their Inner Circle NES origin (Appleby, 2016, p. 761), despite the fact that, as argued earlier, inner circle countries have historically been multiracial and multilingual (Pascoe, 2009b). Furthermore, the author notes that 21 male participants reported being married to Japanese women who were former students or colleagues and that being married to a Japanese spouse raises the participants' social standing and employment opportunities. However, Appleby does not explicitly address issues of interraciality. How does being in an interracial committed relationship impact the teacher identity construction of these 21 male participants? How do their social networks influence their racial identity and pedagogies?

While Appleby and Ellis' respective works strongly demonstrate a desire and commitment to decentralize the binary of NEST and NNEST, the analysis revealed that the notion of race in these studies is absent-present (Prendergast, 1998). Out of the four authors, only Charles and Liggett make race a central focus, albeit perceived within a monoracial ideology (White/People of Color). For example, in Liggett's (2009) study, all her participants are categorized as monoracial White, even though two of her participants have mixed heritage. One of them has an Italian background. Italians, Jews, and Irish people were once considered non-White (Barrett & Roediger, 2016). Another participant was born in Cuba and emigrated to the United States when she was 11. Furthermore, her data revealed that her participants did not recognize white as a race at first, but "they became aware of their racialized identities by referencing other groups" in terms of socioeconomic class and historical standing (e.g., slavery) (Liggett, 2009, p. 36).

Liggett's (2009) research is important because our racial identities as educators influence "what to teach and what to leave unexamined" (p. 27). However, as educators, we need to be careful not to assume that everyone (e.g., students, administrators, other educators) is high race salient, defined as being taught to view the concept of race as an important aspect of self-concept (Patton et al., 2016). Many of the students who enter our classrooms, administrators, and other educators might be low race salient, meaning they grew up in homes or social settings where race played no significant role except for physical features (Patton, 2016) or hold multiple monoracial identities, shifting according to the situation ("I am Mexican and Chinese") (Renn, 2004). Perhaps some even hold extraracial identity, refusing to identify according to institutionalized racial categories (Renn, 2004). Thus, to avoid generalizations in the classroom, instructors should consider using a "get-to-know-you" survey to explore the raciolinguistic identities of their students at the beginning of the semester (Mitchum et al., 2021). Doing this can help instructors gain an understanding of how to tailor class activities.

In the next section, I provide suggestions for teaching and further teacher identity research.

CONCLUSION

Holliday's (2019) article in linguistics seems to be the first of its kind in exploring the way that traditional methodologies have excluded the multiracial population and providing considerations for future research. Holliday draws on sociolinguistic theory to show that race has a tendency to be seen as a "fixed speaker trait" (p. 3). However, like other allied fields, it has begun to question the limits of a monoracial framework. She concludes that in language-oriented fields "it is no longer possible to ignore individuals and groups with multiple and complex racial identities in the 21st century" (Holliday, 2019, p. 9). I concur with Holliday. The time is ripe for language-oriented fields to explicitly include the notion of multiraciality when investigating teacher and student identities in the future.

Incorporating the notion of multiraciality as an analytical lens may help expand teacher identity research and teacher training programs (De Costa, 2010a; De Costa & Norton, 2017b; Hill & Bilge, 2020). Introducing lessons about multiraciality in teacher education programs, for example, could help problematize the 'common sense' understanding of Inner Circle countries as monoracial. For researchers, the notion of multiraciality could assist in exploring how social networks (e.g., interracial marriages, multiracial families) might impact pre-service and in-service teacher identity and how race intersects with teachers' plurilingual learning experiences and other facets of social identity (Ellis, 2016). For instance, through the method of duoethnography, language instructors could explore whether they rearticulate racial issues over time — that is, how they infuse familiar racial concepts and ideas with new meanings and purposes (Daniel et al., 2014; Lawrence & Nagashima, 2020).

As stated earlier, educators and researchers should think critically about how they both describe and classify students and participants racially (Holliday, 2019). Rockquemore et al. (2009) suggest that instead of looking at race as an all-encompassing construct, it is important to "differentiate between *racial identity* (an individual's self-understanding), *racial identification* (how others understand and categorize an individual), and *racial category* (what racial identities are available and chosen in a specific context)" (p. 27). Reflecting on the differences between these practices could help language instructors understand themselves and create spaces in their classrooms for interactions that support students' fluid racial identities and identification in meaningful ways.

REFERENCES

Alim, S. H., Rickford, J. R., & Ball, A. F. (2016). *Raciolinguistics: How language shapes our ideas about race*. Oxford University Press. doi:10.1093/acprof:oso/9780190625696.001.0001

Alsup, J. (2006). *Teacher identity discourses: Negotiating personal and professional spaces*. Lawrence Erlbaum. doi:10.4324/9781410617286

American Psychological Association. (n.d.-a). *Race*. https://dictionary.apa.org/race

American Psychological Association. (n.d.-b). *Ethnicity*. https://dictionary.apa.org/ethnicity

Appleby, R. (2016). Researching privilege in language teacher identity. *TESOL Quarterly, 49(1)*, 755-768. doi:10.1002/tesq.321

Bacha-Garza, R. (2019). Race and ethnicity along the antebellum Rio Grande. In R. Bacha-Garza, C. L. Miller & R. K. Skowronek (Eds.), *The civil war on the Rio Grande, 1846–1876* (Vol. 46, pp. 82-106). Texas A&M University Press.

Barrett, J. E., & Roediger, D. (2016). How white people became white. In P. Rothenberg (Ed.), *White privilege: Essential readings on the other side of racism* (5th ed., pp. 65–70). Worth Publishers.

Basu, S. [Host]. (2022, March 12). *Uncovering slave-ship wrecks, a diver puts lost souls to rest*. [Audio podcast episode]. In Apple News. https://podcasts.apple.com/us/podcast/uncovering-slave-ship-wrecks-a-diver-puts-lost-souls-to-rest/id1577591053?i=1000554506215

Braine, G. (1999). *Non-native educators in English language teaching*. Lawrence Erlbaum Associates.

Braveheart-Jordan, M., & DeBruyn, L. (1995). So she may walk in balance: Integrating the impact of historical trauma in the treatment of Native American Indian women. In J. Adleman & G. Enguidanos-Clark (Eds.), *Racism in the lives of women: Testimony, theory, and guides to antiracist practice* (pp. 345–368). Haworth Press.

Brunsma, D. L., & Rockquemore, K. A. (2001). The new color complex: Appearances and biracial identity. *Identity, 1(3)*, 225–246. doi:10.1207/S1532706XID0103_03

Callister, P., & Didham, R. (2009). Who are we? The human genome project, race and ethnicity. *Social Policy Journal of New Zealand, 36*, 63–76.

Canagarajah, S. A. (1999). Interrogating the 'native speaker fallacy': Non-linguistic roots, non-pedagogical results. In G. Braine (Ed.), *Non-native educators in English language teaching* (pp. 77–92). Lawrence Erlbaum Associates.

Charles. (2019). Black teachers of English in South Korea: Constructing identities as a native English speaker and English language teaching professional. *TESOL Journal, 10(4)*. . doi:10.1002/tesj.478

Cheung, P. K., & Said, S. B. (2015). *Advances and current trends in language teacher identity research*. Routledge. doi:10.4324/9781315775135

Choe, H., & Seo, Y. (2021). Negotiating teacher identity: Experiences of Black teachers of English in Korean ELT: How race and English language teacher identity intersect in the Expanding Circle. *English Today, 37*(3), 148–155. doi:10.1017/S0266078419000531

Clements, J. M. (2011). Sarah and the Puritans: Feminist Contributions to New England Historical Archaeology. *Archaeologies, 7*(1), 97–120. doi:10.100711759-010-9155-3

Crenshaw. (1991). Mapping the margins: Intersectionality, identity politics, and violence against women of color. *Stanford Law Review, 43*(6), 1241–1299. doi:10.2307/1229039

Cruz, B. C., & Berson, M. J. (2001). The American melting pot? Miscegenation laws in the United States. *OAH Magazine of History, 15*(4), 80–84. https://www.jstor.org/stable/25163474

Daniel, R. G., Kina, L., Dariotis, W. M., & Fojas, C. (2014). Emerging paradigms in critical mixed race studies. *Journal of Critical Mixed Raced Studies.* doi:10.5070/C811013868

Davis, A. (1972). Reflections on the Black woman's role in the community of slaves. *The Massachusetts Review, 13*(1/2), 81–100. https://www.jstor.org/stable/25088201

De Costa, P., & Norton, B. (2017b). Introduction: Identity, transdisciplinarity, and the good language teacher. *Modern Language Journal, 101*(S1), 3–14. doi:10.1111/modl.12368

De Costa, P. I. (2010a). Let's collaborate: Using developments in global English research to advance socioculturally-oriented SLA identity work. *Issues in Applied Linguistics, 18*(1), 99–124. doi:10.5070/L4181005125

Diving With a Purpose. (n.d.). *Restoring our oceans. Preserving our heritage.* https://www.nationalgeographic.com/podcasts/into-the-depths

Ellis, E. M. (2016). "I may be a native speaker but I'm not monolingual": Reimagining all teachers' linguistic identities in TESOL. *TESOL Quarterly, 49(1), 597-630.* doi:10.1002/tesq.314

Fairclough, N., & Wodak, R. (1997). Critical discourse analysis. In T. van Dijk (Ed.), *Discourse as social interaction* (pp. 258–284). Sage.

Flores, N., & Rosa, J. (2015). Undoing appropriateness: Raciolinguistic ideologies and language diversity in education. *Harvard Educational Review, 85*(2), 149–171. doi:10.17763/0017-8055.85.2.149

Flores, N., & Rosa, J. (2022). Undoing competence: Coloniality, homogeneity, and the overrepresentation of whiteness in applied linguistics. *Language Learning*, 1–28. doi:10.1111/lang.12528

Gabaccia, D. (1989). *Immigrant women in the United States: A selective annotated multidisciplinary bibliography*. Greenwood Press.

Goebel, D. (1938). British trade to the Spanish colonies, 1796-1823. *The American Historical Review, 43*(2), 288–320. https://www.jstor.org/stable/1839720. doi:10.2307/1839720

Gonzalez, J. (2011). *Harvest of empire: A history of latinos in America* (2nd ed.). Penguin Books. Print

Hallman, H. I. (2009). Teacher identity as dialogic response. In R. Kubota & A. M. Lin (Eds.), *Race, culture, and identities in second language education: Exploring critically engaged practice* (pp. 3–14). Routledge.

Hannah-Jones, N. (2019). The 1619 Project: A new origin story. *The New York Times*.

Harper, S. R., Patton, L. D., & Wooden, O. S. (2009). Access and equity for African American students in higher education: A critical race historical analysis of policy efforts. *The Journal of Higher Education, 80*(4), 389–414. doi:10.1080/00221546.2009.11779022

Hickman, C. B. (1997). The devil and the one drop rule: Racial categories, African Americans, and the U.S. Census. *Michigan Law Review, 5*(95), 1161–1265. doi:10.2307/1290008

Hill Collins, P., & Bilge, S. (2020). *Intersectionality*. Polity Press.

Holliday, N. (2019). Multiracial identity and racial complexity in sociolinguistic variation. *Language and Linguistics Compass, 13*(8), 1–12. doi:10.1111/lnc3.12345

Hollinger, D. (2003). Amalgamation and hypodescent: The question of ethnoracial mixture in the history of the United States. *The American Historical Review, 108*(5), 1363–1390. doi:10.1086/529971

Johnson, C. I. (2010). Still rising: An intricate look at black female slaves. In D. R. Haggard (Ed.), *African Americans in the Nineteenth Century* (pp. 33–45). Bloomsbury Publishing USA. doi:10.5040/9798400608025.ch-003

Johnson, J. G. (1931). The founding of the Spanish colonies in Georgia and South Carolina. *The Georgia Historical Quarterly, 15*(4), 301–312. http://www.jstor.com/stable/40576145

Jordan, W. D. (2014). Historical origins of the one-drop racial rule in the United States. *Journal of Critical Mixed Race Studies, 1*(1), 98–132. doi:10.5070/C811013867

Kendi, I. (2017). *Stamped from the beginning: The definite history of racist ideas in America*. Nation Books.

Kennedy, T., Joyce, I. M., & Ratcliffe, K. (2005). Whiteness studies. *Rhetoric Review, 24*(4), 359–402. doi:10.120715327981rr2404_1

Kolchin, P. (2009). Whiteness studies. *Journal de la Société des Américanistes, 95*(1), 117–163. doi:10.4000/jsa.10769

Kubota, R., & Lin, A. M. Y. (2006). Race and TESOL: Introduction to concepts and theories. *TESOL Quarterly, 40*(3), 471–493. doi:10.2307/40264540

Kubota, R., & Lin, A. M. Y. (2009). *Race, culture, and identities in second language education: Exploring critically engaged practice*. Routledge. doi:10.4324/9780203876657

Kuhlmann, A. (1992). American Indian women of the plains and Northern Woodlands. *Social Thought & Research, 16*(1), 1–28. doi:10.17161/STR.1808.5083

Ladson-Billings, G. (1995b). Toward a theory of culturally relevant pedagogy. *American Educational Research Journal, 32*(3), 465–491. doi:10.3102/00028312032003465

Ladson-Billings, G., & Tate, W. F. (1995a). Toward a critical race theory of education. *Teachers College Record, 97*(1), 47–68. doi:10.1177/016146819509700104

Lawrence, L., & Nagashima, Y. (2020). The Intersectionality of gender, sexuality, race, and native-speakerness: Investigating ELT teacher identity through duoethnography. *Journal of Language, Identity, and Education, 19*(1), 42–55. doi:10.1080/15348458.2019.1672173

Loden, M., & Rosener, J. (1990). *Workforce America! Managing employee diversity as a vital resource*. McGraw-Hill Professional Publishing.

Lowe, R. J., & Kiczkowiak, M. (2016). Native-speakerism and the complexity of personal experience: A duoethnographic study. *Cogent Education, 3*(1), 2–16. doi:10.1080/2331186X.2016.1264171

Marinari, M., Hsu, M. Y., & Garcia, M. C. (Eds.). (2019). *A nation of immigrants reconsidered: US society in an age of restriction 1924–1965*. University of Illinois Press.

Martinez, A. Y. (2014a). A plea for critical race theory counterstory: Stock story versus counterstory dialogues concerning Alejandra's 'fit' in the academy. *Composition Studies, 42*(2), 33–55.

Martínez, A. Y. (2020b). Counterstory: The rhetoric and writing of critical race theory. *Conference on College Composition and Communication & the National Council of Teachers of English.*

Masuoka, N. (2018). *Multiracial identity and racial politics in the United States*. Oxford University Press.

Matsuda, P. K. (2013). It's the wild west out there: A new linguistic frontier in US college composition. *Literacy as Translingual Practice: Between Communities and Classrooms, 6*(2), 128-138.

McKibbin, M. L. (2014). The current state of multiracial discourse. *Journal of Critical Mixed Race Studies, 1*(1). Advance online publication. doi:10.5070/C811012861

Menchaca, M. (2008). The anti-miscegenation history of the American southwest, 1837 To 1970: Transforming racial ideology into law. *Cultural Dynamics, 20*(3), 279–318. doi:10.1177/0921374008096312

Mitchum, C., Hebbard, M., & Morris, J. Expanding instructional contexts: Why student backgrounds matter to online teaching and learning. In W. P. Banks & S. Spanger (Eds.), *English Studies Online: Programs, Practices, Possibilities* (pp. 232–257). Parlor Press.

Motha, S. (2014). *Race, Empire, and English Language Teaching*. Teacher College Press.

Motha, S., Jain, R., & Tecle, T. (2012). Translinguistic identity-as-pedagogy: Implications for language teacher education. *International Journal of Innovation in English Language Teaching, 1*(1), 13–28.

Moussu, L., & Llurda, E. (2008). Non-native English-speaking English language teachers: History and research. *Language Teaching, 41*(3), 315–348. doi:10.1017/S0261444808005028

Nagatomo, D. H. (2012). *Exploring Japanese university English teachers' professional identity*. Multilingual Matters. doi:10.21832/9781847696489

Omi, M., & Winant, H. (1994). *Racial formation in the United States from the 1960s to the 1990s* (2nd ed.). Routledge.

Paris, D., & Alim, H. S. (2017). *Culturally sustaining pedagogies: Teaching and learning for justice in a changing world*. Teacher College Press.

Park, G., Bogdan, S., Rosa, M., & Navarro, J. M. (Eds.). (2023). *Critical pedagogy in the language and writing classroom: Strategies, examples, activities from teacher-scholars*. Routledge. doi:10.4324/9781003357001

Parker, B. A. [Host] (2022, July 20). *Who belongs to the Cherokee nation?* Codeswitch. National Public Radio. Retrieved on August 1, 2023 from https://www.npr.org/transcripts/1110422542

Pascoe, P. (1996). Miscegenation law, court cases, and ideologies of "race" in twentieth-century America. *The Journal of American History*, *83*(1), 44–69. doi:10.2307/2945474

Pascoe, P. (2009). *What comes naturally: Miscegenation law and the making of race in America*. Oxford University Press. doi:10.1093/oso/9780195094633.001.0001

Patton, L. D., Renn, K. A., Guido, F. M., Quaye, J. S., & Evans, N. J. (2016). *Student Development in College: Theory, Research, and Practice* (3rd ed.). Jossey-Bass.

Prendergast, C. (1998). Race: The absent presence in composition studies. *College Composition and Communication*, *50*(1), 36–53. doi:10.2307/358351

"Preparing for the Oath". (n.d.). National Museum of American History (NMAH) and U.S. Citizenship and Immigration Services (USCIS).

Rockquemore, K. A., Brunsma, D. L., & Delgado, D. J. (2009). Racing to theory or retheorizing race? Understanding the struggle to build a multiracial identity theory. *The Journal of Social Issues*, *65*(1), 13–34. doi:10.1111/j.1540-4560.2008.01585.x

Rodríguez-García, D., Solana, M., Ortiz, A., & Ballestín, B. (2021). Blurring of colour lines? Ethnoracially mixed youth in Spain navigating identity. *Journal of Ethnic and Migration Studies*, *47*(4), 838–860. doi:10.1080/1369183X.2019.1654157

Rogers, R. (Ed.). (2004). *An introduction to critical discourse analysis in education*. Lawrence Erlbaum Associates. doi:10.4324/9781410609786

Root, M. (1992). Racially mixed people in America. *Sage (Atlanta, Ga.)*.

Rosa, J., & Flores, N. (2017). Unsettling language and race: Toward a raciolinguistic perspective. *Language in Society*, *46*(5), 621–647. doi:10.1017/S0047404517000562

Rosa, J., & Flores, N. (2021). Decolonization, language, and race in applied linguistics and social justice. *Applied Linguistics*, *42*(6), 1162–1167. doi:10.1093/applin/amab062

Rothenberg, P. S. (Ed.). (2016). *White privilege: Essential readings on the other side of racism* (5th ed.). Worth Publishers.

Rudolph, N., & Yazan, B. (2023). Foreword. In G. Park, S. Bogdan, M. Rosa, & J. Navarro (Eds.), *Critical pedagogy in the Language and writing classroom: Strategies, examples, activities from teacher-scholars*. Routledge.

Ruecker, T. (2011a). Challenging the native and nonnative English speaker hierarchy in ELT: New directions from race theory. *Critical Inquiry in Language Studies*, 8(4), 400–422. doi:10.1080/15427587.2011.615709

Ruecker, T., & Ives, L. (2015). White native English speakers needed: The rhetorical construction of privilege in online teacher recruitment spaces. *TESOL Quarterly*, 49(4), 733–756. doi:10.1002/tesq.195

Ruíz, V., & Sánchez Korrol, V. (2006). *Latinas in the United States a historical encyclopedia*. Indiana University Press.

Russell, C. (2006). *Racial and ethnic diversity: Asians, Blacks, Hispanics, Native Americans and Whites* (5th ed.). New Strategist Publications.

Santoro, N. (2009). Teaching in culturally diverse contexts: what knowledge about "self" and "others: do teachers need? *Journal of Education for Teaching*, 35(1), 33–45. doi:10.1080/02607470802587111

Shuck, G. (2006). Racializing the nonnative English speaker. *Journal of Language, Identity, and Education*, 5(4), 259–276. doi:10.120715327701jlie0504_1

Simon, P. (2017). The failure of the importation of ethno-racial statistics in Europe: Debates and controversies. *Ethnic and Racial Studies*, 40(13), 2326–2332. doi:10.1080/01419870.2017.1344278

Spickard, P. R. (1989). *Mixed blood: Intermarriage and ethnic identity in twentieth century America*. University of Wisconsin Press.

Törngren, S. O., Irastorza, N., & Rodríguez-García, D. (2021). Understanding multiethnic and multiracial experiences globally: Towards a conceptual framework of mixedness. *Journal of Ethnic and Migration Studies*, 47(4), 763–781. doi:10.1080/1369183X.2019.1654150

Trent, J. G. (2015). Towards a multifaceted, multidimensional framework for understanding teacher identity. In Y. L. Cheung & K. Park (Eds.), *Advances and current trends in language teacher identity research* (pp. 44–58). Routledge.

Tsai, A., Straka, B., & Gaither, S. (2021). Mixed-heritage individuals' encounters with raciolinguistic ideologies. *Journal of Multilingual and Multicultural Development*, 1-15. doi:10.1080/01434632.2021.1904964

U.S. Census Bureau. (2020). *Census illuminates racial and ethnic composition of the country*. Retrieved from https://www.census.gov/library/stories/2021/08/improved-race-ethnicity-measures-reveal-united-states-population-much-more-multiracial.html

Varghese, M., Morgan, M. B., Johnston, B., & Johnson, K. A. (2005). Theorizing language teacher identity: Three perspectives and beyond. *Journal of Language, Identity, and Education*, 4(1), 21–44. doi:10.120715327701jlie0401_2

Varghese, M. M., Motha, S., Trent, J., Park, G., & Reeves, J. (2016). Special-Topic Issue of TESOL Quarterly, Language teacher identity in multilingual education. *TESOL Quarterly*, 49(1), 219–220. doi:10.1002/tesq.221

Washington, S. L. (2011). *Hypodescent: A history of the crystallization of the one-drop rule in the United States, 1880–1940*. Princeton University ProQuest Dissertations Publishing. 3480237.

Weaver, H. N. (2009). The colonial context of violence on violence in the lives of Native American women. *Journal of Interpersonal Violence, 24*(9), 1552–1563. doi:10.1177/0886260508323665 PMID:18768738

Weber, D. J. (1992). *The Spanish Frontier in North America*. Yale University Press.

Yazan, B., & Rudolph, N. (Eds.). (2018). Criticality, teacher identity, and (in)equity in English language teaching. *Educational Linguistics, 35*. doi.org/10.1007/978-3-319-72920-6_1

KEY TERMS AND DEFINITIONS

Critical Discourse Analysis: An interdisciplinary approach concerned with the relationships of language, discourse, and power in the construction of and representation of the social world.

Hypodescent: Term used to categorize individuals with even a single trace of African ancestry as racially Black.

Miscegenation: Term used to refer to the blending or mixing of individuals from two or more different racial backgrounds.

Multiraciality: A term used to describe the racial composition or representation of descendants of individuals having parents or ancestors of different races.

Native-Nonnative Dichotomy: The non-objective, often-contested, yet dominant paradigm for distinguishing and making sense of language and language users.

Raciolinguistics: An interdisciplinary field of studies that looks at the ways the majoritized White culture has co-constructed language and race since the colonial era. As a methodology, raciolinguistics examines the intersection between language, race, and power in areas like politics and education.

Teacher Identity: The complex and constantly evolving process a teacher goes through to build, interpret, position, negotiate, and enact their beliefs, values, and multiple subjectivities in a manner consonant with the cultural expectations of the profession across space and time.

Chapter 8
Language, Identity, and Racism in Postsecondary Classrooms

Michael Olayinka Gbadegesin
https://orcid.org/0000-0001-5081-6188
Lead City University, Nigeria

Rachel Oluwafisayo Aluko
https://orcid.org/0000-0001-5395-1203
Lead City University, Nigeria

ABSTRACT

Language, identity, and racism are three concepts that define people's attitudes in all facets of relationship. The system of interrelatedness which exists among the three concepts of language, identity, and racism can therefore be said to be reflective. This study investigated elements of language used in foregrounding identity and racism in multiracial classroom settings. The study gathered data through a self-designed Google questionnaire of a mixed structure. Forty Nigerian graduate students studying in different parts of the world were selected for the research. The study shows that use of language to establish identity and racism is covert in postsecondary classrooms of the selected respondents; hence, expression of racism among learners is mostly done unconsciously and basically unintended.

INTRODUCTION

Language, identity, and racism are three concepts that define a person's attitude in different facets of their relationship. This relationship can be that of the intra-space of one's makeup. At other times, it is with other people in the physical environment. Over time, language has served as a medium through which people communicate what they consider to be their identities. It is also used to express racial prejudices which earmark the identity of *the Other*. Just as a mirror reflects images, language reflects who we are and how we see others. It helps us to create distinction for self as well as establishing desired distance for othering (Charles & Bellinger, 2020). Racism is thus established through *othering*. The system of interrelatedness which exists among the three concepts of language, identity, and racism can therefore be said to be reflective (Brenda et al., 2005). It is in this wise that manifestation of identity and racism are said to be discursive. Language is thus deployed as a tool for discriminatory discourse.

DOI: 10.4018/978-1-6684-9029-7.ch008

The study is projected as being one of the timely interventions of academic scholarship and research in sensitizing all stakeholders of education and diverse races on the global space of the need for a discrimination free learning environment. The study focuses on knowledge of use of language as a tool for promoting racism. It will serve as an insight into measures of linguistic and racial exclusivism among learners in multi-racial postsecondary classroom settings. It is believed that this will evoke a sense of linguistic empathy, mutual responsibility, and conscious resort to deploy a more inclusive language usage among multiracial learners. The study will also help policy makers tagged with the duty of catering for students from diverse racial backgrounds to formulate policies that will help preserve learners' racial diversity without the resultant effect of marginalization of any of the groups. This is integral to the futurity and achievement of sustainability of each race's uniqueness.

Study Objectives

1. The chapter intends to examine the interconnectivity of language and identity as elements of racism in postsecondary classroom.
2. This will be carried out through purposive investigation of elements of language used in foregrounding identity among learners, racism tendencies, and manifestations in classroom interaction.
3. The effects of racism on classroom interaction and collaboration will also be examined.

Research Questions

Guided by the enumerated study objectives, the chapter attempts to answer the following research questions in the course of data analysis:

1. What are the elements of language used in foregrounding interconnectivity of language and identity as elements of racism in postsecondary classroom?
2. What are the racial tendencies and manifestations in classroom interaction among learners in postsecondary classroom?
3. What are the effects of racism on classroom interaction and collaboration among learners in postsecondary classroom?

THEORETICAL FRAMEWORKS

Challenges posed by racism in relation to language use and identity formation is open to studies backed up by theories which give room to a sociolinguistic interrogation of human relationship in a biased system. Raciolinguistics and intersectionality are two of such theories which help in promoting the argument raised in this study. The study deploys raciolinguistic model of language theory with partial dependence on Kimberlé Crenshaw's intersectional theory (Crenshaw, 2017; Flores, 2019). The two theories become eminent in this work based on their abilities in theorizing the historical and contemporary co-naturalization of language and race. The theories also give the much-needed avenue to interrogate overlapping or intersecting social identities, particularly minority identities, related to systems and structures of domination and discrimination respectively.

Raciolinguistics

Flores and García (2019) are the proponents of raciolinguistic theory which is a materialist anti-racist approach to bilingual education. Flores (2019) directly posits that the theory is aimed at describing the co-constructing of language and race in ways that depict language practices of racialized communities as inherently deficient and in need of remediation in order for these communities to overcome their marginalized positions within the broader society. Based on his personal experience as a Latino, in his blog series titled "The Educational Linguist," Flores (2015) affirms that the raciolinguistic perspective of language education makes it impossible to discuss language without race and vice versa. He highlights two major agendas of the theory as, firstly, to examine the co-construction of language and race or the ways that both language and race are inextricably interrelated with one another; secondly, to examine the complex role that language ideologies play in the production of racial differences and the role of racialization in the production of linguistic differences.

Different studies have explored the application of the theory to establish these two early mentioned objectives. Sekaja (2022) carried out a study on raciolinguistic ideologies in the South African higher educational system. Through the study, she tried to examine if racialized individuals are stigmatized as "language deficient" (Sekaja, 2022). She also tried to find out if this group of people had fewer opportunities for inclusion and upward social mobility due to their lower proficiency in the use of "standard" English. The inclusion criteria for her study's population were stated—participants had to be academics of color, using English in their day-to-day academic activities, and working with White academics and/or students. The findings corroborate the concept of raciolinguistics to show that non-White or colored South Africans are denied promotions due to the factor of their inabilities to speak the dominant language fluently. They are also denied access to socioeconomic-related services such as schooling and employment opportunities in South African multiracial settings.

Intersectionality

The second linguistic theory to be deployed is intersectionality (Crenshaw, 2014). Though it was proposed by the black feminist writer—Crenshaw (2014) as a theoretical orientation in women and gender studies, Kelly et al. (2021, p.11) observes that the theory has grown beyond feminist concerns among the Black race to embrace concerns in other areas of human existence. In present use, the theory borders on questions of identity, such as gender, race, sexuality, and the likes with focuses on how they overlap, intersect, and reflect macro-level forms of oppression and privilege, such as sexism, racism, and heteronormativity. The theory here aligns with this study through the study's adaptation of Hankivsky's (2014) definition of intersectionality as a methodology, paradigm, lens, or framework which promotes an understanding of human beings as shaped by the interaction of different social locations such as race/ethnicity to establish interdependent forms of privilege and oppression shaped by racism. In essence, both raciolinguistic and intersectional theories provide the required avenue to understand the interplay of language and race within the historical production of hegemony and the ways colonial distinctions within and between national borders continue to shape contemporary linguistic and racial formations (Adewunmi, 2014; Kelly, et al. 2021). This establishes the relevance of the theories to the stated objectives of this study.

LANGUAGE AND IDENTITY

Besides serving as a means of communication, language plays multiple roles. One of these crucial roles is its ability to operate as an identity marker. The relationship between language and identity is completely intertwined. While language is crucial for interpersonal relations, identity in its multifarious forms is established through language. In other words, language and identity are integral to the continual existence of people's diversity and uniqueness. To this end, Byram (2006) asserts that language is a means of expressing and recognizing the different social identities that a person has (p. 6).

By law of evolution, the first social group that a child identifies with is the family. It is from there that the child learns to speak the shared language of the family. This becomes possible as a result of the child's constant exposure and instinctive practice of older members' styles and use of language. The existence of language, as an identity marker, therefore, takes its course from when a person is born into a family. For newborns, parental diversity, in terms of background, upbringing, and the likes, is infused into a uniquely singular identity inclusive of maternal and paternal identities. In most cases, the child unconsciously imbibes his/her parental identities as one and often expresses it in a language which becomes peculiar to the immediate family rather than two different family backgrounds of each of the parents. Every family can as such be rightly described as a language and identity laboratory. It births not just the individual, but the language and dominant identity. From this point, language learners and users can adopt their learnt language(s) as a measure of acquiring social identity with a sense of belonging to an ethnic region, race, or other social groups.

In the light of this, existing research has established that a group's native language spoken by an individual is likely to be the strongest social identity (Alshammari, 2018). In the larger world, people succumb to the use of language varieties or what is known as registers (Agha & Frog, 2015) (that is the deliberate use of language in ways peculiar to a social group with which one chooses to show one's affiliation) as a means of identification. This explains the strong link between language and identity. The choice in the use of one language out of the different languages people speak as either bilingual or multilingual can therefore serve as a means to identify with one of the social groups they share similar identities with. Sapir (1921) corroborates the link between identity and language by stating that people of the same race which are set off by physical characteristics from other groups are bound by their use of the same language. He notes further that the strong link human identity shares with language is a major factor why anthropologists have been in the habit of studying people under the three rubrics of race, language, and culture. Conflicts can also arise from the connection between language, race, and identity. This is a common world phenomenon in places where people operate with the mindset of creating identity which is a form of othering. Language, in such situations, occasionally serves as an instrument of oppression which dominant groups utilize to isolate and marginalize minority populations. For instance, English has long been used in Western states like the US to marginalize immigrant communities who do not speak it (Sapir, 1921).

It is through identity that individuals show a sense of belonging to any social group. Cahyono et al. (2021) observes that every individual is prone to acquiring new identities which invariably demand the acquisition and use of new languages or language varieties as a life-time process. This makes language use and identity significantly dynamic and evolving in relation to time and human development. Language, therefore, continues to play the role of identity marker for all its ability to connect other individuals with an ethnic or racial group, a professional body, a religious sect, and all other communities of social relations. Over time, the total sum of language varieties a person uses is significant of all the social groups the person belongs to. This strongly applies to racial groups which are the largest and most influential sect of all social sects. This connection can be easily identified in classroom settings among learners. Learners who speak the same language are prone to bond easily than those of diverse linguistic communities (Cahyono, 2021).

Vignoles (2017) interrogates the personal and social dimensions of identity. According to her, these two dimensions provide insight into the relationship between the individual and the larger society respectively. While personal identity is situated in what she calls the "intra-psychic makeup" (Vignoles, 2017) of each individual, social identity is built through interpersonal relations and acceptance. In relation to other studies on the subject matter, she agrees that the major features of identity are broad, multifaceted, fluid, and interconnected. She is also of the opinion that identity is formed and it changes gradually due to its fluid nature. The classroom is notably one of the social structures that contribute to the fluid nature of identity formation. Its function, as a place to instill knowledge and probably assist learners in understanding human uniqueness, often leads to transformation of ideas in areas of personal bias. Vignoles (2017), however, objects to the personal-social dichotomy popularly associated with its distinctive types. Though Vignoles' input to the discussion is premised on the personal and social construct of identity formation, she nevertheless did not do justice to other seemingly existing dichotomies either through giving a clear focus on them or provide more explanation on how they constitute types of identity. Her concern is for future research to do better justice in stating and explaining how these untouched dichotomies add up to types of identity constructs.

Hernández and Darling-Hammond (2022) identify practices that create trusting relationships and interpersonal connection between educators and students as central to cultivating identity safety in classroom settings. Through their study, they seek to promote how practitioners can build inclusive and affirming school environments with keen attention to identity safety. Their findings show that the way students are treated in school and society can trigger or ameliorate social identity threats. They posit that "in cases where social identity threat is triggered, the fight-or-flight response occurs as a result of the sense of threat which is activated, thus leading to challenging behavior for all" (p. 1). This underscores the connectivity between language use to build identity in classroom settings. Both instructors and learners are put on hedge when the fight-or-flight response is manifested in whatever form.

Hernández and Darling-Hammond's (2022) study further shows that the "direct implication of this challenging behavior is that many young people may come to view schools as unsafe spaces" (p. 3). Lasting solutions can be proffered when authorities embrace practices that allow educators and students to identify what they have in common. This helps to build empathy in the duo's relationships and, in turn, affects student achievement positively (p. 4). The study concludes that the antidote to stereotype threat is identity safety. This includes intentionally bringing students' voices and experiences into the classroom as well as deploying strategies that convey respect, care, and concern for students. These steps help students to know that educators care about and believe in them and their futures; hence, they respond with motivation, effort, and accomplishment (p. 12).

Vionny Vransisca (2022) also opines that "formation of self-identity in adolescence ultimately directs behavior and attitudes towards the environment; influencing their world view and making choices about alternatives that arise" (p. 1). Her study addresses identity formation among students and how this close-group syndrome is likely to affect academic achievement. From the findings of the study, she notes that "availability of social support, however, makes individuals feel loved, valued and have a general sense of being part of the group" (p. 5). She concludes that there is a significant relationship with a positive direction between peer social support and self-identity in adolescents based on the study conducted on teenagers in the selected school (p. 7).

Other existing studies show that questions of identity concern individual's definition of self in relation to their environment. Tantum (2016) devises a notable means for understanding personal identity. He simply asks his students to complete the sentence "I am ____," using as many descriptions as they can think of in 60 seconds. His observation in mixed race classrooms is that students of color usually mention their race or ethnic group while White students are more prone to give trait descriptive words, such as "friendly," "shy," "honest," and the likes. It is only White students whom he described as having grown up in strong ethnic enclaves that occasionally give self-descriptions of being Irish or Italian. He implies through the study that members of dominant or advantaged social groups rarely make reference to their social categories in their descriptions of the self. This, according to Tantum, is because the dominant group consciously or subconsciously set parameters within which others operate in any given environment. The classrooms are notably a part of this environment.

Through the study, Tantum (2016) is able to establish that the parts of our identity that captures our attention are the ones people notice and reflect back to us in their descriptions of us. This subsequently triggers our consciousness (of who we are) and invariably becomes our key definition of self. In the light of this, it can be deduced that what sets us apart from others gains more attention in our psychical makeup than what makes us alike. It is however unfortunate that the classroom setting happens to be one of the social structures that earmarks the differences in student and instructor identities. As a result of this, even people within the myriads of mixed-race academic institutions across the globe are more conscious of their points of differences and less bothered about the areas of unity.

RACISM

Racism is a social phenomenon which emanates from people's consciousness of their differences in color and language spoken. Clarke (2023) projects racism as systemic injustice that affects the lives of Black people and all people of color in countless ways. This systemic injustice often takes place in the form of police brutality, racial profiling, microaggressions, or even imposter syndrome. From time immemorial, Black people have been subjected to Western oppression. Grills et al., (2016) affirm that "although the enslavement of Black people in the United States ended nearly a century and a half ago, the attitudes and behaviors that promoted and supported it remain a part of the cultural ethos of this country and the world" (p. 340). The deaths of Eric Garner in New York in 2014 and George Floyd on 25 May 2020 are attributed to racism. Apata (2020) attests that "the death of Floyd provoked unprecedented protest marches around the world and reinvigorated the Black Lives Matter" (p. 241).

Language also remains as one of the vital weapons of White oppression and discrimination against Blacks as Apata (2020) has stated, "For black people racism is not an illusion or indeed a delusion but the reality of lived experience" (p. 249). The constant reference to Black people having accent is a typical measure used by Whites to send the discriminatory message against Black people home. In heterogeneous African nations, however, people's accent is a signifier of ethnicity; hence, it showcases people's diverse ethnic identities. The racist bias of describing Africans as people that speak with accents however remains unjustified. Instead, it earmarks racism as being steep in Western ideology (Grills et al., 2016).

Much of existing research on racism has proven that the tendency to promote one's race in this manner is either deliberate or instinctive. Feagin et al. (2000) identify racism as "the subordination of individuals or groups based on a common characteristic" (p. 96). As discussed earlier, the difference in color and language are integral to this common characteristic. Racism is thus a form of emotive response to identify with other members of one's race. Omi and Winant (2015) define race as a socially constructed identity situated in social structure. As already discussed, all these social structures gain recognition through language use, hence the concept of language and identity.

An interesting illustration of the interplay between language, identity, and race is well captured in the experience Nelson Flores (2015) shares in one of his blog series "The Educational Linguist." Having rushed through a paper presentation due to time constraint, a White audience member connected his rushed-over presentation with his background and asked him why all Latin-Americans spoke with a rush. In other circumstances where the speaker is White, there is a strong possibility that the White audience might have excused the rush as an event related to any of the time factor, the presenter's emotive disposition, or the personal trait among others, but will certainly not identify the experienced behavior as being representative of all White people. The overall effect is that both the listener and the speaker's racial differences have been brought to play through the use of language in the encounter of each other to establish racial discrimination/racism within an academic setting. The interconnectivity of language, identity, and race is well foregrounded in this illustration to clearly show that language and race are measures of identity (Flores, 2015).

Othering, as a racist tendency, is established through the use of language, so people are identified with particular races based on the language they speak and/or how others believe that they should speak. Other instances of this connectivity are seen through the deliberate change in use of language which is popularly referred to as code-switching. Code-switching does take place when the speaker chooses one language over another, thus providing an immediate and universally recognized badge of identity with one's race on the one hand and a natural barrier with those of other races on the other hand. Language, when used as a tool for promoting racism, gives rise to what is generally known as "discriminatory discourse" (Wodak, 2015, p. 367).

DISCRIMINATORY DISCOURSE IN MULTIRACIAL CLASSROOM SETTINGS

Discriminatory discourse in a multiracial classroom setting is one of the ways by which racism is demonstrated with regards to language use. Wodak (2015) opines that discriminatory discourse is a complex phenomenon of discrimination such as racism, either in its occurrence as a social practice and/or as an ideology which manifests itself discursively. Racism, as a social construct, is produced, reproduced, practiced, prepared, implemented, justified, and legitimized by means of discourse. It is unarguably rhetoric which Bellinger (2020) identifies as language use supporting acts of othering at the horizontal/societal level of human operation to generate racial violence. Discriminatory discourse in the multiracial classroom setting refers to the use of language, speech, or communication that perpetuates or reinforces racial discrimination, prejudice, and unequal treatment of individuals or groups based on their racial or ethnic backgrounds. It involves expressing biased views through verbal or written communication, often aiming to demean, stereotype, or marginalize certain racial or ethnic groups.

Discriminatory discourse in a multiracial classroom setting happens in different ways such as *negative stereotyping*, *micro-aggressions,* and *scapegoating*. All these are racist strategies at *Othering*—the potential to portray certain racial or ethnic groups as being different from expected norm, emphasizing their separateness and reinforcing racism within any human space of operation. Bellinger (2020) raises arguments on the act of othering as a sin rather than a way of foregrounding racial and linguistic differences.

Discriminatory discourse can take the form of the use of negative stereotypes to generalize and make derogatory assumptions about entire racial or ethnic groups. Voci (2014) defines negative stereotypes as characteristics which are negative and attributed to a social group as well as its individual members. These stereotypes often perpetuate harmful misconceptions and reinforce biased perspectives in classroom settings. It entails using language in a way that dehumanizes or objectifies individuals based on their race discriminatorily during classroom discourses. Such language reduces people to inferior or subhuman status, making it easier to justify mistreatment or unequal treatment.

Micro-aggressions are other means of demonstrating discriminatory discourse in multiracial classroom settings. According to Sue et al (2007) "micro-aggressions are brief, everyday exchanges that send denigrating messages to people of color because they belong to a racial minority group" (p. 273). As an everyday exchange, it has assumed the state of a subtle, often unintended expression of bias that communicates derogatory messages based on race. These can include comments, jokes, behaviors, or action/inaction that provoke racism.

Racial slurs are also one of the discriminatory discourses in multiracial classroom settings. The use of racial slurs, derogatory terms, or offensive language that targets a particular racial or ethnic group is a clear example of discriminatory discourse related to micro-aggressions. Racial slurs, derogatory terms, or offensive language are intended to demean and insult people of color either directly or indirectly. In the multiracial classroom situation, scapegoating is another discriminatory discourse. It involves blaming specific racial or ethnic groups for broader societal issues or problems. This deflects responsibility away from underlying structural and systemic factors.

METHODOLOGY

All the 40 respondents were Nigerians studying in seven different countries of the world other than their home country—Cote d'Ivoire, Canada, Sweden, Turkey, UK, Malaysia, and the USA, spread across five continents–Asia, Europe, North America, Africa, and Oceanic. 60% of them were female while 40%

Table 1. Background information of respondents

Gender	Male (40%)	Female (60%)					
Continent of study	Africa	Asia	Oceanic	Europe	North America		
Country of study	Cote d'ivoire	Malaysia	UK	USA	Turkey	Sweden	Canada
Number of Races in Class	1 (5%)	2 (12%)	3 (20%)	4 (12%)	5 (3%)	More (48%)	
Religion	Christianity (72%)	Islam (15%)	Others (12%)				
Level of Study	Graduate (100%)	Undergraduate Nil	Others Nil				
Language spoken	Yoruba and English (65%)	Igbo and English (20%)	Hausa and English (10%)	English only (5%)			

were male; they are all graduate students in different fields of studies. The majority of them are Christians (72%), 15% practice Islam while 12% practice other religions. The languages vary depending on their tribes where they grew up as well as their course of study. However, 65% of them speak Yoruba and English, 20% speak Igbo and English; 10% speak Hausa and English while 5% speak English only.

Data Collection and Analysis

The study is a descriptive survey that employed a self-designed questionnaire to elicit responses from Nigerian students studying abroad. The study interrogated their racialized experiences in different postsecondary classroom settings. This was done to seek information about intersectionality and raciolinguistic interpretation of the interplay between the preconceived opinions of the members of their host academic communities and their personal ideologies. The research is quantitative in its bid to identify patterns of racism, rate of occurrence, and the likes to generate statistical results by using the questionnaire that is partly close-ended and multiple-choice in its structure.

The study gathered data through primary and secondary sources. Primary source is a self-designed Google questionnaire of mixed structure while secondary source are books, journals articles and relevant online materials. 40 Nigerian students were purposively selected for the research. Besides the participants' Nigerian nationality, the criteria for eligibility also include having postsecondary education in any other continents besides Africa. The electronic questionnaire with 25 closed and four open-ended questions was sent to the target group to fill and submit online. Our collected data was subjected to graphical and descriptive analysis of the closed and open-ended questions respectively. The result is presented in tables and charts. This study drew inference from the statistics and compared them with existing literature.

FINDINGS

Figure 1 shows that 48% of the respondents have more than five different races in their respective classrooms. In all, about 80% of the respondents have three or more different races in their classrooms. This makes such classroom settings potential places to explore racial experiences.

Figure 1.

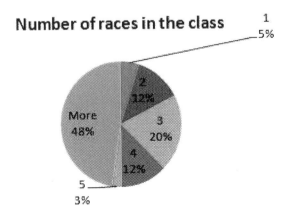

Figure 2 below shows that with the official language of the institution being the dominant language of the learners during their studies, the language of the immediate environment of their study area was not given preference. This might invariably be a major factor for the mild experiences of racism reported by respondents.

Figure 2.

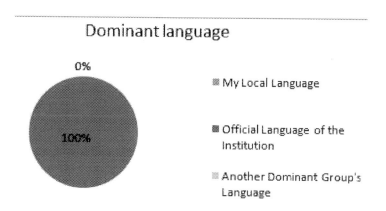

Figure 3.

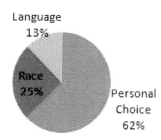

Figure 4 reveals that friendship and relationship beyond classroom setting is largely defined by personal choice (62%) though race (25%) and language (13%) accounts for about 38% of the outside classroom relationships. Therefore, it is difficult to assume that the attestation to one's personal choice as a basis for friendship and relationship beyond the classroom setting is consciously influenced by one's race and language. As such, the role of race and language cannot be overlooked.

RESEARCH QUESTION 1: WHAT ARE THE ELEMENTS OF LANGUAGE USED IN FOREGROUNDING IDENTITY AMONG LEARNERS?

Table 2 reveals that though possibilities of racism exist in multiracial classroom settings, they are not guaranteed to occur in every foreign educational setting. Many universities and educational institutions

Table 2. Elements of language used in foregrounding identity among learners

S/NO	Item/Token	Yes FRQ	Yes %	No FRQ	No %	Undecided FRQ	Undecided %
1	Students from other races are usually discriminated against.	3	7.5	37	92.5	-	-
2	I have been discriminated against by my lecturers.	6	15	32	80	2	5
3	I have been discriminated against by my colleagues.	12	30	28	70	-	-
4	I have been discriminated against by non-teaching staff.	8	20	32	80	-	-
5	I am discriminated against because of my accent.	8	20	32	80	-	-
6	I am discriminated against because of my color.	16	40	24	60	-	-
7	Does language use reveal emotional attachment to racial groups in class situations?	25	62.5	9	22.5	6	15
8	Language plays significant role in deliberate construction of racial identity among learners of the same race.	23	57.5	6	15	11	27.5

are actively working to promote diversity, equity, and inclusivity to create more welcoming and respectful environments for all students, regardless of their backgrounds. The respondents disagreed with major discrimination against students from different races. However, about 15% of the respondents affirmed that they have been discriminated against at one time or the other. The discrimination was largely from their colleagues, followed by non-teaching staff and a few lecturers. Color was the top reason for discrimination against learners in the multiracial classroom setting, followed by the learners' accents.

Table 2 also shows that among the elements of racism in a multiethnic classroom, the emotional attachment is revealed with the way language is used. Most of our respondents (62.5%) agreed that language use in the classroom situation revealed one's emotional attachments to racial groups

It is therefore established that language plays a significant role in deliberate construction of racial identity among learners. Language use—code switching, overlapping which is deliberate interruption of a speaker which is related to racial bias, and vocabulary are elements of language used in foregrounding identity among learners.

RESEARCH QUESTION 2: WHAT ARE THE RACIAL TENDENCIES AND MANIFESTATIONS IN CLASSROOM INTERACTION?

In Figure 4, from the sampled Nigerian graduate students learning in other countries of the world and among other races, it is found that interconnectedness between different races and languages use is low. Learners are easily connected to people of the same race and possibly the same language.

As Figure 5 indicated, class activities and collaboration may be determined by gender, language, race, and official operations. Among these factors, gender has the least effect on class operation and activities with only 2%. This is followed by language with 10%. It is observed that race exerts a mild influence on class activities and collaborations with 20%. The highest determinant of classroom activities and collaboration is official operation with 68%. Learners give preference to official operation during their activities and collaboration than any other factors.

Figure 4.

Figure 5.

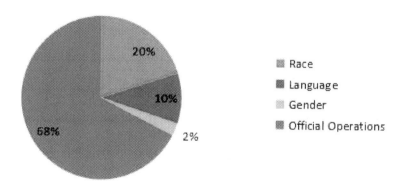

Figure 6.

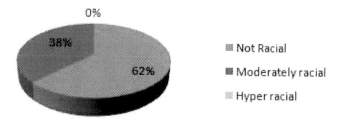

In Figure 6, the majority of the learners perceived that language use in their respective classrooms was not racial. About 62% of the learners attested to this while 38% learners perceived that there was stylishly moderate racial undertone in the use of language in multiracial classrooms. The perceptions of the learners about the racial manifestation in language use were not overt but covert.

Figure 7.

Figure 7 shows that language was used among different learners from different races basically for the exclusion purpose. About 67% of the learners described the use of language among different races in the class as a tool for exclusion.

Figure 8.

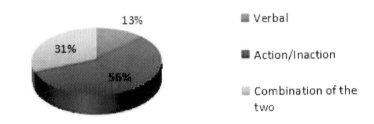

Figure 8 reveals that racism was shown more in action and or inaction (56%) rather than verbal (13%); at times, it is revealed in the combination of verbal and actions/inactions (31%). This epitomizes a dimension of unconscious demonstration of racism in class.

Racial tendencies manifested in classroom interaction through low interaction among different races. It was manifested through offensive utterances and through combination of verbal and actions/inactions.

RESEARCH QUESTION 3: WHAT ARE THE EFFECTS OF RACISM ON CLASSROOM INTERACTION AND COLLABORATION AMONG LEARNERS IN POSTSECONDARY CLASSROOM?

In interrogating the use of discriminatory discourse which is practiced through language deployment, such as language switch, borrowed expressions, communication overlap/deliberate interruption, use of discriminatory discourse, and code-switching among others, the study shows that 35% of the respondents (Nigerian graduate students in Diaspora) unconsciously resorted to language switch, and another

Language, Identity, and Racism in Postsecondary Classrooms

Table 3. Racial tendencies and manifestation in classroom interaction

	Item	Very Often		Seldom		Never	
		FRQ	%	FRQ	%	FRQ	%
1	How often do learners unconsciously resort to language-switch thus creating communication gap during interracial communication?	14	35	15	37.5	11	27.5
2	How often do learners borrow expressions from others' languages to foster interracial acceptance and goodwill in class situations?	9	22.5	21	52.5	10	25
3	How often does individual's race create communication overlap in different classroom situations?	8	20	24	60	8	20
4	How often does discriminatory discourse take place in teaching-learning situations?	13	32.5	15	37.5	12	30
5	How often does discriminatory discourse degenerate into violent or near-violent outbursts during your course?	2	5	9	22.5	29	72.5
6	How often is language deliberately used to promote racial bias?	8	20	20	50	12	30
7	How often does race shape language choice among learners?	22	55	12	30	6	15
8	How often do learners code-switch in class?	10	25	18	45	12	30

37.5% rarely unconsciously sought language-switch while 27.5% never did it. 22.5% of the respondents deployed the use of loanwords and 25% never engaged in it while 52.5% rarely did it. The number of those who did it was low, probably because there was no need. 60% of the respondents believed that individual race seldom created communication overlap in classroom situations. This is followed by 20% of the respondents that observed individual race created communication overlap in classroom situations while 20% perceived that it had never happened in their classrooms. 32.5% respondents alluded to the fact that discriminatory discourses were very likely to take place in teaching-learning situations. 37.5% of the respondents hold that discriminatory discourse seldom occurred while 30% admitted that it never happened in their classes.

Discriminatory discourses that engender violent or near-violent outbursts during course of study in the foreign land is not a common phenomenon as 72.5% attested to the fact that it had never happened. About 22.5% of the respondents believed that it rarely happened while only 5% reported that it was a frequent experience. 50% of the respondents indicated that language was occasionally deliberately used to promote racial bias in the classroom. 30% commented that language had never been deliberately used to promote racial bias while 20% agreed that language was very often deliberately used to promote racial bias. 55% of the respondents believed that their racial affiliation had shaped language choice among learners most of the time. Another 30% believed that occasionally, racial affiliation shaped language choice among learners while only 15% said it never shaped language choice among learners. 70% of the respondents attested to learners' use of code-switching in the classroom; 25.5% said it happened very often while 45% said it happened occasionally. By comparison, 30% stated that it never happened in their classes. The result shows that 45% of the learners rarely code switched in their classrooms and 30% never did so while 25% did codeswitch.

DISCUSSION AND CONCLUSION

Consequently, from the analysis of data, it can be established that one of the reasons for expression of racism through language in multiracial classrooms is cultural identity and affiliation. Discriminatory discourse in the multiracial classroom settings of the respondents is one of the ways by which racism is demonstrated with regards to language use. The overlapping or intersecting cultural identities pinpointed in raciolinguistics is observed in the findings and demonstrated among the learners through code-switching. Another reason displayed in the collected data is inclusion and exclusion. Code-switching can be used as a way to include or exclude certain individuals from a conversation. Switching to a language not understood by everyone can create a sense of exclusion. The learners' attestation to elements of code-switching has implications for how language is used as a tool for expressing racism in postsecondary classroom settings. When learners code switch in a multiracial classroom setting, the minority races represented by the respondents allude to the fact that it signals a sense of discrimination and creates in them the sense of exclusion.

In essence, the study has investigated how racism plays out in multiracial classroom settings through language use and identity expression. This confirms Flores' (2015) assertion that the raciolinguistic perspective of language education makes it impossible to discuss language without race and vice versa. Although, there are no direct and deliberate attempts of racial discrimination among the learners, mild, and unconscious manifestations of racism are observed through language used during learners' interactions and collaboration. The use of discriminatory discourses of different kinds was demonstrated and this of course has a negative influence on learning. Though many of the respondents are hold the opinion that racism is not overtly demonstrated in language usage of members of the dominant/host communities of their study environments, it can however be deduced from the collected data that racism is still rife within the academic system for students studying in foreign nations, such as the U.K., USA, Canada, Turkey, and Sweden.

Furthermore, low interconnectedness among learners of different races in the multi-racial classrooms (see Figure 5) indicates the presence of racism. Low or lack of interaction and interconnectedness between different racial groups can sometimes be a sign of indirect racial bias or divisions, showing that learners are unconsciously biased. Though unconscious bias is not overt racism, but it can affect how individuals perceive others and interact with others. This might also lead to unintentional favoring of certain groups though it is not demonstrated as explicit or intentional racism.

To sum up, effective classroom interaction in all racial settings requires commitment to equity, inclusion, and respect for all students. The averagely low level of interconnection between race and language use which is slated at 50% with the 68% non-racial perception of language use in class as seen in the study are evident of some forms of intervention by educators to curb racism. Educators can further help to create a more just and equitable society for all by fostering open communication, celebrating diversity, and addressing issues of systemic bias and discrimination. Addressing the root causes of racial discrimination is crucial to reducing its prevalence in society. Data from the study shows that there is still a great need for fostering cultural empathy and understanding among learners in multiracial classroom settings. This study will also prove a more holistic way of curbing racism rather than diplomatic silencing with its covert undertone for practicing racism.

Limitations of the Study

The study is limited in a few ways, such as the potential bias of respondents in the survey responses. The research questions gave room for self-identification which might be prone to generate biased opinions that could not be verified in the survey responses. Secondly, the number of subjects in terms of the 40 Nigerian students and the coverage area used in the study were limited. Lastly, the factor of time constraint which did not give room for better exploration of research focus could not be here overruled.

Implications

The study focuses on addressing some factors that are considered to be the root cause of racism in multiracial classroom setting as an addition to ongoing research in education and humanities. It has implications for self-awareness with a sense of embracing objective worldviews and for Black communities to form their study groups in foreign learning environments. Foreign institutions that are open to giving admission to students of other races, especially Blacks, may also find the study useful. This is because school curricula of many institutions admitting foreign students too often fail to reflect on the diversity of contemporary global society. This world system of cross-learning has created multi-tribal classroom settings. Classroom interaction in a multi-tribal setting can be complex and nuanced. It is therefore important for educators, policy makers, and stakeholders in the academia to be aware of the negative effects of the untamed racial bias in classroom interaction.

Recommendations

The study recommends that more research still needs to be carried out on the interconnectedness of language, race and identity. The study population and area of coverage need to be expanded to authenticate the conclusions made in this research. It is also recommended that stakeholders across the world come together to create a body of policy makers that are assigned to carry out thorough investigations on the interconnectivity of language and identity as elements of racism in postsecondary classrooms. The effects of racism on classroom interactions and collaboration should also be given more attention to foster better collaborative activities among learners of different races in every postsecondary classroom setting.

REFERENCES

Adewunmi, B. (2014). Kimberlé Crenshaw on intersectionality: 'I wanted to come up with an everyday metaphor that anyone could use'. *New Statesman*. https://www.newstatesman.com/politics/welfare/2014/kimberl-crenshaw-intersectionality-i-wanted-come-everyday-metaphor-anyone-could

Agha, A., & Frog, S. (Eds.). (2015). *Registers of communication*. Finish Literature Society. doi:10.21435flin.18

Alshammari, S. H. (2018). The relationship between language, identity and cultural differences: A critical review. *Research on Humanities and Social Sciences*, *4*(8), 98–101.

Apata, G. O. (2020). 'I can't breathe': The suffocating nature of racism. *Theory, Culture & Society*, *37*(7-8), 241–254. doi:10.1177/0263276420957718

Byram, M. (2006). *Languages and identities*. Language Policy Division.

Cahyono, H., Bahri, S., Salim, A., Eka, N. M., Fauzi, R., Bayu, J. T., & Purwanti, S. (2021). Language as national identity. *Advances in Social Science, Education and Humanities Research*, *584*, 782–785. doi:10.2991/assehr.k.211102.104

Charles, K., & Bellinger, C. K. (2020). *Othering: The original sin of humanity*. Cascade Books.

Clarke, Z. (2023). *Black people breathe: a mindfulness guide to racial healing*. Ten Speed Press.

Crenshaw, K. W. (2017). *On intersectionality: Essential writings*. The New Press.

Feagin, J., Johnson, J., & Rush, S. (2000). Doing anti-racism toward an egalitarian American society. *Contemporary Sociology*, *29*(1), 95–100. doi:10.2307/2654935

Flores, N. L. (2015). Examining language and race in education: Why we need a raciolinguistic perspective. *The Educational Linguist*. https://educationallinguist.wordpress.com/

Flores, N. L. (2019). Translanguaging into raciolinguistic ideologies: A personal reflection on the legacy of Ofelia García. *Journal of Multilingual Education Research*, *9*(5), 45–60. https://fordham.bepress.com/jmer/vol9/iss1/5

Grills, C. N., Aird, E. G., & Rowe, D. (2016). Breathe, baby, breathe: clearing the way for the emotional emancipation of Black people. *Cultural Studies*, *16*(3), 333–343. doi:10.1177/1532708616634839

Hankivsky, O. (2014). *Intersectionality 101*. The Institute for Intersectionality Research & Policy.

Hernández, L. E., & Darling-Hammond, L. (2022). *Creating identity-safe schools and classrooms*. Learning Policy Institute. doi:10.54300/165.102

Kelly, C., Kasperavicius, D., Duncan, D., Etherington, C., Giangregorio, L., Presseau, J., Sibley, K. M., & Straus, S. (2021). "Doing" or "using" intersectionality? Opportunities and challenges in incorporating intersectionality into knowledge translation theory and practice. *International Journal for Equity in Health*, *20*(187), 187. Advance online publication. doi:10.118612939-021-01509-z PMID:34419053

Omi, M., & Winant, H. (2015). *Racial formation in the United States*. Routledge.

Perera, S. B. (1986). *Scapegoat complex: Toward a mythology of shadow and guilt*. Inner City Books.

Rosa, J., & Flores, N. (2017). Unsettling race and language: Toward a raciolinguistic perspective. *Language in Society*, *46*(5), 621–647. doi:10.1017/S0047404517000562

Sapir, E. (1921). Language, race and culture. In E. Sapir (Ed.), *Language: An introduction to the study of speech* (pp. 207–220). Harcourt, Brace & World.

Sekaja, L., Byron, G. A., & Kutlay, Y. (2022). Raciolinguistic ideologies as experienced by racialized academics in South Africa. *International Journal of Educational Research*, *116*(102092), 102092. Advance online publication. doi:10.1016/j.ijer.2022.102092

Sue, D. W., Capodilupo, C. M., Torino, G. C., Bucceri, J. M., Holder, A. M. B., Nadal, K. L., & Esquilin, M. (2007). Racial microaggressions in everyday life: Implications for clinical practice. *The American Psychologist*, *62*(4), 271–286. doi:10.1037/0003-066X.62.4.271 PMID:17516773

Tatum, B. D. (2016). *The complexity of identity: "Who am I?"* Unitarian Univesalist College of Social Justice. https://uucsj.org/wp-content/uploads/2016/05/The-Complexity-of-identity.pdf

Vignoles, V. L. (2017). *Identity: Personal and social.* https://www.researchgate.net/publication/316790231_Identity_Personal_AND_Social#:~:text=Identity%20refers%20to%20how%20people,to%20others%20or%20to%20oneself

Vionny, V. (2022). The relationship between peer social support and self-identity in adolescents at the SMAK Penabur Harapan Indah. *European Journal of Psychological Research, 9*(3).

Voci, A. (2014). Negative Stereotypes. In A. C. Michalos (Ed.), *Encyclopedia of quality of life and well-being research.* Springer. doi:10.1007/978-94-007-0753-5_1926

Wodak, R. (2015). Discrimination via discourse. In N. Bonvillain (Ed.), *The Routledge Handbook of Linguistic Anthropology* (pp. 366–383). Routledge. https://www.routledgehandbooks.com/doi/10.4324/9780203492741.ch24

KEY TERMS AND DEFINITIONS

Classroom Interactions: Relationship among class members expressed through verbal communication.

Discriminatory Discourse: Creating a sense of otherness through language use in multiracial classroom setting.

Identity: Group that students within a multiracial classroom setting chooses to identify with based on shared language.

Interracial Classroom: Segment of learning environment comprising of learners from multiple race/racial groups.

Language: Medium of verbal communication which differs among learners in multi-racial classroom settings.

Othering: Discriminatory bias or prejudice established through use of language among learners in multiracial classroom setting.

Racism: Discriminatory acts among learners in multiracial classroom setting based on shared language and ethnic background.

APPENDIX

Questionnaire: Section A

Background Information

Country of Study
Continent of Study
Gender
Religion
Language (s)
What is your Level of study?
Number of different races present in your class.
Dominant language used by you during the course of study.

Elements of Language Used in Foregrounding Identity Among Learners

How often do learners code-switch in class?
Friend ties and relationships beyond class setting is largely defined by …
How often does race shape language choice among learners?
Does language use reveal emotional attachment to racial groups in class situation?
How often does discriminatory discourse take place in teaching-learning situation?
Your perception of language usage in class shows that teaching-learning activity is …
Observed dominant language used by all students during the course of study.

Racial Tendencies and Manifestation in Classroom Interaction

Students from other races are usually discriminated against.
I have been discriminated against by my lecturers.
I have been discriminated against by non-teaching staff.
I am discriminated against because of my accent.
I am discriminated against because of my color.
How would you describe use of language among the different races in the class?
Language plays significant role in deliberate construction of racial identify among learners of same race.
How often is language deliberately used to promote racial bias?
How often does discriminatory discourse degenerate into violent or near-violent outbursts during your course? (never, not often, often, very often)?

Effects of Racism on Classroom Interaction and Collaboration

Class activities and collaboration is largely determined by …
Level of interconnection between race and language use among course mates (low, average, high, extremely high)

How often does individual's race create communication overlap in class situation?
How often does racism create significant relational barriers?
How often do learners borrow expressions from other languages among to foster interracial acceptance and goodwill in class situation?
How often do learners unconsciously resort to language-switch thus creating communication gap during interracial communication?
What are the challenges pose by racial discrimination to learner?
What are the challenges pose by racial discrimination to academic collaboration?
What do you think could be solutions to racial discrimination in classroom setting?

Section 3
Interrogating Race and Racism in Postsecondary Language Classrooms

Chapter 9
Empowering Linguistic Diversity:
Theory Into Practice in Multilingual Writing Classrooms

Anita Chaudhuri
University of British Columbia, Canada

Jordan Stouck
University of British Columbia, Canada

ABSTRACT

The chapter uses the case of multilingual students to discuss how teaching and learning practices in Canadian writing classrooms must examine "systems and structures of linguicism, racism, and classism, which are interrelated and continuously shaping one another" to develop an understanding of linguistic racism. A critical dialogic approach was used to listen to the study participants and explore strategies to promote decolonial practice in the writing classroom and inform literature on Canadian multilingual pedagogy. The chapter identifies themes of diversity, curriculum design and instructional practice aligned with linguistic justice practices, and perceptions of success and challenges to recommend theoretical standpoints and examples of classroom practice. Through this process of negotiating theory into practice, the authors move from a focus on linguistically and culturally responsive pedagogy toward sustaining and revitalizing pedagogy. They conclude with macro-level strategies and a call to promote and sustain linguistic justice.

Multilingual learners are appreciated in pedagogical research for their unique voice, diverse identities and language learning practices that are informed by socio-cultural experiences (e.g., Bhowmik & Chaudhuri, 2022; Canagarajah, 2016; Cummins, 2000, 2007; Marshall & Marr, 2018; Norton, 2013). Therefore, it is important that course development and assessment practices have the flexibility to encourage distinctness in student work (Burgess & Rowsell, 2020; Schissel, Leung, López-Gopar & Davis, 2018). How instructors teach and assess should complement diverse linguistic and cultural values and associations,

DOI: 10.4018/978-1-6684-9029-7.ch009

literacy practices, and socio-historical narratives. Researchers have noted that, without such validations, marginalized communities can go through a process of "internalization" that leads to self-devaluation, lack of confidence, and low engagement with learning and institutional expectations (Hudley & Mallinson, 2014). Indeed, to decolonize education, address social justice and sustain culturally distinct ways of learning, all instructors must engage with students to co-create knowledge (Accurso & Mizell, 2020; Gebhard & Accurso, 2023; Motha, 2014). Motha (2014) views such co-constructed knowledge as a way for instructors "to embrace their own identities" (p. 3) in "safe spaces" (p. 4) uninterrupted by institutional hierarchies. We argue that decolonial pedagogical motives can make classrooms safe havens for students to share their unique identities. In fact, such recognition of an engaged self can empower classrooms to "dismantle unequal relations of power between standardized English used by White L1 English users and other... users, many of whom are racialized" (Kubota, 2022, p. 5) and embrace decolonial thinking in knowledge production.

In this chapter, a Canadian case study of an advanced communication course for multilingual students is used to present recommendations for linguistically responsive and culturally sustaining pedagogy. We use a critical dialogic approach to ask instructors about pedagogical choices, reflect on their teaching stances and classroom practice, and assess how forms of linguistic justice are clearly articulated or emerge in their classrooms. As scholar-practitioners, we draw inferences from these dialogic interactions to identify macro-strategies, particularly around assessment, that are applicable in diverse learning contexts.

The Canadian scenario presented in this chapter is particularly interesting because the 2021 Census data revealed that "one in five Canadian households were multilingual" with "a non-official language, alone or with one or both official languages" spoken in "90% of multilingual households" (Statistics Canada, 2023). Multilingualism at home combined with a typically high international student enrollment in post-secondary institutions (The Daily, 2020), lays emphasis on learning practices informed by linguistic diversity. Indeed, Canada's official policies, combined with its historical development of writing instruction in ways that are distinct from the U.S. (see Clary-Lemon, 2009; Wright-Taylor, 2021), means that Canadian classrooms warrant further study. The linguistic justice work already begun in the U.S. offers valuable guidelines; however, as Huo (2020) notes, despite Canada's "camouflage of meritocracy and colorblindness" higher education in this country nevertheless "marginalizes and excludes minorities" (p. 24). Therefore, we use the case of multilingual students, both domestic and international learners, to discuss how teaching and learning practices in the Canadian writing classroom must examine "systems and structures of linguicism, racism, and classism, which are interrelated and continuously shaping one another" (Baker-Bell, 2020b, p. 16) to develop an understanding of linguistic racism. In particular, the chapter analyzes instructor attitudes and, informed by Inoue's (2019a) probing question "How do we language so people stop killing each other, or what do we do about white language supremacy?", identifies pedagogical and assessment strategies to promote linguistic justice.

We also find it important to recognize the role of researcher positionality in qualitative studies such as this. Anita Chaudhuri's scholarship and practice has evolved across multiple locations and learning cultures. Her research and teaching experiences in second language writing, rhetoric and composition represent a negotiated space for diverse voices, learning styles and expectations. Jordan Stouck is a settler scholar with a background in Writing Across the Curriculum and genre theory; she has taught in diverse classrooms for nearly two decades. Our individual positionalities contribute towards an interpretation of linguistic racism as justice focused so that fairness and equity concerns are addressed in classroom practice, cognizant of diverse cultures, multiple learning styles, varied learner expectations, and supportive of learning progression across disciplines. We use our authorial agency, choices in course design and materials development, participation in communities of practice, and institutional leadership roles to rationalize an understanding of linguistic justice as asset-based, motivated by learner goals and objectives, and promoted by resilient networks of practice. The recommendations in this chapter, therefore, are reflective of our interpretation of linguistic justice efforts as stated above and received knowledge from peers that sustains our practice.

For us, Inoue's call for "deep and mindful attending" (2019a, p. 363) is significant and we listen/act to invite participation, feedback, and critical input to balance student learning expectations. We also recognize that institutional systems can control and even limit some changes and, therefore, use Porter et al.'s (2000) approach to institutional critique by reporting on institutional context and a historical purview of systematic changes. For instance, non-credit to credit-based course offering, student placement, and recognition of experienced labor required to design and teach the curriculum are discussed as part of institutional context. Porter et al. also recommend looking for change that "weds research and action" (2000, p. 631). We have addressed, for example, institutional support for a new credit course that also appeals to students as a way to meet their degree requirement. This sort of an investment (institutional and individual) can support transfer from theory to classroom practice. The following quote from Hymes (1996) is a reminder that recognizing language varieties, student agency, institutional history, and sociocultural significance of languages impacts individuals and communities:

It is where linguistic work is connected with practical problems and the circumstances of actual communities that one is most likely to realize the need to stress the potential equality/equivalence of all languages, grounded in human nature, to recognize the actual inequalities that obtain, and to be brought face-to-face with the difference it can make to share with others understandings linguists may take for granted. (p. 221)

Classroom injustices can include requiring students only to speak English, devaluing previous learning, or assessment that privileges monolingualism. By not taking for granted the linguistic repertoire of multilingual students and positioning linguistic justice as reflective of concerns of social justice, questioning the path of justice, how injustice informs and shapes justice, and considering "justice as an imperative" (Tuck & Yang, 2020, p. 11), this chapter demonstrates application of theory "through stories of change and attempted change" (Porter et al. 2000, p. 631). Researchers have also noted that promoting students' "multilingual practices and cultural and linguistic identities" requires "planned and strategic engagement" (Van Viegen & Zappa-Hollman (2020, pp. 183-84) to avoid being viewed as "problematic" (Shin & Sterzuk, 2019, p. 149) or "slowing students' English learning" (Burton & Rajendram, 2019, p. 40). In the context of World Englishes and the lived experiences of multilingual Canadian students (see Huo, 2020), we argue such strategic change is overdue. Therefore, we listened to instructor interviews and join our participants in exploring strategies to both promote linguistic justice in the writing classroom and further the literature on Canadian multilingual pedagogy. Through this process, we move from a focus on linguistically and culturally responsive pedagogy toward sustaining and revitalizing pedagogy, concluding with initial strategies for classroom application which we invite our readers to pursue. We note that our focus in this chapter is on non-Indigenous students; we strongly believe that linguistic justice practices have important implications for Indigenous students and classrooms, but we also believe that residential school legacies require separate and in-depth discussions and applications of linguistic justice. We support and align our work with that of researchers and advocates such as Armstrong (2022),

Battiste and Bouvier (2013), Brunette-Debassige et al. (2022) and Lee and McCarty (2014), who are undertaking this work, and encourage readers to consult resources in this area.

INSTITUTIONAL CONTEXT

The course on which our case study is based evolved from considerable institutional history and discussion. Administratively, the course's position within the institution and various degree requirements required careful consideration. On a course design level, developing calls for linguistic justice and culturally responsive pedagogy that validates students' backgrounds and experiences, which were relatively new to the campus and faculty, needed to be incorporated into existing curricular structures. The narrative of those curricular and administrative processes that follows grounds our case study in a specific context. We recognize that such contexts will vary and that readers will need to carefully negotiate their own institutional histories, structures and discourses; we hope, however, that, in addition to explaining the circumstances for our study, offering this narrative provides a useful example of the ex/changes currently occurring in Canadian institutions and offers some guidance for the application of linguistic justice and culturally responsive pedagogy in these developing contexts. Indeed, before we can turn to classroom praxis, the administrative processes that place students into categories and classrooms based on race and linguistic "ability" must be interrogated and revised (Shapiro & Watson, 2022, p. 294).

To put it succinctly, the course that forms the basis of our study here came with a history: Between 2009 and Spring 2017 courses for students who wanted to "upgrade" (please note we are using the language current at the time) their English writing skills were available first via the Continuing Studies office and later via the university Writing Center. Through the Writing Center, students were able to take a one semester course (Writing 009) which focused on grammar, writing process, and structure, as well as some first-year transition material. This was a not-for-credit course taught by a range of instructors depending on availability (some newly minted MAs or PhDs, some experienced sessional instructors, some Writing Centre staff). Writing 009 had steady enrollment, but presented a significant resource investment for the Centre and occupied an unusual position in the university in that it was an academic course with no credit recognition or home faculty; questions regularly came up regarding how to align the content with first year English curriculum and how to track student progress.

In 2016-17, launching in Fall 2017, members of the English program who were specialists in writing studies were asked to create a new course (English 009) that would be housed in their home department and would be accredited, although ultimately no degree programs elected to recognize the course as counting towards their communication requirement. For every degree except Applied Science (which has its own communications programming), students who achieved an English Language Admission Standard (ELAS) below a certain percentage or test score (depending on how the student fulfilled that admission requirement) were required to take the course before proceeding to the requisite first year English courses. This was monitored and students were removed from first year English if they had a low ELAS score and had not successfully completed the new preparatory course. A wide range of students were impacted by this institution-wide, long-standing practice including multilingual students (domestic and International), Indigenous students, mature students, and students with lower literacy skills but strong academic records in other areas, all resulting in highly diverse classrooms.

English 009 itself was designed with an asset-based approach to multilingualism, emphasizing self-efficacy and knowledge transfer; it was carefully aligned with the first year English courses that were recognized by the campus' degree programs to promote student success. As it was for Writing 009, the instructors were sessionals and limited term lecturers with varying degrees of experience and backgrounds. As part of the implementation, an ethics approved study surveyed the students and interviewed instructors to better understand the course experience, what was working and what was not. That study (Stouck & Shaw, 2019) found the course was positively impacting student confidence, writing skills, and academic socialization, although additional time beyond the 13 weeks of a single semester was noted as a potentially helpful revision by instructors and students; both groups felt that literacy practices take time to develop. However, the study also found that additional and integrated institutional supports for instructors and students were warranted, as was a transition in university discourse around deficiency and belonging; the failure to recognize the course for degree requirements and the monitoring and forced placement of students in the course based on ELAS scores undermined the asset based approach that the course design sought to build. Indeed, the enforced approach to enrollment was not supported by studies such as Silva's (2015) or Caouette and Griggs (2015), which identify directed self-placement as the appropriate way to stream students in higher education literacy contexts (see also Matsuda, 1998). In 2016-17, linguistic justice and culturally responsive pedagogical approaches were developing in the U.S. but not yet widely disseminated in Canada. As Baker et al. (2017) note, at this point many higher education institutions were struggling "in reconciling the aspirational nature of multilingual policy at the national/institutional level with the everyday challenges of enacting such policies on the ground" (p. 180).

Based partly on the study of English 009, but also on changing institutional discourses around multilingualism and student agency, in 2018 curriculum processes began on a revised version of the course. Awareness and discussion around more just and culturally responsive approaches to multiliterate students was becoming part of the institutional and department discourse, resulting in support for the revised version, launched in Fall 2019. The new version was designed with several elements intended to implement a more socially just and culturally responsive learning environment. First and perhaps most significantly, registration was no longer compelled; students were able to choose based on institutional advising, their own past experiences, and perceived needs as to which of nine possible first year courses they registered in. Second, the course was accepted for the communication requirement in most degree programs, with the only exceptions being professional programs that could not commit their students to a two-semester course. Indeed, the two-semester, 6 credit format was the third revision made to address the additional time requested by participants in the first study and to allow students to take all required communication credits in a culturally responsive and cohort-based environment. A fourth important change was occurring campus-wide around recognizing communication as separate from literary studies. The communication focus incorporated knowledge transfer and built on the previous course's asset-based approach. This version included additional culturally responsive pedagogy and assessment practices, and encouraged students to develop a sense of institutional belonging and self-efficacy through transitional exercises. The additional time allowed careful scaffolding, and weekly writing practice and feedback. Institutional investment enabled sections to be capped at 25 students (below the standard writing-intensive class size of 30-35) and provided TA and Writing Centre support for students in the course. Two specialists in writing and communication studies, with backgrounds in multilingual learning, were hired into permanent positions. By year two, demand for the course had increased from 117 to 201 students, leading to a fifth and final element, which was a Community of Learning implemented to support additional instructors from diverse backgrounds in teaching the multiple course sections. As we elaborate below, this Community of Learning played an important role assisting instructors in, as Burton and Rajendram (2019) describe, negotiating institutional demands and adopting a "translanguaging-as-resource orientation" (p. 41) as well as "promoting the bastion of multiracial and multicultural performance-rhetorics" in student compositions (Young, 2021, p. 634). The larger curriculum process, meanwhile, shows a trajectory towards recognizing "linguistic, literate, and cultural pluralism as part of schooling for positive social transformation" (Paris & Alim, 2017, p. 1), although we realize that this is a case study documenting only the first step toward larger systemic change. As in its previous iteration, the implementation was accompanied by an ethics approved study to assess the course's efficacy in achieving its intended outcomes.

METHODS

Our three-year (2019, 2020, 2021) mixed methods study thus sought to investigate the shift to an "asset-oriented mindset" (Van Viegen et al., 2016, p. 498), aligning with recent calls for linguistic justice and facilitated through linguistically and culturally responsive curriculum design (Lucas & Villegas, 2013; Van Viegen & Zappa-Hollman, 2020), (inter)disciplinary navigation, and adaptive knowledge transfer (DePalma & Ringer, 2011). The research questions for the study are:

RQ1: What aspects of the ecological, instructional, and material features of a writing course for multilingual students contribute to academic success?

RQ2: What are students' and instructors' perceptions of effective linguistically responsive pedagogy that facilitates the transfer of writing skills in and across the disciplines?

RQ3: How does the instructional design of a course for multilingual students support their academic navigation and development of learning autonomy and agency?

In this chapter, we focus on pedagogical orientations and assessment approaches derived from instructor interviews, which were conducted during each year of the study (N=12; 7 separate instructors). Other components of the research data included student surveys and analyses of curricular documents and student reflective writing; preliminary results from these other components have been reported on elsewhere (Ravindran & Stouck, 2021) and final analyses are forthcoming. We focus on instructor interviews in this article as a way to better understand how culturally and linguistically responsive pedagogical strategies are applied and where gaps or challenges may exist. In this focus, we follow calls by Baker-Bell (2020b), Canagarajah (2013), Paris and Alim (2017), Tuck and Yang (2018), and several others to move the theory into praxis; as Paris and Alim (2017) suggest, changing pedagogy is a first step toward systemic change. Interview questions explored instructor backgrounds, pedagogical and assessment approaches, and perceptions of student strengths and challenges (see Appendix 1). Please see Table 1 for instructor demographic information:

Transcribed interview data was analyzed using NVivo 14 software and constant comparative inquiry by two researchers and a graduate research assistant. To increase coding reliability, we did an initial round of coding, meeting after to discuss variations and refine the nodes and procedures; we then proceeded with the full analysis. To achieve better reliability, we conducted participant checks both with interview participants and with adminstrative personnel/ faculty involved in the course development, and incorporated any feedback. Coding results prioritized three nodes relating to curriculum design, instructional practice, and instructor perceptions with some inter-coder variation in the granularity of coding (see Hallgren, 2012 on implications); additional information on coding outcomes available on request. We recognize that results are not generalizable to all contexts, but present this as an explor-

Table 1. Instructor backgrounds

Instructor	Educational Background	Institutional Position	Experience Teaching Multilingual Students
A	PhD	Tenured	15+ years
B	PhD	Tenured	20+ years
C	PhD	Tenure-track	10+ years
D	MA, TESL certification	Sessional	15+ years
E	PhD	Contract lecturer	5-10 years
F	PhD	Sessional	10+ years
G	PhD candidate, TESL certification	Sessional	20+ years

atory case study on Canadian multilingual writing course design. We note that the study was conducted between Fall of 2019 and Spring of 2022, during the Covid-19 pandemic, which necessitated a shift to remote, then online, and back to in-person teaching. Results thus cover three different delivery modes, which may have impacted instructor and student experiences. The interviews were conducted between 1 month before and up to 4 months after the end of the course to accommodate instructor schedules and, for sessional instructors, contract agreements. This variation in timing may have had a limited impact on instructor recall.

FINDINGS AND DISCUSSION

Our findings identify three themes which we use as the basis for our recommendations in this chapter. First, instructor perception and background were two of the most frequently coded nodes and included understandings of student backgrounds as well as perceptions of learning. This coding showed that demographics varied significantly, and in some ways unexpectedly, a context demonstrating the need to consider diversity as a theme at all levels. Second, coding around curriculum design and instructional practice revealed emphases on process over product, on transferability of knowledge and developing student agency, and on reflective and multimodal approaches that attend to student needs and interests. Many of these approaches align with linguistically responsive pedagogical strategies and moves to decolonize the classroom. Finally, exploring perceptions around the success of the course in achieving its literacy and culturally and linguistically responsive goals, our participants noted areas of success in skill transfer across genres and disciplines, and in growing student self-efficacy. However, challenges remained for students in terms of academic transition and, for instructors, in developing classroom strategies that fully address the diverse needs and linguistic and cultural contexts of their students. As a result, we conclude our chapter with a discussion of macro and micro strategies for linguistic justice practices, particularly around assessment.

Theme 1: Diversity

Questions about instructor backgrounds and perceptions of student backgrounds revealed a range of linguistic, socio-historical and cultural contexts. Instructors were both multi and monolingual from disciplines including English literature, communication, TESL, education, and labour studies (see also table 1). Most participants articulated positive, asset-based approaches to multilingualism, as well as a focus on student well being (influenced by the Covid context). However, awareness and experience of socially responsible curriculum design varied, a context we suspect is true at other institutions. This led to the development of a Community of Learning for the course, beginning in year 2 of the study, designed to share research and pedagogical strategies among the instructors. The Community of Learning was an effective approach to network and use diverse capabilities as well as interdisciplinary interests of instructors toward informed teaching practices (De Costa & Norton, 2017). To ensure that pedagogical motives can transform and respond to "racial identities [that] can shift across contexts and even within specific interactions" (Alim, 2016, p. 35), communities of learning (Cummings & van Zee, 2005) can be spaces for critical praxis (Waller, Wethers & De Costa, 2017). The application of critical praxis can lead to culturally responsive teaching practices and administrative reform. Lopez (2015) brings up the case, for example, of "fearless" leaders in the K-12 system who reform practices for student success. The same could be argued for the post-secondary context where a culturally responsive leadership can contribute to an inclusive learning environment and community engagement (Johnson, 2014; Horsford, Grosland, & Gunn, 2011).

Perceived student backgrounds were also described as diverse. As participant F notes:

About student demographics in this course I'm teaching: so I notice that they are quite different. It is not a homogeneous group with a singular set of needs. So there are international students and there are native—domestic--students as well.... But within this group of Canadian students, I think there is a slight difference as well. Some students, I think English is their native language or the only language they speak, but a couple of students, they told me that English is not their first language at home--at least their formal language--so these are multilingual students.

Participant B further explains that,

We discovered that the students who had actually preferred to remain in this particular course were not necessarily students for whom English is a second language. So they were mature students, there were students whose first language was English, but they still preferred to take a two-term six-credit course rather than going directly into English X because they felt that this additional time would grant them an opportunity to develop their skills over a period of time. So, this was really interesting for us.

In other words, alongside the multilingual majority, monolingual and mature students added further diversity to the classroom (as in the earlier iteration, the course population initially included Indigenous students, although in 2022, a pair of equivalent courses, taught using Indigenous methodologies and materials, was launched[1]). Such diverse classroom spaces can benefit from linguistically responsive and translingual (understood as "students' agentive, skillful strategic use of their linguistic repertoire" Van Viegen & Zappa Holman, 2020, p. 174) approaches, both to advance students' own learning and to contribute to decolonizing transformations of the academy (Van Viegen & Zappa Holman, 2020; Young, 2011). To inform the discussion on decoloniality, Shapiro and Watson (2022) note, "translingual pedagogies informed by antiracist and decolonial approaches have the advantage of serving a range of racially and linguistically diverse students in a single classroom" (p. 295). Challenges remained, though, as evidenced in instructor comments, regarding how to best advance those approaches. As participant B concludes

How do the instructors see this pedagogical space? Do we allow for, for example, multilingualism, or bilingualism, or translingual processes, you know, code meshing, for example? Are we allowing something like that? Some of those concepts exist in the field of applied linguistics, but how many writing instructors . . . actually incorporate those into their classrooms.

Gutiérrez and Johnson (2017) recommend that "celebrating, affirming, sustaining, and accounting for culture is the central object of pedagogies that seek to redress educational inequities and histories of curricular exclusion and pedagogical malpractice for youth from nondominant communities" (p. 249). Young (2021) points that recognition, commitment, and "active effort" are essential "to root out anti-Black sentiment and racisms" (p. 635). Therefore, drawing on the multifaceted experiences of students is important and including their voice in learning is essential. We observed that participant C, for instance, mentioned that students *"were interested in knowing...different kinds and styles of writing"* and learning about *"different culture," "composition practices"* and exploring layers of meaning: *"What do the expressions mean?" "Why are certain texts written in certain ways?"* and *"What's the historical backdrop?"* We find that when instructional practice invites student questions and their involvement in classroom learning, it creates room for pedagogy that can "sustain culture...particularly those who have been and continue to be racially, linguistically, and otherwise marginalized" (p. 249) as Gutiérrez and Johnson have noted. By mentioning the importance of *"academic socialization,"* use of *"practice-oriented course design,"* and how students can show *"intentionality"* even in their choice of *"sustainability"* as an assignment topic, instructors can affirm diverse learning expectations and acknowledge different interests and experiences.

Theme 2: Curriculum Design and Instructional Practice Aligned with Linguistic Justice Practices

The study participants strategized curriculum design and practice in diverse ways to address student needs, speak to writing issues (for example, comprehension skills, grammar), support development of voice and ownership, create oppotunities to *"co-mingle with other learning expectations"* and utilize their agency to *"explore what they really like to write and learn"* (participant C). The instances listed below show that course design is recognized by the particpants as a way to connect with institutional expectations (for example, academic matters), focus on practice and application of new skills, view learning as incremental, and become cognizant of varied linguistic and cultural backgrounds of learners.

- *the benefit of taking 109... is not just fixing or talking about academic writing but also talking about academic matters (participant C)*
- *...review, then add a new component, then practice, and then do the next assignment, has been my strategy this year (participant D)*
- *we train the students with this scaffolding strategy in mind (participant E)*
- *I try to bring in different materials covering different, for example, cultural topics or culture traditions, and when I ask students to complete these writing assignments, I notice, because they come*

from different cultural linguistic background[s], so they tend to think things in different ways and they really bring in very interesting and creative ideas (participant F)

It is important to note that these approaches to curriculum design respond to the institutional context of the English 109 course discussed in an earlier section of this chapter. The course learning outcomes direct teaching and learning efforts towards development of writing communication as a "tool for exploring, learning, and reflecting on academic values and disciplinary expectations" and "understanding of academic forms and styles" (English 109 syllabus) through introductory application of rhetorical elements such as audience, purpose and context. These two learning outcomes, among others that focus on reading strategies and scholarly research process, stand out as opportunities to include classroom material from multiple disciplines, and to research interdisciplinarity, how academic form and style vary.

As noted in the institutional context section, the course was redesigned to improve learning transfer so that students can skillfully meet academic expectations. Following the Elon Statement on Writing Transfer (2015), the course embedded strategies to promote adaptive knowledge transfer such as extensive practice, first year transition exercises (promoting students' progress toward scholarly identities), genre based analysis (see Cui, 2019), and reflective metacognitive writing, all of which encourage the remixing, repurposing and integration of learning in new contexts. Yancey et al.'s (2018) and Adler-Kassner and Wardle's (2019) work elucidating the complexities and implications of transfer were on-going considerations in course delivery and in exploring the intersections between writing transfer and culturally responsive and sustaining pedagogies, as were James (2009) and Wilson and Soblo's (2020) applications of transfer to second language writing classrooms. English 109 takes an asset-based, transfer oriented approach by teaching learners to negotiate standardized expectations of a syllabus. When viewed as "the racial contract" (Miller 1997, as cited in Baker-Bell, 2020b) standardized versions of learning contracts highlight problems of overlooking minority cultures, practices, and promote a deficit viewpoint. Lee (2017) references such a contract as one that "frames a web of normalized assumptions to which we are continuously having to argue against" (p. 263). Instead, English 109 has learning expectations that encourage "*different perspectives*" and the application of previous knowledge, as noted by participant F,

I tend to share these different perspectives within class and other students had the opportunity to see, "oh this is something I've never thought of before and now I can see that other students bring their diverse backgrounds as assets to contribute to this classroom discussion"

Such sharing of diverse student perspectives as assets has the potential to "disrupt appropriateness-based approaches to language education in ways that might link to larger social movements that challenge the racial status quo" (Rosa & Flores, 2017, p. 187). Participant F's comment also indicates a way to scaffold previous knowledge and find application in current learning context. Recognition of learning as transferable appreciates knowledge pathways as culturally responsive, remains sensitive to other learning cultures, promotes transparency in academic expectations ("*telling them how the course works*"- participant A), focuses on critical thinking and application, and helps learners thrive. In responding to whether students gained confidence in their course because of its structure, participant F noted the value of a two-term course with a "*relaxing pace*" and "*hard work and good efforts*" of both students and the course instructor as equally important. This recognition of the lives and practices of both students and instructors, enabled by both the extended time and adaptive transfer elements of the course design, is viewed by Lee (2017) as part of "ecological framing" (p. 262). According to Lee, students' and teachers' lives inside and outside the classroom intersect and interact with institutional policies, socio-cultural expectations, and other lived experiences. By making these shared social interactions part of classroom experience, one can contribute to what Lee calls "the multidimensional nature of human learning" (p. 269):

Instruction needs to support students in feeling efficacious, in seeing the relevance of targets of learning and of developing relationships that build a sense of belonging, and in socializing beliefs in the power of effort. (Lee, 2017, p. 269)

We found this notion of support for culturally sustaining and linguistically responsive pedagogy in our data set. For instance, participant D addresses a *"daunting"* text analysis exercise by inviting the student to work with them: *"let's do it together and let's talk about how to approach this kind of task."* According to researchers, this kind of shared effort can include a "review [of] various micro-cultures such as genres, rhetorical choices, and disciplinary expectations in academic writing" (Bhowmik & Chaudhuri, 2022, p. 1417) and help students to adjust to a "new academic culture" (Bhowmik et al. 2020). Part of our data set was collected during the COVID-19 pandemic and the challenging circumstances of learning called for a sensitive instructional practice that fostered "a sense of belonging" (Lee, 2017, p. 269). Participant E stated that,

Giving this compassionate feeling to my students--that within this pandemic, they are not alone--there is a human being on the other side of their[learning management platform], where they submit their writing, it has been a good pedagogical practice for me to tell my students compassionately that they need to be thinking of performance and learning [rather] than just submission of an assignment. So that compassion, I don't know how where it comes in, but it resulted in better teaching.

Particpant F also references the pandemic as a *"challenging situation"* to reason why it was important for students to not only learn but also *"find a sense of community or maybe coming together while they[are] still studying apart."* Thus, there was clear recognition that curriculum design and practice should include transparency in skill development and assessment, promote transfer of learning, foster belonging and community participation, and acknowledge distinct learning styles. The challenge in designing such a curriculum is embedded in, for example, participant E's acknowledgement that they knew compassion is important, but they *"don't know where it comes"* from. In challenging circumstances created by a pandemic, perhaps, instructors are more easily reminded of compassion and they are *"diligent about checking in"* (participant A). It is arguably more difficult to be as sensitive and compassionate when the pandemic filter has been lifted: what then? How does one train instructors to consistently utilize these human values? How does one ensure that students feel efficacious and supported by a community of supporters both inside and outside their classroom?

Theme 3: Perceptions of Success and Challenges

Our final theme investigates instructors' perceptions of how successful the course was in advancing student learning, particularly in terms of knowledge transfer and student agency, while also reflecting on their own culturally and linguistically responsive pedagogical practice. When asked about student achievements over the course of the two semesters, instructors indicated general satisfaction with students' progress in understanding, applying, and critically thinking about course material. As participant E notes,

I was really happy with seeing my students in the analysis assignment showing confidence, giving one reason from this source, understanding that they need to respond to that with one sentence from their own, guiding the reader into another source which would be either a support of this or a refutation. . . . So I was happy to see this kind of thing developing.

As this response indicates, a common observation was increased student confidence and agency; students were seen as developing their authorial voice in classroom communities alongside increasing ability to navigate the academic context. Much of this insight came through the reflective writing and extended time embedded in the course design. As Participant F explains, bringing in one student's words:

I particularly notice students' big improvement in their confidence and this is what one student said in her reflection on the improvement, the overall improvement or accomplishments she had made after one semester's studies. So this is what she said: "I have found as the assignments have gone on, I have been able to grasp the topic at hand much better and I am able to think more critically and between the lines of the text. . . . I feel much more confident and satisfied with my finished project. The positive effects I have seen are not just with this class. When I have to do writings for biology or chemistry, I find myself less intimidated than I would have been.

Indeed, multiple instructors observed students adapting their new understandings of genre and research writing to other situations, often with critical awareness of the underlying values embedded in academic genres. Participant E states, *"It is a good feeling to see your students can use narrative to talk about their experiences, the expectation and also frustrations with English."* In reading students' reflective writing and during office hours, instructors learned of adaptive knowledge transfer to courses in the sciences, social sciences, and other humanities areas. Participant C describes such discussions as, *"quite fantastic, illuminating even, because [students] are trying to bring what they are learning or move it to another course, which is the primary purpose of any writing course, for me."* As DePalma and Ringer (2011) suggest, adaptive transfer holds particularly rich implications for multilingual writers in "reshaping prior writing knowledge," leading to "productive lines of inquiry within L2 writing and composition scholarship" (p. 135). Cui (2019) likewise affirms the importance of transfer for second language writers, while noting the opportunities to interrogate hidden curriculum that research in this area provides. Student agency and critical awareness have similarly been embedded within culturally and linguistically responsive pedagogical approaches as ways to affirm difference and begin the process of decolonization (see, for example, Baker-Bell, 2020a; Canagarajah, 2013; Ladson-Billings, 2021; Paris & Alim, 2017, among others).

Despite a generally positive evaluation of the course's approach, instructors noted lingering challenges related to academic transition, exacerbated by the pandemic, and sought additional strategies to bring culturally and linguistically relevant approaches into their teaching. Student learning challenges were typically described in terms of motivational or study habit difficulties; some respondents sympathized with the challenges of transitioning into North American academic culture, with Participant F explaining,

I notice when we started last term, for most of my students, it was their first semester at university, so this is it was a big transition for these high school students to come to university and then they have to [start] this post-secondary education with a new kind of learning. . . . [And particularly] international students, they don't have any previous experience of what a Canadian classroom looks like, so they are unfamiliar with classroom culture and it took them awhile to figure out what's going on in class.

Use of institutional supports, such as TAs and academic success consultants, seemed to be perceived as a sign of weakness by some students, entailing another form of adjustment to the institutional context before students felt comfortable using these resources. What may have also played a part is the conundrum of access paradox (Janks, 2000) where teaching students to learn and "manipulate the dominant language code for empowerment ironically perpetuates inequality" (Kubota, 2022, p. 5). As a result of these transitional challenges, instructors perceived that not all students fully reached their potential. Participant A notes, "*some students made dramatic progress, some students were really slow and steady. There were maybe, I'm just trying to think back, three or four students who I felt probably could've made better progress over the course of the year.*"

Instructors also reflected on their own teaching practices, noting some of the practice-based and linguistically responsive strategies they had used. Participant F gives an example:

I have this activity called doing the cultural and linguistic self-portrait. So what I did was basically ask each student to draw a portrait of themselves and then writ[e] some simple phrases or sentences about their cultures and languages they speak, and just whatever interesting or they want to share with their classmates or with me, and they made that self-portrait and then we spent some time to have that activity as a self introduction activity. So everyone got to know each other, not just as a classmate, but also as a classmate who comes from different backgrounds.

Several instructors articulated the benefits of working in a multilingual classroom, with Participant C, for example, stating:

One of the things I have noticed is that being a multilingual . . . shows in the learning strategies because one is able to transfer a lot of different styles of learning and educational practices when approaching assignments, class discussions, the material—the classroom material. And that's a big advantage, I feel.

But another key element of this reflection was ongoing teaching development and a desire to further their asset-based pedagogical approaches. Participant A explains their changing approach to assessment, for example, stating:

I think, as I think more and work more in this area, my grading approach has changed so that, for example, in addressing things like grammatical and style issues, I've come to recognize that there are sort of different kinds of concerns and levels of concern, I guess, in relation to what students do in their writing. And I've tried to create more space for linguistic difference in my grading and the kind of responses I give to students.

Instructors described continuing work towards linguistically responsive pedagogy or, as this was often more broadly termed "multilingual teaching," with expressed desire for more innovation and collaborative work in this area. As participant G states at the end of one session, "*[next year] I know how I'm going to do it differently . . . having the group of instructors is amazing and we can sort of develop our own resources that are specific to what we're trying to achieve.*" Interestingly, while we coded for references to scholarship on writing and/ or raciolinguistics, this node was not prevalent, suggesting the ongoing need to bridge theory into practice; for the instructors we interviewed, concrete, classroom recommendations and revised assessment practices were at the forefront. This focus on classroom implementation aligns with calls to "dismantle" linguistic racism through critical pedagogies (Baker-Bell, 2020a). Yet the Canadian classroom context is distinct from the U.S. where much antiracist pedagogy originates, so that our participants' desire to develop, as participant G describes, resources *"specific to what [they're] trying to achieve"* becomes understandable. The call for culturally sustaining/ revitalizing pedagogy (Lee & McCarty, 2017) is a worthy mention as it can support student expectations. So, instructors are not just creating "more space for linguistic difference" (participant A) but also helping them "reclaim and revitalize what has been disrupted by colonization" (p. 62) and therefore, achieve a clear sense of self, voice, and ownership in academic writing. The move from culturally responsive to revitalizing approaches may well underlie our instructors' desire for added and innovate pedagogical strategies.

In redesigning the course to include extended time, reflection, development of a learning portfolio, and scaffolded learning opportunities, we posit that ENGL 109 has the capacity for "inward gaze" (Paris & Alim, 2014) and question the impact of colonization on individual identity, thought and learning patterns. Instructors can also take Motha's (2014) cue on "silences around race" perpetuated by "a liberal multiculturalist ideology that professes to be antiracist" (p. 141) and make visible the need for equitable approaches in curriculum design and institutional mechanisms. Therefore, a decolonial approach is vital to speaking about differences in learner expectations and centering equity and justice concerns. The idea of equity in assessment design and response is valuable and as recognized by particpant A in the above quote, it takes experience and reflexive practice to change, for instance, *"grading approach"* and notice *"levels of concern"* in student writing.

RECOMMENDATIONS AND CONCLUSION

In taking a critical dialogic approach (Motha, 2014) for this study and listening carefully to instructor experiences to inform learning goals and expectations for multilingual students, we observe that successful curriculum design and instructional practice are often associated with confident learners who are able to transfer skills and effectively negotiate institutional and discipline-based academic expectations. Instructors related accomplishment with shared knowledge [for example, students *"opened up their... personal interests"* (participant C)] and learners' ability to demonstrate how to *"think things in different ways"* (participant F). The study participants also posited challenging premises which inform the recommendations offered in this section. We respond to these challenges from a theoretical standpoint and underline a linguistically responsive and increasingly culturally sustaining pedagogical approach. Next, we consider praxis in Table 2 and offer macro strategies with examples of class activities and assessment types. These strategies are applicable in composition studies courses that are writing intensive and focus on the development of communication skills. We expect that these strategies can be integrated within other learning spaces and disciplines.

Recommendation 1: Asset-Based and Student-Centered Course Design

"Do we allow for, for example, multilingualism, or bilingualism, or translingual processes...?" (Participant B)

Matsuda's (2006) frequently cited conceptualization of the "myth of linguistic homogeneity" highlighted "the assumption that college students are by default native speakers of a privileged variety of English – is seriously out of sync" (p. 85). This mythic assumption is applicable to the Canadian context (see Huo, 2020). Therefore, like Matsuda we recommend making visible the language differences as a "default" (2006, p. 93) expectation. Tardy and Whittig (2017) state that "multilingual writers write multilingually" (p. 924) to fracture the expectations of monolingual writing practice and make writing classrooms ethical. They also note the importance of discussing "dominant conventions and forms... and genre variation" (p. 925). Curriculum design and instructional practice for linguistic justice asks for a balancing act. Therefore, when designing courses, students should have the opportunity to self-select writing styles, text organization, and embed a translingual process, to name a few options, if they can rhetorically position the content for a perceived audience. In this context, instructors act as expert facilitators who offer frameworks for practice and application of course learning objectives. They are also evaluators. We offer a few instances of assessment design and practice in Table 2, but from a theoretical perspective we see the importance of recognizing personal bias and upholding an asset-based mindset to validate student agency and diverse perspectives. In this case, our recommendation calls for the recognition of student agency and positionality vis-à-vis the course, and how that can inform classroom discussion. As Inoue (2019b) notes, antiracist practice in language classrooms is intertwined with assessment strategies. How teachers respond to "students' multilingual resources" (French, 2019), their "stancetaking" as an identity marker (Podesva, 2016), and multimodal composing practices (Hafner & Ho, 2020; Lim & Polio, 2020) impact linguistic and diverse cultural practice. Thus, course design should consider how to create room for this modular space for student engagement to inform learning. Table 2 can be read as a step in this direction.

Recommendation 2: Reflexive Pedagogy Informed by Learner Motivation

"So that compassion, I don't know how where it comes in, but it resulted in better teaching." (Participant E)

Motha and Lin (2014) propose that "desire can... serve as a tool for compassionate and liberatory pedagogy" (p. 333) and in their framework include five interconnected levels of desire (learners, communities, teachers, institutions, and state). For this recommendation, desires of learners and instructors are particularly relevant. If desires shape learner motivation then one can contend that how a course is designed and received by community stakeholders (student groups and institutional) makes an impact on learner perception. In language and writing courses, desire may be a factor in enrolment, but also in engaging with and responding to course material. The theoretical premise set by Motha and Lin (2014) argues that if learners can " shift... desires from unconscious to conscious planes" (p. 352) then,

Students can develop critical agency in their language learning pursuits. Questioning the accessibility or even desirability of the object of one's desire can lead learners to consciously reject the position of perpetually illegitimate speaker by, for instance, participating in political action to reconceptualize what constitutes an English speaker, critiquing language education policies, and reframing language learning goals from "passing as a native" to intelligibility. (pp. 351-52)

In similar ways, instructors have personal and professional desires and sometimes they may be in conflict with what students desire. In recognizing the value of compassion and desiring a "*better teaching*" scenario, participant E addresses challenges due to the COVID-19 pandemic. To promote a compassion-based pedagogy, researchers (see Motha & Lin, 2014) have proposed reflexive practice and collaboration with students to understand and respond to their desires so that as a community they can participate in thoughtful sharing and critical engagement.

Recommendation 3: Sustain and Empower Practices in Collaborative Networks

"I've tried to create more space for linguistic difference in my grading." (Participant A)

The Community of Learning emerged as an effective way to share and learn about course attributes and instructional practices. The discursive space helped instructors to filter out ineffective practice, inform assessment criteria with an understanding of cultural pluralism and linguistic difference, and use this "structured" space "to contend with internalized oppressions, false choices, and inward gazes" (Paris, 2021, p. 367; Yeo et al., 2019). This supportive network of peers can also be viewed as a source of strength to fulfill culturally sustaining pedagogy's call to "resist and refuse" (Paris, 2021, p. 369) powerful and authoritative demands and respond to Young's (2021) call for a Black Body Acknowledgement (p. 635) by forging a path towards social justice and centering the need for change. By positioning the community of practitioners as change agents, one can begin to visualize identity of self and others, position the group's intent as actively dismantling linguistically strenuous and opressive practices. Such forums can develop sustainable ways to address linguistic difference so that the onus to sustain cultural and linguistic diversity is not on an individual instructor. Therefore, as a space for collective effort, Communities of Learning represent the value of process over product (dialogic, shared interests and objectives are the focus).

The recommendations above take a theoretically informed approach to linguistic justice and culturally sustaining classrooms. The macro strategies in Table 2 offer examples of concrete applications. We raise questions instead of defining the macro concepts to demonstrate how we set up the critical dialogic process for this research. By asking questions, we received valuable reflection and feedback from our study participants and the format can be used to find applications for linguistically and culturally sustaining pedagogies in diverse contexts (recognizing that our readers likely contend with different institutional and locational demands). We respond to the questions in the first column by identifying instances of class activity and assessment practices, some of which may overlap (for instance, flexible modes for course materials both validate diversity and promote student agency). As mentioned towards the beginning of this section, the table is not comprehensive but a starting point. When readers respond to these questions, we anticipate that their disciplinary inclinations and desires will surface to finetune activities and assessment types listed below as well as lead to the creation or identification of further learning engagements.

In conclusion, we found an important takeaway in participant G's statement:

I think that we ignore the fact that university courses are constantly testing literacy but pretending that we don't... literacy is essential to doing well in higher ed. I mean it just is.... so you know, we disadvantage students when we don't help them develop those skills to a high level of competency early in their programs.

Table 2. Strategies to apply linguistically and culturally sustaining pedagogies

Macro Strategies (Learning Outcomes)	Class Activity Examples	Assessment Examples
Agency: How can students be involved in learning? How can instructors encourage student agency?	• Students as partners model e.g. in developing examples, bringing in personally relevant readings/ class materials • Students and instructors negotiate course learning outcomes • Students lead discussions, developing mediation abilities as well as guiding their own learning • Flexibility in how students access materials (e.g. text or video) and in pacing their learning	• Contract based grading or ungrading (see Blum, 2020) • Choice in topic, submission deadlines (as feasible), weighting or grading options, mode of access and/ or submission
Validating diversity: What kind of learning spaces are being created? And how are these spaces efficacious for diverse learners?	• Activities to recognize diversity in the classroom e.g. diverse course materials and perspectives on those materials (while recognizing that not all readers have the same background knowledge) • Multiple languages in the classroom e.g. during groupwork which students then translate for the class, or through translanguaging • Use classroom space in ways that promote accessibility and inclusion (e.g. using the UDL framework)	• Careful consideration of rubrics: What values or "hidden curriculum" are embedded in the rubric? Can it be more transparent/ equitable? Consider Critical Language Awareness (see Gere et al., 2021) • Citation practice: Who is being cited? What cultural and linguistic backgrounds are authors from? • Create space for linguistic diversity in assignments e.g. by allowing writers to use texts written in other languages, translating as needed
Reflexivity/ listening: How can instructors attend to and promote student voices?	• Community engaged learning (see for example, Paris, 2021) • Exercises that critically engage with students' cultures, experiences and goals e.g. participant F's self-portrait • Regular instructor reflection on their own pedagogical practices	• Reflective writing as part of each assignment • Peer review as a regular practice • Topics and assignment genres aligned with students' experiences, dispositions and goals
Process over product: How can instructors develop a learning mindset and promote adaptive transfer?	• Scaffolded learning • Adaptive knowledge transfer e.g. through translating information for different audiences • Extended time for learning and practice e.g. through a two semester course structure	• Labour based grading (see Inoue, 2019b) • Low stakes, formative assignments (may include reflection)

This exposes the deficit model that researchers reference when discussing asset-based pedagogies, the institutional "silences" and desires unconsciously perpetuated by instructors. It also brings to the forefront our central premise that multilingual classrooms must question systems and structures in place to skillfully promote and sustain linguistic justice. The question, though, is what skills we prioritize and how we develop those skills. We hope this study provides evidence for re-thinking discriminatory practices around language and languaging, and offers initial strategies to advance skills around critical literacy, linguistic justice, and transformative diversity both for students and instructors.

ACKNOWLEDGMENT

We would like to recognize and commemorate the work of our third team member, Dr. Aisha Ravindran (1960-2023). Her insights, expertise and dedication were invaluable in developing and collecting the data for this work. She has left us a legacy of exemplary scholarship and collegiality.

We would like to thank our graduate research assistant, Naeem Nedaee, for his invaluable work in organizing and analyzing the interview data. We would also like to acknowledge and appreciate the in-depth reading of the two anonymous reviewers of this chapter.

REFERENCES

Accurso, K., & Mizell, J. D. (2020). Toward an antiracist genre pedagogy: Considerations for a North American context. *TESOL Journal, 11*(4), e554. Advance online publication. doi:10.1002/tesj.554

Adler-Kassner, L., & Wardle, E. (Eds.). (2019). *(Re)Considering what we know: Threshold concepts in writing composition, rhetoric, and literacy*. Utah State University Press.

Alim, H. S. (2016). *Who's afraid of the transracial subject? Raciolinguistics: How language shapes our ideas about race*. Oxford University Press. doi:10.1093/acprof:oso/9780190625696.001.0001

Alim, H. S., Rickford, J. R., & Ball, A. F. (2016). *Raciolinguistics: How language shapes our ideas about race*. Oxford University Press. doi:10.1093/acprof:oso/9780190625696.001.0001

Armstrong, J. C. (2022). The role of indigenous governed institutions of higher adult learning in indigenous language recovery. *Vancouver Institute Lectures*. University of British Columbia.

Baker, B., Palfreyman, D. M., Hiller, G., Poha, W., & Manu, Z. (2017). Biliteracy as policy in academic institutions. In D. Palfreyman & C. Van der Walt (Eds.), *Academic biliteracies: Multilingual repertoires in higher education* (1st ed.). Multilingual Matters. doi:10.21832/9781783097425-012

Baker-Bell, A. (2020a). Dismantling anti-black linguistic racism in English language arts classrooms: Towards an anti-racist black language pedagogy. *Theory into Practice, 59*(1), 8–21. doi:10.1080/00405841.2019.1665415

Baker-Bell, A. (2020b). *Linguistic justice: Black language, literacy, identity, and pedagogy*. Routledge., doi:10.4324/9781315147383

Battiste, M., & Bouvier, R. (2013). *Decolonizing education: Nourishing the learning spirit*. UBC Press.

Bhowmik, S., & Chaudhuri, A. (2022). Addressing culture in L2 writing: Teaching strategies for the EAP classroom. *TESOL Quarterly, 56*(4), 1410–1429. doi:10.1002/tesq.3172

Bhowmik, S. K., Chaudhuri, A., Tweedie, G., Kim, M., & Liu, X. (2020). Culture and L2 writing: Student perceptions of factors affecting academic writing. *Writing & Pedagogy, 12*(2-3), 223. doi:10.1558/wap.19538

Blum, S (2020). *Ungrading: Why Rating Students Undermines Learning (and What to Do Instead)*. West Virginia UP.

Brunette Debassige, C., Wakeham, P., Smithers-Graeme, C., Haque, A., & Chitty, S. M. (2022). Mapping approaches to decolonizing and indigenizing the curriculum at Canadian universities: Critical reflections on current practices, challenges, and possibilities. *International Indigenous Policy Journal, 13*(3), 1–24. doi:10.18584/iipj.2022.13.3.14109

Burgess, J., & Rowsell, J. (2020). Transcultural-affective flows and multimodal engagements: Reimagining pedagogy and assessment with adult language learners. *Language and Education, 34*(2), 173–191. doi:10.1080/09500782.2020.1720226

Burton, J., & Rajendram, S. (2019). Translanguaging-as-resource: University ESL instructors' language orientations and attitudes toward translanguaging. *TESL Canada Journal, 36*(1), 21–47. doi:10.18806/tesl.v36i1.1301

Canagarajah, S. (2013). *Literacy as translingual practice: Between communities and classrooms*. Routledge. doi:10.4324/9780203120293

Canagarajah, S. (2016). Translingual writing and teacher development in composition. *College English, 78*(3), 265–273.

Caouette, B. L., & Griggs, C. (2015). A compelling collaboration: The first year writing program, writing center, and directed self-placement. *Praxis. Writing Center Journal, 12*(2), 17–22.

Clary-Lemon, J. (2009). Shifting tradition: Writing research in Canada. *The American Review of Canadian Studies, 39*(2), 94–111. doi:10.1080/02722010902848128

Cui, W. (2019). Teaching for transfer to first-year L2 writers. *Journal of International Students, 9*(4), 1115–1133. doi:10.32674/jis.v9i4.755

Cummins, J. (2000). Negotiating intercultural identities in the multilingual classroom. *The CATESOL Journal, 12*(1), 163–178.

Cummins, J. (2007). Rethinking monolingual instructional strategies in multilingual classrooms. *Canadian Journal of Applied Linguistics, 10*(2), 221–240. https://journals.lib.unb.ca/index.php/CJAL/article/view/19743

Cummings, S., & van Zee, A. (2005). Communities of practice and networks: Reviewing two perspectives on social learning. *Knowledge Management for Development Journal, 1*(1), 8–22. https://km4djournal.org/index.php/km4dj/article/view/9

De Costa, P. I., & Norton, B. (2017). Introduction: Identity, transdisciplinarity, and the good language teacher. *Modern Language Journal, 101*(S1), 3–14. doi:10.1111/modl.12368

DePalma, M., & Ringer, J. M. (2011). Toward a theory of adaptive transfer: Expanding disciplinary discussions of "transfer" in second-language writing and composition studies. *Journal of Second Language Writing, 20*(2), 134–147. doi:10.1016/j.jslw.2011.02.003

Elon Statement on Writing Transfer. (2015). Retrieved from https://www.centerforengagedlearning.org/elon-statement-on-writing-transfer

French, M. (2019). Multilingual pedagogies in practice. *TESOL in Context*, *28*(1), 21–44. doi:10.21153/tesol2019vol28no1art869

Gebhard, M., & Accurso, K. (Eds.). (2023). *In Pursuit of a multilingual equity agenda: SFL teacher action research* (1st ed.). Routledge. doi:10.4324/9781003162575

Gere, A. R., Curzan, A., Hammond, J. W., Hughes, S., Li, R., Moos, A., Smith, K., Van Zanen, K., Wheeler, K. L., & Zanders, C. J. (2021). Communal justicing: Writing assessment, disciplinary infrastructure, and the case for critical language awareness. *College Composition and Communication*, *72*(3), 384–412. doi:10.58680/ccc202131160

Guttierez, K. D., & Johnson, P. (2017). Understanding identity sampling and cultural repertoires advancing a historicizing and syncretic system of teaching and learning in justice pedagogies. In D. Paris & H. S. Alim (Eds.), *Culturally sustaining pedagogies: Teaching and learning for justice in a changing world* (pp. 247–60). Teachers College Press.

Hafner, C. A., & Ho, W. Y. J. (2020). Assessing digital multimodal composing in second language writing: Towards a process-based model. *Journal of Second Language Writing*, *47*, 100710. doi:10.1016/j.jslw.2020.100710

Hallgren, K. A. (2012). Computing inter-rater reliability for observational data: An overview and tutorial. *Tutorials in Quantitative Methods for Psychology*, *8*(1), 23–34. doi:10.20982/tqmp.08.1.p023 PMID:22833776

Horsford, S. D., Grosland, T., & Gunn, K. M. (2011). Pedagogy of the personal and professional: Toward a framework for culturally relevant leadership. *Journal of School Leadership*, *21*(4), 582–606. doi:10.1177/105268461102100404

Hudley, C., & Mallinson, C. (2014). *We do language: English language variation in the secondary English classroom*. Teachers College Press.

Huo, X. Y. (2020). *Higher education internationalization and English language instruction: Intersectionality of race and language in Canadian universities*. Springer. doi:10.1007/978-3-030-60599-5

Hymes, D. (1996). *Ethnography, linguistics, narrative inequality: Toward an understanding of voice* (1st ed.). Taylor & Francis. doi:10.4324/9780203211816

Inoue, A. B. (2019a). 2019 CCCC chair's letter: How do we language so people stop killing each other, or what do we do about white language supremacy? *College Composition and Communication*, *71*(2), 370–379. doi:10.58680/ccc201930428

Inoue, A. B. (2019b). Classroom writing assessment as an antiracist practice: Confronting white supremacy in the judgments of language. *Pedagogy*, *19*(3), 373–404. doi:10.1215/15314200-7615366

James, M. A. (2009). "Far" transfer of learning outcomes from an ESL writing course: Can the gap be bridged? *Journal of Second Language Writing*, *18*(2), 69–84. doi:10.1016/j.jslw.2009.01.001

Janks, H. (2000). Domination, access, diversity, and design: A synthesis model of critical literacy education. *Educational Review*, *52*(2), 175–186. doi:10.1080/713664035

Johnson, L. (2014). Culturally responsive leadership for community empowerment. *Multicultural Education Review*, *6*(2), 145–170. doi:10.1080/2005615X.2014.11102915

Kubota, R. (2022). Decolonizing second language writing: Possibilities and challenges. *Journal of Second Language Writing*, *58*, 100946. doi:10.1016/j.jslw.2022.100946

Ladson-Billings, G. (2021). *Culturally relevant pedagogy: Asking a different question.* Teachers College Press.

Lee, T. S., & McCarty, T. L. (2017). Upholding Indigenous education sovereignty through critical culturally sustaining/revitalizing pedagogy. In D. Paris & H. S. Alim (Eds.), *Culturally sustaining pedagogies: Teaching and learning for justice in a changing world* (pp. 61–82). Teachers College Press.

Lee, C. D. (2017). An Ecological framework for enacting culturally sustaining pedagogy. In D. Paris & H. S. Alim (Eds.), *Culturally sustaining pedagogies: Teaching and learning for justice in a changing world* (pp. 261–73). Teachers College Press.

Lim, J., & Polio, C. (2020). Multimodal assignments in higher education: Implications for multimodal writing tasks for L2 writers. *Journal of Second Language Writing*, *47*, 100713. doi:10.1016/j.jslw.2020.100713

Lopez, A. E. (2015). Navigating cultural borders in diverse contexts: Building capacity through culturally responsive leadership and critical praxis. *Multicultural Education Review*, *7*(3), 171–184. doi:10.1080/2005615X.2015.1072080

Lucas, T., & Villegas, A. M. (2013). Preparing linguistically responsive teachers: Laying the foundation in preservice teacher education. *Theory into Practice*, *52*(2), 98–109. doi:10.1080/00405841.2013.770327

Marshall, S., & Walsh Marr, J. (2018). Teaching multilingual learners in canadian writing-intensive classrooms: Pedagogy, binaries, and conflicting identities. *Journal of Second Language Writing*, *40*, 32–43. doi:10.1016/j.jslw.2018.01.002

Matsuda, P. K. (2006). The myth of linguistic homogeneity in U.S. college composition. *College English*, *68*(6), 637–651. doi:10.2307/25472180

Matsuda, P. K. (1998). Situating ESL: Writing in a cross-disciplinary context. *Written Communication*, *15*(1), 99–121. doi:10.1177/0741088398015001004

Motha, S. (2014). *Race, empire, and English language teaching: Creating responsible and ethical anti-racist practice.* Teachers College Press.

Motha, S., & Lin, A. (2014). "Non-coercive rearrangements": Theorizing desire in TESOL. *TESOL Quarterly*, *48*(2), 331–359. doi:10.1002/tesq.126

Norton, B. (2013). *Identity and language learning: Extending the conversation* (2nd ed.). Multilingual Matters. doi:10.21832/9781783090563

Paris, D. (2021). Culturally sustaining pedagogies and our futures. *The Educational Forum*, *85*(4), 364-376. 10.1080/00131725.2021.1957634

Paris, D., & Alim, H. S. (2014). What are we seeking to sustain through culturally sustaining pedagogy? A loving critique forward. *Harvard Educational Review, 84*(1), 85–100. doi:10.17763/haer.84.1.982l873k2ht16m77

Paris, D., & Alim, H. S. (2017). *Culturally Sustaining Pedagogies: Teaching and learning for justice in a changing world*. Teachers College Press.

Podesva, R. J. (2016). Stance as a window into the language-race connection. In H. S. Alim, J. R. Rickford, & A. F. Ball (Eds.), *Raciolinguistics: How language shapes our ideas about race* (pp. 203–220). Oxford University Press. doi:10.1093/acprof:oso/9780190625696.003.0012

Porter, J. E., Sullivan, P., Blythe, S., Grabill, J. T., & Miles, L. (2000). Institutional Critique: A Rhetorical Methodology for Change. *College Composition and Communication, 51*(4), 610–642. doi:10.2307/358914

Ravindran, A., & Stouck, J. (2021, Aug. 5). Academic transition and navigation of multilingual students through writing across the curriculum: Building institutional connections through linguistically responsive curriculum design. *International Writing Across the Curriculum (IWAC) Conference*.

Rosa, J., & Flores, N. (2017). Do you hear what I hear? Raciolinguistic ideologies and culturally sustaining pedagogies. In D. Paris & H. S. Alim (Eds.), *Culturally sustaining pedagogies: Teaching and learning for justice in a changing world* (pp. 175–190). Teachers College Press.

Schissel, J. L., Leung, C., López-Gopar, M., & Davis, J. R. (2018). Multilingual learners in language assessment: Assessment design for linguistically diverse communities. *Language and Education, 32*(2), 167–182. doi:10.1080/09500782.2018.1429463

Shapiro, R., & Watson, M. (2022). Translingual praxis: From theorizing language to Antiracist and decolonial pedagogy. *College Composition and Communication, 74*(2), 292–321. doi:10.58680/ccc202232276

Shin, H., & Sterzuk, A. (2019). Discourses, practices, and realities of multilingualism in higher education. *TESL Canada Journal, 36*(1), 147–159. doi:10.18806/tesl.v36i1.1307

Silva, T. (2015). Writing instruction for matriculated International students: A lived case study. In *ESL Readers and Writers in Higher Education* (1st ed., pp. 64–79). Routledge.

Statistics Canada. (2023). *Multilingualism of Canadian households*. https://www12.statcan.gc.ca/census-recensement/2021/as-sa/98-200-X/2021014/98-200-X2021014-eng.cfm

Stouck, J., & Shaw, C. (2019, Feb. 17). A sense of belonging: Studying a foundational academic literacy course. In *38th Annual Conference on the First-Year Experience*. National Resource Center.

Tardy, C. M., & Whittig, E. (2017). On the ethical treatment of EAL writers: An update. *TESOL Quarterly, 51*(4), 920–930. doi:10.1002/tesq.405

The Daily. (2020). *International students accounted for all of the growth in postsecondary enrolments in 2018/2019*. https://www150.statcan.gc.ca/n1/daily-quotidien/201125/dq201125e-eng.htm

Tuck, E., & Yang, K. W. (2018). *Toward what justice?: Describing diverse dreams of justice in education*. Taylor and Francis. doi:10.4324/9781351240932

Van Viegan Stille, S., Bethke, R., Bradley-Brown, J., Giberson, J., & Hall, G. (2016). Broadening educational practice to include translanguaging: An outcome of educator inquiry into multilingual students' learning needs. *Canadian Modern Language Review*, *72*(4), 480–503. doi:10.3138/cmlr.3432

Van Viegen, S., & Zappa-Hollman, S. (2020). Plurilingual pedagogies at the post-secondary level: Possibilities for intentional engagement with students' diverse linguistic repertoires. *Language, Culture and Curriculum*, *33*(2), 172–187. doi:10.1080/07908318.2019.1686512

Waller, L., Wethers, K., & De Costa, P. I. (2017). A critical praxis: Narrowing the gap between identity, theory, and practice. *TESOL Journal*, *8*(1), 4–27. doi:10.1002/tesj.256

Wilson, J. A., & Soblo, H. (2020). Transfer and transformation in multilingual student writing. *Journal of English for Academic Purposes*, *44*, 100812–100813. doi:10.1016/j.jeap.2019.100812

Wright-Taylor, C. (2021). *"Sorry If My Words Aren't Right": Writing studies' partnership with second language writing to support translingual students in the Anglo-Canadian classroom* [Dissertation]. University of Waterloo. http://hdl.handle.net/10012/17684

Yancey, K. B., Davis, M., Robertson, L., Taczak, K., & Workman, E. (2018). Writing across college: Key terms and multiple contexts as factors promoting students' transfer of writing knowledge and practice. *The WAC Journal*, *29*(1), 44–66. doi:10.37514/WAC-J.2018.29.1.02

Yeo, M., Haggarty, L., Wida, W., Ayoungman, K., Pearl, C. M. L., Stogre, T., & Waldie, A. (2019). Unsettling faculty minds: A faculty learning community on indigenization. *New Directions for Teaching and Learning*, *2019*(157), 27–41. doi:10.1002/tl.20328

Young, V. A. (2011). Should writers use they own english? In L. Greenfield & K. Rowan (Eds.), *Writing centers and the new racism* (p. 61). Utah State University Press. doi:10.2307/j.ctt4cgk6s.7

Young, V. A. (2021). 2020 CCCC Chair's address: Say they name in black english: George Floyd, Breonna Taylor, Atatiana Jefferson, Aura Rosser, Trayvon Martin, and the need to move away from writing to literacies in CCCC and rhetoric and composition. *College Composition and Communication*, *72*(4), 623–639. doi:10.58680/ccc202131445

KEY TERMS AND DEFINITIONS

Adaptive Transfer: Application of prior knowledge in new learning contexts to show learning as transferable across diverse learning situations.

Critical Dialogic Approach: Research that is informed by mindful listening of participant observation and critical reflection of participant experiences.

Culturally Responsive Pedagogy: Pedagogy that validates students' backgrounds and experiences, connects with culturally informed learning contexts, and supports a justice focused approach to learning.

Culturally Sustaining/Revitalizing Pedagogy: Recognition of linguistic and cultural differences in teaching practice that supports learners to "reclaim" personal identity and voice disrupted by colonization.

Decolonial Approach: Teaching approach that centres equity and justice to sustain culturally distinct ways of learning. Students and instructors are co-creators of knowledge.

Levels of Desire: Developing associations with communities that interest students can respond to their learning desire. Addressing levels of desire can motivate learners.

Linguistic Justice: Pedagogy that is asset-based, motivated by learner goals and objectives, and promoted by resilient networks of practice.

Multilingual: Multilingual learners represent unique voices, diverse identities and prior learning practices that are informed by myriad socio-cultural experiences. A multilingual teaching approach critically questions prescribed learning expectations and embraces decolonial thinking.

ENDNOTE

[1] While Indigenous students were welcome to enroll in English 109, and some did, the majority of Indigenous students, due to their community funding requirements, were not able to commit to a two-semester course in which they did not receive an official grade until April of the academic year. Consequently, sections of English 009 continued to run for these students until 2022. This situation, alongside our position that Indigenous histories and methodologies require special consideration, led us to focus on non-Indigenous learning experiences.

APPENDIX

Instructor Interview Questions

1. Could you tell me about your educational and teaching background? Have you taught courses similar to English 109? How do you find English 109 to be different from other courses you've taught before?
2. Could you share something about student demographics with regard to multilingual students and how that impacted your teaching strategies?
3. What were the academic strengths of the students when they began the course? What were the challenges faced by the students during the first term? Could you give me a few examples?
4. How effective were the pedagogical strategies, assessment tools, course content and resources, or literacy support that facilitated students' academic progress in the course during the first term? Could you share some examples? How have you scaffolded activities so that students develop their skills incrementally?
5. What was your perception of the students' writing abilities by the end of the first term?
6. What were the successes and challenges of the two-term duration and practice-oriented course design and pedagogy on the learning of the students?
7. What transferable skills have the students acquired in this course to facilitate their navigation in and across the disciplines?
8. How did the academic literacy support for English 109 (TAs, Learning Hub/Library workshops, etc.) support student learning and academic progress?
9. What challenges still remain at the end of the course?
10. Do you have any suggestions regarding the instructional design or resources that will better facilitate academic transition at university and navigation of students in other courses?

Chapter 10
Writing Centers' Praxis Is Not Neutral but Raced:
Collaborative Ethnography

Daniel Chang
Simon Fraser University, Canada

Qinghua Chen
https://orcid.org/0000-0001-5212-2163
The Education University of Hong Kong, Hong Kong

Angel Mei Yi Lin
https://orcid.org/0000-0002-6204-8021
Simon Fraser University, Canada

ABSTRACT

This chapter begins by questioning the existing practices of writing centre tutoring. Based on the first author's writing centre tutoring experience and some artifacts, such as consultation notes, consultation forms, and feedback on student essays, the authors question whether the writing centre is truly a safe and neutral space for post-secondary writers and whether writing tutoring feedback contains some Eurocentric racial discourses that are complicit and coded in a way that sounds so called objective. Drawing on Lemke's principle of intertextuality, the authors highlight how standardized academic writing expectations have been unconsciously normalized and naturalized in writing centre tutoring discussions, thereby reinforcing the tutor's authority. In the end, we are in the position to look for an alternative, transformative change in the writing centre tutoring practice and a structural shift that can go beyond "remedial writing service provider."

DOI: 10.4018/978-1-6684-9029-7.ch010

INTRODUCTION

We want to mention that this chapter is written creatively because we tried to move away from the conventional Eurocentric presentation of research and scholarship. Here is the reason.

In the journey of decolonization, we have been thinking about transformation when we discussed critical scholarship. An important lesson that AL (the third author) taught her students is always, "Okay, now we know, you need to move on and make a change." This was Daniel's (the first author, hereafter referred to as DC) first impression when working with AL (Angel, the third author). So, when DC wrote this chapter, DC thought that maybe he must disrupt the way he writes and think about different ways of presenting the ideas.

As scholars, educators, and researchers deeply rooted in the Eurocentric tradition, we had been told that certain writing is highly preferred, and we needed to write things objectively. We have been educated in a way that we should write in a certain style. We should use the third person pronouns whenever we present research findings. We should use a certain tense structure when we present research ideas. We should not have questions in the opening paragraph. We should have a topic sentence. We should have a thesis statement. We should have an in-text citation; otherwise, the claims are unsupported. Writing has a purpose, and we should know what genre we are writing. A one-sentence paragraph is a big *no-no*.

We know that writing has always been the goal for postsecondary education, and writing centers are the places where writers can go to polish their writing skills with respect to the above-mentioned standards. Writing centers contain a group of writing specialists who can review structures, provide comments, or train writers to conform to the above-mentioned standards. Writing centers have been portrayed as neutral spaces that can hone a student writer's skill. Yes, we agree. But maybe this is a good time to revisit some of the writing center practices and maybe disrupt our knowledge and even the functions of the writing center. Is it true that the writing center is a neutral space? Are there any racial discourses embedded within writing center specialists' discourses? To guide our examination and reformulation of the role of writing center support services in the Canadian context, we turn to the first author's experience within a writing center, as well as several artifacts shared by the first author, DC. Borrowing insights from the perspectives of writing center practices, anti-racism, Culturally Sustaining Pedagogy, and linguistic justice, we hope to present a transformative paradigm that questions the current role of institutional writing centers. This new approach offers enhanced possibilities for writers from marginalized racial backgrounds to actively participate in their writing processes and authentically contest the dominant paradigm of White-standard writing practices. In a nutshell, we hope to present a compelling argument that it may be time to reimagine and reposition the role of writing centers within the Canadian educational framework.

Context

Positionality of the First Author – Daniel (DC)

After being invited to collaborate on this chapter with the other two authors, DC was excited, but at the same time, DC was hesitant and felt unsettled. DC had doubts about the impact of this proposed chapter because DC was worried about how these ideas would splash in this era that seemed to value diversity and inclusion on the surface. However, in fact, a lot of hidden systemic racist practices and policies still lurked behind society's loud voice to be diverse or to be decolonized.

For many years, while working in the writing center, DC never thought about the issue of race in the context of Canadian writing centers. In alignment with his colleagues, he believed his efforts were driven by a genuine desire to help, guided by his compassion, kindness, and generosity (Noddings, 2012). He also thought that his academic background could significantly contribute to the growth of independent undergraduate writers. His rigorous training in applied linguistics and learning sciences, despite its roots in Eurocentric traditions, held the potential to benefit students on their journey to becoming autonomous academic writers. Throughout his time in the writing center, DC received training from the coordinators who oversaw the center's operations. Periodically, the tutors would meet together for writing tutoring workshops or hold meetings to discuss various issues that arose during writing center consultations. In these sessions, DC was instructed not to engage in proofreading students' work or edit their sentences. Instead, he was encouraged to structure writing consultations as sessions that aimed to enhance the writers' independent writing skills. In cases where writers sought assistance with lower-order concerns, such as grammar, he was taught to consistently redirect the focus of consultation toward higher-order concerns, including the structure and the thesis statement.

Having critically reflected on his learning experience, DC realized that he, as a target of racism, had also unconsciously internalized many deficit discourses toward English Language Learners (ELLs) while learning English as a second language. An example is the deficit view on ELLs' grammar and writing skill development. Subtly and gradually, he reproduced such deficit discourses in his teaching as he regarded these deficit discourses as value-free, neutral "knowledge" about learning English that could be helpful to his students. So, racism-embedded Eurocentric views haunted his entire education journey ever since DC was an international student in Canada after working hard, passing this racialized scrutiny, and starting work at the writing center, he continued to reproduce these views. With increasing awareness and knowledge of racism and how it drove the existing system reinforcing inequity and injustice, DC has found this unlearning process to be very uneasy and difficult because his former onto-epistemological perspective was challenged and contested. Tiostanova and Mignolo (2012) once described this learning-to-unlearn process as to "forget what we have been taught, to break free from the thinking programs imposed on us by education, culture, and social environment, always marked by the Western imperial reason" (p. 7). They, in fact, called for our attempt to re-examine our own developed assumptions and beliefs imposed by our prior experience so that we can change "the normalized social-structural process" (Poe, 2022).

The first event that introduced DC to the issue of race in writing center practice was Dr. Julia Lane and her colleague Emily Lam's guide to inclusive and antiracist writing (Lane & Lam, 2021). DC particularly appreciated this inclusive writing practice guide, but at the same time, to be honest, DC doubted the practical value and how anti-racist practice in writing could be useful when many faculty members continued to be unaware of their exclusive subscription to the Eurocentric way of writing, which they often did not see race in it. In many of his conversations with his colleagues who identified themselves as critical scholars, DC often cast doubt on the practical and transformative value of their work despite his appreciation of their good intentions. DC found some of the practical recommendations from critical scholars are, in fact, unlikely to create any impact on the existing social-structural system, as described by Dumontet et al. (2019): "Postsecondary educational institutions are ... still complicit in colonialism" (p.197). This quote generally means, in particular, that many postsecondary educational institutions still seem to prefer teaching and evaluating academic writing in a Eurocentric, standardized way.

As a faculty member now primarily teaching undergraduate writing courses in Education, DC is fully aware of the potential writing improvement students can gain if they visit the university's writing center.

DC has deep knowledge (so-called the *ideology of writing center tutors*) about what writing tutors[1] can do within a live, in-person, and/or online writing tutoring consultation session and what their feedback discourse strategy looks like. Nancy Grimm (2011) also uses the word, *ideology,* and points out three common-sense White principles governing writing center tutor training:

1. A good tutor makes the student do all the work.
2. The ultimate aim of a tutorial is to help develop an independent writer.
3. Our job is to produce better writers, not better writing (Grimm, 2011, p.81).

The term, ideology, implies the "naturalized" process of how "normal people are supposed to think, write, act, speak and believe" (Grimm, 2011, p.82). At writing centers, tutoring practices have been naturalized and normalized through these neutral principles. As Grimm argues, not many people will view these three principles as White writing center ideologies because they have already been naturalized and assumed as neutral and as the most preferred practices in writing center pedagogy. In this chapter, all three authors strive to re-examine these assumptions with other epistemological and ontological perspectives to rethink, restructure, and reconceptualize decolonizing alternatives for writing tutoring in university writing centers. Santos (2015), in the book *Epistemologies of the South*, has proposed a framework for co-journeying with Western epistemologies and ontologies but decentering them and provincializing them among all other possibilities and alternatives. Chen (2010), in his book *Asia as Method*, has emphasized the importance of centring the subjectivity and de-imperializing and decolonizing the subjectivity of racialized individuals like us, the authors of this chapter, as a way to imagine cultural alternatives. Then, in this chapter, we are not aiming to blatantly replace the current writing tutoring practice at the writing center with our approach as the more democratic one; however, we do think it is pivotal to begin implementing alternatives by adding these decolonizing lenses to writing tutor training and the structure.

Literature Context: Racism and Diagnostic Written Assessment

Eurocentric postsecondary education values academic writing and academic literacy, forming an epistemic system that prompted educators working in writing pedagogy to develop a diagnostic perspective toward writing tutoring and assessment. The concept of race, in the literature of writing assessment, has been greatly omitted or avoided (Villanueva, 2006). Inoue (2015) thus writes, *"the influence of the concept of race is in the coded ways we talk about each other, the words we use for race and to avoid its reference"* (p.25). The concept of Whiteness is profoundly ingrained in our current pedagogy to evaluate the literary and writing standards of students. This labelling of failure or incompetency is inequitably imposed upon writers from racially marginalized backgrounds when their expressions deviate from Eurocentric discourse norms (Amin, 1999; Mahboob & Szenes, 2007). Specifically, Baker-Bell's (2020) book underscores the emotional distress and dehumanization experienced by Black students as a consequence of the sustained predominance of white linguistic hegemony. In response to these challenges, Baker-Bell propounds an antiracist Black Language Pedagogy, which seeks to redefine the role of Black Language within the realm of education. Racial structures that support the function of writing assessments are deeply associated with a writing educator's approach to giving feedback and the reality that the writing educator wants to convey to their students.

When DC teaches an undergraduate lesson focusing on the concept of intelligence in his educational psychology course, he guides the students to think critically about the connection between race, the intelligence test, and the person who invented the test. Especially, it is not hard to see that Jean Piaget, a white developmental psychologist coming from a white scholarly family assisted his schools in developing intelligent tests to differentiate students' backgrounds by their ability. Historically, the Intelligence Quotient tests (IQ tests), or any kind of tests or examinations that were created within the Eurocentric context all aimed at differentiating students with special needs and racialized students (Hanson, 1993; Inoue, 2015). So, "race has had a strong connection to assessment generally since assessment tends to confer social and economic privileges" (Inoue, 2015, p. 27). We, therefore, would like to extend and shift Inoue's writing assessment ecologies in classrooms to a larger structural and racial context, re-examining the way writing/literacy educators in higher education (in our case, writing tutors) evaluate writing and how Eurocentric assessment structure realize into "white" writing center tutoring discourses that continue to marginalize immigrant and/or racialized students. Drawing from the lens of writing center practices, anti-racism, Culturally Sustaining Pedagogy, and linguistic justice, we would like to propose a paradigm shift that challenges the prevailing function of institutional writing centers. This shift creates additional opportunities for racially marginalized writers to engage in their own writing practices and to realistically challenge the norm of White standard writing practice.

It is not hard to see that the White writing center tutoring discourse features diagnosing and deficit-orienting students' writing. This practice has been problematized by Peter Carino (1995), as writing centers were once referred to as clinics. For example, diagnostic writing assessment, with the aim of establishing validity and objectivity in assessing students' writing, has been popular since the 1990s (Knoch, 2009). These assessment practices usually include establishing objective rubrics in the form of standardizing assessment tools, against which, students' writing is assessed as if such assessment practice is value-free or neutral. Regardless of being framed as a formative or summative assessment, it is usually a process of finding the deficits in student writing. For example, some students' writing that may not foreground an explicit thesis statement is considered to have a higher-level concern, and students who do not conform to punctuation and spelling conventions are labelled as possessing a lower-level concern issue. As Matsuda argues, the image of a prototypical White student's performance is reflected in any pedagogy and assessment (Matsuda, 2006). The writing assessment embodies a set of assumptions about a student's writing skills and their ways of completing the task. In particular, the assumptions of White performance have been deeply woven into the postsecondary writing assessment system and the practice that institutional faculty members or writing center professionals subscribe to as a way to reinforce the abstract image (in Grimm (2011)'s term, *imagined background*) of a White student's performance and to impose such hegemonic expectations on racialized, international students.

In order to disrupt the prevailing deficit-oriented approach within writing center practices, we propose the integration of Culturally Sustaining Pedagogy as a transformative tool for addressing the existing disparities, linguistic hegemony, and linguistic injustices (Paris, 2012). Culturally Sustaining Pedagogy, according to Paris (2012), sustains "cultural pluralism" in our schooling system (p.95). That is, multiple practices or cultural beliefs coexist within a system of practice, and they are fully supported by the stakeholders in an educational community. As previously noted, writing center tutoring practices have been significantly shaped by a White hegemonic influence that positions White, middle-class values as the superior societal norm. Consequently, the cultural knowledge that racially marginalized writers bring to their expression and writing is often neglected or considered as a subordinate status, deemed in need of assimilation. As suggested by Paris and Alim (2014) and Wynter-Hoyte et al. (2019), educators need to redirect their focus away from pedagogies that endorse or reinforce specific linguistic and cultural hegemonies. Integrating Culturally Sustaining Pedagogy into writing center practices offers a strategic response to the persistent issues within the Eurocentric writing center discourse, which perpetuate linguistic biases and injustices. A recent publication in *The Peer Review* authored by Natarajan et al. (2023) draws on Culturally Sustainable Pedagogy to propose a reshaping of writing center practices. This reshaping entails three key aspects: (1) emphasizing academic success during tutoring sessions, (2) acknowledging and respecting the cultural customs to which writers adhere, and (3) encouraging learners to reflect on the political implications of language usage (Natarajan et al., 2023). While this approach indeed acknowledges and celebrates the multifaceted linguistic and knowledge capital inherent in racially marginalized writers, we contend that it remains somewhat insufficient. Our objective of this chapter extends beyond merely praising or appreciating the merits of diverse cultures; it is not solely about discussing the nuances of language use and exposing the embedded privilege within current academic discourse. What we advocate for is the provision of a platform for writers to authentically express themselves—a writing platform on which the writing center can firmly stand alongside racially marginalized writers or champion their cause in cases of linguistic injustice. By doing so, we can foster a profoundly inclusive and equitable educational environment.

Because of the prevalence of assessment practices, many writing centers housed in North American universities recruited writing tutors to offer feedback that aimed at reproducing White students' performance in the name of helping students achieve course standards on their own (Leibowitz et al., 1997; Moussu, 2013). As Grimm (2011) wrote, "this propensity to describe writing center work as 'helping' neutralizes the hierarchy and power of …[Writing Center's] position within a system of advantage/disadvantage based on race" (p. 79). Such Eurocentric individualistic values are tacit, hidden and unspoken in writing center tutoring and its tutoring discourse. As described earlier, Grimm (2011) also argued that individuality discourse is complicit in writing center tutors' expected conduct and the way they approach a tutoring consultation session. But very often, these tacit standards of Eurocentric white writing tutoring practice may subject the novice writers to harmful scrutiny, especially when "writers whose cultural, racial, or linguistic backgrounds are not congruent with the backgrounds they are imagined to have as college students….this imagined background is 'raced'" (Grimm, 2011, p. 79). Racialized students from a culture that values collectivism over individualism may be interrogated or viewed as deficient due to their cultural writing practice not being aligned with the dominant Eurocentric White standards, and therefore, writing assessments become raced in many of these situations. Furthermore, the binary ideology of collectivism versus individualism that exists within writing discourses needs to be critically examined and problematized. Often, writing center tutors (particularly those with a Eurocentric writing background) tend to stereotype the writing practices of racialized students, assuming they come from a collectivist culture (Wu & Rubin, 2000; Zamel, 1997). This led the tutors to attribute any writing deficiencies to the students' cultural origin during consultations, thereby legitimizing such biases.

These writing centers have been promoted by their institutions as the place to go to improve academic writing and have been used by many ELLs (English Language Learners) writers (Moussu, 2013). In earlier research conducted by Carino (1995), the diagnostic metaphor attributed to a writing center were the subject of contestation and challenge. These metaphors suggested a perception of students' weaknesses, overshadowing their strengths and talents (i.e. writing clinics). In addition, we also interrogate the instrumentality of post-secondary writing centers. While writing centers claim to assist students in developing their academic literacy and language skills, they are often de facto perpetuating a hegemonic, colonial, and assimilative approach to learning and writing. As a result, the writing center inadvertently reinforces the prevalence of these dominant academic practices, requiring racialized students to conform to Eurocentric norms when providing their service. Consequently, the recent paradigm shift towards a critical perspective offers us theoretical lenses to re-examine the writing center tutoring practice and its racial discourse (Hernández, 2016; Reger, 2009). We will do so by questioning the diagnostic and deficit finding practice (Ginting & Barella, 2022), as it seems to be intensifying the deficit perspective towards EAP learners, especially those who use English as an additional language and, oftentimes, students of minorities or racialized individuals. It has become important to explore the existing diagnostic writing assessment practice to find ways to transform writing tutoring at university writing centers to better help racialized individuals achieve academic success while avoiding colluding with them or reproducing the status quo.

CONCEPTUAL FRAMEWORK

In this study, we applied the conceptual framework—the principle of intertextuality to understand discourse. Gordon (2014) defined writing centers as "*a place where students can meet with peer tutors and receive direct feedback on their writing*. Students can ask questions that they might not feel comfortable asking their professors. The writing center, furthermore, offers students more exposure to the academic community while giving writing tutors the chance to augment students' sense of agency in the academic community" (p.1). The function of the writing center is uncontested; we agree that post-secondary students do need a safe space where they can ask questions about writing and negotiate to make meaning (Chang & Goldrick-Jones, 2019). But as Poe (2022) suggested, perhaps, when learning "academic writing" is instrumentalized and institutionalized and being framed as goals and aims for post-secondary education, we may begin to question the assumptions of teaching academic writing, including how faculty members have positioned themselves while assessing students' writing. We thus used the word '*discourse*' as a way to implicate "what we mean by saying and doing, …, the meaning-making resources of our communities, …, the conventions of gesture and depiction, … [and] the typical patterns of actions that other members of our community will recognize and respond to" (Lemke, 1995, p.16). Most importantly, when academic writing expectations are naturalized in writing center tutoring discourse, such discourse is hegemonically legitimized as the power being exercised in "*the interests of the powerful*" (p.17). We are, therefore, particularly drawn to Lemke's call for "a general social theory" and the principle of intertextuality (Lemke, 1995, p. 16). This is because both will help us understand "how the discourse habits of the community around us both shape our own discourses and viewpoints and provide us with resources for saying and doing things that are new but still make sense to others" (Lemke, 1995, p.16).

Drawing on Lemke's (1995) principle of intertextuality, we are in a position to look for, or even create, discourses that can counter the White writing tutoring discourse and feedback discourse commonly used in a Canadian postsecondary writing center. According to Lemke (1995), when one discourse is referred to in any communication, it, in fact, implies "a social act" (p. 20) being particularly valued, prioritized, favoured, and dominated in a community of practice. Such formation of discourse constructs its own epistemology and/or realities of knowledge about *praxis*. Praxis, in Lemke's conceptualization, is constantly changing, "unstable and unpredictable" (p. 111). We, literacy educators, often subscribe to the "I-think-we-are-neutral" discourse, being unaware of the assumptions of our writing center tutoring practices. Lemke (1995), therefore, writes, "We are [in fact] part of the problem, even our most basic beliefs and values should be suspect" (p. 111).

In this case, we thus argue that, while there has been increasing attention to anti-racist writing practices or similar efforts in the academic community, writing center tutoring practice and the way tutors offer templated, diagnostic feedback to writers have been wrongfully assumed as 'neutral'; instead, the writing center tutoring discourse, associated with different rhetorical compositional features, still assumes and favours writers to use their language only with Eurocentric conventions, particularly putting racialized international students at a disadvantaged position. For example, teachers' organic conversations about student writing often focus on specific physical, rhetorical compositional features; intercultural logic, content, and the messages conveyed by students are often assimilated into the standardized praxis (Leibowitz et al., 1997). The organic nature of this discourse regarding teacher feedback often results in a naturalizing and neutralizing of the practice of academic writing as well as of the diagnostic writing discourse as scientifically normed, objective, validated, and useful. These physical categories of academic writing discourse are often raced and, we would argue, they have been unseen and invisible; they are taken for granted by the members of the academic community, including literacy instructors, as a way to give particular meaning to (or judge) student writing so they can "create and maintain a system of power" (Johnson, 2011, p.214). As Villanueva (2006) and Michelle Johnson (2011) suggest, when raced discourse is not recognized, we actually "reify the invisibility of white privileges and power," flourishing 'the new racism' by creating "more subtle, insidious, and blended forms of racial oppression" (Johnson, 2011, p.215). Based on Lemke's principle of intertextuality, it is this "intertextuality" that is important in structuring the power relationships in the dynamics of writing tutoring, making the conversations between the tutor and the students less likely to be dialogic or dialectical because these conversations have to stick to the standardized format.

Instead of employing an objective scientific methodology that aligns with the positivist research paradigm, we would like to frame this chapter as a creative, academic experience-sharing channel. Up to this point, readers may feel that there are mixed narratives of the authors and formal academic registers that may seem to be sporadic to many readers. The main claims of the chapter are spread across the sections in the chapter. Since we aim to examine intersecting social constructs, such as race, discourse, power, and the system of academic writing, we feel that there is a need for us to disrupt the rigid norm of the academic genre and adopt an alternative approach so that we can generate new knowledge for our readers by sharing our arguments, examining the system's writing tutoring discourse and analyzing what we have observed and what we believe to be useful, transformative and practical.

METHODOLOGY

Research Questions

In this chapter, our methodology focuses on a detailed examination of the underlying assumptions in writing center tutoring practices, employing collaborative ethnography as our primary method. In response to the editors' directive and with consideration for the preferences of some readers accustomed to the conventions inherent in traditional research papers, we phrase our research questions as follows:

Figure 1. A proposed methodological approach

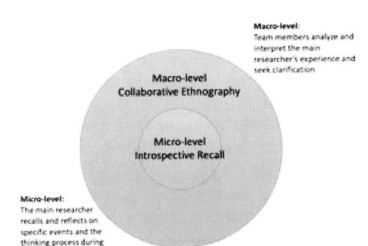

1. What are the specific practices employed in writing center tutoring and tutoring feedback?
2. What implications do these assumptions hold?

Collaborative Introspection

At first, we found it hard to locate a suitable research methodology that would align with our approach to analyzing the experience of the first author. We, therefore, decided to break our methodology into two levels: the micro-level one starts from the subjective recalled experience of the first author DC's writing center tutoring experience, whereas the macro-level one encircles collaboration that interprets DC's experience. The micro-level employs the Introspective Method, while the macro-level utilizes Collaborative Ethnography. Combining the two levels, we therefore call it the Collaborative Introspection (*COIR*) approach. Figure 1, as shown below, summarizes the methodological approach we utilized in this chapter.

Introspective Method

The closest methodology that the first author, DC could relate to was an introspective methodology – the one grounded stimulated recall that has been used in second-language research (Bloom, 1953, as cited in Gass & Mackey, 2017). Borrowing the introspective feature from the stimulated recall method, we employed the introspective recall that occured within our micro level of analysis. We would like to introspectively collect a participant's (DC's) thoughts and recall specific events "they had had while performing a prior task" (Gass & Mackey, 2017, p.14). We found this methodology quite useful when we used it to recall DC's prior experience introspectively. A criticism of introspection was its accuracy and inconsistency; however, in this case, the researcher, DC, is also the participant, and he best knows what he thought and felt while he acted as a writing center tutor and what discourse he had used while tutoring students during a particular time. The criticism will be valid only if a third-person researcher tries to interpret the subjective recalled experience of the other. Gass and Mackey (2017) thus write, "Some tangible (perhaps visual or aural) reminder of the event will stimulate recall of the mental processes in operation during the event itself and will, in essence, aid the participant in mentally re-engaging with the original event" (p. 14).

Collaborative Ethnography

At another broader macro level, we feel that collaboration is needed to derive a complete picture of what has been going on under this raced system of academic writing and praxis. As recommended by the second and the third authors (QC & AL), we propose that at the macro level, we can utilize collaborative ethnography methodology to get broader sociological implications for a writing tutor's praxis (Lassiter, 2005a; Lassiter, 2021). Collaborative ethnography is a team-based approach to examining "social phenomena" involving participants and researchers (May & Pattillo-McCoy, 2000, p.66). As Lassiter (2021) argues, collaborative ethnography fosters "a framework of possibilities for charting newly emergent collaborative research, ... [as it] implicates historical, hermeneutic, and personal trajectories of research and action" (p.70). As a result, by examining DC's own records of writing center tutoring diaries and consultation notes and sharing these with the team members, he can re-construct these events and the team, including DC, possibly help to deconstruct his ideology of writing center tutoring practice. The second author, QC, as a colleague and friend of DC, who has more training in critical discourse studies, has had ample fruitful and insightful conversations with the first author, DC, regarding the tutoring experience of the first author. QC and DC then bring these conversations, ideas, and insights to the third author, AL, an established scholar in the field of language education, who has then provided recommendations, encouragement, and additional insights in analysis, interpretation, and conceptualization.

Data Collection

The data collection process involved gathering various materials from the first author, DC, the writing center tutor, to investigate the practices and discourse surrounding writing center tutoring. The collected data encompassed a book of loose field notes (also referred to as consultation notes), 52-page scripted teaching diaries, and 46 asynchronous tutoring responses provided by DC. We aim to clarify the distinction between consultation notes and traditional field notes, elaborate on the significance of post-consultation forms, and explain the use of asynchronous responses and scripted teaching diaries in the research.

Consultation notes were generated during in-person consultations between DC and his students. They were recorded either on some pages of DC's personal notebooks, or they were recorded loosely on several pieces of scrap paper. While engaging in consultations, DC would make real-time records of the discussions, documenting the writing process and key concerns to be addressed. Unlike conventional field notes typically used in ethnographic research, these consultation notes were not originally intended for research purposes. However, their value as useful data for in-depth analysis of writing center practice later became evident to DC and his co-authors. To avoid confusion, we refer to these as consultation notes rather than field notes. These notes also served as DC's records for the writing center's post-consultation forms (see Figure 3). When DC documented the consultation notes, DC's primary focus was to direct the writers' attention toward structural elements, often referred to as higher-order concerns. Consequently, the consultation notes reveal the discussion led by DC on various aspects, including genre, outlining, paragraph structures, thesis statements, and transitions between ideas and sentences. DC also offered

Figure 2. In-person consultation notes
Note: *These are several pieces of writing consultation notes DC produced while DC was taking a student writer. From the figure, DC explained the outline of an essay and several rhetorical components of an essay, such as thesis statement, body paragraphs and sample phrases that can be used for writing a science report.*

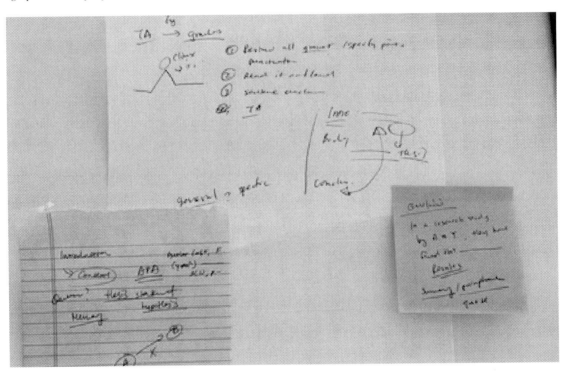

practical strategies to aid writers, such as recommending reading aloud or consulting with a Teaching Assistant (TA). This tutoring approach is underpinned by the prevailing assumption of a writing center within Writing Across the Curriculum (WAC) that frames writing as a social act (McLeod, 1992). This perspective posits that writers need to conform to the social expectations and discourses associated with Whiteness. Unfortunately, the tutoring discussion tends to reinforce these expectations rather than genuinely valuing the cultural perspectives and knowledge writers bring into the process.

The post-consultation feedback form, a standard requirement for all tutors, is completed after each consultation session, see a sample in Figure 3. While not directly having access to the backend system of the post-consultation forms, DC recalled that these forms were qualitative in nature, and we deemed quantifying the number of sessions or consultations conducted by DC unnecessary. Quantification would not contribute substantially to our understanding of writing center tutoring discourse. The writing center where DC worked catered to diverse student populations, including domestic and international students, each with distinct cultural backgrounds. Despite the seemingly random and personalized nature of DC's writing center's artifacts, such as consultation notes, post-consultation forms, and teaching diaries, they contain abundant, rich, contextual, and historical information related to DC's subjective, lived experiences in writing center tutoring. Consequently, we leverage these materials to reflect upon and deconstruct the discourse surrounding writing center tutoring for this study.

Figure 4 and Figure 5 showcase DC's asynchronous responses provided to students through the online writing tutoring platform WriteAway, a cross-institutional asynchronous online writing center platform in

Figure 3. Writing center's post-consultation form
Note: This figure represents the sample post-consultation form that DC was required to fill out after each consultation. The form specifically asked the tutor about the type of assignment, the higher-order issues discussed, the lower-order issues discussed and the corresponding next actions that the student writers should take.

Sample Post-Consultation Form from a Writing Centre
Assignment:
Essay; Memo
Higher Order Concerns:
Structure, coherence, thesis statement
Lower Order Concerns:
Proofreading strategies, vocabulary, collocation
Other suggestions?

Figure 4. The first author's asynchronous online feedback to a student
Note: From the figure, the masked texts are student drafted content in a submission. The texts in bold and bracket is DC's in-text comments offered to students. DC also provided general feedback before the student's drafted content, indicating areas where they need to work on (i.e. higher order concerns and lower order concerns).

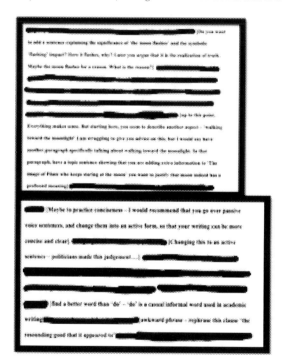
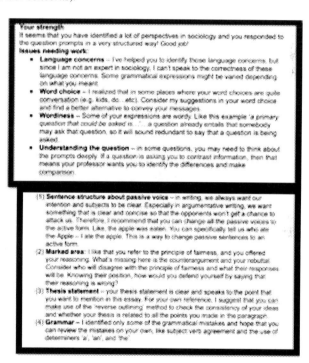

British Columbia and Alberta (https://writeaway.ca). These instances were selected from DC's feedback collection for analysis in this research. Over time, DC organized and classified student writing issues in his teaching diaries despite their initial disorganization. These diaries contained valuable information addressing specific student writing concerns. In the final two years at the writing center, DC further structured these diary entries, categorizing them according to different student issues (see Figure 5). The scripted teaching diaries span 52 pages, with some entries adapted and employed as responses to student essays (see Figure 4).

Figure 5. Writing center scripted tutoring diaries
Note: This figure represents DC's diary. Over the eight years, DC has systematically collected and categorized student writing issues into higher order issues and lower-order issues. Each issue has a corresponding script that can be used and customized for the purpose of feedback.

Higher Order Issues – Essay Elements 9
    Essay Structure 9
    Structure of a business letter 10
    Developing a strong paragraph structure 10
    Paragraph Structure: TEEL 11
    Ways to structure comparative/contrast essays 11
    Missing a warrant when describing research evidence 11
    Making claims and arguments 12
    A hook for narrative essay in the introduction 13
    Having a catchy opening for introduction 13
    Improving thesis statement by using a more sophisticated language 14
    Thesis statement – narrative essay 14
    Making your thesis statement parallel 15

Higher order Issues – Summary writing 22
    Strategies for writing an effective summary for research articles: some tips 22
    Strategies for summarizing a book 22
    Formatting a summary for a book: general guidelines 24
    Formatting a research article summary 24
    Being too broad/general in the summary 25
    History assignment: too much summary; lack of arguments 25

Lower Order Issues – Coherence between sentences 26
    Improving coherence: several tips for solving many standalone sentences 26
    Clarity and Flow of Sentences 26
    Use of transitional words to improve flow between ideas and sentences 27

Lower Order Issues – Word Choice, Tones, Expressions and Styles 27
    Colloquial language 27
    Some strategies to improve clarity 29
    Watch out your tone for Business Communication 30
    Incorrect Word Choice – For EAL students 30
    Wordiness – Cleaning your words 30
    Tips for shortening expressions 31
    Word Choice – Being specific on your words 32

Lower Order Issues – Referencing, citation, and quotes 43
    Avoid citing each sentence in APA 43
    Paraphrase your ideas by not using too many quotes from sources 44
    Paraphrasing versus Quoting 44
    MLA styling guide 45
    Quoting in MLA styles 45
    Too many quotes in MLA: out of context 47
    MLA – Citing electronic sources (social media, newspaper) 47
    When do I need to cite? APA 48
    APA In-text Citation Guide 49
    APA Style Guide 50
    APA – in-text citation combing two or more sources 50
    APA – in-text citation for less than 6 authors 50
    APA – In-text citation for more than 6 authors 51
    APA – missing information on the reference page 51
    APA – Citing a study within a study 51
    APA – in-text citation ordering alphabetically 52
    APA – quoting in APA missing page number 52

FINDINGS AND DISCUSSION

Consultation Notes and Post-Consultation Forms

Upon examining the notes and the post-consultation forms, we realized that it became evident that the term *thesis* appeared twice among the three shared consultation notes in Figure 2. DC's approach to writing consultations consistently emphasized guiding students' attention toward higher-order concerns, including developing structured outlines, thesis statements, introductions, and coherence among paragraphs. Additionally, DC occasionally addressed lower-order concerns such as referencing formatting, sentence structure, and paraphrasing/summarizing articles. DC recalled a prevailing norm in the writing center during their training, wherein tutors were encouraged to prioritize broader compositional issues, such as higher-order concerns, over content accuracy assessment. In cases where student writing exhibited unclear sentence structures or grammatical issues, tutors were prohibited from editing or proofreading the work but could provide examples of errors to facilitate students' self-editing skills.

Furthermore, our examination of the post-consultation form used in the writing center revealed potential framing effects on the tutor-student interaction. The form template, required by the writing center for all tutors to complete during writing feedback sessions, categorized concerns into two main compositional issues: higher-order and lower-order. The higher order category encompassed subcategories related to cohesion, outline, thesis statement, content development, and structure, while the lower order category comprised subcategories involving grammar, sentence structure, reference formatting, and punctuation. It is worth noting that all tutors were required to use the same form for every writing consultation, regardless of the diverse backgrounds of students, including ethnicity, cultural heritage, first language, academic discipline, and learning styles.

By examining the form, the consultation notes, and other artifacts shared by DC, we noted that the distinction between higher-order and lower-order concerns in writing center tutoring reflects a Eurocentric perspective on writing, overlooking the richness and diversity of epistemic viewpoints (Keh, 1990). This framework perpetuates an inherent hierarchy of writing skills, elevating higher-order concerns such as organization and argumentation while downplaying lower-order concerns like grammar and punctuation. Consequently, the Western perspective fails to acknowledge that various cultural and linguistic communities may attribute significance to different aspects of writing and adopt alternative evaluation methods to assess its effectiveness. By adhering to such discourses, writing tutors inadvertently reinforce the dominance of Eurocentric standards, running into marginalizing other valuable epistemic perspectives. To foster a more inclusive and equitable approach to writing assessment, one that respects diverse ways of knowing and communicating, we argue that writing center practice could include a space to disrupt, challenge and dismantle these limited frameworks. Embracing a pluralistic understanding of writing and developing assessment practices that honor the varied cultural and linguistic traditions of writers worldwide becomes necessary.

In another instance, upon examination of DC's consultation records, it was observed that DC's generic feedback templates appeared to structure and guide discussions between DC and the students. Notably, in one of the higher-order writing concerns, DC documented, "Check for the use of 'reflexive' phrases (e.g., "I find that/I feel that") in places that could undermine your thesis statement." The phrase "undermine your thesis statement" signifies a practice of avoiding personal pronouncements to achieve a more objective tone. This statement contains several assumptions, including the devaluation of subjective experiences and ideas and a preference for scientific writing that omits the self and solely "reports" on phenomena. Such assumptions bypass discussions on the complexities of writing and interdisciplinary conventions, potentially causing tutors to overlook opportunities to engage students in conversations about these issues and assist in establishing the author's scholarly voice.

Writing Center Tutoring Diaries and Online Feedback on Student Writing

The tutoring diaries DC shared with the team contain his generic diagnosis of student writing issues based on his eight years of experience working at the writing center. He classified these issues in the last two years of his work at the writing center. These tutoring diaries further classify higher-order concerns and lower-order concerns with respect to genre, common mistakes, group of student characteristics, and writing. DC recalled that he consistently expanded these issues while he was working on a student submission. For example, there was a time when many students submitted their essays on history to a cross-institutional asynchronous online writing center platform in British Columbia and Alberta,. WriteAway is an online writing support service. Undergraduate writers from participating institutions in British Columbia or Alberta can submit their essays to WriteAway and receive feedback from well-trained writing center specialists and consultants. Under each category, DC had specific explanations for these diagnosed issues and had a scripted recommendation that could be copied and pasted to student writing while working on an online writing submission, such as shown in Figure 4 (the figure on the right is an example). That was why DC recalled that under the higher-order concern category, there was an issue called *History Assignments: Too much summary; lack of arguments*. The assumption of this category indicated that students writing for history might present a list of facts in historical events but rather a lack of interpretations or particular views on the historical events. Similarly, working on feedback for international EAL students, DC created a diagnosis category for *Incorrect Word Usage: For EAL students*, assuming several characteristics of racialized students, especially multilingual EAL students. For example, it focuses on the incorrect use of words, and perhaps the choice itself might be implied and framed as 'incorrect'. The specific reference to multilingual EAL students signals the racialized writing discourse being imposed on multilingual EAL students.

From the online feedback that DC provided to his student, DC did not remember specifically whether this student was multilingual EAL or not. From Figure 4, when DC suggested the student writer focus on thesis statement development (Figure 3), he explained that *I suggest you can make use of the 'reverse outlining' method to check the consistency of your ideas and whether your thesis is related to all the points you made in the paragraph*. DC's suggestion to use the 'reverse outlining' method and check the consistency of the points made in reference to the thesis statement reflects a particular epistemological Westernized stance that values linear and hierarchical organization of ideas. In addition, when DC pointed to the student directly on the draft, he indicated, *I would say to have another paragraph specifically talking about walking toward the moonlight. In that paragraph, have a topic sentence showing that you are adding extra information to the image....you want to justify that moon indeed has a profound meaning*. DC's comment about adding another paragraph with specific content implies compliance with standardized academic writing norms that could have prioritized including certain Western compositional elements, such as a topic sentence and specific arguments. This comment perpetuates a one-size-fits-all approach to writing, overlooking the student writer's expression and diverse writing styles.

Also, we can see that DC provided lower-order concerns feedback for the student, centring the issues on language, wordiness, and word choice. Yet, he felt that as a writing tutor, as can be seen from several examples of his feedback, he particularly emphasized the language aspect because he thought these suggestions would foster students' abilities to check their own work and provide effective strategies so that they can pay attention to these lower-order concerns on their own. An example was that the student used too many passive voice structures in their writing. DC directly asked the student to change these instances into active voice structures. His recommendation of changing from passive to active might originate from DC's presumption of English being a subject-prominent language, whereas students using too many passive voice structures might indicate that they have topic-prominence (theme prominence). Using passive voice might be a particular linguistic characteristic in a culture (topic prominence). Yet, the practice of using active voice in English writing (subject prominence) is favoured and dominating the Eurocentric writing community.

Based on what DC shared, we strongly felt that students' language use had been challenged under the system of 'neutralized' academic writing discourse. These writing center practices, at least based on DC's writing tutoring practice, conform to the European individualistic view of learning. Although such writing center practices seemingly position students as the core center of instruction, they encase Eurocentrism and superficially frame the writing center as a neutral place to implicitly reinforce this type of European individualistic discourse, expecting students to comply with the tacit rule of academic writing practice through learning, developing and applying a set of strategies. Instead of negotiating for meaning, writing tutoring and compositions have been reduced and narrowed down into a set of strategies or toolkits offered to students to quickly fix in a short period of time (Zamel, 1997).

CONCLUSION

In this chapter, there are two main arguments we would like to bring forth. First, we contend that despite the growing focus on anti-racist writing approaches within the community, there is a mistaken belief that writing center tutoring practices are inherently "neutral." However, the discourse surrounding writing center tutoring, characterized by various rhetorical elements, presumably might continue to be favoured, particularly placing multilingual racialized international students in a disadvantageous position. Secondly, categorizing academic writing discourse into physical and rhetorical attributes has strong European influences, although these influences often go unnoticed and remain invisible in the praxis of writing centers. These categorizations are commonly taken for granted within the academic writing center community, including literacy instructors, as a means to assign specific interpretations or evaluations to student writing to establish and uphold a system of Eurocentric power in charge.

Through analyzing the first author DC's teaching and tutoring diaries along with several of his personal records from writing center tutoring, we have found that the intertextuality in these writing center tutoring artifacts reflects what Lemke (1995) called "a social act" (p. 20); the formation of these discourses, along with the use of the post-consultation forms and the feedback given to the students, has been neutralized as core writing center praxis. Framing feedback as neutral and objective, writing center tutors reinforce and support the structure of privilege by passing the responsibilities onto those racialized students who are often in the least powerful position in academia, and closes the opportunity for negotiating meaning between writing tutors and students that prevents mutual learning and development (Grimm, 2011). The neutralized writing center praxis, unless intentionally stimulated recalled, is informed and hegemonically dominated by a certain race - Eurocentric White perspectives. Johnson (2011) once mentioned that race signifies the way students read, write, view and speak the language, and these practices informed by race direct our attention to a particular, favored worldview of writing.

As a result, the praxis may have structured and narrowed the discussion between the tutor and students, resulting in the loss of many more pedagogical, intercultural writing conferencing opportunities. At the same time, we feel that there is a need to re-examine the research that emphasizes peer tutoring at writing centers or writing center training and re-identify this widespread knowledge that possibly contains hidden, Eurocentric racial biases.

In addition, we intend to interrogate the current privileged structure of the academic support system in higher education (Inoue, 2015). While we understand the need to position "multilingual racialized students" as the core center of writing center instructions because they need to learn to write on their own, we indeed question whether such pedagogical, individualistic ideology might have been connected to immediate expedient, economic impact in higher education (Johnson, 2011). Writing centers are framed as neutral spaces that foster academic writing and learning in higher education. Such race-neutral branding "becomes important in neoliberal influenced markets," as these writing support programs need to be marketed as "non-threatening" and dissociated with remedial perspectives (Milson-Whyte & Campbell, 2022, p. 124). In particular, when writing tutor training focuses greatly on how to avoid proofreading and editing, how to let students do their own work, or how to diagnose "issues" and align the issues with corresponding strategic writing and learning resources, we feel that the true essence of writing has been, in fact, reduced to a set of sugar-coated, superficial toolkits and skillsets that in fact pressure racialized multilingual students to conform to Eurocentric writing system (Diab et al., 2012). Writing centers, or academic support programs in higher education, become a space that does not resist the privileged Eurocentric writing system, yet they are partners being complicit in this raced system of academic writing (Johnson, 2011). We do hope, standing from literacy educators' and researchers' perspectives, that the future system of writing center pedagogy (or academic support programs) can be more transformative in a way that resists the current raced academic system.

For instance, at the writing tutor training level, the writing feedback could have been focused on collaboratively creating intercultural meaning and diverse discourses instead of just simply suggesting a list of resources that still gear writers to the Eurocentric norms. That means, writing centers should allow a more dialogic, diverse and open space for intercultural conversations between the tutor and students, allowing students to establish the authorship of meaning in their writing assignments while retaining their own ways of writing. Furthermore, it is crucial for writing center tutors to actively prioritize and amplify their students' voices, recognizing its inherent value in facilitating their writing projects. The experience the first author shared in this chapter revealed rich compliance with writing traditions and Western epistemologies. Given this diverse landscape nowadays, it might be more effective that writing center tutoring sessions embrace the concept of co-journeying alongside students rather than coercing them into conforming solely to Western notions of good academic writing. The writing center must not only provide a dialogic space for collaboration but also undergo a fundamental restructuring of its perception. Rather than being viewed as a remedial venue solely for student support, the writing center should be reconceptualized as an environment fostering equitable scholarly exchanges, where a vibrant ecology of epistemologies can flourish.

Lastly, at the structural level, we are proposing a dynamic structural shift of instrumentality of writing centers or academic support systems. We recommend that post-secondary writing centers become a real academic bargaining unit that mediates students' writing voices and instructors' expectations. That is, writing centers can serve as more than just feedback providers or writing and learning skill training agencies. Yet, they can become advocates for all students, addressing any concerns or doubts they may have about their grades in writing. At the same time, writing centers can also play a pivotal role in facilitating conversations between students and instructors regarding grades. This restructuring of writing centers would enable students to have a platform where they can voice their concerns, clarify their understanding, and engage in meaningful discussions about their writing assessments. Furthermore, if the writing center identifies substantial improvements in a student's work through its guidance and support, it can serve as a catalyst for requesting a grade review or re-grading from the instructor, or grade change at a higher departmental level. In this way, writing centers would foster a more anti-racist, inclusive and fair academic environment. They would ensure that the grades assigned to all students accurately reflect their growth, effort, and the quality of their work. This shift would empower students to actively participate in the assessment process and challenge the notion that grades are fixed and unchangeable. Writing centers are no longer places that support the system of oppression, yet they are places for all students to exercise their will to write and voice themselves.

REFERENCES

Amin, N. (1999). Minority women teachers of ESL: Negotiating white English. In G. Braine (Ed.), *Non-native educators in English language teaching* (pp. 93–104). Lawrence Erlbaum Associates, Inc.

Baker-Bell, A. (forthcoming). *Linguistic justice: Black, language, literacy, identity, and pedagogy.* Routledge & National Council of Teachers of English.

Carino, P. (1995). Early writing centers: Toward a history. *Writing Center Journal, 15*(2), 103–115. doi:10.7771/2832-9414.1279

Chang, D., & Goldrick-Jones, A. (2019). EAL writers and peer tutors: Pedagogies that resist the "broken writer" myth. *Discourse and Writing/Rédactologie, 29,* 238-242.

Chen, K-H. (2010). *Asia as method: Toward deimperialization.* Duke University Press.

Diab, R., Godbee, B., Ferrel, T., & Simpkins, N. (2012). A multi-dimensional pedagogy for racial justice in writing centers. *Praxis. Writing Center Journal, 10*(1), 1–8.

Dumontet, M., Kiprop, M., & Loewen, C. (2019). Steps on the path towards decolonization: A reflection on learning, experience, and practice in academic support at the University of Manitoba. *Discourse and Writing/Rédactologie, 29,* 196-216.

Gass, S. M., & Mackey, A. (2017). *Stimulated recall methodology in applied linguistics and L2 research.* Taylor & Francis.

Ginting, D., & Barella, Y. (2022). Academic writing centers and the teaching of academic writing at colleges: Literature review. *Journal of Education and Learning, 16*(3), 350–356.

Gordon, L. M. (2014). Beyond generalist vs. specialist: Making connections between genre theory and writing center pedagogy. *Praxis Writing Center Journal, 11*(2), 1–5.

Grimm, N. (2011). Retheorizing writing center work to transform a system of advantage based on race. *Writing centers and the new racism: A call for sustainable change and dialogue,* 75-99.

Hanson, K. (1993). Facing Facts and Responsibilities: The white man's burden and the burden of proof. In S. Cahn (Ed.), *Affirmative Action and the University: A Philosophical Inquiry* (pp. 174–180). Temple University Press.

Inoue, A. (2015). *Antiracist Writing Assessment Ecologies: Teaching and Assessing Writing for a Socially Just Future*. WAC Clearinghouse/University of Colorado Press. doi:10.37514/PER-B.2015.0698

Johnson, M. (2011). Racial literacy and the writing center. In L. Greenfield & K. Rowan (Eds.), *Writing centers and the new racism: A call for sustainable dialogue and change* (pp. 211–227). Utah State University Press. doi:10.2307/j.ctt4cgk6s.14

Keh, C. L. (1990). Feedback in the writing process: A model and methods for implementation. *ELT Journal, 44*(4), 294–304. doi:10.1093/elt/44.4.294

Knoch, U. (2009). Diagnostic assessment of writing: A comparison of two rating scales. *Language Testing, 26*(2), 275–304. doi:10.1177/0265532208101008

Lane, J., & Lam, E. (2021). *This new SFU writing guide champions inclusivity*. Retrieved from https://www.sfu.ca/sfunews/stories/2021/04/this-new-sfu-writing-guide-champions-inclusivity.html

Lassiter, L. (2005a). Collaborative ethnography and public anthropology. *Current Anthropology, 46*(1), 83–106. doi:10.1086/425658

Lassiter, L. E. (2021). Collaborative ethnography. In B. Diamond, S. Castelo-Branco, & S. Castelo-Branco (Eds.), *Transforming Ethnomusicology* (Vol. 2). Oxford University Press. doi:10.1093/oso/9780197517604.003.0004

Leibowitz, B., Goodman, K., Hannon, P., & Parkerson, A. (1997). The role of a writing center in increasing access to academic discourse in a multilingual university. *Teaching in Higher Education, 2*(1), 5–19. doi:10.1080/1356251970020101

Lemke, J. L. (1995). *Textual politics: Discourse and social dynamics*. Taylor & Francis.

Mahboob, A., & Szenes, E. (2007). Linguicism and racism in assessment practices in higher education. *Linguistics and the Human Sciences, 3*(3), 325–354. doi:10.1558/lhs.v3i3.325

Matsuda, P. K. (2006). The myth of linguistic homogeneity in US college composition. *College English, 68*(6), 637–651. doi:10.2307/25472180

May, R. A. B., & Pattillo-McCoy, M. (2000). Do you see what I see? Examining a collaborative ethnography. *Qualitative Inquiry, 6*(1), 65–87. doi:10.1177/107780040000600105

McLeod, S. (1992). Writing across the curriculum: An introduction. In S. McLeod & M. Soven (Eds.), *Writing across the curriculum: A guide to developing programs* (pp. 1–11). Sage.

Milson-Whyte, V., & Campbell, A. (2022, December). Neoliberal influences and academic writing student support systems in higher education. *UWI Quality Education Forum, 26*, 119-145.

Moussu, L. (2013). Let's talk! ESL students' needs and writing center philosophy. *TESL Canada Journal, 30*(2), 55–68. doi:10.18806/tesl.v30i2.1142

Natarajan, S., Cardona, V. G., Bondi, J., & Yang, T. (2023). What's on our landing page? Writing center policy commonplaces and antiracist critique. *Peer Review : Emerging Trends and Key Debates in Undergraduate Education, 1*(7). https://thepeerreview-iwca.org/issues/issue-7-1-featured-issue-reinvestigate-the-commonplaces-in-writing-centers/whats-on-our-landing-page-writing-center-policy-commonplaces-and-antiracist-critique/

Noddings, N. (2012). The caring relation in teaching. *Oxford Review of Education, 38*(6), 771–781. doi:10.1080/03054985.2012.745047

Paris, D. (2012). Culturally sustaining pedagogy: A needed change in stance, terminology, and practice. *Educational Researcher, 41*(3), 93–97. doi:10.3102/0013189X12441244

Paris, D., & Alim, H. S. (2014). What are we seeking to sustain through culturally sustaining pedagogy? A loving critique forward. *Harvard Educational Review, 84*(1), 85–100. doi:10.17763/haer.84.1.982l873k2ht16m77

Poe, M. (2022). Learning to unlearn the teaching and assessment of academic writing. *Discourse and Writing/Rédactologie, 32,* 161-190.

Santos, B. S. (2015). *Epistemologies of the South: Justice against epistemicide.* Routledge. doi:10.4324/9781315634876

Tiostanova, M. V., & Mignolo, W. (2012). *Learning to unlearn: Decolonial reflections from Eurasia and the Americas.* The Ohio State University Press.

Villanueva, V. (2006). Blind: Talking about the new racism. *Writing Center Journal, 26*(1), 3–19. doi:10.7771/2832-9414.1589

Wu, S. Y., & Rubin, D. L. (2000). Evaluating the impact of collectivism and individualism on argumentative writing by Chinese and North American college students. *Research in the Teaching of English, 35*(2), 148–178.

Wynter-Hoyte, K., Braden, E. G., Rodriguez, S., & Thornton, N. (2019). Disrupting the status quo: Exploring culturally relevant and sustaining pedagogies for young diverse learners. *Race, Ethnicity and Education, 22*(3), 428–447. doi:10.1080/13613324.2017.1382465

Zamel, V. (1997). Toward a model of transculturation. *TESOL Quarterly, 31*(2), 341–352. doi:10.2307/3588050

KEY TERMS AND DEFINITIONS

Collaborative Ethnography: Collaborative ethnography is an introspective research method where the researchers work together in teams to closely examine the research team members' lived experiences.

Culturally Sustaining Pedagogy: It supports and nurtures diversities of linguistic, literacy, and cultural practices within an education system.

Intertextuality: Our way of speaking and thinking is influenced by the shared communication practices of the community we belong to. It shapes our own language and perspectives, and gives us a framework to create expressions and ideas that other members will understand.

Naturalized Ideology: Ideology refers to the ingrained and accepted way in which society expects ordinary individuals to think, write, behave, communicate, and hold their beliefs. It represents the conventional and often unspoken norms that guide our understanding of what is considered 'normal' in our culture.

Paradigm Shift: A transformative way that re-examines the dominant practice and constructively implements alternative strategy or discourse that respects diverse members within educational settings.

Subjectivity: A community member's personal perspective, feelings, beliefs, and experiences based on their lived experiences.

Writing Tutoring Discourse: Writing tutoring discourse refers to the established patterns of interactions and communication that writing consultants are trained to identify and engage in while adhering to the shared community norms and expectations within the context of tutoring.

ENDNOTE

[1] In my institution, they refer to writing tutors as the following job titles based on two academic levels: undergraduate peer educators or graduate writing facilitators.

APPENDIX

Figure 6. Another sample consultation notes

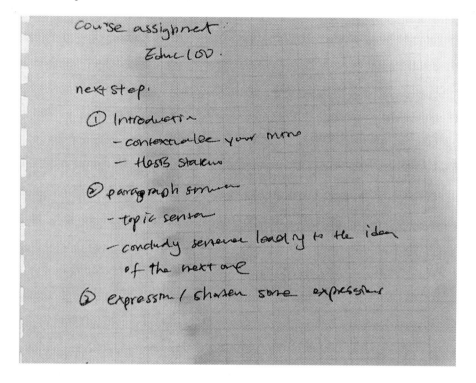

Figure 7. Sample tutoring feedback from the teaching diary 1

Developing a topic sentence

A good topic sentence has a focus, and it relates to the whole essay's thesis statement as well as the examples that you will be talking about. It is because it shows your arguments and how you are going to support your ideas.

Think about some issues here while developing your topic sentence: (1) what is my first idea for supporting my thesis? (2) why is my first idea important/ or how is my first idea supported? (3) what is the connection between my first idea, my thesis statement, and my examples.

The following examples might give you some ideas of how a topic sentence should look like:

- While it is obvious that X..., Y seems to be ....
- Not only does A ...., but B also....
- A uses X to support Y because .....

Figure 8. Sample tutoring feedback from the teaching diary 2

Grammar – Sentence Fragment

Fragments are incomplete sentences. Usually, fragments are pieces of sentences that have become disconnected from the main clause. One of the easiest ways to correct them is to remove the period between the fragment and the main clause. Other kinds of punctuation may be needed for the newly combined sentence.

Below are some examples with the fragments shown in red. Punctuation and/or words added to make corrections are highlighted in blue. Notice that the fragment is frequently a dependent clause or long phrase that follows the main clause.

- Fragment: Purdue offers many majors in engineering. Such as electrical, chemical, and industrial engineering.

Possible Revision: Purdue offers many majors in engineering, such as electrical, chemical, and industrial engineering.

- Fragment: Coach Dietz exemplified this behavior by walking off the field in the middle of a game. Leaving her team at a time when we needed her.

Possible Revision: Coach Dietz exemplified this behavior by walking off the field in the middle of a game, leaving her team at a time when we needed her.

- Fragment: I need to find a new roommate. Because the one I have now isn't working out too well.

Possible Revision: I need to find a new roommate because the one I have now isn't working out too well.

- Fragment: The current city policy on housing is incomplete as it stands. Which is why we believe the proposed amendments should be passed.

Possible Revision: Because the current city policy on housing is incomplete as it stands, we believe the proposed amendments should be passed

Chapter 11
A Textbook Case of Antiracism:
Course Readings and Critical Pedagogy for Multilingual First-Year University Writers

Srividya Natarajan
https://orcid.org/0000-0001-5959-4649
King's University College, Canada

Emily Pez
https://orcid.org/0009-0006-5812-6062
King's University College, Canada

ABSTRACT

The pedagogic assumption that English is not only a target language for international students and other L2 English users, but also a metonym for the desirable culture to which they must assimilate is still prevalent in many Canadian institutions. This chapter discusses how two teacher-practitioners wrote a first-year writing (FYW) textbook for multilingual students, drawing on critical pedagogy to resist this form of white linguistic and epistemic supremacy while also empowering multilingual writers and resolving the vexed question of content in writing textbooks. In this chapter, the authors describe their fruitless search for a suitable textbook, their decision to write their own, their articulation of the principles that would guide their composing process, the frameworks they drew upon, and the secondary research that supported their choices as they created FYW learning materials that were antiracist and anti-linguicist but supportive of the academic success of multilingual students within the prevailing assessment ecologies in their institution.

INTRODUCTION

In this chapter, we—Srividya (Vidya) Natarajan, a Writing program administrator and instructor, and Emily Pez, a Writing instructor[1]—bring a practitioner focus to the issue of textbooks for multilingual international students who are taking first-year university Writing courses in Canada.[2] Our liberal arts college recruits international students from many countries, with by far the largest numbers coming from

DOI: 10.4018/978-1-6684-9029-7.ch011

China, South Korea, and South Asia. As in many other Canadian post-secondary institutions, international students and students who have recently immigrated to Canada from non-English speaking nations are encouraged to take first-year Writing (FYW) courses designed specifically for multilingual writers.[3]

Like many teacher-practitioners who share a growing awareness of

- the extent to which Open Educational Resources (OERs) can mitigate financial hardship among students,
- critiques of commercially produced textbooks and associated pedagogic practices, especially on raciolinguistic grounds (Basabe, 2006; Bori, 2018; Gulliver & Thurrell, 2016; Kumaravadivelu, 2003a; Ndura, 2004; Pennycook, 2012), and
- the ways in which learning materials can be adapted and customized in the digital age (Atkinson & Corbitt, 2023; Mishan, 2022),

we embarked on the work of creating an FYW textbook for our own localized and specific purposes. What we learned in the process may be of interest to colleagues in the field.

Discussing the creation of learning materials, Spiro (2022) observed that "for the teacher the starting point is often a perceived need, and a gap in resources that meet this need" (p. 479). She recommended that practitioners who are creating learning materials learn their craft by engaging with materials scholarship, by trawling through existing textbooks, and, importantly for our chapter, by listening to each other. It is this impulse to share the "pedagogic reasoning" (Pang, 2016; Richards, 2015; Shulman, 1987) behind their textbook creation with a community of practitioners that animated Atkinson and Corbitt's (2023) fascinating discourse analysis of their composing process, which elicits the relationship between their teaching praxis and their textbook choices. As humanities scholars, we offer the pedagogical reasoning behind our choices for an FYW textbook for multilingual writers partly as theorized narrative, which gathers together what Shulman called the "wisdom of practice" (1987, p. 11), and partly in the form of a theorized list of "principles," enumerating what Shulman called "formal scholarship of education" (1987, p. 10).[4]

While many of these choices were intuitive at the time they were made (in 2018–2019), we have since been drawing on existing scholarship and research to interpret, reflect upon, and analyze them. While self-reflection for the purposes of pedagogic improvement has been ongoing since 2019, when we piloted our textbook in our classrooms, focused analysis occurred through Zoom meetings in the spring and summer of 2023. During these meetings, we discussed and took notes on:

- our teaching experiences
- our impressions of textbooks that we had encountered in our searches (and had revisited recently for this project)
- our reading of scholarship in a number of contiguous domains (including antiracist and decolonial pedagogy, linguistic ideology, second language writing, learner identity studies, learning materials creation, and so on).

Our secondary research helped us unpack and frame our notes, and helped us make our pedagogic reasoning explicit. It will also inform our plan for enrichment and enlargement of our textbook, which we hope to make available beyond its current in-house avatar, as an OER.

Drawing on our teaching experiences and our research, we want to argue strongly for textbook *content* that is antiracist[5] and anti-linguicist,[6] transparent about the operations of sociolinguistic and cultural ideologies, and supportive of positive (rather than deficit) understandings of L2 writer identities *as the starting point* for a decolonial approach to learning materials for multilingual university writers. We assert that such empowering content, tied to critical pedagogy, should be the *ground* on which academic literacies are built. Staking out this ground can allow instructors to adopt a "post-method" stance that sees pedagogic approaches through the lens of "principled pragmatism." This lens is wrought from classroom experience and teacher autonomy, and it yields "a systematic, coherent, and relevant alternative to method" (Kumaravadivelu, 2003b, p. 27). With pragmatic and locally-defined learning goals guiding our choice of methods, we anchored our pedagogy in genre-based modelling and writing about writing. We believe that this combination of approaches can support agency and metacognitive capacities in multilingual students, supporting them in successful but critically aware adaptation to North American textual and academic conventions without pressuring them to assimilate to North American cultural norms.[7]

SEARCHING FOR A TEXTBOOK

Srividya Natarajan

When I (Vidya) took over administration of the Writing program at the college where I teach, I found it impossible to leave my identity behind. As a first-generation immigrant and settler in Canada whose country of origin was a British colony, and as a researcher familiar with the scholarship on the role of language in colonial hegemony,[8] I felt immediately at odds with the current-traditional textbooks and the highly prescriptive, monolingual pedagogy that were in place for multilingual students at my institution.[9] I began searching for an FYW textbook with ideological and pedagogic features that I thought would serve L2 writers well. While the ideological and the pedagogic aspects of any educational project are inextricably entangled with each other,[10] I will unpack these two parts of my textbook wish-list (i.e., the "principles" I was trying to apply) to clarify what I mean by "serving L2 writers well."

The *ideological* assumption that English is not only a target language for international students and other L2 English users, but also a metonym for the desirable *culture* to which they must assimilate, is still widely prevalent in many North American post-secondary institutions (Basabe, 2006; Bori, 2018; Gulliver & Thurrell, 2016; Ndura, 2004).[11] This assumption manifests in FYW textbooks, which, like other language and literacy materials, are, as Curdt-Christiansen and Weninger (2015) noted, "the products of complex selective processes reflecting political decisions, educational beliefs and priorities, cultural realities and language policies" (p. 1). English language textbooks in many countries, from the 1990s onwards, began to reflect some resistance to the positioning of Anglo-American culture as the "target culture," and began to place some value on learners' "source cultures" (Basabe, 2006; Bori, 2018; Risager, 2023). Nevertheless, capitalist values, western triumphalism, racist depictions of newcomers, and denial of racism continued to be reflected in language learning materials (Basabe, 2006; Bori, 2018; Gulliver & Thurell, 2016; Ndura, 2004). Basabe (2006) noted that "the world constructed by [English language course books in Argentina] still remains one in which the English-speaking countries are not only linguistic but also cultural 'targets' the globe has to aspire to, imitate, and follow" (pp. 68–69). Fan Shen's (1989) classic essay brilliantly encapsulates how the ethos of white/western supremacy works at the level of individual self-fashioning, and how it pushes international university students in North

American universities to acquire not only the academic literacies valued in their new contexts, but also new *westernized selves* with western ways of looking at the world.

My search for a first-year writing textbook for multilingual and international students thus began with a desire to combat the racism and white (linguistic and epistemic) supremacy implicit in this demand that they absorb and enact western understandings of the connections between selves and knowledges. If nothing else, the cultural swallowing up of the distinct, fluid, emergent, and diverse identities of multilingual students in the writing class subverts the idea of "exchange between equals" that informs the (idealized) framework of internationalization. By trapping racialized international students in the role of perpetual culture-learners, even as they exalt and transform white native speakers into both language instructors and cultural informants, culturally assimilative approaches create a power structure that delegitimizes instead of authorizing (see Bucholtz & Hall, 2005; Canagarajah, 2004; Xiao & Zhao, 2022).

From the point of view of content, then, I was looking for a textbook that contextualized and made transparent the power relations between L1 and L2 in the FYW classroom, that created affordances for the expression of the strengths, submerged resistances, capacity for social critique, and overt subversions associated with L2 writer identities (Canagarajah, 2004). I was searching, a little outrageously, for a textbook that was written from the subject positions of L2 English users who were engaged in a *critique* of neoliberalism and what Meighan (2023) called the colonialingualism of the North American university context.[12] In terms of frameworks for praxis, what I was hoping for was a textbook whose content productively combined and applied elements of critical pedagogy (Canagarajah, 2002; Freire, 2000; Giroux, 2023; hooks, 1994) and elements of Culturally Sustaining Pedagogy (Alim et al., 2020; Ladson-Billings, 2014).

Much as I wished for a textbook that would facilitate critical engagement with academic norms and resistant negotiation of learner identity, I also held on to the pragmatic and instrumental goal of FYW: the goal of supporting writers' development of the university-level literacies that would lead to academic success. Many of the textbooks I examined during my search adopted some version of a current-traditional approach to teaching writing (some use of reading-to-write; discussion of rhetorical modes, paragraph and essay structure, grammar, and citation, along with some attention to writing voice), to which explication of the writing process and sometimes of genre was added.[13] Readings, when provided, were often journalistic rather than academic (thus foreclosing on modelling citation practices, and creating a confusing contradiction for students between what we urged them to do and what they were seeing on the page).[14] The readings were often lexically and syntactically sophisticated (see Schmitt, 2019) but without modelling linguistic diversity within English. For instance, with one exception,[15] there was barely a trace of Black Language or African American Vernacular English (AAVE), whose very rich and distinguished history, and viability as an academic language, are powerfully captured by Smitherman (1977), Baker-Bell (2020), and Young (2011), among others. Nor did the textbooks reference any World Englishes (Kachru, 1986). Even when they showcased multiculturalism or ethnic diversity in authorship, the readings-based textbooks I encountered rarely addressed the concept of ideology, let alone particular raciolinguistic ideologies.[16] Textbooks that were explicitly written for multilingual students discussed the writing process, information literacy, citation, grammar, vocabulary, and so on, and had short readings and genre examples on "neutral"—i.e., non-controversial—topics.[17] I began to see the omission of critical consciousness from FYW textbooks as a problem with a bearing on the second item on my wish-list: a functional *pedagogy* that enabled entry into Canadian university-level disciplinary discourse communities.

Thus, with respect to pedagogy, I was looking for an FYW textbook for multilingual students that supported academic literacy development *through* critical reading materials and critical language awareness.[18] As demanding assimilation to the (white, middle-class, western) "target culture" became increasingly problematic (Canagarajah, 2013), many language learning scholars began describing the empowering effects of intercultural awareness and translingual orientations as pedagogic resources (Canagarajah, 2013; Jain, 2022; McPherron & An, 2023). What if the demystification of academic literacies could be consciously coupled with intercultural and translingual awareness in pedagogy for multilingual students?[19]

Studying the transition to university of "Generation 1.5" students (both students who themselves immigrated to Canada and students who are children of immigrants, with some years of high school in Canada), Roessingh and Douglas (2012) noted that their high levels of communicative competence in everyday contexts did not necessarily prepare them to carry what they called the "linguistic burden" of university-level academic materials, which demand "the ability to engage with problem solving approaches to learning that require the active and collaborative construction of meaning and understanding" (p. 292). Problem-solving and the construction of meaning are essentially culturally inflected activities but are often presented in the Canadian writing classroom as universals. Could raising critical awareness of the relationship between North American academic conventions and North American cultural norms empower students to draw on their own cultural resources more confidently?

As I grew increasingly dissatisfied with the resources I had found, I had to concede, echoing Masuhara (2011), that "my ideal materials only exist[ed] in my dreams" (p. 236). I decided that I would write a textbook for our students, and that it would be accompanied by a selection of additional readings consisting of academic articles by established multilingual Writing Studies scholars. My colleague Emily Pez joined me in this endeavour. Following Tomlinson's (2012a) suggestion that developing learning materials should involve articulating criteria based on theories of effective teaching for a target audience, here is a summary of our principles for an FYW writing textbook for multilingual international students.

Table 1. Criteria for a Year 1 writing textbook for multilingual international students

Ideological Features	Pedagogic Features
● Embodies antiracism and anti-linguicism ● Creates affordances for students to explore and express social and political critique as well as intercultural competence ● Values cultural/rhetorical knowledge from students' home cultures ● Supports positive L2 learner identity and self-concept; no deficit modelling, no radical re-orientation of the writing self ● Raises students' critical awareness of L1 and L2 power relations along with other intersections of power/knowledge	● Learning units support academic literacy development for success in the Canadian/North American university context today ● Syntactically and lexically accessible and friendly, avoids excessive cognitive load ● Genre-based readings model academic conventions, including citation practices, while also explaining these conventions in culturally contextualized ways to promote metacognition ● Describes writing process with step-by-step breakdown of how genre features can be incorporated or invented ● Affordances for writing about writing, self-reflection, positionality, agency ● Low-cost

WRITING THE TEXTBOOK

Srividya Natarajan and Emily Pez

I (Emily) am a postsecondary writing instructor and writing center consultant who speaks English as a first language and is descended from European settlers (both English-speakers and Italian-speakers). My passion for our research is tied to my experiences as an academic peer guide, writing tutor, and friend of international students of raciolinguistically minoritized identities, with whom I lived and studied at my undergraduate institution. Now, working primarily with multilingual students, I constantly feel enthused by the students, their creations, and the talents they share with me. It is important to me to support these students and help them combat any educational barriers that they have faced due to their diverse identities. Srividya truly inspires and guides me as I continue to learn and grow as an educator.

Pushing the Boundaries: Textbook Content and Critical Pedagogy

Nieto (2015), discussing how she was drawn to critical pedagogy, recounted the words of a teacher called Hyung Nam, whom she interviewed:

Hyung took the advocacy function of education very seriously, saying, "I see part of my job is to agitate. You know, if we think about the kind of society, the dominant mainstream society that we have, that's kind of why I'm a teacher is to agitate and make people think and question things." (p. 47)

In planning the content of our textbook, we believed, like Hyung and Nieto, that writing skills did not have to be divorced from a broader critical literacy and concern for social justice. We believed that critical pedagogy (Canagarajah, 2002; Freire, 2000; Giroux, 2023; hooks, 1994; Pennycook, 2017) and Culturally Sustaining Pedagogy (CSP) (Alim et al., 2020; Ladson-Billings, 2014) would raise consciousness in both students and instructors about oppressive ideologies and practices including neoliberal competitiveness, hyperindividualism, and the white linguistic/epistemic supremacy that emerges in the monolingual orientation of writing classrooms, deficit modelling and negative stereotypes of L2 writers, and the overarching expectation that multilingual students will assimilate culturally (Bori, 2018; Davila, 2022; Inoue, 2015; Jain, 2022; Kumaravadivelu 2003a).

Culturally Relevant Pedagogy (CRP) was first theorized by Ladson-Billings (1995) to describe effective pedagogical practices observed in eight teachers' elementary school classrooms of predominantly African-American students. Ladson-Billings' theoretical framework has three major aspects: (1) emphasis on student academic achievements, (2) celebration of students' own diverse cultures along with increased understanding of another culture's practices, and (3) development of students' "sociopolitical consciousness" to enable them to critique inequities within and beyond classroom settings (2014, p. 75). Ladson-Billings (2014) described CSP as "the remix" of this earlier theory (p. 77). Alim et al. (2020) explained that CSP "is necessarily and fundamentally a critical, anti-racist, anti-colonial framework that rejects the white settler capitalist gaze and the kindred cisheteropatriarchal, English-monolingual, ableist, classist, xenophobic and other hegemonic gazes" (p. 262) and seeks to sustain "the cultures, languages and lives of communities" of color (p. 269), including their dynamic, emerging cultural and linguistic practices that intersect with multiple racial identities (p. 267). CSP "draws strength and wisdom from centuries of intergenerational revitalization, resistance and the revolutionary love" in these communities (p. 262).

Defining critical pedagogy, Pennycook (2017) drew on Giroux (2011) to suggest that one of its vital functions is to help us "to understand difference both in terms of how student and teacher identities are formed and how differences between groups are maintained" (p. 298). Accordingly, we decided that the content of our textbook would be a series of short articles that would interrogate the ways in which academic writing instruction places international students, seen both as individuals (i.e., *student identities*) and as collectivities (i.e., *groups*), at a raciolinguistic disadvantage.

The textbook (to which we gave the bland and thoroughly unexciting title *Thinking About Writing*) contains readings written by us, each one no longer than four pages. Each reading either names, contextualizes, and challenges implicit racism and white supremacy in language education, or validates aspects of non-western rhetorical knowledge and L2 writer identity; some readings do both. For instance, one of the readings, an article titled "LEP, ESL, ELL, EL, or Multilingual? Resisting the Deficit Model" problematizes North American institutional labelling of multilingual writers. This article models a research essay and offers the following thesis:

Resisting the "deficit model" approach to users of English as an academic language will not only change the attitudes of instructors in such a way as to result in a positive environment for learning, but it will also psychologically support the students as they handle the stress of trying to succeed academically while using an unfamiliar language. (Natarajan, 2019b, p. 15)

The article also celebrates multilingual students' "rich knowledge and skills in their own language and cultural worlds" (p. 16). Modelling citation justice, this article references articles by racialized scholars on deficit understandings of L2 writers (Li, 2018; Martínez, 2018).

Chun (2016) asserted that critical pedagogies

should not be seen as detracting from language learning; indeed, these approaches can aid in developing English language learners' (ELLs') academic literacy skills by engaging them more deeply with curriculum materials featuring dominant cultural and racialized—and thus already politicized— representations through closer interrogations of their underlying discourses and the language constructing these. Through these engagements, ELLs would have more opportunities to learn how language and discourse work, and thus help expand their own meaning-making in the process. (pp. 110–111)

The article on labelling described above (Natarajan, 2019b) created affordances for a researched argumentative essay assignment that invites students to consider how they respond to deficit representations of L2 writer identities, and to create terminology that they feel more accurately and fairly represents their own positionalities. Judging by the assignments that were submitted for our evaluation, a few of which were adapted and published in one of our institution's own publications (Chen, 2021; Du & Huang, 2020; Yin, 2022), students enjoyed the opportunities for self-reflection and the creation of meaning, coming up with interesting terminology for multilingual writers that identified and sometimes actively subverted the racial and linguistic hierarchies they had encountered. Our informal observations are in line with an analysis by Bucholtz et al. (2017) of the experiences of two students of Mexican-American heritage in a grade 12 California college preparation class,[20] which shows how instructors' CSP-based practices enabled students' appreciation of their own linguistic repertoires, their identity formation, and their application of agency.[21] The class enabled the students to conduct and present research at a conference on the topic of sociolinguistic justice, while deploying and further developing their multilingual skillsets (Bucholtz et al., 2017). Our observations also echo Chen's case analysis of six Chinese international students' genre practices at a US university, which revealed that facilitating self-reflective writing opportunities helped students repurpose skills learned in first-year academic writing courses for discipline-specific writing contexts (2022, p. 62).

Other readings in *Thinking About Writing* present content that draws on critical pedagogic frameworks to question punitive approaches to patchwriting (Howard, 1995) and inadvertent textual borrowing, and on CSP frameworks to validate learning techniques (such as memorization) used by some writers in non-western cultures but devalued in North American classrooms.[22] Overall, the readings invite students to think critically about the very course they are taking, and about their relationship to its goals, pedagogy, instructors, and context. We believe the readings engage the interest of multilingual students because they so directly address their identities and raciolinguistic predicaments. Without resorting to cultural stereotypes or essentialism, the readings capture aspects of L2 writer identity that students are very much in the process of negotiating in complex, dynamic, and sometimes conflicted ways. It is not surprising that they are interested in reflecting on these questions. As Muramatsu (2018) observed, "L2 learners ... do not passively emulate the normative practices of the target language communities or accept undesirable social values and positions being simply imposed on them; instead, they negotiate, resist and shape their learning processes and experiences" (p. 5).

The readings (and associated assignments) position international students as bringing with them significant knowledge of the rhetorical approaches of their home academic contexts and cultures, rather than as being in deficit. They also allow students to showcase critical thinking as defined by North American academic culture. Intrigued by the invitation to interrogate the racism underlying their learning goals, and finding the politics of language meaningful and relevant to their academic lives, many students submit writing that is charged with passion, focus, and fluency.

Toeing the Line: Pedagogic Frameworks and Learning Goals

In creating the readings in our textbook, we engaged critical and Culturally Sustaining Pedagogies to support self-reflexivity and antiracist, anti-linguicist conscientization among L2 writers. Oddly enough, we felt that encouraging students to take a critical stance on institutional expectations and hidden racism was *not* particularly risky. What we did see as burdening multilingual students with risk was any significant redefinition of the academic literacies that they would need for membership in their disciplinary communities. All too familiar with (some) course policies and (some) instructor attitudes in our institution (the marks docked per grammatical "error," the complaints about inadequate citation and "cheating," the frequent bemoaning of the lack of "the most basic skills"), we erred on the side of pedagogic conservatism when we defined the FYW course's learning outcomes, and when we identified the frameworks and classroom practices we would use. As we saw it, we were also working towards raciolinguistic equity by equipping multilingual students to survive and thrive in an academic context where most disciplinary instructors (whose rhadamanthine judgement would be exercised on these students' work in their respective disciplines) were either ignorant of or indifferent to the fierce debates around translingualism, codemeshing, standard language ideology, Students' Right to Their Own Language (SRTOL), and Global Englishes that were taking place in the world of language and writing educators (Baker-Bell, 2020; Canagarajah, 2013; Kachru, 1986; Smitherman, 1977; Young, 2011).

One of the applied implications of Huo's (2020) studies of postsecondary students' orientations toward monolingual standard English-speaking educational norms, as well as of Huo's lived experiences of racism and linguicism as a racialized non-native English-speaking teacher at a writing center, was that institutions need to be transformed so that they "value the capital and resources that minority students bring to the classroom" (p. 153). Institutional change can also shift racist and linguicist attitudes among instructors and students, contributing to the success and well-being of raciolinguistically minoritized students and instructors (p. 153). This work of advocacy should be considered one of the conditions for the viability of a textbook like ours; it is an ongoing project for many writing program administrators and many writing instructors, but we are not there yet.

Learning Outcomes

Toeing a clearly-drawn conventional line, we defined the FYW course's learning outcomes as follows:
Writing 1002 will help students to

- feel that they belong to a supportive community of learners and know how to access campus resources and supports (Toorenburgh & Gaudet, 2023);
- consider their own personal and cultural identities as a writer, and honour diverse cultural modes of communication;
- understand the kinds of reading, thinking, and writing skills needed to succeed in the Canadian university context;
- interpret an essay prompt or question, and identify or define a research problem;
- write a valid hypothesis, thesis, or argument related to a research question;
- find reliable academic sources, and read them selectively and critically;
- organize ideas in well-structured paragraphs, and connect the paragraphs to produce a coherent essay;
- integrate material from research sources through paraphrase, summary, and quotation;
- cite sources in APA style; and
- have an overall sense of how genre governs writing, and produce writing in three genres. (Adapted from Pez, 2023)

Pedagogic Moves

Given these learning outcomes, the textbook had to model the conventions of North American academic writing and facilitate the development of student academic literacies. Here are some of the frameworks we used and the textual choices we made in order to support student academic success:

1. Using Academic Literacies as a Pedagogic Frame. The Academic Literacies approach, as discussed by Lillis et al. (2015), and supported by research from Zhou et al. (2020), opposes the deficit approach to students and instead emphasizes the competencies or academic literacies that students can learn and apply to their new academic context. Performing qualitative analysis of audio data from student focus group discussions and teaching units, as well as student reflective essays from first-year Chinese students completing their English as a Foreign Language (EFL) university studies, Zhou et al. (2020) found that instructors need to explicitly communicate academic- and employment-related learning goals to students as well as convey how each assessment contributes to those goals to help students value academic literacies (pp. 272–277). An intervention study at a UK university supported student learning through an academic literacy model for diverse students (Wingate, 2018). Defining principles of Wingate's model are collaborative, discipline-specific writing instruction and analysis of relevant genres and their social purposes to help create an inclusive learning environment that demystifies the expectations of disciplinary discourse communities (p. 128). The Academic Literacies approach of making the implicit expectations and conventions explicit through the transformation of writing pedagogy promotes antiracism, as opposed to blaming multilingual students for being unfamiliar with the tacit conventions to which they have not had prior access (Lillis & Tuck, 2016). Applying Academic Literacies research, our textbook elucidates how writing in particular genres enables students to practise and develop academic writing competencies outlined in our course learning outcomes. While we emphasize how writing competencies will serve students in their writing across the disciplines, we also link genres (for example, the case analysis) to disciplinary discourse communities (for example, Business studies).

2. Using Genre as a Pedagogic Frame. Genre-based approaches have been valued in the teaching of academic writing because they increase students' understanding of academic genre patterns and help students reproduce them in their own writing (Tardy, 2017, p. 69). Our textbook introduces the concept of genre as well as rationales for specific genres, with genre rationales unpacked to maximize metacognitive understanding of the socio-rhetorical purposes of, and audiences for, different genres in the North American context. The step-by-step writing process by which students might produce writing in a specific genre is also laid out. This is in line with the findings of a study of EFL pre-university students enrolled in an academic writing course in Thailand. In this study, Kitajroonchai et al. (2022) found that process genre-based writing, which combines both the genre-based approach of learning how to write in particular academic genres for specific discourse communities and the process writing approach, which emphasizes obtaining feedback at various stages of the writing process, more positively affected student writing content and language use than a process writing approach in isolation. It is also in keeping with Acar's (2023) point that the process genre-based approach can support students' learning through formative feedback on assessments and self-reflective student involvement in assessments (writing about writing). A case study of an English for Academic Purposes (EAP) course at a US university demonstrated that instructional scaffolding, through classroom analysis and discussion of models from relevant genres, and instructors' clear communication of assessment criteria before students produce writing in particular genres were important for the success of the genre approach (Acar, 2023).

Genre-based teaching can promote linguistic justice for multilingual students. Important for critical pedagogy are opportunities for students not just to apply genre conventions but also to use them in innovative and critical ways. Multilingual scholars can use, "fuse," and "resist" genre conventions to achieve their own communication goals, including critique of mainstream western academic discourses (Canagarajah, 2002, p. 75). Hyon (2018) referred to intentional genre innovations as "genre play" (p. 163), arguing that it may enable "genre learning transfer" (p. 182) by developing students' competencies and experiences in flexibly and skillfully applying genre knowledge to new genre contexts (p. 183). Genre conventions are thus described in our textbook as dynamic rather than static, and explained, wherever possible, in terms of their social context. For instance, we speculate about the possible relationship between capitalist perceptions of time as money and the typical positioning of the thesis at the start of the argumentative essay. As we model and discuss the writing of thesis statements for the Canadian university context, we also acknowledge diverse cultural modes of encapsulating or arriving at an argument, a theme discussed by Zhang (2010).

3. Attending to Transfer. The readings in our textbook engage students in analysis of their own writing identities and in "writing about writing," which, according to Rieman et al. (2019), encourages student agency, participation, and transfer. Cui's (2019) "pedagogic framework for L2 transfer teaching" applies genre-based writing pedagogies, critical literacy, and writing about writing, offering six strategies for facilitating writing transfer, particularly for L2 students at American universities (p. 1124). Research from both Chen (2022) and Pourghasemian and Zarei (2021) shows the creative and innovative potential displayed by multilingual students as they adaptively transferred the skills learned in general academic writing courses to their writing in content courses.

Research on writing transfer has associated anti-linguicist pedagogy with increased transferability of writing competencies. A key strategy in Cui's (2019) framework for improving transfer among multilingual students is to "build on previous cultural and academic knowledge" (p. 1125). Relating L2 course content to students' previous L1 knowledge and experiences, instructors can "help L2 students build up confidence and offer opportunities for them to realize that being an L2 student is an advantage, not a deficiency" (Cui, 2019, p. 1126). Our textbook's readings and accompanying assignments, which encourage students to apply their expertise in their cultures' writing practices, are similarly intended to develop students' confidence and self-efficacy and enable writing transfer.

4. Using Authentic Academic Articles that Include Citation. Wubalem (2021) suggested that transfer could be facilitated through authentic readings, which introduce students to features and conventions of academic writing, and exercises through which students model these texts.[23] Drawing upon an anti-oppressive Academic Literacies approach, our textbook theorizes authentic academic writing as context-specific and reflective of institutional power relations, applying a linguistic register and citation practices approved by a specific academic audience, rather than theorizing academic norms as universal and uncontested (Lillis & Tuck, 2016). The readings model academic authenticity for a North American university context. Largely written by Srividya Natarajan (from her subject position as a racialized woman and a first-generation immigrant/settler) they push for raciolinguistic equality and more diverse academic voices, inviting students' critique and questioning of the monolingual, Eurocentric norms they learn, in line with the advice of Lillis and Tuck (2016).

Each of our readings models a genre (with multiple readings in the research essay genre, since it is so central to expectations in students' disciplines). We capped articles at four pages each, to make them readable, to maximize student engagement with their content, and to minimize cognitive load (see Schütze, 2017). Each reading is conceptually complex and rich without being lexically or syntactically overwhelming. Each section of the textbook invites students to follow the model articles as closely as they like as they go through their apprenticeship in writing for the Canadian university context. Importantly, each article showcases in-text and end-of-text citation practices, contextualizing them within the history of western writing practices (rather than seeing them as universal). In unpacking citation, for instance, we discuss the recent history of individual authorship and intellectual property in the West. As noted above, our citation practices also model citation justice, giving prominence to racialized authors (e.g., Chien, 2014; Gaulee, 2018; Hunjeri, 2015; Li, 2018; Liu, 2018; Martínez, 2018; Shen, 1989; Zhang, 2010). The References list for each reading includes articles by Writing Studies scholars who take a clear antiracist position on topics closely related to the ones in the readings.

EXAMPLE OF A TEXTBOOK READING: THE CASE ANALYSIS CHAPTER

One of the textbook chapters is structured as a case study (Pez, 2019), and is intended to familiarize students with this genre. Its content addresses one of the key issues that international students encounter in Canadian universities, which is lack of familiarity with citation conventions. Institutions often spell out the importance of citing sources and the consequences of failing to do so. In order to introduce the problem of textual borrowing without using moralistic and judgmental language (e.g., "cheating," "dishonesty"), our case study sketches a scenario in which an instructor, who teaches an introductory university writing course for multilingual students, finds that students in his class are patchwriting. The students in the case scenario explain why they are borrowing text without acknowledgement (their reasons echo reasons we have heard from our own students). Students using the textbook are invited (in their case analysis) to imagine how the instructor should respond to this situation. In completing the writing on this assignment, students apply theoretical concepts from multilingual scholars, use their own moral yardsticks, and justify their own decisions that range from the extremely punitive to the extremely compassionate. They also learn more about the sociocultural reasons why citation is accorded so much importance in Canadian universities, and how they can improve their own skills in this area.

Instructors have found that case-based instruction has supported students' development of critical thinking skills (Bandyopadhyay & Szostek, 2019) as well as self-confidence and social skills (Orr & Weekley, 2019). Our case analysis textbook chapter aims to develop the following academic literacies:

Students

1. learn how to showcase their critical thinking skills through a case analysis;
2. understand that complex problems have more than one solution, and that strong solutions are based on sound reasoning and evidence;
3. gain increased confidence with decision making and both oral and written communication;
4. learn how to structure a case analysis so that they present their evidence effectively;
5. learn skills in applying a general theory or concept to a specific situation.

To achieve these learning goals, this chapter provides genre-based modelling of a case analysis. We scaffold the assignment by summarizing the theories that the students will apply; by providing an annotated model case analysis; by offering step-by-step process instructions for how to approach and structure the assignment; and by sharing our own prewriting notes to show how we combined data from the case and theoretical evidence to produce the model case analysis, step-by-step. We also provide students with questions about the model case analysis for small group discussion with their classmates so that they can practise and gain confidence with decision-making through ungraded writing opportunities before they write their own case analysis assignments.

In Wang et al.'s (2021) study of Chinese EFL undergraduate students, which operationalized self-efficacy as "students' confidence in their EFL-related skills with a person-centered approach" (p. 7), it was observed that self-efficacy was associated with students' emotions. Thus, "the more students felt confident in language learning ability, the more pleasant (e.g., enjoyment) and fewer unpleasant feelings (e.g., shame) they reported" (Wang et al., 2021, p. 9). Higher self-efficacy was particularly associated with higher listening and reading language test scores (Wang et al., 2021, p. 9). The study thus supported pedagogical strategies like "providing appropriate positive feedback (e.g., praise, reward), sufficient background knowledge and scaffolding" (p. 9). While Wang et al. did not discover a significant correlation between self-efficacy and writing scores, high academic writing self-efficacy among L2 students has elsewhere been shown to positively impact their writing scores (Teng & Wang, 2023; Zhang et al., 2023). Surveying and interviewing first-year Bachelor of Teaching students at an Australian University, Nallaya et al. (2022) found that first-year students using English as an Additional Language can particularly struggle with developing self-efficacy in relation to using academic literacies, especially in the use of genres such as case analyses (p. 280). Student data from Nallaya et al.'s study also indicated that "[i]nstructor assistance and being shown sufficient examples through scaffolding" would be helpful (p. 280). Our case analysis assignment tries to develop students' confidence and competencies across the disciplines, while allowing them to practise writing in a key genre for Business courses, which are popular among multilingual students at our institution.

Writing instructors' trust and respect for multilingual students through providing assignments that enable students to exercise their decision-making skills can promote writers' agency (Mao, 2021, p. 89). The textbook's case analysis assignment supports students' agency as it allows them to suggest their own strategies for how instructors can better cultivate the confidence and writing transfer of multilingual students such as themselves. It invites students to consider the complexities of the case, including problematic pedagogical practices at western universities as the possible root of the problem, rather than simply blaming students for failing to meet those universities' expectations.

CONCLUSION

Kubota (2022) called attention to a central dilemma faced by decolonially-minded instructors who are guiding students as they attempt "high-stakes academic writing … [at the post-secondary level, which] requires authors to follow established conventions" (p. 5). This is a dilemma "in which helping minoritized students manipulate the dominant linguistic code for empowerment ironically perpetuates inequality between the dominant language and their own" (Kubota, 2022, p. 5). In creating our FYW textbook, we believe we are addressing the conflict many Writing instructors face when they teach raciolinguistically minoritized students: the conflict between preparing them for success in disciplinary discourse communities and supporting and validating their diverse identities and linguistic range. We infuse our curriculum with social justice values through affirmation of minoritized raciolinguistic identities and of resistance, on the one hand; and, on the other, we continue to attend to the academic survival and success of L2 students despite the prevailing assessment ecologies within the white *habitus* (Davila, 2022; Inoue, 2015) of the North American university.

In line with research from Atkinson and Corbitt (2023), our teaching praxis influenced our ideas for the textbook.[24] Conversely, the textbook fed into our teaching praxis. As we used the textbook in the FYW course for multilingual students over the past four years, we observed how students related to the ideas in the textbook and critically engaged with them in their own writing. Instructor observation (through assignment evaluation and class interaction) and anecdotal evidence (through casual conversation with students and other colleagues who are using the textbook) suggest that this textbook has been effective in developing students' critical consciousness and self-reflexive capacities while building their academic literacies.

In addition, so far, we have gathered evidence of our textbook's effectiveness through our institution's (anonymous) Student Questionnaires on Courses and Teaching. For instance, in the questionnaire administered in fall 2022 for the FYW course for multilingual students, 100% of student respondents in the two sections of the course that Emily taught agreed that the course textbook contributed to their learning.[25] In the comment section of the questionnaire, one student referred to the textbook as a "perfect design for this course." A limitation of this chapter is that we have not yet collected empirical evidence of the textbook's effectiveness. We are planning to do qualitative research to explore the successes and shortfalls of this textbook as we begin developing it into a more widely available OER.

We consider this project an ongoing one, both in that we hope to expand the textbook and in that we hope to improve how we use it in our teaching. For instance, collaborating with Srividya to teach and tutor multilingual students increased Emily's understanding of linguicism that the students encounter and taught her about using more accessible writing models, subsequently informing the vocabulary, proposed solutions, and scaffolding of the model case analysis. Important in this process of development, as we solicit additional articles for our proposed OER, is that the authors themselves represent diverse cultures and linguistic backgrounds. In our next iteration of the textbook, we also plan to create affordances for translanguaging pedagogies and classroom practices.

REFERENCES

Acar, A. S. (2023). Genre pedagogy: A writing pedagogy to help L2 writing instructors enact their classroom writing assessment literacy and feedback literacy. *Assessing Writing*, *56*, 100717. Advance online publication. doi:10.1016/j.asw.2023.100717

Alim, H. S. (2012). Interview with Geneva Smitherman. *Journal of English Linguistics*, *40*(4), 357–377. doi:10.1177/0075424212463821

Alim, H. S., Paris, D., & Wong, C. P. (2020). Culturally sustaining pedagogy: A critical framework for centering communities. In N. S. Nasir, C. D. Lee, R. D. Pea, & M. McKinney de Royston (Eds.), *Handbook of the cultural foundations of learning* (pp. 261–276). Taylor & Francis. doi:10.4324/9780203774977-18

Atkinson, D., & Corbitt, S. (2023). Tracing the influences of praxis on the development of an open corequisite writing textbook. *Written Communication*, *40*(2), 754–784. doi:10.1177/07410883221146550

Bailey, S. (2018). *Academic writing: A handbook for international students* (5th ed.). Routledge, Taylor & Francis.

Baker-Bell, A. (2020). *Linguistic justice: Black language, literacy, identity, and pedagogy*. NCTE. doi:10.4324/9781315147383

Bandyopadhyay, S., & Szostek, J. (2019). Thinking critically about critical thinking: Assessing critical thinking of business students using multiple measures. *Journal of Education for Business*, *94*(4), 259–270. doi:10.1080/08832323.2018.1524355

Basabe, E. (2006). From de-Anglicization to internationalization: Cultural representations of the UK and the USA in global, adapted and local ELT textbooks in Argentina. *PROFILE Issues in Teachers' Professional Development (Philadelphia, Pa.)*, *7*(1), 59–75.

Bori, P. (2018). *Language textbooks in the era of neoliberalism* (1st ed.). Taylor and Francis. doi:10.4324/9781315405544

Bucholtz, H., & Hall, K. (2005). Identity and interaction: A sociocultural linguistic approach. *Discourse Studies*, *7*(4-5), 585–614. doi:10.1177/1461445605054407

Bucholtz, M., Casillas, D. I., & Lee, J. S. (2017). Language and culture as sustenance. In D. Paris & H. S. Alim (Eds.), *Culturally sustaining pedagogies: Teaching and learning for justice in a changing world* (pp. 43–59). Teacher's College Press.

Canagarajah, A. S. (2002). *Critical academic writing and multilingual students*. University of Michigan. doi:10.3998/mpub.8903

Canagarajah, A. S. (2004). Subversive identities, pedagogical safe houses, and critical learning. In B. Norton & K. Toohey (Eds.), *Critical pedagogies and language learning* (pp. 116–137). Cambridge University Press. doi:10.1017/CBO9781139524834.007

Canagarajah, A. S. (2013). *Translingual practice: Global Englishes and cosmopolitan relations*. Routledge. doi:10.4324/9780203120293

Chen, D. (2021). How to adapt to academic writing expectations: A challenge for international students. *MEM Insider*, *6*, 20–21. https://www.kings.uwo.ca/academics/school-of-management-economics-and-mathematics/mem-insider/

Chen, X. (2022). L2 students' adaptive transfer beyond first-year writing. *INTESOL Journal*, *19*(1). Advance online publication. doi:10.18060/26359

Chiapello, E., & Fairclough, N. (2002). Understanding the new management ideology: A transdisciplinary contribution from critical discourse analysis and new sociology of capitalism. *Discourse & Society*, *13*(2), 185–208. doi:10.1177/0957926502013002406

Chien, S. (2014). Cultural constructions of plagiarism in student writing: Teachers' perceptions and responses. *Research in the Teaching of English*, *49*(2), 120–140.

Chun, W. C. (2016). Addressing racialized multicultural discourses in an EAP textbook: Working toward a critical pedagogies approach. *TESOL Quarterly*, *50*(1), 109–131. doi:10.1002/tesq.216

Cui, W. (2019). Teaching for transfer to first-year L2 writers. *Journal of International Students*, *9*(4), 1115–1133. doi:10.32674/jis.v9i4.755

Curdt-Christiansen, X. L., & Weninger, C. (2015). Introduction: Ideology and the politics of language textbooks. In X. L. Curdt-Christiansen & C. Weninger (Eds.), *Language, ideology and education: The politics of textbooks in language education* (pp. 1–8). Routledge. doi:10.4324/9781315814223-7

Davila, B. (2022). White language supremacy in course descriptions. *College Composition and Communication*, *73*(4), 640–664. doi:10.58680/ccc202232013

Du, Y., & Huang, Z. (2020). International students reflect on how they would like to be described. *MEM Insider*, *5*, 13. https://www.kings.uwo.ca/academics/school-of-management-economics-and-mathematics/mem-insider/

Flachmann, K., Flachmann, M., MacLennan, A., & Zeppa, J. (2013). *Reader's choice: Essays for thinking, reading, and writing* (7th Canadian ed.). Pearson Canada.

Freire, P. (2000). Pedagogy of the oppressed (30th anniversary ed.) (M. B. Ramos, Trans.). Continuum. (Original work published 1970)

Gaulee, U. (2018). How to understand the international students with whom you work. *Journal of International Students, 8*(2), I–II. doi:10.32674/jis.v8i2.93

Giroux, H. A. (2011). *On critical pedagogy*. Continuum International Publishing Group.

Giroux, H. A. (2023). Fascist culture, critical pedagogy, and resistance in pandemic times. *English Language Notes, 61*(1), 51–62. doi:10.1215/00138282-10293151

Green, B. (2023). Five design principles for language learning materials development. *The ORTESOL Journal, 40*, 4–20.

Gulliver, T., & Thurrell, K. (2016). Denials of racism in Canadian English language textbooks. *TESL Canada Journal, 33*(10), 42–61. doi:10.18806/tesl.v33i0.1245

Hansen Edwards, J. G. (2017). Defining "native speaker" in multilingual settings: English as a native language in Asia. *Journal of Multilingual and Multicultural Development, 38*(9), 757–771. doi:10.1080/01434632.2016.1257627

Henderson, E. (2015). *Writing by choice* (3rd ed.). Oxford University Press.

hooks, b. (1994). *Teaching to transgress: Education as the practice of freedom*. Routledge.

Howard, R. M. (1995). Plagiarisms, authorships, and the academic death penalty. *College English, 57*(7), 788–806. doi:10.2307/378403

Hunjeri, N. (2015). *Broken English*. Poetry Soup. https://www.poetrysoup.com/poem/broken_english_642543

Huo, X. (2020). *Higher education internationalization and English language instruction: Intersectionality of race and language in Canadian universities*. Springer. doi:10.1007/978-3-030-60599-5

Hyon, S. (2018). *Introducing genre and English for specific purposes* (1st ed.). Routledge. doi:10.4324/9781315761152

Inoue, A. B. (2015). *Antiracist writing assessment ecologies: Teaching and assessing writing for a socially just future*. The WAC Clearinghouse. doi:10.37514/PER-B.2015.0698

Jain, R. (2022). Translingual-identity-as-pedagogy: Problematizing monolingually oriented "native-non-native" identity constructions through critical dialogues in EAP classrooms. *TESOL Journal, 13*(3), e666. Advance online publication. doi:10.1002/tesj.666

Johnstone, M., & Lee, E. (2022). Education as a site for the Imperial project to preserve whiteness supremacy from the colonial era to the present: A critical analysis of international education policy in Canada. *Whiteness and Education, 7*(1), 1–17. doi:10.1080/23793406.2020.1784038

Kachru, B. B. (1986). *The alchemy of English: The spread, functions, and models of non-native Englishes* (1st ed.). Pergamon Institute of English.

Kemper, D., Meyer, V., Van Rys, J., Sebranek, J., & Holditch, G. (2016). *Write 2: Paragraphs and essays* (Canadian ed.). Nelson Education.

Kendi, I. X. (2019). *How to be an antiracist* (1st ed.). One World.

Kitajroonchai, N., Kitjaroonchai, T., & Sanitchai, P. (2022). The effects of process genre-based writing and process writing approaches on Asian EFL pre-university students' writing performance. *Journal of Language Teaching and Research, 13*(4), 860–871. doi:10.17507/jltr.1304.19

Kumaravadivelu, B. (2003a). Problematizing cultural stereotypes in TESOL. *TESOL Quarterly, 37*(4), 709–719. doi:10.2307/3588219

Kumaravadivelu, B. (2003b). A postmethod perspective on English language teaching. *World Englishes, 22*(4), 539–550. doi:10.1111/j.1467-971X.2003.00317.x

Ladson-Billings, G. (1995). Toward a theory of culturally relevant pedagogy. *American Educational Research Journal, 32*(3), 465–491. doi:10.3102/00028312032003465

Ladson-Billings, G. (2014). Culturally relevant pedagogy 2.0: A.k.a. the remix. *Harvard Educational Review, 84*(1), 74–84. doi:10.17763/haer.84.1.p2rj131485484751

Lee, E., & Alvarez, S. P. (2020). World Englishes, translingualism, and racialization in the US college composition classroom. *World Englishes, 39*(2), 263–274. doi:10.1111/weng.12459

Li G. (2018). From stigma to strength: A case of ESL program transformation in a greater Vancouver high school. *BC TEAL Journal, 3*(1), 63–76. https://doi.org/ doi:10.14288/bctj.v3i1.303

Lillis, T., Harrington, K., Lea, M. R., & Mitchell, S. (Eds.). (2015). *Working with academic literacies: Case studies towards transformative practice*. The WAC Clearinghouse. https://wac.colostate.edu/books/perspectives/lillis/

Lillis, T., & Tuck, J. (2016). Academic Literacies: A critical lens on writing and reading in the academy. In K. Hyland & P. Shaw (Eds.), *The Routledge handbook of English for Academic Purposes* (pp. 30–43). Routledge.

Liu, J. (2018). Cultivation of critical thinking abilities in English writing teaching. *Theory and Practice in Language Studies, 8*(8), 982–987. doi:10.17507/tpls.0808.09

Mao J. (2021). Thriving through uncertainties: The agency and resourcefulness of first-year Chinese English as an additional language writers in a Canadian University. *BC TEAL Journal, 6*(1), 78–93. doi:10.14288/bctj.v6i1.390

Martínez, R. A. (2018). Beyond the *English learner* label: Recognizing the richness of bi/multilingual students' linguistic repertoires. *The Reading Teacher, 71*(5), 515–522. doi:10.1002/trtr.1679

Masuhara, H. (2011). What do teachers really want from coursebooks? In B. Tomlinson (Ed.), *Materials development in language teaching* (pp. 236–266). Cambridge University Press. doi:10.1017/9781139042789.013

McPherron, P., & An, L. (2023). Supporting Asian American multilingual college students through critical language awareness programming. *Journal of Language, Identity, and Education, 22*(4), 340–358. doi:10.1080/15348458.2023.2202587

Meighan, P. J. (2023). Colonialingualism: Colonial legacies, imperial mindsets, and inequitable practices in English language education. *Diaspora, Indigenous, and Minority Education, 17*(2), 146–155. doi:10.1080/15595692.2022.2082406

Mishan, F. (2022). Language learning materials in the digital era. In J. Norton & H. Buchanan (Eds.), *The Routledge handbook of materials development for language teaching* (pp. 17–29). Routledge. doi:10.4324/b22783-3

Moran, K. M., & Henderson, E. (2022). *The empowered writer: An essential guide to writing, reading and research* (4th ed.). Oxford University Press.

Muramatsu, C. (2018). *Portraits of second language learners: An L2 learner agency perspective*. Multilingual Matters. doi:10.21832/9781783099887

Nallaya, S., Hobson, J. E., & Ulpen, T. (2022). An investigation of first year university students' confidence in using academic literacies. *Issues in Educational Research*, *32*(1), 264–291.

Natarajan, S. (2019a). How I learned to think critically: A reflection on culture and writing identity. In S. Natarajan (Ed.), *Thinking about writing* (pp. 4–5).

Natarajan, S. (2019b). LEP, ESL, ELL, EL, or multilingual? Resisting the deficit model. In S. Natarajan (Ed.), *Thinking about writing* (pp. 15–17).

Natarajan, S., & Pez, E. (2023a). *Random university sample of Universities Canada member institutions Year 1 writing*. https://docs.google.com/spreadsheets/d/1nq6zrXcoNrkJPRvojkdcfo71G_b_nO-5gEyMhUT4ApBQ/edit?usp=sharing

Natarajan, S., & Pez, E. (2023b). *Writing textbook analysis*. https://docs.google.com/document/d/1YEuR0rkquSefZyv5UiyB_ii08DNuONNb/edit?usp=sharing&ouid=107777330223027431718&rtpof=true&sd=true

Ndhlovu, F., & Makalela, L. (2021). *Decolonizing multilingualism in Africa*. Multilingual Matters. doi:10.21832/9781788923361-006

Ndura, E. (2004). ESL and cultural bias: An analysis of elementary through high school textbooks in the Western United States of America. *Language, Culture and Curriculum*, *17*(2), 143–153. doi:10.1080/07908310408666689

Nieto, S. (2015). Language, literacy, and culture: Aha! moments in personal and sociopolitical understanding. In B. Porfilio & D. R. Ford (Eds.), *Leaders in Critical Pedagogy* (pp. 37–48). Sense Publishers. doi:10.1007/978-94-6300-166-3_3

Orr, L., & Weekley, L. (2019). Teaching with case studies in higher education. In A. Baron & K. McNeal (Eds.), *Case study methodology in higher education* (pp. 180–208). IGI Global. doi:10.4018/978-1-5225-9429-1.ch009

Padilla, L. V., & Vana, R. (2019). Ideologies in the foreign language curriculum: Insights from textbooks and instructor interviews. *Language Awareness*, *28*(1), 15–30. doi:10.1080/09658416.2019.1590376

Pang, M. (2016). Pedagogical reasoning in EFL/ESL teaching: Revisiting the importance of teaching lesson planning in second language teacher education. *TESOL Quarterly*, *50*(1), 246–263. doi:10.1002/tesq.283

Pennycook, A. (2012). *Language and mobility: Unexpected places.* Multilingual Matters. doi:10.21832/9781847697653

Pennycook, A. (2017). *The cultural politics of English as an international language.* Routledge. doi:10.4324/9781315225593

Pez, E. (2019). Case analysis: University students and plagiarism. In S. Natarajan (Ed.), *Thinking about writing* (pp. 8–11).

Pez, E. (2023). *WRIT 1002F – Introduction to Writing in English* [Course outline]. King's University College. https://www.kings.uwo.ca/kings/assets/File/outlines/2023/writ/fall/writ_1002F_651_fall_2023.pdf

Pourghasemian, H., & Zarei, G. R. (2021). Adaptivity of learning transfer from theory to practice: A case study of second language writers. *Applied Research on English Language, 10*(4), 1–38. doi:10.22108/are.2021.126760.1675

Richards, J. C. (2015, December 21). Competence and performance #10 – Pedagogical reasoning skills. In *World of better learning.* Cambridge University Press. https://www.cambridge.org/elt/blog/2015/12/21/competence-performance-10-pedagogical-reasoning-skills/

Rieman, J., McCracken, I. M., Downs, D., & Bird, B. (Eds.). (2019). *Next steps: New directions for/in writing about writing.* Utah State University Press.

Risager, K. (2023). Analysing culture in language learning materials. *Language Teaching, 56*(1), 1–21. doi:10.1017/S0261444822000143

Roessingh, H., & Douglas, S. (2012). English language learners' transitional needs from high school to university: An exploratory study. *Journal of International Migration and Integration, 13*(3), 285–301. doi:10.100712134-011-0202-8

Schmitt, N. (2019). Understanding vocabulary acquisition, instruction, and assessment: A research agenda. *Language Teaching, 52*(2), 261–274. doi:10.1017/S0261444819000053

Schütze, U. (2017). *Language learning and the brain: Lexical processing in second language acquisition.* Cambridge University Press.

Shen, F. (1989). The classroom and the wider culture: Identity as a key to learning English composition. *College Composition and Communication, 40*(4), 459–466. doi:10.2307/358245

Shulman, L. S. (1987). Knowledge and teaching: Foundations of the new reform. *Harvard Educational Review, 57*(1), 1–22. doi:10.17763/haer.57.1.j463w79r56455411

Skutnabb-Kangas, T. (1988). Multilingualism and the education of minority children. In T. Skutnabb-Kangas & J. Cummins (Eds.), *Minority education: From shame to struggle* (pp. 9–44). Multilingual Matters. doi:10.21832/9781800418110-002

Sladek, A. (2022). Student-centered grammar feedback in the Basic Writing classroom: Toward a translingual grammar pedagogy. *Journal of Basic Writing, 41*(1), 106–134. doi:10.37514/JBW-J.2022.41.1.05

Smitherman, G. (1977). *Talkin and testifyin: The language of Black America.* Houghton Mifflin.

Spiro, J. (2022). Making the materials writing leap: Scaffolding the journey from teacher to teacher-writer. In J. Norton & H. Buchanan (Eds.), *The Routledge handbook of materials development for language teaching* (pp. 475–482). Routledge. doi:10.4324/b22783-41

Tardy, C. M. (2017). The challenge of genre in the academic writing classroom: Implications for L2 writing teacher education. In J. Bitchener, N. Storch, & R. Wette (Eds.), *Teaching writing for academic purposes to multilingual students: Instructional approaches* (pp. 69–83). Routledge. doi:10.4324/9781315269665-5

Teng, M. F., & Wang, C. (2023). Assessing academic writing self-efficacy belief and writing performance in a foreign language context. *Foreign Language Annals, 56*(1), 144–169. doi:10.1111/flan.12638

Tomlinson, B. (2012a). Materials development. In A. Burns & J. C. Richards (Eds.), *The Cambridge guide to pedagogy and practice in second language teaching* (pp. 269–278). Cambridge University Press. doi:10.1017/9781009024778.034

Tomlinson, B. (2012b). Materials development for language learning and teaching. *Language Teaching, 45*(2), 143–179. doi:10.1017/S0261444811000528

Toorenburgh, L., & Gaudet, L. (2023, May 28–29). *Belonging as a learning outcome: A case for Indigenous-only Writing classrooms* [Conference presentation]. 2023 conference of the Canadian Association for the Study of Discourse and Writing/Association Canadienne de Rédactologie, York University, Toronto, ON, Canada.

Universities Canada. (2022). *Enrolment by university*. https://www.univcan.ca/universities/facts-and-stats/enrolment-by-university/

Viswanathan, G. (2014). Masks of conquest: Literary study and British rule in India (25th anniversary ed.). Columbia University Press. doi:10.7312/visw17169

Wang, Q. (2023). Memorization strategy and foreign language learning: A narrative literature review. *Frontiers in Psychology, 14*, 1261220. Advance online publication. doi:10.3389/fpsyg.2023.1261220 PMID:37767209

Wang, Y., Shen, B., & Yu, X. (2021). A latent profile analysis of EFL learners' self-efficacy: Associations with academic emotions and language proficiency. *System, 103*, 1–9. doi:10.1016/j.system.2021.102633

Wardle, E., & Downs, D. (2020). *Writing about writing: A college reader*. Bedford/St. Martins.

Wingate, U. (2018). *Academic literacy and student diversity: The case for inclusive practice*. Multilingual Matters. doi:10.21832/9781783093496-008

Wubalem, A. Y. (2021). Assessing learning transfer and constraining issues in EAP writing practices. *Asian-Pacific Journal of Second and Foreign Language Education, 6*(1), 1–22. doi:10.118640862-021-00122-5

Xiao, Y., & Zhao, A. (2022). A case study on the impacts of social contexts on a Chinese English as a foreign language learner's L1 and L2 identities development. *Frontiers in Psychology, 12*, 1–10. doi:10.3389/fpsyg.2021.772777 PMID:35069354

Yin, C. (2022). Bridging the gap between Eastern and Western academic writing expectations: Who is responsible? *MEM Insider, 7*, 9–10. https://www.kings.uwo.ca/academics/school-of-management-economics-and-mathematics/mem-insider/

Young, V. A. (2011). Should writers use they own English? In L. Greenfield & K. Rowan (Eds.), *Writing centers and the new racism: A call for sustainable dialogue and change* (pp. 61–72). Utah State University Press. doi:10.2307/j.ctt4cgk6s.7

Zhang, J., Zhang, L. J., & Zhu, Y. (2023). Development and validation of a genre-based second language (L2) writing self-efficacy scale. *Frontiers in Psychology, 14*, 1181196. Advance online publication. doi:10.3389/fpsyg.2023.1181196 PMID:37351429

Zhang, Y. (2010). The impact of ESL writers' prior writing experience on their writing in college. In *Additional essays: Companion site for What is "college-level" writing? Volume 2*. National Council of Teachers of English. https://cdn.ncte.org/nctefiles/resources/books/collegelevel2/yufengzhang_final.pdf?_ga=2.228630740.974481951.1683917960-2141036358.1683917949&_gl=1*18we6es*_ga*MjE0MTAzNjM1OC4xNjgzOTE3OTQ5*_ga_L5Q68NRK05*MTY4MzkxNzk0OS4xLjEuMTY4MzkxNzk5Ny4xMi4wLjA

Zhou, J., Zhao, K., & Dawson, P. (2020). How first-year students perceive and experience assessment of academic literacies. *Assessment & Evaluation in Higher Education, 45*(2), 266–278. doi:10.1080/02602938.2019.1637513

KEY TERMS AND DEFINITIONS

Academic Literacies: Dynamic and critical understanding of discursive conventions and academic methods in social context.
Anti-Linguicism: Intellectual and social arguments and action against systemic discrimination and exclusion based on language.
Antiracism: Intellectual and social arguments and action against systemic discrimination and exclusion based on race.
Decoloniality: Intellectual and social arguments and action against systems and hierarchies set in place by colonialism.
Genre: Types of writing appropriate to specific audiences and contexts.
L2 Learner Identity: Self-concept of writers in a second language.
Learning Materials: Materials that support learning and teaching, in this case in the Year 1 Writing classroom.
Second Language Writing: In this context, academic writing at the university in a second language.
Textbook: An example of materials that support learning and teaching, in this case in the Year 1 Writing classroom.
Translingual Pedagogy: Teaching approaches and methods that use all the learner's languages or full linguistic repertoire as a source of knowledge, identity, and value.
Writing About Writing: Using discursive norms, methods, identities, and processes as the subject of writing instruction.

ENDNOTES

1. Emily is so thankful to Vidya for inviting her to collaborate on this chapter and on the textbook discussed within it. We would also like to thank Xiangying Huo, Clayton Smith, and the anonymous reviewers for their valuable feedback and suggestions for this chapter.

2. Definitions of (ethno)linguistic identity are highly contentious; see, for instance, Hansen Edwards (2017) on the complexities of native/non-native speaker labels for English users in many Asian countries, including India, and Ndhlovu and Makalela's (2021) brilliant deconstruction of the meanings of "multilingualism" in Africa. For the purposes of this article, we use the term "multilingual international" to describe students from non-North American countries who use English primarily for academic purposes while studying in a North American university/college.

3. We created a stratified random sample of 10% of *Universities Canada* member institutions (Natarajan & Pez, 2023a). The 95 member institutions were first grouped according to full-time undergraduate student enrolment (those with above and below 20000 students were separated in two groups, based on enrolment data in the table "Fall 2022 Full-Time and Part-Time Fall Enrolment at Canadian Universities"(Universities Canada, 2022). Then a stratified random sample was created so that five institutions were randomly selected from each group. We found that eight out of the ten institutions in our sample had some form of specialized Writing instruction (including via courses with "English" or "French" in their titles) for multilingual students.

4. Experts in materials creation for the teaching of languages and writing strongly recommend that creators use pedagogically reasoned *principles* in addition to their own intuition and prior experiences or repertoire as instructors (Green, 2023; Tomlinson, 2012b).

5. Kendi (2019) usefully defined an antiracist idea as "any idea that suggests the racial groups are equals in all their apparent differences—that there is nothing right or wrong with any racial group" (p. 20). Importantly, Kendi's understanding of antiracism includes an intersectional lens, an assertion that we must try to "remain at the antiracist intersections where racism is mixed with other bigotries" (p. 228).

6. Anti-linguicist content counteracts linguicism, a form of discrimination defined by Skutnabb-Kangas (1988) as "ideologies, structures and practices which are used to legitimate, effectuate, regulate and reproduce an unequal division of power and resources (both material and immaterial) between groups which are defined on the basis of language" (p. 13).

7. We go into more detail about the difference between successful use of western writing conventions and assimilation to western norms later in our paper. This is a longstanding dilemma for teachers of L2 writers (see, for instance, Sladek, 2022). Geneva Smitherman, in an interview with Alim (2012), expresses it in these powerful terms:

    In Talkin and Testifyin *[1977], I dubbed it linguistic push-pull: pushing toward White American Language and Culture while pulling away from it and toward the embrace of Black Language and Culture. How do you reconcile this fundamental contradiction in the development of the Black psyche? The instrumental, functional need for literate proficiency in White American English with the psycho-cultural love and affinity with the Black Language Thang? (p. 360)*

8. See, for instance, Viswanathan (2014) for an account of English education as a vehicle of colonial rule in India. Canada's colonial language policies seemed all too familiar. Johnstone and Lee (2022) have made some plausible connections between colonial policy and the current approach to international education in Canada.

9   I found myself agreeing with Pennycook (2017), when he argued that

    [t]o teach is to be caught up in an array of questions concerning curriculum (whose knowledges and cultures are given credence?), educational systems (to what extent does an educational system reproduce social and cultural inequalities?) and classroom practices (what understandings of language, culture, education, authority, knowledge or communication do we assume in our teaching?). (p. 295)

10 As Padilla and Vana (2019) noted, "language ideologies are subtle to the extent that they could easily be disseminated in the guise of pedagogical suggestions and consequently, [are] rarely looked at through critical lenses" (p. 16).

11 Defining the term *ideology* in the context of language education, Chiapello and Fairclough (2002) called it "a system of ideas, values and beliefs oriented to explaining a given political order, legitimizing existing hierarchies and power relations and preserving group identities" (p. 187).

12 Meighan wrote,

    Colonialingualism *upholds colonial legacies, imperial mindsets, and inequitable practices in ELE [English Language Education] through its reluctance to question or challenge the dominant western status quo at its epistemic foundations. An epistemic "(un)learning" of the western "epistemological error" is required to enable equitable validation of all languages and knowledge systems, including those Indigenous and minoritized, in ELE.* (2023, p. 152)

13 For a quick overview of the textbooks we explored and what we found, please see our writing textbook analysis table, which is a work-in-progress (Natarajan & Pez, 2023b): https://docs.google.com/document/d/1YEuR0rkquSefZyv5UiyB_ii08DNuONNb/edit?pli=1

14 See, for instance, Flachmann et al. (2013), which was the textbook in use when I began working in my administrative role; Moran and Henderson (2022); Kemper et al. (2016); and Henderson (2015).

15 The very interesting textbook *Writing about Writing* (Wardle & Downs, 2020) was the exception. It discusses writing as a socially situated activity, connected to literacies and identities, including racial and linguistic ones, and models resistance in a number of readings. Some of the readings use AAVE and hybrid forms of English. The textbook seemed too dense, abstract, and syntactically/lexically challenging for an introductory FYW course for multilingual students.

16 For instance, Bailey (2018) targets his textbook towards multilingual students, but does not bring up race or language as contentious questions for his readers.

17 For instance, Bailey (2018, p. 232) models a book review that discusses a (possibly fictitious) book titled *Atlantic Crossing: A Comparison of European and American Society*, edited by M. Montero: surely a missed opportunity to present a review of a book with a theme of more immediate interest to international multilingual students from non-European/North American backgrounds.

18 See McPherron and An (2023): "Critical language awareness (CLA) as a pedagogical approach encourages teachers and students to examine language as social practice and reflect on ideologies and power dynamics embedded within language use" (p. 340).

19 Discussing the harm done by monolingual pedagogies, Lee and Alvarez (2020) argued that engaging with the disciplinary domains of World Englishes and translingualism can affirm the "language ownership" of non-native English users, and can "help us positively shift power dynamics for those students who have been marginalized and racialized in the writing classroom, to the extent that they can feel a sense of ownership of and confidence in their own writing practice" (p 265).

20   This class was part of a program with over 800 students in California called School Kids Investigating Language in Life and Society (SKILLS) (Bucholtz et al., 2017, p. 46).

21   For example, one of the students, supported by the SKILLS instructors, changed her school's English-monolingual policy for commencement ceremony speeches (Bucholtz et al., 2017, p. 53).

22   In the textbook, memorization is discussed in a personal reflection (Natarajan, 2019a) that models the reflective essay genre and discusses the author's own learning techniques. While there has been a tendency to stereotype Asian students as using "rote-learning," recent research suggests that memorization, especially when combined with metacognition, can be a useful technique for language learning. See Wang (2023) for a useful literature review on this subject.

23   Wubalem (2021) conducted qualitative as well as statistical analysis of 58 first-year EFL students, seven EFL teachers, and 14 content area teachers in an Ethiopian postsecondary institution to determine the rate at which the skills demanded in content learning courses aligned with the skills practised in general academic writing courses, the rate at which the skills were transferred, and the variables that impacted transfer.

24   Analyzing data from concurrent verbalization and interviews, Atkinson and Corbitt (2023) tracked their own process of composing four chapters of an open-access technical writing textbook, finding that they applied teaching and nonteaching praxis with the intention of creating readable, meaningful, and authentic content for their target student audience. For example, they drew upon supervisory experience to provide realistic context for workplace documents (p. 760).

25   In response to the statement "The course textbook and/or readings contributed to my learning of the subject matter," students had the option to select one of the following: Strongly Agree, Agree, Agree Somewhat, Neither Agree nor Disagree, Disagree Somewhat, Disagree, or Strongly Disagree. Of the 14 respondents, 100% selected either "Strongly Agree" or "Agree."

Chapter 12
Implications of Multilingual Students' Stories for Promoting Linguistic Justice in Higher Education:
Insights From Oral History Interviews

Kamila Kinyon
University of Denver, USA

ABSTRACT

This chapter explores multilingual students' experiences and addresses ways that institutions of higher learning can best celebrate and support multilingual learners. Challenging the long-standing deficit model, many researchers have used raciolinguistic and translingual concepts to reframe multilingualism as an asset. The author draws on these frameworks in contextualizing her oral history research collecting multilingual students' stories. This year-long study conducted in 2022-23 was funded by an internal grant at a private U.S. university in the Rocky Mountain region. Eleven multilingual students with diverse native languages and countries of origin were interviewed about their perceptions of their native languages as heritage languages, their academic experiences, and other aspects of their lived experiences. After documenting and analyzing these stories, the author offers suggestions for what institutions of higher learning can do to best institute linguistic justice on their increasingly multilingual campuses.

INTRODUCTION

Especially given the steadily growing multilingual student population in Anglophone countries and the call for linguistic justice among educators, it is crucial to foster awareness of the lived experiences of multilingual students and to gather their perceptions of how well their universities are serving their needs. To collect, preserve, and disseminate multilingual students' stories, the author conducted qualitative research at a private U.S. university in the Rocky Mountain region. The university's multilingual popula-

DOI: 10.4018/978-1-6684-9029-7.ch012

tion includes over 800 international students from 80 countries and a growing number of first-generation students (first in their families to attend college) representing over 15% of the overall student population. While the university prides itself in its increasing diversity, it should be noted that it is still a predominantly white institution where most students have been schooled in Standard American English. It is therefore imperative to establish the importance of a multilingual perspective for the university's future.

In a project funded by an internal grant, the author and Juli Parrish, the university's writing center director, recruited interviewees among international students and students of immigrant heritage identifying as speakers of native languages other than English. The author then conducted interviews which became the basis for a series of spotlight articles and podcasts published through the writing center. Sharing these students' stories brings awareness to their lived experiences and shows other members of the university community the benefits of a multilingual campus.

The study was guided by the following central research questions:

1. How do students' native languages connect to their sense of identity and heritage?
2. In what ways do students perceive multilingualism as an advantage for their academic or professional lives?
3. What characterizes multilingual students' lived experiences of educational institutions, and what specific challenges have they faced?
4. How and to what extent do multilingual students feel supported at their current university, and what suggestions do they have for further fostering linguistic justice and/or better support systems?

LITERATURE REVIEW

The imposition of monolingual norms at institutions of higher learning has come under increasing criticism by scholars from fields such as composition and rhetoric, education, sociolinguistics, and critical race and ethnic studies.

Over the past several decades, researchers of raciolinguistics have increasingly recognized that it is a form of racial discrimination to insist on Standard English in educational settings. This commitment to SE is driven by the belief that it is the most proper, sophisticated, and clear way to speak and write, despite linguistic evidence to the contrary (Greenfield, 2011). The privileging of an idealized variety of English denies access to people of color and conceals the inherent racism of viewing multilingual students through a deficit model that devalues the many advantages that linguistic difference can bring to academic environments (Alim, 2016; Howell et.al., 2020; Veronelli, 2015). Placing the burden on minoritized students to acquire the language varieties that are dominant at a given university and larger community, this deficit model may manifest itself in the attitudes and practices of professors, writing center consultants, administrators, or even students' peers. Multilingual speakers and writers with complex linguistic practices may be viewed reductively by those who perceive their language use through raciolinguistic binaries (Rosa, 2018; Sanchez, 2016). For instance, those who inhabit borderlands between the U.S. and Latin America and have self-constructed hybrid identities may be stereotyped as native Spanish speakers who are considered deficient in their role as language learners; this ignores the complexity of their nuanced language practices (Rosa & Florez, 2017). Racialized students whose language is not considered articulate can become dissociated from their communities and culturally rooted practices (Baker-Bell, 2000; Cushman, 2017; Lee & Alvarez, 2020).

In a seminal 2011 manifesto in composition studies, Horner, Lu, and Trimbur called for a "translingual turn" honoring the contribution of multilingual users to shape language to specific ends, recognizing the heterogeneity of language users, and confronting English monolingual expectations (Horner et.al., 2011, p. 305). Since the coining of this term, many researchers have considered practical ramifications of how professors, writing center consultants, and writing program administrators can serve linguistic justice by cultivating a translingual turn (Canagarajah, 2013; Lee, 2017; Lee & Alvarez, 2020). It is important to realize that multilingual writers are capable of negotiating between different languages and dialects to create meaning (Canagarajah, 2006; Garcia & Lee, 2014; Higgins, 2009). By adopting a translingual disposition, educators can come to welcome linguistic difference in their classrooms rather than imposing monocultural and monolingual norms (Alvarez & Lee, 2020; Avineri et.al., 2019; Ayash, 2020; Condon & Ashanti, 2017; Smith & Zhou, 2020). It is crucial to abandon the focus on named standardized languages and to instead engage with students' individuated and unique practices of translanguaging (Wei & Garcia 2022). Opening the space for successful translanguaging practices is an important component of instituting linguistic justice on college campuses (Donahue 2018; Schreiber et.al., 2022).

It is imperative to recognize the value that multilingual students and teachers bring to their institutions and to cultivate linguistically diverse academic communities (Huo, 2020; Marginson & Savir, 2011). However, access to SE can be important for some students' professional success. An "access paradox" (Bourdieu, 1991) results for educators who wish to give multilingual students the access to English that they need but who do not want to further solidify the dominance of SE at the expense of other languages or language variants. It is important to find pedagogical and curricular methods of getting around this paradox by offering access to English while simultaneously celebrating students' native languages as equally important (Janks, 2004).

In moving beyond a deficit-based model to asset-based teaching, one should avoid viewing English language learning as the students' English language problem; rather, one can re-conceptualize this as a problem of Anglophone educators who need to gain more intercultural awareness (Collins, 2018). Anglophone educators often act on a dualistic assumption by viewing the multilingual student as an Other who needs to assimilate to the monolingual SE norm (Lin, 2020). This allows such educators to take on a stance of "privileged irresponsibility" as defined by Tronto (1993, pp. 106-107). Those in a position of privilege may practice willful ignorance of the needs of others, thus perpetuating the system. To move from privileged irresponsibility to caring responsibility, it is necessary to move beyond a dualistic way of thinking (Bozalek & Zembylas, 2023). By taking shifting demographics into account and by perceiving multilingualism rather than monolingualism as the norm, we can then move towards mutual responsibility that involves educators as well as students (Lin, 2020). Taking such responsibility makes it necessary for educators to make changes in how class material is presented and accessed as well as in assessment practices, which should uphold educational equity and social justice by being attentive to learners' language practices (Shohamy, 2011).

Linguistic justice can best be upheld if we encourage multilingual students to situate themselves socially in the world through a close connection to their native languages (Lippi-Green, 2012). It is important to recognize students' multilingual repertoire as an important communicative resource (Canagarajah, 2006). By advocating for marginalized students' languages and literacies, we can help support students' diverse linguistic practices (Schreiber et al., 5-6).

The current study about the experiences and needs of multilingual students is situated within these movements in higher education to welcome and celebrate multiple languages and dialects in academic settings.

METHODS

Research Context

Given the composition of the university's multilingual population, the researchers sought to understand the lived experiences of students from an array of linguistic, cultural, and academic backgrounds. Decisions about recruiting interviewees, conducting interviews, and analyzing interview data were motivated by the goal of representing a broad spectrum of narratives.

Interviewee Recruiting and Demographics

Eleven interviewees with diverse native languages and countries of origin were recruited through advertising in the following places: 1) first-year composition courses (which all first-year students are required to take), 2) the university's interdisciplinary ethnography lab (which is used by both undergraduates and graduate students), 3) the university's international student center, 4) the university's writing center, and 5) a campus center serving first-generation students, many of whom are multilingual. The final interview pool consisted of students from different linguistic and cultural backgrounds who were at varying points in their academic careers. Undergraduate and graduate students from a range of disciplines were represented. Six interviewees were first or second-generation immigrants and five were international students. Table 1 summarizes students' countries of origin and heritage, languages, fields of study, year in school, and role as international students or U.S. residents/citizens (whether born in the U.S. to multilingual parents or first-generation immigrants).

Interview Approach and Analysis

Interviews were informal and interviewees were asked to elaborate on subjects unique to their individual experiences. In conducting interviews, the author followed the typical oral history protocol in making the interview into a dialogue where the interviewee's answers in turn generate the interviewer's questions (Shopes, 1998). Despite this dialogic interview methodology, there were a set of key questions which were covered in all interviews, as summarized in Table 2:

Interviews were transcribed and then manually analyzed through thematic analysis methods as discussed by Braun and Clarke (2006). After reading the transcriptions multiple times, the researcher developed codes from the interviews and then connected these to themes relating to the central research questions outlined in the introduction. When themes were finalized, the researcher selected quotes from the interviews to represent the themes in interviewees' own words, thus linking to students' lived experiences.

Researcher Positionality

The author/researcher is a bilingual immigrant who moved to the United States with her parents following the 1968 Soviet invasion of Czechoslovakia. She has an MA in TESOL/Linguistics from the University of Utah and a PhD in Comparative/Slavic Literatures from the University of Chicago. Since she was immersed in two cultures from an early age and has an extensive background in linguistics and cultural studies, she was able to closely identify with and understand the linguistic and cultural complexities that her interviewees brought into their discussion. She followed up on interviewee comments by bringing

Implications of Multilingual Students' Stories

Table 1. Interviewee data

Pseudonym	Countries	Languages	Field of Study	Level	Residency or Citizenship
Alia	U.S. Sudan	English, Arabic	Biology	Undergraduate (Junior)	Born in U.S.
Maria	U.S. Mexico	English, Spanish	International Relations	Undergraduate (Senior)	Born in U.S.
Sofia	Puerto Rico U.S.	Spanish, English	International Studies	Undergraduate (Junior)	U.S. (First-Generation Immigrant)
Ki	U.S. Korea	Korean, English, Mandarin Chinese	Business (Accounting)	Undergraduate (Junior)	Born in U.S.
Ira	India U.S.	Hindi, Bengali, English	Geography	PhD Student	India (International Student)
Amina	Mali U.S.	Bambara, French, English	International Studies	MA Student	U.S. (First-Generation Immigrant)
Chimwala	Malawi U.S.	Yao, Chichewa, English	Anthropology	MA Student	Malawi (International Student)
Danso	Ghana U.S.	Kusaal, English, Twi, Mampruli, Hausa	Geography	PhD Student	Ghana (International Student)
Majid	Iran U.S.	Farsee, English	Engineering	PhD Student	Iran (International Student)
Hannah	Germany U.S.	German, English	International Studies	MA Student	Germany (International Student)
Manuel	Angola U.S.	English, Portuguese	English	Undergraduate (Senior)	U.S. (First-Generation Immigrant)

Table 2.

Interview Topics:
Interviewees' cultural and linguistic background and memories; Connections between native language and cultural heritage/identity
School and college experiences related to multilingualism, linguistic justice, or ethnicity and language.
Perceived professional and personal advantages of multilingualism
Challenges encountered in speaking, listening, and/or writing in English
Perceived university support and suggestions for improvement
Final thoughts or advice for other multilingual students

in aspects of her own experiences with bilingualism. This led to a sense of rapport with interviewees and helped make interviewees comfortable to speak openly about their experiences and feelings. The author does however acknowledge that her positionality may have affected the interviewees' responses about the writing center and about professors at the university since she is a professor who has worked for the writing center.

RESULTS

Interviewees emphasized the value of their heritage languages and multilingualism's considerable academic and professional advantages. At the same time, they acknowledged challenges connected with speaking, listening, writing, or reading in English within higher education academic contexts. Their experiences of university support and their suggestions for needed changes are pertinent to educators and administrators committed to linguistic justice.

Native Language as Heritage Language

All eleven interviewees valued their native language as an integral element of their home culture and spoke their heritage language to communicate with family and friends. However, educators' attitudes towards their heritage languages in school settings were mixed. Some students were encouraged to engage with their languages and dialects in classes while others were forbidden to do so due to entrenched racist practices.

In some cases, even those interviewees from countries with a colonialist history found that their native languages were valued at school by educators in their home countries, although this was often an exception. Amina, an interviewee from Mali remarked, "We learn a lot about our heritage in school… The fact that we are also able to speak our native language Bambara is so important and so crucial." This joy in speaking the heritage language within a classroom setting was short lived, as she fled to the U.S. with her mother and brother following political unrest in Mali. Amina remained attached to Bambara, spoke it with her mother and brother, and was eventually able to use it in her academic work as she pursued a master's degree that involved social work with refugees from her country. Her story shows how a heritage language can motivate one's eventual career goals and academic choices.

Importantly, the attachment to a heritage language remained strong even for interviewees whose languages were minoritized and looked down upon in their countries. For instance, Chimwala, a student from Malawi, recounted that Yao, the language spoken in the south, formed a bond between her family members despite being regarded in Malawi as a language of the uneducated:

Yao is a language from the southern part (of Malawi) and a lot of people feel shy to speak in public…a lot of people say that it is from the district where a lot of dropouts happen, a lot of witchcraft, a lot of negative things. But then, with my family, we feel lucky to speak that language, so sometimes we speak in public.

This student's experiences give credence to Greenfield's and Veronelli's observations about raciolinguistic stereotyping (Greenfield, 2011; Veronelli, 2015). People come to associate a certain appearance, race, and class with a way of speaking, and when somebody speaks in a way that does not fit the stereotype, people often appear disconcerted and shocked. Nevertheless, to preserve a sense of community and heritage, people often persevere in speaking a dialect that is looked down upon as undesirable or regarded as uneducated by those in power. Furthermore, Chimwala, like Amina, was able to use her attachment to her home language in building a professional identity. She came to the university to study anthropology; in her fieldwork, she used her knowledge of Yao to gain rapport and communicate closely with her informants.

While for Chimwala heritage was associated with a dialect that was considered uneducated and therefore inferior, for Danso, our interviewee from Ghana, indigenous languages were forbidden in school. He and his peers witnessed colonialist suppression of indigenous languages at their worst when they were physically punished for speaking languages other than English in class. Only English, the language of the colonizer, was allowed:

In the 1990's, teachers were allowed to use the cane in class, so you could get some lashes. Additionally, they actually recruited students to spy on each other. So, you had a class captain...write down names of those who spoke local languages. Luckily, schools in Ghana today no longer use these practices.

Despite punishment for speaking his native language in school and despite respect for English as the language of power within the larger community, Danso emphasized that his mother tongue Kusaal was of central importance to his family. It was the only means of communication with grandparents who did not speak English. The role of the native language in maintaining cultural roots is an important embodiment of its value. For Danso, Kusaal had a double function as a heritage language and the language he used for his work as an ethnographer and geography student.

Other students from countries with a colonial past were also required to speak only the colonizer's language at school. This was an implicitly racist demand on the part of educators, even in those cases where it was presented without punishment. For instance, despite her positive experiences later in her education, Amina said that students who spoke their native dialects at her primary school in Mali had to put a coin in a box. These coins were then gifted at the end of the term to students who did not bring their home languages into the classroom. Similarly, Ira, our interviewee from India, relates that students in her elementary school were scolded for speaking English in class or even during recess. Despite the privileging of English in her schools, Ira spoke Bengali at home to stay in touch with her heritage language: "To speak to family, I use my mother tongue Bengali which makes it easier to connect even though everybody knows English as well."

Interviewees born in the U.S. to immigrant parents also felt a mission to preserve their home communities' languages and dialects. This was perceived as essential for continuing links to the home country. For example, Alia's family only spoke Arabic in the home. She emphasized, "I do have a really deep attachment to Sudan and my culture and my language." Maria and Ki also felt closely connected to their native languages, both when living in the U.S. and when traveling to their parents' home countries. Maria mentioned, "Spanish is the language I've used most of my life growing up in Mexico, and even in New Mexico, with my family, who is in the States. Spanish has just always been a really big part of my life." Ki also remained connected to his native language. He was born in the U.S. and subsequently moved between Korea and the U.S. with family. In both countries, his parents consistently spoke Korean with him. In all of these cases, family practices fostered students' fluency in at least two languages.

As these examples demonstrate, students' heritage languages remain central to their identities. As discussed later, encouraging students to engage with their native languages and cultures can motivate curriculum development for many higher education classes. In some cases, students come to institutions of higher learning having experienced linguistic discrimination and racism at school, whether in their home countries or in the United States. Such racism can be overt and extreme, as in the case of Danso's accounts of physical punishment in school for speaking languages other than English. Racism can also take more subtle forms, as in rewarding students for not speaking their native languages in school. To best institute linguistic justice, it is the responsibility of Anglophone institutions of higher learning to counter colonialist attitudes and assumptions that privilege standardized English over other languages and dialects.

Multilingualism as Academic and Professional Advantage

In addition to their central role in shaping students' identities, heritage languages may also hold professional and academic advantages. Multilingualism helps students to communicate with others, whether for academic or occupational purposes. Based on their fields of study, students perceived these advantages in different ways.

For some students, multilingualism was central to their research. For example, as mentioned briefly in the previous section, Danso and Chimwala used their heritage languages as ethnographers when communicating with informants. In addition, being fluent in other languages and dialects was essential for communicating with informants, for gaining their trust, and for motivating them to speak openly about their experiences:

For research purposes, being able to master the language is 50% of the work done. It will feel comfortable—oh yeah he is one of us—so it minimizes the risk of a lying respondent, a respondent who would give answers you want to hear not what is really happening. So, I have had that situation happen in multiple occasions. People give me a transcript and I say if you go back and reinterview that person using that person's language, they are going to tell you something different. (Danso, Geography Graduate Student from Ghana)

When I was doing ethnographic food work people didn't believe I spoke their language, so they thought I only spoke Chichewa, but then in the end I respond in the Yao language, so they all get surprised and sometimes even change the topic; they are oh she can listen to what we say so it is really funny for me, and I just feel grateful to know all those languages. (Chimwala, Anthropology Graduate Student from Malawi)

Multilingualism is also an advantage for students in fields such as international studies and social work. As already mentioned, Amina, a first-generation immigrant from Mali planning to work with immigrants and refugees, emphasized that multilingualism has been essential to her:

I would like to work in refugee resettlement. So, with that it's very important. I had an internship in New York working on refugee resettlement and most of our clients there spoke Spanish, French, and Bambara so knowing that I was fluent in Bambara really helped me in doing intakes and in talking to the clients to really understand what they are going through, so I really hope that in the future I will continue doing that work and being trilingual is going to help me tremendously.

Similarly, Sofia, a first-generation immigrant from Puerto Rico who is studying sustainability, noted that being bilingual in Spanish and English will aid her in helping others:

I'm interested in helping people and also helping the environment... I'm very interested in equitable housing and sustainable housing... with that I'm very interested in helping communities of color and helping communities that are in need. So, being able to find myself in spaces where I can speak for other people that aren't able to and serve as a translator will be very beneficial, I think, in my career.

Maria, a Spanish speaking immigrant from Mexico who was born in the U.S., mentioned that through being bilingual she found a campus position where she can help students of color:

I am the student mentor at the dean's office and basically what I do is to be like the connect between the students and faculty and staff so I meet with a lot of students especially students of color who speak other languages and I focus on how I can assist these students...I got priority in the interview process because I was bilingual.

Ki, a U.S. born Korean student studying business, likewise stressed the importance of knowing multiple languages for his future career. He remarked, "Having or knowing a second or third language is always a benefit for a job environment. For my job, it's going to be important if I open a business and it grows bigger." In a variety of contexts, our interviewees emphasized that multilingualism was an important academic and professional advantage. This was equally true for international students, first-generation immigrants, and students born in the U.S. to multilingual parents.

Although it should come as no surprise that multilingualism holds a high value in an increasingly multilingual global culture, proponents of Standard English working within an implicit deficit model still evidently believe that it is SE rather than multilingualism that is the ticket to success. Greenfield writes that SE is often imposed on students by well-meaning educators who purport to favor diversity, but still think they need to emphasize the value of SE to help students succeed in the job market (Greenfield, 2011). While this may be true in some situations, our interviewees' emphasis on the practical value of their native languages implies that for finding and keeping employment, the multilingual student may often have an edge over the monolingual student versed in SE. This is important for educators to keep in mind. A key component of instituting linguistic justice lies in recognizing the advantages of multilingualism and the value that multilingual students bring to their communities.

Academic Challenges for Multilingual Students and Implications for University Practices

While interviewees perceived their multilingualism as both a personal and a professional advantage, they had to overcome obstacles in listening, speaking, reading, and writing in English. This was accompanied by a further process of adjustment in learning new cultural codes connected with formal and informal registers as well as different practices of nonverbal communication. The nature and extent of students' challenges depended on factors such as their native language, the points in their education at which they learned English, and their course of study.

While acquiring and using a new language is always difficult, some of the obstacles that interviewees encountered stemmed from the attitudes they encountered at this university, a predominantly white institution where, despite shifting demographics, many students are still versed in Standard American English. Even though faculty, administrators, and employees are generally enthusiastic about increasing the school's diversity, there is still a degree of privileged irresponsibility, as defined by Tronto (1998). Instead of assuming that multilingualism is a norm, monolingual speakers may not think to conduct lectures or respond to student work in a way that is sensitive to the needs of an increasingly multilingual campus. As discussed below, linguistic justice can best be served if educators pro-actively change their practices to better reach out to multilingual students.

Listening and Speaking

Interviewees found that it was hard to absorb lectures or to communicate their own thoughts with the same speed as native speakers. Five students (four international students and one first-generation immigrant) remarked that speaking and listening posed an even greater challenge for them than reading or writing in English. Majid noted that professors spoke too quickly in classes for him to fully absorb the lectures. Three other international students—Danso, Chimwala, and Ira—came from countries that were former British colonies; they learned British English from an early age but were unaccustomed to the American regional slang of their university or to the jargon specific to their fields of study. Amina explained that English was her third language, and that she had a hard time following her professors: "I feel like professors speak so fast and it takes me time to actually sometimes understand what they're saying." Although none of the U.S. born students mentioned issues with listening or speaking, it is evident that many international and immigrant students need support in these areas. It is important to provide training for university professors, staff, and administrators so they can better understand how to interact effectively in increasingly multilingual academic settings. Rather than placing the responsibility on multilingual students to better fit in with the demands of their universities, it is the responsibility of monolingual speakers at these universities to change their behavior to suit increasingly multilingual campus cultures. This could be best achieved if universities were to shift from deficit to asset-based models (Lin, 2020).

One area in which multilingual students are an asset to their universities is in their role as teachers. When working as TAs or teaching classes, the multilingual graduate students we interviewed found that their knowledge of more than one language gave them advantages as teachers. Two international students praised their departments for providing training for all new graduate student teachers. This helped to give them confidence as new teachers. They initially feared their accents would not be well understood by Americans, since they learned English in their home countries from teachers educated in British English. When given the opportunity to teach classes, these interviewees had overwhelmingly positive teaching experiences. For instance, Ira explained that her background enabled her to better communicate with other multilingual students who were going through the same experiences:

I tell students my story. I'm from a different country. I speak a different language. I can empathize a lot more. I get that they would need more time to communicate their thoughts. I had a student who is Italian. He used to tell me he was thinking in a different language, and then translating, so I should give him extra time for writing. But then, when he should communicate with me, his problems are he is not understanding a question, because the question is written in such a way. I had to explain to him in English, but in an easier way, so that he would get it. Then I would like, help him construct the sentence so that he could write. I understand better, I guess.

This statement about the value of multilingualism for providing teachers with understanding and empathy is particularly meaningful in the new perspective that it gives on multilingual teachers, who have so often been regarded through a deficit model as less successful than their native speaker counterparts. Multilingual teachers can play an important part in promoting linguistic justice on college campuses.

Reading and Writing

Regarding reading and writing, three major areas of difficulty that our multilingual interviewees identified related to test taking, writing college papers, and academic publishing. Students reached out for help through resources such as the university writing center, their professors, collaborators, or external editors. As discussed below, students sometimes related frustration about the interference between their languages. They struggled to fluently read and write texts in academic jargon and/or to compose in Standard English using expected conventions. However, some also saw the potential for their multiple languages and dialects to enrich their writing and research.

Test Taking

Test taking continues to pose a challenge for many multilingual undergraduate and graduate students. This is especially the case when tests include discipline specific jargon that they did not have the chance to learn. Hannah, an international student from Germany, related her experiences as follows:

I remember I got a C+ my freshman year in Introduction to Public Health because I didn't understand the questions and because I didn't understand the words because they were very specific what they were asking, and I just didn't know them…It wasn't I would say basic English but more advanced higher academic English.

To promote a more positive learning experience for multilingual students and for monolingual students struggling with similar issues, educators should consider adapting their testing practices. For instance, more time could be given for taking tests, or students could prepare notes in advance, or students could be allowed to use dictionaries. It is imperative to remember that an increasing number of multilingual students have English as their second, third, or even fourth language. It is a matter of educational equity to be attentive to learners' language practices when designing and implementing assessment (Shohamy, 2011). Educators could benefit from becoming immersed in recent assessment research focusing on linguistic justice.

Writing College Papers

Multilingual students' difficulties in completing assigned college papers may be compounded by the fact that many professors' assessment practices emphasize conforming to Standard Written English. Some interviewees discussed how their professors tended to emphasize grammatical errors in their grading rubric. Following Standard English grammatical conventions was particularly difficult for students whose languages had radically different structural principles. Ki shared his encounters with English grammar as follows: "Because of my middle school and elementary school, I learned mostly Korean how to write. I was really struggle with the grammars a lot because they use different structure parameters." In the interview, his articulation of this struggle implies that he wanted to become fluent in Standard American English and that a lack of such fluency would be an academic and professional disadvantage to him.

Professors often also mark down papers with semantic errors or imprecise word choice; some insist on formal registers of language and on using only approved Standard English words in a college essay. Multilingual students may not understand the nuances of word choice and register. The process of translating from their native language to English is a time-consuming process, often carried out with the help of a dictionary. Ki's experiences with translation exemplify the complexity that is involved:

Sometimes there is a word only English can describe but sometimes there's a word only Korean has it. For example, 'common sense' in English means societal rules you can abide by. In Korean, common sense is not just about social life but how to behave in a social in-group. There are also differences in words that relate to foods. In English "nutty" evokes a Brownie texture type of thing. In Korean, you would need to use a more specific word that relates to Korean types of foods.

While having to translate back and forth in this way may be perceived by some as a disadvantage, educators could instead capitalize on students' knowledge of two or more languages to encourage translanguaging. As emphasized by Horner et al (2011), we should take a translingual turn in our approaches to multilingual writing. By drawing on their languages and meshing elements of these, students may come to realize how combining different linguistic systems can enrich a text. However, Ki, a student in international business, doesn't recall being encouraged to translanguage in his university classes. It is therefore not surprising that he expresses negative associations with the experience of writing academic essays. He implicitly posits Korean and English as two separate and discreet systems with no possibility of hybrid uses. As emphasized by Wei and Garcia (2022), even educators versed in linguistics often think of bilingualism as a sort of double monolingualism in which each language is seen as a separate discreet entity. To best instantiate linguistic justice on college campuses, it is important to move beyond such a view and to instead encourage translingual approaches.

Academic Publishing

Depending on their fields of study, interviewed multilingual graduate students related various challenges to preparing English language scholarly work for publication. However, in some cases, multilingualism offered a clear advantage for research and for the publishing of scholarly work. Danso's and Majid's experiences with academic publishing reflect differences between publication conventions in their fields, anthropology, and bioengineering respectively.

As addressed earlier, for Danso knowing multiple languages was essential to his anthropological fieldwork studying water access rights in Ghana. Reflecting on linguistic subtleties in his fieldnotes was integral to conveying his findings to English-speaking audiences. Although he explicitly relates to the translation process as a "struggle," he often makes a point of addressing linguistic differences in his writing. For example, he included footnotes in his scholarly work to explain untranslatable idioms to readers:

Sometimes, the local context is not available in English. So sometimes I struggle with that, but I write it in ways even my English-speaking audience would understand what it means. For example, the idiom "eating anger" that one of my informants used does not translate to an eating disorder like it might in

English. It means having to endure the pain of not having access to water. So I need to explain this in a footnote.

For Danso, the discussion of semantic differences between Kusaal and English was seen as an enriching element of his paper. His expertise in different languages and their connotations could be shared as a point of interest with readers. Within the larger context of the interview, negotiating not only between multiple languages but also between dialects within these languages is something that the interviewee values and views as integral to his work as a geographer conducting ethnographic research. However, even though translanguaging is something that is important within his field of study, it was still difficult to convey the results of his ethnographic research in the correct footnote style to an English-speaking audience.

For Majid, an Iranian international student pursuing a doctorate in bioengineering, the challenges of academic publishing took a different form. Learning the specific sociolinguistic conventions for academic publishing in his field was a source of frustration as well as a time drain. He said that paraphrasing was his largest problem in writing English scholarly articles. He explained that the literature review sections of his papers were more difficult to represent than the methods, results, or discussion sections:

I published a paper about cardiovascular engineering technology in English. In the beginning, it's so hard. In the introduction, when you want to have some parts from other articles you cannot exactly copy that sentence. So you need to somehow change, summarize, or paraphrase that. And for a person who is not English it's a little hard to change everything. Overall, I do my best to change or paraphrase the introduction, so it is OK to be published.

It is worth considering that the expectation to extensively rephrase and cite sources to avoid plagiarism is a western tradition and that not all cultures share these expectations (Hendershott et.al., 2000; Macfarlane et.al., 2014). One can perceive this student's problems as stemming from the colonialist perspective underlying much academic publishing, including in his field. Until this unfortunate perspective changes, students pursuing a career in the sciences may still need to work within this set of conventions to succeed. For this reason they must seek support with issues like these. The best way to negotiate the resulting access paradox is to continue giving students access to the privileged variety while still finding ways to value students' native languages (Janks, 2004). This is important for countering linguistic racism on college campuses and for instituting linguistic justice.

As these examples illustrate, the challenges faced by multilingual students often stem from entrenched racist practices in institutions of higher learning. These may have different points of origin, such as individual educators' curricular decisions or presentation habits, programmatic decisions about testing, rubrics for assessing writing, or editorial decisions about publishing. In service of linguistic justice, it is vital to move beyond the deficit model and to realize the value of translingual perspectives (Garcia & Li, 2014; Horner et.al. 2011; Wei & Garcia, 2022). Rather than placing the burden on multilingual students to conform to the dominant dialect of the dominant language, monolingual educators, administrators, editors, and others need to revise their practices to better support an increasingly diverse student body (Janks 2014; Lee, 2017; Lin, 2020). Our interviewees' lived experiences speak to the importance of instituting fundamental changes in the ways that universities respond to international students and to students of immigrant heritage.

INTERVIEWEES' PERCEPTIONS OF THE UNIVERSITY: POSITIVE EXPERIENCES AND SUGGESTIONS FOR IMPROVEMENT

Interactions with Professors: Support and Suggestions for Change

Several interviewees appreciated the support that they received from their professors. Chimwala and Ira remarked that their future advisors went out of their way to help them when they arrived in the country as international graduate students. Ira was invited to stay in her advisor's home for several days while looking for housing. In addition, interviewed international students had multilingual professors who were able to relate to the advantages and challenges offered by speaking more than one language. In responding to their written work, their professors usually encouraged them and gave them positive feedback. For instance, Chimwala emphasized, "My professors assure me I am doing great and that my grammar is great which makes me proud." Interviewees also explained that they were provided with strong teacher training programs, which helped prepare them for working as TA's or for teaching their own classes.

While interviewees' responses to professor support were overwhelmingly positive, students had suggestions for the ways that lectures, peer work, and other delivery of class material could be adjusted. For instance, Majid suggested:

So sometimes I think some professors don't care that in this class maybe there are some students that they are not English people, so it's better to speak a little slower...Some professors talk like all the students are native and they don't need to, for example, maybe change their speed in the classes.

Majid's observations attest to the privileged irresponsibility of many Anglophone professors and other university employees who ignore multilingual students' situations. Instead, professors need to start taking responsibility for their role in a multilingual world, whether by changing the way they conduct class, by making lecture notes or PowerPoints available outside of class or meeting with students more frequently in one-on-one conversations.

Praising Class Content about Culture, Language, and Heritage

U.S. born interviewees of multilingual and multiethnic heritage can benefit from engaging with their native cultures and languages in their college classes. Alia and Maria both mentioned that professors encouraged them to incorporate translingual elements and engage with their linguistic and cultural roots in their academic papers. Alia appreciated the opportunity to connect with her Sudanese-American identity: "Whenever I can write about my culture it sparks this light inside of me...every time I would be given that opportunity, I would immediately jump on it and write about my multilingual perspective. And I did that in writing classes and communication classes that I've had as well." Maria, who is bilingual in Spanish and English, also expressed appreciation for classes where she was able to examine her heritage and her multilingual perspective. This included, for instance, work that she did in a Spanish course for heritage speakers. Students from multicultural backgrounds often welcome course material that allows them to engage with their cultural and linguistic backgrounds.

Foreign Language Requirements

An area of concern for many multilingual students is the additional foreign language requirement that they must fulfill while they are still learning English. For example, Alia reported on the stresses experienced by a multilingual friend who had to take French while still struggling to learn English. She therefore suggested that the university rethink its foreign language requirement. The university's language professors have already taken some steps in this direction. Spanish professor Lina Reznicek-Parrado established a Spanish bilingual heritage program which provides challenging and meaningful classes. Maria and Sofia both expressed enthusiasm for these courses. Maria emphasized, "A lot of people learn Spanish at home, but their entire education is in English, so a lot of people will speak Spanish, but they don't know how to write it well, or they don't know how to read it well." She relates that she used to be embarrassed in regular Spanish classes because her knowledge of the language was too proficient. The Spanish bilingual heritage program provided challenging and meaningful classes. A different type of course that substitutes for the foreign language requirement is now being developed by the University Writing Program. Under the direction of Writing Program Director Sheila Carter-Tod, new English for Academic Purposes (EAP) courses have been established for international students. That way, instead of being required to take an additional language, international students can work on their academic English skills at a level matching their experience and professional goals. These are a few examples of the ways that educators and administrators can work to better respond to student needs in increasingly multilingual campuses.

Perceptions of the Writing Center

In working on their academic papers, interviewees came to the university's writing center, and all eleven praised their experiences there. For example, Amina noted:

I would say that I use the writing center a lot and it has helped me tremendously with my writing, and I've truly had positive experiences with the writing tutors there...They value diverse perspectives and incorporate them in the writing programs and also recognize that multilingual writers bring unique insights and experiences.

In making suggestions for how the writing center could improve further, Danso suggested hiring more multilingual consultants who would know first-hand what multilingual writers go through. In fact, Manuel, an English major from Angola and a native speaker of Portuguese, said that his own role as a multilingual student helped him in his position as a writing center consultant: "It's about knowing what it's like to be somebody who has moved to the U.S. and being expected to read and write in English as an outsider...People are doing way better than they think they are, and I can empathize." As comments like these imply, writing centers with multilingual consultants and/or consultants trained to work with international and immigrant students play a significant role in providing needed feedback and support for multilingual writers.

The writing center trains consultants how to work effectively with multilingual students. For example, consultants are taught that different countries have different rhetorical conventions. They also practice how to prioritize global meanings in a text over Standard American English conventions. Interviewees' generally positive views of the feedback they received at the writing center may be linked to these factors in consultant education as well as to increasing hiring of multilingual consultants.

SUPPORT FROM UNIVERSITY ORGANIZATIONS AND SUGGESTIONS FOR FURTHER OUTREACH

Students also appreciated the university organizations through which they could meet with other students speaking their languages, or, more broadly, could communicate with other international students, first-generation students, and multilingual students.

Ira felt that as an international student, she would have appreciated more outreach while she was still living in her home country. As an Indian student, she would have liked to contact other Indian international students, so she could consult about practical logistics of moving to the U.S. or perhaps even find somebody with whom to share housing. She said:

I would like to see a bridge of communication between students coming from the same country. I have seen other universities reaching out to students. There could be a Facebook page through which students could find a way to share housing and a way to connect. Knowing of other international students from the same country could make the whole process much easier in terms of passports, visas, and ways to go about it.

As Ira's comments indicate, universities can improve students' transition into college life by facilitating avenues of communication and helping students of similar cultural and linguistic backgrounds to meet.

Overall, interviewees had a generally positive assessment of their student experience and of the levels of support they received. However, their suggestions for improvement are important and implementing these could further contribute to a linguistically just campus.

DISCUSSION: RECOMMENDATIONS FOR INSTITUTIONS OF HIGHER LEARNING

As this study has shown, it is important for institutions of higher learning to embrace an asset-based model in responding to multilingual students. Multilingualism is an advantage to students both professionally and personally as well as bringing considerable assets to their universities. However, it can pose challenges for multilingual students to fully leverage their multilingualism in universities that are still unconsciously rooted in the deficit model. To facilitate linguistic justice on their campuses, institutions of higher learning need to make changes for better and more equitable education.

Foster Asset-Based Response Strategies to Student Writing

As illustrated by the featured interviews, multilingual writers often encounter challenges when composing an English language text for their classes. While grammar is one area of concern, when asked about their difficulties in writing, interviewees generally focused more on semantic challenges to ensure that

English speakers could fully understood their meaning. In seeking help in the writing center or from their professors and peers, making sure that they had a sound argument was a dominant focus.

Teachers, tutors, and peers who are untrained in responding to multilingual writing often tend to focus on surface level errors, directing their comments on making the text more closely conform to the expectations of SE, which in the case of the author's university is Standard American English. The author has, for instance, noticed this during peer reviews in her writing classes. Without specific training on how to do peer reviews, monolingual English speakers often respond to multilingual writers by pinpointing mechanical errors instead of engaging with larger issues of meaning making. Admittedly, there is still a place for line editing for errors, especially in giving feedback on texts intended for a particular audience or publication venue that requires SE texts. In case this is an issue for students, this should, however, be relegated to the later stages of the composition process and not foregrounded in comments at stages when meaning making is still at stake.

Overall, understanding the access paradox (Janks, 2004) could help professors, writing center consultants, or other members of the university community to better respond to multilingual students. As already explained, this paradox relates to the fact that giving access to SE may offer a practical professional advantage for multilingual students while at the same time unfortunately bolstering the status of SE the expense of other equally valuable variants and languages. We need a pedagogy that can provide access while still placing a strong emphasis on the value of other languages and variants.

Institutions of higher learning need to realize that many students negotiate between multiple languages. For U.S. educators, Standard American English should be perceived as a variant that can offer practical capital to students in some occupational settings that value it., However, it is not a variant that is in any way more logical or superior to other variants (Greenfield, 2011). Professors, writing center consultants, and even peers could use more training in the asset-based model, whether through workshops, classes, or reading of relevant articles.

Changing Assessment Practices

Over the past several decades, there has been much valuable research about ways in which universities can alter their assessment practices to better serve an increasingly multilingual student body. As indicated by Shohamy (2011), it is crucial to develop assessment practices that recognize the language practices of learners. In light of changes in the student body, professors and others who assess student performance should consider the following practices: 1) Adhere to grading principles for written work that allow for different language varieties and avoid privileging Standard American English over other varieties; 2) offer additional time to complete course assignments; 3) give additional time on tests; 4) make lecture material available, such as posting PowerPoints, lecture notes, or audio recordings of lectures; 5) adjust pronunciation or speed of delivery of course material to make it more easily understandable for multilingual students and/or enable a written transcript of spoken material; 6) change the university's foreign language requirements to better account for multilingual students' needs. Students can be tested for proficiency in their native language in those institutions that do not offer courses in the students' languages. In cases where there are many multilingual students of a single language group, institutions of higher learning can consider establishing heritage speaker courses where students speaking the given language can complete their language requirement at a higher level, together with other heritage speakers. Alternately, universities can establish English for Academic Purposes courses where students can work on improving their academic English rather than being required to study additional languages.

Curriculum and Assignment Design

With opportunities for new assignment design and larger curricular changes within composition programs, administrators and individual faculty members can consider creating assignments or assignment sequences where multilingualism and other aspects of cultural heritage could be addressed in class assignments. For example, the author has found that ethnographic, oral history, and literacy narrative assignments, or open-ended journalistic assignments enable students in writing courses to discuss their own linguistic, racial, or cultural heritage, or to explore other people's experiences with racial and linguistic identity. Curricular changes encouraging translanguaging and exploration of cultural heritage could be considered by faculty in a variety of departments.

Teacher Training for International Graduate Students

Judging from interviewee comments, speaking along with listening can pose a larger problem than writing for many multilingual writers. For example, this seems to be a pattern among multilingual international students from countries that were former British colonies, including some African countries and India, where British English is taught from an early age. Such students tend to have strong writing skills but may be unfamiliar with their university's regional pronunciation, slang, and jargon. For graduate students who will be teaching their own classes or working as TA's, effective teacher training is essential. At the same time, it is important that this training should not be approached from the deficit model perspective. Indeed, multilingualism gives an advantage to instructors who work with multilingual students in their classes.

Create Organizations and/or Sites That Connect Multilingual Students

According to this study, multilingual students often seek out other multilingual students with whom to interact. While meeting others speaking their native language helps foster a sense of community, our interviewees also expressed their wishes to socialize with multilingual students from other ethnic and language groups. International students wanted to be part of a larger international student community. Likewise, first-generation students of immigrant background wanted to meet others in a comparable situation. It is important for institutions of higher learning to create organizations where students can communicate, both before they leave home to move to a new city and once they arrive on campus. Creating sites where international students can contact others online could also facilitate their transition to starting college in a new country.

Recruit International and First-Generation Students as Well as Multilingual Faculty

Due largely to shifting demographics, there is already a substantial increase in enrollments of multilingual students at most institutions of higher learning. Recognizing that multilingualism enriches university communities, postsecondary institutions should strive to further recruit international and first-generation students through advertising and offering scholarships or employment to qualified multilingual students. As this study has demonstrated, multilingual students feel more welcome at their institutions if they can interact with other multilingual speakers. They feel an affinity with those who are going through similar experiences, such as moving to a new country or negotiating several languages. In addition to creating a community of multilingual students, it is also beneficial for these students to be able to interact with multilingual faculty members, and universities could make a special effort to hire more multilingual faculty.

Support Language Programs and Study Abroad Programs

Our interviewees' final words of advice to other students at their university often included the encouragement to value their languages and to consider learning another language. In the United States, many people only speak a single language and have not made the effort to learn a second or a third language. It could benefit higher education institutions to put more resources into building and maintaining strong language programs that provide a wide choice of languages for students to study. Study abroad programs are another way that monolingual students can move towards a multilingual experience. For multilingual students within an institution of higher learning, as already mentioned, heritage classes can offer a meaningful way to study their native language and its literature together with others from the same background.

Collecting Stories of Multilingual Students, Faculty, and Staff

This study has centered on collecting and sharing multilingual students' stories. Gathering the firsthand lived experiences of a university's multilingual members fosters understanding of the assets that multilingualism brings to institutions of higher learning. Individuals and groups within a university can initiate oral history projects documenting the multilingual experience. Whenever feasible, universities should fund such projects through internal grants. Recorded in-depth interviews can encapsulate the experiences of multilingual speakers and writers. Recordings can then be preserved in stable campus archives thus making the lived experiences of multilingual community members available for future study. More immediately, it is important to share multilingual students' experiences with others at the same institution. This can be done through journalistic articles, such as spotlights, or through podcasts where multilingual voices can directly be represented. It is furthermore valuable to share these stories between institutions through conferences and scholarly publications.

CONCLUSION

It is vital to counter the colonialist tendencies of educational institutions by making a move towards linguistic justice. This can be best achieved by creating an environment where multilingual students can have their voices heard. By collecting and archiving multilingual speakers' and writers' stories, we can acquire the knowledge and understanding through which we can push for change.

Although our interviewees viewed their university as generally supportive, they still encountered stresses stemming from some educators' implicitly racist Anglophone assumptions. Professors, administrators, and others sometimes acted from the implicit assumption that Standard American English is the norm. This was manifested, for instance, in styles and speed of teaching presentations, in the imposition of deadlines that disadvantage multilingual speakers, in timed tests that do not give multilingual students the opportunity to use dictionaries, or in the imposition of foreign language requirements that do not give multilingual students the opportunity to focus their attention on learning the English language necessary for their academic work. These types of decisions at institutions of higher learning can be seen as stemming from privileged irresponsibility (Bozalek & Zemblylas, 2023) as those who use the language and variety in power may feel it unnecessary to change their practices.

To best serve the increasingly multilingual student population, educators at Anglophone institutions need to be the ones to reach out and adapt their practices and requirements. While educators should realize that giving access to English may be needed to facilitate students' professional success, the insistence on Standard English should not come at the expense of devaluing students' native languages and dialects (Janks, 2014). Educators can best navigate the access paradox by simultaneously giving students access and placing a high value on multilingualism.

It is imperative to recognize the assets that multilingual students bring to college campuses and to move beyond the deficit model by embracing the asset-based approach (Lin, 2020). The lived experiences of multilingual students reveal a strong attachment to heritage languages while also speaking to the rich potential of combining multiple languages in personal, academic, and professional spheres. Listening to these stories can inspire us to foster linguistically just campus communities where students' diverse ethnicities and languages are valued and celebrated.

REFERENCES

Alim, S., Rickford, J. R., & Ball, A. F. (Eds.). (2016). *Raciolinguistics: How language shapes our ideas about race*. Oxford University Press. doi:10.1093/acprof:oso/9780190625696.001.0001

Alvarez, S. P., & Lee, E. (2020). Ordinary difference, extraordinary dispositions: Sustaining multilingualism in the writing classroom. In J. W. Lee & S. Dovchin (Eds.), *Translinguistics: Negotiating innovation and ordinariness* (pp. 61–72). Routledge.

Avineri, N., Graham, L. R., Johnson, E. J., Riner, R. C., & Rosa, J. (Eds.). (2019). *Language and social justice in practice*. Routledge.

Ayash, N. B. (2020). Critical translation and paratextuality: Translingual and anti-racist pedagogical possibilities for multilingual writers. *Composition Forum*, 44. https://compositionforum.com/issue/44/critical-translation.php

Baker-Bell, A. (2020). *Linguistic justice: Black language, literacy, identity, and pedagogy*. Routledge. doi:10.4324/9781315147383

Bernal, D. D., & Villalpando, O. (2002). An apartheid of knowledge in academia: The struggle over the "legitimate" knowledge of faculty of color. *Equity & Excellence in Education*, 35(2), 169–180. doi:10.1080/713845282

Blommaert, J., & Rampton, B. (2011). Language and superdiversity. *Diversities*, 13(2), 1–22.

Bourdieu, P. (1991). *Language and symbolic power*. Polity Press.

Bozalek, V., & Zembylas, M. (2023). *Responsibility, privileged irresponsibility and response-ability: Higher education, coloniality and ecological damage*. Springer Nature. doi:10.1007/978-3-031-34996-6

Braun, V., & Clarke, V. (2006). Using thematic analysis in psychology. *Qualitative Research in Psychology*, 3(2), 77–101. doi:10.1191/1478088706qp063oa

Canagarajah, A. S. (2006). The place of world Englishes in composition: The pluralization continued. *College Composition and Communication*, *57*(4), 586–619.

Canagarajah, A. S. (2013). *Translingual practice: Global Englishes and cosmopolitan relations*. Routledge. doi:10.4324/9780203120293

Cenoz, J., & Gorter, D. (2011). A holistic approach to multilingual education: Introduction. *Modern Language Journal*, *95*(3), 339–343. doi:10.1111/j.1540-4781.2011.01204.x

Collins, H. (2018). Interculturality from above and below: Navigating uneven discourses in a neoliberal university system. *Language and Intercultural Communication*, *18*(2), 167–183. doi:10.1080/14708477.2017.1354867

Condon, F., & Ashanti, V. (2017). *Performing antiracist pedagogy in rhetoric, writing, and communication*. WAC Clearinghouse.

Cushman, E. (2016). Translingual and decolonial approaches to meaning making. *College English*, *78*(3), 234–242.

Donahue, C. (2018). Rhetorical and linguistic flexibility: Valuing heterogeneity in academic writing education. In D. Martin (Ed.), *Transnational Writing Education* (pp. 21–40). Routledge. doi:10.4324/9781351205955-2

Flores, N., & Rosa, J. (2015). Undoing appropriateness: Raciolinguistic ideologies and language diversity in education. *Harvard Educational Review*, *85*(2), 149–171. doi:10.17763/0017-8055.85.2.149

García, O. (2009). Emergent bilinguals and TESOL: What's in a name? *TESOL Quarterly*, *43*(2), 322–326. doi:10.1002/j.1545-7249.2009.tb00172.x

García, O., & Li, W. (2014). *Translanguaging: Language, bilingualism, and education*. Palgrave Macmillan. doi:10.1057/9781137385765

Garcia-Sanchez, I.M. (2016). Multiculturalism and its discontents. *Raciolinguistics: How language shapes our ideas about race*, 291.

Greenfield, L. (2011). The 'standard English' fairy tale: A rhetorical analysis of racist pedagogies and commonplace assumptions about language diversity. In L. Greenfield & K. Rowan (Eds.), *Writing centers and the new racism: A call for sustainable change and dialogue* (pp. 33–60). Utah State UP. doi:10.2307/j.ctt4cgk6s.6

Hendershott, A., Drinan, P., & Cross, M. (2000). Toward enhancing a culture of academic integrity. *NASPA Journal*, *37*(4), 587–598. doi:10.2202/1949-6605.1119

Higgins, C. (2009). English as a local language: Post-colonial identities and multilingual practices *Multilingual Matters 2*.

Horner, B., Lu, M. Z., Royster, J. J., & Trimbur, J. (2011). Language difference in writing: Toward a translingual approach. *College English*, *73*(3), 303–321.

Howell, N. G., Navickas, K., Shapiro, R., Shapiro, S., & Watson, M. (2020, June). Embracing the perpetual 'but' in raciolinguistic justice work: When idealism meets practice. In *Composition Forum 44*. Association of Teachers of Advanced Composition.

Huo, X. (2020). *Higher education internationalization and English language instruction: Intersectionality of race and language in Canadian universities.* Springer. doi:10.1007/978-3-030-60599-5

Inoue, A. B. (2017). *Antiracist writing assessment ecologies: Teaching and assessing writing for a socially just future.* WAC Clearninghouse.

Janks, H. (2004). The access paradox. *Literacy Learning: The Middle Years, 12*(1), 33–42.

Lee, E., & Alvarez, S. P. (2020). World Englishes, translingualism, and racialization in the US college composition classroom. *World Englishes, 39*(2), 263–274. doi:10.1111/weng.12459

Lee, J. W. (2017). *The politics of translingualism: After Englishes.* Routledge. doi:10.4324/9781315310534

Lin, A. M. (2020). From deficit-based teaching to asset-based teaching in higher education in BANA countries: Cutting through 'either-or' binaries with a heteroglossic plurilingual lens. *Language, Culture and Curriculum, 33*(2), 203–212. doi:10.1080/07908318.2020.1723927

Lippi-Green, R. (2012). *English with an accent. Language, ideology, and discrimination in the United States* (2nd ed.). Routledge. doi:10.4324/9780203348802

Macfarlane, B., Zhang, J., & Pun, A. (2014). Academic integrity: A review of the literature. *Studies in Higher Education, 39*(2), 339–358. doi:10.1080/03075079.2012.709495

Marginson, S., & Sawir, E. (2011). *Ideas for intercultural education.* Palgrave Macmillan.

Rosa, J. (2018). *Looking like a language, sounding like a race: Raciolinguistic ideologies and the learning of latinidad.* Oxford University Press.

Rosa, J., & Flores, N. (2017). Unsettling race and language: Toward a raciolinguistic perspective. *Language in Society, 46*(5), 1–27. doi:10.1017/S0047404517000562

Schreiber, B.R., Lee, E., Johnson, J.T. & Fahim, N. (2022). Linguistic justice on campus: Pedagogy and advocacy for multilingual students. *New Perspectives on Language and Education, 96.*

Shohamy, E. (2011). Assessing multilingual competencies: Adopting construct valid assessment policies. *Modern Language Journal, 95*(3), 418–429. doi:10.1111/j.1540-4781.2011.01210.x

Shopes, L. (1998). What is oral history? *History matters: The U.S. survey on the web.* http://historymatters.gmu.edu

Smith, C., & Zhou, G. (Eds.). (2022). *Handbook of research on teaching strategies for culturally and linguistically diverse international students.* IGI-Global. doi:10.4018/978-1-7998-8921-2

Tronto, J. (1993). *1993: Moral boundaries: a political argument for an ethic of care.* Routledge.

Veronelli, G. A. (2015). Five: The coloniality of language: Race, expressivity, power, and the darker side of modernity. *Wagadu: A Journal of Transnational Women's and Gender Studies, 13*, 108-134.

Wei, L., & García, O. (2022). Not a first language but one repertoire: Translanguaging as a decolonizing project. *RELC Journal, 53*(2), 313–324. doi:10.1177/00336882221092841

KEY TERMS AND DEFINITIONS

Access Paradox: On the one hand, multilingual students should be given access to privileged English variants, since this could provide them with social or economic power. On the other hand, giving them this access could unfortunately solidify the dominance of Standard English at the expense of other languages or variants of English.

Deficit Model: The assumption that being a nonnative speaker of English implies a lack of skills that the given speaker needs to make up for. This model has been challenged as the benefits of multilingualism have increasingly been recognized.

Immigrants: People who are residents of a country where they were not born.

International Students: Students pursuing their education outside of their country of birth.

Monolingual: Speaking only one language fluently.

Multilingual: Speaking two or more languages with some degree of fluency.

Native Speakers: Those who learned a given language as children rather than as a foreign language.

Oral History: An interview methodology based on in-depth interviews with the purpose of preserving some aspect of the past that interviewer and interviewee consider of historical significance.

Privileged Irresponsibility: A stance of avoiding responsibility taken by those in power vis a vis those from underrepresented groups. In the case of linguistic justice, this may take the form of imposing a dominant dialect of a dominant language, such as Standard American English.

Raciolinguistics: The study of how language shapes our ideas about race.

Standard English: A variety of English that is commonly regarded as "correct" and that is generally spoken and written by white middle and upper classes.

Translingualism: Recognizing linguistic difference as a resource rather than a deficit.

APPENDIX

Sample Interview Questions

1. *Cultural Background and Native Language*: To start out with today, could you tell us about your cultural background? Where did you grow up and what language/s did you speak at home as a child? How is your native language connected for you with your sense of heritage and cultural or ethnic identity? What stories stand out from your early experiences with language?
2. *Memories of Becoming Multilingual or Becoming Versed in More than One Dialect*: What other languages or dialects do you speak and at what point did you learn these? Can you share some stories or experiences about using multiple languages and/or dialects and the contexts in which you have used these?
    a. *Code meshing or other hybrid language uses*: Have you ever combined languages when you speak or write, such as using words or grammar from one language when you talk or write in a different language? If you do this, is it accepted or even admired by others or is it criticized?
    b. *Fluency*: How fluent are you in the different languages that you speak? Which language is dominant in the sense that you think in that language? Has this changed over time based on where you live or whom you interact with?
3. *Elementary and Secondary School Experiences:* Where did you go to school, and what primary language or languages were used in your school? Was the official school language the same as the language/s you spoke at home? If not, how did the private language of your home and the public language of your school intersect? For example, did your teachers ever make you feel out of place or disadvantaged because of your multilingualism or was your multilingualism seen as an advantage? Did you ever experience racism related to your ethnicity and language use?
4. *Advantages of Multilingualism:* What are some ways that you perceive multilingualism as an advantage in your personal or professional life? What are some concrete examples?
5. *College/University Experiences as Multilingual Student:* How has knowing multiple languages affected your college experience? If relevant, relate this to how you use multiple languages for classes in your major or how you might use these in your future professional life?
    a. Speaking
    b. Listening
    c. Reading
    d. Writing
6. *University Perceptions of Multilingualism and Cultural/Linguistic Diversity:* How did professors, tutors, or others perceive your multilingualism? Do you believe that the university does enough to foster cultural and linguistic diversity? Did you ever experience any racism or discrimination based on your ethnic and cultural background or your language use?
7. *University Support for Multilingual Students:* To what extent have you felt supported as a multilingual student at this university? What are some concrete examples of the support you received? For example, what steps did teachers, writing center tutors, or administrators take to be mindful of your needs as a multilingual student?
8. *Approaches to Teaching and Assessment:* To what extent were professors mindful of the multilingual experience in their approaches to teaching and assessment? For instance, to what extent were you

required to follow the rules of Standard American English in your writing? Were you encouraged to incorporate or draw on your different languages and/or dialects in your course work?
9. *Linguistic Justice and Suggestions for Improvement:* What suggestions do you have for how the university could further foster linguistic justice? How could the university better support and celebrate multilingual students?
10. *Final Thoughts*: Do you have anything else you'd like to share? Do you have any advice for other students at our university?

Chapter 13
Translanguaging or English Monolanguaging?
Exploring Postsecondary Students' Perceptions of Linguistic Human Rights in Pakistan's Sindh Province

Ameer Ali
Government Arts and Commerce College, Larkano, Pakistan

Maya Khemlani David
University of Malaya, Malaysia

Shahnawaz Tunio
 https://orcid.org/0000-0003-3855-8045
Government Arts and Commerce College, Larkano, Pakistan

ABSTRACT

This study explores postsecondary students' perceptions of translanguaging and its nexus with linguistic human rights in Pakistan's Sindh province. English monolanguaging policy in higher educational institutions in Sindh has been seen as a ladder for upward social mobility. This monolingualism has posed challenges to linguistic diversity and linguistic human rights in the province (Sindh) that is multilingual. Interviews conducted via WhatsApp with postsecondary students in Sindh showed the popularity of translanguaging in contrast to English monolanguaging. Responses provided by participants were coded and qualitatively analyzed. Findings demonstrated how translanguaging could help provide and protect linguistic human rights.

DOI: 10.4018/978-1-6684-9029-7.ch013

INTRODUCTION

Sindh, a multilingual province in Pakistan, is home to the Sindhi language. Pakistan including all its provinces, such as Baluchistan, Khyber Pakhtunkhwa, Punjab, and Sindh, was once a British colony, and the language of the colonial masters (i.e., English) was and has always been prioritized over the local languages.

Even today in Sindh and Pakistan, the English language is a tool of power, in the hands of linguistic gatekeepers and the dominant class (Ali & David, 2023). The role of the English language has been discussed by many researchers (Kachru, 1986; Quijano, 2000; Veronelli, 2015). English, as a colonial language, has replaced linguistic diversity in many formal, educational domains in the form of imposing monolingual hegemony, instilling raciolinguistic ideologies of White native speakerism or banning the use of L1 in English language classrooms in Sindh.

Currently, the field of linguistic human rights is contesting linguistic colonial legacy in a number of countries (Ali & David, 2023). Language human rights or linguistic human rights protect a person's or a group's right to use their language or languages in the private and public domains (Minority Rights Group International, 2015). Linguistic human rights involve the right to speak one's own language in legal, judicial, and administrative sites, the right to get education in one's own language, and the right for media to be on air in one's own language (Minority Rights Group International, 2015).

Previous research has focused on individual and collective aspects of linguistic human rights (Skutnabb-Kangas, 2012). Looking at languages from an instrumental perspective, Skutnabb-Kangass (2012) defines languages as instruments of communication and markers of identity, and thus these are fundamental for a dignified life (Paz, 2014). Embedded in the area of linguistic human rights, this study postulates how access to linguistic human rights through translanguaging can be fundamental for a linguistically free, dignified life. Earlier studies have discussed how linguistic human rights can either prevent linguistic discrimination or affirm the use of L1 (Organization for Security and Co-operation in Europe, 1999), how language policy and planning provide access or very little or completely no access to linguistic human rights (Grin, 2000), how discourses on linguistic human rights are constructed in the global south and the global north (Paulsrud & Rosén, 2019), and how such discourses clash in the context of private schools in Pakistan's Sindh province (Ali & David, 2023). However, there is not much research conducted on how postsecondary students perceive translanguaging and how translanguaging can replace English monolanguaging by instilling the ideology of linguistic human rights and linguistic emancipation in postsecondary English language teaching contexts in Sindh.

Literature Review

Translanguaging

The origin of translanguaging is traced to the Welsh bilingual education system (Lewis et. al., 2012). Cen Williams, a Welsh bilingual educationist, coined the Welsh term "trwasieithu" which translates into its English equivalent "translanguaging" (Conteh, 2019). Its purpose was to function as a cross-curricular strategy for the use of two languages for teaching and learning inside the same classroom (Conteh, 2019). It is currently receiving much appraisal because it advocates learners' first language inside the classroom (Hall & Cook, 2012). Translanguaging is a pedagogical act of emancipation (Mbirimi-Hungwe, 2021) and it involves meshing of two or more than two languages while speaking or writing (Canagarajah,

2021). The pedagogical act enables foreign language learners to use multiple languages at their disposal to achieve their learning and communicative goals (Canagarajah, 2011).

Using semi-structured individual interviews and ethnographic observations, Prada (2019) discussed how translanguaging at tertiary level can help Spanish heritage speakers achieve linguistic, ideological, and attitudinal reconfigurations. In other words, his study demonstrates how translanguaging can help Spanish heritage speakers challenge traditional monoglossic ideologies. Other researchers have discussed the role of translanguaging in security and justice education (Charalambous et al., 2020), in cultural and linguistic maintenance (Ali & Mangrio, under review) and in multilingual turn (Prada & Turnbull, 2018). However, none of these studies have provided the view of translanguaging and human rights from the perspective of postsecondary school learners in English language classrooms in Sindh. Therefore, this study seeks to explore postsecondary students' perceptions of translanguaging, the role of translanguaging in accessing linguistic human rights, and question the monolingual hegemony of the English language.

In a study conducted by Paulsrud and Rosén (2019), the focus is on critical pedagogy and translanguaging. However, their study does not correlate translanguaging with linguistic human rights. Using a perspective based on critical pedagogy, Paulsrud and Rosén (2019) present and critically analyze empirical studies from the global north and the global south to explain how ideologies are demonstrated through classroom policies. Focusing on the studies of translanguaging in the primary classrooms in Europe, in secondary schools in Scandinavia, and in higher education institutions in South Africa, they show how language ideologies are manifested, negotiated, and challenged through translanguaging.

Apart from critical pedagogical approaches, post-colonial approach has assisted in legitimizing translanguaging as a social justice strategy in Chinese language classrooms in Hong Kong (Wang, 2022). For instance, students can use both Chinese and English to achieve their communication goals. Additionally, Wang's post-colonial approach towards translanguaging discusses diversity and inclusion. In other words, students' culture and language are valued and practiced respectively in the classroom; such a post-colonial approach that questions and challenges power relations can be made more comprehensive by including discourse on linguistic human rights to the discussion on translanguaging.

Heltai and Tarsoly's (2023) multi-authored monograph, based in the junction of translanguaging research and Romani studies, provides a robust analysis of the ways in which translanguaging assists bilingual Roma students' learning in monolingual school systems. This study is based on long-term participatory ethnographic research and a pedagogical implementation project undertaken in Hungary and Slovakia by a group of teachers, bilingual Roma (Roma students belong to the Romani community in Europe) participants, and researchers. Furthermore, the role of translanguaging in teacher education has been examined in a special volume by Pablo and Christain (2023). Pablo and Christian (2023) explore how teachers enact translanguaging pedagogy in linguistically and culturally diverse classrooms and community settings. The study investigates some of the current debates in the arena of multilingual education and teacher education in the ways that illustrate new ideas and provide new approaches linked to translanguaging.

Linguistic Human Rights and Translanguaging

Linguistic human rights have been recognized in international covenants and declarations. For instance, Article 27 of the International Covenant on Civil and Political Rights enables minority communities to use their language in a range of contexts:

In those States in which ethnic, religious or linguistic minorities exist, persons belonging to such minorities shall not be denied the right, in community with the other members of their group, to enjoy their own culture, to profess and practice their own religion, or to use their own language. (United Nations, 1976)

Furthermore, Article 2 of Universal Declarations of Human Rights states that:

Everyone is entitled to all the rights and freedoms set forth in this Declaration, without distinction of any kind, such as race, color, sex, language, religion, political or other opinion, national or social origin, property, birth or other status. (United Nations, 1948)

In her qualitative review, Skutnabb-Kangas (2012) postulates how linguistic human rights can be discussed using an instrumental perspective, and she argues that languages can either be communication tools or markers of identity. In academic traditions, there have been three kinds of discourses on linguistic rights in Sindh. The first type of discourse calls for Sindhi as a medium of instruction (Gopang et al., 2020); the second type of discourse advocates Urdu as a medium of instruction (Ali & David, 2023). The third one supports English as a medium of instruction in schools (Channa, 2014). Moreover, the clash of such diverging discourses on linguistic human rights in Sindh has been discussed by Ali and David (2023).

Methodology

Research Questions

1. What are postsecondary students' perceptions of translanguaging?
2. How do postsecondary students view English Monolanguaging?
3. How does translanguaging protect linguistic human rights?

This study used the qualitative method of data collection and analysis. The research was conducted in the context of the district—Larkana in Pakistan's Sindh province. Data was collected using ethnography which included the use of WhatsApp calls and voice notes. Ethnography was appropriate for this study because it helped in data collection from participants living in different areas in Larkana. Researchers shared questions via WhatsApp voice notes in the Sindhi language and participants provided responses via voice notes. When needed, WhatsApp calls were used for clarification, though the calls were not recorded. Data collected through purposive sampling and narrative inquiry was manually transcribed and translated for analysis.

Participants

Participants and researchers were multilinguals as they could speak Sindhi, English, and Urdu languages. Thirty postsecondary students (15 males and 15 females) from three public sector universities in Larkana were selected for interviews, and these prospective participants were contacted and their selection was finalized only after they agreed to share their responses. Besides, the prospective students were pursuing their graduate degrees and their first language was Sindhi. The average age of the participants was 26 years. The selected students were well-aware of translanguaging and their awareness was checked by asking a few questions related to translanguaging.

Since the prospective participants lived in different areas in district Larkana, interviews were conducted via WhatsApp voice notes and phone calls using open-ended questions in the Sindhi language. In total, 30 interviews were conducted, and each interview lasted about half an hour. Only 30 relevant chunks were taken from the interviews and their rigorous coding was conducted. The interviews were conducted in July, 2023 and were manually transcribed and translated. Translation was conducted by a bilingual speaker that was one of the researchers who received much training and possessed much experience in translating Sindhi and English languages. Furthermore, the expert was a professor of Linguistics in a university in Malaysia.

The translations of the interviews were verified by this bilingual speaker, read, reread, and codified to identify general patterns and generate themes. Qualitative coding is a process of classifying excerpts to find themes and patterns. Deductive coding, a top-down approach, was used to develop an initial set of codes which were based on research questions. Data was then read through, and codes were assigned to excerpts. Four steps were followed in the process of coding. First, data was read carefully and codes were assigned to various excerpts. In this step, value coding was conducted. Second, excerpts were organized into codes and sub codes. Thirdly, the created categories were reexamined to reduce any resulting inconsistency. Content analysis coding also helped in the re-examination. Fourth, the categories were classified into broader final themes. Moreover, the audit trial of the data was conducted by presenting research findings in tables. The qualitative thematic analysis of the codified and tabulated findings was conducted to demonstrate how postsecondary students perceive translanguaging in the wake of monoglossic ideologies. Ethical protocols were followed by giving pseudonyms to participants to hide their identities.

Researchers' Positionalities

Researchers of this study had diverse educational and national backgrounds. First author was a Pakistani multilingual as he could speak Sindhi, Urdu and English languages. He was a graduate in Applied Linguistics and worked as English lecturer in a government college in Pakistan. Second writer worked as Honorary Professor in a university in Malaysia. She was multilingually proficient in English, Sindhi, Malay, and Urdu. Moreover, third author possessed expertise in Education and Psychology and worked as Assistant Professor in a government college in Pakistan. Such diverse experience was used to conduct this study.

Findings

Findings in this section are discussed based on three main headings: *postsecondary students' perceptions of translanguaging, postsecondary students' perceptions of English monolanguaging, and translanguaging: the protector of linguistic human rights.*

Postsecondary Students' Perceptions of Translanguaging

Postsecondary students' perceptions of translanguaging are presented in Table 1 and analysis of their perceptions is provided after the table.

Table 1. Translanguaging

Participant Name	Participant's Response	Gender
Azad	I think translanguaging should be the medium of instruction. It makes understanding course content easier. I sometimes find it difficult to put my thoughts in the foreign language (English). So, I translanguage and communication becomes much easier. Moreover, I feel good using my language along with English to convey my ideas. The use of translanguaging should be encouraged.	Male
Fatima	Translanguaging is very helpful for students. Apart from making learning easier, it promotes local languages and cultures. Translanguaging is student friendly. It provides confidence and makes learning meaningful. You know…confident students are active learners. So, I think translanguaging activates students' capability of learning both language and content.	Female
Shafquat	Translanguaging is a pedagogical strategy. It makes students creatively engage in class activities. This strategy is inclusive. It makes all students participate inside the classroom. It is equally good for both introvert and extrovert students. I endorse the idea of using translanguaging inside the classroom.	Male
Sana	Translanguaging is a tool that helps in democratizing the process of learning. I mean to say that it gives you an opportunity to make use of a wide range of linguistic repertoire that is at your disposal. In other words, you can use your choice linguistic items or languages that you like and that you think can make learning easy for you.	Female
Atahar	In my opinion, translanguaging can help us in bringing our local culture, personal experience and social understanding to the class. It can help in bridging the gap between outside (social) knowledge and classroom learning. It can be a good link between society and classroom.	Male
Sania	The use of mother tongue along with English (a foreign language) can help us understand what we read and talk about inside the class. Translanguaging provided the role of explaining and translation to both teachers and learners. Both explanation and translation are important for successful learning outcomes.	Female
Tanveer	Translanguaging makes us feel welcome inside the classroom. We don't feel alien in the class. We feel like we belong to the classroom and the classroom belongs to us. We can use any language that we like and convey our message much more easily. We feel more comfortable when we can translanguage.	Male
Mahira	For me, translanguaging is a learner friendly technique. It makes us feel confident and articulate our message effectively and fluently. It empowers the learner and helps them feel proud of their identity by using their language inside the classroom.	Female
Asif	I think translanguaging is not the demonstration of language deficiency. It is in fact language competence. When we use different languages at our disposal, it shows how deftly we are making linguistic choices to achieve communicative goals. It makes communication more convenient and easier.	Male
Sabina	Translanguaging helps us redefine language competence. The richer and more diverse linguistic repertoire a person has means they have a higher degree of language competence. In contrast, if a person's linguistic repertoire is not diverse, they can be said to have a lower degree of language competence.	Female

Azad viewed translanguaging as a learner friendly mechanism that made learning course content much easier. According to Hall and Cook (2012), translanguaging advocates learners' own language use and Azad's response also shows how he demands linguistic human rights by supporting translanguaging. Such ease in content learning is achieved through translanguaging because it allows learners to use their L1 in expressing their ideas and understanding key concepts in the course. Likewise, this ease of expression and understanding makes learners feel positive about their academic progress as Azad remarked, "I feel good using my language along with English to convey my ideas. The use of translanguaging should be encouraged."

Another positive view of translanguaging was provided by Fatima. She believed that it helps in promoting languages and cultures. Following Prada (2019), translanguaging helps in preserving linguistic and cultural heritage and using the heritage in successful learning of content and language. Similarly, this study demonstrates how translanguaging enables students to link their social knowledge with the classroom learning, develop their linguistic repertoire, knowledge base and social competence, and thus makes students feel confident about their academic and social progress.

Although Azad and Fatima emphasized the benefits of translanguaging, it is important to acknowledge that depending too heavily on translanguaging can hinder students' language development in the foreign language (English, in this case) up to some extent. Consequently, it is essential to strike a balance between using the native language for comprehension and gradually improving foreign/second language skills.

Translanguaging can accommodate language and learning preferences of students. According to Shafquat, translanguaging inclusively accommodates learning preferences of both extrovert and introvert students. Accommodating students' learning preferences can result in their creative engagement in classroom activities, and these, learning preferences through translanguaging, according to Mbirimi-Hungwe (2021), can be described as an example of a pedagogical act of emancipation.

In addition, Sana thought that translanguaging democratized learning by providing access to a wide range of linguistic repertoire. Democratization of learning involves the process of providing free choice to learners to select one or more languages and use such languages in learning and expressing their ideas. Evidently, this democratization of learning can also help challenge the discourse on standardization of course and language as such discourse often excludes local languages and cultures from the process of teaching and learning. The democratization of learning through translanguaging can also play an important role in security and justice education (Charalambous et. al., 2020).

Integration of outside knowledge and classroom learning is brought about with translanguaging. Atahar mentioned how the integrative role of translanguaging could help mainstream local experiences, narratives, and mother tongues (see also Sania's response in Table 1). Through integration of institutional (formal) and non-institutional (informal) forms of knowledge, translanguaging can help in preserving cultural diversity and establishing social justice (Wang, 2022). As Tanveer articulated, "Mainstreaming local knowledge can help teachers and learners diversify their course content and make it socially and culturally relevant." It is also important to critically evaluate whether this integration always increases learning or if it might sometimes introduce distractions or off-topic discussions.

The continual emphasis on the use of translanguaging by Tanveer set forth how it could reduce the feelings of alienation in students. Linguistic freedom given through translanguaging enables students to feel at home and develop a sense of belonging. This sense of belonging brings forth the sense of comfort in such students who can strategically use their linguistic repertoire. However, as Mahira suggested, "it should be emphasized that such belonging and comfort may not result in students predominantly using their native languages and missing out on opportunities to improve their proficiency in the foreign/second language".

Mahira also discussed the ways translanguaging could enhance learners' feelings of pride and how it could increase their communicative effectiveness and fluency. Communicative effectiveness and fluency make students feel empowered and such empowered students can cherish their identities and proudly introduce such identities inside and outside the classroom.

An insightful suggestion to look at the practice of translanguaging inside the classroom was provided by Asif and Sabina. These responses suggest that diverse linguistic repertoire signifies higher language competence while the lack of such diverse repertoire implies lower linguistic competence. It is important to consider that language competence should be evaluated not only in terms of mastery and fluency in the primary language of instruction, but also in terms of the diversity of linguistic repertoires in multiple languages used inside the classroom.

There are some similarities and differences in the responses provided by participants. According to Azad, translanguaging could facilitate an easy way of expressing ideas. By contrast, Fatima commented that translanguaging could facilitate promotion of local languages and cultures. Moreover, Shafquat's and Sana's responses were similar as they both discussed the ways translanguaging could democratize learning by making it inclusive. Additionally, Atahar postulated that translanguaging could link social experience and classroom learning while Sania stated that translanguaging helped with explanation and translation of texts. Finally, Asif and Sabeena shared their views and re-conceptualized linguistic competence as translingual competence.

Postsecondary Students' Perceptions of English Monolanguaging

Postsecondary students' perceptions of English monolanguaging are provided in Table 2, and analysis of their responses is conducted after the table.

Table 2. English monolanguaging

Participant Name	Participant's Response	Gender
Yaseen	The use of only English inside the class can reduce the level of confidence. We feel we have not much confidence to convey our thoughts in English. Lack of confidence can be challenging in the process of learning and makes us feel inferior to those who can speak and write good English. I think this should not be the case in the classroom, and there ought to be linguistic freedom in the classroom.	Male
Jannat	English monolanguaging inside the classroom is a symbol of linguistic hegemony. In such a scenario, English is imposed from the top echelons of power, and the use of local languages is completely banned and penalized. This linguistic dictatorship can result in many of us (students) losing faith in their local languages and in the probable extinction of minor languages.	Female
Farman	In English monolanguaging, English is seen as a language of education, while other local languages are seen as languages of the ignorant people, and the use of such languages is strictly prohibited inside the classroom. Language is just a tool of communication, and it should not be linked with education or ignorance. All languages are important, and they should be respected.	Male
Fehmida	English monolanguaging creates social segregation both inside the classroom and outside the classroom. Those who can speak and write good English are seen as sophisticated, modern, and well educated. In contrast, those who speak or use their mother tongues inside the classroom are seen as outcast ignorant.	Female
Ahmed	The aim of English monolanguaging is to provide education to those fewer students who are good at reading and writing English. Otherwise, those who cannot read and write good English are denied the right to learn in their mother tongue. Education should be the right given to all without any linguistic discrimination.	Male
Asma	English monolanguaging is a mechanism of exclusion. English speaking students are included in the process of learning, teaching, and getting good jobs. In contrast, non-English speaking students are excluded from educational process and job market. In result, many such students become disappointed and are forced to lead a struggling life.	Female
Asim	English monolanguaging creates a system of linguistic discrimination. Those who are able to read and write in English are appreciated and rewarded. Those who cannot read and write in English are discouraged and demotivated.	Male
Maira	In this, expressing ideas and sharing answers are not easy tasks. Many students struggle in English monolanguaging. English monolanguaging creates many hurdles for learners, and these hurdles include difficulty in speaking, discussing, and debating. In other words, it makes learning a difficult process, especially for those who are not comfortable in speaking and writing English.	Female
Tahir	If English is imposed inside the classroom and other languages are banned, this can suppress many ideas that many learners can comfortably express in their mother tongues. Suppression of ideas is perhaps not a good thing when it comes to teaching and learning. Therefore, I would like to suggest the use of translanguaging instead of monolanguaging.	Male
Sabeena	Content understanding becomes much harder. Learners cannot fully grasp the process of learning if it takes place in a language in which he/she is not comfortable. A learner must be made to feel comfortable, and this can be done through the use of translanguaging inside the classroom.	Female

Opposing to English monolanguaging was expressed by participants as a form of advocacy for linguistic human rights. Yaseen highlighted a fact that the lack of linguistic freedom could be a problem for learners. Yaseen continued that the imposition of English monolanguaging prevented learners from using their L1 along with English in the classroom. According to Kachru (1986), preventing learners' L1 and encouraging the use of English inside the classroom is an example of English as a colonial language. Such linguistic restrictions not only limit the language choices of learners, but also have decreased their confidence. The issue of reduced confidence when English is the sole language used in the classroom underscores the psychological impact of monolanguaging on students' self-esteem. In short, English monolanguaging can diminish students' linguistic freedom and self-esteem.

Strong criticism of English monolanguaging was expressed by Jannat. She noted that English monolanguaging had resulted in linguistic hegemony or dictatorship and probable extinction of minor languages. This phenomenon has been described as coloniality of language (English) by Veronelli (2015). In such a scenario, rather than becoming a breeding ground of linguistic diversity, classroom has become, as Fehmida reported, "a graveyard of minor languages." In other words, this response critically examines the power dynamics associated with monolanguaging and its broader societal impact.

The idea behind the English monolanguaging policy has been looked at from a critical point of view. Farman provided critical assessment of the notion of "English" as the language of education and "local languages" as languages of ignorance. Moreover, this process of negatively describing regional languages has been described by Kachru (1986) as colonization through the English language. Farman insisted upon the importance of respecting all languages and challenged the idea of language being linked solely to education. This response stresses the need for linguistic equality. Moreover, Fehmida raised concerns about social segregation resulting from English monolanguaging, stressing the stigmatization of those who used their mother tongues. This response critically examines how language choices can affect social perceptions and identities within and outside the classroom.

Yet, in another critical evaluation of English monolanguaging policy, Ahmed revealed that it was based on linguistic discrimination. The linguistic discrimination violates Article 2 of Universal Declarations of Human Rights that prevents discrimination on linguistic and other grounds (United Nations, 1948). Ahmed asserted that education should be inclusive and should not discriminate based on one's language proficiency. Otherwise, education provided through English monolanguaging becomes a mechanism of exclusion, leading to disparities in educational and job opportunities (see Asma and Asim's responses in Table 2). These responses emphasize the social and economic implications of English monolanguaging, particularly for non-native speakers of English. Asim also underscored how language proficiency can impact students' motivation and achievements.

Those students who were not comfortable with English faced pedagogical challenges associated with a monolingual approach (See Maira's response in Table 2). By contrast, a multilingual approach adopted through translanguaging can reduce such pedagogical challenges and help students actively engage in learning and problem solving. In other words, Maira pressed the need of facilitating her learning through translanguaging. By comparison, English monolanguaging takes away the comfort of learning from students as it suppresses such students' ideas. Tahir protested against the suppression of ideas while suggesting the use of translanguaging. In addition, Sabeena indicated the challenges in content understanding caused by monolanguaging and pointed out that comprehension and learning were hindered when students were not at ease with the language of instruction and advocated for translanguaging to improve students' understanding. In summary, these responses collectively provided detailed insights into English monolanguaging, emphasizing problems of confidence, power dynamics, social segregation, discrimination, practical difficulties, and the negative impact on the learning process. These respondents (e.g., Sabeena & Maira) advocated for more inclusive and equitable language practices, such as translanguaging within the classroom.

Participants' views of English monolanguaging have also indicated some interesting similarities and differences. For example, Yaseen perceived English monolanguaging as a tool of creating inferiority and a lack of confidence in non-English speaking students. Contrarily, Jannat believed that English monolanguaging was an example of linguistic hegemony and it could endanger local languages. Furthermore, Farman thought that language should be seen as a tool of communication while Fehmida suggested that langugae should be seen as a way of social segregation. Tahir noted how English monolanguaging suppressed students' ideas whereas Sabeen commented that it caused difficulty in content learning.

Translanguaging: The Protector of Linguistic Human Rights

Translanguaging is also seen as a tool to protect linguistic human rights by participants. Responses of the participants and the analysis of their responses are provided in this section. See Table 3.

Table 3. Linguistic human rights

Participant Name	Participant's Response	Gender
Hamza	Translanguaging can protect and provide linguistic human rights as it can challenge and counter linguistic dictatorship inside the classroom. Linguistic dictatorship is a phenomenon in which one language is imposed at the cost of other languages inside or outside the classroom. Translanguaging is a mechanism through which such dictatorial language policies can be questioned and challenged.	Male
Iqra	To translanguage, is to be free. It gives us linguistic freedom. It gives us freedom to use our mother tongues in learning and teaching. It gives us choices to use any language to make learning of content and language happen successfully. Through linguistic freedom we can have our linguistic human rights provided and protected.	Female
Muhammad Khan	Translanguaging is a pedagogical tool that has a remarkable potential to liberalize learning through linguistic freedom. Linguistic freedom involvesa free choice that is given to a person allowing him/her to use the language of their choice in all social domains.	Male
Saqiba	Linguistic human rights can be protected through translanguaging. It gives us freedom to choose any linguistic item from a wide range of linguistic repertoire that is at our disposal.	Female
Karamat	It is very helpful for our cognitive processes. If we can use more than one language in learning and teaching, we will be more successful learners and teachers. The students who are multilingual speakers are more competent than those students who are monolingual speakers. Multilingual speakers can not only preserve their linguistic human rights but also perform well in languages of wider communication.	Male
Bakhtawar	Translanguaging is a tool that can reconciliate the clashing discourses on linguistic human rights. It can redefine the concept of linguistic human rights through the use of multilingual repertoire.	Female
Musawar	Translanguaging can protect linguistic human rights by preserving local languages and cultures.	Male
Dariya	It helps us challenge and prevent linguistic hegemony. It seeks to establish equality among learners by encouraging the use of learners' mother tongues.	Female
Qamar	We feel like there is no more threat to our mother tongue because in translanguaging, I can use it inside the classroom and wherever I like.	Male
Urooj	Linguistic human rights can be provided and protected through translanguaging especially in a context where there is language policy conflict. It can reduce such conflicts and preserve minor languages.	Female

Linguistic human rights can protect a person's or a group's right to use their language (Minority Rights Group International, 2015). Similarly, Hamza remarked that translanguaging allowed for protecting and preserving learners' rights to learn in their mother tongues with the probable assistance of a foreign or second language. This response places linguistic diversity and freedom at the center of linguistic human rights because such rights, as Hamza implies, are difficult to get to some extent without free linguistic choice and diversity.

Also, translanguaging is not an end, but a means to protect linguistic human rights (see Iqra's response in Table 3). In the same manner, Iqra optimized the potential of translanguaging as it sought to link linguistic freedom to the protection of linguistic human rights. Linguistically free, students can not only perform much better in their academic domain, but also exercise their influence to negotiate language policies in the classroom and protect their linguistic human rights (see Saqiba's response in Table 3). Achieving such linguistic rights can help students use their choice languages in various social domains (see Muhammad Khan's response in Table 3).

Additionally, protecting linguistic human rights through translanguaging can have many potential, cognitive benefits for learners (see Karamat's response in Table 3). Multilingual speakers are cognitively more active and better academic performers than monolingual speakers. Proponents of translanguaging, by demanding their linguistic human rights, seek to protect their multilingual repertoire because realization of such demands can result in many benefits for students. Hence, translanguaging can preserve linguistic human rights while improving knowledge proficiency, particularly for multilingual speakers.

Translanguaging can also play a reconciliatory role by reducing conflict between clashing discourses on linguistic human rights (see Bakhtawar's response in Table 3). In other words, it can accommodate the linguistic preferences of supporters of English and activists of mother tongue (Ali & David, 2023). Moreover, translanguaging can help redefine the concept of linguistic human rights through the use of multilingual repertoires. Discussing the cultural aspect of linguistic human rights, Musawar makes the connection of these rights with translanguaging. In contrast, Dariya describes the social justice aspect of translanguaging and linguistic human rights. The former discusses how preserving local cultures and languages can help protect linguistic human rights. The latter demonstrates how social justice can be established by encouraging the use of mother tongue in education, and how such use of mother tongue is linked with linguistic human rights. These trends of preventing linguistic discrimination and preserving languages are central to the discourse on linguistic human rights (Organization for Security and Co-operation in Europe, 1999). Translanguaging also helps establish the sense of linguistic security in learners (see Qamar's response in Table 3).

In summary, the participants' responses demonstrate translanguaging's benefits in promoting linguistic freedom, protecting linguistic diversity, challenging language hegemony, and preserving local languages and cultures. The respondents link translanguaging to the concept of linguistic human rights, underscoring its potential to increase language education and empower students to choose the language of their choice in a range of contexts. Although participants have linked translanguaging to linguistic human rights, there are both shared traits and variations as commented by our respondents. According to Hamza, translanguaging could provide linguistic human rights by challenging dictatorial language policies while Iqra believed that it could help achieve linguistic human rights by giving linguistic freedom to students. Besides, Karamat contended that translanguaging was students' linguistic human right and it was conducive to the improvement of cognitive processes. Echoing Karamat's views, Bakhtawar articulated that translanguaging reconciliated the clashing discourses on linguistic human rights. However, there are also similarities between these responses.

DISCUSSION

The discussion places the findings of this study in the context of existing research on linguistic human rights and translanguaging. Research studies (Grin, 2000; Organization for Security and Co-operation in Europe, 1999; Skutnabb-Kangas, 2012) have focused on individual and collective aspects of linguistic human rights and the negative and positive dimensions of these rights. Research has also examined language policies' impact on linguistic human rights (Ali & David, 2023). Some studies (Pablo & Christain, 2023; Prada, 2019) have discussed the role of translanguaging in various educational contexts, such as heritage language speakers or security and justice education, but not necessarily in the context of linguistic human rights.

Unlike Ali and David's (2023) qualitative study that investigated the clash of discourses on linguistic human rights, this study underlines how translanguaging can be seen by students as a means of safeguarding linguistic human rights. It highlights the promotion of linguistic freedom, inclusivity, and respect for all languages, countering potential language dominance. It raises the importance of linguistic diversity, suggesting that translanguaging is necessary to counteract linguistic hegemony and the potential extinction of minor languages.

The discussion also acknowledges the challenges of balancing language policies in education. Much like Wang's (2022) study that described translanguaging as a social justice strategy, this study discusses postsecondary learners' views on how translanguaging can help achieve linguistic human rights. In addition, again from the perspective of learners, this study emphasizes the protection of linguistic human rights while also considering the importance of foreign language proficiency. The discussion also highlights the importance of ensuring that students fully understand and engage with educational content which translanguaging can facilitate. It highlights that educational policies should support linguistic human rights and protect students' diverse ideas and expressions. Moreover, this study provides valuable insights into the complex dynamics of language policies, translanguaging, and education.

In the context of linguistic human rights, our study aligns with the principle of respecting linguistic diversity. Linguistic human rights entail the right to use one's native language and the preservation of linguistic diversity (Skutnabb-Kangas, 2012). Translanguaging, as advocated in our study, can serve as a counterforce to linguistic hegemony by allowing students to draw upon their varied linguistic repertoire without suppressing their native languages.

Students' Perspectives of Translanguaging and English Monolanguaging

Responses from students in our study suggest that translanguaging, as compared with English monolanguaging, plays a vital role in improving their confidence and academic performance. Besides, translanguaging, as suggested in our study, can contribute to breaking down language barriers to learning by fostering inclusivity and respecting all languages. Furthermore, our findings based on students' perceptions collectively underscore the complexity of language policies in educational contexts. However, it is a multifaceted challenge of balancing the need to develop proficiency in a foreign language with the promotion of translanguaging, inclusivity, and the preservation of linguistic diversity. The role of language in education and its impact on societal perceptions cannot be underestimated.

Analyzing participants' responses, our findings also show that the social segregation and discrimination can result from English monolanguaging. Students proficient in English may be perceived as sophisticated and educated while those who primarily use their native languages may face discrimination.

The practical challenges posed by English monolanguaging to the learning process are also revealed by our study. Students may struggle with speaking, discussing, and debating in English, hindering their overall learning experience.

Based on our interview data, translanguaging, provides students with a means to communicate effectively, reducing the barriers imposed by the lack of language proficiency in the target language. However, it is important to strike a balance between the benefits of translanguaging in terms of confidence and linguistic freedom and the need to develop proficiency in the foreign language, in this case, English.

Intersection of Translanguaging and Linguistic Human Rights

As well, the findings from our study demonstrate a significant intersection between translanguaging and linguistic human rights in that the suppression of ideas expressed in native languages is contrary to the principles of linguistic human rights which advocate for the free expression of ideas in one's native language. This perspective is not only theoretically compelling, but also carries practical implications for language policies in educational contexts, especially in linguistically diverse regions like Sindh. Our findings also resonate with the broader concept of linguistic human rights, where individuals should not be judged, marginalized, or discriminated based on their lack of language proficiency in the target language. In the context of linguistic human rights, such linguistic discrimination raises questions about equal access and opportunities. Linguistic human rights should encompass not just the right to use one's language, but also the right to access educational and employment opportunities without language-based discrimination.

CONCLUDING REMARKS

In conclusion, our study's findings combat monolanguaging and provide valuable insights into the intersection of translanguaging and linguistic human rights. Translanguaging, as a powerful tool for protecting linguistic human rights by fostering confidence, promotes inclusivity, challenges linguistic hegemony, and respects linguistic diversity. However, it is crucial to strike a balance between the benefits of translanguaging and the need for language proficiency in educational settings. Achieving this balance is essential for ensuring that all students can access education without language-based discrimination and feel comfortable in the learning process. Ultimately, this study highlights the pivotal role that translanguaging can play in safeguarding linguistic human rights and shaping more equitable and inclusive language policies in education.

REFERENCES

Ali, A., & David, M. K. (2023). Investigating the Clash of Discourses on Linguistic Human Rights: Focus on the Private Schools in Sindh, Pakistan. *Forma Y Funcion*, *36*(2). Advance online publication. doi:10.15446/fyf.v36n2.101898

Ali, A., & Mangrio, M. A. (forthcoming). Exploring sociocultural benefits of translanguaging in ELT in Pakistan's Sindh province. *European Journal of TEFL and Applied Linguistics*.

Canagarajah, S. (2011). Codemeshing in academic writing: Identifying teachable strategies of translanguaging. *Modern Language Journal, 95*(3), 401–417. doi:10.1111/j.1540-4781.2011.01207.x

Channa, L. (2014). *English Medium for the government primary schools of Sindh, Pakistan: an exploration of government primary school teachers' attitudes* [Doctoral dissertation]. The University of Georgia.

Charalambous, C., Charalambous, P., Zembylas, M., & Theodorou, E. (2020). Translanguaging, (In)Security and Social Justice Education. In J. A. Panagiotopoulou, L. Rosen, & J. Strzykala (Eds.), *Inclusion, Education and Translanguaging. Inklusion und Bildung in Migrationsgesellschaften* (pp. 105–123). Springer. doi:10.1007/978-3-658-28128-1_7

Conteh, J. (2019). Translanguaging. *ELT Journal, 72*(4), 445–447. doi:10.1093/elt/ccy034

Gopang, A. S., Panhwar, A. H., &Nizamani, H. A. (2020). Issue of language as the medium of instruction in Pakistan: An analytical study. *The Shield, 11*.

Grin, F. (2000). *Evaluating policy measures for minority languages in Europe: Towards effective, cost-effective and democratic implementation. ECMI Report 6, October 2000*. ECMI.

Heltai, J., & Tarsoly, E. (2023). *Translanguaging for Equal Opportunities: Speaking Romani at School.* De Gruyter Mouton. doi:10.1515/9783110769609

Kachru, B. R. (1986). *The alchemy of English: The spread, functions, and models of non-native Englishes.* Pergamon Institute of English Oxford. doi:10.1080/13803611.2012.718488

Lewis, G., Jones, B., & Baker, C. (2012). Translanguaging: origins and development from school to street and beyond. *Educational Research and Evaluation, 18*(7), 641–654. doi:10.1080/13803611.2012.718488

Mbirimi-Hungwe, V. (2021). Translanguaging as an act of emancipation: rethinking assessment tools in multilingual pedagogy in South Africa. *Per Linguam, 37*(1), 97-108.

Minority Rights Group International. (2020). *Linguistic rights.* Minority Rights Group. https://minorityrights.org/law/linguistic-rights/

Organization for Security and Co-operation in Europe. (1999). *Report on the linguistic rights of persons belonging to national minorities in the OSCE area. + Annex.* Replies from OSCE Participating States. OSCE High Commissioner on National Minorities.

Pablo, R., & Christian, F. (2023). Re-Exploring translanguaging in teacher education. *Language and Education, 37*(5), 551–556. doi:10.1080/09500782.2023.2240299

Paulsrud, B., & Rosén, J. (2019). Translanguaging and Language Ideologies in Education: Northern and Southern Perspectives. In S. Brunn & R. Kehrein (Eds.), *Handbook of the changing world language map.* Springer. doi:10.1007/978-3-319-73400-2_124-1

Paz, M. (2014). The Tower of Babel: Human rights and the paradox of language. *European Journal of International Law, 25*(2), 473–496. doi:10.1093/ejil/chu037

Prada, J. (2019). Exploring the role of translanguaging in linguistic ideological and attitudinal reconfigurations in the Spanish classroom for heritage speakers. *Classroom Discourse, 10*(3-4).

Prada, J., & Turnbull, B. (2018). The role of translanguaging in the multilingual turn: Driving philosophical and conceptual renewal in language education. *EuroAmerican Journal of Applied Linguistics and Languages*, *5*(2), 8–23. doi:10.21283/2376905X.9.151

Quijano, A. (2000). Coloniality of power and Eurocentrism in Latin America. *International Sociology*, *15*(2), 215–232. doi:10.1177/0268580900015002005

Skutnabb-Kangas, T. (2012). Linguistic Human Rights. In L. M. Solan & P. M. Tiersma (Eds.), *The Oxford Handbook of Language and Law* (pp. 235-247). OUP Oxford.

United Nations. (1948). *Universal Declaration of Human Rights*. https://www.un.org/en/aboutus/universal-declaration-of-human-rights

United Nations. (1976). *International covenant on civil and political rights*. https://www.ohchr.org/en/professionalinterest/pages/ccpr.aspx

Veronelli, G. A. (2015). The coloniality of language: Race, expressivity, power, and the darker side of modernity. *Wagadu*, *13*, 108–133.

Wang, D. (2022). Translanguaging as a social justice strategy: The case of teaching Chinese to ethnic minority students in Hong Kong. *Asia Pacific Education Review*, *24*(3), 473–486. doi:10.100712564-022-09795-0

KEY TERMS AND DEFINITIONS

English Monolanguaging: The practice of speaking and writing only in the English language.

Linguistic Diversity: It refers to a variety of languages and a variety of communication methods used by people.

Linguistic Human Rights: These rights involve people's freedom of using their own language in a range of contexts.

Translanguaging: A fluid movement between two or more than two languages in teaching or learning.

APPENDIX

These are our interview questions:

1. What language is used by teachers in class?
2. How much space is given to local languages/mother tongues by teachers?
3. How much space is given to English by teachers?
4. Up to what extent are your language preferences accommodated by teachers?
5. Which medium of instruction would you prefer inside the class?
6. How do you perceive monolanguaging?
7. How do you perceive translanguaging?
8. How can your linguistic human rights be preserved?

Chapter 14
A Systematized Review of Anti-Racist Pedagogical Strategies

Teresa Holden
https://orcid.org/0009-0008-6746-1967
University of Windsor, Canada

Clayton Smith
https://orcid.org/0000-0002-7611-9193
University of Windsor, Canada

ABSTRACT

Racism permeates postsecondary language classrooms around the world which affects the experiences and learning outcomes of language students, namely those who study English as an additional language and English as a foreign language, referred to as additional language learners (ALLs), English as a second language (ESL), or English language learners (ELLs). Through an interrogation of the connection between race and language instruction, this chapter discusses anti-racist practices that interfere with language teaching in higher education. It presents a systematized review that aims to critically examine existing literature on the interrogation of racism within higher education with a focus on anti-racist pedagogical strategies. Critical Race Theory (CRT) guides the analysis and highlights the underlying power structures and systemic racism that shape language education. This review finds evidence of epistemological racism, linguistic biases, White supremacy, and English language dominance in the higher education language classroom. Recommendations for teacher practice are made.

INTRODUCTION

Regarding English language education, research demonstrates that Teaching English to Speakers of Other Languages (TESOL) practices focus on assimilating immigrants into the dominant English language and culture, rather than disrupting hierarchies of power (Pavlenko, 2002; Philipson, 1992). Historically, the English language has been perceived as fixed and unchanging, with teachers assuming the role of possessors of English knowledge that students were expected to attain. Teachers commonly made refer-

DOI: 10.4018/978-1-6684-9029-7.ch014

ences to "Standard English" (or variations like "good English" or "correct English"), which reflects the influence of standard language ideology that prioritizes certain linguistic practices as more authoritative or valid, compared to other languages (Swift, 2021). Research also indicates that there is a connection between race and language instruction, but more pointedly, racist and colonial underpinnings thrive in the language classroom (Kubota & Lin, 2006). Issues of epistemological racism, White supremacy, and social hierarchical power structures are part of this dynamic. According to Suraweera (2020), teaching approaches, inherent in TESOL, reproduce and affirm unequal power structures that are underpinned by settler-colonial attitudes that marginalize non-White and non-native English speakers.

THEORETICAL FRAMEWORK

Critical Race Theory (CRT)

In crafting this chapter, the authors deliberately chose to exclusively employ Critical Race Theory (CRT) as a theoretical foundation recognizing its unparalleled analytical strength to illuminate the interconnection between language and race. CRT's well-established and comprehensive framework extends beyond individual linguistic experience allowing for an in-depth exploration of the systemic nature of linguistic inequities and emphasizing how race shapes the essence of language. CRT's principal message is to emphasize and analyze how systemic racism is ingrained in social structures and institutions, impacting individuals based on their racial identity. In addition, intersectionality, a concept closely associated with CRT stresses the interconnected nature of social categories of race, gender, class, and more, acknowledging that individuals experience multiple layers of privilege and oppression simultaneously. While some critics argue that CRT may employ essentialist viewpoints oversimplifying complex issues by generalizing experiences and perspectives within racial groups and that CRT identifies problems with existing systems without always providing concrete and practical solutions for addressing these issues, it stands as a winning choice for this review. The strategic decision to choose CRT aligns with the study's goal of providing a comprehensive synthesis, advancing understanding of the impact of racial dynamics on linguistic structures and practices in higher education.

While raciolinguistics, as highlighted by Alim et al., (2016), underscores the importance of recognizing race construction through language and discourse, the theoretical framework proposed by Flores and Rosa (2015, 2017) primarily emphasizes educational approaches perpetuating racial normativity. However, CRT's broader systemic focus better aligns with the study's objective to comprehensively address racial and linguistic inequalities (Alim at al., 2016; Flores & Rosa, 2015, 2017). In response to the normalization of Whiteness in language studies, scholars in TESOL turn to CRT. Crump (2014a) introduces LangCrit as an emerging framework, yet CRT's more established literature and broader applicability to systemic analysis in educational contexts justify the exclusive focus on CRT in this chapter (Crump, 2014a).

To interrogate race and racism in the postsecondary language question, one must first define racism. According to Miles and Brown (2003), racism may be defined as a "representational form which by designing discrete human collectivities, necessarily functions as an ideology of inclusion and exclusion" (p. 104). Solorzano (1998) identified three prominent features of racism: (a) the belief that one group is superior; (b) this "superior" group has the power to carry out racist acts, and (c) various racial/ethnic groups are affected (p. 124).

As elucidated by Kubota (2002), epistemological racism, as one of the major forms of racism, produces a profound perspective on the manifestations of racism, highlighting its intellectual dimensions and emphasizing the critical role of knowledge system in perpetuating discriminatory ideologies. Scheurich (1997) argues that it is based on the epistemologies, knowledges, and practices that privilege the European modernist White civilization. Referring to influential philosophers, social scientists, and educators, who have been virtually all White males, Scheurich argues that the world ontological categories and epistemologies that we are used to think, analyze, socialize, and educate have been largely developed within this racial and cultural tradition, including "the legitimated ways of knowing (for example, positivism, neo-realism, post-positivisms, interpretivisms, constructivism, the critical tradition, and postmodernisms/poststructuralisms) that we use" (Kubota & Lin, 2006, p. 140). Epistemological racism is reflected in North American textbooks for various disciplines, such as biology, history, and English, which construct and perpetuate racial stereotypes and the hegemony of Whiteness stemming from Western imperialism (Willinsky, 1998). The hegemony of Whiteness is also reflected in ESL/EFL textbooks when constructing the norm about what is legitimate linguistic and cultural knowledge (Matsuda, 2002). Another effect of epistemological racism is the construction of what is considered more rigorous and valued in academic work (Kubota & Lin, 2006).

Due to the discussion of race and language, a fitting theoretical framework, with which to view this review, would be via Critical Race Theory (CRT). With its origins in the United States legal system, it investigates and transforms the relationship between race ideas, racism, and power (Delgado & Stefancic, 2001). CRT is a powerful framework for interrogating anti-racism in the classroom because it addresses the complexities of race, racism, and power dynamics within educational settings. CRT originated in legal scholarship, but has been applied to various disciplines, including education, to understand and challenge systemic racism and social inequalities. The following are basic tenets of CRT:

1. Racism is deeply ingrained in the ordinary ways in which everyday life in our society operates; thus, it cannot be fixed by color-blind policies of superficial equality.
2. Racism benefits "both White elites (materially) and working-class people (physically)- large segments of society have little incentive to eradicate it" (p. 7). That is, a sizable portion of the working class and White elites have little motivation to eradicate it both in terms of material wealth and physical health.
3. "Races are categories that society invents, manipulates, or retires when convenient" (p. 7).
4. The forms of racialization or racial discrimination are in flux; the socioeconomic needs of the dominant society influence them.
5. Antiessentialist understandings of racialized groups (i.e., recognizing various kinds of diversity that exist within a racialized group, rather than viewing it as homogeneous or static) is vital; and
6. The unique voice of the People of Color about their experiences can be communicated to White people through storytelling, which exposes and challenges hidden forms of racism in everyday interactions (Ladson-Billings, 1999). The last point is referred to as counter storytelling (Delgado, 2000) or counter-story (Solórzano & Yosso, 2002), which is defined as a method of telling the stories of those people whose experiences are on the margins of society.

CRT and Teaching English as a Second Language (TESOL)

This chapter engages with the consciousness of various language environments recognizing the dynamics of power, identity, and racialization within TESOL that are reflective of broader issues in language education worldwide. By addressing the awareness of these diverse language contexts, the chapter seeks to contribute insights that are not only applicable to TESOL but resonate with educators and researchers working across a spectrum of linguistic and cultural landscapes to promote more inclusive and globally informed approaches to language teaching and learning.

The international focus on TESOL in this chapter arises from TESOL's unique position at the intersection of language acquisition and socio-cultural dynamics especially within diverse language learning contexts. It can be acknowledged that TESOL classrooms function as microcosms of linguistic and racial diversity becoming fertile ground for applying CRT principles. This chapter delves into the intricate connections between language education, race, equity, and social justice demonstrating how CRT can reshape pedagogical practices. This focus provides implications for CRT integration in global language education offering insights that can be extended to educators, policymakers, and researchers working in language teaching spaces. This approach which is rooted in TESOL complements the framework for growing equitable and culturally responsible language education practices across the globe.

The pedagogies proposed in this chapter speak to the transferability beyond the realm of TESOL extending their application to diverse language teaching contexts. Whether in English as a Second Language (ESL) instruction, teacher education programs, or more broad language teaching spaces including non-English teaching settings, the research derived from the intersection of CRT with TESOL principles offers a strong framework for promoting cultural responsiveness, inclusivity, and addressing racialization.

Liggett (2014) provides a theoretical explanation for how the fields of Teaching English as a Second Language (TESL) and Critical Race Theory (CRT) overlap when language is a discriminatory factor and discusses cultural differences in contemporary racial discourse with racial differences. Liggett maintains that English learners and non-native English speakers are governed by their linguistic ability and accent. This is a result of a long and complicated process that can be traced to racism. Liggett found that native speakers were placed at the top of the social hierarchy, and non-native speakers and non-Whites were placed at the bottom, proliferating the existing social order. This finding is consistent with Creese and Kambere (2003) in their study of accentism in Canada.

In English language teacher education, such inquiry could work to broaden teacher candidates' knowledge and understanding of the ways that linguistic and racial membership inform student learning and raise awareness about the range of perspectives and cultural interpretations that linguistic minorities may hold (Liggett, 2013). In looking to CRT to inform and expand critical approaches to English language teaching, the goal is to closely tie English language learning to issues of race to better understand the intersectionality of these identity factors in the educational context of language teaching and learning (Liggett, 2013). The connection between CRT and TESOL is further delineated. It can overlap since the idea that linguicism is an everyday, permanent feature of life for English language learners, and non-native speakers of English, runs parallel to the normalization of racism as a commonplace, unremitting phenomenon (Delgado & Stefancic, 2012). Any discrimination against English language learners based on their race, accent, or country of origin, in this situation, is related to their level of language proficiency. Compared to non-English speakers, who typically come from the working class or lower social classes, they enjoy privileges in their home countries. By setting boundaries between regional English varieties, they attempt to preserve their privileged position. They no longer enjoy the privilege of living in expanding-circle countries when they relocate to inner-circle nations, but they may still be in a better position linguistically than other non-native English speakers.

As English language methodology courses do not attempt to minimize the effects of European colonialism ingrained in the process of English language learning that alienates English learners, colonial practices rooted in ELT methods and curricula relate to CRT. For instance, the strongly advocated English-only policy in the classroom, backed by a monolingual and monocultural ideology, may have disastrous effects on multicultural societies, because "the binary native-non-native categories that emerge from this monolingual model not only frame social hierarchies of race, class, and ethnicity, they also inform existing cultural models of educational and political systems" (Shuck, 2001; Urciuoli, 1996, as cited in Ligget, 2014, p.114). The fact that a person's English proficiency is valued more highly than their subject-matter expertise leads to a situation in which intelligence is mistakenly linked to the English language, which raises questions about subjectivity and social justice. Third, Liggett (2014) emphasizes the value of narratives and storytelling in educating and validating the oppression experiences that second language speakers encounter. CRT is used as a theoretical orientation by Kubota and Lin (2006, 2009b) to describe how racial inequalities and power relations have an impact on the development of curricula, the hiring of teachers, state policies, and scholarship.

Despite seeing CRT as a crucial analytical tool, they are aware of its shortcomings due to its inability to explain how racism is related to material circumstances, like wealth and poverty. Additionally, they criticize CRT's tendency to place too much emphasis on the powerful and the marginalized, which allows liberal discourse to obtrusively reappear as individualism. Kubota and Lin (2006) further assert that "these criticisms address a need for TESOL professionals to be cognizant of the conceptual diversity, complexity, and potential problems in critical inquiries" (p. 485). Greater focus is placed on racial superiority or inferiority as the primary factors determining one's fate, even though CRT provides a foundation upon which we can understand the role played by individuals' phenotype in experiencing the world differently. CRT accounts for racial experiences, offers innovative solutions, and can be used for strategic analysis in this educational context.

White Supremacy

Transitioning from the critiques of CRT, the examination now extends to its intersections with the issue of White Supremacy highlighting how these criticisms align with broader discussions surrounding systemic racial hierarchies and power structures. Stinson and Migliarini (2022) investigated how White English teachers (monolingual and monocultural) conceptualize the racial identities of students who are socially and racially marginalized in the classroom. This aligns with the understanding of how supremacy has been a strategy for historically dispossessing, assimilating, and eliminating negatively racialized and linguistically marginalized communities through mechanisms of Western settler-colonial hegemony and English language teaching. Despite their efforts for inclusive teaching, White English language teachers reproduce White supremacist beliefs, values, and knowledge. Certainly, as in this finding, English language teaching is plagued with White supremacist attitudes, and in the process, actively co-creates negatively racialized and language-minoritized identities. Gilborn (2008) considered White supremacy and White privilege as the fundamental aspects of systematic racism. Crenshaw (1988) argues that White supremacy is implicitly exercised through contemporary stereotypes based on notions of culture, rather than genetics. Bell and Roberts (2010) maintain that racism is systematic patterns and social hierarchies in which Whites benefit at the expense of other racialized groups. Other scholars such as Dixson and

A Systematized Review of Anti-Racist Pedagogical Strategies

Rousseau (2005) question systematic manifestations of power imbalances between Whites and non-Whites that occur daily. Confronting the enduring challenges of White supremacy, a detailed examination of linguisticism takes center stage revealing intersections between language, power dynamics, and systemic biases that profoundly shape the educational landscape.

Linguisticism

Linguisticism is a key component in the discussion of the language classroom. Skutnabb-Kangas (1995) define it as akin to other negative-isms: racism, classism, sexism, ageism. They explain that these are all

Ideologies and structures which are used to legitimate, effectuate and reproduce an unequal division of power and resources (both material and non-material) between groups which are defined on the basis of language (on the basis of their mother tongues). (p. 42)

Research in language education has increasingly explored the idea of race as a social construct seen through the work of Kubota and Lin (2006). This research exposed the socially and discursively created notions of racial differences and hierarchies. However, the leading liberal discourse of human differences obscures the reason why and how race still matters in today's language classrooms. In our society, race takes on different forms, such as linguistic proficiency or cultural competence disguising its true impact (Stoler, 1997). Racialized social structures perpetuate the notion of White privilege, which confers social and material advantages to the dominant racial group (Bonilla-Silva, 2010). When seen in educational settings, racism often becomes institutionalized through the incorporation of everyday values and 'normal practices' into the curriculum, teaching methods, assessment, and attitudes and assumptions of educators. These practices fail to reflect the historical and experiential realities of racial minority students (Cummins, 2001; Henry & Tator, 2005).

Cho (2017) argues that linguicism involves the attribution of differences of native English speakers of a certain language or dialect-- standard English-- in an advantageous position. In this way, like racism, linguicism is a social construct or process in which differences are used to make and reinforce a hierarchy of power and dominance. Austin (2009) points out that linguicism has become "naturalized to perpetuate notions of inferiority" in diverse students and teachers (p. 264), while Phillipson (1992) states that linguicism "has taken over from racism as a more subtle way of hierarchizing social groups in the contemporary world" (p. 241). Linguicism normalizes native (monolingual) speaker values, beliefs, and experiences, while racism positions "Whites as the entitled beneficiaries of unearned social privilege and status" (Huber et al., 2008, p. 41).

The objective of this systematic review is to investigate to what extent race and racism are embedded in the postsecondary language classroom. The review seeks to answer the following research questions:

1. How does anti-racist pedagogy manifest in a postsecondary ESL classroom?
2. What recommendations for practice to combat anti-racist education practices in language classrooms have been endorsed by leading scholars?

This paper offers a discussion of anti-racist pedagogy in the postsecondary language classroom. This review also offers educational implications and critical considerations that researchers, teachers, and practitioners should consider in promoting equity and fairness in their classrooms. The next section

Figure 1. Guidance on conducting a systemic literature review
Source: Xiao and Watson (2017)

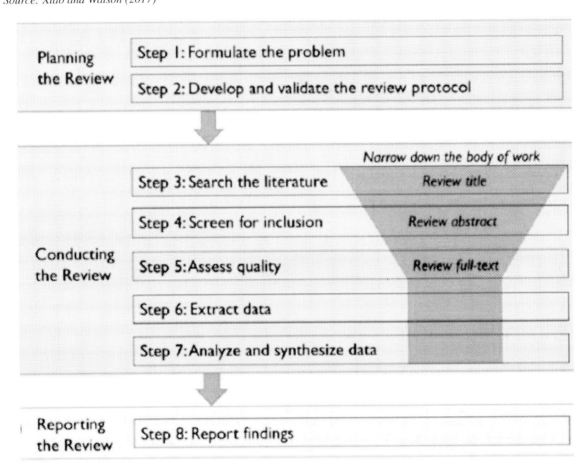

describes the methodology, followed by a section that presents and discusses the major findings from selected papers, and how they connect with the research questions. The last section concludes the paper with a summary, followed by some educational implications and strategies for teachers.

METHODOLOGY

The chosen methodology for this review was modelled on the framework of Xiao and Watson (2017) by following three main stages with eight steps.

Step 1: Formulate the Research Problems

The principal researcher of the paper, a student in the doctoral program at a university in Canada, has several years of experience teaching in an ESL classroom with international students at the college level. As there is an established connection between English language teachers and learners in the language classroom, the researcher acknowledges the need to raise awareness of interrogating race and racism and implement ways in which anti-racist strategies could be implemented to benefit students and teachers alike.

Step 2: Develop and Validate the Review Protocol

The development and validation of the review protocol were necessary to help establish the review's rigor and improve its quality. The researchers defined the study objectives, research questions, inclusion/exclusion criteria, and methods for data extraction during this phase. Exclusions were made for studies that were conducted in elementary, middle, or secondary schools to limit information to higher education (college and university classrooms).

Step 3: Searching for Literature

A range of 10-year investigations between 2013 and 2023 were considered. However, seminal sources that fell outside of that period have been included on the basis that they are foundational and pioneering in understanding race and racism in the English language classroom. The articles were collected from various peer-reviewed journals such as Scopus, Academic Search Complete (Ebsco Host), and ERIC (ProQuest), with the following codes: title search, abstract search, and subject search. The way the sources were extracted was by first conducting a search bearing in mind the population, concept, and context.

Step 4: Screening for Inclusion and Step 5: Assessing Quality

Based on the research objectives, questions, and methodology, the researchers screened the titles, abstracts, subject terms, and keywords according to the inclusion and exclusion criteria that were stated in Step Two. The articles were selected with the following requirements in mind: (a) methodology designs could be a literature review, qualitative, quantitative, or mixed methods; (b) research participants must be postsecondary language students, and (c) the study context was racism in the English language classroom. Inclusions were any country to keep a global perspective. The countries which were reflected in the review are the United States, Canada, Mexico, the United Kingdom, Brazil, China, and Korea. In assessing the quality of literature, articles that discussed secondary school classrooms were disregarded.

Step 6: Extract Data and Step 7: Analyze and Synthesize Data

The researchers meticulously reviewed, categorized, and analyzed the identified and chosen papers used with clearly defined parameters. Author, publication year, study design/methods, and major themes were among the information retrieved.

Step 8: Report Findings

As the last step, key themes such as racism, linguicism, and English language dominance for the ESL learner in higher education emerged. See Table 1 for a list of collected studies.

Figure 2. Query academic search premier

#	Query	Limiters/Expanders	Last Run Via	Results
S11	S3 AND S6 AND S9	Expanders - Apply equivalent subjects Narrow by Language: - english Search modes - Boolean/Phrase	Interface - EBSCOhost Research Databases Search Screen - Advanced Search Database - Academic Search Complete	133
S10	S3 AND S6 AND S9	Expanders - Apply equivalent subjects Search modes - Boolean/Phrase	Interface - EBSCOhost Research Databases Search Screen - Advanced Search Database - Academic Search Complete	134
S9	S7 OR S8	Expanders - Apply equivalent subjects Search modes - Boolean/Phrase	Interface - EBSCOhost Research Databases Search Screen - Advanced Search Database - Academic Search Complete	22,981
S8	DE "ENGLISH as a foreign language"	Expanders - Apply equivalent subjects Search modes - Boolean/Phrase	Interface - EBSCOhost Research Databases Search Screen - Advanced Search Database - Academic Search Complete	8,450
S7	(TI("post secondary" OR post-secondary OR universit* OR colleg*) AND language* AND (class* OR cours*)) OR "English language education" OR linguicism OR "English second language" OR "english as a second language" OR ESL OR "english additional language" OR "english as an additional language" OR EAL OR "additional language learner" OR "additional language learners" OR AAL OR "english as a foreign language" OR EFL OR OR "teaching English as a second language" OR "teaching english as a second other language" OR TESOL)) OR (AB("post secondary" OR post-secondary OR universit* OR colleg*) AND language* AND (class* OR cours*)) OR "English language education" OR linguicism OR "English second language" OR "english as a second language" OR ESL OR "english additional language" OR "english as an additional language" OR EAL OR "additional language learner" OR "additional language learners" OR AAL OR "english as a foreign language" OR EFL OR OR "teaching English as a second language" OR "teaching english as a second other language" OR TESOL))	Expanders - Apply equivalent subjects Search modes - Boolean/Phrase	Interface - EBSCOhost Research Databases Search Screen - Advanced Search Database - Academic Search Complete	17,298
S6	S4 OR S5	Expanders - Apply equivalent subjects Search modes - Boolean/Phrase	Interface - EBSCOhost Research Databases Search Screen - Advanced Search Database - Academic Search Complete	303,909
S5	DE("ANTI-racism" OR "ANTI-racism education" OR "critical race theory")	Expanders - Apply equivalent subjects Search modes - Boolean/Phrase	Interface - EBSCOhost Research Databases Search Screen - Advanced Search Database - Academic Search Complete	4,229
S4	(TI(racism OR anti-racism OR race* OR "racial identity" OR "racial identities" OR racialization OR anti-racist OR "critical race theory" OR CRT)) OR (AB(racism OR anti-racism OR race* OR "racial identity" OR "racial identities" OR racialization OR anti-racist OR "critical race theory" OR CRT))	Expanders - Apply equivalent subjects Search modes - Boolean/Phrase	Interface - EBSCOhost Research Databases Search Screen - Advanced Search Database - Academic Search Complete	301,022
S3	S1 OR S2	Expanders - Apply equivalent subjects Search modes - Boolean/Phrase	Interface - EBSCOhost Research Databases Search Screen - Advanced Search Database - Academic Search Complete	1,301,236
S2	DE("TEACHERS" OR "STUDENTS" OR "GRADUATE teaching assistants" OR "Teachers' assistants")	Expanders - Apply equivalent subjects Search modes - Boolean/Phrase	Interface - EBSCOhost Research Databases Search Screen - Advanced Search Database - Academic Search Complete	126,426
S1	(TI(professor* OR student* OR instructor* OR educator* OR pupil* OR "teaching assistant" OR "teaching assistants" OR "TA" OR "graduate assistant" OR "graduate assistants" OR "GA")) OR (AB(professor* OR student* OR instructor* OR educator* OR pupil* OR "teaching assistant" OR "teaching assistants" OR "TA" OR "graduate assistant" OR "graduate assistants" OR "GA"))	Expanders - Apply equivalent subjects Search modes - Boolean/Phrase	Interface - EBSCOhost Research Databases Search Screen - Advanced Search Database - Academic Search Complete	1,262,437

Table 1.

No.	Articles	Quantitative	Qualitative	Literature Review	Major Topic Areas	Data Collection Tools	Geographical Area/Country	Geographical Area/Country
1	Chen & Lo (2017)		Yes		Examines how three primary TEFL (Teaching English as a Foreign Language) teachers construct identities as inclusive practitioners as they enact inclusive education policy in Hong Kong schools	Reflective inquiry for teacher professional development	China	China
2	Cho (2017)		Yes		Examines how language minority pre-service teachers engage in the discussion of racism and linguicism through counter-storytelling informed by Critical Race Theory (CRT)	Data draws on co-teaching experiences with white teacher educators	United States	United States
3	Creese & Kambere (2003)		Yes		Explores how accents form a site through which racialized power relations are negotiated and "Others" are reproduced materially and figuratively in Canada	Preliminary research with African women	Canada	Canada
4	Gray (2023)		Yes		Explores discriminatory practices in ESL hiring, self-efficacy issues surrounding authenticity, racialized interactions, the influence of race on professional identity, and an absence of diversity in curricular materials	Data collection relied on three interviews and four forum posts.	United States	United States
5	Hume & Callahan (2018)		Yes		Examines two schools' responses to native EB (Emergent Bilingual) population growth via the intersecting racial and language ideologies informing and influenced by programmatic changes, educator perceptions, and pedagogical practices	Data included semistructured interviews, focus group interviews, and participant observations.	United States	United States
6	Liao & Li (2023)	Yes	Yes		Explores the potential of culturally responsive teaching (CRT) as a pedagogical approach to intercultural foreign language teaching. Implementing 14 CRT sessions with English as a foreign language (EFL) learners in a Chinese university, this study examined and assessed students'	Data based on a mixed-methods analysis of students' learning journals, interviews, intercultural assignments, and assessment results.	China	China
7	Liggett (2014)			Yes	Explores intersections between critical race theory (CRT) in synthesis with English language learning as a way to examine linguistic and racial identity in English language teaching	Personal inquiry	United States	United States
8	Marx & Moss (2011)		Yes		Provides a qualitative examination of university student experiences with culture, language, and race in a short-term study abroad program in Cuernavaca, Mexico	White teacher education student interviews.	Mexico	Mexico
9	Sonnyox (2020)				Explores how adult ESL instructors promote culturally responsive pedagogy and guided by CRT.	Data was collected through face-to-face semistructured interviews, journal entries, and classroom observations.	United States	United States
10	Santos & Windle (2021)		Yes		Racialized senses of being as an analytical category allow for connections to be made between political economy and language education, including as part of anti-racial pedagogical efforts	Data is the experiences of two Black, first-generation university students	Brazil	Brazil
11	Shin (2018)		Yes		Explores English language learners who recently returned to South Korea after learning English in the U.S. for more than two years.	Case study. Data were collected through the researcher's field notes and semi-structured interviews with five participants and their	Korea	Korea
12	Smith (2022)		Yes		Examines linguistic authority centralized through the practitioners of a closed linguistic system and a focus on the replication of semiotic languages. This allows for the drawing of linguistic borders by pathologizing forms traditionally associated with racialized varieties of English pointing to the persistence of raciolinguistic ideologies.	Ethnographic observation and interviews.	United States	United States
13	Wedgley (2023)		Yes		Explores three main areas that emerged as crucial to a deeper and critical engagement with English as an Additional Language and the experience of students: (1) the need for a critical reflection on ideas of inclusion and mainstreaming, (2) active anti-racial work in schools and initial teacher training, and (3) decolonizing assessment	Dialogues and co-analysis with EAL practitioners.	United Kingdom	United Kingdom

FINDINGS

One of the first concepts in this debate is that linguicism is a typical, normal, and permanent feature of society that requires us to investigate how English language learners experience prejudice based on accent and language ability both in and out of classroom communities. The second concept is to examine the repercussions of European colonialism, which includes a curriculum on the history of colonialism in connection to language and educational policies, as well as how such policies are implemented in the way that is now taught. In addition, helping to validate the unique experiences that English language learners bring to their learning is the way that CRT uses narrative and storytelling to explain histories of oppression (Liggett, 2013).

The breadth and quality of research findings were ensured by the research design (quantitative or qualitative) and research strategy. Since there were only 13 sources that met selection criteria and were generated using the systematic review process, Table 1 would be useful for researchers to target distinct geographical areas/countries where research was conducted. This reflects a global viewpoint that underscores how this research is purposeful and visible in a global scale, and to demonstrate how anti-racist pedagogy manifests itself in a postsecondary ESL classroom. Another objective of having a table is to condense findings to ascertain how CRT, linguicism, settler colonialism, intersectionality, and other related themes affect students in higher educational settings across the world. The data was captured from North America, South America, United Kingdom, and Asia. Moreover, this information, which clearly outlines major topic areas and research designs, would be helpful to gain a better understanding of the issue. As noted in Table 1, country, research methods, major topics, authors, publication year, research design, data collection tools, and geographical area are included for reference.

DISCUSSION

The first research question that guides this systematic review concerns itself with anti-racist pedagogy that is evident in the postsecondary ESL classroom. The research that emerges from the search reveals that this experience is not confined to one country. In other words, similar student experiences in language education can be found in the United States, Brazil, China, and Korea. Based on these readings, themes that spoke about racism, linguicism, and power/hierarchy surfaced.

The literature presented findings that revolved around the need to offer a decolonial perspective on curriculum, language, and pedagogical practice inspired by CRT (Welply, 2023). It requires a deeper dive into the relationship between EAL (English as a Second Language) learners and the experience of students, as well as an anti-racist positioning in schools, teacher training and decolonizing assessment. Gras (2022), reports that in EFL (English as a Foreign Language) hiring, there are discriminatory practices, issues regarding racialized interactions, race as an influencer on identity, and a lack of diversity in curricula materials. This brings us to another related point having to do with linguistic authority. In other words, English is treated as a fixed linguistic system connected to an authority centrally located in the text and in teacher expertise (Swift, 2021). Freire (1970) remarked that teachers and textbook authors-imposed English in the spirit of the banking model of education – their primary role was to pass knowledge to students excluding student knowledge of English rarely included or referenced in classroom activities, or even excluded altogether (Swift, 2021). This discriminatory practice positioned teachers as figures of linguistic authority and were therefore actors in creating linguistic boundaries.

Studies in adult ESL teaching revealed that teachers did not have adequate knowledge about their student populations, avoided integrating cultural topics, relied on superficial cultural values, rarely supplemented curriculum, and did not encourage student autonomy (Borjigin, 2017; Johnson & Chang, 2012; Rhodes, 2013). As opposed to Sleeter's (2012) claim that culturally responsive pedagogy is being "simplified, trivialized, and essentialized" (p. 570) in classrooms, most participants in the Sancyzk (2020) study successfully incorporated their students' individual strengths and experiences into their classrooms rather than relying solely on surface-level tactics like cultural celebrations.

In revisiting the second important research question in this systematic review, it is necessary to explore a combination of pedagogical strategies that emerged from the readings. Beyond knowing one's own racial identity, anti-racist pedagogy requires the practice of self-reflection on the part of the faculty to reflect upon their social position with the realization that it is dynamic and changing (Tatum, 1992). Another discriminant is that they are privileged, and their socialization and intersecting identities (internalized racialized superiority or inferiority) can impact their output be it through teaching, research, community work, or outreach (Hurtado, 1996). These are important steps to take in anti-racist work. Self-reflection requires that faculty have the humility to understand that they are consistently improving and changing as individuals and professionals, scholars, or researchers. Faculty members can analyze concepts of power, privilege, and oppression in others; however, it is much more complex when asked to look at themselves. This psychological work comes from within, per say. As a supporter for anti-oppressive education, Kishimoto (2000) shows us that "for White people, and People of Color, it is easier to succumb to the oppressor/oppressed dichotomy, identify with the oppressed identities, and blame them for problems" (p. 543). A striking comment that was highlighted in the research is that faculty cannot ask students to become aware and self-reflect on their social if we are unwilling to do so ourselves.

Anti-Racist Pedagogy

Anti-Racist Pedagogy is a paradigm located within critical theory utilized to explain and counteract the persistence and impact of racism (Blakeney, 2005). An instructor may apply an anti-racist pedagogy to any field of study. While an anti-racist pedagogy may employ several tools and praxis to build a more inclusive and representative course design, the heart of an anti-racist pedagogy is the intent to actively acknowledge and oppose racism in all aspects of the course. Instructors can foster the conditions necessary for positive change by carefully selecting which authorial voices to highlight, purposefully establishing communication expectations and power dynamics in the classroom, using discussion to look at and challenge the racist forces influencing the subject matter, and incorporating ongoing feedback and iteration into the course design (Chew et al, 2020).

Kishimoto (2018) cautions that "anti-racist pedagogy is an intentional and strategic organizing effort in which we incorporate anti-racist approaches into our teaching as well as apply anti-racist values into our various spheres of influence. It requires the "professor's humility, critical reflection of our social position, and commitment as we begin and continue to confront our internalized racial oppression or internalized racial superiority and how those impact our teaching, research, and work in the university and community" (p. 551). Furthermore, anti-racist pedagogy attempts to teach about race and racism in a way that fosters critical analytical skills, which reveal the power relations behind racism and how race has been institutionalized to create and justify inequalities (Kishimoto, 2018). Anti-racist pedagogy is not about simply incorporating racial content into courses, curriculum, and discipline. It is also about how one teaches, even in courses where race is not the subject matter. It begins with the faculty's awareness and self-reflection of their social position, and leads to the application of this analysis, not just in their teaching, but also in their discipline, research, and department, university, and community work (Phillips 2013; Rodriguez & Drew, 2009- 2014).

Kumashiro (2000) explores anti-oppressive education in the form of four approaches: education for others, education about others, education that critiques privilege and difference, and education that changes students and society. By that standard, to effectively address the diversity and the location of oppression, and the oppression and complexity of teaching and learning, educators must consistently look beyond educational research to explore theories. Kumashiro suggests looking beyond marginalized theories, including post-structural and psychoanalytic perspectives.

Anti-racist pedagogy, which is informed by Critical Race Theory (CRT), focuses more in-depth on the analysis of structural racism, power relations, and social justice. Since some of its tenets are race and racism which are present in the normal operation of society, racism persists because there are those who benefit from it ('interest convergence'), and because race is a social construct through the process of racialization (Delgado & Stefancic, 2012). CRT is also anti-essentialist, because it focuses on the intersectionality of identities and recognizes the unique voices of People of Color. Labels like "academic language" go unquestioned, but "the fact that White people consider themselves the 'standard' by which 'Others' are measured – has real and tangible effects on the lives of People of Color" (Alim & Smitherman, 2012, p. 171).

CONCLUSION

This review offers an evidence-based rationale as to the current climate of race and racism in the English language classroom, but it also provides a new direction in adopting anti-racist pedagogical strategies to help reduce, and ideally, eliminate this way of thinking. In the context of ESL, CRT prompts a critical analysis of how language curriculum and instructional materials may affirm dominant cultural norms and narratives, while oppressing the experiences and perspectives of English language learners. By introducing CRT into language classrooms, teachers can foster a more inclusive and equitable learning environment that encourages students to critically examine societal biases, challenge stereotypes, and engage in meaningful dialogue about race, power, and language. By doing so, this approach enhances linguistic proficiency and equips students with the critical thinking skills for active participation in a diverse world. As a result, language classrooms can grow into transformative spaces cultivating social justice and empowering students to become change agents. In the spirit of Liggett (2013), professionals in education are called to examine the intersectionality of language and race to understand linguicism and the historical contextual basis that frames discourse around English language education, and how it interplays and intertwines with race, racial identity, and racialization.

RECOMMENDATIONS FOR FUTURE RESEARCH AND TEACHING PRACTICE

According to De Costa (2021), silence on behalf of TESOL practitioners and teacher educators is not an acceptable response, because something must be done about racism and xenophobia. Equipping teachers with pedagogical and policy strategies to respond to inequities is tantamount. Kubota and Lin (2006) argue that in the field of TESOL, where teachers and students are racialized globally, hegemonic racialized norms should be challenged in relation to Whiteness, but also in relation to racial/ethnic dynamics. Their viewpoint is that racism is not limited to the inferiorization of people of color in the White dominant society; rather, it is observed in Japanese discrimination against non-White people including other Asians. Therefore, race ideas and racism cannot be reduced to White versus non-White issues. Theories about them are not exclusively Anglo-European. It is necessary to overcome epistemological racism in this arena.

Chan and Lo (2017) show how resourceful EFL teachers are at supporting the diverse needs of learners that they teach, but at the same time, their expertise is not always recognized as valid knowledge within the education community. That collaborative project gave three EFL teachers in Hong Kong a space to share their expertise with teachers and teacher educators outside their schools. One of the challenges educators continue to face is how to advance our education system to one that truly embraces the uniqueness of the diversity of learners in the community. A recent study has shown that Hong Kong's education system is still failing learners from ethnic minority groups in Hong Kong (Kapai, 2015).

Cho (2017) puts forth the idea that there is much to learn regarding in-class collaboration and the intentional creation of a space to dialogue with learners. This would be an effective tool that requires empathy without sameness. Via empathetic engagement, it is possible to undo racism and linguicism that flourish in social structures and in institutions. Learning from multiple perspectives allows for new awareness and transformative alliances between White anti-racist instructors as well as minority instructors and their students. Teacher educators can employ counter storytelling (related to CRT), as a pedagogical tool in the postsecondary classroom. They can challenge assumptions of racial and linguistic neutrality in teaching practices and discourse. Through this technique, deeply ingrained racial and linguistic biases in classrooms can be brought to attention. Counter storytelling is a strategy for gaining an understanding of how racism and linguistic biases contribute to the marginalization of learners (Brown & Jackson, 2013). Milner (2007) stated that it is important for teacher educators to examine their own daily discourses and practices because what they do, say, and model in the classroom influence future teachers and their students. Additionally, as Hurie and Callhan (2019) point out, "ESL research and practice would benefit from an explicit questioning of racializing discourses and boundaries of academic disciplines as part of a racially literate critical practice designed to counter the normalization of Whiteness" (p. 1). Marx (2004) argues that ignoring Whiteness, White racism, and the role that they play in education will only do a disservice to all involved, including teachers, educators, and children. Researchers and teacher educators are responsible for ensuring that future teachers have the training to recognize how their limitations--cultural, racial, and linguistic--can be challenged.

Regarding the educational experiences of Korean ESA students, specifically, and other racial minority students, Shin (2018) states the goal is to assist teachers and policymakers to gain a better grasp of the complexities regarding racism and racialization in the era of globalization. The analysis demonstrated that racialized linguistic ideologies have significant material consequences in the language learning experiences of the students, which is why teachers need to understand why and how race matters in today's classroom. Given the complex and elusive nature of contemporary racism in educational settings, an anti-racist pedagogy for language minority students in multilingual settings will need to adequately reflect the history and experiences of racial minority students. A wise first step would be the acknowledgment by teachers and policymakers that race still matters in education, and work needs to be undertaken based on that awareness to see common struggles among various racial minorities and to seek solidarity.

In the context of Black language learners, the answer appears to be found in active self-awareness and critical reflection: "For teachers to move toward dispositions and language and literacy pedagogical practices that are inclusive, just and anti-racist, they must become aware of and interrogate their real trouble with BL (Black Language) through guided and continuous critical, introspective, and reflexivity" (McMurty & Williamson, 2021, p.1).

Strategies and recommendations derive from ESL nursing students that could be applied to language students. Peter (2005) conducted research to demonstrate that a mentorship program with faculty and peers, writing consultation, and tutoring for academic support helps combat anti-racism in the classroom. In fact, a University of Southern California program called "Learn for Strategies for Success" (LFS), addresses student mentoring and retention issues for racial, ethnic, and minority students. This program pairs faculty mentors for writing and test-taking with students (Peter, 2005). This proves that students can succeed in passing their ESL courses at the same rate as non-at-risk students. Along a similar vein, Salamonson (2009) found that writing skills can improve with one-on-one consultation, tutoring, and support. Condrey and Derico (2012) affirm that it is educators who should be responsible to acculturate language students into the discipline that is specific to their chosen profession, which faculty can achieve through the careful consideration of unique approaches to meet the needs of diverse learners.

FUTURE RESEARCH

Future research could focus on how intersectional identities (race, gender, class, immigration status, etc.,) intersect to shape the experiences of ELLs in the ESL classroom and how these intersections influence educational outcomes. Another concept worthy of exploration would be teacher training and anti-racist practices by examining the effectiveness of teacher training programs in encouraging anti-racist practices in ESL classrooms and identifying the best practices for equipping teachers with tools to address racism and cultural biases. Future research could also analyze curriculum to assess whether there is representation of diverse cultural perspectives, histories, and contributions, which could explore how culturally inclusive curricula impact students' sense of belonging and engagement. A move towards decolonization would be appropriate to allow for greater student empowerment. In fact, counter-narratives and empowerment could challenge stereotypes, dismantle racism, and promote a positive racial identity for ELLs. This research could inform policy changes, instructional policies, and interventions to promote anti-racist education and empower ELLs to thrive academically and personally.

Combatting racism in the language classroom takes on a combination of multiple approaches. With the complete disruption of racism in the language classroom being the end goal, however lofty that might be, the literature reveals that the impetus should first originate from the individual in the role of teacher or faculty. It comes from faculty who set the tone, pace, and stage for anti-racist English language learning to occur. In so doing, faculty can explore areas where there is a manifestation of negative stereotypes or discrimination. First, faculty must be critically aware of how the English language can perpetuate racism and discrimination. Second, the anti-racist classroom involves the creation of a supportive environment where language learners feel comfortable expressing their thoughts and engaging in dialogue. This means active encouragement of learners to share their personal stories, experiences, and perspectives on race, identity, and social justice. Third, the act of decolonizing the English language is another recommendation to draw upon culturally diverse literature and texts. It is also important to engage in discussions of how the cultural and historical context in literature promotes critical thinking and empathy. The goal is to facilitate honest discussions, particularly for ESL or EAL learners, on language biases, microaggressions, and/or stereotypes embedded in the English language. Last, faculty could also explore how language affects power dynamics and representation. To ignore that this exists would be doing a disservice to ESL students who deserve better. They have an awareness that more work needs to be done to balance the equity scales in the postsecondary language classroom, which could become a space to inspire empathy, critical thinking, and positive change.

REFERENCES

Alim, H. S., Rickford, J. R., & Ball, A. F. (2016). *Raciolinguistics: How language shapes our ideas about race*. Oxford University Press. doi:10.1093/acprof:oso/9780190625696.001.0001

Alim, H. S., & Smitherman, G. (2012). *Articulate while Black: Barack Obama, language, and race in the US*. Oxford University Press.

Austin, T. (2009). Linguicism and race in the United States. *Race, culture, and identities in second language education: Exploring critically engaged practice*. Routledge.

Bell, L. A., & Roberts, R. A. (2010). The storytelling project model: A theoretical framework for critical examination of racism through the arts. *Teachers College Record*, *112*(9), 2295–2319. doi:10.1177/016146811011200907

Blakeney, A. M. (2005). Antiracist pedagogy: Definition, theory, and professional development. *Journal of Curriculum and Pedagogy*, *2*(1), 119–132. doi:10.1080/15505170.2005.10411532

Bonilla-Silva, E. (2010). *Racism without racists. Color-blind racism & racial inequality in contemporary America* (3rd ed.). Rowman and Littlefield.

Borjigin, A. (2017). *Culturally relevant pedagogy in adult ESL classrooms: A case study of a university intensive English program*. Electronic Theses and Dissertations. 1267. https://digitalcommons.du.edu/etd/1267

Chan, C., & Lo, M. (2017). Exploring inclusive pedagogical practices in Hong Kong primary EFL classrooms. *International Journal of Inclusive Education*, *21*(7), 714–729. doi:10.1080/13603116.2016.1252798

Chew, S., Houston, A., & Cooper, A. (2020). *The anti-racist discussion pedagogy: An introductory guide to building an anti-racist pedagogy in any discipline through instructor reflection, clear communication guidelines, and inquiry-based discussion*. The University of North Carolina at Chapel Hill.

Cho, H. (2017). Racism and linguicism: Engaging language minority pre-service teachers in counter-storytelling. *Race, Ethnicity and Education*, *20*(5), 666–680. doi:10.1080/13613324.2016.1150827

Condrey, T., & Derico, S. (2012). Strategies for success for English as a second language (ESL) students in the post-secondary setting. *Perspectives In Learning*, *13*(1). https://csuepress.columbusstate.edu/pil/vol13/iss1/6

Creese, G., & Kambere, E. N. (2003). What colour is your English? *Canadian Review of Sociology*, *40*(5), 565–573. doi:10.1111/j.1755-618X.2003.tb00005.x

Crenshaw, K. (1988). Race, reform, and retrenchment: Transformation and legitimation in antidiscrimination law. *Harvard Law Review, 101*(7), 1331–1387. doi:10.2307/1341398

Cummins, J. (2001). *Negotiating identities: Education for empowerment in a diverse society* (2nd ed.). California Association for Bilingual Education.

De Costa, P. I. (2021). Anti-Asian racism: How it affects TESOL professionals like you and me. *TESOL Journal, 12*(3), e620. Advance online publication. doi:10.1002/tesj.620

Delgado, R., & Stefancic, J. (Eds.). (2000). *Critical race theory: The cutting edge*. Temple University Press.

Delgado, R., & Stefancic, J. (2001). *Critical race theory: An introduction*. NYU Press.

Delgado, R., Stefancic, J., & Harris, A. (2012). *Critical race theory: An introduction* (2nd ed.). NYU Press. https://www.jstor.org/stable/j.ctt9qg9h2

Dixson, A. D., & Rousseau, C. K. (2005). And we are still not saved: Critical race theory in education ten years later. *Race, Ethnicity and Education, 8*(1), 7–27. doi:10.1080/1361332052000340971

Dos Santos, G. N., & Windle, J. (2021). The nexus of race and class in ELT: From interaction orders to orders of being. *Applied Linguistics, 42*(3), 473–491. doi:10.1093/applin/amaa031

Flores, N., & Rosa, J. (2015). Undoing appropriateness: Raciolinguistic ideologies and language diversity in education. *Harvard Educational Review, 85*(2), 149–171. doi:10.17763/0017-8055.85.2.149

Freire, P. (1970). *Pedagogy of the oppressed*. Seabury Press.

Gras, C. (2022). Narratives of race and identity in English language teaching. *Language Learning Journal*, 1–15. doi:10.1080/09571736.2022.2107693

Henry, F., & Tator, C. (2005). *The colour of democracy: Racism in Canadian society* (3rd ed.). Thomson Nelson.

Huber, L. P., Lopez, C. B., Malagon, M., Velez, V., & Solorzano, D. G. (2008). Getting beyond the "symptom," acknowledging the "disease": Theorizing nativism. *Contemporary Justice Review: Issues in Criminal, Social, and Restorative Justice, 11*(1), 39-51. https://www.tandfonline.com/doi/full/10.1080/10282580701850397

Hurie, A. H., & Callahan, R. M. (2019). Integration as perpetuation: Learning from race evasive approaches to ESL program reform. *Teachers College Record, 121*(9), 1–38. doi:10.1177/016146811912100904 PMID:32508373

Hurtado, A. (1996). *The color of privilege: Three blasphemies on race and feminism*. University of Michigan Press. doi:10.3998/mpub.9839

Johnson, M. A., & Chang, D. I. (2012). Balancing act: Addressing culture and gender in ESL classrooms. *Journal of Adult Education, 41*, 19–26.

Kapai, P. (2015). Status of ethnic minorities in Hong Kong 1997–2014. Hong Kong: Centre for Comparative and Public Law. Hong Kong University Press.

Kishimoto, K. (2018). Anti-racist pedagogy: From faculty's self-reflection to organizing within and beyond the classroom. *Race, Ethnicity and Education, 21*(4), 540–554. doi:10.1080/13613324.2016.1248824

Kubota, R., & Lin, A. (2006). Race and TESOL: Introduction to concepts and theories. *TESOL Quarterly, 40*(3), 471–493. doi:10.2307/40264540

Kumashiro, K. K. (2000). Toward a theory of anti-oppressive education. *Review of Educational Research, 70*(1), 25–53. doi:10.3102/00346543070001025

Ladson-Billings, G. J. (1999). Preparing teachers for diverse student populations: A critical race theory perspective. *Review of Research in Education, 24*, 211–247. doi:10.2307/1167271

Liggett, T. (2013). The mapping of a framework: Critical race theory and TESOL. *The Urban Review, 46*(1). doi:10.1007/s11256-013-0254-5

Marx, S. (2004). Regarding Whiteness: Exploring and intervening in the effects of White racism in teacher education. *Equity & Excellence in Education, 37*(1), 31–43. doi:10.1080/10665680490422089

Marx, S., & Pray, L. (2011). Living and learning in Mexico: Developing empathy for English language learners through study abroad. *Race, Ethnicity and Education, 14*(4), 507–535. doi:10.1080/13613324.2011.558894

Matsuda, A. (2002), International understanding through teaching world Englishes. *World Englishes, 21*, 436-440. doi:10.1111/1467-971X.00262

McMurtry, T., & Williamson, T. (2021). With liberty and Black linguistic justice for all: Pledging allegiance to anti-racist language pedagogy. *Journal of Adolescent & Adult Literacy, 65*(2), 175–178. doi:10.1002/jaal.1187

Miles, R., & Brown, M. (2003). *Racism* (2nd ed.). Routledge.

Milner, H. R. IV. (2007). Race, culture, and researcher positionality: Working through dangers seen, unseen, and unforeseen. *Educational Researcher, 36*(7), 388–400. doi:10.3102/0013189X07309471

Pavlenko, A. (2002). Bilingualism and emotions. *Journal of Cross-Cultural and Interlanguage Communication, 21*(1), 4-78. doi:10.1515/mult.2002.004

Peter, C. (2005). Learning-whose responsibility is it? *Nurse Educator, 30*(4), 159–165. doi:10.1097/00006223-200507000-00008 PMID:16030452

Phillipson, R. (1992). *Linguistic imperialism.* Oxford University Press.

Rhodes, C. M. (2013). *Culturally responsive teaching practices of adult education English for speakers of other languages and English for academic purposes teachers* [Doctoral dissertation]. https://scholarcommons.usf.edu/etd/4568/

Rodriguez, V., Drew, E., & Phillips, A. (2009-2014). *Anti-racist pedagogy across the curriculum workshop.* St. Cloud State University.

Rosa, J., & Flores, N. (2017). Unsettling race and language: Toward a raciolinguistic perspective. *Language in Society, 46*(5), 621–647. doi:10.1017/S0047404517000562

Salamonson, Y., Koch, J., Weaver, R., Everett, B., & Jackson, D. (2009). Embedded academic writing support for nursing students with English as a second language. *Journal of Advanced Nursing, 66*(2), 413–421. doi:10.1111/j.1365-2648.2009.05158.x PMID:20423424

Sanczyk, A. (2021). Creating inclusive adult ESL classrooms through promoting culturally responsive pedagogy. *Coalition on Basic Adult Education, 9*(2), 5–16.

Santos, G. N. D., & Windle, J. (2021). The nexus of race and class in ELT: From interaction orders to orders of being. *Applied Linguistics, 42*(3), 473–491.

Scheurich, J. J. (1997). *Research method in the postmodern.* Falmer Press.

Shin, J. (2018). *From ESL learners to EFL learners: A case study of adolescent Korean returnees.* Georgia State University.

Skutnabb-Kangas, T., Phillipson, R., & Rannut, M. (1995). *Linguistic human rights.* De Gruyter Mouton.
Sleeter, C. E. (2012). Confronting the marginalization of culturally responsive pedagogy. *Urban Education, 47*(3), 562–584. doi:10.1177/0042085911431472

Solorzano, D., & Yosso, T. (2000). Toward a critical race theory of Chicana and Chicano education. *Charting New Terrains of Chicana (o)/Latina (o) Education*, 35-65. doi:psycnet.apa.org/doi/10.1525/eth.1997.25.1.101

Solorzano, D. G. (1998). Critical Race Theory, race and gender microaggressions, and the experience of Chicana and Chicano scholars. *International Journal of Qualitative Studies in Education : QSE, 11*(1), 121–136. doi:10.1080/095183998236926

Stinson, C., & Migliarini, V. (2022). "Race had never been an issue": Examining White supremacy in English language teaching. *British Journal of Sociology of Education*. Advance online publication. doi:10.1080/01425692.2022.2145933

Stoler, A. L. (1997). On political and psychological essentialisms. *Ethos (Berkeley, Calif.), 25*(1), 101–106. doi:10.1525/eth.1997.25.1.101

Suraweera, D. (2020). *Towards integrating antiracism into TESL programs in Ontario.* Doctoral dissertation. University of Toronto.

Swift, K. (2022). "The good English": The ideological construction of the target language in adult ESOL. *Language in Society, 51*(2), 309–331. doi:10.1017/S0047404521000427

Tatum, B. D. (1992). Talking about race, learning about racism: The application of racial identity development theory in the classroom. *Harvard Educational Review, 62*(1), 1–25. doi:10.17763/haer.62.1.146k5v980r703023

Von Esch, K., Motha, S., & Kubota, R. (2020). Race and language teaching. *Language Teaching, 53*(4), 391–421. doi:10.1017/S0261444820000269

Welply, O. (2023). English as an additional language (EAL): Decolonising provision and practice. *Curriculum Journal, 34*(1), 62–82. doi:10.1002/curj.182

Willinsky, J. (1998). *Learning to divide the world: Education at empire's end.* University of Minnesota Press.

Zinga, D., & Styres, S. (2019). Decolonizing curriculum: Student resistances to anti-oppressive pedagogy. *Power and Education, 11*(1), 30–50.

KEY TERMS AND DEFINITIONS

Anti-Racist Pedagogy: Anti-racist pedagogy refers to an approach to teaching and education that actively works against and challenges racism. It aims to create inclusive and equitable learning environments that empower students to recognize, confront, and dismantle systemic racial injustices.

Critical Race Theory (CRT): Critical Race Theory is an academic framework that emerged in legal studies and later expanded to other disciplines. It critically examines how race and racism intersect with social structures, institutions, and everyday practices, emphasizing the role of power and historical context in shaping racial inequalities.

English as a Second Language (ESL): ESL stands for English as a Second Language and refers to programs or courses designed for individuals who are learning English in a country where English is the dominant language.

English Language Learner (ELL): ELL refers to students who are learning English as an additional language, often in a setting where English is the primary language of instruction.

Epistemological Racism: Epistemological racism refers to how racial biases and prejudices influence knowledge production, dissemination, and validation. It explores how dominant cultural perspectives can marginalize and undermine the knowledge systems of certain racial or ethnic groups.

Higher Education: Higher education typically refers to post-secondary education beyond the high school level, including universities and colleges. It involves advanced academic and professional learning and often includes undergraduate and graduate programs.

People of Color (POC): An inclusive term that collectively refers to individuals who do not identify as White, encompassing a diverse array of ethnic and racial backgrounds such as Black, Indigenous, Latinx, Asian, Pacific Islander, and others from non-European ethnic or racial groups.

White Privilege: White privilege refers to the unearned advantages and societal benefits that individuals perceived as white may experience due to their racial identity. These advantages are often systemic and may include better access to opportunities and less exposure to negative stereotypes.

White Supremacy: White supremacy is a belief system or ideology that asserts the superiority of white people over people of other racial backgrounds. It can manifest in discriminatory practices, policies, and structures that uphold and perpetuate racial hierarchies.

Compilation of References

Acar, A. S. (2023). Genre pedagogy: A writing pedagogy to help L2 writing instructors enact their classroom writing assessment literacy and feedback literacy. *Assessing Writing*, *56*, 100717. Advance online publication. doi:10.1016/j.asw.2023.100717

Accurso, K., & Mizell, J. D. (2020). Toward an antiracist genre pedagogy: Considerations for a North American context. *TESOL Journal*, *11*(4), e554. Advance online publication. doi:10.1002/tesj.554

Adewunmi, B. (2014). Kimberlé Crenshaw on intersectionality: 'I wanted to come up with an everyday metaphor that anyone could use'. *New Statesman*. https://www.newstatesman.com/politics/welfare/2014/kimberl-crenshaw-intersectionality-i-wanted-come-everyday-metaphor-anyone-could

Adler-Kassner, L., & Wardle, E. (Eds.). (2019). *(Re)Considering what we know: Threshold concepts in writing composition, rhetoric, and literacy*. Utah State University Press.

Agha, A., & Frog, S. (Eds.). (2015). *Registers of communication*. Finish Literature Society. doi:10.21435flin.18

Ajayi, L. (2011). Exploring how ESL teachers related their ethnic and social backgrounds to practice. *Race, Ethnicity and Education*, *14*(2), 253–275. doi:10.1080/13613324.2010.488900

Ali, A., & Mangrio, M. A. (forthcoming). Exploring sociocultural benefits of translanguaging in ELT in Pakistan's Sindh province. *European Journal of TEFL and Applied Linguistics*.

Ali, A., & David, M. K. (2023). Investigating the Clash of Discourses on Linguistic Human Rights: Focus on the Private Schools in Sindh, Pakistan. *Forma Y Funcion*, *36*(2). Advance online publication. doi:10.15446/fyf.v36n2.101898

Alim, H. S. (2010). Critical language awareness. In N. H. Hornberger & S. L. McKay (Eds.), *Sociolinguistics and language education: New perspectives on language and education* (pp. 205–231). Multilingual Matters. doi:10.21832/9781847692849-010

Alim, H. S. (2012). Interview with Geneva Smitherman. *Journal of English Linguistics*, *40*(4), 357–377. doi:10.1177/0075424212463821

Alim, H. S., Paris, D., & Wong, C. P. (2020). Culturally sustaining pedagogy: A critical framework for centering communities. In N. S. Nasir, C. D. Lee, R. D. Pea, & M. McKinney de Royston (Eds.), *Handbook of the cultural foundations of learning* (pp. 261–276). Taylor & Francis. doi:10.4324/9780203774977-18

Alim, H. S., Rickford, J. R., & Ball, A. F. (2016). *Raciolinguistics: How language shapes our ideas about race*. Oxford University Press. doi:10.1093/acprof:oso/9780190625696.001.0001

Alim, H. S., & Smitherman, G. (2012). *Articulate while Black: Barack Obama, language, and race in the US*. Oxford University Press.

Alshammari, S. H. (2018). The relationship between language, identity and cultural differences: A critical review. *Research on Humanities and Social Sciences, 4*(8), 98–101.

Alsup, J. (2006). *Teacher identity discourses: Negotiating personal and professional spaces*. Routledge. doi:10.4324/9781410617286

Alvarez, S. P., & Lee, E. (2020). Ordinary difference, extraordinary dispositions: Sustaining multilingualism in the writing classroom. In J. W. Lee & S. Dovchin (Eds.), *Translinguistics: Negotiating innovation and ordinariness* (pp. 61–72). Routledge.

American Psychological Association. (n.d.-a). *Race*. https://dictionary.apa.org/race

American Psychological Association. (n.d.-b). *Ethnicity*. https://dictionary.apa.org/ethnicity

Amin, N. (1999). Minority women teachers of ESL: Negotiating white English. In G. Braine (Ed.), *Non-native educators in English language teaching* (pp. 93–104). Lawrence Erlbaum Associates, Inc.

Anderson, A., & Aronson, B. (2019). Teacher education, diversity, and the interest convergence conundrum. How the demographic divide shapes teacher education. In K. T. Han & J. Laughter, (Eds.), Critical race theory in teacher education informing classroom culture and practice (pp. 26-35). Teachers College.

Anzaldúa, G. (1999). *Borderlands/La Frontera: The new mestiza*. Academic Press.

Apata, G. O. (2020). 'I can't breathe': The suffocating nature of racism. *Theory, Culture & Society, 37*(7-8), 241–254. doi:10.1177/0263276420957718

Appiah, A. (2006). *Cosmopolitanism: Ethics in a world of strangers*. Norton.

Appleby, R. (2016). Researching privilege in language teacher identity. *TESOL Quarterly, 49*(1), 755-768. doi:10.1002/tesq.321

Armstrong, J. C. (2022). The role of indigenous governed institutions of higher adult learning in indigenous language recovery. Vancouver Institute Lectures. University of British Columbia.

Arroyo-Romano, J. E. (2022). My Spanish feels like my second language: Addressing the challenges of the academic language of bilingual teachers. *Journal of Latinos and Education*, 1–21. doi:10.1080/15348431.2022.2146118

Atkinson, D., & Corbitt, S. (2023). Tracing the influences of praxis on the development of an open corequisite writing textbook. *Written Communication, 40*(2), 754–784. doi:10.1177/07410883221146550

Austin, T. (2009). Linguicism and race in the United States. Race, culture, and identities in second language education: Exploring critically engaged practice. Routledge.

Avineri, N., Graham, L. R., Johnson, E. J., Riner, R. C., & Rosa, J. (Eds.). (2019). *Language and social justice in practice*. Routledge.

Ayash, N. B. (2020). Critical translation and paratextuality: Translingual and anti-racist pedagogical possibilities for multilingual writers. *Composition Forum*, 44. https://compositionforum.com/issue/44/critical-translation.php

Azulai, A. (2020). Are grounded theory and action research compatible? considerations for methodological triangulation. *The Canadian Journal of Action Research, 21*(2), 4–24. doi:10.33524/cjar.v21i2.485

Babino, A., & Stewart, M. A. (2023). Whose bilingualism counts? Juxtaposing the sanctioned and subaltern languaging of two dual language teachers. *Journal of Language, Identity, and Education*, 1–18. Advance online publication. doi:10.1080/15348458.2023.2169697

Bacha-Garza, R. (2019). Race and ethnicity along the antebellum Rio Grande. In R. Bacha-Garza, C. L. Miller & R. K. Skowronek (Eds.), The civil war on the Rio Grande, 1846–1876 (Vol. 46, pp. 82-106). Texas A&M University Press.

Bailey, S. (2018). *Academic writing: A handbook for international students* (5th ed.). Routledge, Taylor & Francis.

Baker, B., Palfreyman, D. M., Hiller, G., Poha, W., & Manu, Z. (2017). Biliteracy as policy in academic institutions. In D. Palfreyman & C. Van der Walt (Eds.), *Academic biliteracies: Multilingual repertoires in higher education* (1st ed.). Multilingual Matters. doi:10.21832/9781783097425-012

Baker-Bell, A. (forthcoming). *Linguistic justice: Black, language, literacy, identity, and pedagogy.* Routledge & National Council of Teachers of English.

Baker-Bell, A. (2020a). Dismantling anti-black linguistic racism in English language arts classrooms: Towards an antiracist black language pedagogy. *Theory into Practice*, 59(1), 8–21. doi:10.1080/00405841.2019.1665415

Baker-Bell, A. (2020b). *Linguistic justice: Black language, literacy, identity, and pedagogy.* Routledge., doi:10.4324/9781315147383

Bandyopadhyay, S., & Szostek, J. (2019). Thinking critically about critical thinking: Assessing critical thinking of business students using multiple measures. *Journal of Education for Business*, 94(4), 259–270. doi:10.1080/08832323.2018.1524355

Barkhuizen, G. (2014). Narrative research in language teaching and learning. *Language Teaching*, 47(4), 450–466. doi:10.1017/S0261444814000172

Barkhuizen, G. (2016). Language teacher identity research: An introduction. In G. Barkhuizen (Ed.), *Reflections on language teacher identity research* (pp. 9–19). Routledge. doi:10.4324/9781315643465-5

Barone, T., & Eisner, E. W. (2011). Arts based research. *Sage (Atlanta, Ga.).*

Barrett, J. E., & Roediger, D. (2016). How white people became white. In P. Rothenberg (Ed.), *White privilege: Essential readings on the other side of racism* (5th ed., pp. 65–70). Worth Publishers.

Basabe, E. (2006). From de-Anglicization to internationalization: Cultural representations of the UK and the USA in global, adapted and local ELT textbooks in Argentina. *PROFILE Issues in Teachers' Professional Development (Philadelphia, Pa.)*, 7(1), 59–75.

Basu, S. [Host]. (2022, March 12). *Uncovering slave-ship wrecks, a diver puts lost souls to rest.* [Audio podcast episode]. In Apple News. https://podcasts.apple.com/us/podcast/uncovering-slave-ship-wrecks-a-diver-puts-lost-souls-to-rest/id1577591053?i=1000554506215

Battiste, M., & Bouvier, R. (2013). *Decolonizing education: Nourishing the learning spirit.* UBC Press.

Baumeister, R. F., & Leary, M. R. (2017). The need to belong: Desire for interpersonal attachments as a fundamental human motivation. *Interpersonal Development*, 57-89.

Bell, L. A., & Roberts, R. A. (2010). The storytelling project model: A theoretical framework for critical examination of racism through the arts. *Teachers College Record*, 112(9), 2295–2319. doi:10.1177/016146811011200907

Bernal, D. D., & Villalpando, O. (2002). An apartheid of knowledge in academia: The struggle over the "legitimate" knowledge of faculty of color. *Equity & Excellence in Education*, 35(2), 169–180. doi:10.1080/713845282

Bhowmik, S. K., Chaudhuri, A., Tweedie, G., Kim, M., & Liu, X. (2020). Culture and L2 writing: Student perceptions of factors affecting academic writing. *Writing & Pedagogy*, 12(2-3), 223. doi:10.1558/wap.19538

Bhowmik, S., & Chaudhuri, A. (2022). Addressing culture in L2 writing: Teaching strategies for the EAP classroom. *TESOL Quarterly*, *56*(4), 1410–1429. doi:10.1002/tesq.3172

Blakeney, A. M. (2005). Antiracist pedagogy: Definition, theory, and professional development. *Journal of Curriculum and Pedagogy*, *2*(1), 119–132. doi:10.1080/15505170.2005.10411532

Blommaert, J. (2013). Citizenship, language, and superdiversity: Towards complexity. *Journal of Language, Identity, and Education*, *12*(3), 193–196. doi:10.1080/15348458.2013.797276

Blommaert, J., & Rampton, B. (2011). Language and superdiversity. *Diversities*, *13*(2), 1–22.

Blum, S (2020). *Ungrading: Why Rating Students Undermines Learning (and What to Do Instead)*. West Virginia UP.

Bonilla-Silva, E. (2010). *Racism without racists. Color-blind racism & racial inequality in contemporary America* (3rd ed.). Rowman and Littlefield.

Bonilla-Silva, E. (2012). The invisible weight of whiteness: The racial grammar of everyday life in contemporary America. *Ethnic and Racial Studies*, *35*(2), 173–194. doi:10.1080/01419870.2011.613997

Bori, P. (2018). *Language textbooks in the era of neoliberalism* (1st ed.). Taylor and Francis. doi:10.4324/9781315405544

Borjigin, A. (2017). *Culturally relevant pedagogy in adult ESL classrooms: A case study of a university intensive English program*. Electronic Theses and Dissertations. 1267. https://digitalcommons.du.edu/etd/1267

Bourdieu, P. (1991). Language and symbolic power. Polity Press.

Bourdieu, P., & Passeron, J.-C. (1970). *La reproduction: éléments pour une théorie du système d'enseignement*. Édition Minuit.

Bozalek, V., & Zembylas, M. (2023). *Responsibility, privileged irresponsibility and response-ability: Higher education, coloniality and ecological damage*. Springer Nature. doi:10.1007/978-3-031-34996-6

Braine, G. (1999). *Non-native educators in English language teaching*. Lawrence Erlbaum Associates.

Braun, V., & Clarke, V. (2006). Using thematic analysis in psychology. *Qualitative Research in Psychology*, *3*(2), 77–101. doi:10.1191/1478088706qp063oa

Braveheart-Jordan, M., & DeBruyn, L. (1995). So she may walk in balance: Integrating the impact of historical trauma in the treatment of Native American Indian women. In J. Adleman & G. Enguidanos-Clark (Eds.), *Racism in the lives of women: Testimony, theory, and guides to antiracist practice* (pp. 345–368). Haworth Press.

Briceño, A., Rodriguez-Mojica, C., & Muñoz-Muñoz, E. (2018). From English learner to Spanish learner: Raciolinguistic beliefs that influence heritage Spanish speaking teacher candidates. *Language and Education*, *32*(3), 212–226. doi:10.1080/09500782.2018.1429464

Brunette Debassige, C., Wakeham, P., Smithers-Graeme, C., Haque, A., & Chitty, S. M. (2022). Mapping approaches to decolonizing and indigenizing the curriculum at Canadian universities: Critical reflections on current practices, challenges, and possibilities. *International Indigenous Policy Journal*, *13*(3), 1–24. doi:10.18584/iipj.2022.13.3.14109

Brunsma, D. L., & Rockquemore, K. A. (2001). The new color complex: Appearances and biracial identity. *Identity*, *1*(3), 225–246. doi:10.1207/S1532706XID0103_03

Bryant, A., & Charmaz, K. (2007). Grounded theory research: methods and practices. In A. Bryant & K. Charmaz (Eds.), *The Sage handbook of grounded theory* (pp. 1–28). Sage. doi:10.4135/9781848607941

Compilation of References

Bucholtz, M., Casillas, D. I., & Lee, J. S. (2017). Language and culture as sustenance. In D. Paris & H. S. Alim (Eds.), *Culturally sustaining pedagogies: Teaching and learning for justice in a changing world* (pp. 43–59). Teacher's College Press.

Bucholtz, H., & Hall, K. (2005). Identity and interaction: A sociocultural linguistic approach. *Discourse Studies, 7*(4-5), 585–614. doi:10.1177/1461445605054407

Burgess, J., & Rowsell, J. (2020). Transcultural-affective flows and multimodal engagements: Reimagining pedagogy and assessment with adult language learners. *Language and Education, 34*(2), 173–191. doi:10.1080/09500782.2020.1720226

Burns, A., & Roberts, C. (2010, September). Migration and adult language learning: Global flows and local transpositions. *TESOL Quarterly, 44*(3), 409–419. doi:10.5054/tq.2010.232478

Burton, J., & Rajendram, S. (2019). Translanguaging-as-resource: University ESL instructors' language orientations and attitudes toward translanguaging. *TESL Canada Journal, 36*(1), 21–47. doi:10.18806/tesl.v36i1.1301

Butler-Kisber, L. (2010). *Qualitative inquiry: Thematic, narrative and arts-informed perspectives*. Sage Publications. doi:10.4135/9781526435408

Byram, M. (2006). *Languages and identities*. Language Policy Division.

Byrd Clark, J. (2010). Making "wiggle room" in French as a Second Language/Français langue seconde: Reconfiguring identity, language, and policy. *Canadian Journal of Education, 33*(2), 379–406.

Cabrera, N. L. (2019). *White guys on campus: Racism, White immunity, and the myth of "post-racial" higher education*. Rutgers University Press. doi:10.36019/9780813599106

Cahyono, H., Bahri, S., Salim, A., Eka, N. M., Fauzi, R., Bayu, J. T., & Purwanti, S. (2021). Language as national identity. *Advances in Social Science, Education and Humanities Research, 584*, 782–785. doi:10.2991/assehr.k.211102.104

Caldas, B. (2021). Spanish language development and support in a bilingual teacher preparation program. *Journal of Language, Identity, and Education, 20*(1), 18–29. doi:10.1080/15348458.2021.1864206

Callister, P., & Didham, R. (2009). Who are we? The human genome project, race and ethnicity. *Social Policy Journal of New Zealand, 36*, 63–76.

Canagarajah, A. S. (2002). *Critical academic writing and multilingual students*. University of Michigan. doi:10.3998/mpub.8903

Canagarajah, A. S. (2004). Subversive identities, pedagogical safe houses, and critical learning. In B. Norton & K. Toohey (Eds.), *Critical pedagogies and language learning* (pp. 116–137). Cambridge University Press. doi:10.1017/CBO9781139524834.007

Canagarajah, A. S. (2006). The place of world Englishes in composition: The pluralization continued. *College Composition and Communication, 57*(4), 586–619.

Canagarajah, S. (2011). Codemeshing in academic writing: Identifying teachable strategies of translanguaging. *Modern Language Journal, 95*(3), 401–417. doi:10.1111/j.1540-4781.2011.01207.x

Canagarajah, S. (2013). *Literacy as translingual practice: Between communities and classrooms*. Routledge. doi:10.4324/9780203120293

Canagarajah, S. (2016). Translingual writing and teacher development in composition. *College English, 78*(3), 265–273.

Canagarajah, S. A. (1999). Interrogating the 'native speaker fallacy': Non-linguistic roots, non-pedagogical results. In G. Braine (Ed.), *Non-native educators in English language teaching* (pp. 77–92). Lawrence Erlbaum Associates.

Caouette, B. L., & Griggs, C. (2015). A compelling collaboration: The first year writing program, writing center, and directed self-placement. *Praxis. Writing Center Journal*, *12*(2), 17–22.

Carino, P. (1995). Early writing centers: Toward a history. *Writing Center Journal*, *15*(2), 103–115. doi:10.7771/2832-9414.1279

Cenoz, J., & Gorter, D. (2011). A holistic approach to multilingual education: Introduction. *Modern Language Journal*, *95*(3), 339–343. doi:10.1111/j.1540-4781.2011.01204.x

Chan, A. (2020). Superdiversity and critical multicultural pedagogies: Working with migrant. *Policy Futures in Education*, *18*(5), 560–573. doi:10.1177/1478210319873773

Chan, C., & Lo, M. (2017). Exploring inclusive pedagogical practices in Hong Kong primary EFL classrooms. *International Journal of Inclusive Education*, *21*(7), 714–729. doi:10.1080/13603116.2016.1252798

Chang, D., & Goldrick-Jones, A. (2019). EAL writers and peer tutors: Pedagogies that resist the "broken writer" myth. *Discourse and Writing/Rédactologie*, *29*, 238-242.

Channa, L. (2014). *English Medium for the government primary schools of Sindh, Pakistan: an exploration of government primary school teachers' attitudes* [Doctoral dissertation]. The University of Georgia.

Charalambous, C., Zembylas, M., & Charalambous, P. (2015). Superdiversity and discourses of conflict: Interaction in a Greek-Cypriot literacy class. *Working Papers in Urban Language & Literacies*.

Charalambous, C., Charalambous, P., Zembylas, M., & Theodorou, E. (2020). Translanguaging, (In)Security and Social Justice Education. In J. A. Panagiotopoulou, L. Rosen, & J. Strzykala (Eds.), *Inclusion, Education and Translanguaging. Inklusion und Bildung in Migrationsgesellschaften* (pp. 105–123). Springer. doi:10.1007/978-3-658-28128-1_7

Charles. (2019). Black teachers of English in South Korea: Constructing identities as a native English speaker and English language teaching professional. *TESOL Journal*, *10*(4). . doi:10.1002/tesj.478

Charles, K., & Bellinger, C. K. (2020). *Othering: The original sin of humanity*. Cascade Books.

Charmaz, K. (2005). Grounded theory in the 21st century: Applications for advancing social justice studies. In N. K. Denzin & Y. S. Lincoln (Eds.), *Sage handbook of qualitative research* (pp. 507–535). Sage Publications.

Charmaz, K. (2006). Constructing grounded theory: A practical guide through qualitative analysis. *Sage (Atlanta, Ga.)*.

Chen, D. (2021). How to adapt to academic writing expectations: A challenge for international students. *MEM Insider*, *6*, 20–21. https://www.kings.uwo.ca/academics/school-of-management-economics-and-mathematics/mem-insider/

Chen, K-H. (2010). *Asia as method: Toward deimperialization*. Duke University Press.

Chen, X. (2022). L2 students' adaptive transfer beyond first-year writing. *INTESOL Journal*, *19*(1). Advance online publication. doi:10.18060/26359

Cheung, P. K., & Said, S. B. (2015). *Advances and current trends in language teacher identity research*. Routledge. doi:10.4324/9781315775135

Chew, S., Houston, A., & Cooper, A. (2020). *The anti-racist discussion pedagogy: An introductory guide to building an anti-racist pedagogy in any discipline through instructor reflection, clear communication guidelines, and inquiry-based discussion*. The University of North Carolina at Chapel Hill.

Chiapello, E., & Fairclough, N. (2002). Understanding the new management ideology: A transdisciplinary contribution from critical discourse analysis and new sociology of capitalism. *Discourse & Society*, *13*(2), 185–208. doi:10.1177/0957926502013002406

Chien, S. (2014). Cultural constructions of plagiarism in student writing: Teachers' perceptions and responses. *Research in the Teaching of English*, *49*(2), 120–140.

Choe, H., & Seo, Y. (2021). Negotiating teacher identity: Experiences of Black teachers of English in Korean ELT: How race and English language teacher identity intersect in the Expanding Circle. *English Today*, *37*(3), 148–155. doi:10.1017/S0266078419000531

Cho, H. (2014). Enacting critical literacy: The case of a language minority preservice teacher. *Curriculum Inquiry*, *44*(5), 677–699. doi:10.1111/curi.12066

Cho, H. (2017). Racism and linguicism: Engaging language minority pre-service teachers in counter-storytelling. *Race, Ethnicity and Education*, *20*(5), 666–680. doi:10.1080/13613324.2016.1150827

Chun, W. C. (2016). Addressing racialized multicultural discourses in an EAP textbook: Working toward a critical pedagogies approach. *TESOL Quarterly*, *50*(1), 109–131. doi:10.1002/tesq.216

Ciriza, M. del P. (2023). Comparing Spanish certification exams for bilingual teachers: Test design and other pedagogical considerations. *International Journal of Bilingual Education and Bilingualism*, *26*(2), 114–130. doi:10.1080/13670050.2020.1791046

Clandinin, D. J., & Connelly, F. M. (2000). *Narrative inquiry: Experience and story in qualitative research*. Jossey-Bass Publishing.

Clarke, Z. (2023). *Black people breathe: a mindfulness guide to racial healing*. Ten Speed Press.

Clary-Lemon, J. (2009). Shifting tradition: Writing research in Canada. *The American Review of Canadian Studies*, *39*(2), 94–111. doi:10.1080/02722010902848128

Clements, J. M. (2011). Sarah and the Puritans: Feminist Contributions to New England Historical Archaeology. *Archaeologies*, *7*(1), 97–120. doi:10.100711759-010-9155-3

College factual. (n.d.). *Clemson University graduate school report*. https://www.collegefactual.com/graduate-schools/clemson-university

Collins, B. A., Sánchez, M., & España, C. (2023). Sustaining and developing teachers' dynamic bilingualism in a redesigned bilingual teacher preparation program. *International Journal of Bilingual Education and Bilingualism*, *26*(2), 97–113. doi:10.1080/13670050.2019.1610354

Collins, H. (2018). Interculturality from above and below: Navigating uneven discourses in a neoliberal university system. *Language and Intercultural Communication*, *18*(2), 167–183. doi:10.1080/14708477.2017.1354867

Compton-Lilly, C., & Hawkins, M. R. (2023). Global flows and critical cosmopolitanism: A longitudinal case study. *Harvard Educational Review*, *93*(1), 26–52. doi:10.17763/1943-5045-93.1.26

Condon, F., & Ashanti, V. (2017). *Performing antiracist pedagogy in rhetoric, writing, and communication*. WAC Clearinghouse.

Condrey, T., & Derico, S. (2012). Strategies for success for English as a second language (ESL) students in the postsecondary setting. *Perspectives In Learning*, *13*(1). https://csuepress.columbusstate.edu/pil/vol13/iss1/6

Conteh, J. (2019). Translanguaging. *ELT Journal*, *72*(4), 445–447. doi:10.1093/elt/ccy034

Cook, V. (1999). Going beyond the native speaker in language teaching. *TESOL Quarterly*, *33*(2), 185–209. doi:10.2307/3587717

Creese, G., & Kambere, E. N. (2003). What colour is your English? *Canadian Review of Sociology*, *40*(5), 565–573. doi:10.1111/j.1755-618X.2003.tb00005.x

Crenshaw. (1991). Mapping the margins: Intersectionality, identity politics, and violence against women of color. *Stanford Law Review*, *43*(6), 1241–1299. doi:10.2307/1229039

Crenshaw, K. (1988). Race, reform, and retrenchment: Transformation and legitimation in antidiscrimination law. *Harvard Law Review*, *101*(7), 1331–1387. doi:10.2307/1341398

Crenshaw, K. W. (2017). *On intersectionality: Essential writings*. The New Press.

Creswell, J. W., & Poth, C. N. (2018). *Qualitative inquiry & research design: Choosing among five approaches* (4th ed.). Sage.

Crul, M. (2016). Super-diversity vs. assimilation: How complex diversity in majority-minority cities challenge the assumptions of assimilation. *Journal of Ethnic and Migration Studies*, *42*(1), 54–68. doi:10.1080/1369183X.2015.1061425

Crump, A. (2014b). *"But your face, it looks like you're English:" LangCrit and the experiences of multilingual Japanese-Canadian children in Montréal* [Unpublished doctoral thesis]. McGill University.

Crump, A. (2014a). Introducing LangCrit: Critical language and race theory. *Critical Inquiry in Language Studies*, *11*(3), 207–224. doi:10.1080/15427587.2014.936243

Cruz, B. C., & Berson, M. J. (2001). The American melting pot? Miscegenation laws in the United States. *OAH Magazine of History*, *15*(4), 80–84. https://www.jstor.org/stable/25163474

Cui, W. (2019). Teaching for transfer to first-year L2 writers. *Journal of International Students*, *9*(4), 1115–1133. doi:10.32674/jis.v9i4.755

Culligan, K., Battistuzzi, A., Wernicke, M., & Masson, M. (2023). Teaching French as a second language in Canada: Convergence points of language, professional knowledge, and mentorship from teacher preparation through the beginning years. *Canadian Modern Language Review*, *79*(4), 352–370. doi:10.3138/cmlr-2022-0059

Cummings, S., & van Zee, A. (2005). Communities of practice and networks: Reviewing two perspectives on social learning. *Knowledge Management for Development Journal*, *1*(1), 8–22. https://km4djournal.org/index.php/km4dj/article/view/9

Cummins, J. (2000). Negotiating intercultural identities in the multilingual classroom. *The CATESOL Journal*, *12*(1), 163–178.

Cummins, J. (2001). *Negotiating identities: Education for empowerment in a diverse society* (2nd ed.). California Association for Bilingual Education.

Cummins, J. (2007). Rethinking monolingual instructional strategies in multilingual classrooms. *Canadian Journal of Applied Linguistics*, *10*(2), 221–240. https://journals.lib.unb.ca/index.php/CJAL/article/view/19743

Curdt-Christiansen, X. L., & Weninger, C. (2015). Introduction: Ideology and the politics of language textbooks. In X. L. Curdt-Christiansen & C. Weninger (Eds.), *Language, ideology and education: The politics of textbooks in language education* (pp. 1–8). Routledge. doi:10.4324/9781315814223-7

Cushman, E. (2016). Translingual and decolonial approaches to meaning making. *College English*, *78*(3), 234–242.

Compilation of References

Daniel, R. G., Kina, L., Dariotis, W. M., & Fojas, C. (2014). Emerging paradigms in critical mixed race studies. *Journal of Critical Mixed Raced Studies*. doi:10.5070/C811013868

Darbes, T. (2023). Constructing deficit from diversity: Assessment and placement networks and the raciolinguistic enaction of ESL. *Language and Education*, 1–15. doi:10.1080/09500782.2023.2239774

Data, U. S. A. (n.d.-a). *Bob Jones University*. https://datausa.io/profile/university/bob-jones-university

Data, U. S. A. (n.d.-b). *Charleston Southern University*. https://datausa.io/profile/university/charleston-southern-university

Data, U. S. A. (n.d.-c). *Greenville Technical College*. https://datausa.io/profile/university/greenville-technical-college

Data, U. S. A. (n.d.-d). *Midlands Technical College*. https://datausa.io/profile/university/midlands-technical-college

Data, U. S. A. (n.d.-e). *North Greenville University*. https://datausa.io/profile/university/north-greenville-university

Data, U. S. A. (n.d.-f). *University of South Carolina Aiken*. https://datausa.io/profile/university/university-of-south-carolina-aiken

Data, U. S. A. (n.d.-g). *University of South Carolina Upstate*. https://datausa.io/university-of-south-carolina-upstate

Davey, R. (2013). *The professional identity of teacher educators: Career on the cusp?* Routledge. doi:10.4324/9780203584934

Davies, B. (2005). Communities of practice: Legitimacy not choice. *Journal of Sociolinguistics*, 9(4), 557–581. doi:10.1111/j.1360-6441.2005.00306.x

Davila, B. (2022). White language supremacy in course descriptions. *College Composition and Communication*, 73(4), 640–664. doi:10.58680/ccc202232013

Davis, S. (2023). Multilingual Learners in Canadian French Immersion Programs: Looking Back and Moving Forward. *Canadian Modern Language Review*.

Davis, A. (1972). Reflections on the Black woman's role in the community of slaves. *The Massachusetts Review*, 13(1/2), 81–100. https://www.jstor.org/stable/25088201

De Costa, P. I. (2010a). Let's collaborate: Using developments in global English research to advance socioculturally-oriented SLA identity work. *Issues in Applied Linguistics*, 18(1), 99–124. doi:10.5070/L4181005125

De Costa, P. I. (2021). Anti-Asian racism: How it affects TESOL professionals like you and me. *TESOL Journal*, 12(3), e620. Advance online publication. doi:10.1002/tesj.620

De Costa, P., & Norton, B. (2017b). Introduction: Identity, transdisciplinarity, and the good language teacher. *Modern Language Journal*, 101(S1), 3–14. doi:10.1111/modl.12368

de los Ríos, C. V., Martinez, D. C., Musser, A. D., Canady, A., Camangian, P., & Quijada, P. D. (2019). Upending colonial practices: Toward repairing harm in English education. *Theory into Practice*, 58(4), 359–367. doi:10.1080/00405841.2019.1626615

Dei, G. J. S., & Asgharzadeh, A. (2001). The power of social theory: The anti-colonial discursive framework. *The Journal of Educational Thought*, 35(3), 297–323.

Delgado, R., & Stefancic, J. (2023). *Critical race theory: An introduction* (4th ed.). NYU Press.

Delgado, R., & Stefancic, J. (Eds.). (2000). *Critical race theory: The cutting edge*. Temple University Press.

DePalma, M., & Ringer, J. M. (2011). Toward a theory of adaptive transfer: Expanding disciplinary discussions of "transfer" in second-language writing and composition studies. *Journal of Second Language Writing, 20*(2), 134–147. doi:10.1016/j.jslw.2011.02.003

Diab, R., Godbee, B., Ferrel, T., & Simpkins, N. (2012). A multi-dimensional pedagogy for racial justice in writing centers. *Praxis. Writing Center Journal, 10*(1), 1–8.

Diving With a Purpose. (n.d.). *Restoring our oceans. Preserving our heritage.* https://www.nationalgeographic.com/podcasts/into-the-depths

Dixson, A. D., & Rousseau, C. K. (2005). And we are still not saved: Critical race theory in education ten years later. *Race, Ethnicity and Education, 8*(1), 7–27. doi:10.1080/1361332052000340971

Donahue, C. (2018). Rhetorical and linguistic flexibility: Valuing heterogeneity in academic writing education. In D. Martin (Ed.), *Transnational Writing Education* (pp. 21–40). Routledge. doi:10.4324/9781351205955-2

Dos Santos, G. N., & Windle, J. (2021). The nexus of race and class in ELT: From interaction orders to orders of being. *Applied Linguistics, 42*(3), 473–491. doi:10.1093/applin/amaa031

Du, Y., & Huang, Z. (2020). International students reflect on how they would like to be described. *MEM Insider, 5*, 13. https://www.kings.uwo.ca/academics/school-of-management-economics-and-mathematics/mem-insider/

Dumontet, M., Kiprop, M., & Loewen, C. (2019). Steps on the path towards decolonization: A reflection on learning, experience, and practice in academic support at the University of Manitoba. *Discourse and Writing/Rédactologie, 29*, 196-216.

Edwards, J. J. (2015). *Superchurch: The rhetoric and politics of American fundamentalism*. doi:10.5860/CHOICE.191900

Ellis, E. M. (2016). "I may be a native speaker but I'm not monolingual": Reimagining all teachers' linguistic identities in TESOL. *TESOL Quarterly, 49(1), 597-630.* doi:10.1002/tesq.314

Elon Statement on Writing Transfer. (2015). Retrieved from https://www.centerforengagedlearning.org/elon-statement-on-writing-transfer

Ergas, O. (2020). Education and cosmopolitanism: Liberating our non-cosmopolitan minds through mindfulness. *Policy Futures in Education, 18*(5), 610–627. doi:10.1177/1478210319876512

Fairclough, N., & Wodak, R. (1997). Critical discourse analysis. In T. van Dijk (Ed.), *Discourse as social interaction* (pp. 258–284). Sage.

Fallas-Escobar, C. (2023). "Se me sale el Español y se me pega el Spanglish!": Latina/o bilingual teacher candidates' racialized notions of bilingualism. *Critical Inquiry in Language Studies*, 1–20. Advance online publication. doi:10.1080/15427587.2023.2218507

Fallas-Escobar, C., & Herrera, L. J. P. (2022). Examining raciolinguistic struggles in institutional settings: A duoethnography. *Linguistics and Education, 67*, 101012. doi:10.1016/j.linged.2022.101012

Fallas-Escobar, C., & Treviño, A. (2021). Two Latina bilingual teacher candidates' perceptions of language proficiency and language choice options: Ideological encounters with listening and speaking others. *Bilingual Research Journal, 44*(1), 124–143. doi:10.1080/15235882.2021.1877213

Feagin, J., Johnson, J., & Rush, S. (2000). Doing anti-racism toward an egalitarian American society. *Contemporary Sociology, 29*(1), 95–100. doi:10.2307/2654935

Fedoration, S., & Tang, M. (2023, February 14). *The contradiction of being a French L+ teacher: Issues to consider to support immersion teachers.* CASLT Online Professional Learning Webinars.

Field, J. (2018). *An illustrated field guide to the elements and principles of art + design.* Lulu.com.

Fillol, V., Razafimandimbimanana, E., & Geneix-Rabault, S. (2019). La créativité en formation professionnalisante: un processus émancipateur. *Contextes et didactiques: Revue semestrielle en sciences de l'éducation*, (14). doi:10.4000/ced.1497

Flachmann, K., Flachmann, M., MacLennan, A., & Zeppa, J. (2013). *Reader's choice: Essays for thinking, reading, and writing* (7th Canadian ed.). Pearson Canada.

Fletcher, D., & Sarkar, M. (2013). Psychological resilience. *European Psychologist*, *18*(1), 12–23. doi:10.1027/1016-9040/a000124

Flores, N. L. (2015). Examining language and race in education: Why we need a raciolinguistic perspective. *The Educational Linguist.* https://educationallinguist.wordpress.com/

Flores, N. L. (2019). Translanguaging into raciolinguistic ideologies: A personal reflection on the legacy of Ofelia García. *Journal of Multilingual Education Research*, *9*(5), 45–60. https://fordham.bepress.com/jmer/vol9/iss1/5

Flores, N., Lewis, M. C., & Phuong, J. (2018). Raciolinguistic chronotopes and the education of Latinx students: Resistance and anxiety in a bilingual school. *Language & Communication*, *62*, 15–25. doi:10.1016/j.langcom.2018.06.002

Flores, N., & Rosa, J. (2015). Undoing appropriateness: Raciologinguistic ideologies and language diversity in education. *Harvard Educational Review*, *85*(2), 149–171. doi:10.17763/0017-8055.85.2.149

Flores, N., & Rosa, J. (2022). Undoing competence: Coloniality, homogeneity, and the overrepresentation of whiteness in applied linguistics. *Language Learning.* Advance online publication. doi:10.1111/lang.12528

Forbes Magazine. (n.d.). *Erskine College.* Forbes. https://www.forbes.com/colleges/erskine-college-and-seminary/?sh=5f6b126465dc

Freire, P. (2000). Pedagogy of the oppressed (30th anniversary ed.) (M. B. Ramos, Trans.). Continuum. (Original work published 1970)

Freire, P. (1970). *Pedagogy of the oppressed.* Seabury Press.

French, M. (2019). Multilingual pedagogies in practice. *TESOL in Context*, *28*(1), 21–44. doi:10.21153/tesol2019vol28no1art869

Freynet, N., & Clément, R. (2019). Perceived accent discrimination: Psychosocial consequences and perceived legitimacy. *Journal of Language and Social Psychology*, *38*(4), 496–513. doi:10.1177/0261927X19865775

Gabaccia, D. (1989). *Immigrant women in the United States: A selective annotated multidisciplinary bibliography.* Greenwood Press.

Galindo, R., & Olguín, M. (1996). Reclaiming bilingual educators' cultural resources: An autobiographical approach. *Urban Education*, *31*(1), 29–56. doi:10.1177/0042085996031001002

García, O. (2009). Education, multilingualism and translanguaging in the 21st century. *Social Justice through Multilingual Education*, 140-158.

García, O. (2009). Emergent bilinguals and TESOL: What's in a name? *TESOL Quarterly*, *43*(2), 322–326. doi:10.1002/j.1545-7249.2009.tb00172.x

García, O. (2014). Countering the dual: Transglossia, dynamic bilingualism and translanguaging in education. In R. Rubdy & L. Alsagoff (Eds.), *The global-local interface, language choice and hybridity* (pp. 100–118). Multilingual Matters. doi:10.21832/9781783090860-007

Garcia, O., & Kleifgen, J. A. (2018). *Educating emergent bilinguals: Policies, programs, and practices for English learners*. Teachers College Press.

García, O., & Li, W. (2014). *Translanguaging: Language, bilingualism, and education*. Palgrave Macmillan. doi:10.1057/9781137385765

Garcia-Sanchez, I.M. (2016). Multiculturalism and its discontents. *Raciolinguistics: How language shapes our ideas about race*, 291.

Gass, S. M., & Mackey, A. (2017). *Stimulated recall methodology in applied linguistics and L2 research*. Taylor & Francis.

Gaulee, U. (2018). How to understand the international students with whom you work. *Journal of International Students*, *8*(2), I–II. doi:10.32674/jis.v8i2.93

Gauna, L. M., Beaudry, C., & Cooper, J. (2022). The leaking Spanish bilingual education teacher pipeline: Stories of PK-20 challenges told by Latinx becoming bilingual teachers in the U.S. *Journal of Latinos and Education*, *22*(5), 1885–1899. doi:10.1080/15348431.2022.2057989

Gauna, L. M., Márquez, J., Weaver, L., & Cooper, J. (2023). Bilingual teacher candidates and their professors: Efforts to pass a Spanish proficiency certification exam. *Bilingual Research Journal*, *46*(1-2), 158–175. doi:10.1080/15235882.2023.2225460

Gearon, L. (2013). The King James Bible and the politics of religious education. *Religious Education (Chicago, Ill.)*, *108*(1), 9–27. doi:10.1080/00344087.2013.747838

Gearon, L., Kuusisto, A., Matemba, Y., Benjamin, S., du Preez, P., Koirikivi, P., & Simmonds, S. (2020). Decolonizing the religious education curriculum. *British Journal of Religious Education*, *43*(1), 1–8. doi:10.1080/01416200.2020.1819734

Gebhard, M., & Accurso, K. (Eds.). (2023). *In Pursuit of a multilingual equity agenda: SFL teacher action research* (1st ed.). Routledge. doi:10.4324/9781003162575

Gee, J. P. (2014). *An introduction to discourse analysis: Theory and method*. Routledge. doi:10.4324/9781315819679

Gere, A. R., Curzan, A., Hammond, J. W., Hughes, S., Li, R., Moos, A., Smith, K., Van Zanen, K., Wheeler, K. L., & Zanders, C. J. (2021). Communal justicing: Writing assessment, disciplinary infrastructure, and the case for critical language awareness. *College Composition and Communication*, *72*(3), 384–412. doi:10.58680/ccc202131160

Ginting, D., & Barella, Y. (2022). Academic writing centers and the teaching of academic writing at colleges: Literature review. *Journal of Education and Learning*, *16*(3), 350–356.

Giroux, H. A. (2011). *On critical pedagogy*. Continuum International Publishing Group.

Giroux, H. A. (2023). Fascist culture, critical pedagogy, and resistance in pandemic times. *English Language Notes*, *61*(1), 51–62. doi:10.1215/00138282-10293151

Goebel, D. (1938). British trade to the Spanish colonies, 1796-1823. *The American Historical Review*, *43*(2), 288–320. https://www.jstor.org/stable/1839720. doi:10.2307/1839720

Gonzalez, G. (2001). *Education is the great equalizer in a democratic society*. https://www.indiana.edu/~ocmhp/092801/text/gonzalez.htm

Compilation of References

Gonzalez, J. (2011). *Harvest of empire: A history of latinos in America* (2nd ed.). Penguin Books. Print

Gopang, A. S., Panhwar, A. H., &Nizamani, H. A. (2020). Issue of language as the medium of instruction in Pakistan: An analytical study. *The Shield, 11*.

Gordon, L. M. (2014). Beyond generalist vs. specialist: Making connections between genre theory and writing center pedagogy. *Praxis Writing Center Journal, 11*(2), 1–5.

Gorski, P. C. (2011). Unlearning deficit ideology and the scornful gaze: Thoughts on authenticating the class discourse in education. *Counterpoints, 402,* 152–173. https://www.jstor.org/stable/42981081

Gras, C. (2022). Narratives of race and identity in English language teaching. *Language Learning Journal*, 1–15. doi: 10.1080/09571736.2022.2107693

Green, B. (2023). Five design principles for language learning materials development. *The ORTESOL Journal, 40,* 4–20.

Greenfield, L. (2011). The 'standard English' fairy tale: A rhetorical analysis of racist pedagogies and commonplace assumptions about language diversity. In L. Greenfield & K. Rowan (Eds.), *Writing centers and the new racism: A call for sustainable change and dialogue* (pp. 33–60). Utah State UP. doi:10.2307/j.ctt4cgk6s.6

Grills, C. N., Aird, E. G., & Rowe, D. (2016). Breathe, baby, breathe: clearing the way for the emotional emancipation of Black people. *Cultural Studies, 16*(3), 333–343. doi:10.1177/1532708616634839

Grimm, N. (2011). Retheorizing writing center work to transform a system of advantage based on race. *Writing centers and the new racism: A call for sustainable change and dialogue,* 75-99.

Grin, F. (2000). *Evaluating policy measures for minority languages in Europe: Towards effective, cost-effective and democratic implementation. ECMI Report 6, October 2000.* ECMI.

Growe, R., & Montgomery, P. S. (2003). Educational equity in America: Is education the great equalizer? *Professional Educator, 25*(2), 23–29.

Guardado, M. (2010). Heritage language development: Preserving a mythic past or envisioning the future of Canadian identity? *Journal of Language, Identity, and Education, 5*(9), 329–346. doi:10.1080/15348458.2010.517699

Guerrero, M. D. (2023). State of the art: A forty-year reflection on the Spanish language preparation of Spanish-English bilingual-dual language teachers in the U.S. *International Journal of Bilingual Education and Bilingualism, 26*(2), 146–157. doi:10.1080/13670050.2020.1865257

Gulliver, T., & Thurrell, K. (2016). Denials of racism in Canadian English language textbooks. *TESL Canada Journal, 33*(10), 42–61. doi:10.18806/tesl.v33i0.1245

Gusa, D. L. (2010). White institutional presence: The impact of Whiteness on campus climate. *Harvard Educational Review, 80*(4), 464–489. doi:10.17763/haer.80.4.p5j483825u110002

Guttierez, K. D., & Johnson, P. (2017). Understanding identity sampling and cultural repertoires advancing a historicizing and syncretic system of teaching and learning in justice pedagogies. In D. Paris & H. S. Alim (Eds.), *Culturally sustaining pedagogies: Teaching and learning for justice in a changing world* (pp. 247–60). Teachers College Press.

Hafner, C. A., & Ho, W. Y. J. (2020). Assessing digital multimodal composing in second language writing: Towards a process-based model. *Journal of Second Language Writing, 47,* 100710. doi:10.1016/j.jslw.2020.100710

Hallgren, K. A. (2012). Computing inter-rater reliability for observational data: An overview and tutorial. *Tutorials in Quantitative Methods for Psychology, 8*(1), 23–34. doi:10.20982/tqmp.08.1.p023 PMID:22833776

Hallman, H. I. (2009). Teacher identity as dialogic response. In R. Kubota & A. M. Lin (Eds.), *Race, culture, and identities in second language education: Exploring critically engaged practice* (pp. 3–14). Routledge.

Han, H., & Varghese, M. (2019). Language ideology, Christianity, and identity: Critical empirical examinations of Christian institutions as alternative spaces. *Journal of Language, Identity, and Education*, *18*(1), 1–9. doi:10.1080/15348458.2019.1569525

Hankivsky, O. (2014). *Intersectionality 101*. The Institute for Intersectionality Research & Policy.

Hannah-Jones, N. (2019). The 1619 Project: A new origin story. *The New York Times*.

Hannerz, U. (1990). Cosmopolitans and locals in world culture. In M. Featherstone (Ed.), *Global culture: Nationalism, globalization, and modernity* (pp. 237–252). Sage Publications.

Hansen Edwards, J. G. (2017). Defining "native speaker" in multilingual settings: English as a native language in Asia. *Journal of Multilingual and Multicultural Development*, *38*(9), 757–771. doi:10.1080/01434632.2016.1257627

Hanson, K. (1993). Facing Facts and Responsibilities: The white man's burden and the burden of proof. In S. Cahn (Ed.), *Affirmative Action and the University: A Philosophical Inquiry* (pp. 174–180). Temple University Press.

Haque, E. (2012). *Multiculturalism within a bilingual framework: Language, race, and belonging in Canada*. University of Toronto Press. doi:10.3138/9781442686083

Harper, S. R., Patton, L. D., & Wooden, O. S. (2009). Access and equity for African American students in higher education: A critical race historical analysis of policy efforts. *The Journal of Higher Education*, *80*(4), 389–414. doi:10.1080/00221546.2009.11779022

Heidemann, K. A. (2019). Close, yet so far apart: Bridging social movement theory with popular education. *Australian Journal of Adult Learning*, *59*(3), 309–318.

Heltai, J., & Tarsoly, E. (2023). *Translanguaging for Equal Opportunities: Speaking Romani at School*. De Gruyter Mouton. doi:10.1515/9783110769609

Hendershott, A., Drinan, P., & Cross, M. (2000). Toward enhancing a culture of academic integrity. *NASPA Journal*, *37*(4), 587–598. doi:10.2202/1949-6605.1119

Henderson, E. (2015). *Writing by choice* (3rd ed.). Oxford University Press.

Henry, F., & Tator, C. (2005). *The colour of democracy: Racism in Canadian society* (3rd ed.). Thomson Nelson.

Hernández, L. E., & Darling-Hammond, L. (2022). *Creating identity-safe schools and classrooms*. Learning Policy Institute. doi:10.54300/165.102

Hernández-Truyol, B. E. (1997). Borders (en)gendered: Normativities, Latinas, and a LatCrit paradigm. *New York University Law Review*, *72*, 882–927.

Hickman, C. B. (1997). The devil and the one drop rule: Racial categories, African Americans, and the U.S. Census. *Michigan Law Review*, *5*(95), 1161–1265. doi:10.2307/1290008

Higgins, C. (2009). English as a local language: Post-colonial identities and multilingual practices *Multilingual Matters 2*.

Hill Collins, P., & Bilge, S. (2020). *Intersectionality*. Polity Press.

Holliday, N. (2019). Multiracial identity and racial complexity in sociolinguistic variation. *Language and Linguistics Compass*, *13*(8), 1–12. doi:10.1111/lnc3.12345

Holliday, N. R., & Squires, L. (2021). Sociolinguistic labor, linguistic climate, and race (ism) on campus: Black college students' experiences with language at predominantly white institutions. *Journal of Sociolinguistics*, *25*(3), 418–437. doi:10.1111/josl.12438

Hollinger, D. (2003). Amalgamation and hypodescent: The question of ethnoracial mixture in the history of the United States. *The American Historical Review*, *108*(5), 1363–1390. doi:10.1086/529971

hooks, b. (1994). *Teaching to transgress: Education as the practice of freedom*. Routledge.

Horn, C., Burnett, C., Lowery, S., & White, C. (2021). *Texas Teacher Workforce Report*. https://www.raiseyourhandtexas.org/wp-content/uploads/2020/11/Texas-Teacher-Workforce-Report.pdf

Horner, B., Lu, M. Z., Royster, J. J., & Trimbur, J. (2011). Language difference in writing: Toward a translingual approach. *College English*, *73*(3), 303–321.

Horsford, S. D., Grosland, T., & Gunn, K. M. (2011). Pedagogy of the personal and professional: Toward a framework for culturally relevant leadership. *Journal of School Leadership*, *21*(4), 582–606. doi:10.1177/105268461102100404

Ho, W. Y. J. (2023). Discursive construction of online teacher identity and legitimacy in English language teaching. *Learning, Media and Technology*, 1–16. doi:10.1080/17439884.2023.2259295

Howard, R. M. (1995). Plagiarisms, authorships, and the academic death penalty. *College English*, *57*(7), 788–806. doi:10.2307/378403

Howell, N. G., Navickas, K., Shapiro, R., Shapiro, S., & Watson, M. (2020, June). Embracing the perpetual 'but' in raciolinguistic justice work: When idealism meets practice. In *Composition Forum 44*. Association of Teachers of Advanced Composition.

Huber, L. P., Lopez, C. B., Malagon, M., Velez, V., & Solorzano, D. G. (2008). Getting beyond the "symptom," acknowledging the "disease": Theorizing nativism. *Contemporary Justice Review: Issues in Criminal, Social, and Restorative Justice*, *11*(1), 39-51. https://www.tandfonline.com/doi/full/10.1080/10282580701850397

Hudley, C., & Mallinson, C. (2014). *We do language: English language variation in the secondary English classroom*. Teachers College Press.

Hunjeri, N. (2015). *Broken English*. Poetry Soup. https://www.poetrysoup.com/poem/broken_english_642543

Huo, X. Y. (2020). *Higher education internationalization and English language instruction: Intersectionality of race and language in Canadian universities*. Springer. doi:10.1007/978-3-030-60599-5

Hurie, A. H., & Callahan, R. M. (2019). Integration as perpetuation: Learning from race evasive approaches to ESL program reform. *Teachers College Record*, *121*(9), 1–38. doi:10.1177/016146811912100904 PMID:32508373

Hurtado, A. (1996). *The color of privilege: Three blasphemies on race and feminism*. University of Michigan Press. doi:10.3998/mpub.9839

Hymes, D. (1996). *Ethnography, linguistics, narrative inequality: Toward an understanding of voice* (1st ed.). Taylor & Francis. doi:10.4324/9780203211816

Hyon, S. (2018). *Introducing genre and English for specific purposes* (1st ed.). Routledge. doi:10.4324/9781315761152

Inoue, A. (2015). *Antiracist Writing Assessment Ecologies: Teaching and Assessing Writing for a Socially Just Future*. WAC Clearinghouse/University of Colorado Press. doi:10.37514/PER-B.2015.0698

Inoue, A. B. (2017). *Antiracist writing assessment ecologies: Teaching and assessing writing for a socially just future*. WAC Clearninghouse.

Inoue, A. B. (2019a). 2019 CCCC chair's letter: How do we language so people stop killing each other, or what do we do about white language supremacy? *College Composition and Communication, 71*(2), 370–379. doi:10.58680/ccc201930428

Inoue, A. B. (2019b). Classroom writing assessment as an antiracist practice: Confronting white supremacy in the judgments of language. *Pedagogy, 19*(3), 373–404. doi:10.1215/15314200-7615366

Inoue, M. (2003). The listening subject of Japanese modernity and his auditory double: Citing, sighting, and siting the modern Japanese woman. *Cultural Anthropology, 18*(2), 156–193. doi:10.1525/can.2003.18.2.156

Jack, D., & Nyman, J. (2019). Meeting labor market needs for French as a second language instruction in Ontario. *American Journal of Educational Research, 7*(7), 428–438. doi:10.12691/education-7-7-1

Jain, R. (2022). Translingual-identity-as-pedagogy: Problematizing monolingually oriented "native-nonnative" identity constructions through critical dialogues in EAP classrooms. *TESOL Journal, 13*(3), e666. Advance online publication. doi:10.1002/tesj.666

James, M. A. (2009). "Far" transfer of learning outcomes from an ESL writing course: Can the gap be bridged? *Journal of Second Language Writing, 18*(2), 69–84. doi:10.1016/j.jslw.2009.01.001

Janks, H. (2000). Domination, access, diversity, and design: A synthesis model of critical literacy education. *Educational Review, 52*(2), 175–186. doi:10.1080/713664035

Janks, H. (2004). The access paradox. *Literacy Learning: The Middle Years, 12*(1), 33–42.

Johnson, C. I. (2010). Still rising: An intricate look at black female slaves. In D. R. Haggard (Ed.), *African Americans in the Nineteenth Century* (pp. 33–45). Bloomsbury Publishing USA. doi:10.5040/9798400608025.ch-003

Johnson, J. G. (1931). The founding of the Spanish colonies in Georgia and South Carolina. *The Georgia Historical Quarterly, 15*(4), 301–312. http://www.jstor.com/stable/40576145

Johnson, L. (2014). Culturally responsive leadership for community empowerment. *Multicultural Education Review, 6*(2), 145–170. doi:10.1080/2005615X.2014.11102915

Johnson, M. (2011). Racial literacy and the writing center. In L. Greenfield & K. Rowan (Eds.), *Writing centers and the new racism: A call for sustainable dialogue and change* (pp. 211–227). Utah State University Press. doi:10.2307/j.ctt4cgk6s.14

Johnson, M. A., & Chang, D. I. (2012). Balancing act: Addressing culture and gender in ESL classrooms. *Journal of Adult Education, 41*, 19–26.

Johnston, B. (2017). *English teaching and Protestant mission: The case of Lighthouse School*. Multilingual Matters.

Johnston, B., & Varghese, M. (2006). Neo-imperialism, evangelism, and ELT: Modernist missions and a postmodern profession. In J. Edge (Ed.), *Re-)locating TESOL in an age of empire* (pp. 195–207). Palgrave Macmillan.

Johnstone, M., & Lee, E. (2022). Education as a site for the Imperial project to preserve whiteness supremacy from the colonial era to the present: A critical analysis of international education policy in Canada. *Whiteness and Education, 7*(1), 1–17. doi:10.1080/23793406.2020.1784038

Jordan, W. D. (2014). Historical origins of the one-drop racial rule in the United States. *Journal of Critical Mixed Race Studies, 1*(1), 98–132. doi:10.5070/C811013867

Compilation of References

Kachru, B. B. (1986). *The alchemy of English: The spread, functions, and models of non-native Englishes* (1st ed.). Pergamon Institute of English.

Kachru, B. R. (1986). *The alchemy of English: The spread, functions, and models of non-native Englishes.* Pergamon Institute of English Oxford. doi:10.1080/13803611.2012.718488

Kapai, P. (2015). Status of ethnic minorities in Hong Kong 1997–2014. Hong Kong: Centre for Comparative and Public Law. Hong Kong University Press.

Kastoryano, R. (2000). Global trends and issues: Settlement, transnational communities and citizenship. *International Social Science Journal*, *52*(165), 307–312. doi:10.1111/1468-2451.00261

Keh, C. L. (1990). Feedback in the writing process: A model and methods for implementation. *ELT Journal*, *44*(4), 294–304. doi:10.1093/elt/44.4.294

Keicho, M. (2021). *Raciolinguistic socialization and subversion at a predominantly white institution* [Unpublished bachelor's thesis]. Swarthmore College.

Kelly, C., Kasperavicius, D., Duncan, D., Etherington, C., Giangregorio, L., Presseau, J., Sibley, K. M., & Straus, S. (2021). "Doing" or "using" intersectionality? Opportunities and challenges in incorporating intersectionality into knowledge translation theory and practice. *International Journal for Equity in Health*, *20*(187), 187. Advance online publication. doi:10.118612939-021-01509-z PMID:34419053

Kemper, D., Meyer, V., Van Rys, J., Sebranek, J., & Holditch, G. (2016). *Write 2: Paragraphs and essays* (Canadian ed.). Nelson Education.

Kendi, I. (2017). *Stamped from the beginning: The definite history of racist ideas in America.* Nation Books.

Kendi, I. X. (2019). *How to be an antiracist* (1st ed.). One World.

Kennedy, T., Joyce, I. M., & Ratcliffe, K. (2005). Whiteness studies. *Rhetoric Review*, *24*(4), 359–402. doi:10.120715327981rr2404_1

Kim, E. Y. (2019). English as a site of evangelical contact: A critical ethnography of missionary English teaching between South and North Koreans. *Journal of Language, Identity, and Education*, *18*(1), 10–24. doi:10.1080/15348458.2019.1575739

Kishimoto, K. (2018). Anti-racist pedagogy: From faculty's self-reflection to organizing within and beyond the classroom. *Race, Ethnicity and Education*, *21*(4), 540–554. doi:10.1080/13613324.2016.1248824

Kitajroonchai, N., Kitjaroonchai, T., & Sanitchai, P. (2022). The effects of process genre-based writing and process writing approaches on Asian EFL pre-university students' writing performance. *Journal of Language Teaching and Research*, *13*(4), 860–871. doi:10.17507/jltr.1304.19

Knoch, U. (2009). Diagnostic assessment of writing: A comparison of two rating scales. *Language Testing*, *26*(2), 275–304. doi:10.1177/0265532208101008

Kolchin, P. (2009). Whiteness studies. *Journal de la Société des Américanistes*, *95*(1), 117–163. doi:10.4000/jsa.10769

Kubota, R. (2001). Discursive construction of the images of U.S. classrooms. *TESOL Quarterly*, *35*(1), 9–38. doi:10.2307/3587858

Kubota, R. (2021). Critical antiracist pedagogy in ELT. *ELT Journal*, *75*(3), 237–246. doi:10.1093/elt/ccab015

Kubota, R. (2022). Decolonizing second language writing: Possibilities and challenges. *Journal of Second Language Writing*, *58*, 100946. doi:10.1016/j.jslw.2022.100946

Kubota, R., & Lin, A. (2009). *Race, culture, and identities in second language education: Exploring critically engaged practice*. Routledge. doi:10.4324/9780203876657

Kubota, R., & Lin, A. M. Y. (2006). Race and TESOL: Introduction to concepts and theories. *TESOL Quarterly*, *40*(3), 471–493. doi:10.2307/40264540

Kuhlmann, A. (1992). American Indian women of the plains and Northern Woodlands. *Social Thought & Research*, *16*(1), 1–28. doi:10.17161/STR.1808.5083

Kumaravadivelu, B. (2003a). Problematizing cultural stereotypes in TESOL. *TESOL Quarterly*, *37*(4), 709–719. doi:10.2307/3588219

Kumaravadivelu, B. (2003b). A postmethod perspective on English language teaching. *World Englishes*, *22*(4), 539–550. doi:10.1111/j.1467-971X.2003.00317.x

Kumashiro, K. K. (2000). Toward a theory of anti-oppressive education. *Review of Educational Research*, *70*(1), 25–53. doi:10.3102/00346543070001025

Kunnas, R. M. (2019). *Inequities in black et blanc: Textual constructions of the French immersion student* [Unpublished master's thesis]. University of Toronto.

Lachenicht, S., Henneton, L., & Lignereux, Y. (2016). Spiritual geopolitics in the early modern imperial age. An introduction. *Itinerario*, *40*(2), 181–187. doi:10.1017/S0165115316000309

Ladson-Billings, G. (2020). Just what is critical race theory and what's it doing in a nice field like education? In L. Parker & D. Gillborn (Eds.), Critical race theory in education (pp. 9–26). Routledge. doi:10.4324/9781003005995-2

Ladson-Billings, G. J. (1999). Preparing teachers for diverse student populations: A critical race theory perspective. *Review of Research in Education*, *24*, 211–247. doi:10.2307/1167271

Ladson-Billings, G. (1995b). Toward a theory of culturally relevant pedagogy. *American Educational Research Journal*, *32*(3), 465–491. doi:10.3102/00028312032003465

Ladson-Billings, G. (2014). Culturally relevant pedagogy 2.0: A.k.a. the remix. *Harvard Educational Review*, *84*(1), 74–84. doi:10.17763/haer.84.1.p2rj131485484751

Ladson-Billings, G. (2021). *Culturally relevant pedagogy: Asking a different question*. Teachers College Press.

Ladson-Billings, G., & Tate, W. F. (1995a). Toward a critical race theory of education. *Teachers College Record*, *97*(1), 47–68. doi:10.1177/016146819509700104

Lah, M. (2017). "Vous avez un petit accent": Enseignement de la prononciation aux apprenants de Français langue étrangère. *Lingüística*, *57*(1), 171–183. doi:10.4312/linguistica.57.1.171-183

Lane, J., & Lam, E. (2021). *This new SFU writing guide champions inclusivity*. Retrieved from https://www.sfu.ca/sfunews/stories/2021/04/this-new-sfu-writing-guide-champions-inclusivity.html

Lassiter, L. (2005a). Collaborative ethnography and public anthropology. *Current Anthropology*, *46*(1), 83–106. doi:10.1086/425658

Lassiter, L. E. (2021). Collaborative ethnography. In B. Diamond, S. Castelo-Branco, & S. Castelo-Branco (Eds.), *Transforming Ethnomusicology* (Vol. 2). Oxford University Press. doi:10.1093/oso/9780197517604.003.0004

Compilation of References

Lave, J., & Wenger, E. (1991). *Situated learning: Legitimate peripheral participation*. Cambridge University Press. doi:10.1017/CBO9780511815355

Lavoie, C. (2015). Trois stratégies efficaces pour enseigner le vocabulaire: Une expérience en contexte scolaire innu. *Canadian Journal of Applied Linguistics*, *18*(1), 1–20.

Lawrence, L., & Nagashima, Y. (2020). The Intersectionality of gender, sexuality, race, and native-speakerness: Investigating ELT teacher identity through duoethnography. *Journal of Language, Identity, and Education*, *19*(1), 42–55. doi:10.1080/15348458.2019.1672173

Lee, C. D. (2017). An Ecological framework for enacting culturally sustaining pedagogy. In D. Paris & H. S. Alim (Eds.), Culturally sustaining pedagogies: Teaching and learning for justice in a changing world (pp. 261–73). Teachers College Press.

Lee, T. S., & McCarty, T. L. (2017). Upholding Indigenous education sovereignty through critical culturally sustaining/revitalizing pedagogy. In D. Paris & H. S. Alim (Eds.), Culturally sustaining pedagogies: Teaching and learning for justice in a changing world (pp. 61–82). Teachers College Press.

Lee, E. (2015). Doing culture, doing race: Everyday discourses of 'culture' and 'cultural difference' in the English as a second language classroom. *Journal of Multilingual and Multicultural Development*, *36*(1), 80–93. doi:10.1080/01434632.2014.892503

Lee, E., & Alvarez, S. P. (2020). World Englishes, translingualism, and racialization in the US college composition classroom. *World Englishes*, *39*(2), 263–274. doi:10.1111/weng.12459

Lee, J. W. (2017). *The politics of translingualism: After Englishes*. Routledge. doi:10.4324/9781315310534

Leibowitz, B., Goodman, K., Hannon, P., & Parkerson, A. (1997). The role of a writing center in increasing access to academic discourse in a multilingual university. *Teaching in Higher Education*, *2*(1), 5–19. doi:10.1080/1356251970020101

Leitch, R. (2006). Limitations of language: Developing arts-based creative narrative in stories of teachers' identities. *Teachers and Teaching*, *12*(5), 549–569. doi:10.1080/13540600600832270

Lemke, J. L. (1995). *Textual politics: Discourse and social dynamics*. Taylor & Francis.

Lewis, C. S. (1956). *Surprised by joy: The shape of my early life*. Harcourt Brace.

LiG. (2018). From stigma to strength: A case of ESL program transformation in a greater Vancouver high school. *BC TEAL Journal*, *3*(1), 63–76. https://doi.org/ doi:10.14288/bctj.v3i1.303

Liggett, T. (2009). Unpacking white racial identity in English language teacher education. In R. Kubota & A. Lin (Eds.), *Race, culture, and identities in second language education: Exploring critically engaged practice* (pp. 27–43). Routledge.

Liggett, T. (2010, September). Postpositivist realist theory of identity: Expanding notions of gender in teacher education. *Journal of Curriculum Theorizing*, *26*(2), 90–101.

Liggett, T. (2014). The mapping of a framework: Critical race theory and TESOL. *The Urban Review*, *46*(1), 112–124. doi:10.100711256-013-0254-5

Liggett, T., Watson, D., & Griffin, L. (2017, March). Language use and racial redirect in the educational landscape of "just good teaching." *Teaching Education*, *28*(4), 393–405. doi:10.1080/10476210.2017.1306506

Lillis, T., & Tuck, J. (2016). Academic Literacies: A critical lens on writing and reading in the academy. In K. Hyland & P. Shaw (Eds.), The Routledge handbook of English for Academic Purposes (pp. 30–43). Routledge.

Lillis, T., Harrington, K., Lea, M. R., & Mitchell, S. (Eds.). (2015). *Working with academic literacies: Case studies towards transformative practice*. The WAC Clearinghouse. https://wac.colostate.edu/books/perspectives/lillis/

Lim, J., & Polio, C. (2020). Multimodal assignments in higher education: Implications for multimodal writing tasks for L2 writers. *Journal of Second Language Writing, 47*, 100713. doi:10.1016/j.jslw.2020.100713

Lin H. (2018). *Super-diversity*. doi:10.6191/JPS.201812_57.0003

Lin, A. M. (2020). From deficit-based teaching to asset-based teaching in higher education in BANA countries: Cutting through 'either-or' binaries with a heteroglossic plurilingual lens. *Language, Culture and Curriculum, 33*(2), 203–212. doi:10.1080/07908318.2020.1723927

Lippi-Green, R. (1997). *English with an accent: Language, ideology, and discrimination in the United States*. Routledge.

Lippi-Green, R. (2012). *English with an accent. Language, ideology, and discrimination in the United States* (2nd ed.). Routledge. doi:10.4324/9780203348802

Liu, J. (2018). Cultivation of critical thinking abilities in English writing teaching. *Theory and Practice in Language Studies, 8*(8), 982–987. doi:10.17507/tpls.0808.09

Loden, M., & Rosener, J. (1990). *Workforce America! Managing employee diversity as a vital resource*. McGraw-Hill Professional Publishing.

Lopez, A. E. (2015). Navigating cultural borders in diverse contexts: Building capacity through culturally responsive leadership and critical praxis. *Multicultural Education Review, 7*(3), 171–184. doi:10.1080/2005615X.2015.1072080

Lowe, R. J., & Kiczkowiak, M. (2016). Native-speakerism and the complexity of personal experience: A duoethnographic study. *Cogent Education, 3*(1), 2–16. doi:10.1080/2331186X.2016.1264171

Lucas, T., & Villegas, A. M. (2013). Preparing linguistically responsive teachers: Laying the foundation in preservice teacher education. *Theory into Practice, 52*(2), 98–109. doi:10.1080/00405841.2013.770327

Macfarlane, B., Zhang, J., & Pun, A. (2014). Academic integrity: A review of the literature. *Studies in Higher Education, 39*(2), 339–358. doi:10.1080/03075079.2012.709495

Madibbo, A. (2021). *Blackness and la Francophonie: Anti-black racism, linguicism and the construction and negotiation of multiple minority identities*. Presses de l'Université Laval. doi:10.2307/j.ctv23khnb5

Mahboob, A., & Szenes, E. (2007). Linguicism and racism in assessment practices in higher education. *Linguistics and the Human Sciences, 3*(3), 325–354. doi:10.1558/lhs.v3i3.325

Makoni, S., & Pennycook, A. (Eds.). (2006). *Disinventing and reconstituting languages*. Multilingual Matters. doi:10.21832/9781853599255

Makropoulos, J. (2004). Speak White! Language and race in the social construction of Frenchness in Canada. In C. Nelson & C. Nelson (Eds.), Racism, eh? A critical inter-disciplinary anthology of race and racism in Canada (pp. 242-257). Captus Press.

MaoJ. (2021). Thriving through uncertainties: The agency and resourcefulness of first-year Chinese English as an additional language writers in a Canadian University. *BC TEAL Journal, 6*(1), 78–93. doi:10.14288/bctj.v6i1.390

Marginson, S., & Sawir, E. (2011). *Ideas for intercultural education*. Palgrave Macmillan.

Marinari, M., Hsu, M. Y., & Garcia, M. C. (Eds.). (2019). *A nation of immigrants reconsidered: US society in an age of restriction 1924–1965*. University of Illinois Press.

Marshall, S., & Walsh Marr, J. (2018). Teaching multilingual learners in canadian writing-intensive classrooms: Pedagogy, binaries, and conflicting identities. *Journal of Second Language Writing*, *40*, 32–43. doi:10.1016/j.jslw.2018.01.002

Martinez, A. Y. (2014a). A plea for critical race theory counterstory: Stock story versus counterstory dialogues concerning Alejandra's 'fit' in the academy. *Composition Studies*, *42*(2), 33–55.

Martínez, A. Y. (2020b). Counterstory: The rhetoric and writing of critical race theory. *Conference on College Composition and Communication & the National Council of Teachers of English*.

Martínez, R. A. (2018). Beyond the *English learner* label: Recognizing the richness of bi/multilingual students' linguistic repertoires. *The Reading Teacher*, *71*(5), 515–522. doi:10.1002/trtr.1679

Marx, S. (2004). Regarding Whiteness: Exploring and intervening in the effects of White racism in teacher education. *Equity & Excellence in Education*, *37*(1), 31–43. doi:10.1080/10665680490422089

Marx, S., & Pray, L. (2011). Living and learning in Mexico: Developing empathy for English language learners through study abroad. *Race, Ethnicity and Education*, *14*(4), 507–535. doi:10.1080/13613324.2011.558894

Massey, D. (1994). *Space, place, and gender*. University of Minnesota Press.

Masson, M., Grant, R., & Keunne, E., & Carroll, S. (2023, April 13). *Anticolonial feminist critical discourse analysis: Race, gender, culture and capitalism in the second language curriculum*. American Educational Research Association (AERA).

Masson, M., Larson, E. J., Desgroseilliers, P., Carr, W., & Lapkin, S. (2019). *Accessing opportunity: A study on challenges in French-as-a-second-language education teacher supply and demand in Canada*. Office of the Commissioner of Official Languages. https://www.clo-ocol.gc.ca/en/publications/studies-other-reports/2019/accessing-opportunity-study-challenges-french-second

Masson, M. (2018). Reframing FSL teacher learning: Small stories of (re) professionalization and identity formation. *Journal of Belonging, Identity, Language, and Diversity*, *2*(2), 77–102.

Masson, M., Knouzi, I., Arnott, S., & Lapkin, S. (2021). A critical interpretive synthesis of post-millennial Canadian French as a second language research across stakeholders and programs. *Canadian Modern Language Review*, *77*(2), 154–188. doi:10.3138/cmlr-2020-0025

Masson, M., Kunnas, M., Boreland, T., & Prasad, G. (2022). Developing an anti-biased, anti-racist stance in second language teacher education programs. *Canadian Modern Language Review*, *78*(4), 385–414. doi:10.3138/cmlr-2021-0100

Masuhara, H. (2011). What do teachers really want from coursebooks? In B. Tomlinson (Ed.), *Materials development in language teaching* (pp. 236–266). Cambridge University Press. doi:10.1017/9781139042789.013

Masuoka, N. (2018). *Multiracial identity and racial politics in the United States*. Oxford University Press.

Matias, C. E. (2013). Check yo'self before you wreck yo'self and our kids: Counterstories from culturally responsive White teachers? ... to culturally responsive White teachers! *Interdisciplinary Journal of Teaching and Learning*, *3*(2), 68–81.

Matias, C. E. (2016). *Feeling White: Whiteness, emotionality, and education*. Sense Publishers. doi:10.1007/978-94-6300-450-3

Matsuda, A. (2002), International understanding through teaching world Englishes. *World Englishes*, *21*, 436-440. doi:10.1111/1467-971X.00262

Matsuda, P. K. (2013). It's the wild west out there: A new linguistic frontier in US college composition. *Literacy as Translingual Practice: Between Communities and Classrooms*, *6*(2), 128-138.

Matsuda, A. (Ed.). (2017). *Preparing teachers to teach English as an international language*. Multilingual Matters. doi:10.21832/9781783097036

Matsuda, P. K. (1998). Situating ESL: Writing in a cross-disciplinary context. *Written Communication*, *15*(1), 99–121. doi:10.1177/0741088398015001004

Matsuda, P. K. (2006). The myth of linguistic homogeneity in U.S. college composition. *College English*, *68*(6), 637–651. doi:10.2307/25472180

May, R. A. B., & Pattillo-McCoy, M. (2000). Do you see what I see? Examining a collaborative ethnography. *Qualitative Inquiry*, *6*(1), 65–87. doi:10.1177/107780040000600105

Mbirimi-Hungwe, V. (2021). Translanguaging as an act of emancipation: rethinking assessment tools in multilingual pedagogy in South Africa. *Per Linguam*, *37*(1), 97-108.

McKibbin, M. L. (2014). The current state of multiracial discourse. *Journal of Critical Mixed Race Studies*, *1*(1). Advance online publication. doi:10.5070/C811012861

McLeod, S. (1992). Writing across the curriculum: An introduction. In S. McLeod & M. Soven (Eds.), *Writing across the curriculum: A guide to developing programs* (pp. 1–11). Sage.

McMurtry, T., & Williamson, T. (2021). With liberty and Black linguistic justice for all: Pledging allegiance to anti-racist language pedagogy. *Journal of Adolescent & Adult Literacy*, *65*(2), 175–178. doi:10.1002/jaal.1187

McPherron, P., & An, L. (2023). Supporting Asian American multilingual college students through critical language awareness programming. *Journal of Language, Identity, and Education*, *22*(4), 340–358. doi:10.1080/15348458.2023.2202587

Meighan, P. J. (2023). Colonialingualism: Colonial legacies, imperial mindsets, and inequitable practices in English language education. *Diaspora, Indigenous, and Minority Education*, *17*(2), 146–155. doi:10.1080/15595692.2022.2082406

Meissner, F., & Vertovec, S. (2014). Comparing super-diversity. *Ethnic and Racial Studies*, *38*(4), 541–555. doi:10.1080/01419870.2015.980295

Melo-Pfeifer, S. M. (2019). Comprendre les représentations des enseignants de langues à travers des récits visuels. La mise en images du développement professionnel des futurs enseignants de français langue étrangère. *EL. LE*, *8*(3), 587-610.

Menchaca, M. (2008). The anti-miscegenation history of the American southwest, 1837 To 1970: Transforming racial ideology into law. *Cultural Dynamics*, *20*(3), 279–318. doi:10.1177/0921374008096312

Mendoza, B. (2016). Coloniality of gender and power: From postcoloniality to decoloniality. In L. Disch & M. Hawkesworth (Eds.), *The Oxford handbook of feminist theory* (pp. 100–121). Oxford University Press.

Menezes de Oliveira e Paiva, V. L. (2016). Language teaching identity: A fractal system. In G. Barkhuizen (Ed.), Reflections on language teacher identity research (pp. 258-263). Routledge.

Mertova, P., & Webster, L. (2020). *Using narrative inquiry as research method: An introduction to critical event narrative analysis in research, teaching and professional practice*. Routledge.

Migration Policy Institute. (n.d.). [Frequently Requested Statistics-Immigrants Now Historically]. Retrieved May 5, 2023, from https://www.migrationpolicy.org/article/frequently-requested-statistics-immigrants-and-immigration-united-states#immigrants_now_historically

Migration Policy Institute. (n.d.-a). *Largest Immigrant Groups Over Time*. Retrieved May 5, 2023, from https://www.migrationpolicy.org/programs/data-hub/charts/largest-immigrant-groups-over-time

Compilation of References

Migration Policy Institute. (n.d.-b). *Frequently Requested Statistics-Demographic-Educational-Linguistic.* Retrieved May 17, 2023, from https://www.migrationpolicy.org/article/frequently-requested-statistics-immigrants-and-immigration-united-states-2020#demographic-educational-linguistic

Migration Policy Institute. (n.d.-c). *ELL Information Center.* Retrieved June, 21, 2023, from https://www.migrationpolicy.org/programs/ell-information-center

Migration Policy Institute. (n.d.-d). *ELs K-12 per State.* Retrieved on July 13, 2023, from https://www.migrationpolicy.org/programs/data-hub/charts/english-learners-k-12-education-state

Migration Policy Institute. (n.d.-e). *Immigrant Population Metro Area.* Retrieved July 13, 2023 from https://www.migrationpolicy.org/programs/data-hub/charts/us-immigrant-population-metropolitan-area?width=1000&height=850&iframe=true

Miles, R., & Brown, M. (2003). *Racism* (2nd ed.). Routledge.

Miller, J. (2009). Teacher identity. In A. Burns & J. Richards (Eds.), *The Cambridge guide to second language teacher education* (pp. 172–181). Cambridge University Press. doi:10.1017/9781139042710.023

Milner, H. R. IV. (2007). Race, culture, and researcher positionality: Working through dangers seen, unseen, and unforeseen. *Educational Researcher*, *36*(7), 388–400. doi:10.3102/0013189X07309471

Milner, H. R. IV. (2020). *Start where you are, but don't stay there* (2nd ed.). Harvard Education Press.

Milson-Whyte, V., & Campbell, A. (2022, December). Neoliberal influences and academic writing student support systems in higher education. *UWI Quality Education Forum*, *26*, 119-145.

Minority Rights Group International. (2020). *Linguistic rights.* Minority Rights Group. https://minorityrights.org/law/linguistic-rights/

Mishan, F. (2022). Language learning materials in the digital era. In J. Norton & H. Buchanan (Eds.), *The Routledge handbook of materials development for language teaching* (pp. 17–29). Routledge. doi:10.4324/b22783-3

Mitchum, C., Hebbard, M., & Morris, J. Expanding instructional contexts: Why student backgrounds matter to online teaching and learning. In W. P. Banks & S. Spanger (Eds.), *English Studies Online: Programs, Practices, Possibilities* (pp. 232–257). Parlor Press.

Molinié, M. (2009). *Le dessin réflexif: élément d'une herméneutique du sujet plurilingue.* Encrages-Belles Lettres.

Molinié, M. (2011). *Démarches portfolio en didactique des langues et des cultures. Enjeux de formation par la recherche-action.* Encrages-Belles Lettres.

Moran, K. M., & Henderson, E. (2022). *The empowered writer: An essential guide to writing, reading and research* (4th ed.). Oxford University Press.

Morgan, B. (2004). Teacher identity as pedagogy: Towards a field-internal conceptualisation in bilingual and second language education. *International Journal of Bilingual Education and Bilingualism*, *7*(2-3), 172–188. doi:10.1080/13670050408667807

Motha, S. (2014). *Race, Empire, and English Language Teaching.* Teacher College Press.

Motha, S. (2014). *Race, empire, and English language teaching.* Teachers College Press.

Motha, S. (2014). *Race, empire, and English language teaching: Creating responsible and ethical anti-racist practice.* Teachers College Press.

Motha, S., Jain, R., & Tecle, T. (2012). Translinguistic identity-as-pedagogy: Implications for language teacher education. *International Journal of Innovation in English Language Teaching, 1*(1), 13–28.

Motha, S., & Lin, A. (2014). "Non-coercive rearrangements": Theorizing desire in TESOL. *TESOL Quarterly, 48*(2), 331–359. doi:10.1002/tesq.126

Moussu, L. (2013). Let's talk! ESL students' needs and writing center philosophy. *TESL Canada Journal, 30*(2), 55–68. doi:10.18806/tesl.v30i2.1142

Moussu, L., & Llurda, E. (2008). Non-native English-speaking English language teachers: History and research. *Language Teaching, 41*(3), 315–348. doi:10.1017/S0261444808005028

Muramatsu, C. (2018). *Portraits of second language learners: An L2 learner agency perspective*. Multilingual Matters. doi:10.21832/9781783099887

Musanti, S. I. (2014). "Porque sé los dos idiomas:" Biliteracy beliefs and bilingual preservice teacher identity. In Y. Freeman & D. Freeman (Eds.), *Research on preparing preservice teachers to work effectively with emergent bilinguals*. Emerald Group Publishing Limited. doi:10.1108/S1479-368720140000021002

Nagatomo, D. H. (2012). *Exploring Japanese university English teachers' professional identity*. Multilingual Matters. doi:10.21832/9781847696489

Nallaya, S., Hobson, J. E., & Ulpen, T. (2022). An investigation of first year university students' confidence in using academic literacies. *Issues in Educational Research, 32*(1), 264–291.

Natarajan, S., & Pez, E. (2023a). *Random university sample of Universities Canada member institutions Year 1 writing*. https://docs.google.com/spreadsheets/d/1nq6zrXcoNrkJPRvojkdcfo71G_b_nO5gEyMhUT4ApBQ/edit?usp=sharing

Natarajan, S., & Pez, E. (2023b). *Writing textbook analysis*. https://docs.google.com/document/d/1YEuR0rkquSefZyv5UiyB_ii08DNuONNb/edit?usp=sharing&ouid=107777330223027431718&rtpof=true&sd=true

Natarajan, S. (2019a). How I learned to think critically: A reflection on culture and writing identity. In S. Natarajan (Ed.), *Thinking about writing* (pp. 4–5).

Natarajan, S. (2019b). LEP, ESL, ELL, EL, or multilingual? Resisting the deficit model. In S. Natarajan (Ed.), *Thinking about writing* (pp. 15–17).

Natarajan, S., Cardona, V. G., Bondi, J., & Yang, T. (2023). What's on our landing page? Writing center policy commonplaces and antiracist critique. *Peer Review : Emerging Trends and Key Debates in Undergraduate Education, 1*(7). https://thepeerreview-iwca.org/issues/issue-7-1-featured-issue-reinvestigate-the-commonplaces-in-writing-centers/whats-on-our-landing-page-writing-center-policy-commonplaces-and-antiracist-critique/

National Center for Children in Poverty. (n.d.). *Children Living in Poverty*. Retrieved July, 7, 2021, from www.nccp.org

National Center for Education Statistics. (n.d.). *English Learners in Public Schools*. Retrieved May, 17, 2023, from https://nces.ed.gov/programs/coe/indicator/cgf

Ndhlovu, F., & Makalela, L. (2021). *Decolonizing multilingualism in Africa*. Multilingual Matters. doi:10.21832/9781788923361-006

Ndura, E. (2004). ESL and cultural bias: An analysis of elementary through high school textbooks in the Western United States of America. *Language, Culture and Curriculum, 17*(2), 143–153. doi:10.1080/07908310408666689

Nieto, S. (2015). Language, literacy, and culture: Aha! moments in personal and sociopolitical understanding. In B. Porfilio & D. R. Ford (Eds.), *Leaders in Critical Pedagogy* (pp. 37–48). Sense Publishers. doi:10.1007/978-94-6300-166-3_3

Compilation of References

Noddings, N. (2012). The caring relation in teaching. *Oxford Review of Education*, *38*(6), 771–781. doi:10.1080/03054985.2012.745047

Norton, B. (2013). *Identity and language learning: Extending the conversation* (2nd ed.). Multilingual Matters. doi:10.21832/9781783090563

O'Regan, J. P. (2021). *Global English and political economy*. Routledge. doi:10.4324/9781315749334

Office of the Commissioner of Official Languages. (2022). *Cross-Canada Official Languages Consultation 2022*. https://www.canada.ca/en/canadian-heritage/campaigns/consultation-official-languages-2022/report.html

Omi, M., & Winant, H. (1994). *Racial formation in the United States from the 1960s to the 1990s* (2nd ed.). Routledge.

Omi, M., & Winant, H. (2015). *Racial formation in the United States*. Routledge.

Ong, A. (1999). *Flexible citizenship: The cultural logics of transnationality*. Duke University Press.

Organization for Security and Co-operation in Europe. (1999). *Report on the linguistic rights of persons belonging to national minorities in the OSCE area. + Annex*. Replies from OSCE Participating States. OSCE High Commissioner on National Minorities.

Orr, L., & Weekley, L. (2019). Teaching with case studies in higher education. In A. Baron & K. McNeal (Eds.), *Case study methodology in higher education* (pp. 180–208). IGI Global. doi:10.4018/978-1-5225-9429-1.ch009

Pablo, R., & Christian, F. (2023). Re-Exploring translanguaging in teacher education. *Language and Education*, *37*(5), 551–556. doi:10.1080/09500782.2023.2240299

Padilla, L. V., & Vana, R. (2019). Ideologies in the foreign language curriculum: Insights from textbooks and instructor interviews. *Language Awareness*, *28*(1), 15–30. doi:10.1080/09658416.2019.1590376

Pang, M. (2016). Pedagogical reasoning in EFL/ESL teaching: Revisiting the importance of teaching lesson planning in second language teacher education. *TESOL Quarterly*, *50*(1), 246–263. doi:10.1002/tesq.283

Paris, D. (2021). Culturally sustaining pedagogies and our futures. *The Educational Forum*, *85*(4), 364-376. 10.1080/00131725.2021.1957634

Paris, D., & Alim, H. S. (2017). What is culturally sustaining pedagogy and why does it matter? In D. Paris & H. S. Alim (Eds.), Culturally sustaining pedagogies: Teaching and learning for justice in a changing world (pp. 1–21). Teachers College Press.

Paris, D. (2012). Culturally sustaining pedagogy: A needed change in stance, terminology, and practice. *Educational Researcher*, *41*(3), 93–97. doi:10.3102/0013189X12441244

Paris, D., & Alim, H. S. (2014). What are we seeking to sustain through culturally sustaining pedagogy? A loving critique forward. *Harvard Educational Review*, *84*(1), 85–100. doi:10.17763/haer.84.1.982l873k2ht16m77

Paris, D., & Alim, H. S. (2017). *Culturally sustaining pedagogies: Teaching and learning for justice in a changing world*. Teacher College Press.

Paris, D., & Alim, H. S. (2017). *Culturally Sustaining Pedagogies: Teaching and learning for justice in a changing world*. Teachers College Press.

Parker, B. A. [Host] (2022, July 20). *Who belongs to the Cherokee nation?* Codeswitch. National Public Radio. Retrieved on August 1, 2023 from https://www.npr.org/transcripts/1110422542

Park, G., Bogdan, S., Rosa, M., & Navarro, J. M. (Eds.). (2023). *Critical pedagogy in the language and writing classroom: Strategies, examples, activities from teacher-scholars*. Routledge. doi:10.4324/9781003357001

Pascoe, P. (1996). Miscegenation law, court cases, and ideologies of "race" in twentieth-century America. *The Journal of American History, 83*(1), 44–69. doi:10.2307/2945474

Pascoe, P. (2009). *What comes naturally: Miscegenation law and the making of race in America*. Oxford University Press. doi:10.1093/oso/9780195094633.001.0001

Patel, L. L. (2014). Countering coloniality in educational research: From ownership to answerability. *Educational Studies (Ames), 50*(4), 357–377. doi:10.1080/00131946.2014.924942

Patton, L. D., Renn, K. A., Guido, F. M., Quaye, J. S., & Evans, N. J. (2016). *Student Development in College: Theory, Research, and Practice* (3rd ed.). Jossey-Bass.

Paulsrud, B., & Rosén, J. (2019). Translanguaging and Language Ideologies in Education: Northern and Southern Perspectives. In S. Brunn & R. Kehrein (Eds.), *Handbook of the changing world language map*. Springer. doi:10.1007/978-3-319-73400-2_124-1

Pavlenko, A. (2002). Bilingualism and emotions. *Journal of Cross-Cultural and Interlanguage Communication, 21*(1), 4-78. doi:10.1515/mult.2002.004

Paz, M. (2014). The Tower of Babel: Human rights and the paradox of language. *European Journal of International Law, 25*(2), 473–496. doi:10.1093/ejil/chu037

Pennycook, A. (2002). *English and the discourses of colonialism*. Routledge., doi:10.4324/9780203006344

Pennycook, A. (2012). *Language and mobility: Unexpected places*. Multilingual Matters. doi:10.21832/9781847697653

Pennycook, A. (2017). *The cultural politics of English as an international language*. Routledge. doi:10.4324/9781315225593

Pennycook, A., & Makoni, S. (2005). The modern mission: The language effects of Christianity. *Journal of Language, Identity, and Education, 4*(2), 137–155. doi:10.120715327701jlie0402_5

Peregoy, S. F., & Boyle, O. F. (2016). *Reading, writing, and learning in ESL: A resource book for teaching K-12 English learners* (7th ed.). Pearson.

Perera, S. B. (1986). *Scapegoat complex: Toward a mythology of shadow and guilt*. Inner City Books.

Pérez Huber, L., Benavides Lopez, C., Malagón, M., Velez, V., & Solórzano, D. (2008). Getting beyond the "symptom," acknowledging the "disease": Theorizing racist nativism. *Contemporary Justice Review, 11*(1), 39–51. doi:10.1080/10282580701850397

Peter, C. (2005). Learning-whose responsibility is it? *Nurse Educator, 30*(4), 159–165. doi:10.1097/00006223-200507000-00008 PMID:16030452

Pez, E. (2023). *WRIT 1002F –Introduction to Writing in English* [Course outline]. King's University College. https://www.kings.uwo.ca/kings/assets/File/outlines/2023/writ/fall/writ_1002F_651_fall_2023.pdf

Pez, E. (2019). Case analysis: University students and plagiarism. In S. Natarajan (Ed.), *Thinking about writing* (pp. 8–11).

Phillipson, R. (1992). *Linguistic imperialism*. Oxford University Press.

Podesva, R. J. (2016). Stance as a window into the language-race connection. In H. S. Alim, J. R. Rickford, & A. F. Ball (Eds.), *Raciolinguistics: How language shapes our ideas about race* (pp. 203–220). Oxford University Press. doi:10.1093/acprof:oso/9780190625696.003.0012

Compilation of References

Poe, M. (2022). Learning to unlearn the teaching and assessment of academic writing. *Discourse and Writing/Rédactologie, 32*, 161-190.

Pollock, M. (2017). *Schooltalk: Rethinking what we say about and to students every day*. The New Press.

Porter, J. E., Sullivan, P., Blythe, S., Grabill, J. T., & Miles, L. (2000). Institutional Critique: A Rhetorical Methodology for Change. *College Composition and Communication, 51*(4), 610–642. doi:10.2307/358914

Portes, A., & Fumbaut, R. G. (2014). *Immigrant America: A portrait* (4th ed.). University of California Press. doi:10.1525/9780520959156

Pourghasemian, H., & Zarei, G. R. (2021). Adaptivity of learning transfer from theory to practice: A case study of second language writers. *Applied Research on English Language, 10*(4), 1–38. doi:10.22108/are.2021.126760.1675

Prada, J. (2019). Exploring the role of translanguaging in linguistic ideological and attitudinal reconfigurations in the Spanish classroom for heritage speakers. *Classroom Discourse, 10*(3-4).

Prada, J., & Turnbull, B. (2018). The role of translanguaging in the multilingual turn: Driving philosophical and conceptual renewal in language education. *EuroAmerican Journal of Applied Linguistics and Languages, 5*(2), 8–23. doi:10.21283/2376905X.9.151

Prendergast, C. (1998). Race: The absent presence in composition studies. *College Composition and Communication, 50*(1), 36–53. doi:10.2307/358351

Prince, Z. (2016, June 15). Eleven o'clock on Sundays is still the most segregated hour in America. *The Louisiana Weekly*. http://www.louisianaweekly.com/eleven-oclock-on-sundays-is-still-the-most-segregated-hour-in-america/

Quijano, A. (2000). Coloniality of power and Eurocentrism in Latin America. *International Sociology, 15*(2), 215–232. doi:10.1177/0268580900015002005

Ravindran, A., & Stouck, J. (2021, Aug. 5). Academic transition and navigation of multilingual students through writing across the curriculum: Building institutional connections through linguistically responsive curriculum design. *International Writing Across the Curriculum (IWAC) Conference*.

Rhodes, C. M. (2013). *Culturally responsive teaching practices of adult education English for speakers of other languages and English for academic purposes teachers* [Doctoral dissertation]. https://scholarcommons.usf.edu/etd/4568/

Richards, J. C. (2015, December 21). Competence and performance #10 – Pedagogical reasoning skills. In *World of better learning*. Cambridge University Press. https://www.cambridge.org/elt/blog/2015/12/21/competence-performance-10-pedagogical-reasoning-skills/

Riches, C., & Parks, P. (2021). Navigating linguistic identities: ESL teaching contexts in Quebec. *TESL Canada Journal, 38*(1), 28–48. doi:10.18806/tesl.v38i1.1367

Rieman, J., McCracken, I. M., Downs, D., & Bird, B. (Eds.). (2019). Next steps: New directions for/in writing about writing. Utah State University Press.

Risager, K. (2023). Analysing culture in language learning materials. *Language Teaching, 56*(1), 1–21. doi:10.1017/S0261444822000143

Rocafort, M. C. (2019). The development of plurilingual education through multimodal narrative reflection in teacher education: A case study of a pre-service teacher's beliefs about language education. *Canadian Modern Language Review, 75*(1), 40–64. doi:10.3138/cmlr.2017-0080

Rockquemore, K. A., Brunsma, D. L., & Delgado, D. J. (2009). Racing to theory or retheorizing race? Understanding the struggle to build a multiracial identity theory. *The Journal of Social Issues*, *65*(1), 13–34. doi:10.1111/j.1540-4560.2008.01585.x

Rodriguez, V., Drew, E., & Phillips, A. (2009-2014). *Anti-racist pedagogy across the curriculum workshop*. St. Cloud State University.

Rodríguez-García, D., Solana, M., Ortiz, A., & Ballestín, B. (2021). Blurring of colour lines? Ethnoracially mixed youth in Spain navigating identity. *Journal of Ethnic and Migration Studies*, *47*(4), 838–860. doi:10.1080/1369183X.2019.1654157

Roessingh, H., & Douglas, S. (2012). English language learners' transitional needs from high school to university: An exploratory study. *Journal of International Migration and Integration*, *13*(3), 285–301. doi:10.100712134-011-0202-8

Rogaly, B. (2020). *Stories from a migrant city: Living and working together in the shadow of Brexit*. Manchester University Press. ProQuest Ebook Central, https://ebookcentral.proquest.com/lib/linfield/detail.action?docID=6144184

Rogers, R. (Ed.). (2004). *An introduction to critical discourse analysis in education*. Lawrence Erlbaum Associates. doi:10.4324/9781410609786

Root, M. (1992). Racially mixed people in America. *Sage (Atlanta, Ga.)*.

Rosa, J., & Flores, N. (2017). Do you hear what I hear? Raciolinguistic ideologies and culturally sustaining pedagogies. In D. Paris & H. S. Alim (Eds.), Culturally sustaining pedagogies: Teaching and learning for justice in a changing world (pp. 175–190). Teachers College Press.

Rosa, J. (2016). Standardization, racialization, languagelessness: Raciolinguistic ideologies across communicative contexts. *Journal of Linguistic Anthropology*, *26*(2), 162–183. doi:10.1111/jola.12116

Rosa, J. (2018). *Looking like a language, sounding like a race: Raciolinguistic ideologies and the learning of latinidad*. Oxford University Press.

Rosa, J., & Flores, N. (2017). Unsettling race and language: Toward a raciolinguistic perspective. *Language in Society*, *46*(5), 621–647. doi:10.1017/S0047404517000562

Rosa, J., & Flores, N. (2021). Decolonization, language, and race in applied linguistics and social justice. *Applied Linguistics*, *42*(6), 1162–1167. doi:10.1093/applin/amab062

Rothenberg, P. S. (Ed.). (2016). *White privilege: Essential readings on the other side of racism* (5th ed.). Worth Publishers.

Roudometof, V. (2020). Globalization, cosmopolitanism and 21st century populism. *Protosociology*, *37*(165).

Roy, S., & Galiev, A. (2011). Discourses on bilingualism in Canadian French immersion programs. *Canadian Modern Language Review*, *67*(3), 351–376. doi:10.3138/cmlr.67.3.351

Rudolph, N., & Yazan, B. (2023). Foreword. In G. Park, S. Bogdan, M. Rosa, & J. Navarro (Eds.), *Critical pedagogy in the Language and writing classroom: Strategies, examples, activities from teacher-scholars*. Routledge.

Ruecker, T. (2011a). Challenging the native and nonnative English speaker hierarchy in ELT: New directions from race theory. *Critical Inquiry in Language Studies*, *8*(4), 400–422. doi:10.1080/15427587.2011.615709

Ruecker, T., & Ives, L. (2015). White native English speakers needed: The rhetorical construction of privilege in online teacher recruitment spaces. *TESOL Quarterly*, *49*(4), 733–756. doi:10.1002/tesq.195

Ruíz, V., & Sánchez Korrol, V. (2006). *Latinas in the United States a historical encyclopedia*. Indiana University Press.

Compilation of References

Russell, C. (2006). *Racial and ethnic diversity: Asians, Blacks, Hispanics, Native Americans and Whites* (5th ed.). New Strategist Publications.

Salamonson, Y., Koch, J., Weaver, R., Everett, B., & Jackson, D. (2009). Embedded academic writing support for nursing students with English as a second language. *Journal of Advanced Nursing*, *66*(2), 413–421. doi:10.1111/j.1365-2648.2009.05158.x PMID:20423424

Saldaña, J. M. (2016). *The coding manual for qualitative researchers* (3rd ed.). Sage.

Sanczyk, A. (2021). Creating inclusive adult ESL classrooms through promoting culturally responsive pedagogy. *Coalition on Basic Adult Education*, *9*(2), 5–16.

Santoro, N. (2009). Teaching in culturally diverse contexts: what knowledge about "self" and "others: do teachers need? *Journal of Education for Teaching*, *35*(1), 33–45. doi:10.1080/02607470802587111

Santos, B. S. (2015). *Epistemologies of the South: Justice against epistemicide*. Routledge. doi:10.4324/9781315634876

Sapir, E. (1921). Language, race and culture. In E. Sapir (Ed.), *Language: An introduction to the study of speech* (pp. 207–220). Harcourt, Brace & World.

Sarkar, M., Low, B., & Winer, L. (2007). "Pour connecter avec les peeps": Quebequicité and the Quebec hip-hop community. In M. Mantero (Ed.), *Identity and second language learning: Culture, inquiry, and dialogic activity in educational contexts* (pp. 351–372). Information Age Publishing.

Schaefer, L., & Clandinin, D. J. (2019). Sustaining teachers' stories to live by: Implications for teacher education. *Teachers and Teaching*, *25*(1), 54–68. doi:10.1080/13540602.2018.1532407

Scheurich, J. J. (1997). *Research method in the postmodern*. Falmer Press.

Schissel, J. L., Leung, C., López-Gopar, M., & Davis, J. R. (2018). Multilingual learners in language assessment: Assessment design for linguistically diverse communities. *Language and Education*, *32*(2), 167–182. doi:10.1080/09500782.2018.1429463

Schmitt, N. (2019). Understanding vocabulary acquisition, instruction, and assessment: A research agenda. *Language Teaching*, *52*(2), 261–274. doi:10.1017/S0261444819000053

Schreiber, B.R., Lee, E., Johnson, J.T. & Fahim, N. (2022). Linguistic justice on campus: Pedagogy and advocacy for multilingual students. *New Perspectives on Language and Education*, 96.

Schütze, U. (2017). *Language learning and the brain: Lexical processing in second language acquisition*. Cambridge University Press.

Sekaja, L., Adams, B. G., & Yağmur, K. (2022). Raciolinguistic ideologies as experienced by racialized academics in South Africa. *International Journal of Educational Research*, *116*, 102092. doi:10.1016/j.ijer.2022.102092

Sensoy, O., & DiAngelo, R. (2017). *Is everyone really equal? An introduction to key concepts in social justice education* (2nd ed.). Teachers College Press.

Seror, J., & Weinberg, A. (2021). Exploring the longitudinal impact of university immersion: Bilingual spaces, multilingual values. *System*, *99*, 102523. doi:10.1016/j.system.2021.102523

Shapiro, R., & Watson, M. (2022). Translingual praxis: From theorizing language to Antiracist and decolonial pedagogy. *College Composition and Communication*, *74*(2), 292–321. doi:10.58680/ccc202232276

Shen, F. (1989). The classroom and the wider culture: Identity as a key to learning English composition. *College Composition and Communication*, *40*(4), 459–466. doi:10.2307/358245

Shiller, N. G., & Irving, A. (2014). *Whose cosmopolitanism? Critical perspectives, relationalities and discontents*. Berghahn Books.

Shin, H., & Sterzuk, A. (2019). Discourses, practices, and realities of multilingualism in higher education. *TESL Canada Journal*, *36*(1), 147–159. doi:10.18806/tesl.v36i1.1307

Shin, J. (2018). *From ESL learners to EFL learners: A case study of adolescent Korean returnees*. Georgia State University.

Shohamy, E. (2011). Assessing multilingual competencies: Adopting construct valid assessment policies. *Modern Language Journal*, *95*(3), 418–429. doi:10.1111/j.1540-4781.2011.01210.x

Shopes, L. (1998). What is oral history? *History matters: The U.S. survey on the web*. http://historymatters.gmu.edu

Shuck, G. (2006). Racializing the nonnative English speaker. *Journal of Language, Identity, and Education*, *5*(4), 259–276. doi:10.120715327701jlie0504_1

Shulman, L. S. (1987). Knowledge and teaching: Foundations of the new reform. *Harvard Educational Review*, *57*(1), 1–22. doi:10.17763/haer.57.1.j463w79r56455411

Silva, T. (2015). Writing instruction for matriculated International students: A lived case study. In *ESL Readers and Writers in Higher Education* (1st ed., pp. 64–79). Routledge.

Simon, P. (2017). The failure of the importation of ethno-racial statistics in Europe: Debates and controversies. *Ethnic and Racial Studies*, *40*(13), 2326–2332. doi:10.1080/01419870.2017.1344278

Skies, C. L., & Villanueva, C. (2021). Creating a more bilingual Texas: A closer look at bilingual education in the Lone Star State. *Every Texan*, 1-32. https://files.eric.ed.gov/fulltext/ED614323.pdf

Skutnabb-Kangas, T. (2012). Linguistic Human Rights. In L. M. Solan & P. M. Tiersma (Eds.), The Oxford Handbook of Language and Law (pp. 235-247). OUP Oxford.

Skutnabb-Kangas, T. (1988). Multilingualism and the education of minority children. In T. Skutnabb-Kangas & J. Cummins (Eds.), *Minority education: From shame to struggle* (pp. 9–44). Multilingual Matters. doi:10.21832/9781800418110-002

Skutnabb-Kangas, T., Phillipson, R., & Rannut, M. (1995). *Linguistic human rights*. De Gruyter Mouton.Sleeter, C. E. (2012). Confronting the marginalization of culturally responsive pedagogy. *Urban Education*, *47*(3), 562–584. doi:10.1177/0042085911431472

Sladek, A. (2022). Student-centered grammar feedback in the Basic Writing classroom: Toward a translingual grammar pedagogy. *Journal of Basic Writing*, *41*(1), 106–134. doi:10.37514/JBW-J.2022.41.1.05

Sleeter, C. E. (2004). Context-conscious portraits and context-blind policy. *Anthropology & Education Quarterly*, *35*(1), 132–136. doi:10.1525/aeq.2004.35.1.132

Smith, C., Masson, M., Spiliotopoulos, V., & Kristmanson, P. (2023). A course or a pathway? Addressing French as a Second Language teacher recruitment and retention in Canadian BEd programs. *Canadian Journal of Education*, *46*(2), 412–440.

Smith, C., & Zhou, G. (Eds.). (2022). *Handbook of research on teaching strategies for culturally and linguistically diverse international students*. IGI-Global. doi:10.4018/978-1-7998-8921-2

Smitherman, G. (1977). *Talkin and testifyin: The language of Black America*. Houghton Mifflin.

Compilation of References

Snyder, S., & Fenner, D. S. (2021). *Culturally responsive teaching for multilingual learners: Tools for equity.* Corwin Publishing.

Solorzano, D., & Yosso, T. (2000). Toward a critical race theory of Chicana and Chicano education. *Charting New Terrains of Chicana (o)/Latina (o) Education*, 35-65. doi:psycnet.apa.org/doi/10.1525/eth.1997.25.1.101

Solorzano, D. G. (1998). Critical Race Theory, race and gender microaggressions, and the experience of Chicana and Chicano scholars. *International Journal of Qualitative Studies in Education: QSE*, *11*(1), 121–136. doi:10.1080/095183998236926

Solórzano, D. G., & Yosso, T. J. (2001). From racial stereotyping and deficit discourse toward a critical race theory in teacher education. *Multicultural Education*, *9*(1), 2–8.

Sonday, A., Ramugondo, E., & Kathard, H. (2020). Case study and narrative inquiry as merged methodologies: A critical narrative perspective. *International Journal of Qualitative Methods*, *19*. doi:10.1177/1609406920937880

Spickard, P. R. (1989). *Mixed blood: Intermarriage and ethnic identity in twentieth century America.* University of Wisconsin Press.

Spiro, J. (2022). Making the materials writing leap: Scaffolding the journey from teacher to teacher-writer. In J. Norton & H. Buchanan (Eds.), *The Routledge handbook of materials development for language teaching* (pp. 475–482). Routledge. doi:10.4324/b22783-41

Spoonley, P., & Bedford, R. (2012). *Welcome to our world? Immigration and the reshaping of New Zealand.* Dunmore Publishing.

Srivastava, P., & Hopwood, N. (2009). A practical iterative framework for qualitative data analysis. *International Journal of Qualitative Methods*, *8*(1), 76–84. doi:10.1177/160940690900800107

Statistics Canada. (2023). *Key facts on the French language in Ontario in 2021.* https://www150.statcan.gc.ca/n1/pub/89-657-x/89-657-x2023017-eng.htm

Statistics Canada. (2023). *Multilingualism of Canadian households.* https://www12.statcan.gc.ca/census-recensement/2021/as-sa/98-200-X/2021014/98-200-X2021014-eng.cfm

Stinson, C., & Migliarini, V. (2022). "Race had never been an issue": Examining White supremacy in English language teaching. *British Journal of Sociology of Education*. Advance online publication. doi:10.1080/01425692.2022.2145933

Stoler, A. L. (1997). On political and psychological essentialisms. *Ethos (Berkeley, Calif.)*, *25*(1), 101–106. doi:10.1525/eth.1997.25.1.101

Stouck, J., & Shaw, C. (2019, Feb. 17). A sense of belonging: Studying a foundational academic literacy course. In *38th Annual Conference on the First-Year Experience*. National Resource Center.

Sue, D. W., Capodilupo, C. M., Torino, G. C., Bucceri, J. M., Holder, A. M. B., Nadal, K. L., & Esquilin, M. (2007). Racial microaggressions in everyday life: Implications for clinical practice. *The American Psychologist*, *62*(4), 271–286. doi:10.1037/0003-066X.62.4.271 PMID:17516773

Suraweera, D. (2020). *Towards integrating antiracism into TESL programs in Ontario.* Doctoral dissertation. University of Toronto.

Swift, K. (2022). "The good English": The ideological construction of the target language in adult ESOL. *Language in Society*, *51*(2), 309–331. doi:10.1017/S0047404521000427

Tang, M. (2020). *D'apprenant à enseignant: la construction identitaire et l'accès à la communauté professionnelle des enseignants de français en Colombie-Britannique* [Unpublished Doctoral thesis]. Simon Fraser University.

Tang, M., & Fedoration, S. (2022, November 3). *The contradiction that is an L+ teacher: A guide to help me thrive.* Congrès de l'ACPI.

Tardy, C. M. (2017). The challenge of genre in the academic writing classroom: Implications for L2 writing teacher education. In J. Bitchener, N. Storch, & R. Wette (Eds.), *Teaching writing for academic purposes to multilingual students: Instructional approaches* (pp. 69–83). Routledge. doi:10.4324/9781315269665-5

Tardy, C. M., & Whittig, E. (2017). On the ethical treatment of EAL writers: An update. *TESOL Quarterly*, *51*(4), 920–930. doi:10.1002/tesq.405

Tatum, B. D. (2016). *The complexity of identity: "Who am I?"* Unitarian Univesalist College of Social Justice. https://uucsj.org/wp-content/uploads/2016/05/The-Complexity-of-identity.pdf

Tatum, B. D. (1992). Talking about race, learning about racism: The application of racial identity development theory in the classroom. *Harvard Educational Review*, *62*(1), 1–25. doi:10.17763/haer.62.1.146k5v980r703023

Taylor, A. (2017). Putting race on the table: How teachers make sense of the role of race in their practice. *Harvard Educational Review*, *87*(1), 50–73. doi:10.17763/1943-5045-87.1.50

Tedeschi, M., Ekaterina, V., & Jauhiainen, J. S. (2022). Transnationalism: Current debates and new perspectives. *GeoJournal*, *87*(2), 603–619. doi:10.100710708-020-10271-8

Telles, E. E., & Ortiz, V. (2008). *Generations of exclusion: Mexican-Americans, assimilation, and race*. Russell Sage Foundation.

Teng, M. F., & Wang, C. (2023). Assessing academic writing self-efficacy belief and writing performance in a foreign language context. *Foreign Language Annals*, *56*(1), 144–169. doi:10.1111/flan.12638

The Canadian Encyclopedia. (2023). *Confederation*. https://thecanadianencyclopedia.ca/en/article/confederation-plain-language-summary

The Daily. (2020). *International students accounted for all of the growth in postsecondary enrolments in 2018/2019*. https://www150.statcan.gc.ca/n1/daily-quotidien/201125/dq201125e-eng.htm

Tiostanova, M. V., & Mignolo, W. (2012). *Learning to unlearn: Decolonial reflections from Eurasia and the Americas*. The Ohio State University Press.

Tomlinson, B. (2012a). Materials development. In A. Burns & J. C. Richards (Eds.), *The Cambridge guide to pedagogy and practice in second language teaching* (pp. 269–278). Cambridge University Press. doi:10.1017/9781009024778.034

Tomlinson, B. (2012b). Materials development for language learning and teaching. *Language Teaching*, *45*(2), 143–179. doi:10.1017/S0261444811000528

Toorenburgh, L., & Gaudet, L. (2023, May 28–29). *Belonging as a learning outcome: A case for Indigenous-only Writing classrooms* [Conference presentation]. 2023 conference of the Canadian Association for the Study of Discourse and Writing/Association Canadienne de Rédactologie, York University, Toronto, ON, Canada.

Törngren, S. O., Irastorza, N., & Rodríguez-García, D. (2021). Understanding multiethnic and multiracial experiences globally: Towards a conceptual framework of mixedness. *Journal of Ethnic and Migration Studies*, *47*(4), 763–781. doi:10.1080/1369183X.2019.1654150

Trent, J. G. (2015). Towards a multifaceted, multidimensional framework for understanding teacher identity. In Y. L. Cheung & K. Park (Eds.), *Advances and current trends in language teacher identity research* (pp. 44–58). Routledge.

Tronto, J. (1993). *1993: Moral boundaries: a political argument for an ethic of care*. Routledge.

Compilation of References

Tsai, A., Straka, B., & Gaither, S. (2021). Mixed-heritage individuals' encounters with raciolinguistic ideologies. *Journal of Multilingual and Multicultural Development*, 1-15. doi:10.1080/01434632.2021.1904964

Tuck, E., & Yang, K. W. (2018). *Toward what justice?: Describing diverse dreams of justice in education*. Taylor and Francis. doi:10.4324/9781351240932

U.S. Census Bureau. (2020). *Census illuminates racial and ethnic composition of the country*. Retrieved from https://www.census.gov/library/stories/2021/08/improved-race-ethnicity-measures-reveal-united-states-population-much-more-multiracial.html

United Nations. (1948). *Universal Declaration of Human Rights*. https://www.un.org/en/aboutus/universal-declaration-of-human-rights

United Nations. (1976). *International covenant on civil and political rights*. https://www.ohchr.org/en/professionalinterest/pages/ccpr.aspx

United States Census Bureau. (n.d.). *Bachelor's Degree or Higher*. Retrieved June, 21, 2023, from https://data.census.gov/cedsci/profile?g=0100000US

Universities Canada. (2022). *Enrolment by university*. https://www.univcan.ca/universities/facts-and-stats/enrolment-by-university/

US News Best Colleges. (n.d.). *Limestone University*. US News. https://www.usnews.com/best-colleges/limestone-college-3436

Valenzuela, A. (1999). *Subtractive schooling: U.S.-Mexican youth and the politics of caring*. State University of New York Press.

Vallente, J. P. C. (2020). Framing pre-service English language teachers' identity formation within the theory of alignment as mode of belonging in community of practice. *Teaching and Teacher Education*, *96*, 103177. doi:10.1016/j.tate.2020.103177

Van Leeuwen, T. (2011). Semiotics and iconography. In T. Van Leeuwen & C. Jewitt (Eds.), *The Handbook of Visual Analysis* (pp. 92–118). Sage.

Van Viegan Stille, S., Bethke, R., Bradley-Brown, J., Giberson, J., & Hall, G. (2016). Broadening educational practice to include translanguaging: An outcome of educator inquiry into multilingual students' learning needs. *Canadian Modern Language Review*, *72*(4), 480–503. doi:10.3138/cmlr.3432

Van Viegen, S., & Zappa-Hollman, S. (2020). Plurilingual pedagogies at the post-secondary level: Possibilities for intentional engagement with students' diverse linguistic repertoires. *Language, Culture and Curriculum*, *33*(2), 172–187. doi:10.1080/07908318.2019.1686512

Vandrick, S. (1999). ESL and the colonial legacy: A teacher faces her 'missionary kid' past. In G. Haroian-Guerin (Ed.), *The personal narrative: Casting ourselves as teachers and scholars* (pp. 63–74). Calendar Islands. doi:10.4324/9781410606273-34

Varghese, M., & Johnston, B. (2007). Evangelical Christians and English language teaching. *TESOL Quarterly*, *41*(1), 5–31. doi:10.1002/j.1545-7249.2007.tb00038.x

Varghese, M., Morgan, M. B., Johnston, B., & Johnson, K. A. (2005). Theorizing language teacher identity: Three perspectives and beyond. *Journal of Language, Identity, and Education*, *4*(1), 21–44. doi:10.120715327701jlie0401_2

Varghese, M., Motha, S., Trent, J., Park, G., & Reeves, J. (2016). Language teacher identity in multilingual education. *TESOL Quarterly*, *49*(1), 219–220. doi:10.1002/tesq.221

Veronelli, G. A. (2015). Five: The coloniality of language: Race, expressivity, power, and the darker side of modernity. *Wagadu: A Journal of Transnational Women's and Gender Studies*, *13*, 108-134.

Veronelli, G. A. (2015). The coloniality of language: Race, expressivity, power, and the darker side of modernity. *A Journal of Transnational Women's & Gender Studies*, *13*, 108–134.

Veronelli, G. A. (2015). The coloniality of language: Race, expressivity, power, and the darker side of modernity. *Wagadu*, *13*, 108–133.

Vertovec, S. (2007). Super-diversity and its implications. *Ethnic and Racial Studies*, *30*(6), 1024–1054. doi:10.1080/01419870701599465

Vertovec, S. (2019). Talking around super-diversity. *Ethnic and Racial Studies*, *42*(1), 125–139. doi:10.1080/01419870.2017.1406128

Vignoles, V. L. (2017). *Identity: Personal and social*. https://www.researchgate.net /publica tion/316790231_Identity_Personal_AND_Social#:~:text=Identity%20refers%20to%20how%20people,to%20others%20or%20to%20oneself

Vigouroux, C. B. (2017). The discursive pathway of two centuries of raciolinguistic stereotyping: 'Africans as incapable of speaking French'. *Language in Society*, *46*(1), 5–21. doi:10.1017/S0047404516000804

Villalpando, O. (2004). Practical considerations of critical race theory and Latino critical theory for Latino college students. *New Directions for Student Services*, *105*(105), 41–50. doi:10.1002s.115

Villanueva, V. (2006). Blind: Talking about the new racism. *Writing Center Journal*, *26*(1), 3–19. doi:10.7771/2832-9414.1589

Vionny, V. (2022). The relationship between peer social support and self-identity in adolescents at the SMAK Penabur Harapan Indah. *European Journal of Psychological Research*, *9*(3).

Viswanathan, G. (2014). *Masks of conquest: Literary study and British rule in India* (25th anniversary ed.). Columbia University Press. doi:10.7312/visw17169

Vitanova, G. (2016). Exploring second-language teachers' identities through multimodal narratives: Gender and race discourses. *Critical Inquiry in Language Studies*, *13*(4), 261–288. doi:10.1080/15427587.2016.1165074

Voci, A. (2014). Negative Stereotypes. In A. C. Michalos (Ed.), *Encyclopedia of quality of life and well-being research*. Springer. doi:10.1007/978-94-007-0753-5_1926

Von Esch, K. S., Motha, S., & Kubota, R. (2020). Race and language teaching. *Language Teaching*, *53*(4), 391–421. doi:10.1017/S0261444820000269

Waller, L., Wethers, K., & De Costa, P. I. (2017). A critical praxis: Narrowing the gap between identity, theory, and practice. *TESOL Journal*, *8*(1), 4–27. doi:10.1002/tesj.256

Wang, D. (2022). Translanguaging as a social justice strategy: The case of teaching Chinese to ethnic minority students in Hong Kong. *Asia Pacific Education Review*, *24*(3), 473–486. doi:10.100712564-022-09795-0

Wang, Q. (2023). Memorization strategy and foreign language learning: A narrative literature review. *Frontiers in Psychology*, *14*, 1261220. Advance online publication. doi:10.3389/fpsyg.2023.1261220 PMID:37767209

Wang, Y., Shen, B., & Yu, X. (2021). A latent profile analysis of EFL learners' self-efficacy: Associations with academic emotions and language proficiency. *System, 103*, 1–9. doi:10.1016/j.system.2021.102633

Wardle, E., & Downs, D. (2020). *Writing about writing: A college reader*. Bedford/St. Martins.

Washington, S. L. (2011). *Hypodescent: A history of the crystallization of the one-drop rule in the United States, 1880–1940*. Princeton University ProQuest Dissertations Publishing. 3480237.

Weaver, H. N. (2009). The colonial context of violence on violence in the lives of Native American women. *Journal of Interpersonal Violence, 24*(9), 1552–1563. doi:10.1177/0886260508323665 PMID:18768738

Weber, D. J. (1992). *The Spanish Frontier in North America*. Yale University Press.

Wei, L., & García, O. (2022). Not a first language but one repertoire: Translanguaging as a decolonizing project. *RELC Journal, 53*(2), 313–324. doi:10.1177/00336882221092841

Welply, O. (2023). English as an additional language (EAL): Decolonising provision and practice. *Curriculum Journal, 34*(1), 62–82. doi:10.1002/curj.182

Wenger, E. (1998). Communities of practice: Learning as a social system. *The Systems Thinker, 9*(5), 2–3.

Werbner, P. (1999). Global pathways: Working class cosmopolitans and the creation of transnational ethnic worlds. *Social Anthropology, 7*(1), 17–35. doi:10.1017/S0964028299000026

Wernicke, M., Masson, M., Kunnas, M., & Adatia, S. (forthcoming). Moving beyond erasure of race in French second language education. In R. Kubota & S. Motha (Eds.), Race, racism and antiracism in Language Education. Routledge.

Wernicke, M. (2018). Plurilingualism as agentive resource in L2 teacher identity. *System, 79*, 91–102. doi:10.1016/j.system.2018.07.005

Wernicke, M. (2020). Orientations to French language varieties among Western Canadian French-as-a-second-language teachers. *Critical Multilingualism Studies, 8*(1), 165–190.

Wernicke, M. (2022). "I'm trilingual–so what?": Official French/English bilingualism, race, and French language teachers' linguistic identities in Canada. *Canadian Modern Language Review, 78*(4), 344–362. doi:10.3138/cmlr-2021-0074

Widodo, H. P., Fang, F., & Elyas, T. (2020). The construction of language teacher professional identity in the Global Englishes territory: "we are legitimate language teachers". *Asian Englishes, 22*(3), 309–316. doi:10.1080/13488678.2020.1732683

Willinsky, J. (1998). *Learning to divide the world: Education at empire's end*. University of Minnesota Press.

Wilson, J. A., & Soblo, H. (2020). Transfer and transformation in multilingual student writing. *Journal of English for Academic Purposes, 44*, 100812–100813. doi:10.1016/j.jeap.2019.100812

Winchcombe, R. (2021). *Commercializing America: Religion, trade, and the challenges of English colonialism*. Encountering Early America. doi:10.7765/9781526145789.00007

Wingate, U. (2018). *Academic literacy and student diversity: The case for inclusive practice*. Multilingual Matters. doi:10.21832/9781783093496-008

Wise, A. (2016). Becoming cosmopolitan: Encountering difference in a city of mobile labour. *Journal of Ethnic and Migration Studies, 42*(14), 2280–2299. doi:10.1080/1369183X.2016.1205807

Wodak, R. (2015). Discrimination via discourse. In N. Bonvillain (Ed.), *The Routledge Handbook of Linguistic Anthropology* (pp. 366–383). Routledge. https://www.routledgehandbooks.com/doi/10.4324/9780203492741.ch24

Wright-Taylor, C. (2021). *"Sorry If My Words Aren't Right": Writing studies' partnership with second language writing to support translingual students in the Anglo-Canadian classroom* [Dissertation]. University of Waterloo. http://hdl.handle.net/10012/17684

Wright, W. E. (2019). *Foundations for teaching English language learners: Research, theory, policy, and practice* (3rd ed.). Caslon.

Wubalem, A. Y. (2021). Assessing learning transfer and constraining issues in EAP writing practices. *Asian-Pacific Journal of Second and Foreign Language Education*, *6*(1), 1–22. doi:10.118640862-021-00122-5

Wu, S. Y., & Rubin, D. L. (2000). Evaluating the impact of collectivism and individualism on argumentative writing by Chinese and North American college students. *Research in the Teaching of English*, *35*(2), 148–178.

Wynter-Hoyte, K., Braden, E. G., Rodriguez, S., & Thornton, N. (2019). Disrupting the status quo: Exploring culturally relevant and sustaining pedagogies for young diverse learners. *Race, Ethnicity and Education*, *22*(3), 428–447. doi:10.1080/13613324.2017.1382465

Xiao, Y., & Zhao, A. (2022). A case study on the impacts of social contexts on a Chinese English as a foreign language learner's L1 and L2 identities development. *Frontiers in Psychology*, *12*, 1–10. doi:10.3389/fpsyg.2021.772777 PMID:35069354

Xu, Y. (2017). Becoming a researcher: A journey of inquiry. In G. Barkhuizen (Ed.), *Reflections on Language Teacher Identity Research* (pp. 120–125). Routledge.

Yancey, K. B., Davis, M., Robertson, L., Taczak, K., & Workman, E. (2018). Writing across college: Key terms and multiple contexts as factors promoting students' transfer of writing knowledge and practice. *The WAC Journal*, *29*(1), 44–66. doi:10.37514/WAC-J.2018.29.1.02

Yazan, B., & Rudolph, N. (Eds.). (2018). Criticality, teacher identity, and (in)equity in English language teaching. *Educational Linguistics*, *35*. doi.org/10.1007/978-3-319-72920-6_1

Yeo, M., Haggarty, L., Wida, W., Ayoungman, K., Pearl, C. M. L., Stogre, T., & Waldie, A. (2019). Unsettling faculty minds: A faculty learning community on indigenization. *New Directions for Teaching and Learning*, *2019*(157), 27–41. doi:10.1002/tl.20328

Yin, C. (2022). Bridging the gap between Eastern and Western academic writing expectations: Who is responsible? *MEM Insider*, *7*, 9–10. https://www.kings.uwo.ca/academics/school-of-management-economics-and-mathematics/mem-insider/

Yoon, I. H. (2012). The paradoxical nature of whiteness-at-work in the daily life of schools and teacher communities. *Race, Ethnicity and Education*, *15*(5), 587–613. doi:10.1080/13613324.2011.624506

Young, V. A. (2011). Should writers use they own english? In L. Greenfield & K. Rowan (Eds.), *Writing centers and the new racism* (p. 61). Utah State University Press. doi:10.2307/j.ctt4cgk6s.7

Young, V. A. (2021). 2020 CCCC Chair's address: Say they name in black english: George Floyd, Breonna Taylor, Atatiana Jefferson, Aura Rosser, Trayvon Martin, and the need to move away from writing to literacies in CCCC and rhetoric and composition. *College Composition and Communication*, *72*(4), 623–639. doi:10.58680/ccc202131445

Zamel, V. (1997). Toward a model of transculturation. *TESOL Quarterly*, *31*(2), 341–352. doi:10.2307/3588050

Compilation of References

Zhang, Y. (2010). The impact of ESL writers' prior writing experience on their writing in college. In *Additional essays: Companion site for What is "college-level" writing? Volume 2*. National Council of Teachers of English. https://cdn.ncte.org/nctefiles/resources/books/collegelevel2/yufengzhang_final.pdf?_ga=2.228630740.974481951.1683917960-2141036358.1683917949&_gl=1*18we6es*_ga*MjE0MTAzNjM1OC4xNjgzOTE3OTQ5*_ga_L5Q68NRK05*MTY4MzkxNzk0OS4xLjEuMTY4MzkxNzk5Ny4xMi4wLjA

Zhang, J., Zhang, L. J., & Zhu, Y. (2023). Development and validation of a genre-based second language (L2) writing self-efficacy scale. *Frontiers in Psychology, 14*, 1181196. Advance online publication. doi:10.3389/fpsyg.2023.1181196 PMID:37351429

Zhou, J., Zhao, K., & Dawson, P. (2020). How first-year students perceive and experience assessment of academic literacies. *Assessment & Evaluation in Higher Education, 45*(2), 266–278. doi:10.1080/02602938.2019.1637513

Zinga, D., & Styres, S. (2019). Decolonizing curriculum: Student resistances to anti-oppressive pedagogy. *Power and Education, 11*(1), 30–50.

About the Contributors

Xiangying Huo, Ph.D., Assistant Professor at the University of Toronto, is a writing specialist and English language learning specialist. She has taught writing across the curriculum at the University of Toronto, York University, and OCAD Art and Design University. She has presented widely at national and international conferences on writing studies, anti-racist education, applied linguistics, ESL/EFL policy and pedagogy, internationalization in higher education, language ideology, and World Englishes. Dr. Huo is the author of *Higher Education Internationalization and English Language Instruction: Intersectionality of Race and Language in Canadian Universities* (2020, Springer) which was nominated by the International Writing Centers Association (IWCA) for the IWCA Outstanding Book Award in 2021.

Clayton Smith is professor at the University of Windsor in the Faculty of Education where he teaches at both the undergraduate and graduate levels. Over the course of his career, Dr. Smith has amassed significant knowledge and expertise in the areas of enrolment management, internationalization of higher education, and student success. He is the co-editor for the IGI-Global book, *Handbook on Research on Teaching Strategies for Culturally and Linguistically Diverse International Students*. His current research focuses on the promising practices for teaching linguistically and culturally diverse international students, microaggression experienced by international students in postsecondary educational institutions, and international students' sense of belonging in secondary schools.

* * *

Ameer Ali is working as English lecturer in the College Education Department, Government of Sindh, Pakistan. He is a solidarity member of the Foundation for Endangered Languages. His areas of interest include sociolinguistics, forensic linguistics, discourse studies, language shift and maintenance, language and ageism, and English language teaching. He has published many research papers and book chapters on Sociolinguistics in Pakistan's Sindh province.

Rachel Oluwafisayo Aluko is a Lecturer at Lead City University Ibadan, Nigeria. She bagged her PhD in European literature from the University of Ibadan, Nigeria where she earlier obtained a Master's degree with focus on African literature in 2008. Her areas of interest include comparative literature, Gender studies, Literature and Sustainability among others. She has published in different journals: High School Literature-in-English 2021-2025- a collection of poems; questions with answers on all literary texts for the 2021-2025 WASSCE is part of her contribution to secondary education in West Africa.

About the Contributors

Lucy Arellano Jr. is an associate professor of higher education in The Gevirtz School of Education at the University of California, Santa Barbara. She has almost twenty years of experience in the field of higher education. Her research focuses on persistence, retention, and degree completion for emerging majority students. Concepts of diversity, campus climates, engagement, and student co-curricular involvement ground her work. She examines campus environments and how institutional agency impacts student success.

Delia Carrizales is an Assistant Professor and Special Populations Curriculum Program Anchor at Texas Tech University in the Teacher Education Department. Dr. Carrizales' research is focused in (1) developing preservice teachers' pedagogical Spanish, (2) preparing bilingual preservice teachers to teach in various dual language settings, and (3) preparing preservice teachers to teach emergent bilinguals with learning disabilities.

Daniel Chang is currently a teaching faculty in the Faculty of Education at Simon Fraser University. Daniel Chang's scholarly expertise brings composition studies, argumentation, teaching multilingual students, and instructional design and technology together. For example, the three main areas are: writing instructions and writing pedagogy, multilingual international students' academic literacy, and the use of educational technology in designing and supporting teaching, learning, and writing.

Anita Chaudhuri is an Assistant Professor of Teaching in the Faculty of Creative and Critical Studies at the University of British Columbia, Okanagan campus. Her research in the areas of identity construction of language learners and their development in writing and communication has been published in academic journals such as, TESOL Quarterly, BC TEAL Journal, and Writing & Pedagogy. She is UBC Okanagan's Faculty Advisor on Academic Integrity, chairs the EDI sub-committee for STLHE's Contract Cheating and Academic Integrity Committee, and supports the development of an educative approach in this area.

Qinghua Chen is a postdoctoral fellow at the English Language Education Department of the Education University of Hong Kong. His current research interests include subjectivity, emotions, and identity of pre-service teachers and English language learners. He is particularly interested in exploring how these factors shape teaching and learning experiences in multicultural and multilingual contexts.

Simone Côté holds a Master of Arts in Education and Society from McGill University and a Bachelor of Arts in Sociology from Toronto Metropolitan University (formely Ryerson University). Supported by the Joseph Armand Bombardier Canadian Graduate Scholarship and the P. Lantz Graduate Fellowship for Excellence in Education and the Arts, her Master's thesis, "Student distress on Canadian post-secondary campuses: Arts-based approaches and positive affect", reviews the literature on arts communities and art-making modalities in ameliorating student distress and in promoting mental health and well-being. Côté is an independently motivated community-engaged scholar and instructor, facilitating arts-based wellness workshops at the Yeates School of Graduate and Postdoctoral Studies at Toronto Metropolitan University and through her non-profit volunteer work.

Maya Khemlani David is Honorary Professor at Asia Europe Institute in University of Malaya and Adjunct Professor 2017-2020 Jaipuria Institute of Management, Lucknow. She is also an Associate member of the International Institute of Public Policy and Management (IMPUMA) University of Malaya. Moreover, she also works as an Associate Section Editor for *Journal of English and Applied Linguistics* and for a number of other journals. ().

Michael Olayinka Gbadegesin is a lecturer in the department of English and Literary Studies, Lead City University, Ibadan Nigeria. His areas of specialization are Phonetics and Phonology, Sociolinguistics, Applied Linguistics.

Marcela Hebbard is a Senior Lecturer at the University of Texas Rio Grande Valley where she teaches composition, linguistic and teacher preparedness courses. Her research interests include online writing pedagogies, language and mixed race identities, first-year composition, and writing across the curriculum. She has co-author multiple book chapters and several articles in academic journals. She holds five master's degrees, one doctoral degree in Women's Studies, and is currently a PhD Candidate (ABD) in the Composition and Applied Linguistics Program at the Indiana University of Pennsylvania.

Teresa Holden is a Ph.D. student in Educational Studies, specializing in Educational Policy and Leadership, at the University of Windsor. A former E.S.L. instructor and adjunct faculty in the Ontario college system, she is passionate about critical pedagogy, culturally responsive teaching, assessment, and educational equity issues.

Ruthanne Hughes is an emerging scholar in her field, having graduated with her PhD in second language acquisition in May 2023 from the University of South Carolina. Her research interests focus on second language acquisition through a sociolinguistic lens, particularly engaging with raciolinguistic dynamics in the English as a second/foreign language classroom. Her dissertation focused on ideologies of race, gender, and religion in evangelical ESL programs in South Carolina. After graduation, Dr. Hughes moved to Shaanxi Province, China, where she teaches English at Weinan Normal University. Her current and future research plans focus on native-speakerism in the classroom.

Kamila Kinyon is a Teaching Associate Professor in the University of Denver Writing Program. She has a doctorate in Comparative Literature from the University of Chicago (2000) and an MA in TESOL/Linguistics from the University of Utah (1987). Her teaching at DU has focused on the rhetoric of journalism, oral history, and ethnography, which has also been a subject of her recent service and research—including a 2021 article in Annals of Anthropological Practice and a chapter for the Proceedings for the International Writing Across the Curriculum Conference 2020/2021. Other teaching and research interests include multilingual writing, WAC, and visual rhetoric.

Thu Thi-Kim Le is a Ph.D. Candidate in Educational Studies, the Joint Ph.D. Program at the University of Windsor, Canada. Before commencing her doctoral program, she was a faculty member at the Faculty of Foreign Languages, Ho Chi Minh City University of Technology and Education, Vietnam for ten years. She holds a master's degree in TESOL at the HCM Open University. Her major research interests lie in TESOL, Educational Technology, Education Aspiration, Internationalization in Higher Education, and International Student Learning Experience.

About the Contributors

Tonda Liggett is an Associate Professor and Graduate ESOL Program Director at Linfield University. Dr. Liggett's research focuses on the intersections of race and language in English language teacher education. Within this nexus, she weaves in aspects of critical multicultural education and contemporary immigration to broaden understandings of the varied ways that issues of race, language and culture inform teacher identity and teaching. Most recently she has been examining the role of immigration in multilingual student learning to better prepare teachers for the complex and dynamic experiences that these learners bring to their education.

Angel M. Y. Lin is Professor and Tier 1 Canada Research Chair in Plurilingual and Intercultural Education. Her research interests include translanguaging and trans-semiotizing (TL-TS), Content and Language Integrated Learning (CLIL), languages and literacies in science and mathematics education, critical media literacies, and social semiotics in plurilingual and pluricultural education. Her research and development of the Multimodalities-Entextualization Cycle (MEC) serves as a critical pragmatic heuristic to navigate and disrupt the often monoglossic institutional spaces by both valuing and enabling translingual, multimodal, and multisensory meaning making actions with implications for equity, diversity and inclusion in education. She is the current Chair of the American Educational Research Association's Special Interest Group (SIG), Semiotics in Education. She also started the TL-TS Research Channel on Youtube and has organized over 30 research seminars featuring both seasoned and emergent scholars in applied linguistics and education from all over the world.

Mimi Masson is an Assistant Professor at the Faculty of Education at the Université de Sherbrooke. Her research focuses on the language teacher identity development, specifically through the lens of anti-oppressive and antiracist education. She specializes in using critical discourse analysis and arts-based research methodologies.

Srividya (Vidya) Natarajan teaches writing and coordinates the Writing Program at King's University College, London, Ontario. Her research and writing focus on writing and writing center pedagogy in relation to racial, gender, caste, and disability justice. She recently co-edited a special section of Discourse and Writing/Rédactologie with contributions from the 2021 CWCA/ACCR conference, and a special issue of *The Peer Review* on changing writing center commonplaces in response to anti-oppressive frameworks.

Emily Pez holds a Ph.D. in English literature from Western University and works as a writing center consultant and part-time instructor in the Department of English, French, and Writing at King's University College (Western University).

Ana K. Soltero López is an Education instructor at Fresno City College in the Central Valley of California. She has been a teacher educator for nine years and espouses an educator philosophy that is firmly grounded in equity-centered, student-centered, asset-based, social justice, anti-racist, and anti-deficit perspectives and application. Her courses centralize culturally and linguistically sustaining pedagogies, critical teacher inquiry and reflexivity, and community-building and empowerment. Her general research focus is K-20 BIPOC educational access, retention, and persistence. Her research agenda is informed by her teaching and work with youth, educators, and BIPOC communities and lies at the intersection of disciplines such as Education, Ethnic Studies, Sociology, and Immigration Studies.

Jordan Stouck is an Associate Professor of Teaching in the Faculty of Creative and Critical Studies at the University of British Columbia, Okanagan campus. She is the co-author of two Canadian editions of the composition textbook, Writing Today, as well as articles on blended learning and graduate writing.

Elena Tran has accumulated more than a decade of teaching experience at the tertiary level. She holds a TESL Diploma from the Canadian College of Educators and a master's degree in TESOL from Victoria University in Melbourne, Australia, where she proudly served as the valedictorian in 2016. Currently, she is teaching Business Communications at both Sheridan College and Niagara College Toronto.

Shahnawaz Tunio holds a PhD degree in Education Economics and Management from Zhengzhou University, China and works as an Assistant Professor at College Education Department, Government of Sindh Pakistan. His areas of interest include Clinical Psychology, Psychology and Education.

Index

A

Academic Literacies 27, 241, 243-245, 248-253, 257-258, 261
Access Paradox 205, 267, 277, 281, 284, 286-287
Adaptive Transfer 193, 202, 204, 211, 215, 255
Anti-Linguicism 241, 261
Antiracism 145, 241, 250, 261-262, 323
Anti-Racist Pedagogy 306, 311, 315-318, 320, 322, 324
Arts-Based Research 116, 123, 145
Assimilation 10, 14, 34, 80, 84-85, 90-91, 93, 112, 114, 157, 222, 245, 262
Autoethnography 52-53, 61, 68-69, 71-72

B

Bilingual Certification 28
Bilingual Licensure 50
Bilingual Preservice Teacher 37-38, 49-50

C

Classroom Interactions 187, 189
Collaborative Autoethnography 52-53, 61, 69, 72
Collaborative Ethnography 218, 225-227, 236, 238
Colonialism 2-3, 14, 56, 73-75, 84, 90-94, 116-117, 130, 137, 220, 261, 310, 315
Common European Framework of Reference 73, 79, 93
Critical 1-7, 10-27, 29-30, 33, 46-50, 69-70, 74, 90-92, 101, 111-112, 114, 120-121, 125, 136, 138, 140, 142, 145, 150-151, 153, 157-159, 163, 166-171, 187, 193-195, 200, 202, 204, 206-209, 211-213, 215, 219-220, 224, 227, 241, 243-248, 250-258, 261, 263, 266, 284, 292, 298, 306-311, 316-324
Critical Dialogic Approach 193-194, 206, 215
Critical Discourse Analysis 13-14, 142, 150-151, 153, 158, 166, 169, 171, 255
Critical Race Theory (CRT) 1, 3-4, 30, 151, 157, 306-309, 317, 324

Culturally Responsive Pedagogy 14-15, 21, 98, 193, 195-197, 215, 316, 323
Culturally Sustaining 11, 14-15, 17, 24, 49, 157, 169, 193-194, 203, 206, 208-209, 212-215, 219, 222-223, 237-238, 244, 246, 248, 254-255
Culturally Sustaining Pedagogy 11, 14-15, 17, 24, 49, 194, 208, 213-214, 219, 222-223, 237-238, 244, 246, 254

D

Decolonial Approach 206, 215, 243
Decoloniality 143, 200, 241, 261
Deficit Model 209, 247, 258, 265-266, 273, 275, 277, 280, 282, 284, 287
Discriminatory Discourse 172, 178-179, 184-186, 189-190

E

ELL 113, 247, 258, 306, 324
Employment Discrimination 52, 56, 69, 72
English as a Second Language (ESL) 52-53, 73, 306, 309, 320, 324
English Language Learner (ELL) 324
English Language Teacher Education 23, 98, 102, 112, 115, 309
English Learner Education 98
English Monolanguaging 290-291, 293-294, 297-299, 301-302, 304
Epistemological Racism 2, 306-308, 318, 324
ESL 6, 10, 21, 32, 52-54, 56-58, 60, 62-68, 70-77, 88, 90-91, 93, 111, 113, 137, 140, 143, 211-214, 235-236, 247, 257-258, 261, 308-309, 311-313, 315, 317-321, 323-324

F

French as a Second Language 23, 116, 118, 123, 140-

142, 144-145

G

Genre 194, 202, 204, 207, 210, 219, 225, 227, 232, 235, 241, 244, 248-251, 253-254, 256, 260-261, 264

H

Hegemony 8, 15-17, 43, 73, 93, 174, 221-222, 243, 291-292, 298-302, 308, 310

Hierarchy 4, 7-9, 29-30, 153, 170, 223, 231, 309, 311, 315

Higher Education 1, 8, 10, 21, 23, 40, 44-47, 53, 65, 70, 78, 82, 153, 157, 167, 194, 197, 210, 212-214, 222, 234, 236, 256, 258, 261, 265, 267, 270, 272, 283-284, 286, 292, 306-307, 313, 324

Hypodescent 150-153, 155-157, 167, 171

I

Identity 1, 6-7, 9-10, 12-16, 18, 23-26, 29-31, 34, 43, 45, 47, 49, 60, 68, 70-71, 92-93, 95, 98-99, 101-105, 107-112, 114-123, 125, 127, 129-131, 134-145, 149, 151-153, 156-178, 181-182, 186-190, 206-208, 210-213, 215, 235, 242-244, 247-248, 254, 256-259, 261-262, 266, 271, 278, 282, 284, 288, 291, 293, 307, 309, 315-317, 319, 321, 323-324

Ideology 1, 3, 5, 7-9, 12, 14-15, 17, 30-31, 46, 48, 71, 75, 88, 92-93, 102, 122, 128, 131, 135, 138, 142, 151, 153, 155-157, 163, 168, 177-178, 206, 221, 223, 227, 234, 238, 242, 244, 248, 255, 263, 286, 291, 307, 310, 324

Immigrant 39, 41, 55-56, 67-68, 70-71, 98, 100-101, 104, 106-107, 109-110, 113, 123, 134, 155-156, 166, 175, 222, 243, 251, 266, 268, 271-274, 277, 279, 282

Immigrants 31, 34, 40, 46, 54-55, 66, 69, 71-72, 82, 98, 100, 103, 106-107, 109, 113, 155, 163, 168, 245, 268, 272-273, 287, 306

Immigration 30-31, 39, 45, 55, 58, 71, 98-101, 103-110, 114-115, 163, 169, 319

Institutional 2, 35, 49, 52-53, 59, 63, 72, 76-77, 80, 87, 110, 122, 139, 141, 152, 157, 160, 194-197, 201-203, 205-209, 214, 219, 222, 247-249, 251, 296

Institutional Challenges 72

International Student 82, 194, 220, 268, 275, 277, 280, 282

International Students 21, 54, 57, 137, 200, 204, 211, 214, 222, 225, 228, 233, 241-248, 251, 254-256, 266, 268, 273-274, 277-280, 282, 286-287, 312

Interpersonal Challenges 72

Interracial Classroom 189

Interracial Settings 172

Intersectionality 1, 3-5, 7, 9, 21, 29, 43-44, 101, 104, 110, 150-151, 166-168, 173-174, 180, 187-188, 212, 256, 286, 307, 309, 315, 317

Intertextuality 218, 224-225, 233, 238

J

Justice 1, 4, 6, 13, 15, 17-18, 23, 25, 30, 46, 49, 82, 92, 98, 110-111, 114, 169, 176, 189, 193-199, 201, 206-210, 212-216, 219, 222, 235, 237, 246-247, 250-251, 253-255, 265-267, 270, 272-277, 280, 283-287, 289, 292, 296, 300-301, 303-304, 309-310, 317, 319, 321-322

L

L2 Learner Identity 261

LangCrit 6-7, 19, 26, 116, 121, 140, 145, 307

Language 2-3, 5-26, 28-31, 33-38, 41-50, 52-53, 55-56, 58-60, 68-78, 80, 82, 84, 87-96, 98-99, 101-103, 106-124, 127-133, 135-146, 148, 150-153, 157-179, 181-190, 193-196, 200, 202, 204-205, 207, 209-215, 220-221, 223-225, 227, 231-233, 235-236, 238, 241-250, 252-264, 266-267, 270-288, 291-296, 298-313, 315, 317-324

Language Classrooms 1, 5-6, 15, 150, 207, 291-292, 306, 311, 317

Language Teacher Identity 18, 114, 116, 120-121, 140, 143, 145, 151, 159, 165-166, 170

Language Teaching 5, 9-11, 16-19, 21-24, 69-70, 72, 93, 98-99, 113-114, 118-120, 140-141, 143, 145, 148, 165, 168, 171, 213, 235, 257-260, 291, 306, 309-310, 321, 323

Languages 2-3, 7-9, 11-13, 15-16, 18, 20, 23, 28-31, 34, 43-44, 63, 73-74, 76, 79-80, 84, 90, 93-94, 101, 104, 117, 119, 125-127, 129, 131-133, 138, 142-143, 146, 148, 150, 162, 172, 175, 180, 182, 188, 191, 194-195, 205, 246, 261-263, 265-268, 270-273, 275-278, 280-281, 283-284, 287-289, 291-307, 322

Latina 5, 28-30, 34-37, 41-42, 44-45, 47-48, 50-51, 323

Learning Materials 241-243, 245, 256, 258-259, 261

Levels of Desire 207, 216

Linguicism 1, 3, 15, 142, 193-194, 236, 249, 254, 262, 309, 311, 313, 315, 317-318, 320

Linguistic Diversity 17, 193-194, 208, 244, 288, 290-291, 298, 300-302, 304

Linguistic Human Rights 13, 290-295, 298-302, 304-

Index

305, 323
Linguistic Justice 6, 15, 17, 193-199, 201, 207-210, 216, 219, 222, 235, 250, 254, 265-267, 270, 272-277, 280, 283-284, 286-287, 289, 322
Linguistic Terrorism 28-32, 34, 36-37, 39, 41, 44-46, 50

M

Migration Channels 98, 100-101, 105-106, 110-111
Minoritized Students 1, 6, 9, 14, 249, 253, 266
Miscegenation 150, 153, 166, 169, 171
Missionary 78, 88-90, 92-94
Missions 73-74, 77, 87-94
Monolingual 3, 10, 15-16, 84, 109, 151, 154, 161-162, 166, 199-200, 207, 211, 243, 246, 248, 251, 263, 265-267, 273-275, 277, 281, 283, 287, 291-292, 298, 300, 310-311
Multiculturalism 14, 19, 22, 84-85, 93, 141, 244, 285
Multilingual 1, 8-18, 20, 22-24, 28-29, 31-33, 43-44, 84, 92-93, 98-99, 102-103, 105-106, 108-112, 114-115, 121, 138, 140-144, 163, 168, 170, 175, 188, 193-200, 204-207, 209-217, 232-234, 236, 241-248, 250-260, 262-263, 265-268, 273-292, 294, 298, 300, 303-304, 318
Multilingual Learner Education 98
Multiraciality 150-154, 158, 164, 171

N

Native Speakers 8, 10, 16, 53, 59, 76, 120, 122, 158, 207, 244, 265, 274, 287, 309
Native-Nonnative Dichotomy 150, 171
Nativism 34, 42, 44, 46, 49, 52, 56, 59, 68, 72, 321
Naturalized Ideology 238

O

Oral History 265, 268, 282-283, 286-287
Organizational 52-53, 63, 65, 72
Organizational Challenges 72
Othering 31, 172, 175, 178-179, 188-189

P

Paradigm Shift 157, 222, 224, 238
Pedagogy 1, 10-15, 17-19, 21-25, 27, 43, 49, 92, 98, 143, 157, 167, 169, 193-198, 201, 203, 205-208, 210-217, 219, 221-223, 234-235, 237-238, 241-248, 250-251, 254-261, 281, 284-286, 292, 303, 306, 311, 315-318, 320-324
People of Color (POC) 324

Positionality 33, 36, 77, 101, 105, 115, 125, 152, 159, 162, 194, 207, 219, 268, 270, 322
Power 2-4, 6-8, 13-15, 19, 24-26, 29, 31, 33, 41, 46, 59, 67, 69, 71, 75-76, 90-91, 93, 98-99, 103, 122, 141, 143, 152, 158, 162-163, 171, 194, 203, 223-225, 233, 244, 251, 262-263, 271, 284, 286-287, 291-292, 298, 304, 306-311, 315-317, 319, 324
Preservice Teachers 6, 28-30, 32-35, 37-39, 43-45, 47, 49-50
Privileged Irresponsibility 267, 274, 278, 284, 287

R

Race 1-11, 15-30, 33-34, 36, 39-40, 44-51, 53, 59, 67-68, 70, 77, 80, 82, 84, 90, 93, 98-99, 101, 104, 107, 109-115, 117, 121, 125, 127, 138, 140-142, 144-145, 150-159, 161-171, 173-175, 177-179, 181-182, 185-191, 196, 206, 210, 212-214, 220-223, 225, 233, 235, 237, 256, 261, 263, 266, 270, 284-287, 293, 304, 306-311, 313, 315-324
Race and Language 2-3, 6-8, 15, 19, 21, 25, 29, 45-46, 49, 93, 98, 107, 114, 144-145, 181, 186, 188, 190, 212, 256, 286, 306-308, 322-323
Racialization 1-7, 9, 19-20, 23, 25, 30, 36, 39-41, 46, 49, 104, 107, 121, 151, 174, 257, 286, 308-309, 317-318
Raciolinguistic 5-10, 13, 19, 25, 28-30, 34, 41, 44, 46-47, 49, 73, 75-76, 90-91, 93, 116-117, 119, 121-123, 125, 127, 136-137, 140-142, 144-145, 152, 157, 162-164, 166, 169-170, 173-174, 180, 186, 188, 214, 242, 244, 247-248, 251, 253, 265-266, 270, 285-286, 291, 321-322
Raciolinguistics 1, 3, 6-7, 15-17, 23, 25, 29, 47, 116, 121, 145, 150-151, 165, 171, 173-174, 186, 206, 210, 214, 265-266, 284-285, 287, 307, 320
Racism 1-7, 11, 14-17, 19, 28, 30-34, 36, 39-42, 44-47, 50, 52, 56, 59, 68, 75, 98, 101, 103-105, 111, 116-117, 121, 142, 145, 151, 165, 169, 172-174, 177-182, 184, 186-187, 189-191, 193-194, 206, 210, 215, 218, 220-221, 225, 235-237, 243-244, 247, 249, 256, 261-262, 266, 272, 277, 285, 288, 306-311, 313, 315-324

S

Second Language Writing 18, 194, 202, 211-213, 215, 242, 261
Social Movement Theory 98-105, 111-112, 115
Standard English 8, 11, 14-15, 24, 26, 29, 75, 265-266, 273, 275-276, 284-285, 287, 307
Subjectivity 4, 221, 238, 310

Super-Diversity 98, 101-102, 112-114

T

Teacher Education 6, 13, 23, 25-26, 28, 32-34, 46-47, 49-50, 69-70, 98, 102, 112, 115-116, 121, 123, 136-139, 142-145, 147, 164, 168, 213, 258, 260, 292, 303, 309, 322

Teacher Identity 10, 16, 18, 24, 49, 98, 114, 116-118, 120-122, 138-141, 143, 145, 151, 153, 157-159, 163-168, 170-171

TESL 56, 64, 70-71, 143, 200, 211, 214, 236, 256, 309, 323

Textbook 241-252, 254-255, 258, 261-264, 315

Transformative Change 218

Translanguaging 1, 10-13, 15, 20, 23, 38, 45, 73, 84, 90, 92-93, 123, 188, 211, 215, 254, 267, 276-277, 282, 285-286, 290-305

Translingual Pedagogy 1, 11, 261

Translingualism 10-11, 16, 248, 257, 263, 265, 286-287

Transnationalism 98, 105, 108, 111, 114

W

White Listening Subject 16, 73, 75-76, 80, 82, 84, 90, 93, 121, 130-131, 136, 157

White Privilege 4, 7, 165, 169, 310-311, 324

White Supremacy 2, 4-6, 8, 14-15, 20, 30, 72-74, 90-91, 159, 212, 247, 306-307, 310-311, 323-324

Writing About Writing 243, 250-251, 259-261, 263

Writing Center 17, 19, 196, 211, 218-237, 246, 249, 266-268, 270, 275, 279-281, 288

Writing Tutoring 218, 220-221, 223-225, 228, 233, 238

Writing Tutoring Discourse 224-225, 238

Recommended Reference Books

IGI Global's reference books are available in three unique pricing formats:
Print Only, E-Book Only, or Print + E-Book.

Order direct through IGI Global's Online Bookstore at
www.igi-global.com or through your preferred provider.

ISBN: 9781799897064
EISBN: 9781799897088
© 2022; 302 pp.
List Price: US$ 215

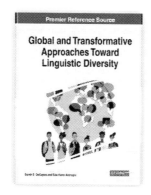

ISBN: 9781799889854
EISBN: 9781799889878
© 2022; 383 pp.
List Price: US$ 215

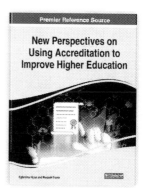

ISBN: 9781668451953
EISBN: 9781668451960
© 2022; 300 pp.
List Price: US$ 195

ISBN: 9781799852001
EISBN: 9781799852018
© 2022; 355 pp.
List Price: US$ 215

ISBN: 9781799897507
EISBN: 9781799897521
© 2022; 304 pp.
List Price: US$ 215

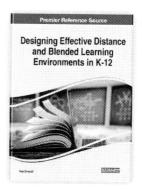

ISBN: 9781799868293
EISBN: 9781799868316
© 2022; 389 pp.
List Price: US$ 215

Do you want to stay current on the latest research trends, product announcements, news, and special offers?
Join IGI Global's mailing list to receive customized recommendations, exclusive discounts, and more.
Sign up at: **www.igi-global.com/newsletters.**

Publisher of Timely, Peer-Reviewed Inclusive Research Since 1988

www.igi-global.com   Sign up at www.igi-global.com/newsletters   facebook.com/igiglobal   twitter.com/igiglobal   linkedin.com/igiglobal

Ensure Quality Research is Introduced to the Academic Community

Become an Evaluator for IGI Global Authored Book Projects

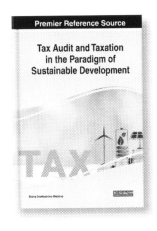   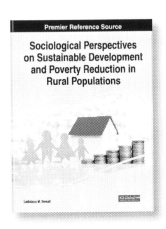

The overall success of an authored book project is dependent on quality and timely manuscript evaluations.

Applications and Inquiries may be sent to:
development@igi-global.com

Applicants must have a doctorate (or equivalent degree) as well as publishing, research, and reviewing experience. Authored Book Evaluators are appointed for one-year terms and are expected to complete at least three evaluations per term. Upon successful completion of this term, evaluators can be considered for an additional term.

If you have a colleague that may be interested in this opportunity, we encourage you to share this information with them.

Easily Identify, Acquire, and Utilize Published
Peer-Reviewed Findings in Support of Your Current Research

IGI Global OnDemand

Purchase Individual IGI Global OnDemand Book Chapters and Journal Articles

For More Information:
www.igi-global.com/e-resources/ondemand/

Browse through 150,000+ Articles and Chapters!

Find specific research related to your current studies and projects that have been contributed by international researchers from prestigious institutions, including:

- Accurate and Advanced Search
- Affordably Acquire Research
- Instantly Access Your Content
- Benefit from the InfoSci Platform Features

"It really provides *an excellent entry into the research literature of the field*. It presents a manageable number of *highly relevant sources* on topics of interest to a wide range of researchers. The sources are *scholarly, but also accessible* to 'practitioners'."

- Ms. Lisa Stimatz, MLS, University of North Carolina at Chapel Hill, USA

Interested in Additional Savings?

Subscribe to
IGI Global OnDemand *Plus*

Learn More

Acquire content from over 128,000+ research-focused book chapters and 33,000+ scholarly journal articles for as low as US$ 5 per article/chapter (original retail price for an article/chapter: US$ 37.50).

7,300+ E-BOOKS.
ADVANCED RESEARCH.
INCLUSIVE & AFFORDABLE.

IGI Global e-Book Collection

- **Flexible Purchasing Options** (Perpetual, Subscription, EBA, etc.)
- Multi-Year Agreements with **No Price Increases** Guaranteed
- **No Additional Charge** for Multi-User Licensing
- No Maintenance, Hosting, or Archiving Fees
- Continually Enhanced & Innovated **Accessibility Compliance Features** (WCAG)

Handbook of Research on Digital Transformation, Industry Use Cases, and the Impact of Disruptive Technologies
ISBN: 9781799877127
EISBN: 9781799877141

Handbook of Research on New Investigations in Artificial Life, AI, and Machine Learning
ISBN: 9781799886860
EISBN: 9781799886877

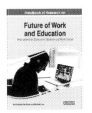

Handbook of Research on Future of Work and Education
ISBN: 9781799882756
EISBN: 9781799882770

Research Anthology on Physical and Intellectual Disabilities in an Inclusive Society (4 Vols.)
ISBN: 9781668435427
EISBN: 9781668435434

Innovative Economic, Social, and Environmental Practices for Progressing Future Sustainability
ISBN: 9781799895909
EISBN: 9781799895923

Applied Guide for Event Study Research in Supply Chain Management
ISBN: 9781799889694
EISBN: 9781799889717

Mental Health and Wellness in Healthcare Workers
ISBN: 9781799888130
EISBN: 9781799888147

Clean Technologies and Sustainable Development in Civil Engineering
ISBN: 9781799898108
EISBN: 9781799898122

Request More Information, or Recommend the IGI Global e-Book Collection to Your Institution's Librarian

For More Information or to Request a Free Trial, Contact IGI Global's e-Collections Team: eresources@igi-global.com | 1-866-342-6657 ext. 100 | 717-533-8845 ext. 100

Are You Ready to Publish Your Research?

IGI Global offers book authorship and editorship opportunities across 11 subject areas, including business, computer science, education, science and engineering, social sciences, and more!

Benefits of Publishing with IGI Global:

- Free one-on-one editorial and promotional support.
- Expedited publishing timelines that can take your book from start to finish in less than one (1) year.
- Choose from a variety of formats, including Edited and Authored References, Handbooks of Research, Encyclopedias, and Research Insights.
- Utilize IGI Global's eEditorial Discovery® submission system in support of conducting the submission and double-blind peer review process.
- IGI Global maintains a strict adherence to ethical practices due in part to our full membership with the Committee on Publication Ethics (COPE).
- Indexing potential in prestigious indices such as Scopus®, Web of Science™, PsycINFO®, and ERIC – Education Resources Information Center.
- Ability to connect your ORCID iD to your IGI Global publications.
- Earn honorariums and royalties on your full book publications as well as complimentary content and exclusive discounts.

Join Your Colleagues from Prestigious Institutions, Including:

Learn More at: www.igi-global.com/publish
or Contact IGI Global's Aquisitions Team at: acquisition@igi-global.com